A Selective Index to Theatre Magazine

by

Stan Cornyn

The Scarecrow Press, Inc.
New York and London
1964

L. C. Card No. 64-11778

For Thomas Guy Cornyn

Table of Contents

INTRODUCTION

From 1900 to 1930, the monthly periodical, Theatre Magazine,[1] chronicled the events, personalities, ideas, indeed everything that was theatre in America. Its 360 issues preserve a pictorial and verbal record of this period in American theatre history.

Because it presents this unique record of a vital span of theatre history, Theatre Magazine can prove invaluable to the scholar interested in the period.

Blanche M. Ganahl devoted a lengthy section of her thesis, "The Commercial Theatre Magazine in the United States from 1900 to 1958,"[2] to a description of Theatre Magazine, its editors, aims, policies, format, and contents; any reiteration of such material in this work is unnecessary.

Theatre Magazine contains articles by George Bernard Shaw, John Barrymore, George M. Cohan, Sherwood Anderson, George Jean Nathan, David Belasco, Charles Chaplin, George Gershwin, Raymond Hitchcock, Weber and Fields, Theodore Dreiser, Al Jolson, Will Rogers, D.W. Griffith, and a hundred other popular figures of the time. Critical reviews of every production opening on Broadway, as well as records of such foreign theatre activity as that of the Theatre Libre and Moscow Art Theatre, are found in the volumes. It records the early history of films, together with vaudeville, opera, chatauqua, radio, and burlesque. Interviews by the scores with important foreign and American actors--Duse, Bernhardt,

Skinner, Warfield, Arliss, Eagels, Cowl, Nazimova, Maeterlinck, Caruso, and Galsworthy to name a few--present a broad panorama of the theatre. Histories of theatre houses are presented, as are articles on earlier actors and theatre history.

No important or even vaguely notable theatrical personality or production goes undocumented by the photographer's camera. Theatre Magazine is unique among its contemporaries in this regard, and this record is of special values.

Form of the Index

Selectivity. This index includes approximately 45,000 references to authors, subjects, and dramatic works, arranged alphabetically according to American Library Association indexing practice.[3]

This index is selective. Although various criteria have been applied in determining whether each entry should be included, the most important criterion was that of possible scholarly interest. It was resolved to omit approximately 5,000 article titles, since each one of these had been covered by author and subjects. Selectivity was also applied to material such as the names of individual actors in complete cast lists, titles of plays in length-of-run charts, allusions of no interest to the subject entry, and the like. Such material is more readily available in other works, such as the Burns Mantle annuals.[4]

Also omitted from this index are those departments of Theatre Magazine which are not germane to theatre history, e.g., Fashions, Dining Out, and to some extent, Concerts. Regional theatre activity has been included only when it covers more than a calendar of productions.

Form of page references. Aside from the exceptions noted below, each reference will be found in the form of two numbers divided by a comma, e.g., "245,76." The first of these is the issue number, while the second refers to the page in that issue. The Issue Numbering Code, see p. 11 to 14, gives the year and volume number corresponding to each issue number.

Certain exceptions occur. The first two issues of Theatre Magazine were largely pictorial souvenir booklets, and were issued under the title Our Players Gallery, with consecutive paging. When references to these issues are made, they are in the form of "PG," followed by the page number.

Suffixed numbers--e.g., "179,4c"--correspond to those used in Theatre Magazine for insert pages.

Pagination by Roman numerals--e.g., "96, xxxiv"--follows the practice of pagination found in some issues of Theatre Magazine.

A suffixed "f"--e.g., "68,13f"--indicates that the entry falls on an unnumbered page facing page 13.

Abbreviations. The following abbreviations are used in this index:

(A) ..... The autograph of the subject reference.

(B) ..... Critical review of a book.

(C) ..... Caricature of or by subject reference.

c ..... Cover of issue.

(D) ..... Drawing or design of or by subject reference.

(F) ..... Film.

f ..... Facing page.

(FI) ..... Fiction.

(OP)..... Opera.

PG ....Our Players Gallery (Vol. I, Nos. 1 and 2 of Theatre Magazine).

(R) .....Play review, followed by year of production.

(S) .....Synopsis of play, with dialogue.

(V) .....Verse.

(W) .....By-line article appearing under the name of the subject reference.

Spelling. Spellings of names is based on reference works by Browne and Koch, Odell, Kolodin, Lang, Ambriere, Mantle and Sherwood, Parker, Slonimsky, and Blum, which are listed in the Bibliography to this work.

Subject References. Subject entries, which are underscored, are limited to material that would be especially useful to the researcher. The subject headings chosen conform either to those used in other theatrical indices[5] or are cross-referenced therefrom. However, because of certain individualities in Theatre Magazine, occasional departures from conventional indexing practice have been made.

Regular round-up articles, covering entire seasons of dramatic activity, are listed under the generic title, Review of the Season--(Year). Since each play for which a review appears in Theatre Magazine is also followed by the date of production--e.g., "(R'17)"--which indicates that the play was reviewed (R) in 1917--the scholar interested in placing an individual play within the scope of the season should refer to the Review of the Season references.

Book reviews are listed by title of the book.

Play reviews are listed by title and, normally, not by author.

Scholars interested in reviews of the works of a given playwright should also check under the titles of plays by that author. The Shaw scholar, for example, should check listings under "Arms and the Man," "Androcles and the Lion," etc.

Broad subject listings have been restricted or eliminated. Such entries as those for American Theatre and Theatre History, are omitted.

Author references. In every case, authorship is indicated by the symbol "(W)" either directly following the main entry--e.g., "COHAN, ELIZABETH (W):"--which indicates that she is author of all successive references, or immediately preceding a particular page reference within a listing of other entries--e.g., "36,45; 37, 52; (W) 64,113; 71,11"--which indicates that the entry was author of the material in issue number 64 only.

Conclusion

Throughout the work that has gone into the compilation of this index, it has been the author's goal to present an effective key to the research resource available in Theatre Magazine. This work is, however, not a complete index of Theatre Magazine.

Notes

1. Theatre Magazine is used throughout this work as the title covering the series of magazines which appeared under the following titles: Our Players Gallery, Vol. I, Nos. 1-2; The Theatre, through the July, 1917 issue; and Theatre Magazine from August, 1917 until publication was suspended.

2. Blanche M. Ganahl, "The Commercial Theatre Magazine in the United States from 1900 to 1958" (unpublished Master's thesis, Southern Illinois University, 1959.

3. Sophie K. Hiss, A.L.A. Rules for Filing Catalog Cards (Chicago: American Library Association, 1942).

4. Burns Mantle and Garrison P. Sherwood, The Best Plays of [various years] (New York: Dodd, Mead and Co.).

5. William Wolf Melnitz, Theatre Arts Publications in the United States, 1945-1952 (AETA Monograph, no. 1; Dubuque: Brown, c. 1959); David Welker, Educational Theatre Journal, a Ten-Year Index: 1949-1958 (Michigan: AETA, [n.d.]).

Issue Numbering Code

The table below lists the issue numbers used throughout this index, together with the month and year of the appearance of each issue and the volume number in which the issues are customarily bound.

No.	Date	Vol.	No.	Date	Vol.
PG	'01	I	39	MAY,'04	IV
3	MAY,'01	I	40	JUN, '04	IV
4	JUN, '01	I	41	JUL, '04	IV
5	JUL, '01	I	42	AUG, '04	IV
6	AUG, '01	I	43	SEP, '04	IV
7	SEP, '01	I	44	OCT, '04	IV
8	OCT, '01	I	45	NOV, '04	IV
9	NOV, '01	I	46	DEC, '04	IV
10	DEC, '01	I	47	JAN, '05	V
11	JAN, '02	II	48	FEB, '05	V
12	FEB, '02	II	49	MAR,'05	V
13	MAR,'02	II	50	APR, '05	V
14	APR, '02	II	51	MAY,'05	V
15	MAY,'02	II	52	JUN, '05	V
16	JUN, '02	II	53	JUL, '05	V
17	JUL, '02	II	54	AUG, '05	V
18	AUG, '02	II	55	SEP, '05	V
19	SEP, '02	II	56	OCT, '05	V
20	OCT, '02	II	57	NOV, '05	V
21	NOV, '02	II	58	DEC, '05	V
22	DEC, '02	II	59	JAN, '06	VI
23	JAN, '03	III	60	FEB, '06	VI
24	FEB, '03	III	61	MAR,'06	VI
25	MAR,'03	III	62	APR, '06	VI
26	APR, '03	III	63	MAY,'06	VI
27	MAY,'03	III	64	JUN, '06	VI
28	JUN, '03	III	65	JUL, '06	VI
29	JUL, '03	III	66	AUG, '06	VI
30	AUG, '03	III	67	SEP, '06	VI
31	SEP, '03	III	68	OCT, '06	VI
32	OCT, '03	III	69	NOV, '06	VI
33	NOV, '03	III	70	DEC, '06	VI
34	DEC, '03	III	71	JAN, '07	VII
35	JAN, '04	IV	72	FEB, '07	VII
36	FEB, '04	IV	73	MAR,'07	VII
37	MAR,'04	IV	74	APR, '07	VII
38	APR, '04	IV	75	MAY,'07	VII

No.	Date	Vol.	No.	Date	Vol.
76	JUN, '07	VII	128	OCT, '11	XIV
77	JUL, '07	VII	129	NOV, '11	XIV
78	AUG, '07	VII	130	DEC, '11	XIV
79	SEP, '07	VII	131	JAN, '12	XV
80	OCT, '07	VII	132	FEB, '12	XV
81	NOV, '07	VII	133	MAR, '12	XV
82	DEC, '07	VII	134	APR, '12	XV
83	JAN, '08	VIII	135	MAY, '12	XV
84	FEB, '08	VIII	136	JUN, '12	XV
85	MAR, '08	VIII	137	JUL, '12	XVI
86	APR, '08	VIII	138	AUG, '12	XVI
87	MAY, '08	VIII	139	SEP, '12	XVI
88	JUN, '08	VIII	140	OCT, '12	XVI
89	JUL, '08	VIII	141	NOV, '12	XVI
90	AUG, '08	VIII	142	DEC, '12	XVI
91	SEP, '08	VIII	143	JAN, '13	XVII
92	OCT, '08	VIII	144	FEB, '13	XVII
93	NOV, '08	VIII	145	MAR, '13	XVII
94	DEC, '08	VIII	146	APR, '13	XVII
95	JAN, '09	IX	147	MAY, '13	XVII
96	FEB, '09	IX	148	JUN, '13	XVII
97	MAR, '09	IX	149	JUL, '13	XVIII
98	APR, '09	IX	150	AUG, '13	XVIII
99	MAY, '09	IX	151	SEP, '13	XVIII
100	JUN, '09	IX	152	OCT, '13	XVIII
101	JUL, '09	X	153	NOV, '13	XVIII
102	AUG, '09	X	154	DEC, '13	XVIII
103	SEP, '09	X	155	JAN, '14	XIX
104	OCT, '09	X	156	FEB, '14	XIX
105	NOV, '09	X	157	MAR, '14	XIX
106	DEC, '09	X	158	APR, '14	XIX
107	JAN, '10	XI	159	MAY, '14	XIX
108	FEB, '10	XI	160	JUN, '14	XIX
109	MAR, '10	XI	161	JUL, '14	XX
110	APR, '10	XI	162	AUG, '14	XX
111	MAY, '10	XI	163	SEP, '14	XX
112	JUN, '10	XI	164	OCT, '14	XX
113	JUL, '10	XII	165	NOV, '14	XX
114	AUG, '10	XII	166	DEC, '14	XX
115	SEP, '10	XII	167	JAN, '15	XXI
116	OCT, '10	XII	168	FEB, '15	XXI
117	NOV, '10	XII	169	MAR, '15	XXI
118	DEC, '10	XII	170	APR, '15	XXI
119	JAN, '11	XIII	171	MAY, '15	XXI
120	FEB, '11	XIII	172	JUN, '15	XXI
121	MAR, '11	XIII	173	JUL, '15	XXII
122	APR, '11	XIII	174	AUG, '15	XXII
123	MAY, '11	XIII	175	SEP, '15	XXII
124	JUN, '11	XIII	176	OCT, '15	XXII
125	JUL, '11	XIV	177	NOV, '15	XXII
126	AUG, '11	XIV	178	DEC, '15	XXII
127	SEP, '11	XIV	179	JAN, '16	XXIII

No.	Date	Vol.
180	FEB, '16	XXIII
181	MAR,'16	XXIII
182	APR, '16	XXIII
183	MAY,'16	XXIII
184	JUN, '16	XXIII
185	JUL, '16	XXIV
186	AUG, '16	XXIV
187	SEP, '16	XXIV
188	OCT, '16	XXIV
189	NOV, '16	XXIV
190	DEC, '16	XXIV
191	JAN, '17	XXV
192	FEB, '17	XXV
193	MAR,'17	XXV
194	APR, '17	XXV
195	MAY,'17	XXV
196	JUN, '17	XXV
197	JUL, '17	XXVI
198	AUG, '17	XXVI
199	SEP, '17	XXVI
200	OCT, '17	XXVI
201	NOV, '17	XXVI
202	DEC, '17	XXVI
203	JAN, '18	XXVII
204	FEB, '18	XXVII
205	MAR,'18	XXVII
206	APR, '18	XXVII
207	MAY,'18	XXVII
208	JUN, '18	XXVII
209	JUL, '18	XXVIII
210	AUG, '18	XXVIII
211	SEP, '18	XXVIII
212	OCT, '18	XXVIII
213	NOV, '18	XXVIII
214	DEC, '18	XXVIII
215	JAN, '19	XXIX
216	FEB, '19	XXIX
217	MAR,'19	XXIX
218	APR, '19	XXIX
219	MAY,'19	XXIX
220	JUN, '19	XXIX
221	JUL, '19	XXX
222	AUG, '19	XXX
223	SEP, '19	XXX
224	OCT, '19	XXX
225	NOV, '19	XXX
226	DEC, '19	XXX
227	JAN, '20	XXXI
228	FEB, '20	XXXI
229	MAR,'20	XXXI
230	APR, '20	XXXI
231	MAY,'20	XXXI

No.	Date	Vol.
232	JUN, '20	XXXI
233	MIDSUM'R,'20	XXXII
234	SEP, '20	XXXII
235	OCT, '20	XXXII
236	NOV, '20	XXXII
237	DEC, '20	XXXII
238	JAN, '21	XXXIII
239	FEB, '21	XXXIII
240	MAR,'21	XXXIII
241	APR, '21	XXXIII
242	MAY,'21	XXXIII
243	JUN, '21	XXXIII
244	JUL, '21	XXXIV
245	AUG, '21	XXXIV
246	SEP, '21	XXXIV
247	OCT, '21	XXXIV
248	NOV, '21	XXXIV
249	DEC, '21	XXXIV
250	JAN, '22	XXXV
251	FEB, '22	XXXV
252	MAR,'22	XXXV
253	APR, '22	XXXV
254	MAY,'22	XXXV
255	JUN, '22	XXXV
256	JUL, '22	XXXVI
257	AUG, '22	XXXVI
258	SEP, '22	XXXVI
259	OCT, '22	XXXVI
260	NOV, '22	XXXVI
261	DEC, '22	XXXVI
262	JAN, '23	XXXVII
263	FEB, '23	XXXVII
264	MAR,'23	XXXVII
265	APR, '23	XXXVII
266	MAY,'23	XXXVII
267	JUN, '23	XXXVII
268	JUL, '23	XXXVIII
269	AUG, '23	XXXVIII
270	SEP, '23	XXXVIII
271	OCT, '23	XXXVIII
272	NOV, '23	XXXVIII
273	DEC, '23	XXXVIII
274	JAN, '24	XXXIX
275	FEB, '24	XXXIX
276	MAR,'24	XXXIX
277	APR, '24	XXXIX
278	MAY,'24	XXXIX
279	JUN, '24	XXXIX
280	JUL, '24	XL
281	AUG, '24	XL
282	SEP, '24	XL
283	OCT, '24	XL

No.	Date	Vol.	No.	Date	Vol.
284	NOV, '24	XL	322	JAN, '28	XLVII
285	DEC, '24	XL	323	FEB, '28	XLVII
286	JAN, '25	XLI	324	MAR, '28	XLVII
287	FEB, '25	XLI	325	APR, '28	XLVII
288	MAR, '25	XLI	326	MAY, '28	XLVII
289	APR, '25	XLI	327	JUN, '28	XLVII
290	MAY, '25	XLI	328	JUL, '28	XLVIII
291	JUN, '25	XLI	329	AUG, '28	XLVIII
292	JUL, '25	XLII	330	SEP, '28	XLVIII
293	AUG, '25	XLII	331	OCT, '28	XLVIII
294	SEP, '25	XLII	332	NOV, '28	XLVIII
295	OCT, '25	XLII	333	DEC, '28	XLVIII
296	NOV, '25	XLII	334	JAN, '29	XLIX
297	DEC, '25	XLII	335	FEB, '29	XLIX
298	JAN, '26	XLIII	336	MAR, '29	XLIX
299	FEB, '26	XLIII	337	APR, '29	XLIX
300	MAR, '26	XLIII	338	MAY, '29	XLIX
301	APR, '26	XLIII	339	JUN, '29	XLIX
302	MAY, '26	XLIII	340	JUL, '29	L
303	JUN, '26	XLIII	341	AUG, '29	L
304	JUL, '26	XLIV	342	SEP, '29	L
305	AUG, '26	XLIV	343	OCT, '29	L
306	SEP, '26	XLIV	344	NOV, '29	L
307	OCT, '26	XLIV	345	DEC, '29	L
308	NOV, '26	XLIV	346	JAN, '30	LI
309	DEC, '26	XLIV	347	FEB, '30	LI
310	JAN, '27	XLV	348	MAR, '30	LI
311	FEB, '27	XLV	349	APR, '30	LI
312	MAR, '27	XLV	350	MAY, '30	LI
313	APR, '27	XLV	351	JUN, '30	LI
314	MAY, '27	XLV	352	JUL, '30	LII
315	JUN, '27	XLV	353	AUG, '30	LII
316	JUL, '27	XLVI	354	SEP, '30	LII
317	AUG, '27	XLVI	355	OCT, '30	LII
318	SEP, '27	XLVI	356	NOV, '30	LII
319	OCT, '27	XLVI	357	DEC, '30	LII
320	NOV, '27	XLVI	358	JAN, '31	LIII
321	DEC, '27	XLVI	359	FEB, '31	LIII
			360	MAR, '31	LIII
			361	APR, '31	LIII

Selective Index

--A--

"A La Carte": (R'27) 319,23.
Aarons, Alex: 291,36; 361,31.
Abales, Edward: 20,3.
"Abagail": (R'05) 50,81; 50,103.
Abarbanell, Lina: 69,296; 83,vi; 89,196; 90,207; 112,179; 112,180; 115,94; 117,154; 139,91; 144,38; 147,133; 160,317; 189,280; 219,281; 250,25.
Abbe, Charles: 96,69; 179,8.
Abbe, James: 290,49.
Abbey, Beatrice: 40,147.
Abbey, Henry E.: 78,215; 168, 75.
Abbey Theatre (see Irish Players).
Abbott, Charles: 24,33.
Abbott, George: 288,27; 289,14; 310,33; 328,29; 333,49; (W) 338,42.
Abbott, Marion: 44,252; 65,189; 114,34.
Abbott, Muriel: 259,214.
Abbott, Ruth: 345,47.
"Abduction from the Seraglio, The" (OP): 315,25.
Abdullah, Achmed: (W) 326,9.
"Abe and Mawruss": 178,299; (R'15) 178,320.
Abel, Walter: 277,18; 289,39; 297,19.
Abeles, Edward: 39,121; 48,33; 56,247; 72,30; 74,92; 93, 295; 205,143.
Abell-Brinker, UNA: 42,204.
"Abie's Irish Rose": (R'22) 257, 95; 280,18; 291,10; 306,7; 316,7; 316,8.
"Abigail": (R'18) 206,219.
Abingdon, William: 61,56.
Abington, Frances: 32,261.
Aborn, Milton: 152,131; 265,213; 294,63.
Aborn, Sargent: 165,212.
Aborn Opera Co.: 83,xiv; 136,xi.
Abott, Bessie: 57,282; 61,77; 70,342; 82,350; 106,176; 114, 58; 116,109; 139,83; 145,80; 153,157; 156,77; 161,19.
"About Town": (R'06) 68,xiii.
"Abraham and Isaac": 196,333.
"Abraham Lincoln": 225,310; 227,7; (R'19) 228,97; 243, 394; (F) 356,47.
Abramowitz, Bina: 265,14.
Abthorpe, Ray: (W) 222,102.
"Abyssinia": (R'06) 62,xiv.
Academy of Music (Berlin): 46, 301.
Academy of Music (New York): 59,16; 99,146.
Academy Theatre (Chicago): 116,122.
"Accused": (R'25) 297,16.
Achron, Isidor: (C) 325,43.
Acker, Edward (W): 130,208; 138,36.
Acker, Mabel: 164,163; 174,67.
Ackerman, Jean: 320,61; 327, 47; 340,7.
Ackte, Aino: 30,183; 30,208.
Acord, Art: 305,46.
"Acquittal, The": (R'20) 228, 101; 228,103.
"Across the Border": 167,9; (R'14) 167,44; 168,78.
Acting Technique (see also "Actor in the Street, The"): 8,17; 10,12; 10,13; 11,12; 14,19; 16,9; 46,303; 54,196; 63,116; 70,324; 70,330; 85,70; 85,70; 109,71; 149,25; 151,86; 160, 306; 173,25; 181,145; 194, 160; 195,283; 198,74; 199, 128; 211,146; 221,10; 221,18; 222,88; 232,516; 255,368; 296,12; 311,24; 325,32; 335, 22; 337,15; 350,36.
"Actor in the Street, The" by W.P. Dodge:

George Arliss: 106,199.
George M. Cohan: 120,60.
Arnold Daly: 94,326.
Henry E. Dixey: 98,114.
J.E. Dodson: 101,20.
Lew Fields: 89,178.
Wilton Lackaye: 96,49.
Ermete Novelli: 92,271.
James T. Powers: 100,182.
Otis Skinner: 88,156.
Actors' and Authors' Theatre, The: 208,348; 209,22; 209,24.
Actors' Church Alliance of America: 48,48.
Actors, Conditions of (see also Actors Equity Association; "Confessions of a Stage Struck Girl"; Salaries; Stock; Touring): 18,10; 22,18; 89,186; 90, 202; 94,325; 106,180; 157, 128; 158,192; 161,43; 176, 174; 178,290; 205,168; 222, 90; 223,6; 227,34; 246,142; 253,216; 276,24; 295,30; 298, 10; 314,10; 323,32; 348,15; 358,18.
Actors, Conditions of--Film: 158,186.
Actors' Corner (Cohasset): 105, 162.
Actors Equity Association: 223, 172; 224,216; 224,221; 225, 296; 228,96; 232,573; 244, 34; 245,76; 248,296; 251,102; 253,210; 253,214; 254,70; 263,25; 278,7; 281,43; 342,34.
Actors' Fund: 41,163; 54,vii; 54, 186; 74,xv.
Actors' Fund Fair: 75,118; 76, xviii; 109,72; 111,iv; 137,10; 183,294; 193,183; 196,359; 219,281; 225,296; 309,7; 333, 30; 353,74.
Actors' Homes: 35,14; 105,162; 114,52; 191,42; 196,359; 222, 92; 333,30; 361,45.
Actors' Theatre: 294,7.
Adair, Alice: 320,54.
Adair, Janet: 240,165.
Adair, Jean: 334,34.
Adair, Josephine: 242,332.
Adair, Ronald: 249,395.
Adaire, Anne: 79,233.
"Adam and Eva": (R'19) 225,344; 226,375.
Adams, Annie: 58,301.
Adams, Edwin: 17,19; 111,163.
Adams, Isabel: 235,182.
Adams, J.K.: 22,20; 132,48.
Adams, John Quincy: 139,94.
Adams, Justin: 19,7.
Adams, Lionel: 69,301.
Adams, Maude: PG,11; PG,27; PG,28; 5,12; 7,11; 8,3; 9,3; 10,c; 10,1; 10,2; 11,14; 29, 174; 31,218; (D) 34,298; 34, 306; 35,17; 48,c; 49,55; 50, 93; 51,105; 54,200; 54,201; 58,288; 28,289; 28,301; 60,c; 64,164; 68,267; 73,63; 77,xi; 79,228; 84,ix; 94,33; 84,43; 84,58; 86,c; 90,205; 90,206; 90,219; 95,17; 96,38; 97,xxvi; 97,xxviii; 97,88; 98,118; 100, xiii; 101,c; 101,8; 101,9; 101,10; 101,33; 102,iii; 102, 38; 106,185; 113,1; 113,2; 113,24; 115,66; 121,69; 121,81; 121,90; 125,19; 127,77; 139, 66; 141,146; 142,199; 144,vi; 145,75; 151,78; 154,189; 156, 58; (D) 157,c; (D) 157,125; 163,98; 168,75; 170,173; 170, 191; (A) 173,31; 175,108; 176, 176; 178,288; 181,141; 186,73; 187,127; 192,86; 192,89; 193, 155; 195,283; 198,80; 199,137; 206,235; 216,84; 221,36; 231, 348; 231,349; 231,383; 234,81; 237,356; 275,32; 286,19; 287, 26; 290,12; 336,40; 354,29;
Adams, Suzanne: 10,33.
Adams, William P.: (W) 210,76.
Adamson, Robert: (W) 187,146.
"Adam's Rib": (F,R) 266,72.
Adamy, Daisy: 172,300.
Adaptations (see also Playwriting): 345,23; 361,42.
Ade, George: 24,34 (W) 28,145; 31,235; 35,7; 45,271; 45,287; 46,322; 48,34; 55,227; 56,xiv; 56,242; 57,267; 61,lb; 82,xviii; 97,xiii; 106,186; 118,196; 123, 173; 124,xi; 274,32; (W) 317,5.
Adelaide (See also Adelaide and Hughes): 271,35; 287,37.
Adelaide and Hughes: 177,229; 178,301; 183,286; 202,365;

219,365.
"Adele": (R'13) 152,xi; 152,117; 152,127; 166,283.
Adelphi Theatre (Philadelphia): 81,iv; 82,xiv.
Addams, Jane (see Hull House Players).
"Adding Machine, The": (R'23) 266,19; (S) 267,30; 347,50.
Addison, Victoria: 37,62.
Adkins, Morton: 152,132.
Adleman, Rose (W): 328,15; 353,21; 359,15.
Adler, Adeline: PG,16.
Adler, Celia: 237,352; 251,91.
Adler, Else: 178,278; 196, 349; 198,78; 244,9.
Adler, Jacob: 9,8; 11,17; 21,18; 23,8; 29,160; 29,169; 44,249; 52,137; 168,81.
Adler, Lola: 262,20.
"Admirable Crichton, The": (R'02) 22,12; 27,110; 361,16.
Adolf Philipp Theatre (New York): 115,20.
"Adorable Liar, The": 307,27; (R'26) 308,16.
Adoree, Renee: 225,306; 230, 281; 294,33; 300,43; 311, 35; 313,49; 323,16; 324,34.
"Adrea": (R'05) 48, 28; 49,70; (C) 51,126; 51,127.
"Adrienne": (R'23) 269,16.
"Adrienne Lecouvreur": 54,ix; 75,124.
"Adrift in the Roaring Forties" by B. de Casseres: 255, 370; 259,236; 260,306; 261, 366.
Advance Men: 55,234.
"Adventure": (F,R) 292,32.
"Adventure of Lady Ursula, The": 170,170 (R'15) 170,172.
Advertising (see also Pressagentry): 260,359.
"Advertising of Kate, The": (R'22) 256,30.
Adye, Oscar: 103,72.
Aerial Gardens (New York): 41, 160; 53,158.
"Aero Club, The": 73,60; (R'07) 73,62.
"Affairs of Anatol, The": (R-12) 141,ix; (R'31) 360,24; 141,131.
"Affaires Sont Les Affaires, Les" (see also "Business Is Business"): 37,72.
"Affinity, The": 108,34.
"Afgar": 238,11; (R'20) 238,74.
"After Dark": (R'28) 335,51; 354, 44.
"After Five": (R'13) 154,xviii.
"Agamemnon": 65,173.
Agents: 53,163; 152,126.
"Age of Innocence, The": (R'28) 335,78; 340,15.
"Age of Reason, The": (R'16) 183,277; 183,283.
"Agnes": (R'18) 94,xv.
Agnew, Beatrice: 60,37; 60,42; 98,119.
Agoust, Emile: 136,179.
Aguglia [-Ferrau], Mini: (C) 86,96; 95,xiv; 95,4; 156,104; 170,194; 192,394; 246,153; 228,96.
Aguilar Lute Quartet: (D) 343,51.
"Ah Sin": 296,70.
Ahearn, John: 208,359.
Aherne, Brian: 361,34.
Ahlberg, Irene: 353,29.
Ahren, Nils: 268,38.
Ahrendt, Carl: 70,319.
"Aida" (OP): 136,177; (R'13) 152,131.
Ainley, Henry: 35,17; 43,220; 270,12; 282,13.
Ainsworth, Grace: 51,viii.
Ainsworth Sydney: 49,59; 80,279; 105,147.
Aitken, Spottiswoode: 118,199.
"Adjax": (R'04) 39,123.
Akins, Zoe: (W,V) 111,148; 246, 167; 251,76.
"Alabama": 71,10.
Alabama Theatre: 299,40; 322,53.
Aladjalov, Constantain (D) 315, 27.
"Aladdin and the Wonderful Lamp": (F,R) 201,316.
"Alaskan, The": (R'07) 79,230; 79,233; 80,280.
Albaugh, J.W., Jr.: 20,11; 38,88; 61,65.
Albee, E.F.: 162,72; 222,126; (W) 231,408; 231,485; 250, 36; 252,187; 275,36; 277,36;

288,58.
Albee Theatre (Brooklyn):296,50.
Alberni, Luis: 284,14.
Alberti, Fleeda: 334,43.
Albertson, Arthur: 247,231.
Albertson, Lillian: 86,105; 87, 130; 97,94; 132,45; 177,230; 177,242; 180,68; 249,375.
Albin, Charles: 290,49.
Albright, Claude: 37,iv.
Alcazar Theatre (San Francisco): 138,51; 334,31.
Alcock, Merle: 279,35.
Alda, De Lyle: 276,37.
Alda, Frances: 93,308; 97,76; 107,10; 110,106; 114,57;121, 83; 141,140; 146,106; 153, 148; 157,116; 159,229;167,17; 180,89; (A) 180,111; 181,127; 190,345; 192,94; 198,78; 286, 35; 298,35.
Alden, Hortense: 245,80;353,35; 359,35.
Alden, Mary: 169,116.
Alder, Else: 196,363.
Alderman, James: 279,14.
Alderson, Erville: 138,53; 168, 61.
Aldrich, Mariska: 93,308.
Aldrich, Mildred (W): 57,280; 58,311.
Aldrich, Richard (W): 231,366.
Aldridge, Arthur: 125,13; 137, 3.
Aldridge, Ira: 202,356.
Alessandro, Jose: 275,24.
Alexander, Benjamin: 33,288.
Alexander, Eleanor: 86,iii.
Alexander, George: (W) 54,198; 62,ii.
Alexander, John W.: 101,10; 122,113.
Alexander, [Mrs.] John W.: 196, 339.
Alexander, Katherine: 221,35; 295,19; 201,52b; 310,27; 324,33; 326,29; 337,11; 352, 17; 356,23; 359,28.
Alexander, Louise: 95,4.
Alexandresco: 280,30.
Alexandroviez, Marie: 120,62.
"Algeria" (see also "Rose of Algeria, The"): (R'08) 92, xxiv; 92,263.
Ali, Sie Hassan Ben: 135,168.
"Alias Jimmy Valentine": (R'10) 108,41; 109,vii; 131,23; 231, 351; (R'21) 251,99.
"Alias the Deacon": 301,27; (R'26) 301,72.
"Alice in Wonderland": 171,231.
"Alice of Old Vincennes": (R'01) 11,6; 11,7.
"Alice Sit-By-The-Fire": (R'05) 60,31; 60,37; 60,43; 95,24.
"Alien, The": 173,7.
Alison, George; 249,376.
"Alison's House": (R'30) 359,25.
"All Aboard": (R'13) 149,xx.
"All Dressed Up": (R'25) 296,16.
"All for a Girl": (R'08) 92,260; 92,277.
"All for the Ladies": 144,iii; (R'12) 144,xii.
"All For You": 298,38.
"All God's Children Got Wings": (R'24) 280,15.
"All-Of-A-Sudden Peggy": (R'07) 73,xvi; 74,62.
"All Over Town": 174,63.
"All Quiet on the Western Front": (F,R) 352,44.
"All Soul's Eve": (R'20) 232,526.
Allan, Mabel: 199,129.
Allan, Maud: 191,39.
Allan Sisters [Betty & Dorothy]: 218,211.
"Allegiance": 211,131; (R'18) 211,143; 212,226.
Allen, A. Hylton: 106,181; 131, 30; 141,134.
Allen, Amelia: 270,21.
Allen, Arthur: 221,35.
Allen, Beatrice: 151,88; 162, 72; 174,63; 177,242; 201, 289; 215,35.
Allen, Billie: 216,85.
Allen, Diana: 207,303; 231,412.
Allen, Fred: 279,14; 281,17; 336,52; (W) 340,31; 341,34; 357,33.
Allen, Joanna: 353,28.
Allen, Joseph: 90,222; 153,156; 153,161; (D) 352,4.
Allen, Kelcey: (C) 335,43.
Allen, [C] Leslie: 48,41; 58, 301; 62,93; 70,337; (W) 210, 88; (C) 318,25.

Allen, Lewis (W): 178,287; 179,20; (V) 190,341; 204, 96; 205,164; 207,276; 209, 32.
Allen, Lillian: 183,278.
Allen, Louise: 32,243; 216,76; 235,179.
Allen, Marie: 76,150.
Allen, Marsh: 238,7.
Allen, Martha Bryan: 252,164; 254,291; 258,139; 272,27; 294,19; 300,25.
Allen, Maud: 88,164; 91,235; 98, 130; 109,87; 127,93; 127, 96.
Allen, Robert: 360,46.
Allen, Vera: 330,26.
Allen, Very: 294,21.
Allen, Viola: PG,18;PG,19;PG, 30; 8,19; 8,20; 10,11; 10, 12; 11,c; 15,2; 17,1; 17,2; 20,6; 22,7; (W) 22,32; 24, 44; 32,237; 34,c; 34,292; 34, 207; 37,56; 41,175; 44,239; 45,266; 48,29; 48,41; 55,229; 58,301; 58,314; 59,15; (W) 62,93; 67,245; 69,281; (W) 70,322; 70,337; 85,63; 89,i; 90,205; 90,206; 90,213; 91, 236; 98,105; 105,164; 113, 17; 127,76; 139,67; 141,129; 142,200; 146,115; 167,10; 177,239; 280,62; (A) 182,222; 183,276; 221,9; 236,276; 290, 12.
Allen, Walter: 12,10.
Allen, Winifred: 202,405.
"Allez-Oop": (R'27) 319,23.
Allgood, Sara: 129,157; 131,11; 146,108; 146,110.
Allison, May: 162,60; 163,106; 207,333; 212,257; 216,123; 222,114; 231,409; 231,496; 288,46.
"Alloy": (R'24) 286,20.
"Alma, Where Do You Live?": 117,159.
"Almanac--1880-1930, John Murray Anderson's": (C) 343, 40; (R'30) 343,42.
"Aloma of the South Seas": (R'25) 292,15.
"Alone at Last": (R'15) 178,320.
"Along Came Ruth": 158,172; 158,211.
Alsop, Martin C.: 38,88.
Alsop, Martin L.: 153,161.
Alt, Natalie: 152,117; 152,127; 176,170; 184,373; 190,390.
"Alt Heidelberg": (R'03) 23,8, 24,36.
Alta, Gladys: 335,46.
Alten, Bella: 59,25; 129,155; 133,78; 136,173; 159,228.
Alter, Lottie: 24,32.
"Alter of Friendship, The": (R'03) 23,6; 23,7.
Althouse, Paul: 141,140; 147, 140; 157,116; 338,43.
"Altruism": (R'16) 191,21; 191,29.
Alviene School of Stage Arts: 128, xv.
"Always You": (R'20) 299,184.
Amateur Comedy Club (New York): 14,26; 194,228; 198,88.
"Amateur Cracksman, The": 33,265.
<u>Amateur Nights</u>: 295,24; (D) 295,25.
<u>Amateur Theatre</u> (<u>see also Little Theatre</u>): 207,334; 211,124 <u>and monthly thereafter</u>; (C) 272,8.
Amato, Pasquale: 94,344; 129, 155; 142,166; 146,106; 155, 14; 156,66; 168,65; 169,118; 170,183; 178,285; 180,89; 184,351; 190,345; (A) 214, 379.
"Amazons, The": (R'13) 148,162; 148,163.
Ambassador Theatre (New York): 242,345.
Ambassador Theatre (Wash., D.C.): 294,56.
"Amber Express, The": (R'16) 189,281.
Amberg, Gustav: 188,191.
"Ambitious Mrs. Alcott, The": (R'07) 75,xx; 75,116.
"Ambush": (R'21) 249,426; (S) 254,292.
"America": (R-13) 152,xiv;152,129; (F) 276,33; (F,R) 278,30; 278,31.
American Academy of Dramatic Arts: 47,ix; 60,i; 66,viii; 70,xxix; 75,xxiv; 86,viii; 87,iii; 87xv; 98,xiii;98,117;

110,xiii; 134,xvi; 145,xvi; 147,xx; 170,211; 182,187; 192,126; 193,188; 207,288.
"American Age, An": (R'18) 207, 288.
American Drama (see also Playwriting): 31,214; 193,135; 236,254; 291,12.
"American Dramatist, The" (Moses) (B): 133,xxvi.
American Dramatists Club: 123, 146.
American Federation of Musicians: 353,57; 358,63.
"American Idea, The": (R'08) 93,xi.
"American Invasion, An": (R'02) 22,14.
American Laboratory Theatre: 300,22; 300,23; 319,41.
"American Lord, The": (R'05) 64,143; 67,v.
"American Maid, The": (R'13) 146,xv; 146,99.
American Playgoer's Society: 62,xx.
"American Playwright, The": (magazine) 135,xi.
American Society of Dramatists and Composers: 123,146.
"American Stage of To-Day, The" (Eaton) (B): 101,vii.
"American Tragedy, An": (R'26) 309,15; 309,29; 350,31.
"American Widow, An": (R'09) 104,xii; 104,102.
"Americana": (R'26) 307,14; 307,15.
"Americans in France, The": (R'20) 235,185.
"America's Answer": (F,R) 211,183.
"America's Greatest Players" by Alfred Ayers
1. Edwin Forrest: 10,21.
2. Charlotte Cushman: 11,19.
3. Edwin Booth: 12,19.
4. James E. Murdoch, John McCullough, and Cecilia Rush: 13,22.
5. Charlotte Crabtree, Charles Fechter, James H. Hackett, and Lawrence Barrett: 14,21.
6. J.E. Owens, J.W. Wallack Jr., and Mrs. D.P. Bowers: 15,24.
7. E.L. Davenport, John Gilbert, and James Booth Roberts: 16,13.
8. Edwin Adams, Frank Mayo, and Junius Brutus Booth: 17, 19.
"America's Sweetheart": (R'31) 361,25; (C) 361,27.
Amero, Emilio: (D) 304,17; (D) 306,11.
Ames, Amy: 113,10.
Ames, Florenz: 286,18.
Ames, Joseph B.: (W) 58,300.
Ames, Percy F.: 59,10; 121,74; 133,85; 288,38.
Ames, Robert: 244,22; 250,16; 266,32; 243,398.
Ames, Winthrop (see also New Theatre [New York]): 102, 58; 105,145; 108,vi; 120,38; 128,xv; 133,77; 146,122; 147, 136; 154,xxix; 154,175; 161, 11; 163,99; 165,255; 167,34; 168,102; (W) 185,2; 199,122; 208,346; 208,347; 215;17; (A) 231,346; 264,13; 303,6; 319, 14; 323,44; (W) 331,17.
"Among Those Present": (R'02) 22,8.
"Amorous Antic, The": (R'29) 346, 49.
Amos and Andy: (D) 353,9.
Amos, Ruth: 335,46.
Amsden, Elizabeth: 154,183.
Amusement Parks (see also Coney Island): 101,18.
"Analysis of Play Construction and Dramatic Principle, The" (Price) (B): 93,iii.
Ananian, Paolo: 159,228.
"Anatol": (S) 140,106.
"Ancient Mariner, The": (R'24) 279,19.
Ancona, Mario: 71,9; 75,140; 83, 11.
"And So To Bed": 309,22; (R'27) 322,38.
Ander, Charlotte: 298,23.
Anders, Glenn: 226,371; 263,24; 271,13; (D) 277,38; 285,14; 288,18; 288,27; 293,28; 311, 19; 312,29; 325,40; 337,43;

356,17; 359,24.
Andersen, Robert: 217,187.
Anderson, Bronco Billy (G.W.): 184,356.
Anderson, Charlotte: 120,44.
Anderson, Dallas: 114,54; 335, 23.
Anderson, George: 187,147; 313,19.
Anderson, John; 196,347; (D,W) 306,10; (W) 316,28; (W) 317,14; (W) 320,44; (C) 333, 33; (W) 346,21; (W) 348,18; (W) 349,19; (W) 350,24; (W) 357,47; (W) 361,15.
Anderson, John Murray (see also "Almanac"; "Greenwich Village Follies"): 192,78; 216, 85; 229,182; 235,181; 237, 374; 247,215; 294,7; (W) 335,17; 343,40.
Anderson, Judith: 280,21; (W) 283,22; 283,26; 283,63; 288,13; 290,15; 291,39; 306,46; 324,58; 325,29; 330,41; 331,68; 360,29; 294,25.
Anderson, Mary: 34,298f; 50, 92; 57,286; 68,x; 68,280b; 71,24; 90,208; 97,90; 116, 113; 130,194; 138,45; 142, 199; 153,167; 168,75; 179, 22; 182,192; 182,225; 241, 260.
Anderson, Maxwell: 285,28; (C) 339,39.
Anderson, P.A.: 132,46; 132,48.
Anderson, Sherwood: (W) 330,13.
"Andre Charlot's Revue of 1924": (R) 276,16; 276,18.
Andrews, A.G.: 86,103; 108,38; 154,176; 191,25.
Andrews, Ann: 195,273; 205,153; 205,167; 226,379; 232,544; 237,354; 242,356; 309,44; 310,27; 324,29; 325,57; 332, 55; 337,57; (D) 240,c.
Andrews, Carlton (W): (V) 125,34; 137,32; 149,20; 182, 206; 186,84; 187,154; 191,27; 192,102; 193,154; 195,268; 198,76; 205,144; 206,212; 207,304; 208,372; 212,204; 213,288; 215,36; 221,28; 228,88; 235,177.
Andrews, Frank: 145,73; 319, 23.
Andrews, Lyle D.: 299,22.
Andrews, Talleur: 44,246.
Andreyev, Leonid: 171,259; 181, 163; 193,149.
"Androcles and the Lion": 154, xxvi; (R'15) 169,110; (R'25) 299,16; 299,17.
Andrus, Albert: 237,357.
<u>Anecdotes, Stage</u>: (see also "Anecdotes of the Stage"): 80,viii; 302,38; 314,32.
"Anecdotes of the Stage": 139, 94; 141,136; 150,52.
"Anethema": 265,14.
"Angel in the House, The": (R'15) 178,324.
Angeles, Aimee: 53,176; 56,viii.
Angelini-Gattini Opera Co. (Milan): 148,xi.
<u>Angels</u>: 124,195; 191,10; 228,92; 284,22; 326,14; 359,37.
"Angels on Earth": (D) 350,56.
Anger, Lou: 113,25.
Anglin, Margaret: 3,2; 3,3; 4,3; 12,12; 13,3; 14,c; 14,1; 14,2; 14,12; 24,29; 26,79, 39,108; 46,294; 48,49; 56,255; 57,269; 58,314; 59,c; 66,217; 67,245; 69,285; 69,298; 71,13; 71,28; 75,118; 78,iii; 78,208; 79, 228; 87,133; 90,206; 90,220; 99,163; 103,79; 105,150; 105, 151;114,xx; 114,48; 115,87; 122,131; 124,201; 125,20; 127,76; 129,148; 129,171; 133,88; 134,135; 138,62; 141, 132; 142,198; 145,75; 149,25; 150,70; 151,78; 152,133; 158, 169; 159,224; 159,225; 159, 260; 160,290; 160,324; 161,6; 161,16; 167,10; 171,247; 172, 281; 172,287; 175,116; (A) 182,222; 184,334; 184,340; 189,273; (W) 190,352; 190, 353; 204,73; 205,132; 205, 152; 206,211; 206,217; (A) 214,379; 228,87; 231,383; 236, 255; 237,364; 243,415; 270,16; 273,12; 317,29; 325,39; (D) 330,57; 336,21; 242,315.
Anglin, Winifred: 241,257.

"Animal Crackers": (F,R) 356,47.
Animation (see Cartoons, Animated).
"Ann Boyd": 125,32; (R'13) 147, xiv.
"Anna Ascends": (R'20) 237, 370.
"Anna Christie": (R'21) 250,29; (D) 250,33; 252,162; (S) 253,220; (F,R) 275,32; 289,20.
"Anna Karenina": (R'05) 51,110; (R'07) 80,260; 81,309; (C) 82,xxiv.
"Anna Pedersdotter": (R'26) 311, 18.
"Annals of Covent Garden Theatre" (Wyndham) (B): 82,ii.
Annapolis Naval Academy: 231, 418; 247,245.
"Anne of Green Gables": (F,R) 228,106.
"Annie Dear": (R'24) 286,22.
"Another Man's Shoes": (R'18) 213,279.
"Another Way Out": (R'16) 191, 21; 191,29.
Ansermet, Ernest: 178,286.
Ansky, S.: 300,31.
Anson, A.E.: 107,9; 118,169; 122,109; 168,55; 215,35; 264,18; 268,31; 343,13; 344, 39.
Anson, George W.: 120,53.
Antheil, Georges: 356,43.
Anthes, Georg: 22,34.
Anthony, Carl: 211,131; 345,48.
Anthony, Pauline: 87,132.
Anthony, Susan B.: 121,78.
"Anthony in Wonderland": (R'17) 202,351.
"Anthony and Cleopatra": (R'09) 106,166; 107,9; (F) 160,282; (R'24) 277,62; (D) 182,219.
"Anti-Matrimony": (R'10) 117,xi.
"Antick, The": (R'15) 177,223.
"Antigone": 114,48; (R'13) 269,16.
Antoine, Andre (see also Theatre Antoine): 21,8; 24,47; 36,vi; 48,51; 50,87; 152,xvii; 164, 177.
Antona-Traversi, Giannio: 147, 158.
Antonio: 286,11.
"Any House": 181,121; (R'16) 182,198.
"Any Night": (R'13) 146,xvi; 147, 155.
"Anybody's War": (F,R) 353,47; 353,48.
"Anybody's Woman": (F,R) 355,48.
"Anything May Happen": (R'23) 265,16.
"Apache, The": (R'23) 268,19.
Apache Dances: 108,xvi; 114,36; 126,40; 127,94; 204,112; 323, 40.
"Apartment 12-K": (R'14) 163, 139.
"Aphrodite": 227,16; (R'19) 227, 61.
"Apothecary, The": 303,13.
"Appearances": (R'29) 339,44.
"Apple Blossoms": 225,312; (R'19) 225,350
"Apple Cart, The": 344,21; 345, 31; 349,15; 349,45; 350,24; 351,20.
"Apple Sauce": (R'25) 297,70.
Appleby, Dorothy: 350,46.
Appleton, Charles L.: (W) 326, 18.
Appleton, George J.: 299,22.
"Appreciation of the Drama, The" (Caffin) (B); 94,xviii.
"April": (R'18) 207,287.
"Apron Strings": (R'30) 349,47; 350,48.
"Arab, The": (R'11) 129,xiv; 129, 163.
Arab in Drama: 135,168.
"Arabesque": (R'25) 297,44; 300, 32.
Aragon, Pepita: 37,68.
Arbell, Lucy: 121,102.
Arbuckle, Maclyn: 4,7; 28,132; 28,156; 32,244; 35,16; (C) 37, 58; 37,62; 41,178; 44,251; (A) 52,131f; 76,145; 77,191; 80,xiv; 101,7; 115,v; 137,13; 160,293; 183,292; 201,291; 205,157; 239,109; 244,21; 268, 3; 290,19.
Arbuckle, Roscoe: 203,59; 212,255; 213,319; 235,234; 239,114.
"Arcadians, The": (R'10) 109,xi; 109,70; 109,94; 109,96; 115, 74; 116,114.

Arcaro, Flavia: 99,158; 136, 172; 192,84; 297,17.
Archer, Ann: 14,7; 31,216.
Archer, Harry: 298,36.
Archer, Stella: 144,41.
Archer, William: 98,111; 138, 42; 236,273; 245,84; 271,20; 271,32; 240,224.
Archibald, Anna: 141,152.
Archibald, Jean: 238,15.
Archibald, Phyllis: 323,33.
Archie, Will: 160,321.
Architecture, Theatre (see Theatres).
Ardeck, Agnes: 36,35.
Ardell, Franklyn: 152,117.
Arden, Cecil: 214,353; 219, 268; 228,94; (A) 251,121; 268,37; 337,36.
Arden, Edwin: PG,11; 19,7; 35,18; 35,19; 53,166; 55,222; 62,89; 68,270; 106,177; 112, 183; 134,124; 154,178; 181, 121.
Ardini, Miriam: 191,42.
Ardwani, Kathryn: 55,225.
"Are Parents People?": (F,R) 293,34.
"Are You a Crook?": (R'13) 148, x; 148,181.
"Are You a Mason?": 3,2.
"Aren't We All?": 269,14; 269, 15; 270,26.
Argentina, La: 181,134; 182, 198; 335,53; 342,47.
Argonne Players: 222,84.
"Argyle Case, The": (R'12) 144, 37; 144,41.
Ari, Carina: 272,11.
"Ariadne": (R'25) 290,32.
"Ariane et Barbe-Bleue" (OP): 123,iii; 123,148.
Arimondi, Vittorio: 72,37; 75, 140; 81,314; 96,42.
"Aristocracy" (F): 170,178.
"Arizona": (R'13) 148,xi; 148, 171.
Arjamont: 222,75.
Arlen, Michael: 290,10; 294,8.
Arlen, Richard: 329,17.
Arliss, George: 23,2; 27,110; 28,134; 42,198; 47,7; (A) 51,i,f; 51,112; 70,324; 91, 228; 92,262; 92,269; 103, 70; 106,199; 107,7; 107,16; 123,141; 124,192; 124,205; 127, 76; 129,xiii; 131,12; 157,130; 179,7; 182,295; (A) 191,31;195, 289; 199,125; 200,190; 201, 277; 201,281; 203,30; 217, 161; 239,101; 241,265; 241,270; 241,271; 244,34; 245,84; 248, 324; 253,219; 271,33; 281,32; 288,16; 288,24; 292,26; 295, 22; (W,A) 314,5; 323,36; 323, 44; 323,45; (W) 335,22; 343, 38; (D) 346,57; (D) 350,63.
Armfield, Maxwell: (D) 220,337; (D) 240,182.
"Armide" (OP): 118,167.
Armin, Walter: 155,6.
Armitage, Pauline: 287,45.
"Arms and the Girl": (R'16) 189,283; 190,365.
"Arms and the Man": (R'15) 172, 280; (R'25) 296,18.
Armsby, Reginald: (W) 262,17.
Armstrong, Andrew: (W,V) 211, 132.
Armstrong, Harrison: 94,331.
Armstrong, Paul: 54,187; 55, 227; 73,60; 85,xii; 165,252.
Armstrong, Robert: 289,17.
Armstrong, William: (W) 123, 152; (W,V) 124,193; (W) 128, 140; (W) 130,221; (W) 134, 119; (W) 136,185; (W) 155, 30; (W) 158,183; (W) 177,226.
"Army with Banners, The": 207,285.
Arnaud, Yvonne: 324,59.
Arnault Brothers: 270,35.
Arnold, Dorothy: 260,293.
Arnold, Edward: 225,309; 230, 257; 306,25; 335,23.
Arnold, Eugene P.: 92,263.
Arnold, Florine: 123,143; 155,7; 155,51; 189,297; 194,231; 224, 222.
Arnold, Hattie: 68,260; 130,217.
Arnold, Indiola: 48,vi.
Arnold, Joseph (W) 232,528; 339, 33.
Arnold, Leroy: (W,V) 78,218.
Arnold, Peggy: 200,221.
Arnold, Roberta: 238,12; 238, 27; 243,402; 247,218; 248, 303; 251,83; 273,13; 280,13;

333, 40.
Arnolds, Billy: (D) 294, 29.
Arnst, Bobbe: 307, 54; 331, 45.
Aronson, Boris: (D) 350, 56.
Aronson, Rudolph: (W) 149, 19; (W) 194, 230; 339, 16.
"Around the Map": 178, 278; (R' 15) 178, 279.
"Around the World": (R' 11) 128, xiv; 106 xiv; 128, 125.
"Arrah-Na-Pogue": (R' 03) 32, 244.
Arral, Blanche: 105, 139.
Arrow, Margaret: 344, 13.
"Arrow Maker, The": (R' 11) 122, 106; 122, 129.
"Arsene Lupin": (R' 09) 104, xiv; 104, 125.
"Art and Mrs. Bottle": 358, 25; (R' 30) 358, 26; (C) 369, 2.
"Art and Opportunity": (R' 17) 203, 51.
"Art of Playwriting, The" (Quinn) (B): 338, 4.
Art Theatre (see also National Theatre): 78, 202; 90, 214; 269, 9; 289, 9.
Arthur, Johnny: 312, 49.
Arthur, Julia: 72, 45; 113, 23; 142, 200; 168, 74; 177, 227; 178, 277; 179, 29; 192, 73; 194, 225; 198, 90; 241, 250; 265, 42.
"Artie": (R' 07) 82, xviii; 82, 322.
"Artists and Models": (R' 24) 285, 64; 278, 39; (R' 25) 294, 15; 294, 3; (' 27) 323, 40; (R' 30) 353, 25.
Arts and Crafts Theatre Detroit: 196, 332.
"Art's Rejuvenation": (R' 18) 209, 24.
."As a Man Thinks": 122, 107; (R' 11) 122, 108.
"As the Sun Went Down": (F, R) 217, 191.
"As Ye Sow": 58, 307; (R' 05) 60, viii.
"As You Desire Me": 360, 28; (R' 31) 361, 26.
"As You Like It": (R' 03) 28, 132; 30, 195; 34, 307; 42, 211; 72, 45; 94, 320; (D) 108, 45; 137, 9; (R' 14) 159, 224; (D) 182, 211; 184, 340; (R' 18) 206, 219; (R' 19) 218, 207; 222, 102; 225, 313; (R' 23) 267, 15.
"As You Were": 229, 171; (R' 20) 299, 185.
Ascarra, Maria: 235, 189; 241, 257.
Asch, Scholom: 104, 132.
Asche, Oscar: 54, 184.
Ascher, Anton: 188, 204.
Ash, Gordon: 257, 83.
Ash, Paul: 330, 47.
Ash, Sam: 236, 281; 303, 46.
Asher, Anthony: 82, 329.
"Ashes": (R' 24) 285, 76.
"Ashes of Love": (F, R) 212, 250.
Ashford, Daisy: 239, 87.
Ashford, Harry: 202, 353; 269, 14.
Ashley, Arthur: 270, 34.
Ashley, Helen: 54, 191.
Ashley, Minnie: 193, 157.
Ashton, Herbert: 213, 267.
Ashton, Lucy: 51, 118.
Ashton, Marie: 138, 44.
Ashlyn, Belle: 52, 152.
Ashwell, Lena: 66, 201; 66, 215; 69, 306; 71, 28; 82, 321.
Askenasy, Betty: 145, 70.
Aspell, Seddie (D): 243, 397; 244, 11; 245, 103; 246, 147; 247, 235; 248, 295.
Astaire, Adele (see also Astaires, The): 211, 145; 233, 14; 256, 33; 265, 33; 320, 63; 354, 52.
Astaire, Fred: 211, 145.
Astaires, The: 355, 358; 287, 16; 289, 13; 323, 7; (C) 358, 16.
Asther, Nils: 319, 45.
Astley, John: 250, 17.
Astor, Mary: 270, 30; 290, 37; 293, 35; 293, 50; 307, 40; 319, 15; 325, 12; 353, 47.
Astor Place Opera House: 137, 28.
Astor Place Riots: 61, 75; (D) 131, 28; 131, 30; 280, 20.
Astor Theatre (New York): 110, 121.
"At Bay": 153, 141; (R' 13) 153, 143.
"At Mrs. Beam's": (R' 26) 304, 16.
"At 9:45": (R' 19) 222, 81; 223, 169.
"At the Barn": (R' 14) 167, 6.
"At the Bottom": (R' 30) 348, 48.
"Athalie": 235, 176.
Athelson, Edith: PG, 17.

Atherton, Gertrude: (W) 204, 102.
Atkins, Zoe: (W, V) 82, 352; 245, 74.
Atkinson, Brooks: 320, 40; 328, 45; (C) 335, 42.
Atlas Club Minstrels (Chicago): 100, 176.
"Attack, The": 136, 174; (R'12) 141, 131.
Atwell, Roy: 93, 296; 143, 3; 217, 164; 307, 14; (C) 343, 40.
Atwill, Lionel: 194, 231; 203, 13; 207, 273; 208, 349; 208, 354; 215, 29; 239, 81; 240, 172; 250, 25; (D) 250, 33; 250, 50; 266, 14; 275, 36; 278, 14; 278, 38; 290, 33; 328, 26; 344, 41.
Aubert, Jeannie: 360, 17; (C) 361, 27.
"Auctioneer, The": (R'01) 9, 4; 13, 17; 231, 348.
<u>Audiences, Manners of</u>: 6, 16; 29, 181; 38, 101; 74, vii; 75, xxvi; 78, iii; 109, 87; 125, 15; 150, 48; 158, 174; 159, 241; 204, 90; 213, 286; 218, 224; 226, 478; 229, 160; 230, 246; 234, 100; 252, 148; 256, 16; 257, 78; 274, 8; (D) 279, 25; 280, 20; (D) 281, 29; 286, 7; 297, 11; (C) 302, 11; 308, 30; 320, 16; 321, 25; 324, 23; 324, 27; 326, 16; 328, 16; 330, 14; 333, 36; 335, 52; 337, 29; (C) 342, 28; 343, 25.
<u>Audiences, Tastes of</u>: 38, 88; 43, 224; 78, 200; 82, 324; 87, xiv; 116, 127; 125, 33; 150, 49; 186, 84; 191, 27; 192, 102; 198, 63; 204, 104; 205, 154; 206, 226; 207, 292; 208, 374; 210, 114; 212, 214; 225, 294; 234, 82; 235, 162; 236, 254; 251, 104; 252, 144; 267, 22; (D) 274, 25; 275, 13; (D) 294, 11; 303, 9; 306, 7; 311, 9; 316, 41; 321, 21; 331, 28; 342, 43.
"Audrey": (R'03) 23, 6; 23, 10.
Auer, Leopold: 335, 39.
Aug, Edna: 30, 207
Augarde, Adrienne: 94, 312; 96, 41; 96, 56; 105, 163; 110, c; 136, 175.
Augier, Emile: 11, 2; 28, 96.
Aulick, W.W.: (W) 110, 121.
"Aulis Difficulty, The": (R'19) 219, 274.
"Aunt Jeannie": (R'02) 20, 5.
Austen, Leslie: 192, 93.
Austin, Fred A. (W): 256, 16; 257, 74; 308, 12; 310, 22.
Austin, J.W.: 312, 20; 320, 28.
Austin, Mary: 176, 180.
Austin, Nat: 54, 193.
Austin, Ralph: 82, vii.
Austin, W.W. (W): 126, 64; 138, 57.
<u>Austrian Theatre</u>: 160, 305; 299, 20; 304, 20.
<u>Australian Theatre</u>: 334, 22.
"Author's Apology, The" (Shaw) (B): 64, xvii.
Authors' League of America: 203, lf.
<u>Authors' Societies</u>: 123, 146.
<u>Automobiles and Actors</u>: 52, 140; 61, 57; 83, 6; 95, ii; 95, 5; 116, 102; 125, 34; 133, ii; 145, 78; 178, 310; 191, 16; 234, 144; 235, 234; 259, 252; 292, 38; <u>and monthly thereafter</u>.
<u>Automobile Theatres</u>: 123, 169.
"Autumn Fire": (R'26) 310, 16.
"Avalanche, The": (F) 221, 65.
"Avenue, The": 202, 347; (R'17) 202, 352.
Avery, Patricia: 313, 39.
"Aviator, The": 118, 199; (R'10) 119, xi.
Avril, Nancy: 101, 23; 136, 198.
Avril, Suzanne: 47, 25.
"Awakening, The": (R'08) 85, ix; 70, 323; (R'18) 213, 279.
"Awakening of Helena Richie, The": 105, 150; 105, 151.
"Awakening of Spring" (<u>see</u> "Erdgeist").
"Awful Truth, The": (R'22) 260, 299; 261, 372; (F) 344, 37.
Aylesworth, Arthur: 176, 186; 213, 275; 234, 83.
Ayling, Herbert: 20, 7; 32, 243; 59, 16; 87, 122; 135, 148.
Aylmer, Felix: 261, 370.
Aylwin, Jean: 123, 172.
Ayers, Agnes: 207, 325; 239, 115; 260, 311; 286, 32; 274, 33.

Ayers, Alfred (see also "America's Greatest Players"): 13,12; 15,19; 22,16; (W) 22,26.
Ayrton, Randle: 237,365.
Azi, Carina: 302,29.

--B--

"B.J. One": 351,31; 352,31.
"Bab": 238,27; (R'20) 238,32.
"Babbitt": (F,R) 283,32.
Babcock, Bertrand (W); 115,94.
Babcock, Louette: 66,210.
"Babes and the Baron, The": (R'05) 60,ix.
"Babes in the Wood": 58,306.
"Babes in Toyland": (R'03) 30, 188; 30,189; 42,ii.
"Bab's Diary": (F,R) 201,316.
"Baby Cyclone, The": (R'27) 320, 23.
"Baby Mine" (see also "Rock-A-Bye Baby"): 116,vii; (R'10) 116,99; 116,125; (R'27) 317,18.
Bach, Reginald: 304,23.
Bachaus, Wilhelm: 132,52; 266, 37; 284,35.
"Bachelor, The": (R'09) 99,136; 99,166.
"Bachelor Belles, The": (R'10) 118,xxi.
"Bachelor Father, The": (R'28) 325,62; (S) 327,24.
"Bachelors and Benedicts": (R'12) 142,xvi.
"Bachelor's Baby, The": (R'09) 108,xv.
"Back Pay": (R'21) 248,315.
"Back Again": 208,363.
"Back to Earth": (R'18) 216,79.
"Back to Methuselah": 254,291; (R'22) 254,305; (D) 254, 309.
Backers (see Angels).
"Backfire": (R'16) 189,284.
Backus, E.Y.: 12,12.
Backus, George: 37,62; 45,279; (A) 54,183f; (W) 89,195; 117, 135; 137,10; 190,347; 223, 169; 23,6.
Backus, Georgia: 357,42; 359, 40.
Bacon, Bessie: 212,203.
Bacon, Francis (see also Bacon vs. Shakespeare): 79,xii.
Bacon, Frank: 165,217; 181, 129; 188,203; 212,203; 212, 209; 213,290; (A) 214,379; 217,164; 225,354; (A) 226, 438; (D) 230,261; (A) 231,347; 231,372; 236,272; 244,34; 247, 206a; 248,292; (A) 250,63; (D) 262,7; 290,12.
Bacon, Josephine Dascom: (W) 340,11.
Bacon vs. Shakespeare: 76,150; 123,176; 149,20; 182,192; 182, 222.
"Bad Girl": 357,28; (S) 358,32; 359,40.
"Bad Habits of 1926": (R) 304,16.
"Bad Man, The": (R'20) 236, 278; (F,R) 273,30.
"Bad Samaritan, The": 55,238; (R'05) 56,242.
Bada, Angelo: 287,35; 299,35.
Baddely, Sophia: 32,261.
Bade, Annette: 221,31.
Badet, Regina: 121,104; 127, 97; 197,35.
"Badges": (R'25) 288,62.
Badillo, Mario: 339,46.
"Badman, The" (see also "Bad Man, The"): 354,61.
Bailey, Consuelo Yznaga: 66, 207; 88,163; 96,45; 98,123; 99,141; 180,73.
Bailey, Fred: 82,vii.
Bailey, James A.: 54,192.
Bailey, Loretto Carroll: 335,57.
Bailey, Ralph Sargent (W): 352, 23; 360,19.
Bailey, William: 304,25.
Baille, Joanna: 27,116.
Baine, Ruth: 83,28.
Bainter, Fay: 190,365; 194,236; 195,271; 195,281; 198,96; 208,356; 208,357; 209,9; 216, 67; 216,95; 221,24; 223,189; 258,144; 264,21; 273,21; 278, 6; 282,14; 284,21; 291,27; 297,19; (C) 326,80; 334,46; 335,30; 335,40; 361,16.
Baird, Dorothea: 66,204.
Baird, Ethel: 176,188.
Baird, Stewart: 124,195; 127,88; 156,59.
Bairnsfather, Bruce (W): 347,21.

Baker, Belle: 342,24.
Baker, Edith Ellis: 27,106; 27,109; 75,119.
Baker, Edythe: 236,284; 266,43.
Baker, Edna: 129,163; 129,164.
Baker, Ellis: 334,45.
Baker, Eugene Blaisdell (W,V): 119,12.
Baker, George Pierce: 82,345; 135,154; 159,249; 292,20; 296,44; 298,20; 311,42; 328, 45.
Baker, Guelma: 72,56.
Baker, Hettie Gray (W): 65,173; 73,73; 77,176; 84,55; 102, 40; 114,50.
Baker, Lee: 111,167; 118,169; 165, 221; 190,347; 207,305; 249,365.
Baker, Lorin: 222,82; 247,239.
Baker, Marie: 173,24.
Baker, Phil: 279,36; 298,27; 317,3; (C) 338,37; 349,70.
Baker, Richard: 5,3.
Baker, Ward: 166,281.
Baklanoff, Georges: 203,39.
Baklanova, Olga: 259,217; 294, 12; 296,14; 298,23; 302, 34; 320,45; 330,44.
Bakst, Leon: 155,10; 178,294; (C) 263,10; 271,72.
Balboni, Sylvano: 310,38.
Balderston, John L.: 342,20.
Baldina, Marie: 125,4.
Baldwin, George: 176,170.
Balfour, William: 183,273.
Balieff, Nikita: 255,381; 256, 28; 258,167; (C) 263,10; 265, 38; 276,9; 287,18; (C) 316, 31; (C) 339,41.
"Balkan Princess, The": (R'11) 121,ix; 121,74.
"Ballad of Reading Gaol": 136, 199.
Ballantine, E.J.: 214,359; 280, 5; 336,51.
Ballard, A.H. (W,V): 222,76.
Ballard, Frederick: 177,228; 342,20.
Ballentine, Lucille: 268,43.
Ballester, Vincente: 236,271; 283,35.
Ballet (see Dance).
"Ballet-Intime": (R'17) 200, 205.
Ballet Russe (see also Russian Ballet: Russian Dance): 181, 128.
Ballet Suedois: 272,10.
Ballew, Julia: 220,347.
Ballin, Mabel: 250,39; 290,37.
Ballin, Marian: 171,253.
Ballou, Peggy: 79,254.
"Ballyhoo": (R'30) 359,26.
Balsamo, Arthur: 181,143.
Balsar, Charles: 87,118; 105, 144; 111,145.
Baltimore Theatre: 197,32; 307, 41.
Balzac, Honore De: 114,60.
Balzerit, Edward: 184,349; 189, 269.
Banastar, [Mrs.] Jack: (see Fischer, Alice).
"Banco": (R'22) 260,297; 261,374.
Bancroft, George: 320,17; 322, 60.
"Bandana Land": (R'08) 85,xii; 86,97.
Bandbox Theatre (New York): 174,64.
Bandmann, Daniel E.: 186,79.
Bang, Ole: 47,12; 48,49.
Bankhead, Tallulah: 223,181; 233,22; 244,47; 261,399; 263,47.
Bankoff, Ivan: 236,259.
Banks, Estar: 164,165.
Banks, Leslie: 346,15; 349,44.
Banky, Vilma: 306,40; 307,40; (D) 312,41; 313,49; 321,40; 338,38; 356,33; 296,31.
Banton, Travis: 247,256.
Bara, Theda: 177,246; 200, 253; 207,331; 208,403; 212, 258; 213,320; 224,254; 229, 170; 231,401; 249,384.
Barbakoff, Tatjana: (D) 347,28.
"Barbara's Millions": (R'06) 69,xiv.
"Barbary Sheep" (F); 200,253.
Barbee, Richard: 219,295; 240, 181.
Barber, Richard: 314,22.
"Barber of New Orleans, The": (R'09) 97,xiv; 97,92.
"Barber of Seville, The" (OP): 36,43.
Barbier, George W.: 14,2; 307,

23; 329,24; 341,42; 356, 19; (D) 357,2.
Barbour, Grace A.: 142,165.
Barbour, Iva: 121,98.
Barbour, Joyce: 284,18.
Barclay, Don: 186,71.
Barclay, John: 311,31; 323,23.
Barclay, Lila: 141,133.
Barclay, McClelland: 241,249.
Barclay, Patricia: 344,47.
Bard, Wilkie: 272,35.
Barescu, Agathe: 123,xii; 124,190.
"Bargain, The": (R'15) 177,223.
Baring, Isabel: (D) 352,4.
Barker, Albert W.: (W,D) 317, 12; 319,18; 320,16.
Barker, Corinne: 203,c; 246, 195.
Barker, Edith: 48,33; 119,14; 201,276.
Barker, Granville: 79,235; 86, 91; 86,92; 168,63; 169,110; 170,196; 170,198; 171,228; 171,251; 171,258; 172,283; 173,12; 178,276; 194,213; (W) 223,142; 139,167; (W) 224,236; 245,98.
Barker, Irene: 228,90.
Barker, Julia: 284,27.
Barker, Margaret: 361,34.
Barker, Mary: 9,11.
Barker, Nell: 260,300.
Barker, Reginald: 310,38.
"Barker, The": (S) 313,24; (F) 329,4b.
Barlow, Reginald: 142,165; 162, 71; 164,165; 165,234; 201, 272; 229,167; 259,226.
Barnabee, Henry Clay: 13,23; 159,276.
Barnard, Ivor: 341,24.
Barnard, Sophie: 113,25; 206, 261.
Barnard College: 64,162; 182, 227; 184,339; 245,109.
Barnes, Helen: 185,34.
Barnes, Howard (W): 342,11; 343,19; 344,15; 345,20; 346, 17; 347,19; 348,25; 349,38; 350,19; 351,24; 352,36; 353, 14; 356,15; 357,20; 360,15; 361,18.
Barnes, T. Roy: 176,194; 183,281.
Barnett, Jean: 174,65.
Barnett, Zoe: 155,23.
Barney, Marion: 39,128; 76,170; 239,90; (D) 275,27.
Barney, Violet: 52,152.
Barnhart, Harry: 203,42.
Barnitz, Wirt W.: (W) 268,10; 270,24.
Barnum, David: 304,25.
Barnum, George W.: 130,220.
Barnum, Phineas Taylor: 113, 19.
Barnum and Bailey: 135,146.
Barnum's Museum: 19,21.
"Barnyard Romeo, The": 113,iii.
Baron, Alice: 104,115; 105,139.
Baron, Henry: 294,7.
"Baron Trenck": (R'12) 134,xiii; 134,105.
Barr Twins: 199,149; 279,38.
Barrand, George H.: 261,372.
Barrat, Robert: 216,69; 223, 169.
Barratt, Watson: 299,38.
Barre, Felix: 226,396.
Barrell, Charles Wisner (W): 99,144; 104,117.
Barrett, Edith: 347,46; 348,47; (C) 351,4; 354,29; 357,28; 358,30; (D) 359,c; 359,28.
Barrett, Elizabeth: 360,12.
Barrett, Jean: 122,119.
Barrett, Lawrence: 14,21; 49,61; 56,250; 69,295; 103,82; 105, 162; 111,163; 145,74; 232, 502; 238,28.
Barrett, Lillian (W): 303,9; 305, 20; 306,20; 317,16.
Barrett, Mildred: 137,8.
Barrett, Minnette: 110,104.
"Barretts of Wimpole Street": 360,8; 360,19; (R'31) 361, 24; (S) 361,33.
Barretto, Gertrude: 124,187.
Barrie, James M.: 10,2; 13,7; 22,12; 54,200; 58,288; 60, 31; 60,32; 86,91; 96,38; 133, xii; 153,143; 153,146; 153, 150; 156,58; 156,81; 187,131; 192,86; 194,215; 205,140; 216, 77; 233,32; 237,356; 240,177; 334,15; 334,16.
Barrientos, Maria: 178,284; 181, 134; 205,147; 207,275.
"Barrier, The": (R'10) 108,xiii;

108,33.
Barrington, Lillian: 67,250.
Barrington, Rutland: 136,171.
Barriscale, Bessie: 156,62; 165, 227; 200,247; 208,399; 208, 402; 211,181; 215,64; 223, 182; 247,228; 247,257.
Barriscale, Charles: 37,75.
Barrison, Mabel: 88,vii; 88,154; 95,29; 96,xx; 111,133; 112, 177; 113,17; 125,34.
Barrows, Mabel Hay: 39,123; 50,88.
Barroy, Earl (W): 246,148; 247,238.
Barroy, Michael: 294,21.
Barry, Bobbie: 7,18.
Barry, Charles: 30,188.
Barry, Elizabeth: 28,138.
Barry, Katie: 17,4; 45,273; 71, 28.
Barry, Philip: 265,16; 266,38; (D) 268,28; 328,29; (C) 339, 29.
Barrymore, Diana: 306,33.
Barrymore, Ethel: (see also Barrymore Family): PG,24; 3,4; 3,12; 6,1; 9,c; 9,22; 21,7; 21,8; 21,20; 34,290; 44,253; 46,293; 46,297; 52, 133; 54,183; 59,8; 60,32; 60,37; 60,43; 63,119; 66,c; 67,244; 71,18; 73,57; 75,114; 75,129; 78,205; 79,228; 83, 9; 84,34; 90,206; 94,xi; 94,311; 95,311; 95,24; 95, 26; 96,xxii; 100,177; 106, 187; 109,69; 109,72; 109,73; 111,xx; 117,157; 120,42; 120, 45; 121,xiii; 122,111; 127,76; 131,ix; 131,2; 133,75; 139, 67; 139,94; 149,16; 151,79; 154,173; 158,197; 160,281; 160,318; 160,319; 160,326; 163,99; 167,10; 169,111; 169, 121; 172,298; 175,110; 178, 287; 178,305; 178,307; 178, 335; (D) 180,80; 183,292; 195,285; 197,17; 201,268; 204,85; 210,95; 205,145; 206,218; 206,221; 208,375; (C) 209,22; 210,112; 214,354; 222,97; 224,222; 225,305; (D) 228,85; 228,96; 231, 383; 243,393; 243,417; 244, 18; 244,32; 245,92; 263,12; 264,20; 264,39; 266,17; 269, 18; 270,34; 286,20; 290,23; 297,5; 313,11; (C) 313,17; 317,31; 317,64; 333,14; 336, 40; 336,49; 339,9; 358,17; 358,37; 361,14.
Barrymore Family: 111,143; 174,72; 206,210; 247,211; 281,23; 361,14.
Barrymore, George M.: 215,61.
Barrymore, Georgiana Drew: 287,25.
Barrymore, John: 39,121; 55,233; 59,8; 60,37; 87,viii; 97,97; 104,xiii; 104,106; 105,147; 130,xiii; 133,75; 139,69; 141, 131; 149,16; 151,81; 152, 113; 152,135; 156,64; 157,129; (W) 160,304; 166,265; 182, 229; 183,294; 183,296; 185, 23; 196,345; 197,15; 202,355; 210,117; 213,277; 214,359; 215,28; 217,191; 220,353; 221,22; 221,24; 223,150; 228, 96; 228,107; 230,309; 230,315; 231,343; 231,410; 232,502; 243; 417; 244,19; 245,92; 259,222; 260,306; 261,386; 262,21; 263,5; (D) 263,10; 264,39; 267,25; 274,33; 282, 64; 286,25; 290,22; 291,24; 293,35; 296,c; 304,37; 305, 17; 307,7; 307,40; 308,37; 309,8; (D) 324,c; (C) 325, 23; 331,75; 339,36; 347,20; (D) 348,61; 354,59; 355,47; 357,20; 361,47.
Barrymore, Lionel: 20,4; 36,47; 55,233; 60,40; 196,345; 197, 15; 206,221; 207,271; 220, 353; 223,150; 224,222; 230, 253; 238,38; 241,251; 249, 365; 259,222; 273,31; 274, 32; 275,15; 277,39; 288,27; 307,35; (C) 316,31.
Barrymore, [Mrs.] Lionel: 256, 35.
Barrymore, Maurice: 34,306; 34,307; 43,225; 51,130; 54, 189; 84,43; 90,205; 149,16; 168,74; 288,28; 357,20.
Bart, Jean: 311,29; (W) 323,31.

Bart and Mallia: 201,287.
Barte, Leo: 265,8.
Bartels, Louis: (D) 278,38; 279,18; 282,28.
"Bartered Bride, The" (OP): 98,109.
Bartet, Jeanne: 48,40.
Barth, Hans: 297,35.
Barthel, Louise: 108,37; 137,3; 149,2.
Barthelmess, Richard: 227,43; 254,297; 258,167; 265, 35; 270,31; 278,31; 285,33; 288,32; 290,37; 306,39; 308, 36; 309,37; 310,48; 320,31; 345,22; 353,61.
Barthold, Gertrude: 114,56.
Barholomae, Philip H.: 151, 100; 176,179.
Bartholomew, Agnes: 141,133.
Barti, Perle: 138,64.
Bartlett, Elise: 213,291; 218, 204; 226,369; 234,101; 265, 18; 267,38.
Bartlett, Josephine: 13,23.
Bartlette, Andree: 183,280.
Bartox, Bela: 326,45.
Bartol, Henry G.: 198,89.
Barton, Bruce (W): 327,5.
Barton, Buzz: 320,45.
Barton, James: 245,80; 245,101; 255,365; 270,29; 284,26; 305,23; 307,19; (C) 358,44.
Barton, Jane: 185,20.
Barton, Julian: 119,19.
Barton, Mary: 141,149.
Barton, Roxane: 153,142.
"Barton Mystery, The": (R'17) 202,350.
Barwell, Edith: 104,101.
Baskcomb, A.W.: 140,123.
"Basker, The": (R'16) 199,357.
Baskette, William: 202,358.
Basque Theatre: 43,219.
Basquette, Lina: 269,8; 293, c; 327,16; 333,26; 341,38.
Bassett, Peter: 143,7.
Bassi, Amadeo: 72,38; 73,65; 75,140; 81,315; 134,110; 177,248.
"Bat, The": 234,111; (R'20) 235,240; 250,28.
Bataille, Felix Henry: 99,140; 159,242.
Bateman, Kate: 246,164.
Bateman-Hunter, Leah: 105,144; 107,9; 108,48; 122,129.
Bates, Anna L.: 103,75.
Bates, Blanche: 3,3; 9,18; 15,c; 19,6; 23,2; 23,3; 25,75; 29, 164; 32,c; (W) 46,xviii; (W) 52,138; 58,292; 58,301; 59, 18; 59,19; 63,116; 67,246; 70,c; 73,63; 75,119; 82,346; 93,284; 93,288; 93,291; 94, 325; 95,10; 103,87; 113,17; 115,73; 118,162; 118,185; 119,28; 121,96; 124,c; 125, 29; 136,188; 136,190; 137,15; 139,69; 142,196; 145,78; 149, 22; 150,70; 151,79; 156,77; 159,237; 165,214; 167,11; 169,142; 172,299; 173,25; 183,292; 187,127; 190,372; 211,183; 212,207; 213,270; (A) 214,379; (D) 220,361; 219, 285; 226,438; 231,368; (W,V) 231,384; 231,385; 233,8; (A) 238,72; 260,295; (A) 272,67; 273,26; 290,20f; 306,33; (A) 322,3; 344,23.
Bates, Edna: 149,11; 171,256; 233,17.
Bates, Marie: 45,274; 58,301; 82,349; 180,87; 190,359.
Bates, Sally: 360,55.
Battista, Miriam; 204,101;232,517.
Battista, William: 214,351.
"Battle, The": (R'08) 96,39; 96,49; 96,57; (S) 98,120.
Battle, George Gordon: 359,39.
"Battle Cry, The": (R'14) 166, 300.
"Battle Cry of Peace, The": (F) 175,114.
Bauer, "Daddy": 35,14.
Bauer, Harold: 154,184; 168, 66; 273,36; 296,34; 339,30.
Bauer, Inez: 224,217.
Bauer, Marion (W): 354,30; 356, 42.
Baum, L. Frank: 102,62; 103,77.
Baume, Edgar: 40,144.
Baumfeld, Maurice: 81,311; 93, 289.
Bavagnoli, Gaetano: 178,284.
"Bavu": (R'22) 254,334.
Baxter, Barry: 250,40.

Baxter, Ernest: 93,287.
Baxter, F. Owen: 23,7.
Baxter, George: 314,17.
Baxter, Helen: 338,48.
Baxter, Marie: 136,192.
Baxter, Warner: 325,50.
"Baxter's Partner": (R'11) 126, 41.
Bay Sisters: 279,38.
Bayard, Beatrice: 238,25.
Bayes, Nora (see also Norworth and Bayes): 90,199; 91, 245; 101,15; 102,c; 108,xiv; 109,72; (A) 115,iv; 116,123; 123,ix; 123,145; 169,124; 185,47; 197,35; 198,90; 199, 128; (W) 202,364; 202,365; 205,137; 216,108; 240,159; 240,180; 241,258; 245,99.
Bayley, Caroline: 166,280.
Bayne, Beverly: 247,228; 282, 31.
Bayne, S.G.: (W) 256,12.
Bayreuth Festival: 44,255; 79, 244; 88,151; 178,304.
Bazzi, Maria: 258,167; 296, 38,
"Be Calm, Camilla": (R'18) 214, 380; 215,29.
"Be Yourself": (R'24) 284,19.
Beach, Lewis: 277,29.
Beach, Rex: (A,D) 184,365; 223,182.
Beach, Stewart: (W) 299,24; 342,9; (A) 353,13; 360,39.
Beach, William: 7,5; 91,231.
Beagard, Jeanette: 40,143.
Beal, George Binton (W): 354, 45.
Bean, Theodore (W); 150,60.
Beane, George: 43,233.
Beardsley, Stella: 42,vii.
Beardsley, Virginia: 273,22.
Beasley, Byron: 131,27; 218, 209.
Beaston, Frank: 308,14.
Beatty, Roberta: 269,14; 272, 29; 314,47; 333,55.
"Beau Brummel": 3,13; (R'16) 184,334; 184,350; (F) 274, 33; (F,R) 279,32.
"Beau Geste": (F) 305,37.
"Beau Marriage, Un": 143,23.
"Beau Strings": (R'26) 304,16.
Beaubien, Julian: 137,8; 160, 285.
"Beaucaire": (R'19) 228,98.
Beaulieu Theatre (Vanderbilt Estate): 20,18.
Beaumont, Lucy: 166,269.
Beaumont, Nellie: 41,184.
Beaumonte, Bertee: 230,266; 245, 80.
"Beautiful Adventure, The": (R'14), 164,158.
"Beauty and the Barge, The": (R'05) 56,242; (R'13) 154, xxii.
"Beauty and the Beast": 10,6.
"Beauty Shop, The": 155,12; (R'14) 160,282; 160,289.
"Beauty Spot, The": (R'09) 99, xi; 99,137.
Beban, George: 102,61; 129, xiv; 133,74; 156,104.
Bechert, Paul (W): 267,13; 299,20; 304,20; 308,20.
Beck, Cornish: 214,351.
Beck, Martin: 258,178; 282,7.
Beck, William: 104,116; 105, 139; 121,83; (A) 117,xviii; 131,30.
Beckett, Harry: 242,338.
Beckley, Beatrice: 196,355; 212, 201; 213,281; 228,86; 230, 289; 259,209.
Beckley, Zoe (W): 214,360; 215, 28; 304,12; 307,12; 308,32.
"Becky Sharp": 43,225.
Becman, Edgar: 179,11.
"Bedfellows": (R'29) 342,39.
Bedford, Barbara: 239,116.
Bedford, Cornelia: 21,9.
Bedford, Eleanore: 259,16.
"Bedford's Hope": 61,57; (R'06) 61,58.
Bedouin, John: 179,19.
Beebe, Irving: 208,345; 253, 229.
Beecham, Thomas: 333,25.
Beecher, Janet: 50,84; 99,166; 106,170; 107,iii; 108,54; 112, 197; 117,131; 147,136; 150, 69; 152,136; 153,142; 161,14; 161,21; 179,16; 187,127; 190, 354; 203,25; 213,295; 217, 157; 235,170; 236,255; 250, 17; 306,33; (W) 333,22; 334,

54.
Beechwood Players (New York): 255,386.
Beechwood School (Pennsylvania): 216,100.
Beegle, Mary Porter: 181,136.
Beer, Rudolf: 297,25.
Beerbohm, Calude: 180,71.
Beerbohm, Evelyn: 132,38.
Beerbohm, Max: 76,163.
Beery, Noah: 294,1; 305,37.
Beery, Wallace: 274,32; (D) 295,2a; 322,50; (D,W) 324,32; 335,44.
"Beethoven": (S) 99,140; 99,142; 101,5; (D) 101,26; (R'10) 111,xxvii; 111,129.
"Before and After": (R'05) 59, xii; 59,6.
"Beggar on Horseback": (R'24) 277,19; (F'R) 293,32; 359, 49.
"Beggar Student, The": (R'13) 147, 132; 147,139.
"Beggar's Opera, The": (D) 239,88; 240,157; (R'20) 240,179; 251,77.
Behan, George: 173,7; 174,62.
"Behavior of Mrs. Crane, The": (R'28) 327,39.
"Behind a Watteau Picture": (R'17) 203,22; 203,35.
"Behind the Door": (F,R) 228, 106.
Behn, Aphra: 27,116; 164,194.
Behnke, Hattie (W): 200,196.
"Behold the Bridegroom": (R'28) 324,38; (S) 325,28.
"Behold This Dreamer": (R'27) 322,38.
Behrman, Samuel Nathaniel: (C) 339,39; 342,20.
Bekefi, Theodore: 271,34; 271,35.
Bekifi, Julie: 275,37.
Belasco, David: 3,4; 8,19; 9,4; 9,13; 9,15; 12,7; 14,11; 21, 14; (W) 22,31; 23,2; 35,2; 43,226; 47,18; 48,28; 48, 42; 51,115; 53,159; 55,227; 57,288; 58,xxiii; 58,291; 65, 186; 66,xi; 67,227; 27,247; 70,xxv; 70,321; 71,4; 72,50; 76,165; 78,viii; 80,v; 82, xxvii; 82,318; 83,xi; 84, 42; 84,48; 89,172; 93,284; 94,xxxiii; 102,64; 103,70; 104,104; 105,149; 106,xxxv; 111,144; 115,xii; 115,66; 117, 132; 118,xxxv; 119,4; 119,12; (A) 120,52; 121,92; 121,97; 123, 164; 127,77; 127,88; 129,xi; 130,xxxiv; 134,124; 137,11; 138,45; 140,103; 140,111;142, xxv; 143,vii; 143,6; 144,57; 145,xii; 145,75; 150,54; (W) 151,86; 152,122; 153,160; 154,xxix; 156,99; 157,160; 159,230;161,6; 162,68; 163, 99; 166,313; 169,111; 169, 135; 170,191; 171,229; 171, 260; 175,108; 178,341; 180,88; 183,272; 184,359; 187,132; 187,172; 189,267; 190,413; 195,292; 196,320; 197,40; 198,64; 198,85; 202,410; 206, 228; 209,14; 211,130; 212, 198; 214,351; 214,398; 216, 84; 216,122; 223,162; 224, 222; 226,443; (A) 231,346; 231, 348; 231,368; (W) 231,378; 232,365f; 234,84; 241,244; 246,165; 249,435; 253,212; 253,228; 258,149; 259,225; 260,295; 262,67; 263,16; 264, 13; 265,38; (C) 266,10; 266, 38; 268,10; 268,38; 269,34; (W) 273,11; 273,20; 273,79; 274,39; 278,10; (C) 279,11; 287,27; 289,5; 290,18; 290, 93; 292,29; 294,7; 296,6; 306,15; 316,34; (A) 316,59; 323,44; 331,75; (W) 336,22; 343,22; 343,33.
Belasco, Frederick: 9,19.
Belasco Theatre (New York): 202,345; (D) 290,50.
Belasco Theatre (Wash.D.C.): 57,288; 87,120; 134,177.
Belch, Leo: 133,78.
Belge, Tavie: 213,293; 215,24.
Bel-Geddes, Norman: 277,20; 296,38.
"Belgian, The": (F,R) 202,394.
Belgian Theatre: 193,162; 327, 19.
"Belgium, The Kingdom of Grief": (F) 215,62.
"Believe Me Xantippe" (R'13)

152,113; 152,117; 152,135.
"Belinda": (R'18) 208,355; 208, 375.
Bell, Archie (W) (See also "Famous Women Who Have Been Dramatized"): 67,234; 69,xviii; 73,66; 75,122; 78, 216; 80,271; 82,323; 105, 158; 113,18; 114,62; 115,93; 118,196; 119,12; 122,132; 123,164; 127,85; 129,163; 131,17; 150,39; 155,32; 156, 76; 174,80; 176,189; 177,246; 178,304; 179,24; 183,298; 187,148; 188,218; 191,36; 255,366; 256,34; 284,20; 285,20; 286,24; 293,30; 298, 10.
Bell, Benedict (W): 143,31.
Bell, Charles J.: 111,134.
Bell, Digby: 7,4; 22,20; 50, 84; 40,144; (A) 51,if; 96, 68; 111,136; 132,46; 137, 10; 137,13.
Bell, E. Hamilton: 105,145.
Bell, Hillary: 7,13; 27,107.
Bell, Jean: 159,236.
Bell, Laura Joyce: 22,20; 132, 46.
Bell, Lisle (W):208,374; 211, 160; 212,196; 214,352; 215, 26; 218,224; 252,148; 253, 244; 254,288.
Bell, Monte: 300,42.
Bell, Norma: 54,204.
Bell, Virginia: 247,221; 253, 227.
Bella, Maria La: 136,178.
"Bella Donna": (R'12) 142,xx; 142,163.
Bellamy, Anne: 37,65.
Bellamy, Madge: 307,31; 309,2. 313,38; 321,50; 322,12; 324, 12.
Bellamy, Ralph: 335,47.
Belle, Ma: 224,243.
"Belle Marseillaise, La": (R'05) 59,5; 59,13.
"Belle of Bond Street, The": (R'14) 159,261; 160,279; 160,298.
"Belle of Brittany, The": (R'09) 106,v; 106,xvii.
"Belle of Mayfair, The": (R'06) 71,xv.
"Belle of New York, The": 216,84.
Bellew, J.C.M.: 221,56.
Bellew, Kyrle: 5,5; 10,8f; 11,11; 12,10; 13,8; 15,1; 16,11; 17,10; 23,16; 28,132; 28,136; 28,143; 33,265; 35,5; 39,124; 41,174; 43,c; 50,92; 52,142; 52,143; 53,viii; (W) 69,304; 75,115; 79,228; 80,257; 81, 297; (C) 82,xxiv; 86,106; 103,70; 106,171; 126,65; 127, 77; 231,363; 231,397; 243, 232; 290,22.
Bellows, [Mrs.] George (W): 304, 18.
"Bells, The": (R'26) 303,50.
Belmont, Frances: 39,113; 40,149.
Belmont, [Mrs.] Morgan: 236, 289.
Belmont, O.H.P.:181,127.
Belmore, Daisy: 195,267.
Belmore, Herbert: 190,374.
Belmore, Lionel: 131,30.
Beloit College: 271,42.
Belostotsky, Boris: 294,12.
"Beloved Rogue, The": (F) 309, 8; (D) 311,39.
Belreva, Beatrice: 304,8.
Belwin, Alma: 146,105; 162,57; 171,236; 250,11; 250,16.
Belyakova, Lydia: 303,8.
"Ben Hur": PG,16; 31,226; 134, 128; (F) 277,32.
Ben Ami, Jacob: 230,260; 234, 98; 238,58; 239,89; 241,247; 253,219; 274,14; (D) 278,38; 285,36; 325,39; (D) 346,29; 347,27.
Benassi, Memo: 275,24.
Benavente, Jacinto: (D) 266,9.
Benchley, Robert: (C) 267,11; 288,36; 321,41.
Benda, W.T.: 239,93.
Bendel, Henry: (W) 286,28; 293,42.
Bender, Blanche: 136,190.
Bender, Paul: 118,182; 299, 35.
Bendix, Max: 188,206.
Benedict, Howard S.: 331,49.
Benelli, Sam: 220,352; 248, 352; 300,31.

Benham, Earl: 227,25.
Benham, Harry: 207,277.
Benjamin, Glelia: 257,71.
Bennet, Violet: 236,265.
Bennett, Arnold:131,17; 163,116.
Bennett, Barbara: 275,23.
Bennett, Belle: 202,405; 238, 12.
Bennett, Constance: 346,61; 350,23.
Bennett, Edith: (A) 260,331.
Bennett, Ella Costillo (W): 80,274; 93,297; 131,23; 159, 241; 160,306.
Bennett, Enid: 183,278; 205,195; 207,329; 215,57; 221,63; 259, 243; 284,33.
Bennett, Evelyn: 307,14.
Bennett, Gertrude: 4,10; 116, 124.
Bennett, Joan: 334,40; 349,37; 355,47; 361,46.
Bennett, Leila: 238,27; 249,382; 343,34; 343,43; (C) 344,44.
Bennett, Lois: 304,19; 304,64; 320,23; 323,23.
Bennett, Mickey: 275,33.
Bennett, Richard: 59,24; 68,259; 28,280; 85,79; 96,39; 96, 64; 98,118; 115,65; 115,70; 115,75; 128,117; 136,187; 139,69; 144,43; 145,78; 147, 134; (D) 163,108; 168,61; 183,295; 199,129; 210,83; 213,267; 218;222; 218,223; 228,103; 233,15; 250,16; 252, 141; 253,231; (D) 253,237; 254,303; 255,356; (W) 278, 12; 288,18; 290,19; 293,26; 307,12; 307,13; 317,20; 328, 23; 329,40; 331,41; 334,36; 343,29; 356,24; 357,27.
Bennett, Wilda: 122,119; 166, 263; 173,5; 199,155; 201, 267; 215,13; 219,281; 225, 312; 250,34; 253,239; 254, 326; 257,c; 267,33; 286,18; 320,51.
Bennett, Zoe: 238,19.
Bennison, Louis: 179,25; 195,271.
Benny, Jack: 279,36; 353,24.
Benrimo, J. Harry: 49,70; 123,147; 333,49.
Benson, E. F.: 20,5.
Benson, Frank R.: (D) 118,188; 153,158; 161,16;182,221; 184, 332.
Benson, Ruth: 50,103; 177,231.
Bentley, Irene: (W) 7,16; 16,4; 16,5; 17,5; 31,c; 32,250; 33,277; 40,148; 71,6; 80,274.
Bentley, Marjorie: 170,200; 221, 7.
Bentley, Walter E.: (W) 48,48.
Benton, Ben: 124,203.
Benton, Joy Kime: (W,V) 281,44.
Benton, Leila: 36,42; 57,288.
Benton, Percy: 233,7; 263,21.
Benzinger, Ernest: 147,160.
Beranger, Clara (W): 219,300.
Berat, Louise: 134,110.
Berber, Anita: 267,23.
Beresford, Alice: 120,42.
Beresford, Edmond: 129,152.
Beresford, Harry: 230,275; 232, 520; 233,15; 260,296; 262, 8; 347,46.
Beresford, J. Cooke: 144,45.
Beresford, Vera: 179,35; 243,408.
Bergen, Nella: 42,208; 64,143; 118,196.
Bergen, Thurlow: 109,iii; 111, 134; 111,136; 200,197.
Bergengren, Ralph: (W) 82,345.
Berger, Rudolf: 153,148.
Bergere, Ouida: 132,39; 307,29.
Bergere, Valerie: 160,293.
Bergman, Gustav: 152,131; 163, 103.
Bergman, Henry: 96,58; 136, 194; 152,123.
Bergman, Leonard E.: 299,23.
Bergner, Elizabeth: 289,29.
Bergstrom, Hjalmar: 205,152.
Beri, Beth: 277,17; 284,43; 305, 23.
Berkeley, Ruth: 10,22; 15,17.
Berkeley (California) (see California, University of).
"Berkeley Square": 346,32; (S) 346,33; (R'29) 346,45; (C) 347,2; 348,20; (D) 349,c; 350, 27; 351,13; 351,21; 351,39.
Berkett, Viva: 347,13.
Berla, Emil: 108,37.
Berlein, Annie Mack: 131,27; 166, 265; 227,19.
Berlin, Irving: 167,9; 168,67;

179,26; 184,351; 212,222; 212,223; 214,335; 218,227; 260,320; 285,27; 300,36; 331, 75; 344,30.
Berlin Theatre (see German Theatre).
Berlioz, Hector: 70,327.
Bernard, Barney: 152,133; (W) 157,136; 178,299; 183,294; 200,221; 225,315; 228,91; 259,252.
Bernard, Jean Jacques: 300,31.
Bernard, Sam: (A) 16,19; 33,272; (A) 51,i,f; 52,135; 52,137; 54,196; 70,338; 79,228; 86, xii; 86,91; 89,193; 103,71; 105,137; 105,141; 117,xv; 117,153; 144,xii; 144,34; 149, 15; 154,xvi; 186,87; 187,136; 194,225; 210,87; 229,171; 231,363; 231,398; 250,34; 253,214; 256,28.
Bernhardt, Sarah: PG,23; 8,15; 9,21; 10,27; 11,12; 16,8; 17,12; 31,224; 36,vi; 37, 61; 50,104; 54,ix; 55,219; 57, 263; 59,2; 59,3; 63,114; 63, 115; 65,v; 65,181; 70,332; 72, vi; 72,55; (D) 75,114; 75, 132; 78,viii; 80,286; 85,62; 87,127; 90,205; 90,223; 107, 5; 111,172; 112,189; 115,xii; 116,115; 117,152; (A) 119, xxiii; 119,7; 199,24; 125,1; 125,18; 127,104; 128,vi; 138, 34; 143,2; 147,xx; 148,161; 148,164; 151,92; 156,83; 174, 75; 175,132; 176,133; 176, 172; 178,305; 180,62; 181,182; 189,286; 190,342; 190,343; 191,64; 199,150; 199,155; 200,206; 204,95; 205,158; 208, 372; 209,10; 211,154; 221, 56; 235,176; 235,177; 260, 303; 261,379; 266,7; 266,12; 352,18; 221,24.
Bernie, Ben: 279,36; 282,23; 298,3; 339,36.
Bernstein, Alice: 351,48.
Bernstein, Elsa: 27,115.
Bernstein, Henry: 80,258; 91,234; 94,xvi; 94,314; 96,48; 99, 155; 107,4; 117,152; (C) 136,174; 143,20; 148,169; 152,xvii.
Bernstein, Karl N.: 331,49.
Berri, Maude Lillian: 75,141.
Berry, Marion: 282,27.
Bersebach, Clara: 249,348.
Bersenieff, Ivan: 259,216.
Bert, Mabel: 69,277; 101,11; 131,8.
Bertram, Helen: 56,248.
Bertrand, Beatrice: 130,222.
Bertrand, Claire: 157,141.
Bertrand, Mary: 103,81.
Beryl, Nelly: 123,179.
Besant, Reginald: 156,65.
Besier, Rudolph: 108,35.
Besley, Madeline: 30,207.
Best, Bert: 222,99.
Best, Edna: 295,27; 298,14; 310,33; 333,56; 338,39.
Best, Susie M.: (W,V) 130,196.
"Best People, The": (R'24) 283, 16; 283,25.
"Best Sellers, The": (R'18) 209, 24.
"Bethlehem": 64,155.
"Betrothal, The": (R'18) 215,17; 215,21.
"Betsy": (R'11) 131,xiii.
"Betsy Ross": (S) 4,8; 4,16.
"Better 'Ole, The": 214,344; (R'18) 214,345; 219,284; (D) 222,82.
"Better Times": (R'22) 261,377; 261,383.
Betterton, Thomas: 142,174; 142,175; 221,8.
Betty, [Master] William Henry W.: 77,176; 221,8; 253, 212.
"Betty": (R'16) 189,284.
"Betty At Bay": 215,15; (R'18) 215,20.
"Betty, Be Good": 232,505; (R'20) 232,525.
Beveridge, J.D.; 56,247.
Beveridge, Ray: 97,94.
"Beverly's Balance": (R'15) 172,281; 172,287.
"Beware of Dogs": (R'21) 249, 440.
"Beware of Smooth Water": (R'03) 26,101.
"Beware of Widows": (R'25) 299, 16.

"Bewitched": 285,14; (R'24) 285, 19.
Beyer, Robert: 335,46.
Beyer, William: 294,21.
"Beyond": 45,288.
"Beyond Human Power": 12,3.
"Beyond the Horizon": (R'20) 299, 185.
Bianco, Pamela: (D) 292,11.
Bickel, George: 114,45; 143,6.
Bickford, Charles: 296,16; 296, 29.
Biddle, Craig Jr.: 271,23.
Biensfeld, Paul: 142,191.
Bierwald, Benjamin: 151,xii.
"Biff-Bang": (R'18) 209,23; 20,96.
"Big Boy": (R'25) 288,19.
"Big Chance, The": 214,339; (R'18) 214,380.
"Big Fight, The": (R'28) 332,47.
"Big Game": 229,167; (R'20) 229,182.
"Big House": (F,R) 353,48.
"Big Idea, The": (R'14) 167,7; 167,31.
"Big Jim Garrity": (R'14) 166, 306.
"Big Parade, The": (F) 294,33.
"Big Pond, The": (R'28) 331,41; 332,32.
"Big Scene, The": (R'18) 208, 356; 208,359.
"Big Shot, The": (R'29) 344, 70.
"Big Show, The": (R'16) 188,246; 189,275.
"Big Trail, The": (F,R) 358, 48.
Bigelow, Charles A.: 40,137; 85,75; 117,159; 150,69.
Bijou Dream Theatre (Boston): 144,59.
Bijou Theatre (New York): 110,121; 231,352; 290,50.
"Bill of Divorcement, A": (R'21) 249,385; 250,17; (D) 250, 35; (S) 251,84.
"Billeted": 204,73; (R'17) 204,86; (R'22) 256,32.
"Billie": (R'28) 334,60.
Billings, George: 277,31.
"Billionaire, The": (R'03) 24,34.
"Billy": (R'09) 103,73; 103,76.
Billy, Little: 181,124; 183,286; 229,187.
Binder, Sybille: 289,29.
Bingham, A.E. (W): 30,201.
Bingham, Amelia: 3,11; 4,2; 12,9; 13,12; 15,3; 15,4; 15, 5; 25,56; 26,84; 34,307; 36, 31; 37,77; 38,v; (A) 39,viii; 50,101; 58,291; 64,141; 67, 246; 78,212; 81,290; 83,16; 106,188; 132,47; 139,72; 156,78; (A) 214,379; 229, 187; 274,21; 306,32.
Bingham, Joseph: 145,72.
Binney, Constance: 215,63; 218,211; 219,277; 220,349; 224,255; 228,109; 231,410; 233,13; 237,380; 244,37; 278, 23; 279,27; 280,27.
Binney, Faire: 223,145; 229,170; 248,309; 255,398.
Birch-Pfeifer, Charlotte: 27, 116.
Bird, Carol (W) (see also "Men Who Write the Hits, The"): 236,258; 237,374; 239,92; 241,242; 242,322; 244,8; 245, 104; 246,146; 249,390; 250, 22; 251,80; 252,162; 254, 286; 257,72; 257,102; 259, 241; 270,20; 279,9; 291,31; 294,18.
Bird, Richard: 289,39; 322,40; 355,27.
Bird, Robert M.: (D) 197,14.
"Bird in Hand": (S) 341,24; (R'29) 341,43; 350,20;
"Bird in the Cage, The": (R'03) 24,30.
"Bird of Paradise, The": (R'12) 132,42; 132,59.
"Bird's Christmas Carol, The": 357,51; 357,52.
Birkett, Phyllis: 204,73.
Birkett, Viva: 189,273.
Birmingham, Alan: 269,13.
Birmingham [Alabama] Little Theatre: 296,21; 299,40; 322,53.
Biron, Lillian: 209,60.
"Birth of a Nation, The": (F,R) 170,212.
"Birthday of the Infanta, The": 228,93.

Birthdays of Actors: 215,26; 216,96; 217,154; 219,282.
Bischoff, Johannes: 44,240.
Bishof, Mariel: 131,14.
Bishop, Anna: 65,196.
"Bishop's Emeralds, The": (F) 220,390; 220,391; 220,400.
"Bishop's Move, The": (R,03) 26, 83; 26,88.
Bissett, Esther: 129,164; 134, 126.
Bispham, David: 12,21; 40,ix; 60,54; 125,21; 141,148; 158, 199; 177,234; 197,31; 202, 369.
Bisson, Alexandre: 107,4.
"Bit O'Love, A": (R'25) 293,15.
"Bitter Sweet": (R'29) 346,44; (D) 347,c.
Bjornsen, Bjornstjerne: 12,3; 26,100; 37,v; 110,112; 161, 27.
Black, Hazel: 171,238.
Black, Nettie: 39,128.
"Black Boy": (R'26) 309,68.
"Black Crook, The": (D) 134, 131; 191,44; 197,34; (R'29) 338,46; 340,38; 354,44.
"Black Mask, The": (R'13) 153,xv; 153,143.
Blackath, Clara: 331,53.
"Blackbirds": (R'13) 144,38.
"Blackbirds of 1928": (R'28) 328,39.
Blackburn, Arline: 305,52; 307,33.
Blackmer, Sydney: 232,523; 243, 407; 251,106; 258,139; 266, 25; 268,3; 287,27; 288,38; 292,30; 298,16; 303,45; 304, 33; 320,60; 352,44.
Blackstone, Nan: 352,42.
Blackstone Theatre (Chicago): 121,80.
Blackwell, Carlyle: 210,120.
Blackwell, Irene: 210,75; (A) 214,379.
Blaire, John: 21,12; 59,5; 104, 132; 146,98; 253,231; 278, 14.
Blaire, Marie: 225,313.
Blaire, Mary: 242,343; 281,42.
Blaire, Eugene: (D) 250,33.
Blake, William Dorsey (W): 331, 52.
Blake, Rodney (W): 144,60.
Blake, Warren Barton (W): 124, 202; 133,89; 164,166.
Blakeley, James: 92,281.
Blakemore, Harry: 269,31.
Blakeslee, Fred Gilbert (W): 22,16; 96,45; 101,16; 216, 96; 234,96.
Blance, Julia: 6,17.
Blanchard, Kitty: 38,100; 111, 158.
Blancke, Kate: 91,238.
Blandick, Clara: 87,123; 88,166; 89,180.
Blane, Sally: 322,22.
"Blank Page, A": 9,10.
Blass, Robert: 74,110.
Blauvelt, Lillian: 13,26; 72,34.
Blayney, May: 57,279; 64,158; 115,66; 121,81; 124,14.
Bledsoe, Jules: 310,11; 336,47.
"Blessed Ones, The": 268,23.
"Blind Alleys": (R'17) 202,352.
"Blind Youth": 203,20; (R'17) 203,24.
"Blindness of Virtue, The": (R'12) 142,xviii.
Blinn, Beatrice: 307,27; 336, 27.
Blinn, Holbrook: 51,114; 67, 237; 73,77; 85,69; 90,209; 95,19; 96,54; 103,71; 111, 139; 121,72; 124,191; 131, 13; 147,155; 148,186; 153, 143; 157,113; 157,119; 166, 267; 170,170; 175,110; 177, 230; 182,192; 184, 334; (A,D) 184,365; 203,13; 207,283; 219,285; 220,333; 233,35; (D) 237,351; 242,337; 273, 33; (C) 290,31; 291,39; (C,W) 307,22; 310,14; 311, 28; (A) 314,50; 319,20; (C) 324,82; 330,72.
Bliss, Lillian: 61,66.
Blitz, Henry: 93,289.
Bloch, Alexander: 155,8.
Bloch, Andre (W): 339,25.
Bloch, Ernest: 196,352.
Block, Stella: 318,36.
Block, Adele: 61,74; 92,276.
Block, Bertram (W): 312,16b.
Block, Ralph (W): 299,32.
Block, Sheridan: 45,279.

Blocki, Fritz (W): 331,39.
Blockz, Jan: 98,109.
"Blonde in Black, The": (R'03) 29,161.
Blondell, Libby Arnold: 54,206.
"Blood and Sand": (R'21) 249, 385; 250,24; (F) 260,306.
"Blood Money": (R'27) 319,22; (S) 319,26.
Bloodgood, Clara: 10,3; 24,33; 25,57; 27,118; 45,282; (W) 46,304; 56,247; 72,33.
"Blood-Stained Russia": (F,R) 203, 57.
Bloom, Sol (W): 331,25.
Bloom, Vera (W): 198,96; 200, 212; 204,100; 206,214; 209, 14; 210,96; 211,152; 214, 342; 218,226; 310,33.
Bloomfield, Estelle: 73,61.
Bloomfield-Zeisler, Fanny: 10, 34.
"Blooming Angel, The": (F,R) 229,100.
Blore, Eric: 272,29.
Blossom, Henry: 38,84; 55,277; 267,13; 196,344.
"Blossom Time": 249,367; (R'21) 249,388; (D) 249,389.
"Blot in the 'Scutcheon, A": (R'05) 51,111.
"Bludgeon, The: (R'14) 164,196.
Blue, Monte: 285,31; 309,40; 312,23; 316,50.
"Blue Bird, The": (S) 72,55; 108,51; 116,121; (R'10) 117, 130; 117,132; 117,133; 118, 170; (F) 204,119; (F) 204, 124.
"Blue Bonnet, The": 236,283; (R'20) 236,328.
"Blue Envelope, The": (R'16) 183, 275.
"Blue Eyes": (R'21) 242,340; 242,341.
"Blue Flame, The": (R'20) 231, 401.
"Blue Grass": 94,xii; 94,316.
"Blue Kitten, The": (R'22) 253, 264.
Blue Laws: 265,7; 301,7; 341, 16.
"Blue Moon, The": (R'06) 70, xix.
"Blue Mouse, The": (R'08) 95, 5; 95,29; 100,190.
"Blue Paradise, The": (R'13) 175,113.
"Blue Pearl, The": (R'18) 211, 144.
"Blue Peter, The": 291,14; 291, 15.
"Bluebeard's Eighth Wife": (R'21) 249,386.
"Bluffs": (R'08) 87, ix.
"Blushing Bride, The": 253,229; (R'22) 253,262.
Blythe, Betty: 206,255; 214, 391; 230,281; 243,423; 272, 31.
Blythe, Veronica: 353,21.
Boag, William: 45,274.
Boardman, Eleanor: 295,39; 305, 35; 312,39; 317,38; (A) 353,58.
"Bobby Burnit": (R'10) 116,xiv.
"Boccaccio": 225,320.
Bochert, George: 331,48.
Bodansky, Artur: 172,288; 178, 284; 223,163; 238,35; 264, 36; (D) 273,27.
Bodenheim, Maxwell: 199,143.
Bogaert, Lucienne: 215,25.
Bogart, Humphrey: 293,44; 297, 26; (C) 319,72.
Bogel, Claus: 17,6; 142,163.
Bohemian Club: 103,88; 125,21; 132,62; 141,148.
"Bohemian Princess, The": 122, iii.
Bohemian Theatre: 137,31.
Bohnen, Michael: 260,318; 277, 35; 301,35.
Bois, Jules: 100,191; 173,34.
Boker, George H.: 197,14.
Boland, Mary: 56,254; 63,116; 80,269; 80,281; 92,255; 94, 330; 95,24; 99,147; 102,36; 105,155; 111,171; 117,c; 126, 48; 128,124; 139,90; 140, 100; 143,c; 149,33; 152,110; 153,143; 160,326; 165,224; 166,268; 166,269; 186,87; 189,284; 195,276; 196,329; 206,216; 206,229; 207,310; 226,365; 226,410; 260,298; 260,329; 260, 330; 269,43; 277,25; 296,19; 297,26; 299,

31; 312,30; 331,47; 333,55; 358,25; 359,28.
Bolce, Harold (W); 315,13; 333, 18; 337,33.
"Bold Soger Boy, The": (R'03) 25,59.
Boles, John: 308,38; 335,28.
Boleslawsky, Richard: (W) 265, 27; 300,22; 302,21; 306, 53; 319,41; 333,49.
Boley, May: 43,233.
Bolles, William: (W) 194,200.
Bolling, Arline: 144,44; 169, 115.
Bolm, Adolph: 127,97; 176,166; 178,294; 178,295; 178,296; 181,128; 188,199; 200,201; 217,133; 226,393; 228,94; 239,102; 243,403; 253,232; 260,315; 261,392; 283,23; 291,29; 310,8; 326,36.
Bolton, Guy: 202,368; 220, 339; 228,96; 249,396; 280,10; 331, 27.
Bolton, Helen: 219,281; (A) 226,438; 230,291; 238,51; 244,14.
Bolton, Linda: 174,67.
"Bombasters Furioso": (R'24) 282,15.
"Bombo": (R'21) 249,424.
Bonci, Alessandro: 67,232; 71,8; 79,xiii; 82,350; 94,346; 265, 9.
Bond, Frederic: 64,160; 64,161; 77,185.
Bond, Helen: 126,67; 128,139; 190,354.
Bond, Lillian: 354,36.
Bond, Raymond: 84,48.
Bondi, Beulah: 304,28; 324,40; 352,15.
"Bonds of Interest, The": (R'19) 220,341; (D) 292,12; (R'29) 345,66.
Bonefeld, Mirele: 119,14.
Bonelli, Richard: 282,35.
Bonetti, Mary: 285,35.
Bonfanti, Marie: 52,144; 340,38.
Bonfield, Edward: 120,36.
Bonheur, Celine: 119,8.
Boniface, George C. Jr.: 76,167; 120,42.
Bonita: 132,71.
Bonn, Ferdinand: 15,14; 13,19.
Bonn, Francis: 49,59.
Bonnet, Joseph: 194,229.
"Bonnie Brier Bush, The": (R'01) 9,11.
Bonstelle, Jessie: 91,232; 94, 315; 109,81; 141,142; 164,166; 269,23; 331,20.
Bonstelle Playhouse (Detroit): 298,36; (D) 331,20.
"Book of Charm, The": (R'25) 296,16.
"Book of Job, The": 206,205; 206,213; (R'18) 206,217; (R'19) 218,208.
Booking Agency (see Agents).
"Boom Boom": 338,25; (R'29) 338,47.
"Boomerang, The": 175,105; (R'15) 175,112; 176,181; 180, 83; 184,359; 190,364.
Boone, John A.: 200,209.
"Boot-Leggers, The": (R'22) 263,20.
Booth, Agnes: 34,307; 62,101; 84,42; 108,ix; 168,72; 171,234.
Booth, Charles Stewart (W): 35, 26; (V) 113,25.
Booth, Doris: 191,42; 204,101.
Booth, Edwin: 12,19; 14,20; 34,310f; 39,114; 46,305; 46, 311; 49,60; 55,226; 58,xii; 63, vii; 67,xiii; 69,311; 81,298; 84,50; 103,82; 106,184; (A) 111,162; 126,64; 132,69; 138, 43; 139,94; 144,60; 145,74; 179,18; 180,79; 182,217; 185, 6; 190,360; 197,30; 212,202; 215,34; 231,399; 244,28; (D) 266,10; 302,37.
Booth, John H.: 55,234.
Booth, John Wilkes: 34,299; 39, 114; (A) 39,115; 57,288; 87, 130; 103,82; 148,179.
Booth, Julia: 39,111.
Booth, Junius Brutus: 17,19; 39, 114; 232,507.
Booth, Sydney: 155,6; 161,46; 176,194.
Booth Family: 143,31; 211,154; 232,502.
Booth Theatre (New York): 153, 146; (D) 206,236; 290,17.

Boothe, Earle: 291,36; 302,21.
Borchard, Adolphe: 116,109.
Borden, Eugene: (D) 255,375.
Borden, Joyce: 303,25.
Borden, Olive: 307,40; 309,2; 314,41; 321,12; 322,12.
"Border Legion, The": (F,R) 211, 183.
"Borderland": 233,35.
Bordini: 153,159.
Bordini, Irene: 179,11; 179,88; 198,83; 207,291; 210,110; (A) 214,379; 215,5; 216,109; 225,323; 229,171; 230,245; (A) 231,455; 233,51; (A) 253, 255; 254,285; (D) 255,375; 257,87; (D) 258,155; 264,29; 271,27; 286,46; 290,13; 291, 44; 296,38; 298,16; 299,c; 300,45; 301,42; 306,40; (C) 316,31; (A) 322,3; 323,53; 334,56; 336,66; (D) 339,c; 342,55; 343,35; 344,73.
Boreo, Emil: 281,27; 305,14.
Bori, Lucrezia: 141,138; 142, 166; 153,149; 155,14; 156,66; 157,117; 159,228; 169,107; 170,183; 178,285; 188,199; 238,35; 260,319; 264,37; 280, 35; 287,35; 298,35; 303,35; 361,21.
"Boris Godunoff" (OP): 147,140.
Borland, Barlowe: 200,209.
Borlin, Jean: 272,11.
Borowski, Vera: 266,21.
Borras, Enrique: 107,32.
Boscacci, Romeo: 248,317.
Boshell, Ada: 192,89; 260,320.
"Bosom Friends": (R'17) 196, 341.
"Boss, The": (R'11) 121,vii; 121, 72.
Boss, Matilda: 218,211.
Bosse-Strindberg, Harriet: 50, 89.
Boston Museum: 178,314.
Boston Opera House: (D) 88, 167; 119,8.
Boston Theatre: 88,168; 155, 28; 216,102; 245,100; 299, 24; 302,37; 354,45.
Bostwick, Elwood F.: 271,18.
Bosworth, Hobart: 33,268; 171, 245.
Botsford, Rosamund: 163,109.
Botta, Luca: 169,107.
Botti, Rose: 38,95.
"Bottled": (R'28) 327,38.
"Bottom of the Cup, The": 315,25.
Bottomley, Roland: 231,407.
Bouchier, Arthur: 187,131.
Boucicault, Aubrey: PG,21; 4,6; 4.7; 4,9; 12,6; 17,2; 20,7; 23,8; 26,101; 49,72; 56,257.
Boucicault, Dion: 25,64; 49,72; 51,109; 52,155; 55,226; 58, xii; (A) 58,302; 74,89; 84, 42; 88,169; 138,45; 138,58; 168,73; 258,142; 286,16.
Boucicault, Ruth Holt: 109,68.
"Bought and Paid for": (R'11) 129,149; 129,169; 231,351; (R'21) 251,99.
Boulanger, Louise: 334,56.
"Bound East for Cardiff": (R'24) 286,22.
"Bound in Morocco": (F,R) 211, 183.
"Boundary Line, The": (R'29) 349,48.
Bouquet, Renee: 214,343; 215, 25.
"Bourbouroche": (R'21) 251,100.
Bourchier, Arthur: 116,128; 118, 197; (D) 129,173.
Bourdelle, Joan: 317,6.
Bourdet, Edouard: 308,33.
Bourke, Fan: 227,19.
Bourne, Adeline: 80,270.
Bourne, Margaret: 8,13; 93, 269.
Bourne, Nettie: 6,15.
Bourskaya, Ina: 266,37; 281, 35.
Bourskaya, Maria: 299,35.
Boutet, Anne F.H.: 118,175.
Bow, Clara: 272,33; (D) 319, c; (W) 320,42.
Bowen, Elgie: 103,74; 104,111;
Bowers, [Mrs.] D.P.: 15,24; 86, 98.
Bowers, John: 167,27; 190,354. 293,39.
Bowery Theatre (New York): 19,20; (D) 136,197; 137,27; (D) 205,160; 250,10.
Bowes, E.J.: 135,142.
Bowes, [Major] Edward: 314,37.

Bowhan, Sibylla: 238,33.
Bowley, Flora Juliet: 47,15; 64, 164; 69,290; 80,279; 82,334.
Bowman, Carrie: 33,282; 89, 184.
Box Office (see also Speculators, Tickets; Tickets, Theatre: 38,90; 88,166; 110,118; 118, xvi; 128,121; 145,74; 161, 22; 189,272; 205,164; 208, 366; 244,7; 253,244; 274, 12; 283,24; 288,7; 294,24; 299,22; 312,24; 316,16; 327, 23.
"Boy and the Girl, The": 101, iii; (R'09) 101,3.
Boyd, Archie: 155,36.
Boyd, Ernest: (W) 295,10.
Boyd, Ruth: 208,359; 219,293.
Boyd, William: 172,287; 284, 14; 284,23; 317,39; 320,66; 321,75; 322,6; 323,4b; 324, 8; 325,81; 326,77; 345,65.
Boyer, Lucien: (D) 251,87.
Boyle, Francis J.: 8,6; 170, 192.
Boyne, Eva Leonard: 143,16; 162,80.
Boyne, Leonard: 35,9.
"Boys and Betty, The": (R'08) 94,313; 94,324.
"Boys of Company B, The": (R'07) 75,115; 75,127.
Bozo: 275,29.
Bracco, Roberto: 76,144.
Brackett, Parmlee (W,V): 126, 70; 152,125; 153,169; 156, 74; 207,303.
Bracy, Clara T.: 120,62; 197, 25; 213,287; 250,24.
Bracy, Sidney: 136,173.
Bradbury, J.H.: 10,4.
Bradbury, James: 105,149; 140, 113; 226,366; 226,379; 272, 29.
Bradbury, Jessie: 120,59.
Bradford, Edith: 105,159; 108, 54.
Bradford, Margaret: (W) 121,78.
Bradish, C.R. (W): 330,21; 334,22.
Bradley, Alice: 176,192.
Bradley, Alma: 37,iv.
Bradley, Anne: 113,20.
Bradley, Florence: 89,185.
Bradley, Lillian Trimble: 230, 261; 235,180; 269,23.
Brady, Adele: 232,534.
Brady, Alice: 124,183; 125,13; 136,170; 137,3; 137,6; 141, 143; 146,124; 152,130; 153, 154; 155,5; 155,7; 157,134; 162,74; 163,101; 168,62; 171,268; (A) 185,49; 199, 155; 213,271; 215,43; 218, 219; (D) 220,361; (A) 221, 47; 223,159; 225,301; 229, 190; 235,171; 235,194; 237, 362; 237,391; 242,333; 248, 305; 251,118; 252,155; (D) 252,169; 256,9; 266,33; 267, 14; 272,66; 273,12; 294,44; 295,14; 296,45; 302,42; 303, 5; 305,27; (C) 308,11; 311, 18; 311,24; 313,46; (C) 317, 31; (A) 324,7; 335,60; (D) 339,37; (W) 345,30; 346, 46; (D) 347,52; 354,55.
Brady, Diamond Jim: (W) 190, 346.
Brady, Eva: 233,27.
Brady, Florence: 270,34; 289, 37; 311,25.
Brady, James Buchanan: 111, xviii.
Brady, W.J.: 93,287; 123,161.
Brady, William A.: 60,42; 62, 89; 65,187; 67,ix; 94,xxxiv; 103,71; 120,xi; 124,viii; 130,xxxv; 141,xviii; 142,xxii; 145,75; 147,ix; 151,81; 151, 102; 154,xxviii; 163,101; 175, 111; 178,310; 180,62; 188, 198; 203,55; 206,254; 215,6; 223,144; 224,221; 231,379; 234,148; 246,166; (W) 275, 9; 289,22; 294,64; 307,6; (W) 338,13.
Bragdon, Claude: (W) 356,20.
Braham, Dave Jr.: 37,58.
Braham, Florence: 193,141.
Braham, Horace: 165,204; 170, 197; 340,50.
Braham, Lionel: 170,196; 184, 386; 185,9; 219,281.
Braidon, Thomas A.: 349,45.
Brailowsky, Alexander; 289,35; 332,27.

"Braisley Diamond, The": (R'06) 60,27.
Braithwaite, Lillian: 187,131; 296,17; 298,28.
Bramhall Playhouse (New York): 171,240; 174,64; 191,21.
Bramson, Karen: 286,25.
Bramwell, William: 24,38; 53, 180.
"Brand": 146,114.
"Branded": (R'17) 201,278.
Brandell, Josephine: 101,14.
Brandon, Helen: 55,225.
Brandon, Lina: 250,22.
Brandon, Mary: 239,90.
Brandon, Philip: 335,46.
Brandt, Edwin: 14,2.
Brandt, Kaethe: 13,20.
Brandt, Sophia: 116,109; 117, 138.
Branigan, A.H.: (W) 113,19.
Branzell, Karin: 277,35.
Braslau, Sophie: 158,183; 167, 17; 180,85; 197,9; 204,105; 207,275; 262,43; 326,45; 153, 148.
"Brass Bottle, The": 115,65; (R'10) 115,70.
"Brat, The": (R'17) 194,216; 195,276; (F) 223,179.
Braun, Carl: 141,139; 145,70; 190,345.
Braun, Toni: 90,207.
Bray, Will H.: 32,259.
Brayton, Lily: 54,184; 70,337.
"Bread": (F,R) 283,32.
"Breakfast in Bed": 229,187; (R'20) 229,220.
"Breaking Point, The": (R'23) 271,16.
Breamer, Sylvia: 223,176; 231,433.
Breese, Edmund: 39,110; 49,59; 55,217; 58,287; 59,24; 67, 252; (W) 75,135; 90,i; 92, 280; 95,33; 112,194; 121,85; 128,xi; 129,162; 131,13; 135, 147; 146,100; 177,231; 204, 103; 245,83; (W) 360,45.
Breitsamter, Melchoir: 255,378.
Brenau College: 230,282.
Brendel, El.: 277,37.
Brennan, Jay (see Savoy and Brennan).
Brennan, John E.: 92,277.
Brennan, Nan: 129,175.
Brenner, Dorothy: 137,24.
Brenon, Herbert: 199,175; 199, 178; 204,124; (W) 317,37.
Brennard, Lillian: 197,25.
Brent, Eleanor: 164,184.
Brent, Evelyn: 334,44; 340,40.
Brent, Romney: 293,19; 299,17; 311,64; 321,52; 337,48.
Breslau, Sophie: 153,148.
Bressler-Gianoli, Clotilde: 72, 38; 73,64; 82,251.
Breston, Gladys: 147,147.
Breton, Ruth: 284,35.
Breval, Lucienne: 121,101.
Brewer, J.H.: 216,81.
Brewster, Betty: 142,165.
Brewster, Harold L.: (W) 292,44.
Brewster, Mary: (W) 232,530.
Brewster, Nellie: 91,244.
"Brewster's Millions": 72,30; (R'06) 72,31; 74,92.
Breyer, Maggie: 196,359.
Brian, Donald: 81,313; (C) 82,xxiv; 82,330; 84,c; 105, 157; 128,120; 128,135; 139, 95; 149,18; 151,80; 153,145; 156,80; 164,167; 166,282; 181,135; 183,294; 184,361; 186,87; 198,104; 199,127; 199,148; 213,271; 214,340; (A) 214,379; 219,281; 225, 312; 231,354; 232,504; 301, 38.
Brian, Mary: 313,49; 341,28.
Brice, Elizabeth: 90,209; 103,98; 105,156; 159,241; 164,174; 221,25; 234,107.
Brice, Fannie: 114,45; 166,281; 186,71; (D) 247,211; 248, 310; 262,36; 263,43; 308,15; 316,34; 323,53; 328,25; 330, 59; 332,35; (D) 336,73; 337, 30; (W) 339,31; (C) 358,44.
Brice, Lew: 307,14.
"Bride, The": (R'13) 153,xvii; 153,153; (R'24) 280,16; 281, 14.
"Bride and the Bridegroom, The": 3 44,xiii.
"Bride of the Lamb": (R'26) 303,15; (S) 305,26; 305, 27.

"Bride of the Regiment": (F, R0 352, 47; (F) 352, 61.
"Bride Retires, The": (R'25) 293, 15.
"Bridge, The": 102, 46; 102, 47; (R'09) 104, 108.
"Bridge Builder": 102, 46.
Bridgeport, Alleta: 112, 187.
Bridger, Anita: 28, 134.
"Bridges": (R'21) 242, 342.
Bridges, Ann Preston: 328, 29.
Bridges, Ruby: 42, 202; 88, 160.
Brieux, Eugene: (W) 56, 246; 76, viii; 88, viii; 117, 160; 145, 92; 151, xii; 167, 24; (A) 167, 25; 168, 56.
"Brigadier Gerard": (R'06) 70, 317.
Briggs, Harlan: 343, 33; (C) 344, 44.
Bright, Cecilia: 160, 326.
Bright, Ione: 116, 122; 138, 44; 158, 198.
Bright, Martha: 88, 155.
"Bright Eyes": 110, vii; 110, 101; (R'10) 110, 127.
"Brighter Side, The": (R'05) 49, 57.
Brighton Beach Park: 53, 178.
Brincken, Val: 357, 48.
Brink, Lily: 35, 12.
Brinkley, Grace: 332, 49; 349, 29.
Briscoe, Lottie: 87, 118; 166, 275.
"British and American Drama of To-Day, The" (Clark): (B) 178, 314.
British Columbia, University of: 214, 366.
Britting, Charles H.: 104, 117.
Britton, Dorothy: 340, 54; 341, 7.
"Brixton Burglary, The": 4, 2; 5, 3.
Broad, Bertha: 206, 207; 247, 225; 260, 305.
Broad Street Theatre (Philadelphia): 37, 79.
Broadcasting (see Radio).
Broadfoot, Eleanor (see De Cisneros, Eleanora).
Broadhurst, George H.: 27, 107; 74, 89; 75, 128; 130, xii; 145, 75; 153, 150; 159, 230; 181, 151; (W) 193, 140; 200, 220; 224, 222; (W) 231, 382; 231, 395; 231, 494; 234, 84; (W) 248, 296; 251, 102; (W) 276, 22.
Broadhurst, Thomas W.: 30, 205.
Broadway (see Rialto, The).
"Broadway": (R'26) 308, 66; 309, 19; (S) 310, 26; 310, 28; 310, 32; 342, 37; (C) 346, 39.
"Broadway and Buttermilk": 186, 59; 187, 133; (R'16) 187, 140.
"Broadway Babies": (F) 342, 67.
"Broadway Brevities: (R'20) 237, 371.
"Broadway Jones": (R'12) 141, 134.
"Broadway Nights": 342, 39; (R'29) 342, 41.
Broadway Theatre (New York): 38, 90; 61, 73; 110, 121; 202, 344; 336, 42.
"Broadway to Paris": (R'12) 143, 5; 143, 6.
"Broadway Whirl, The": (R'21) 245, 98.
Brockwell, Gladys: 204, 127; 211, 187; 228, 147.
Broader, Frank: 128, 114.
Broderick, Robert: 218, 256; 220, 390; 220, 391.
Brodinova, Todya: 196, 357.
Broeck, Helen Ten (W): 183, 285; 184, 352; 185, 23; 186, 69; 187, 150; 190, 372; 191, 28; 192, 74; 193, 164; 194, 202; 195, 274; 196, 354; 197, 16; 198, 86; 199, 150; 200, 224; 201, 282; 206, 210; 209, 40; 212, 226; 231, 406; 232, 532; 233, 24; 240, 184; 259, 220.
"Broken Blossoms": (F) 220, 400; 220, 401.
"Broken Branches": (R'22) 254, 336.
"Broken Dishes": (R'29) 346, 45; 346, 48.
"Broken Hearts": 71, 10.
"Broken Idol, A": 104, iii; 104, xiii.
"Broken Threads": (R'17) 202, 352.
"Broken Wing, The": (R'20) 239, 106; 240, 159.
Brokers, Ticket (see Speculators,

Ticket).
Bromley, George: 150,70.
Bronaugh, Anne: 314,30.
Brommer, Cleveland: 223,159; 236,265.
Bronson, Betty: 284,31; 292, 35; (D) 293,4; 293,34; 295, 34; 296,32; 338,31.
Bronson, Edgar Beecher: (W) 111, 162.
Bronson, Edna: 39,130.
Bronson, Llewellyn (W): 198, 66; 200,214.
Bronson, Percy: 80,273.
"Bronx Express, The": 256,7; (R'22) 256,31.
Brook, Katharine: 202,341; 252,151.
Brooke, Claude: 153,161.
Brooke, Clifford: 333,49.
Brooke, Cynthia: 183,274; 204, 79; 238,7.
Brooks, Alan: 193,166; 238,15; 280,14.
Brooks, Joseph: 166,311; 175,110; 187,178.
Brooks, Louise: 283,21; 320,45; 325,46.
Brooks, Myra: 112,180.
Brooks, Virginia Fox: 178,275; 179,19; 179,21; 190,374; 191,32; 211,151; 226,390.
Broske, Octavia: 112,187; 141, 155.
"Brother Jacques": (R'05) 47,5.
"Brothers Karamazov." (R'18) 205,151; (R'19) 217,143; 312,21.
Brough, Fanny: 39,111; 41,172; 44,243.
Brough, Sidney: 10,1; 10,2.
Brougham, John: 126,64; 205, 166; 246,164.
Broun, Heywood: (C) 193,138; (C) 266,11; (W) 327,7; (C) 333,33.
Browdy, Louis N.: (W) 322, 49.
Brown, A. Seymour: 179,26.
Brown, Agnes Cain: 73,61; 79, 233.
Brown, Albert: 160,283; 163, 101.
Brown, Alice: 161,11.
Brown, Charles: 120,44; 143, 24; 226,371; 307,23; 344,57.
Brown, Eddy: 249,391.
Brown, Eleanor: 171,239.
Brown, Elizabeth: 287,37.
Brown, F.C. (W): 120,43; 209, 36; 245,100.
Brown, Gilmor: (W) 253,247; 325,83; 273,41; 320,49; 331, 55; (W) 348,50; 349,9.
Brown, Harry C.: 177,235; 210, 115.
Brown, Jessica: 220,340; 243, 408; 233,25.
Brown, Joe E.: 298,27; 314,35; (C) 352,59; 358,46; (C) 359, 3.
Brown, John: 178,294.
Brown, John Mack: 324,12.
Brown, Josephine: 147,159.
Brown, Karl: 316,40.
Brown, Kitty: 190,347.
Brown, Lawrence: 293,24.
Brown, Louise: 268,24; 306,47; 329,41.
Brown, Martin: 136,186; 140, 123; 284,10.
Brown, Maud: 79,237.
Brown, Maxine: 278,23.
Brown, Norma: 101,17.
Brown, Pearl: 83,27.
Brown, Reed Jr.: 356,35.
Brown, Seymour: 90,212.
Brown, Southard (W): 161,22.
Brown, [Col.] T. Allston: 18,11; 46,ii.
Brown, W. Graham: 183,274; 192,79.
Brown, Warren Wilmer (W): 134,135; 197,32.
"Brown of Harvard": (R'06) 62, 87; 62,94.
Brown University: 168,86; 258,169.
Browne, Earle: 73,77; 106, 186; 165,217; 189,277.
Browne, Graham: 98,123; 106, 177; 112,183.
Browne, Lewis Allen (W): 221, 6; 214,334; 226,382.
Browne, Maurice: 127,89; 145, 84; 231,403; 243,419; 255, 379; 353,30.
Browne, Porter Emerson: 101, 32; 115,81; 174,71.

Browne, Walter (W): 33,275; 35, 14; 122,118.
Brownell, Mabel: 110,122.
Browning, Edith: 93,299.
Browning, Ethel: 89,176.
Browning, Joe: 275,37.
Browning, Robert: 70,xxiii.
Brownlow, Wallace: 45,276.
Brown-Potter, [Mrs.]: PG,7; 142,200.
Bruce, Dorothy: 284,26.
Bruce, Langdon: 204,73.
Bruguiere, Francis: 290,49.
Bruna, Eda: 64,162.
Brune, Minnie Tittell: 89,180.
Bruner, R.W.: (W,V) 148, 170.
Brunette, Fritzi: 218,251.
Bruning, Albert: 96,38; 100,183; 105,144; 105,145; 107,9; 118, 169; 118,172; 141,137; 216, 94; 221,21; 250,7; 254,291; 276,14; 309,27.
Bruns, Edna: 112,199.
Bruns, Julia: 161,43; 207,291.
"Brute, The": (R'12) 141,xii.
Bryan, Alfred: 179,26.
Bryan, Gertrude: 131,29; 139, 75; 186,73; 280,39; 281,41; 287,13.
Bryan-Allen, Martha: 302,c.
Bryant, Charles: 142,163; 207, 310; 208,349; 223,179.
Bryant, Dan: 192,104.
Bryant, Frances: 230,275.
Bryant, J.V.: 166,264.
Bryant, Nana: 286,21; 286,27; 290,28; 321,43.
Bryn Mawr College: 103,97; 144,63; 233,43.
Bryton, Frederic: 62,101.
"Bubble, The": (R'15) 171,228.
"Buccaneer, The": (R'25) 297,16.
Buchanan, Harry J.: 90,i.
Buchanan, Jack: 276,18; 308, 36; 356,48.
Buchanan, McKean: 78,215.
Buchanan, Thompson: 101,32; 115,81; 115,82.
Buck, Gene: 217,149; 254,327; 285,27; 303,36; 313,32.
Buck, Inez: 159,238; 176,194.
"Buckaroo": (R'29) 338,47.
Buckingham, Inez: 155,21.
Buckingham, Lillian: 116,126.
Buckley, Dot: 233,28.
Buckley, Guy: 240,155.
Buckler, Henry: 206,213.
Buckler, Hugh: 336,31; 349,42.
Buckler, John: 320,28.
Buckley, Joseph: 128,114.
Buckley, May: 39,109; 39,110; 50,98; 62,101; 115,69; 117, 136; 159,267; 299,19.
Bucklin, Margart: 78,209.
Buckner, Blanche: 45,288.
Buckstone, Rowland: 86,117; 105,144; 105,145; 182,230.
Budd, Herbert: 104,113.
"Buddies": 225,312; (R'19) 227, 18.
Buers, Willy: 141,138.
Bufano, Remo: 301,36.
Buffalo Bill (see Cody, William F.).
"Builder of Bridges, The": 106, 171; (R'09) 106,xiii.
"Builders, The": (R'07) 77,iii.
Bulgakov, Barbara: 318,27.
Bulgakov, Leo: 348,28; 264,14.
Bulger, Harry: 53,159; (A) 54, 183f; 68,260.
Bull, Walter: 194,201.
Bullard, F. Lauriston (W): 133,84.
"Bulldog Drummond": 252,155; (R'22) 252,166; (D) 252, 169.
Bulwer-Lytton, Edward: 16,3; 145,74; 57,270.
Bunce, Alan: 314,24.
"Bunch and Judy, The": (R'22) 263,20.
Bunchuk, Yasha: 341,47.
"Bunk": (R'19) 219,274.
"Bunk of 1926": (R'26) 302,14; 302,18.
Bunker, Ralph: 176,170; 319, 23; 325,39.
"Bunny": (R'15) 180,64; 180,71.
Bunny, John: 56,252; 65,185; 140,112; 163,112.
Bunston, Herbert: 298,19.
"Bunty Pulls the Strings": (R'11) 129,152; 135,150; 139,74; 231,351.
Bunyea, Mabel: 103,74; 216,91.
Bunzl, Josef: 274,22.

Burbage, Richard: (D) 182,208; 221,8.
Burbank Theatre (Los Angeles): 153,x.
Burbeck, Frank: 36,47; 66,200; 90,219; 104,127; 129,177; 286,13.
Burby, Gordon: 233,23; 323,41.
Burby, Jane: 53,180.
Burdict, Rose: 266,49.
Buress, William: 172,301.
Burg, Ellen: 22,25; 65,178.
Burg, Eugen: 96,70.
Burgess, Dorothy: 290,55; 307,27; 308,31; 313,15; 321,60.
Burgess, Grover: 300,22.
Burgess, Neil: 209,10.
Burgess, Tom: 35,14.
"Burgomaster of Belgium, A": 218,200; (R'19) 219,273.
Burgstaller, Alois: 74,110.
Burke, Billie: 79,227; 79,230; 80,265; (C) 82,xxiv; 85,c; 90,205; 90,224; 92,xiv; 92,259; 93,292; 93,300; 94,325; 106, 183; 106,189; 109,66; 111,171; 112,184; 113,21; 118,vii; 120, 53; 127,77; 129,150; 129,165; 133,83; 139,66; 140,98; 140, 11; 143,28; 148,163; 149,3; 149,25; 150,43; 151,xxiv; 151,79; 154,189; 156,77; 156, 79; 156,99; 159,225; 159, 253; 159,272; 160,303; 173, 32; 175,138; 176,174; 178, 280; 178,319; 178,333; 180,c; 180,59; 180,63; 182,246; 182, 247; 186,66; 186,73; 186,87; 187,122; (W) 187,123; 188, 220; 188,248; 191,11; 191, 17; 194,205; 198,65; 199, 118; (W) 199,144; 200,256; 202,353; 202,399; 204,121; 205,191; 207,293; 208,343; 211,185; 214,357; 217,185; 219,294; 220,399; 223,178; 224,229; 227,19; 227,21; 228, 95; 229,149; 232,556; 233, 22; 246,186; 250,53; 251,71; 263,38; 264,5; (D) 266,6; 266,38; 270,23; 270,50; 272, 22; 279,39; 285,17; 288,61; 290,23; 298,43; 309,5; (C) 323,29; 324,57; (D) 328, 27; 330,54; (A) 336,71; 342, 10; (W) 347,30; 353,22.
Burke, Ethel: 91,244.
Burke, John J.: (W) 192,71; 193,140; 193,190.
Burke, Johnny: 262,37.
Burke, Katherine: 288,49.
Burke, Verna: 236,284.
Burke, William E.: 175,138.
Burkell, John; 216,95.
Burkhardt, Harry: 30,205; 85,59; 91,250: 128,137.
Burkhardt, Lillian: 39,131.
Burkitt, Viva: 197,15.
Burks, Hattie: 186,83.
Burleigh, Harry T,: 26,96.
"Burlesque": (R'27) 320,22; 320,24; 327,41.
<u>Burlesque</u>: 273,24; (D) 299, 36; 321,34; 347,36.
<u>Burlesques</u> (<u>see also</u> Weber and Fields): 73,63; 90,200; 94,338; 232,512.
<u>Burmese Theatre</u>: 303,13.
Burnand, Lylia: 246,157.
Burnett, Francis Hodgeson: 25, 77.
Burnley, Martine: 210,97.
Burnham, Charles (W) (<u>see also</u> "New York's Historic Theatres"): 75,118; 109,72; 168,72; 187, 134; 191,7; 197,34; 198, 68; 201,272; 209,16; 211, 150; 212,202; 215,38; 220, 356; 294,16.
Burnham, Frances: 214,395.
Burnham, Nicholas: 91,231.
Burns, Edmund: 315,56.
Burns, Julia: 212,213; 212,225.
Burns, Lillian: 55,214.
Burns, Maud: 124,212.
Burns, R.K.: 273,29.
Burnside, R.H.: 65,188; 171, 239; (W) 201,290; (W) 231, 399; (W) 235,164.
Burnside, S. Cameron: 37,80.
Burr, Margery: (W) 188,214.
Burrows, Wilson A.: (W) 138, 46.
Burress, William: 17,4.
Burrian, Carl: 70,342; 129,155.
Burroughs, Marie: 84,42; 165, 215; 168,74; 203,27.
Burrows-Fontaine, Evan: 203,

33; 233,14.
Burt, Frederic: 177,235; 218, 217; 261,376; 285,18; 303, 14.
Burt, Harriet: 79,237; 95,22; 140,iii.
Burt, Laura: 40,142; 75,119; 136,191.
Burton, Alberta: 212,208; 240, 175; 245,87.
Burton, Audrey: 171,239.
Burton, David: 261,368.
Burton, Frederick: 45,289; 147, 142.
Burton, Janet: 77,178.
Burton, Mickey: 353,23.
Burton, Richard (W): 215,22; 311,9.
Busby, Florence: 60,37; 78,221.
Busch, Mae: 272,33; 275,33; 300,43.
Buschner, Dorothy: 71,7.
Bush Temple Theatre (Chicago): 74,92.
"Bushido": (R'16) 191,21; 191,29; 192,90.
"Business Before Pleasure": (R'17) 199,136; 200,221.
"Business Is Business": (R'03) 30,190; (R'04) 45,272; 45, 279.
"Business Widow, The": (R'23) 275,19.
Busley, Jessie: 5,3; 14,8; 20,9; 21,6; 78,221; 83,8; 105, 144; 105,145; 107,9; 109,93; 156,77; 175,126; 189,277; 191,16.
Busoni, Ferhucio: (A) 114,iv; (A) 119,iv; 120,48; 124, ix; 170,184.
Bussert, Anna: 103,74; 103,85; 138,46.
"Buster Brown": (R'05) 49,60; 75, 133.
"Busybody, The": (R'24) 285,70.
Butcher, A.B.C.: 195,272.
Butler, Alice: 48,49.
Butler, Ellis Parker (W): 330, 11.
Butler, Henry: 30,202.
Butler, Irene: 314,38.
Butler, Laura: 82,319.
Butler, Rachel Barton: 229,173.
Butt, Archibald: 134,117.
Butt, Clara: 157,141.
Butterfield, Everett: 226,379.
Butterfield, Walton: (W) 312, 12; (W) 309,10.
"Butterflies, The": 34,306.
"Butterfly on the Wheel, A": 131,24; (R'12) 132,38.
Butterworth, Charles: 307,14; 309,24; 312,29; (W) 332,20; (D) 343,23.
"Buzzin' Around": (R'20) 234, 106; 234,107.
"By Pigeon Post": (R'18) 215,19.
Byers, Gladys: 132,59.
Byford, Roy: 334,37.
Byington, Spring: 357,36; 338, 52; 337,48.
Byrd, Adelaide: 203,31.
Byrne, Francis: 75,117; 104, 109; 121,94; 158,170; 218, 209; 224,225; (A) 226,438; 261,374.
Byrne, Helena: 95,30.
Byron, Arthur: 14,8; 15,4; 15, 5; 33,282; 34,291; 43,228; 44,256; (D) 49,55; (A) 51, i,f; 67,252; 94,333; 99,141; 104,123; 106,iv; 109,92; 128,115; 175,105; 176,181; 214,349; 240,181; 243,411; 274,17; 280,24; 313,30; 345,42; 345,62; 352,20; 353,38; 360,25.
Byron, Oliver Doud: 154,176.
Byton, Dorothy: 283,37.

--C--

"C.O.D.": (R'12) 142,xx; 143, 24.
Cabaret Theatre; (D) 142,183; 152,126; (D) 271,29; 311,20; 345,45.
Cabaret Des Quatz-Arts (Paris): 79,235.
"Cabiria": (F) 161,48; (F) 163, 111.
Cable, George W.: 23,5.
Cabot, Elliot: 312,19; 323,24; 340,24; 350,45.
Cadell, Jean: 129,153.
Cadman, Ethel: 109,94; 114,iii; 116,114.

Cadman, S. Parkes: (W) 315,11.
"Caesar and Cleopatra": (R'06) 70, 312; 153,iii; 155,13; 155,24; (R'25) 291,17.
"Ceasar's Wife": 227,19; (R'19) 227,21.
Cahier, [Mme.] Charles: 135,145; 277,35.
Cahill, Billy: 139,96.
Cahill, Lily: 161,13; 164,154; 164,180; 164,190; 167,23; 184,374; 186,84; 192,84; 217,135; 228,75; 234,111.
Cahill, Marie: 16,5; 20,10; 26, 82; 26,83; 28,146; 39,117; 40,150; 58,xviii; 68,256; 70, 331; 94,314; 94,315; 117,130; 118,xxxii; 125,4; 125,11; 131, 3; 132,58; 133,xi; 169,120; 217,144; 302,24; 302,25.
Caillavet, Armand: 113,28.
"Cain": (R'25) 292,16.
Caine, Georgia: 31,235; 32,242; 70,338; 102,36; 102,63; 103, 98; 152,127; 175,126; 177, 234; 238,33; 136,189.
Caine, Hall: 23,9; 56,241; 106, 186; 115,84.
Caine, Henry: 172,289.
Cajatti, Ida: 178,285.
Calder, Chester T. (W): 145,74; 148,182; 155,28; 161,15; 165,222; 168,86.
Caldara, Orme: 112,175; 123, 167; 124,200; 140,97; 176, 171; 214,349; 73,60.
Calderon, Pedro: 26,101.
Caldwell, Anne: 121,90; 172,305; 191,42.
Caldwell, Gladys: 145,79; 229, 159.
Caldwell, Orville H.: 237,349.
Calhern, Louis: 283,26; 303, 27; 361,12.
Calhoun, Alice: 238,39; 242, 369.
Calhoun, Catherine: 51,126; 340, 25.
Calhoun, Jean: 228,108.
Calhoun, R. (W): 149,10.
"Caliban": (R'16) 185,8; 185,9; 199,132.
"Caliban by the Yellow Sands": (D) 183,269; 184,386.
California, University of: 33, 288; 65,182; 82,v; 113,9; 114,48; 125,18; 175,116; 209,41; 212,228; 219,307; 240,183; 284,42; 324,53.
California Theatre (see also Bohemian Club)
California Theatre: 9,18; 60, 41; 103,88; 128,122; 131, 23; 131,24; 142,185; 147, 153; 160,290; 163,123; 186, 86; 223,171; 229,195; 229, 197; 236,274; 263,22; 269, 44; 293,22; 301,40; 334,30.
California Theatre (San Francisco): 207,328.
California Theatre Stock Co.: 138,43.
Calion, Du: 289,37.
"Call of the Cricket, The": (R'10) 112,x.
"Call of Life, The": (R'25) 297,44.
"Call of the North, The": (R'08) 92,xxiv; (F) 164,161.
"Call of the Wild, The": (F,R) 273,32.
"Call the Doctor": 236,255; (R'20) 236,328.
Callahan, Joseph: 36,35.
Callahan, Marie: 332,49.
Callahan, Nellie: 53,182.
Callaway, Emily: 187,139.
Callender, Romaine: 250,24.
Callish, Betty: 157,113; 203, 11; 204,97.
Caloara, Orme: 73,60.
Calthrop, Donald: 305,14.
Calve, Emma: 10,29; 11,20; 12,20; 12,23; 13,1; 75,140; 82,335; 94,325; 134,112; 189, 286; 229,186; 231,367; 273, 37.
Calvert, Catherine: 122,135; 151,xx; 205,176; 208,376; 221,63; 223,182; 227,40; 231,438; 244,40; (D) 245, 116; (A) 249,360; (D) 249, 404; 250,24; 254,332; 254, 335; 284,36.
Calvert, [Mrs.] Charles: 231,363; 250,8.
Calvert, Louis: 105,145; 107,8; 107,9; 108,64; 118,169; 118,

172; 177,223; 184,353; 200, 193; 208,355; 208,359; 209,30; 212,198; 262,18.
Calvert, Patricia: 291,23; 321, 52.
Cambridge, Cynthia: 267,49.
Cambridge Theatre (England): 356,37.
"Camel Through The Needle's Eye, The": (S) 340,24; (R'29) 340,41.
"Cameo Kirby": (R'10) 108,xiv.
Cameo Theatre (New York): 255, 394.
Cameramen: 205,189.
Cameron, Audrey: 232,528.
Cameron, Beatrice: 67,244; 114,43; 297,36.
Cameron, Cammie: 264,43.
Cameron, Cecil: 170,197.
Cameron, Donald: 281,14.
Cameron, Frances: 81,313; 138, 44; 141,157; 143,14.
Cameron, Madeline: 316,46; 336,60.
Cameron, Rhoda: 8,13.
Cameron Sisters: 215,13; 230, 266.
"Camille": 39,108; (R'04) 39, 108; (R'04) 40,135; 61,64; (D) 134,130; 176,173; 231, 377; (F) 245,107; (R'31) 361,26.
Campanari, Guiseppe: 62,110; 129,155.
Campanini, Cleofonte: 67,233; 75,139; 76,169; 81,315; 116, 109; 177,248; 202,391; 205, 167; (D) 207,278; 265,9.
Campbell, Celeste: 140,108.
Campbell, Colin: 222,82.
Campbell, Craig: 143,3; 216,86; 229,159.
Campbell, Elizabeth: 165,212.
Campbell, Evelyn: (D) 247,211.
Campbell, Fanchon: 87,131.
Campbell, Nan: 159,232; 159, 272; 160,321; 162,49.
Campbell, [Mrs.] Patrick: 10,9; 12,2; 12,3; 16,20; 19,1; 20, 5; 22,13; 23,22; 43,216; 44, c; 45,265; 47,23; 50,93; 82, xxiv; 85,60; 102,48; 120,34; 120,57; 127,77; 142,198; 163,98; 166,262; 167,11; 201, 264; 240,153; 246,143; 313, 19; 360,39; 81,288.
Campeau, Frank: 36,35; 152,135; 183,294.
Canadian Theatre: 89,189; 218, 229; 246,171; 261,395; 268, 45; 304,40; 316,42.
"Canary, The": (R'18) 214,378; 215,37.
"Canary Cottage": (R'17) 193, 150; 193,153.
"Canary Dutch": (R'25) 296,16.
"Candida": (R'04) 35,5; (R'04) 36,39; 40,141; (R'22) 255, 374; 255,379; (R'24) 287, 64.
"Candle Light": 344,17.
"Candy Shop, The": (R'09) 100, 168; 100,193.
Cannell, Catharine: 198,92.
Cannon, Fanny (W): 163,115.
Cansinos, The: 264,43.
"Canterbury Pilgrims, The": 28,150; 103,96.
Cantor, Eddie: (A) 214,379; 223,159; (A) 238,72; 257,7; 270,29; 270,50; 273,39; 277,17; 290,13; 305,47; (C) 319,4; (D) 335,41; 336,28; 342,50; 357,50.
"Cape Smoke": (R'25) 290,34.
Capek, Karel: 266,38.
Capellani, Albert: 220,388.
Capellani, Paul: 177,225.
Capitol Theatre (New York): 297,61; 298,55.
"Caponsacchi": (R'26) 310,18.
Capoul, Victor: (A) 66,199.
Cappiello, Leonetto: 262,17.
"Cappy Ricks": (R'19) 217, 143; 217,163.
"Caprice": (R'29) 336,49; 336,51; 340,15.
Caprice, June: 205,195; 210, 117; 234,135.
"Captain Applejack": 252,155; (R'21) 252,165; (D) 252, 169; 253,226.
"Captain Barrington": (R'04) 35,4.
"Captain Brassbound's Conversion": 67,237; (R'07) 73, 58; 73,69; 183,273; (R'16) 183,274.

"Captain Dieppe": (R'03) 32,240; 33,263; 42,ii.
"Captain Jinks of the Horse Marines": 3,4; 3,12; 143, 21; 216,84; 231,348; 231, 383; (R'25) 296,16.
"Captain Kidd, Jr.": (R'16) 192, 394; 195,270.
"Captain Molly": (R'02) 20,10; 20,11.
"Captive, The": (F) 172,295; 309,14; 309,16; 311,22.
Capus, Alfred: 24,49.
Carasa, Federico: 97,xxviii; 101,16; 104,114; 105,139; 106,202.
Carb, David: (W) 276,10.
"Cardinal, The": (R'02) 12,8; 12,13.
Carens, Elise: 115,67.
Carew, Edwin: 297,43; 215,63.
Carew, James: 73,69; 135,161; 74,105.
Carew, Ona: 211,181; 224,252.
Carewe, Edwin: 215,63; 297, 43.
Carewe, Rita: 313,39.
Carey, Harry: 218,258; (A) 257, 123.
Carey, Joyce: 361,34.
Carillo, Leo: 201,281; 235,189; 245,83; 285,38; 289,37; 304, 35; 334,31.
Carle, Billie: 91,243.
Carle, Richard: 29,181; 71,20; 89,v; 89,190; 139,75; 152, 114; 152,136; 169,120; 171, 258.
Carleton, Carl E.: 208,395.
Carlisle, Alexandra: 88,144; 92,257; 92,279; 154,181; (D) 156,c; 162,51; 164,190; 165,208; 180,61; 184,333; 191,37; 195,290; 199,132; 200,203; 230,271; 230,272; 255,351; 255,353.
Carlisle, Gertrude: 55,213.
Carlisle, Henry Wilson (W): 108, 49.
Carlisle, Sybil: 120,61.
Carlisle, Sydney; 207,301.
Carlson, Violet: 313,35; (D) 343,23; 349,48.
Carlton, Henry Fish: 301,36.
Carlton, William P.: 199,129.
Carlton Academy (New Jersey): 215,42.
Carltons, The: 340,23.
Carlyle, Beatrice: 232,518.
Carlyle, Francis: 4,14; 86,103; 104,113; 137,11; 137,13.
Carlysle, Sydney: 40,147.
Carmel (California) Theatre: 142,185.
"Carmen": 59,7.
"Carmen" (OP): 130,191; 134, 123; 136,178; 165,213; 167, 16; (F) 175,130; (F) 184, 357.
Carmen, Jewel: 203,63; 208,393.
Carmen, Josie: 222,99.
Carmen, Sybil: 181,125; 190, 363; 195,291.
"Carmencita And The Soldier": 296,14.
Carmi, Maria: 132,44; 163, 109; 267,12.
Carminati, Tullio: 308,40; 344, 20; (C) 345,4.
Carnahan, Thomas B., Jr.: 159,252.
Carnegie, Andrew: 4,10; 6,13; 11,9; 38,87; 40,ix; 170, 181.
Carnegie Institute of Technology: 208,350; 208,351; 218, 230; 218,231; 305,40.
"Carnival": 143,26; (R'19) 228, 144; (R'24) 288,15.
Carnovsky, Morris: 327,37; 340, 24; 351,44.
Carnwright, Frances: 115,72.
Carol, Sue: 326,77.
Carolina Playmakers (see also Koch, Frederick H.): 235, 200; 250,41; 259,245; 265, 46; 271,40; 277,40; 279,56; 290,52; 292,42; 298,40; 323, 50; 324,52; 329,45; 335,57; 336,2; 353,51.
"Caroline": 189,273; (R'16) 189, 282; (R'23) 265,19.
"Carolinian, The": (R'25) 298, 16.
Carpen, Remy: 260,328.
Carpenger, Anne: 283,29.
Carpenter, Betty: 243,440.
Carpenter, Constance: 323,41;

324, 47.
Carpenter, Edward Childs: (W) 5, 10; 185, 29; 328, 29; (W) 330, 14; 356, 31.
Carpenter, Frederick: 327, 29.
Carpenter, John Alden: 300, 34; 302, 34.
Carpentier, Georges: 261, 392.
Carr, Alexander: 71, 6; 73, 63; 80, 275; 81, 289; 118, 199; 129, 177; 152, 133; (W) 157, 136; 193, 166; 200, 221.
Carr, Comyns: 86, 91.
Carr, George: 170, 197.
Carr, Herbert: 63, 112.
Carr, Mary: 238, 41.
Carra, Dean: (W, V) 147, 152.
Carre, Albert: 119, xx.
Carre, Marguerite: 119, xx; 122, 138.
Carreno, Teresa: 102, 68; 154, 184.
Carrera, Liane: 158, 199.
Carrier, Mabel: 30, 200.
Carrigan, Thomas Jay: 208, 354.
Carrington, Evelyn Carter: 252, 151.
Carrington, Helen: 309, 21.
Carrington, Murray: 172, 289.
Carroll, Albert: 207, 295; 246, 145; 252, 151; 303, 13; 330, 31; (W) 332, 28; (D) 339, 17; 351, 15; 332, 42.
Carroll, Earl (see also "Sketchbook") F: 235, 178; 253, 232; (W, V) 282, 66; (W, V) 283, 50; 297, 42; 308, 48; 313, 30; (W) 337, 24.
Carroll, George: 69, 292.
Carroll, Harry: 179, 26; 274, 34.
Carroll, Jeanne: 223, 153.
Carroll, Leo G.: 284, 18.
Carroll, Marie: 176, 186; 219, 271; 230, 309; 235, 165; 236, 262; 237, 389.
Carroll, Mary: 280, 44; 321, 60.
Carroll, Nancy: 299, 45; 325, 38; 354, 41.
Carroll College (Wisconsin): 310, 44.
"Carrots": (R'02) 21, 8.
Carson, Adele: 73, 79; 83, 20.
Carson, Doris: (C) 348, 36.
Carson, Frances: 239, 104; 239, 122; 243, 300; 253, 225.
Carson, James B.: 117, 130.
Carson, Murray: 50, 84.
Carter, Frank: 202, 343.
Carter, Harrison: 161, 6.
Carter, Hubert: 59, 17; 60, 48.
Carter, Jessie: 133, 97.
Carter, Joan: 344, 74.
Carter, John; 79, vi.
Carter, [Mrs.] Leslie: 8, 19; 10, 5; 11, 3; 12, 1; 12, 4; (D) 13, 9; 19, 9; 20, c; 20, 20; 25, 69; 41, 173; 48, 28; 49, 70; (C) 51, 127; 57, 268; 67, 227; 72, 46; 79, 229; 83, 17; 90, 205; 96, 37; 97, 72; 97, 101; 103, 69; 106, 183; 115, 93; 119, xi; 119, 23; 128, 127; 139, 69; 139, 86; 145, xxix; 169, 126; 191, 14; 245, 95; 248, 319; (D) 249, 389; 287, 36; 290, 29; (C) 326, 80.
Carter, Mary: 138, 47.
Carter, R. Peyton: 65, 189; 90, 219; 98, 118; 192, 89.
Cartier, Jacques: 299, 8; 318, 36; 326, 36.
Cartoons, Animated: 322, 32.
Cartwright, Charles: 47, 7; (A) 54, 183, f; 105, 144; 105, 145; 108, 42.
Carus, Emma: 37, 76; 54, 190; 83, 6; 115, 85; 119, 22; 130, 187.
Caruske, Raphael: 57, 266.
Caruso, Enrico: 33, 285; 35, 24; 36, 52; 46, 291; (A) 48, iii; 49, xv; 58, 316; 60, 34; 61, 81; 65, 184; 79, xiii; 81, 314; 82, 343; 87, ix; 87, 119; 93, 309; 94, 346; 116, iv; 118, 167; 118, 173; 119, 4; 120, 55; 121, 82; 129, viii; 129, 154; 132, 52; 141, 138; 142, c; (D) 142, 167; 144, 55; 145, 79; 153, 149; 154, 182; 157, 120; (C) 157, 123; 158, 178; 159, 229; (A, C) 159, 254; (A) 161, 2; 166, 271; 167, 16; 178, 284; (C) 183, 300; 190, 340; (D) 193, 132; 197, 35; 211, 180; 212, 255; (A) 214, 379; 215, 62; 216, 125; 218, 202; (A) 226, 438; (D) 239, 80; 240, 161;

(A) 247,216; 306,33.
Caruso, [Mme.] Enrico: 79,vii.
Caruso Theatre (New York): 289,10.
Caruth, Burr: 341,37.
Carvill, Henry: 261,370.
Cary, Annie Louise: 243,452.
Casadesus, Robert: 226,396.
Casajuana, Maria: 316,39.
Casals, Pablo: 170,184; 290, 43; 332,27.
"Casanova": 272,13; (R'23) 272, 15.
Casanova, Emmita: 363,29.
Casanova, Eve: 265,18.
Casara, Frederico: 101,x.
Casavant, Nina: 233,41.
Casazza, Gatti: 94,343.
Case, Anna: 147,140; 180,35; 186,89; 195,295; 200,215; 202, 372; 213,315; (A) 214,379; 221,25; 272,37; 298,35; (A) 322,3; 155,12.
Case, Paul T. (W): 162,58.
"Case of Arson, A": (R'06) 60,26; 60,27; 62,91.
"Case of Becky, The": 141,iii; (R'12) 141,131; 141,137; 143, 9.
"Case of Frenzied Finance, A": (R'05) 51,109.
"Case of Lady Camber, The": 195, 276; (R'17) 195,279.
Casey, Arthur J.: 332,18.
Casey, John M.: 354,45.
"Cashel Byron's Profession": (R'06) 60,v; 60,28.
Cashman, Charlotte: 164,182.
Casion Theatre (New York): 39, 126; 82,322; 110,121; 149, 17.
Caslova, Marie: 166,272.
Caspary, Vera: (W) 321,27.
Cass, Maurice: 112,180; 215, 21.
Cassinelli, Dolores: 216,119; 221, 63; (D) 223,c; 284,36.
Casson, Lewis: 146,111.
"Caste": (R'10) 112,174; 112, 183; 129,168.
Castelle, Cecilia: 40,158.
Casting: 126,42; 135,168; 139, 74; (C) 179,12; 195,284; 206,222; 216,90; 250,8; 260, 286; (D) 288,11; 297,20; 320, 43; 331,43; 333,52; 345,30.
Casting - Film: 180,75; 201, 326; 311,38.
Castle, Egerton: 5,8.
Castle, Irene (see also Castles, The): (D) 163,108; 169,c; 169,107; 169,159; 169,163; 171,267; 186,85; 195,300; 196,328; 196,366; 197,48; 199,162; 199,179; 200,232; 201,295; 201,326; 211,158; 212,215; 214,356; 214,395; (D) 219,267; 221,41; 229, 200; 230,280; 240,195; 246, 183.
Castle, Vernon (see also Castles, The): 105,156; 113,3; (A) 157,107; 208,344.
Castle, William: 102,67.
Castle Garden Theatre (New York): 19,19; (D) 136,197.
Castle Square Theatre (Boston): 24,39.
Castles, Dolly: 143,22.
Castles, Eileen: 216,86.
"Castles in the Air": (R'26) 308,68.
Castles, The (see also Castle, Irene; Castle, Vernon): 161, 28; 157,126; 167,9; 169, 112; 197,38.
Castleton, Barbara: 207,329.
"Cat and the Cherub, The": 166, 267; (R'14) 166,299.
"Cat and the Canary, The": 253, 215; (R'22) 253,234; (D) 254,309.
"Cat-Bird, The": (R'20) 230,269.
"Catch of the Season, The": 54, 186; (R'05) 56,244; 56,259; 57,279.
"Catherine": (R'16) 190,356.
"Cathleen Ni-Hoolihan": (R'03) 29,158; (R'20) 234,108.
Catholic Actor's Guild: 256,28.
Catholic Theatre Movement: 192, 71; 193,140.
Catlett, Walter L.: 198,87; 206, 216; 240,176; 256,28.
"Catskill Dutch": (R'24) 280,15.
Caubet, Suzanne: 216,97; 226, 396; 299,42; 311,33; 315, 40; 331,31.

Cauble, Becky: 249,392.
"Caught in the Rain": (R'06) 72, 34; 72,41.
"Cavalier, The": 23,1; (R) 23,5; 25,61.
Cavalieri, Lina: 66,200; 69,289; 81,315; 104,124; 106,201; 108,58; 147,145; 161,4; 161, 48; 198,98; 202,408; 208,c; 210,81; 216,125; 255,366; 293,30.
"Cavalleria Rusticana (OP): 20, 24; 339,16.
Cavanaugh, Lilian: 185,10.
Cavanagh, Lucille: 150,49; 171, 252; 173,17; 178,306; 185,15; 196,357; 201,267; 201,294; 205,169; 209,c; 219,291; 157,151.
Cavanaugh, Robert: 338,48.
"Cave Girl, The": (R'20) 235,242.
"Cave Man, The": (R'11) 130,xv; 130,222.
Cavan, Marie: 125,10.
Caven, Taylor: (W) 227,8.
Cavendish, Cecil (W,V): 21,23; 34,318; 40,150.
Cavendish, Charles: (W) 254,302.
Cavera: 279,14.
Cawthorne, Joseph: 57,xiii; 64, 143; 94,327; 149,24; 164, 167; 181,135; 184,361; 201, 281; 253,229.
Cayvan, Georgia: 22,3; 100,188; 290,18.
Cazauran, Leon: 82,351.
Cazeneuve, Paul: 41,162.
"Celebrated Case, A": (R'15) 171,229; 171,232; 171,233; 231,363.
"Celebrity": (R'28) 324,39.
Celeste, Fay: 234,93.
Cellini, Benvenuto: (D) 255,384.
Celtic Players: 234,108.
"Cenci, The": (D) 171,248.
"Cendrillon" (OP): (R'12) 134,111.
Centanini, M.: (W) 20,24.
Censorship (see also Morality): 17,16; 57,v; 58,296; 58,298; 60,35; 66,198; 86,91; 87,134; 150,49; 152,116; 247,210; 247, 210; 247,215; 252,204; 256,6; 256,10; 272,9; 273,9; 274,6; 290,25; 291,7; 296,24; 305,7; 310,7; 312,37; 313,23; 314, 7; 316,21; 326,11; 326,34; 327,7; 335,35; 354,45; 360, 13.
"Century Girl, The": (R'16) 190, 392; 191,10; 191,12.
Century Music Hall: 177,229.
Century Opera (see also Opera; "Opera, At The"): 152,131; 162,91; 163,102; 165,212.
Century Players: 38,86.
"Century Revue, The": (R'20) 234, 137.
Century Theatre (New York): 124,xi; 178,276; 184,332; 193,136.
Century Theatre Club: 141,vi.
Century Theatre Co.: 35,1.
"'Ception Shoals": (R'17) 192, 88.
"Certain Party, A": (R'10) 113, 10; (R'11) 124,183; 124, 196.
Chadal, Georges: 117,138; 117, 139; (A) 118,xxiv.
Chadwick, Cyril: 105,160; 208, 357.
Chadwick, Helene: 220,399; 236,288.
Chain, Dell: 245,97.
"Chains": (R'12) 144,xv; 272, 14; (R) 272,16.
Chais-Bonheur, Celine: (A) 123,xvi.
Chalfont, Lucille: 225,299; 236, 284; 249,393; 259,252; 293, 21; 316,3.
Chaliapin, Feodor: 80,267; 81, 314; 121,101; 242,327; 249, 396; 260,318; (D) 263,37; 264,37; 273,37; 286,35; 303, 34; (C) 317,31; 330,23.
Chaliapine, Lydie: 279,23.
Chalif School of Dancing: 220,355.
Challee, William: 324,39.
"Challenge, The": (R'19) 224, 223; 224,225.
Chalmers, Helen: 290,35.
Chalmers, Kelmett: 55,227.
Chalmers, Thomas: 165,212; 176,191; 197,31; 290,35.
Chamberlin, Mary: (W) 147, xvii.
Chamberlain, Winthrop: 138,59.

Chamberlyn, A.H.: 18,v.
Chambers, C. Haddon: 12,13; 15, 3.
Chambers, Howard: 66,209.
Chambers, Lyster: 207,273; 243,402.
Chambers, Marie: 203,20; 205,172; 207,306; (A) 214,379; 226, 390; 292,45.
Chamlee, Mario: 242,335; 275, 35; 303,35.
Chamlee, Ruth Miller: 282,35.
"Champion, The": 240,181; (R' 21) 240,222.
Chandler, Arthur: (W) 170,178.
Chandler, Helen: 214,351; 290, 32; 292,25; 311,19; (C) 317, 31; 320,23; 325,44; (C) 333, 41; 333,45; 337,55.
Chandler, Howard: 214,335.
Chandler, Julia: (W) 202,335; 315,38.
Chaney, Lon: 239,114; 264,35; 271,31; 275,39; 287,30; 294, 30; 295,32; 296,32; 297,30; 305,37; 313,36; (W) 319,37; 327,18.
Chanfrau, F.S.: 86,99; 191,8.
Chanfrau, Henrietta: 105,ii.
"Change": (R'14) 157,158; (R'14) 159,262; (R'14) 159,268.
"Changelings, The": (R'23) 272, 16; (S) 273,26; 273,29.
"Changing Woman, The": (F) 212,253.
"Channel Road, The": 345,24.
"Chantecler": 94,338; (C) 98, 134; 101,x; 107,vi; 109,78; 110,116; 112,185; 115,66; 121,69; (R'11) 121,70; 121,81; 122,113; 123,142; 124,xii.
"Chaperon, The": (R'08) 96,41; 96, 47.
"Chaperons, The": (R'02) 17,5.
Chapin, Benjamin: 62,92; 63, 123; (W) 97,xvi; 196,328; 200,251; 204,128.
Chapin, Harold: 243,419.
Chapine: 133,103; 137,24; 149, 11.
Chaplin, Charles: (W) 175,120; 188,218; 197,10; 221,61; 224, 249; 231,489; 239,97; 241, 270; 241,272; 249,394; 249, 430; 265,38; 266,34; 270,33; 272,33; 273,30; 274,20; 276, 32; 277,24; 279,33; 293,34; 296,30; 296,45; 300,36; 308, 37; (D) 323,29; 324,50; 330, 22; (D) 361,47.
Chaplin, Sydney: 290,37; 297, 32; 307,38; 307,49; 311,48.
Chapman, Betty: 65,171; 137,7.
Chapman, Blanche: 24,30.
Chapman, Edythe: 9,18; 9,19; 36,49; 69,301.
Chapman, George: 22,20.
Chapman, Wm.: 30,204.
"Chapters of Opera" (Krehbiel) (B): 96,70.
Chard, Evelyn: 247,226.
"Charity Girl, The": (R'12) 141,xii.
"Charlatan, The": 256,21; (R'22) 256,31.
Charlebois, Sofia: 248,317.
Charles, Lucile Hoerr: (W) 358,18.
Charles Frohman Co. (see Frohman, Charles).
"Charley's Aunt": 63,136; (F,R) 290,37.
Charlot, Andre: 270,22; 285,10.
"Charlot's Revue" (see also "Andre Charlot's Revue").
"Charlot Revue of 1925": (R) 300,18.
"Charlot's Revue": 270,22; 283, 33.
Charlotte: 177,221; 178,291; 182,244; 189,275; 344,36.
Charlotte Cushman Club: 164,182.
Carlton, Frank: 237,357.
Charlton, George J.: 108,38.
"Charm of Isabel, The": (R'14) 160,283.
"Charm School, The": 235,165; (R'20) 235,186; (R'25) 295, 16.
Charpentier, George: 84,40; 261, 392.
Carpentier, Gustave: 158,178.
Charsky, Boris: (D) 330,29.
Chart, Nye: 120,35; 120,36.
Charters, Spencer: 237,352.
Chase, Arline: 200,201; 221, 19; 242,332.
Chase, Arthur B.: 152,140.
Chase, Cora: 242,335.

Chase, Edna: 88,155; 101,15.
Chase, Pauline: 9,21; 116,c; 116,101; 116,118; 116,126; 173,26.
Chase, William Sheafe: (W) 256, 10.
"Chaser, The": (F) 322,7.
Chastunoff, Vladimir: 303,10.
Chatauqua Association: 258,194.
"Chatelaine, The": (S) 24,49.
Chats With Players:
by Edward Fales Coward:
Viola Allen; 24,44;
Blanche Bates; 29,164;
Amelia Bingham; 26,90;
Edward H. Sothern; 25,66.
by W. De Wagstaffe;
Margaret Anglin; 14,12;
Ethel Barrymore; 21,20;
Kyrle Bellew; 16,10;
[Mrs.] Patrick Campbell; 23, 22;
[Mrs.] Leslie Carter; 20,20;
John Drew; 10,17;
Robert Edeson; 22,22;
Louis James, An Actor of Tradition; 19,22;
Annie Russell; 10,10;
Effie Shannon and Mr. Herbert Kelcey; 15,20;
Mary Mannering; 17,9;
E.S. Willard; 12,13;
Francis Wilson; 13,13.
by Lewis J. Hillhouse;
Richard Mansfield; 65,190.
by Hollis Lorraine;
Henrietta Crosman; 30,195.
by Harry P. Manson;
Clara Bloodgood; 27,118.
by Henry Tyrrell;
Edith Wynne Matthison; 28, 139;
Mary Shaw; 18,21;
Otis Skinner; 35,8.
by Ada Patterson;
Maclyn Arbuckle; 44,251;
Edwin Arden; 55,222;
Sam Bernard; 54,196;
Billie Burke; 93,300;
Marie Cahill; 70,331;
Alex Carr; 80,277;
William Collier; 77,184;
William H. Crane; 66,213;
Arnold Daly; 40,141;
J. E. Dodson; 51,125;
Dorothy Donnelly; 41,171;
Maxine Elliott; 33,270;
Dustin Farnum; 68,272;
William Fayersham; 43,221;
William J. Ferguson; 87,129;
Grace George; 59,14;
Nathaniel C. Goodwin; 36, 40;
Virginia Harned; 38,93;
Annie Irish; 45,277;
May Irwin; 56,258;
Wilton Lackaye; 39,119;
Robert Loraine; 61,70;
Louis Mann; 50,96;
Edna May; 57,276;
Henry Miller; 52,154;
Jessie Millward; 74,106;
Alla Nazimova; 78,219;
Carlotta Nillson; 46,308;
Nance O'Neil; 49,62;
James O'Neill; 86,101;
John Forbes Robertson; 73, 74;
Eleanor Robson; 53,170;
Lillian Russell; 48,44;
Fritzi Scheff; 63,128;
Frances Starr; 84,47;
Mabel Taliaferro; 42,197;
Marie Tempest; 108,60;
Ellen Terry; 76,162;
Denman Thompson; 89,192;
David Warfield; 47,17;
Thomas A. Wise; 94,336.
"Chatterton": (R'19) 217,144.
Chatterton, Ruth: 129,168; 134, 108; 136,200; 138,c; 140, 128; 148,184; 162,84; 164,c; 164,151; 165,205; 167,11; 167,50; 173,25; 175,126; 175, 137; 190,369; 194,225; 195, 283; 211,129; 214,344; 214, 346; 226,371; 231,353; 240, 155; 244,26; 258,144; 263, 29; 273,26; 287,44; 292,25; 295,36; 297,14; 342,38.
"Chauve Souris, The": 250,28; 253,209; (R'22) 253,236; (D) 253,237; 256,28; (R'22) 258,151; 258,162; (R'22) 261, 375; (D) 262,10; (D) 264, 10; 265,23; 272,34; 287,18; (C) 339,41; 356,42.
"Cheaper To Mary": (R'24) 279,19.

"Cheater, The": (R'10) 114,34; 114,37.
Cheatham, Kitty: 110,102; 124, 209; 135,165; 143,32; 153, 159; 161,20; 169,138.
"Cheating Cheaters": (R'16) 187,137; 187,149; 189,268; (F,R) 217, 191.
"Checkerboard, The": (R'20) 235,242.
"Checkmate": (S) 259,247; (S) 260,344.
"Cheer Up": (R'12) 144,xiv; (R'17) 200,242; 201,287.
Chekov, Anton: 185,10; 351, 18.
Chekov, Olga Knipper: 262,14; 268, 38.
Chemet, Renee: 275,35; 349, 56.
"Chemineau, Le": (OP) 86,95.
Cheney, Sheldon (W): 156,81; 161,6; 162,68; 163,120; 250, 42; 261,360; 274,22; 325,4; 345,6.
Chenkin, Victor: 338,19.
Chenko and Alexa: 299,29.
Cherber-Bekefi, Maria: 292,19.
Cherry, Charles: 33,271; 55, 245; 79,242; 84,34; 87,131; 99,166; 112,193; 122,136; 136,171; 139,88; 148,174; 164,158; 183,274; 183,281; 188,204; 191,33; 204,93; 219, 281; (W) 219,290; 223,147; 226,370; 228,96; 252,143; (D) 252,169; 255,360; 276,36.
Cherry, James: 112,194.
"Cherry Orchard, The": (R' 23) 264,15.
Cherry Sisters: 269,19; 282, 39.
Cherryman, Rex; 310,21; 312, 29; 320,22; (C) 320,76; 321, 29; 331,80.
Cheshire, Harmon: 203,31.
Chesmond, Dorothy: 203,31.
Chesney, Ronald: 195,287.
Chester, Ruth: 99,135; 101,24; 188,205; 188,216; 200,281.
Chesterfield, Henry: (W) 231,480; 231,491.
Chesterton, G.K.: 115,88; 241,265.
Chestnut Street Theatre (Philadelphia): 37,79; 82,xiv.
Chestnutt, Charles: 26,96.
Chevalier, Albert: 68,274; 119, xiii; 119,29.
Chevalier, Maurice: 308,33; (D) 330,46; 352,8; 356,6.
Chiarelli, Luigi: 302,20.
"Chicago": 312,20.
Chicago, University of: 182,227; 182,263; 220,365; 220,380.
Chicago Arts Club: 224,245; 224,246.
Chicago Civic Opera House: 119, 9: 347,38.
Chicago Opera Ballet: 251,71.
Chicago Theatre: 29,180; 30, 188; 65,194; 87,126; 112, 178; 124,198; 129,176; 145, 84; 151,xix; 175,122; 199, 142; 220,367; 226,430; 263, 22; 297,74; 303,37; 347,39.
"Chicken Feed": (R'23) 272,56.
"Chief, The": (R'15) 179,9.
"Chief Thing, The": (R'26) 303,16.
"Chienne Du Roi, La": (D) 146, 103.
Child Actors: 40,146; 47,18; 71, 18; 76,154; 77,176; 100,178; 118,170; 124,203; 127,106; 164,173; 188,192; 204,100; 214,350; 216,101; 218,227; 334,29.
"Child Stealer, The": (D) 134, 131.
Childers, Naomi: 175,131; 183, 278.
"Children": (R'16) 183,277.
"Children of Darkness": 347,14; (R'30) 347,72; 348,48; (S) 349,32; 351,21.
"Children of Destiny": (R'10) 110,xii.
"Children of Earth": 161,11; 167, 35; 168,55; (R'15) 168,102.
"Children of Kings, The": (R'02) 22,9.
"Children of the Ghetto, The": 48,33.
"Children of the Moon": 271, 14; (R'23) 271,15; (S) 272, 26.
"Children of To-Day": (R'13) 155,46.

Children's Theatre: 21,24; 76, 154; 85,xvi; 127,106; 144, 46; 144,47; 161,34; 223, 174; 226,399; 233,31; 254, 318; 262,46; 276,41; 282, 41; 317,43; 330,53; 338,35; 353,40.
"Children's Tragedy, The": (R'21) 249,438.
Childs' Restaurant: 140,103.
"Chin-Chin": 166,265; (R'14) 166,304; 171,238; 171,239; 172,305.
"Chinese Honeymoon, A": (R'02) 17,4; 42,ii; 45,viii.
"Chinese Love": (R'21) 242,342.
Chinese Theatre: 29,170; 29, 173; 42,192; 135,138; 142, 163; 144,62; 223,168; 265, 38; 289,10; 290,51; 326,18; (D) 326,18; (D) 326,19; 334, 18; 349,21.
Chisholm, Nina: 86,iii.
Chisholm, Robert: (D) 343,23.
"Chivalry": (R'25) 300,16.
"Chocolate Dandies": (R'24) 284, 70.
"Chocolate Soldier, The": (R'09) 105,xiii; (R'30) 348,72.
"Choir Rehearsal, The": (R 21) 242, 342.
Chong, Goo: 334,45.
Chorus Boys: 294,18; 295,72.
Chorus Girls: 10,5; 62,96; 80,274; 90,209; 118,196; 129,172; 147,146; 171,238; 190,362; 200,214; 205,136; 209,32; 219,282; 220,338; 222,74; (D) 223,143; 223,158; 223,170; 226,393; 231,404; (D) 234, 102; 236,264; 238,16; 241, 248; 243,420; 244,6; 245, 75; 273,22; 313,22; 317,16; 321,27; 329,16; 342,29.
"Chorus Lady, The": 68,257; (R'06) 68,258.
Chotin, Andre: 263,27.
"Christian Pilgrim, The": 81, 288; (R'07) 82,xvi; (C) 82,xxiv.
Christians, Rudolf: 38,88.
Christie, Adele: 171,238.
Christie, Al: 319,11.
Christie, George S.: 181,124.
Christie, Grace: 232,513; 296, 36.
Christmas Plays: 35,28; 345,53.
"Chu Chin Chow": 198,109; 200, 198; 202,337; (R'17) 202, 392; 290,36f.
Church, Minnie: 53,182.
Church, Virginia (W): 112,181; 171,255.
Church and Stage: 48,48; 124, x; 143,30; 192,71; 227,38; 228,74; 244,6; 248,326; 315,11; 321,46; 212,206.
Churchill, Berton: 132,41; 274,5; 301,27; 356,24; 360, 25.
Churchill, Marguerite: 311,29; 316,9; 330,15.
Churchill, Winston: 23,9; 59, 2; 60,viii.
Ciannelli, Eduardo: (D) 351,18.
Ciaparelli-Viafora, Gina: 199, 166.
Ciccolini, Guido: 217,137.
"Cid, Le": 221,28.
"Cielo Espanol": (R'19) 220, 343; 220,357.
Cilea, Francesco: 80,266.
"Cimeron": (F) 358,48.
Cincinnati School of Expression: 86,vi.
Cincinatti Theatre: 177,220.
"Cinderella": (F) 167,18.
"Cinderella Man, The" (R'16) 181,125; 181,137; 185, 29.
"Cinderella on Broadway": (R'20) 234,106.
Cinema (see Films).
"Cingalee, The": (R'04) 46,296; 46,320.
"Circle, The": (S) 248,300; (R'21) 248,316; 248,319; (D) 249, 389; 336,57.
Circus: 44,x; 54,192; 113,19; 135,146; 164,176; 292,10; (D) 292,11.
"Circus Girl, The": 334,23.
"Circus Princess, The": 304,20; (R'27) 316,20.
"Citizen's Home, A": (R'09) 105, xv.
"Citta Morta, La": (R'02) 22,7.
"City, The": 107,ix; (R'09) 108,

34; 108,55.
City Club, The: 149,3.
"City Haul": (R'29) 347,66.
Civic Repertory Theatre: 346,28; 347,18.
Civic Theatre (see Community Theatre; Little Theatre).
"Civilian Clothes": (R'19) 225, 340; 226,371.
"Civilization": (F) 185,12.
"Claim, The": (R'17) 202,350.
"Clair De Lune": (R'21) 243, 417; 245,92.
Claire, Bernice: 351,56.
Claire, Ina: 129,150; 130,218; 137,28; 139,87; 150,55; 172, 295; 174,90; 175,c; 175, 105; 175,148; 176,205; 186,70; 193,180; 198,62; 200,197; 200, 242; 201,262; 202,359; 207, 308; 209,14; 209,15; 214,361; (A) 214,379; 221,45; 224, 233; 224,258; 226,370; (A) 226,438; 227,56; 229,168; 231,358; 231,496; 232,547; 239,121; 248,298; 249,402; 251, 103; 251,123; 261,372; 263,6; (D) 263,11; 283,18; 285,46; 299,19; 299,44; 300,c; (D) 327,c; (D) 335,18; 343,36.
Claire, Willis: 200,221.
"Claire Adams": (R'29) 346, 46.
"Clancy Name, The": 146,110.
"Clansman, The": 59,20; 59,21; 59,22; (R'06) 60,27; (F) 168,68; 170,212; (F) 267, 34.
Clare, Jesse G.: (W) 149,25.
Clare, Mary: 252,160.
"Clarence": (R'19) 225,342; 226, 365.
Clarence, O.B.: 109,92.
Clarens, Juliette: 131,36; 189, 289.
Claretie, Jules: 37,74; (W) 38, 96; 122,137; 156,72.
"Clari": 332,50.
"Clarice": (R'06) 70,xxiii; 70, 338.
Clark, Alexander: 28,135; 71, 7; 178,302; 339,23.
Clark, Barrett H. (W): 264, 25; 279,22; 320,47; 326, 4d; 340,4; 349,6.
Clark, Bobby (see also Clark and Mc Cullough).
Clark, Bobby: 259,223; (C) 263, 11.
Clark, Cathryn: 125,26.
Clark, Charles D.: 134,124.
Clark, Dorothy: 245,94.
Clark, Eva: 286,18.
Clark, J. Mitchell: 41,182.
Clark, Lois F.: 55,247.
Clark, Mae: 320,51.
Clark, Marguerite: 22,20; 34, 303; 39,116; 57,287; 71,25; 95,7; 99,137; 100,c; 108, 36; 115,79; 116,125; 119,17; 137,29; 142,195; 148,167; 148,181; 154,197; (W) 158, 188; 166,275; 167,19; 180, 74; 186,73; 197,20; 198,74; 201,316; 201,321; 201,322; 202,408; 203,63; 204,122; 205,196; 206,255; 207,324; 210,119; (D) 220,c; 220,387; 222,112; (A) 238,72; 242, 350.
Clark, Maurice: 309,34.
Clark, Myrtle: (D) 357,2.
Clark, Rose: 34,315.
Clark, Sylvia: 288,37.
Clark, Trilby: 247,229.
Clark, W.H.: 49,74.
Clark, W. Hutchison: 72,52.
Clark, Wallis: 247,237; 249, 374.
Clark and Mc Cullough: (C) 262,27; 280,36; 280,37; 310, 19; 346,42; (C) 348,36.
Clarke, Burke: 70,336.
Clarke, Carree: 159,245; 162, 70.
Clarke, Creston: 28,132; 28, 135.
Clarke, Crichton: (W) 316,16.
Clarke, George; 53,175; 63, 123.
Clarke, Grant: 285,27.
Clarke, Harry: 130,186; 143, 23; 208,357.
Clarke, Helen: 173,22; 217,151; 221,7.
Clarke, Herbert: 292,21.
Clarke, John Sleeper: 232, 507.

Clarke, Joseph I.C.: 18,8; (W) 23,11; (W) 24,35; 55,227.
Clasper, Edith: 283,37.
"Classmates": (R'07) 80,xiii; 80,279.
Claudel, Paul: 350,8.
Claudius, Dave: 261,383.
Claussen, Julia: 141,140.
"Claw, The": 249,365; (R'21) 250,31.
Claxton, Kate: 25,63; 38,100; 52,150; 111,157; 111,158; 237,368.
Clayton, Bessie: (A) 16,19; 52, 145; 71,6; 82,328; 102,53; 133,95; 203,18; 231,363.
Clayton, Estelle: 62,101.
Clayton, Ethel: 107,7; 165,227; 208,395; 211,185; 221,66; 231,416; 233,41; 235,236; 257,109.
Clayton, Margaret: 209,26.
Clayton, Jackson and Durante: (C) 360,32; (C) 341,23.
Clayworth, June: 356,35.
Cleaves, Freeman: (W) 356,30.
Cleggett, Helen: 140,108.
Clemens, Clara: 310,33.
Clemens, Le Roy: 150,60.
Clemens, Samuel: (A) 286,12.
Clement, Clay: 205,137.
Clement, Edmond: 107,12; 105, 138; 109,84; 116,109; 133,80.
Clement, Jean: 293,51.
Clement, Joan: 253,221.
Clements, Colin Campbell: 297, 40.
Clements, Dudley: 226,379.
Clements, Miriam: 140,99; 148, 163.
Clemmons, Katherine: 34,306.
"Cleopatra": 125,2; (F) 200, 253; (F,R) 201,316.
Clerget, Paul: 188,209.
Cleugh, Dennis: 252,151.
Cleveland Playhouse: 321,54.
Cleveland (Ohio) Theatre: 81, 310; 257,85.
"Clever Mrs. Carfax, The": (R,F) 202,394.
"Clever Ones, The": (R'15) 169,111; 169,114; 170,176.
Cliffe, Alice Belmore: 257, 83; 273,17.
Cliffe, Genevieve: 113,20.
Cliffe, H. Cooper: 96,69; 122, 118; 126,54; 216,69; 217, 152; 266,31; 286,23.
Clifford, Jack: 193,166.
Clifford, Kathleen: 82,vii; 128, 138; 186,73; 188,207; 194, 219; 198,75; 200,246; 201, 321; (D) 213,289; 220,399; 228,107.
Clifford, Ruth: 307,36.
Clifton, Chalmers: 261,34.
Clifton, Marion B.: 196,359.
Clifton, William: 99,158.
"Climax, The": (R'09) 99,ix; 100,183; 173,9; (R'19) 217, 141.
"Climbers, The": 3,3; 3,4; 3,11; 3,13.
Cline, Maggie: 302,25.
"Clinging Vine, The": (R'22) 264,19; 282,24.
Clinton Theatre (Iowa): 61,xiv.
Clive, Colin: 349,31; 354,29; 359,13.
Clive, Kittie: 77,189.
"Clock, Shop, The": 173,3.
"Clod, The": (R'15) 180,116; 181, 143; 188,212.
"Close the Book": (R'18) 208, 358.
"Clothes": (R'06) 68,xi; 69,294; 70,321.
"Clouds, The": (R'11) 124,vii.
Clownes, Louise: 36,34.
Clowns: 82,336; 104,107; 113, 30; 259,229.
"Club Friend, The": (R'04) 40, xiii.
Clubs, Theatrical (see also Lambs' Club): 33,278; 35, 14; 83,30; 91,243; 164,182; 174,67; 191,40; 231,398; 337,42.
Clugston, Robert: 114,56.
Clute, Chester: 308,14.
"Clyde Fitch That I Knew, The" [Bell] (B): 114,x.
Coakley, Marion: 204,91; 218, 221; 236,266; 237,349; 239, 130; 245,87; 284,23; 295, 17; 295,44; 306,46; 323,39; 323,52; 324,37.
Coasley, Marian: 200,203.

"Coat Tails": (R'16) 187,137; 187,147.
Coates, Albert: 340,27.
Coates, Robert M.: (W) 318, 37.
Coates, "Romeo": 34,317.
Cobb, Irvin S.: (W) 205,138.
"Cobra": (R'24) 280,16; 283, 22; (S) 283,26.
Coburn, Charles (see also Coburn Players; Coburns, The): 103,96; 103,97; 216,94; (W) 219,284; 222,82; (A) 226,438; 256, 31; 285,19; (W) 304,9; 325, 39; (A) 336,23; 353,43.
Coburn, [Mrs.] Charles (see also Coburns, The): 119,11; 142,200; 216,89; 242,324; 285,38; 300,22.
Coburn Players: 103,96; 114,40; 114,59; 119,10; 151,xi; 194, 201; 194,214.
Coburns, The: 194,201; 219, 284; 238,11; 302,17; 333,19.
Cochran, Charles B.: 351,30.
Cochran, June: 293,19; 321,43.
"Cochran Revue": 304,30.
Cochrane, Frank: 282,13.
Cochrane, Madeline: 219,294.
Cochrane, May: 183,278.
"Cock O' The Walk": (R'15) 180,64; 180,67.
"Cock Robin": 324,40.
Cocroft, Thoda (W): 304,32; 305,18; 307,10; 310,12; 312, 17; 314,10; 316,16; 353,20; 358,37.
Codd, Ethel: 314,25.
Cody, Lew: 261,392; 270,30; 294,39; 300,42; 315,56; (W) 323,32.
Cody, William F.: 41,173.
Coffin, Harriet E.: (W) 98,130.
Coghlan, Bertha: 67,252.
Coghlan, Charles: 54,188; 79,248; 171,232; 175,129; 224,222; 243,414.
Coghlan, Gertrude: 48,42; 69, 290; 79,234; 91,231; 105, 160; 105,161.
Coghlan, Rose: 33,281; 34,307; 71,19; 81,298; 92,255; 94, 330; 105,144; 105,145; 107, 9; 108,62; 118,169; 126,64; 165,214; 168,73; 171,243; 195,287; 199,148; 209,10; 247,232; 256,36; 261,392.
Cohan, George M. (see also Cohan and Harris; Cohans,[The] Four): 28,134; 60,vi; 61, xii; 62,86; 62,103; 65,170; (W) 72,52; 73,63; 83,xii; 85,62; 88,145; 88,165; (A) 92,xix; 93,xi; 105,xiv; 117, xiv; 120,60; 126,43; 129, xvi; 129,174; 141,134; 151,xi; 151,81; 151,82; (W) 160, 286; 165,205; 167,7; 168,101; 169,132; 171,258; 177,239; 177,240; 178,298; 187,126; 195,270; 195,285; 199,183; 200,245; (W) 201,284; 204, 87; 204,121; 207,319; 209, 40; 215,61; 216,79; 222,76; 224,221; 234,84; (W) 236, 254; 237,349; 246,165; 247, 214; 249,406; 253,214; (D) 254,309; 254,312; 254,336; 257,86; 276,16; 276,19; 277, 22; (W) 278,9; (C) 280,11; 290,19; (C) 290,97; 293,44; 301,55; 307,66; (W,C) 324, 17; (A) 324,18; (A,D) 324, 69; 344,49; 347,25; 351,25; 351,27; 351,43; (D) 352,4; 352,24.
Cohans, (The) Four: 28,134; 31,232; 72,50; 88,146; 88, 165; 171,258; 216,84; 281, 23.
Cohan, Georgette: 237,361; 255, 379; 325,39.
Cohan, Helen: 79,232; 155,32; (W) 254,312; 331,80.
Cohan, Jerry: 63,119; 79, 232; 88,165.
Cohan, Josephine: 88,165.
Cohan and Harris: 154,xxviii; 163,101; 166,310; 178,340; 187,178; 199,171; 202,411; 214,398; 234,84; 242,317; 353,31.
"Cohan Revue of 1916, The": 181,124; (R'16) 181,164.
"Cohan Revue of 1918, The": (R'17) 204,87; (R) 205, 137; 206,235.
Cohen, A.J.: 7,13.

Cohen, Bella (W): 289,28; 293, 16.
Cohen, Octavus Roy: (W) 224, 238; 235,178.
Cohen, Sammy: 325,6.
Coini, Jacques: 215,27.
Colbert, Claudette: 312,3a; 313, 48; 322,57; 325,44; 332,25; 343,17; 344,13; 346,52; (D) 346,53.
Colbourne, Maurice: 276,14; 278, 29.
Colbron, Grace Isabel: 73,84; (W,V) 225,295.
Colcord, Mabel: 176,171.
"Cold Feet": (R) 268,16.
Cole, Walter: (D) 247,211.
Coleman, Alta May (W): 226, 388; 230,264; 257,96; 261, 388.
Coleman, Charles: 168,60.
Coleman, John: 46,320.
Coleman, Majel: 305,47.
Coleman, Willis (W): 280,20; 294,10.
Colesium Garden Theatre (Raton, New Mexico): 64,xiv.
"Colleen Bawn, The": (D) 134, 131.
"College Widow, The": 44,240; (R'04) 45,271; 45,289.
"College Widower, The": (R'05) 48,34.
Collenette, Beatrice: 241,243.
Collier, Constance: 93,293; 94, 332; 94,333; 103,70; 106, 177; 120,42; 121,70; 121,91; 122,106; 134,127; 182,182; 185,27; 186,86; 213,281; 231, 363; 335,21.
Collier, Edmund: 77,186.
Collier, Lizzie Hudson: 40,138; 44,252; 90,219;121,79; 129, 168; 167,15.
Collier, Willie (see also Collier, William, Jr.): 14,3; 14,8; 32,241; 32,243; 39,111; 39, 121; 68,266; 72,34; 72,41; 77,184; 94,323; 95,30; 100, 171; 100,173; 100,175; 100, 180; 109,vi; 110,114; 119, xiii; 120,49; 127,76; 131,xi; 131,12; 131,32; 133,74; 143,18; 151,xi; 152,xi; 152,113; 156, 60; 156,62; 160,286; 169, 132; 188,246; 189,285; (W) 194,226; (A) 197,346; 214, 349; 217,149; 230,258; 230, 309; 232,504; 233,8; 233,24; 247,254; 260,320; 303,47; 317,59.
Collier, [Mrs.] Willie: 25,60.
Collier, William Jr. (see also Collier, Willie): 124,203; 143,18; 233,36; 292,34; 308, 40; 353,66.
Collier-Garrick, Helena: 95,30.
Collinge, Patricia: 122,118; 122,119; 122,120; 156,78; 157,160; 163,100; 164,156; 164,190; 168,58; 169,132; 170,195; 174,81; 175,111; 189,277; 189,281; 191,19; 197,27; 216,69; 217,139; 219, 281; 238,7; (A) 238,72; 239, 103; 291,27; 304,14; 305,21.
Collins, Charles W. (W): 96, 58; 129,176; 130,192.
Collins, Dolly: 114,56.
Collins, Jose: 133,86; 136,186; 140,123; 151,97; 161,35; 166, 265; 176,188.
Collins, Lillian Foster: 337,49.
Collins, Lottie: 127,93; 160, 298; 161,9; 170,172.
Collins, May: 215,21; 239,104; 297,23.
Collins, Miriam: 189,293; 217, 151.
Collins, Ray: 308,19.
Collyer, Dan: 32,259.
Collyer, June: 322,12; 325,22; 336,27.
Colman, George: (D) 314,8.
Colman, Ronald: 272,30; 296, 31; 283,31; 305,37; 306,40; 307,40; 307,48; 308,36; (D) 351,29; 359,48.
"Colonel Newcome": (R'17) 196,341; 196,345.
Colonial Theatre (Boston): 68, xviii.
Colonial Theatre (New York): 166,281.
Colonne, Edouard: 34,322.
Colorado University of: 297,39.
Colosseum (Rome): 77,197.
Colt, Ethel Barrymore (see also

Barrymore, Ethel): 356,15; 359,23; 361,14.

Colt, John Drew: 361,14.

Colt, Joseph: 4,15.

Colton, John: 300,36.

Columbia Theatre (San Francisco): 138,51.

Columbia University: 94,321; 121,92; 139,92; 194,214; 255, 373; 287,ii.

Colombini, Ugo: 93,309.

Columbus (Ohio) Theatre: 50,xii.

Coman, Maude: 83,13.

Coman, Morgan: 75,127; 239,109.

"Come Along": (R'19) 219,276.

"Come on In": (R,F) 213,320.

"Come-On Man, The": (R'29) 339,45.

"Come Out of the Kitchen": (R'16) 199,356.

"Come Seven": 234,83; (R'20) 234,105.

"Come To Bohemia": 184,329; (R'16) 184,366.

"Come Watch With Me The Passing Night": (F) 224,251.

"Comedian, The": 266,14; (R) 266,19.

Comedie Francaise: 30,190; 38, 96; 77,181; 90,xi; 100,191; 122,137; 152,xvii; 156,72; 301,24.

Comedy and Comedians: 54,196; 82,348; 124,188; 127,85; 166, 290; 184,389; 193,160; 197, 7; 197,12; 204,74; 224,230; 229,158; 231,396; 233,16; 235, 172; 277,10; 309,9; 318,18; 321,22; 325,17; 327,10; 343, 19; 345,33.

"Comedy of Errors, The": (R'03) 27,109; 151,98.

Comedy Theatre (New York): 105,146.

Comegys, Kathleen: 249,375; 307,23; 308,31.

"Comet, The": (R'07) 84,33; 84,39.

"Comic, The": (R'27) 316,20.

Comic Opera (see Musical Comedy).

"Coming of Mrs. Patrick, The": (R'07) 82,xvi.

"Coming Thro' The Rye": (R'06) 60,ix.

"Command To Love, The": 320, 24; (R'27) 321,82; 323,39.

"Commanding Officer, The": 106, 198; (R'09) 108,36.

"Commencement Days": 92,258.

"Commodore Marries, The": 343, 41; (R'29) 344,46.

"Common Clay": (R'15) 176,167; 176,171; (F) 218,255; (F,R) 355,47.

"Common Sense Bracket": (R'05) 48,32; 48,38.

Community Theatre (see also Amateur Theatre; Little Theatre): 239,120; 240,190.

"Commuters, The": (R'10) 115,xv; 116,127.

Compson, Betty: 236,288; 241, 270; 246,173; 252,175; 256, 40; 277,33; 286,32; 292, 39; 307,14; 314,11; 329,41; 331,53; 337,44.

Compton, Fay: 172,309; 300,30; 303,21; 307,21; 333,47.

Compton, Juliette: 231,405.

Compton, Mary: 216,97.

Comstock, F. Ray: 273,79.

Comstock, Nancy: 13,11; 66, 200.

Comstock, Nanette: 32,243; 39,121; 42,204; 52,148; 72, 41; 91,246.

"Comtesse Coquette": (R'07) 76,144; 76,151; 78,219.

"Con & Co.": 116,99; (R'10) 117,xi.

"Concert, The": 117,131; (R'10) 117,132; 210,91.

Condon, Eva: 158,177; 159, 272.

Condon, Kate: 147,139.

Conductors, Musical: 188,206.

Cone, Margaret: 171,234.

Conesa Sisters: 107,32.

Coney Island (New York): 31, 224; 40,156; 41,181; 42, 199; 44,v; 64,ii; 65,171; 65, 172; 101,18; 53,169; 65,170; 76,xiv.

"Confession, The": (R'11) 122,x; 123,160; 123,161.

"Confessions of a Playwright" by S. Rosenfeld: 286,12; 287, 25; 288,25; 289,25; 293,38;

296, 70.
"Confessions of a Stage Struck Girl by Julia Wemple (FI): 38, 102; 39, 129; 40, 157; 41, 183; 42, 209; 43, 237.
"Conflict, The": (R'09) 99, xiii; 99, 162.
"Congai": 334, 47; 336, 37.
Conger, Richard: (W) 76, 148.
"Congressman, The": (R'06) 70, xxix.
Congreve, William: (D) 285, 12.
Conheim, Martha Morton: 27, 116.
Conkey, Thomas: 213, 293.
Conkling, Chester: 321, 50.
Conlan, Frank: 351, 47.
Conlon, Francis X.: 140, 109.
Conlon, Paul Hubert: (W) 186, 86.
Connard, Phyllis: 312, 20.
Connecticut Theatre: 323, 49.
"Connecticut Yankee, A": 321, 43; (R'27) 322, 39; 323, 41; (F) 243, 426.
Connolly, Bob: (C) 341, 23.
Connelly, E.J.: 137, 10; 137, 13; 144, 35; 160, 317; 199, 175; 207, 273.
Connelly, (Mrs.) Erwin: 186, 83.
Connelly, Jane: 197, 36.
Connelly, Marc: 302, 30; 308, 29; 350, 27; (W) 357, 16; 360, 14.
Conness, L.E.: 200, 209.
Conness, Robert: 81, 293.
Connolly, (Mrs.) Francis A.: 197, 9.
Connolly, Walter: (D) 351, 19; 351, 45; 352, 43; 360, 26.
Connor, Barry: 302, 21.
Connor, Edmon S.: 10, 22.
Connor, Frank: 48, x; 152, 123.
Connor, W.F.: (W) 176, 172.
Connor, William: 299, 23.
Conor, Harry: 95, 29; 111, 133; 202, 353.
Conover, Charlotte Reeve: (W) 118, 186.
Conover, Teresa Maxwell: 135, 165; 158, 195; 236, 281.
Conquest, Ida: 4, 14; 8, 1; 8, 3; 21, 6; 35, 11; 40, c; 48, 31; 51, 110; 60, 46; 64, xiv; 87, 115; 88, 157; 108, 35; 111, 166; 115, 78; 128, 127; 229, 186.
Conrad, Con: 285, 27.
Conrad, Edith: 72, 47.
Conrad, Robert T.: (D) 197, 14.
Conradt-Eberlin, Eve M.: 356, 39.
Conried, Heinrich: 13, 18; 21, 11; 24, 36; 25, 77; 32, 252; 43, 227; (W) 46, 306; 54, 185; 58, 294; 62, 108; 59, 7; 61, 61; 81, 311; 96, 70; 100, vi; 106, 194; 124, 190; 287, 28.
Conron, Florence: 37, 75.
Conroy, Ethel: 114, 37.
Conroy, Frank: 151, 89; 183, 273; 203, 22; 203, 35; 204, 83; 207, 301; 208, 359; 227, 23; (D) 237, 351; 244, 27; 301, 14.
Conroy, Susan: 321, 27.
"Conscience": (R'24) 284, 62.
"Consequences": (R'14) 165, 204.
Conservatoire Orchestra (Paris): 213, 268.
Considine, Geoffrey: 272, 17.
"Conspiracy, The": (R'12) 144, 38; 145, 86.
Constable, Clifford: 41, 183.
"Constant Nymph, The": (R'26) 311, 15; 311, 19.
"Constant Wife, The": (R'26) 311, 16; (S) 312, 26; 312, 50.
Constantino, Florencio: 88, 167; 95, 36.
"Consuelo": (R'03) 26, 86.
"Consul, The": (R'03) 25, 59.
"Contrast, The": 188, 208; 215, 36.
Convell, May: 55, 224.
Conway, Evelyn: 165, 232; 236, 330.
Conway, Ferry: 236, 273.
Conway, Lizzie: 73, 60.
Conway, Minnie: 54, 189.
Conway, Peggy: 292, 30.
Conway, Mary: 67, 250.
Conwell, May: 40, 145.
Coogan, Jackie: 244, 38; 262, 34; 266, 10; 270, 33; 271, 32; 275, 30; 279, 32; 284, 32; 291, 35; 305, 46; 306, 38; 314, 38.
Cook, Augustus: 21, 9.
Cook, Burr C. (W): 174, 67;

184,359; 188,206; 233,16; 234,10; 257,98; 264,27; 274, 10; 281,43; 284,22; 324,41.
Cook, Charles Emerson: 55,227.
Cook, Donn: 336,52; (C) 349,4.
Cook, Francis: 159,238.
Cook, Helen: 125,21.
Cook, J.F.: 10,20.
Cook, Joe: 262,37; (D) 270,10; 270,15; 283,8; 290,46; 306, 12; 306,13; 318,18; (A) 322, 3; 325,13; 326,53; (W) 329, 10; 329,40; 354,23; 354,31; 356,28; 357,64; 358,32.
Cook, Louise: 341,43.
Cook, Madge Carr: 30,194; 33,288; 41,159; 58,301; 155,32.
Cook, Olga: 249,367; 255,365; 284,26; 284,27.
Cook, Roy A.: (W) 28,151.
Cook, Wm. Marion: 26,97.
Cooke, Beach: 295,28.
Cooke, Emma: 116,116.
Cooke, George Frederick: (D) 97,86.
Cooksey, Curtis: 192,84; 205, 148; 239,83.
Coolidge, Calvin: 286,10.
Coolus, Romain: 117,154.
Coombs, Frank: 117,138.
Cooper, Bigelow: 123,161.
Cooper, Catherine: 88,163.
Cooper, Claude: 303,17; 303,27; 329,24.
Cooper, Frank Kemble: 195,267.
Cooper, George: 309,48.
Cooper, Gladys: 187,131; 307, 20.
Cooper, Jane: 180,87; 190,359; 204,84.
Cooper, Lillian Kemble: (D) 224, 241; 253,250; 268,18.
Cooper, Miriam C.: 206,264; 224, 254; (D) 239,c; 316,40.
Cooper, Opal: 196,350.
Cooper, Scott: 47,7; 140,113; 262,20.
Cooper, Thomas A.: (D) 173, 19; (D) 232,506.
Cooper, Violet Kemble: 158,174; 204,73; 216,81; 244,33; 245, 92; 246,182; 249,383; (D) 249,404; 252,152; 266,17; 269,18; 292,27; 353,33.
Cope, John: 128,116; 155,51; 181,153; 206,221; 213,287; 224,222.
Copeau, Jacques: 195,288; 202, 342; 203,21; 205,152; 212, 198; 212,205; 213,292; 218, 199; 218,206; 287,20; 311,29; 312,21; 319,41.
Coppee, Francois: 90,223.
Copland, Aaron: 356,43.
Copley Theatre (Boston): 245, 100.
"Copperhead, The": (R'18) 206, 218; 206,221.
Copyright (see also Plagarism): 37,72; 115,84; 275,12; 331, 25; 341,11.
Coquelin, Alexandre Honore Emert: 37,74; 97,ii.
Coquelin, Benoit Constant: PG, 10; (A) 3,17; 6,15; 10,12; 12,17; 38,96; 54,186; 60, 38; 90,206; 94,338; (A) 97, 85; 98,134; 107,x; 109,79; 112,xiv; 196,347.
Coquelin, Jean: 38,96; 110,116.
"Coquette": (S) 323,24; (R'27) 323,39.
"Cora": 94,318.
Corallo, Pietro: 248,317.
Corbett, James J.: 38,iv; 60,28; 183,294; 222,109; 288,36.
Corbin, John: (W) 220,334; (C) 268,21; 271,58.
Corcoran, Jane: 92,277; 262,20.
Corda, Maria: 318,40.
"Cordelia Blossom": (R'14) 164, 195.
Corder, Leeta: 286,18.
Corelli, Marie: 283,7.
"Co-Respondent, The": (R'16) 183,277; 184,334.
Corey, Arthur: 241,249; 244, 25; 248,299.
Corey, Madison (see also Corey and Ritter): 202,411; 187, 175.
"Coriolanus": 5,5.
Cornell, Gerald: 353,44.
Cornell, Grace: 333,39.
Cornell, Katherine: 194,223; 195,287; 203,15; 250,17; (D) 250,33; 250,40; 267,17; 272,13; (D) 273,10; 273,12;

277,6; 277,64; 278,14; 278, 22; (D) 278,38; 287,64; 291, 22; 292,9; 293,8; 294,14; (D) 295,11; 297,9; (D) 298,c; (D) 320,10; 320,28; 329,27; 334,21; 340,15; 341,36; 348, 14; 349,24; 350,43; 352,21; 358,37; 360,20; 361,24; 361, 32; 361,33.
Cornell University: 228,112; 231, 420; 263,44; 287,43; 288,40; 297,41; 313,43; 317,45; 337, 50; 351,50.
Cornelys, Pauline: 282,35.
"Cornered": (R'20) 239,105; 239, 109.
Cornwall, Anne: 237,379.
"Coronet and the Duchess, The": (R'04) 45,206; 45,282.
Corrigan, Emmett: 120,58; 121, 92; 140,103; 156,40; 157, 129; 165,208; 190,370; 212, 221; 214,340; 243,395.
"Corsican Brothers, The": (D) 134,130.
Corson, Frances: 124,187.
Cort, Harry L.: 221,27.
Cort, John: 115,72; 118,xxxvi; 139,xi; 142,xxi; 153,viii; 154, xxviii; 163,141; (A) 165, 245; 175,110; 178,341; (A) 199,169; 226,442.
Cort Theatre (Chicago): 124, 198.
Cort Theatre (San Francisco): (D) 138,50.
Cort Theatre (New York): 144, 42.
Cortelyou, Alida: 39,131.
Cortez, Ricardo: (D) 295,2a; 296,41; 306,37.
Cortez and Peggy: 286,11; 338, 25.
Corthell, Herbert: 49,59; 219, 277.
Cortot, Alfred: 216,73; 347,31.
"Cosi Sia": (R'23) 274,16.
"Cossacks, The": (F) 324,34.
Cossart, Ernest: 170,197; 263, 18; 276,14; 327,38; 336, 61; 353,44.
Costa Rica, Teatro Nacional De: 18,14.
Costa, Tessa: 287,13.
Costello, Dolores: 307,38; 310, 35; 322,60; 324,26; 331,38; (D) 333,9f; 337,69; 338,63.
Costello, Helene: 313,39; 329, 14.
Costello, Maurice: 140,112.
Costumes: 21,15; 46,302; 70, 321; 83,15; 95,xvi; 97,xviii; 102,44; 166,283; 173,203; 177,232; 186,73; 200,196; 211,158; 213,282; 220,358; 231,393; 234,96; (D) 240, 182; 255,372; 262,47; (D) 285,13; 286,28; 297,27; 297, 76; 314,44; 336,2; 351,74; 353,21.
Costumes - Opera: 123,152.
"Cottage in the Air, The": (R'09) 106,166; 107,9.
Cottlow, Augusta: 11,24.
Cotton, Idalene: 223,169.
Cotton, Lucy: 163,112; 188, 205; 200,232; 223,180; 230, 281.
Cottrelly, Mathilde: 48,42; 114, 37; 146,105; 147,144; 171, 228; 178,299; 210,87; 289, 26.
Coughlan, Junior: 314,38.
"Could We Do Without The Dramatic Critic?" (Symposium): 111,150.
Couldock, C.W.: 46,305; 182,217.
Coulom, Robert: (W) 346,39.
"Count of Luxembourg, The": (R'12) 140,xiii; 141,157; (R'30) 349,74.
Countiss, Catherine: 55,232; 75,119; 75,137; 95,22; 109, iii; 153,172; 159,237.
"Countess Maritza": (R'26) 308, 15.
Countess of Pembroke: 154,194.
"Country Boy, The": (R'10) 116,100; 116,124.
"Country Cousin, The": 200,203; (R'17) 200,207.
"Country Girl, A": 21,8; (R'02) 21,10; 42,ii; 125,iii.
"Country Mouse, A": (R'02) 21,8.
"County Chairman, The": (R'04) 35,7; 35,16; 42,ii.
"Courage": 333,22; (R'28) 333, 47.

Court, Florence: 226,393.
"Courting": (R'25) 296,18.
"Courtisan, La": 70,xvi.
Courtleigh, William: PG,17; 6,4; 11,7; 45,282; 49,56; 68,252; 137,11; 137,13; 147,131; 152, 115; 182,197; 189,285; 201, 275; 229,192; 262,24.
Courtenay, Fay: 145,80; 308,14.
Courtenay, Vera: 119,30; 168,66.
Courtnay, Marion: 136,63.
Courtweidge, Charles: 312,20.
Courtneidge, Cicely: 300,29; 302,19.
Courtney, Inez: 270,35; (C) 361, 27.
Courtney, Irene: 339,49.
Courtney, Martha: 241,243.
Courtney, William: 12,12; 40,135; 48,30; 59,13; 88,157; 90, 205; 104,106; 104,125; 124, 191; 140,113; 143,32; 145, 65; 154,203; 161,12; 161,13; 164,154; 169,139; 175,111; 175,113; 185,28; 194,231; 204,79; 213,271; 217,149; 217,163; 248,293; 277,36; 288,14.
"Cousin Billy": (R'05) 48,32; 48, 33.
"Cousin Kate": 34,290; 86,vi.
"Cousin Louisa": (R'06) 64,141.
"Cousin Lucy": (R'16) 176,168.
Coute, Sally: 167,19.
Couzinou, Robert: 216,72.
Covarrubias, Miguel: (D) 290, 31; 298,16.
Covent Gardens: (D) 131,28.
Coverdale, Minerva: 217,135.
"Covered Wagon, The": (F,R) 267,34; 267,35.
Covey, Edna: 311,49.
Coward, Edward Fales (W): 15, 19; 22,25; 24,44; 25,66; 26, 90; 29,164; 35,21; (V) 37, 70; 38,vii; 44,249; 51,114; 60,44; 65,186; 89,196; 98, 108; 102,58; 112,202; 124,211; 139,79; 161,11; 170,196; 182,202; 183,289; 198,89; 200, 198; 202,356; 203,28.
Coward, Noel: 279,27; 292,22; 296,17; 297,12; 297,36; 298, 28; (W) 299,7; 299,47; 303, 9; (W,C) 310,10; 310,33; 346,20; 360,21; 360,22; 360,41; (C) 361,2.
Cowell, Sidney: 3,12; 35,15.
Cowie, Laura: 171,256.
Cowl, Jane: 104,104; 104,106; 105,156; 114,41; 117,135; 118,192; 120,c; 139,68; 140, xiv; 140,97; 159,246; 167, 11; 170,190; 176,171; 177, 233; 177,259; 178,288; (W) 181,145; (C) 183,292; 187, 135; (W) 189,270; 191,41; 193,145; 193,152; 196,329; 196,354; 197,46; 198,108; 199,136; 199,180; 200,204; 206,214; 206,215; 211,135; 213,278; 214,335; 214,349; (A) 214,379; 216,83; 217, 157; (W) 218,210; 218, 228; 226,361; (A) 226,438; 227,10; 228,97; (W) 230, 274; 231,349; 231,426; 231, 426; (A) 238,72; 244,36; 250,11; 256,15; 257,87; 260, 320; 261,376; 264,16; 265, 17; 265,29; 267,26; (C) 271,22; 271,38; 275,14; 276, 5; 277,62; 289,19; 290,13; 295,c; 299,17; 300,12; 309,4; (C) 313,17; 315,28; (D) 317,c; (W) 320,11; (A) 322,3; 335,c; (W) 342,12; 345,15; 356,12; 358,25; (C) 359,2.
Cowles, Eugene: 47,14; 125, 13; 137,3; 137,13.
Cowley, Eric: (C) 359,22.
Cowley, Harry: 83,15; 145, 72.
Cowper, Gwendolyn: 40,147.
Cox, Baby: 341,43.
Cox, Dail: 303,25.
Cox, Elinor M.: 183,283; 191, 29.
Cox, Hazel: 150,66; (A) 226, 438.
Cox, Louise: 141,139; 180,85; 206,216.
Cox, Ray: 164,163; 165,234; 213,321; 214,335.
Coyne, Helene: 191,39.
Coyne, Joseph: 13,8; 50,103; 69,298; 90,215; 92,279;

95,x; 294,20.
Coyne, Oliver: (W) 360,21.
Cozzens, Ethel: 230,275.
Crabtree, Charlotte [Lotta]: 14,21; 29,176; 138,50; 140,114; 180, 90; 232,508; 237,368; 285, 26; 359,18.
"Cradle Snatchers": (R'25) 296, 18; 296,19; (S) 297,26.
"Cradle Song": (R'21) 242,340.
Craft, Marcella: 163,103; 225, 320.
Crafts and Haley: 273,35.
Craig, [Mrs.] Charles G.: 172, 287; 217,140.
Craig, Edward Gordon: 52,147; (W) 64,155; 136,xiii; 151, xvi; 155,32; (D) 163,120; 170,197; 194,218; (D) 218, 218; 332,22; (D) 332,23; 335,61; 356,8.
Craig, John: 24,39; 30,187; 155, 28; 194,212; 196,360; 243, 395; 245,100; 257,101; 268, 3; 271,18.
Craig, Robert W.: 301,19.
"Craig's Wife": (R'25) 297,15; 298,29; (S) 301,26; 307,9.
Cram, Mildred (W): 197,10; 204,90; 206,228; 208,362; 211,146; 213,282; 217,158; 257,78.
Cramer, Richard: (D) 275, 27.
Cramer, Ruth: 180,76.
Crampton, Charlotte: 185,31.
Crandell, Edward: 298,19; 310, 14; 311,28; 314,17.
Crandell, Catherine: 296,25; 322,33.
Crane, Donald: 191,39.
Crane, Frank: 199,119.
Crane, Harold: 110,127.
Crane, James L.: 221,27; 223, 159; 234,111; 242,337.
Crane, Virginia: 273,23.
Crane, William H.: 33,268; 34, 306; 41,175; 43,229; 44,249; 45,279; 63,132; 66,213; 67,v; 67,245; 68,277; 74,91; 79, 228; 79,229; 82,322; 85,83; 86,viii; 86,xi; 105,162; 131, 2; 131,8; 156,78; 167,11; 169,129; 169,142; 187,127; 193,146; 233,24; 235,184; 235,218; 287,28.
Craske, Ivy: 107,12.
Crater, Aline: 69,293; 70,328.
Craven, Frank: 129,169; 137, 10; 158,170; 158,177; 160, 296; 187,137; 187,139; 199, 146; 199,147; 200,206; 204, 88; 204,93; (A) 207,312; 219,281; 232,505; 238,27; 243,402; 317,56; (D) 357,2; 322,39.
Craven, H.T.: (W) 83,14.
Craven, Ruby: 195,287.
Craven, Scott: 22,16.
Crawford, Clifton: 90,209; 90, 222; 140,iii; 170,192; 177,239; 233,8; 233,69.
Crawford, Edna Archer: 91, 252.
Crawford, F. Marion: 16,8; 26, 80; (C) 37,56; 55,227; 99, ii; 99,166.
Crawford, Joan: 300,42; 325, 34; 353,46.
Crawford, Margaret: 200,201; 210,75.
Crawford, Mary Caroline (W): 88,167; 90,218; 129,157; 133,87; 135,154; 119,8.
Crawford, Shirley M.: (W) 18, 14.
Crawley, John Snyder: 38,99.
"Creaking Chair": (R'26) 302,18.
Creative Dramatics (see Children's Theatre).
"Creative Theatre" [Mitchell] (B): 345,6.
Creighton, Walter: 141,149.
Cressy, Will M.: 62,103; 86, xv.
Crews, Laura Hope: 14,19; 19, 8; 38,105; 51,108; 57,283; 62,94; 91,252; 112,175; 121, 94; 146,120; 149,30; 150,37; 152,109; 152,110; 165,209; 165,246; 166,277; 173,10; 179,9; 186,87; 192,79; 201, 285; 202,353; 207,283; 225, 309; 242,319; 245,87; 246, 152; 249,390; 277,12; (D) 277,13; 286,66; 289,27; 297, 36; 307,28; (C) 316,31; 333, 47.

Crichton, Madge: 69,292.
"Crime": 314,20; (R) 314,21; (S) 318,26.
"Crime and Punishment": (R'26) 309,70.
"Crimes of a Cynical City": 42, 192.
Crimi, Giulio: 203,39; 216,73.
"Criminal Code, The": (S) 345, 41; (R'29) 345,47; 351,14; 351,20.
Crimmins, Agnes: 135,155.
"Crimson Alibi, The": (R'19) 223, 149; 223,169; 224,238.
"Crimson Gardenia": (F) 223,178.
"Crinoline Girl, The": (R'14) 159, 227; 159,240.
Cripps, Florence: 171,239; 211, 159.
"Crisis, The": 16,1; 16,4; 16,5; (R'03) 23,9; 29,163.
Crisp, Harry: 106,182.
Cristalli, Italo: 155,14; 159,228.
Criterion Club: 181,180.
Criterion Theatre (New York): 39,126.
"Critic, The": 96,50; (R'15) 169,149.
Criticism (see also Critics): 25, 71; 26,84; 45,282; 62,89; 80, 264; 82,331; 84,39; 112,195; 125,8; (C) 133,98; 162,72; 167,12; 176,164; 187,154; 203, 14; 231,364; 256,8; 265,22; 267,9; 281,20; 283,20; 310, 20; 313,8; 313,10; 326,37; 348,22.
Criticism - Film: 184,344; 357, 23.
Criticism - Music: 22,36; 226, 392.
Critics (see also Criticism; ("Those Who Sit In Judgment"): 7,12; 26,88; 46,xxii; 53,159; 67,230; 73,79; 75,xiv; 84,54; 91,249; 182,230; 186,82; (C) 193,138; 209,30; 231,362; 244, 10; 255,370; 262,9; (C) 266, 11; (C) 267,11; (C) 268,21; (C) 269,21; 271,20; 286,7; (C) 290,21; 305,9; 312,16b; 324,23; 325,20; (C) 333,33; (C) 335,42; 361,13.
"Critic's Comedy, The": 203,15; (R'17) 203,23.
Cromer, Lord: 315,20.
Crompton, W.H.: 93,292.
Cromwell, John: 158,177; 223, 169; 323,39.
"Crooked Friday, The": 294,20; (R'25) 297,15.
"Crooked Gamblers": (R'20) 235, 187.
"Crooked Square, The" (R'23) 272,19.
Crooks, Richard: 331,23.
Cropper, Harriet: 46,315.
"Crops and Croppers": (R'18) 213,279.
Crosby, Charles: 57,271.
Crosby, Edward H.: 159,219.
Crosby, Juliette: 9,19; 254, 322; 256,9; 263,31; 277, 25; 277,44; 279,18; 282,28.
Crosby, M.R. (W): 48,47; 77, 188.
Crosman, Henrietta: PG,15; 3,2; 4,8; 4,9; 13,11; (A,D) 14,9; 21,c; 21,5; 21,9; (W) 22,18; 23,18; 30,195; 35, 2; 36,41; 36,45; 41,175; 59, 4; 72,31; 73,xvi; 79,252; 81,287; 82,xvi; (C) 82,xxiv; 89,177; 99,149; 116,105; 117, xi; 126,42; 127,iii; 127,78; 127,79; 136,188; 142,198; 147,157; 73,62; 154,xvi; 156, 77; 172,307; 183,276; 185, 27; 186,87; 190,374; 191,33; (W) 193,160; 193,161; 220, 345; 271,14; 277,21; 278, 36; 290,29; 333,40.
Cross, Mary: 114,56.
Cross, Milton J.: 299,37.
Cross, Wellington: 151,89; 263, 42; (W) 300,24; 301,38.
Cross and Josephine: 151,89.
"Cross My Heart": (R'28) 332, 48.
"Cross Roads": (R'29) 346, 46.
"Cross-Ways, The": 24,33.
"Crossing, The": 59,2; 59,5; (R'06) 60,viii.
Crossley, [Mrs.] G. Reginald: 337,42.
Crothers, Rachel: 70,316; 71,5; 73,84; 111,134; 154,xviii;

156,60; (W) 203,34; 221,27; 230,275; (W) 244,16; 269,23; (W) 304,34; (C) 339,39; 360, 32.
"Crowded Hour, The": (R'18) 215, 20; 217,157.
Crowell, Josepha: 13,5.
"Crown Prince, The": 36,48; (R'04) 37,60; 42,ii; 315,26.
"Crucible, The": (F) 167,19.
Cruikshank, Herbert Knight: (W) 344,26.
"Cruise of the Speejack, The": (F,R) 275,30.
Crume, Camilla: 133,85.
Crumit, Frank: 232,505; 255, 365.
Cruze, James: (D) 289,2; 295, 34; 297,32.
"Cub, The": (R'10) 118,xx.
Cuban Theatre: 138,40.
Cugat, Francis: 207,278.
Cukor, George: 295,66; 304,35.
Culver, A.E.: 64,xvi.
Cumberland, John: 155,21; 164, 163; 178,279; 179,16; 179,21; 204,93; 225,315; 234,83; (W) 309,9; 315,40; 319,23.
Cumming, Dorothy: 215,16.
Cummings, Robert: 87,118; 203,19.
Cunningham, Arthur: 113,15; 147, 139; 152,111.
Cunningham, Cecil: 165,216.
Cunningham, Leon: 217,155; 277, 29.
Curci, Luigi: 206,232.
"Cure For Curables, A": (R'18) 206,220; 206,231.
"Curiosity": (R'19) 228,144.
Currier, Frank: 145,71; 145, 73; 149,vi.
Curry, Helen: 229,173.
Curtain Calls: 58,303; 63,135; 100,190; 159,253; 200,192; 212,198; 263,7; 299,10; 318, 14.
Curtains, Theatre: 261,422.
Curtis, Edward S.: 167,20.
Curtis, Leslie (W): 104,101; 114,46; 115,81; 116,120; 118, 196; 120,54; 122,128; 126,40; 142,182; 147,131; 216,74; 219,294; 220,338; 222,100; 223,170; 225,318; 290,6.
Curtis, Vera: 141,140; 150,72; 153,159; 155,15; 168,66.
Curtis, William A. (W): 219,292.
Cushing, Catherine Chisholm: 160,300.
Cushman, Charlotte: 11,19; 46,305; 48,50; 50,93; 57, 286; 66,206; 72,45; 78,222; 95,24; 103,82; 106,180; 131, 28; 145,74; 180,79; 198,80; 232,507; 242,338; 290,80.
Cushman, Edwin: 190,374.
Cushman, Susan: 48,50.
Cutti, Berta: (W) 302,20.
Cutting, Justine: 11,15; 50,103.
"Cymbeline": (R'06) 70,314; 70, 336; 70,337; (R.23) 273,19; 273,25.
"Cynthia": (R'03) 26,81; 27, 109.
"Cyrano": (OP) (R'13) 146,106.
"Cyrano De Bergerac": PG,12; 17,13; (R'23) 274,16; 274,23; 336,36.
"Cytherea": (F,R) 281,32.
"Czarina, The": 253,211; (R'22) 253,235; (D) 253,237.
Czech Theatre: 137,30.

--D--

D'Abdank, Charles (W): 161, 27.
Daboll, William S.: 149,17.
Da Bubna, Augusta (W): 26,96; 60,52.
Daddi, Francesco: 152,131.
"Daddies": (R'18) 212,211; 213, 287; 214,350; 214,351.
"Daddy Dufard": (R'10) 119, xiii.
"Daddy Dumplins": (R'20) 239, 106.
"Daddy Goes A-Hunting": (F,R) 289,31.
"Daddy Long-Legs": (R'14) 165, 205; 167,50.
"Daddy's Gone A-Hunting": (R'21) 248,315; 249,365.
Dae, Frank: 360,25.
"Daffy Dill": (R'22) 259,228.
"Dagmar": (R'23) 264,16; 270, 18.
Dagwell, Natalie: 88,155.

Dahl, Cyrene: 239,97.
Dahl, Magda: 85,75.
Dahlen, Brenda: 356,24.
Dailey, Joseph: 327,39.
Dailey, Peter F.: 59,xii; 89,vi.
Dainton,Marie: 112,180.
"Dairymaids, The": 80,270
"Daisy Mayme": (R'26) 310,16.
Dakin, Beatrice: 180,79.
Dalberg, Camilla: 121,71.
Dale, Alan (see also Cohen, A.J.) (W): 176,164; 177,232; 178, 281; 179,13; 180,69; 181, 133; 182,224; 183,279; 184, 344; 185,13; 186,65; 187,130; 262,12; (C) 269,21; 319,40.
Dale, Audray: 350,48; 354,17; 359,17; 359,25.
Dale, Charles (W): 354,15; 356, 14; 358,14; 359,14; 360,14.
Dale, Ethel: 306,21.
Dale, J.B.: 139,96.
Dales, James; 261,370; (C) 262, 30.
Dale, Margaret; 14,3; 20,3; 33,263; 44,243; 56,251; 67, 236; 28,277; 76,159; 78,204; 82,322; 85,83; 88,145; 107, 27; 115,88; 124,205; 126,41; 199,135; 200,226; 217,163; 227,19; 283,25; 296,19; 297, 27.
Dale, Reba: 90,207.
Dale, Violet: 36,38; 183,298.
D'Algry, Antonio: 307,38.
D'Algy, Helena: 273,23.
Dallas, Gertrude: 121,79; 124,195; 213,295.
Dallas Little Theatre (Texas): 300,40; 347,50; 361,49.
Dallerup, Ellen: 177,221; 189,275.
Dal Monte, Toti: 283,34.
Dalmores, Aimee: 189,299; 193, 143; 194,209; 201,270; 205, 153; 206,238.
Dalmores, Charles: 71,8; 72,37; 73,64; 74,140; 82,351; 85,84; 95,34; 96,42; 97,77; 108,47; 121,83; 134,111; 136,198; 141, 139.
Dalnert, Colle: 136,198.
Dalton, Charles: 10,5; 10,8; 11,5; 11,8; 86,89; 109,73; 120, 42; 189,273; 228,96; 256, 21; 297,19; 349,34.
Dalton, Dorothy: 201,317; 206, 255; 212,251; 219,301; 224, 250; (D) 225,c; 227,16; 228, 120; 230,237; 231,424; 234, 116; 234,144.
Dalton, Gertrude: 96,68.
D'Alverez, Marguerite: 104,115; 252,163.
Daly, Arnold: 18,2 27,109; 35,7; 36,39; 38,86; 38,89; 40,141; 45,271; 48,28; 51,121; 56, 261; 57,271; 65,188; 75,127; 76,144; 82,xxiii; (W) 83,25; 85,69; 89,197; 94,325; 94, 326; 96,38; 108,xv; 108,35; 120,63; 136,199; 141,xii; 154,176; 157,130; 160,293; 160,294; 172,280; 177,220; 180,62; 184,334; 184,350; 191,9; (W) 192,98; 195,273; 197,40; 203,7; 205,137; 205, 149; 205,153; 205,185; 205, 192; 205,194; 206,219; (D) 237,351; 237,370; 237,373; 243,404; 249,440; (D) 251, 101; 255,367; 255,373; 262, 36; 264,42; 309,27.
Daly, Augustin: 7,10; 22,26; 29,173; 51,130; 52,150; 53, 169; 56,260; 62,101; 68, 276; 77,186; 78,201; 78,210; 83,xii; 126,64; 129,xxxi; 138, 45; 141,136; 145,74; 168,73; 169,136; 177,250; 195,263; 196,346; 205,180; 231,379; 232,504; 235,166; (A) 286,14; 288,25; 293,38; 302,36.
Daly, Blythe: 214,363; 275,23; 308,70; 339,49; 359,39.
Daly, Dan: 9,8; 29,160; 39,112; 141,ix.
Daly, Orlando: 140,109; 146, 123; 181,129; 212,213; 217, 140; 278,17.
Daly, Owen: 89,191.
Daly's Theatre (New York): 10,18; 39,127; 110,121; (D) 231,352; (D) 235,166.
Damacco, Giacomo: 178,284.
"Damaged Goods" 147,134; 149, 2.
Dambois, Maurice: 202,372.
D'Ambricourt, Adrienne: (D)

255,375.
Damita, Lily: 328,31; (D) 346, 27; 347,17; 347,45; (D) 350, 53.
"Damn Your Honor": (R'29) 347, 66.
"Damnation of Faust": (OP) 70, 327; 83,22.
Damrosch, Polly: 300,36.
Damrosch, Walter: (A) 3,17; 17,26; 119,6; 146,106; 178, 286; 229,173; 290,43; 333,25.
Dana, Rita: 234,103.
Dana, Viola: 145,71; 145,72; 145,73; 149,c; 149,vi; 162, 82; 162,83; 177,240; 207,331; 214,391; 231,416; 231,496; 234,144; 236,289; 258,197; 282,32; 296,41.
Dance: 52,144; 61,62; 68,278; 77,192; 88,164; 92,iii; 96,62; 102,51; 106,172; 107,13; 118, 178; 125,2; 127,92; 134,136; 145,90; 146,115; 159,231; 159, 266; 161,28; 165,226; 167,30; 188,212; 188,213; 192,82; 198, 71; 199,140; 213,294; 220,355; (D) 238,9; 242,342; 250,22; 256,13; 258,148; 258,192; 277,27; 282,17; 284,12; 286, 11; (C) 287,29; (C) 291,13; (C) 291,30; 291,31; 295,12; 302,34; 305,30; (C) 307,17; 308,12; (D) 347,28; 350,40; 357,44; 358,45; 360,37.
Dance, Reginald: 156,65.
"Dance of Death, The": 232,503; (R'20) 233,30.
"Dancer, The": (R'19) 227,20.
"Dancers, The": (R'23) 273,16.
"Dancing Around": (R'14) 165,255; 166,259.
"Dancing Duchess, The": 163,95.
"Dancing Girl, The": (F) 170,178.
"Dancing Mothers": (R'24) 283, 15; 283,17; (S) 284,28.
"Dancing Partner": (R'30) 354, 24; 354,25; (S) 354,33.
D'Andrea, Cecile: 250,23; 291, 6.
Dandy, Jess: (A) 54,183f; 56, 260; 129,175.
Dane, Clemence: 251,84; 252,158.
Danforth, Will: 152,127; 176, 170; 216,86; 229,159; 250, 35.
"Danger!": (R'21) 252,167.
Dangerfield, Clinton: (W,V) 106, 198.
"Dangerous Age, The": (F,R) 265,70.
"Dangerous Hours": (F,R) 229, 190.
Dangon, Victor: 32,256.
"Daniel": (R'20) 233,30.
Daniell, Henry: 336,50.
Daniels, Bebe: 231,411; 233, 40; 245,106; 280,27; 285, 31; 292,38; 297,32; 303,47; (W) 328,22.
Daniels, Eleanor: 160,322; 163, 106,221,7.
Daniels, Frank: 13,4; 13,6; 41,174; 52,134; (W) 52, 140; (A) 54,183f; (W) 55,216; 74,90; 83,30; 125,29; 145, 79; (C) 183,292; 287,52b.
Daniels, Mark: 344,53.
Daniels, Thelma: 307,38.
Danise, Giuseppe: 286,35.
Dannenburg, Joseph: (W) 66,219.
D'Annunzio, Antonio: (C) 53, 160; 57,273.
D'Annunzio, Gabrielle (see also Duse, Eleanora): 6,2; 12,18; 18,18; 18,19; 20,13; 22,6; 22,12; 38,89; (C) 53,160; 55,215; 57,273; 62,106; 69, viii; 72,xi; 86,110; 110,xiv; 125,5; 163,111.
"Dante": (S) 25,73; 27,112; (R'03) 34,288.
Daoust, Edmond: 15,12.
Daoust, Julien: 15,12.
D'Aranyi, Yelli: 337,36.
Darby, Myrna: 320,61.
Darch, Edna: 11,22; 12,23.
D'Arcy, Roy: 300,43; 310,40.
D'Arcy, Lynn: 88,155.
"D'Arcy of the Guards": (R'02) 12,9; 12,10.
"Dark, The": (R'27) 313,19.
"Dark Angel, The": (R'25) 289, 15; (F,R) 297,32.
"Dark Rosaleen": (R'19) 220, 340; 220,345.
D'Arle, Yvonne: 299,46; 304,46; 308,27; 309,46; (A) 322,3;

329,41.
Darling, Beatrice: 244,17.
Darling, Edward V.: 283,33.
Darling, Elizabeth: 244,17.
Darling, Grace: 194,208; 223, 154; 223,190.
Darling, Ida: 140,113.
Darling, Lucille: 210,97.
"Darling of the Gods, The": (R'03) 23,2; 23,3; 24,42; 29,164.
D'Armond, Isabel: 91,232; 91, 239; 95,26; 101,22.
Darnton, Charles: (C) 193,138; (D) 270,11.
Darragh, Miss: 83,21.
Darrell, Maisie: 344,56; (D) 345,18.
Darst, Doris: 167,34.
Dartmouth College: 231,419; 350, 50.
Darvas, Lily: 298,23; 323,38.
D'Arville, Camille: 46,316.
D'Arville, Marcelle: 247,258.
Das, Nirmal A.: (W) 353,39.
D'Aubigne, Lloyd: 41,iv.
Daudet, Alphone: 151,92.
"Daughter of Heaven, The": (S) 139,70; (R'12) 141,xviii; 141, 129.
"Daughters of Men": 70,319; (R'06) 71,3.
Davenport, Butler: 241,265.
Davenport, Edgar: 22,19.
Davenport, Edward Loomis: 16, 13; 55,231; 69,295; 111,163; 145,74; (D) 182,217; 241,260.
Davenport, Eva: 39,117; 116,102; 125,28; 160,293; 160,318.
Davenport, Fanny: 52,151; 55, 231; 90,205; 126,64; 130, 219; 195,265; 231,397; 237, 368.
Davenport, Harry: 21,7; 212,203; 215,9; 250,35; 251,103; 351, 35.
Davenport, Millia: 291,23.
Davenport Family: 55,231.
"David Copperfield": 132,47; (D) 165,228.
"David Garrick": (R'04) 46,294; 180,61; (R'16) 180,66.
"David Harum": 169,129; 254, 310.
Davidge, William T. Jr.: 63, 119.
Davidoff, Vladimir N.: 161,21.
Davidson, Dore: 42,192.
Davidson, Jo: (D) 262,3; 283, 33; 300,36.
Davidson, John: 212,195.
Davidson, Lucretia (W): 44, 255; 50,102; 64,144; 67, 240; 79,255; 107,26; 123, 170.
Davidson, W.B.: 223,182.
Davies, Ethel: 138,60; (A) 214,379.
Davies, Gwendolyn: 307,21.
Davies, Herbert Henry: 26,81.
Davies, Margaret: 237,367.
Davies, Marion: 171,239; 185, 34; 194,207; 195,309; 208, 390; 209,58; 210,c; 219,299; 255,326; (A) 229,217; 229, 228; 231,390; 231,415; 231, 428; (D) 232,c; 236,300; 247, 241; 263,59; 268,35; 271, 30; 277,33; 277,64; 278,30; 282,33; 283,30; 297,50; 298, 32; 310,40; 310,49; 320,54; (A) 322,3.
Davies, Olive Wilmot: 166,262.
Davies, Phoebe: 4,16; 34,306.
Davies, Reine: 161,10; 175, 131; 193,163; 194,242; 195, c; (D) 195,307; (A) 214,379.
Davies, Rose: 196,335.
Davis, Ann: 269,26; 280,38.
Davis, Baby: 108,36; 128,177.
Davis, Burton: 331,49.
Davis, Bessie Mc Coy (see also Mc Coy, Bessie): 217,180b; 228,73.
Davis, Bette: 346,48.
Davis, Bob: (W) 342,17.
Davis, C. Jack: 335,47.
Davis, C.T.: 263,14.
Davis, Caridad: 220,357.
Davis, Dolly: 336,59.
Davis, Edwards: 231,491.
Davis, Fay: 22,11; 23,7; 41, 162; 48,30; 56,247; 56,249; 61,54; 67,229; 90,205.
Davis, Florence: 51,120.
Davis, George Ade: (W) 102, 67.
Davis, Gordon: 302,40; 322,55.

Davis, J. Frank: (W) 332,15.
Davis, James J.: (W) 323,11.
Davis, Jessie Bartlett: 32,248.
Davis, Lael: 217,155.
Davis, Lyman Edwyn: (W) 141, 145.
Davis, Mary: 191,42.
Davis, Owen: 133,xiv; 152,x; 176,179; 248,313; 254,300; 263,40; (D) 289,12; 308,29; 315,43; 339,40; 342,17; 356,24; 361,4.
Davis, Paul: (W) 127,102.
Davis, Ray: 330,36.
Davis, Rees: 223,165.
Davis, Richard Harding: 14,6; 22,22; 27,108; 37,71; 61, xiii; 79,249; 115,87.
D'Avril, Yola: 321,50.
"Davy Crockett": 64,149.
Daw, Marjorie: 209,57; 223, 180; 229,189; 230,278; 243, 440.
Dawe, Jessie: 200,221.
Dawley, J. Searle: 204,121.
"Dawn": (F,R) 228,106; (R'24) 287,15; (F) 326,42.
Dawn, Allan: 310,38.
Dawn, Dorothy: 301,47.
Dawn, Eleanor: 235,182.
Dawn, Hazel: 122,132; 123,144; 125,c; 126,iii; (A) 127,xiv; 149,35; 151,81; 155,3; 160, 326; 161,21; 162,c; 162,49; 167,3; 167,47; 182,229; 190, 379; 191,c; 192,111; 198,69; 198,78; (A) 199,163; 199,176; 207,308; 209,39; 210,107; 213, 270; 217,159; (W) 219,278; 234,89; 247,239; 305,19; 313, 30; 317,59.
"Dawn of To-Morrow, The": (R'09) 97,75; 97,99.
"Dawn Patrol, The":(F,R) 353,48; (F) 353,61.
Dawson, Hal K.: 334,32; 334,59.
Dawson, Thomas: (W) 289,10.
Day, Edith: 204,93; 204,117; 224, 252; (D) 226,c; 228,118; 234, 97; 266,49; 269,17; 270,27; (D) 271,44.
Day, Edmund: 80,xiv.
Day, Edward: 62,103.
Day, Juliette: 122,118; 122,120; 142,165; 155,31; 175,131; 190,365; 201,265; 217,151; 235,165; 241,257; 333,32.
Day, Marceline: 314,49; 321,31.
Day, Marie L.: 110,118.
Day, Sharon: 264,35.
Day, Wilson: 132,45.
"Day of Dupes, The": (R'14) 158, 172.
"Daybreak": 199,135; (R'17) 199,136.
Dayton, Ruth: (D) 278,19.
Dazie [Mlle.] Belle: 72,36; 75, 140; 83,29; 94,334; 122,108; 124,185; 140,123; 158,199; 161,36; 164,178; 169,137; 172,299; 193,166; 194,224; 232,513; 242,349.
"Deacon and the Lady, The": (R'10) 117,x.
"Deadlock, The": (R'14) 157,158.
Deagon, Arthur: 79,237.
Deagon, Gracie: 268,42.
Dean, Barbara: 238,54.
Dean, Basil: 295,9.
Dean, Fanny: 215,38.
Dean, John W.: 81,291.
Dean, Julia (1830-86): 55,228.
Dean, Julia: 23,7; 55,217; 55, 228; 61,65; 77,191; 108,42; 113,17; 125,29; 129,169; 136, 191; 138,62; 142,196; 143, 21; 149,12; 151,82; 152,112; 165,207; 165,248; 167,29; 171,258; (D) 172,322; 174,69; 175,127; (C) 183,292; 186, 87.
Dean, Priscilla: 281,32; 293,31.
Dean, Ralph: 111,133.
Dean, Rita: 61,66.
Deane, Barbara: 274,27.
Deane, Gladys: 276,18.
Deane, Sidney: 23,12.
De Angelis, Jefferson: 20,10; 45,273; (A) 52,131f; (W) 52,141; (W) 54,205; 73,61; 74,99; 81,289; 82,xxi; 113, 15; 133,xv; 137,10; 137,11; 149,25; 287,58; 302,38; 324, 30; (W) 330,17; 350,48.
"Dear Brutus": (R'18) 216,77; 216,81; (S) 217,156; 221, 36.
"Dear Fool, The": (R'14) 157,

156.
"Dear Me": (R'21) 240,222.
"Dear Unfair Sex, The": (R'06) 68, xv.
"Dearest Enemy": 297,17; (R'25) 297,44.
"Death of Tintagiles, The": (R'17) 194,213; 194,223.
"Death Takes a Holiday": 347,13; (R'29) 347,49.
De Barry, Katherine: 96,45; 99,141; 100,174; 192,73.
De Basi, Pietro: 296,35.
De Becker, Harold: 195,281.
De Becker, Marie: 252,151.
De Beers, Clara: 101,15.
De Belleville, Frederic: PG,4; 16,6; 17,6; 50,101; (A) 52, 131,f; 81,vii; 122,119; 126, 65; 152,115; 171,233; 231, 363.
De Bray, Yvonne: 123,178.
Debrennes, Lucienne: 226,396.
"Debtors, The": (R'09) 106, xviii.
De Bubna, Augusta: (W) 60,52; (W) 26,96.
"Deburau": 239,82; 240,172; (R'20) 240,178.
Deburau, Jean Baptiste: (D) 239,82.
De Busey, Agatha: 229,169.
Debussy, Claude: 77,174; 116,108; 125,5.
"Debutante, The": 167,3; (R'14) 167,47.
De Caillavet, Gaston Armand: 168,98.
"Decameron": (F) 260,308.
De Casseres, Benjamin (W) (see also "Adrift in the Roaring Forties"): 58,303; 73,67; 74, 96; 79,234; 82,348; 251,78; 312,9; 313,8; 314,16; 315,16; 316,7; 317,10; 318,16; 321, 21; 322,23; 323,12; 324,23; 325, 20; 327,10; 328,12; 329,7; 330,18; 331,22; 331,52; 332, 22; 333,20; 334,20; 335,24; 336,24; 337,20; 338,24; 339, 27; 340,14; 341,16; 342,30.
"Deception": (F,R) 244,38; (F) 244,39; (F,R) 277,32.
"Decision": (R'29) 340,42.
De Cisneros, Eleanora: 68, 261; 71,8; 73,64; 75,138; 82,350; 84,40; 85,84; 119, 9; 146,114; 155,27; 180,85.
Decker, Edith: 98,115; 99,136; 113,17; 130,187.
Decker, John: (D) 273,10; (C) 276,11; (C) 277,11; (C) 278,11; (C) 279,11; (C) 280, 11; (C) 281,11; (C) 282,11; (C) 283,13; (D) 290,91; (D) 295,31; (D) 316,31.
Decker, Paul: 176,170.
"Declasse": 225,305; (R'19) 226,440.
"Decorating Clementine": (R'10) 117,xvii; 117,151.
De Cordobar, Pedro: 110,99; 114,39; 116,101; 117,132; 140,118; 146,105; 172,287; 188,215; 200,251; 201,275; 243,395; 244,27; 249,377; 253,219; 271,13; (A) 322,3.
De Cordova, Rienzi; 202,347.
De Croisset, Francis: 115,71.
"Dedale, Le": 48,40.
Dreen, Marjorie: 219,293.
"Deep Purple, The": (R'10) 120, xxviii; 120,58.
"Deep River": (R'26) 309,18.
"Defender, The": (R'02) 18,2.
De Feraudy, Maurice: 278,5; 278,16; 289,40; 340,22.
De Fina, Dolores: (A) 343,64.
De Flers, Robert: 113,28.
De Foe, Louis, V.: 167,12; (C) 193,138; (W) 198,64; (W) 210,86; (W) 222,74; (W) 231, 348.
De Fontenay, Hortense: 34,304.
De Fornaro, Carlo: (W) 20,13.
De Forrest, Hal: 93,287.
Defreyn, Henry: (D) 293,11.
De Gonzales, Carmen: 140,109.
De Grove, E. Ritzema: 111, xviii.
De Haven, Carter: 160,293; 196,340.
De Haven, Charles: 151,89.
De Haven, Flora Parker: 150, 49.
De Hidalgo, Elvira: 110,107; 277,35.
Dehner, Virginia: 22,26.

De Holtoir, Beatrice: 181,144; 230,261.
Deisha: 241,245.
De Jade, [Mlle.] Diane: 10,24.
De Koven, Reginald, 12,4; 15,18; 93,xiii; 203,36; 229,230.
Delacy, Phillippe: 309,35; 314, 38.
De La Motte, Marguerite: 312, 22; 314,49.
"De Lancey": (R'05) 56,239; 56,251.
Delannoy, Henriette: 226,396.
De Lanux, Pierre: 241,249.
De Lany, Gwendoline: 266,18.
De Lara, Isidore: 123,179.
Delaunois, Raymonde: 167,16; 168,64; 179,12; 230,262.
Delf, Harry: 158,182; 207,277.
Delgado, F.P.: (W) 40,153.
De Lievin, Lucette: 119,8.
De Lipsky, Nicholas: 251,80.
Dell, Eleanor: 160,285; 197,39.
Dell, Floyd: (C) 339,39.
Dellenbaugh, Harriet Otis: 24,33; 37,75; 92,277; 118,172; 169, 131.
Delmar, Louise: 37,62.
D'Elmar, Mabel: 147,146.
Delmar, Madeline: 181,129; 181,153; 206,244; 215,29; 232,529; 250,24.
Delmar, Thomas: 45,289.
Delmarr, Nora: 276,20.
Delmore, Herbert: 151,96.
Delmore, Ralph: 6,5; 36,47; 70,319; 73,77; 95,33; 129, 162.
Delna, Marie: 103,95; 105,138; 109,76.
De Lorde, Andre: 54,202.
Delour, Pamela: 270,35.
Del Rio, Dolores: 306,36; 308,40; 311,37; 313,40; 318,45; 320, 54; (C) 321,33; 322,12; (W) 323,18; (D) 330,29.
Delroy, Irene: 279,14; (A) 322, 3; (D) 323,29; 327,9; 328, 39; 328,47; 335,33; 336,60; (A) 345,70.
De Luca, Guiseppe: 178,285; 280,35; 287,35; 303,34.
"Deluge, The": 199,121; (R'17) 200,205; 253,215; (R'22) 253,233; (D) 253,237.
"De Luxe Annie": 200,197; (R'17) 200,208.
Delysia, Alice: 238,11.
Delza, Monna: 121,102; 122,140.
De Mar, Carrie: 138,58.
De Marco, Nina: 286,11.
De Mare, Rolf: (D) 294,29.
Demarest, Florence: 175,113.
Demarest, Frances: 112,180; 116,102; 170,172; 175,123; 186,63; 202,357.
Demarest, Frederich: 218,201.
Demarest, William: 342,50.
De Max, M.: 100,172; 240, 169.
Demblon, Celestin: 155,12.
De Merode, Cleo: 106,178.
De Mette, Stella: 141,138.
De Mille, Cecil B.: 45,278; 69,287; 87,viii; 147,xx; 154, xviii; 203,58; 208,398; 216, 121; 217,184; 271,32; 276, 32; (D) 287,2; (W) 315,45; 319,68; 342,34.
De Mille, Henry: 45,278; 290,18.
De Mille, [Mrs.] H.C.: 53,164.
De Mille, William C.: 45,278; 49,55; 55,227; 69,287; 80, xiii; 83,xi; 84,48; 87,viii; 128,x; 143,6; 147,xx; 154, xviii; 239,114; 240,186.
De Mille Studio: 319,54.
"Demi-Monde, Le": 49,xviii.
Deming, Will: 248,293.
"Demi-Tasse": 150,39.
"Demi-Tasse Revue": 226,393.
De Montesquiou-Fezensac, Count Robert: (W,V) 26,89.
Dempsey, Clifford: 292,14.
Dempsey, Louise: 136,176.
Dempster, Carol: 243,426; 259,243; 276,31; 287,30.
Dempster, Robert: 76,147.
De Musset, Alfred: 142,168.
De Navarro, Mary Anderson: (D) 119,18.
Denham, G.W.: 71,17.
Denig, Lynde (W) (<u>see also</u> "Vicissitudes of a Playwright"): 165,227; 166,274; 167,18; 168,68; 170,186; 183,282; 184,362; 185,18; 186,92.
Denise, Mary: 307,8; 315,29.
Denishawn, Thessally Niles:

211, 137.
Denishawn Dancers: 210, 71.
Denizon, Helene: 278, 27; 282, 25; 289, 11; 292, 19; 305, 31.
D'Ennery, Guy: 279, 18.
Dennis, Amy Leah: 220, 363.
Dennison, Eva: 88, 162; 88, 163.
Denny, Reginald: 237, 380; 290, 37; 293, 34; 322, 48; (C) 321, 33; (W) 332, 24.
Denny, W.H.: 109, 81.
Denver Theatre: 30, 201; 243, 427; 263, 22.
Denver, University of: 360, 42.
De Pachmann, Vladimir: 130, 190; (D) 276, 27.
"Departmental Case": (F, R) 199, 176.
De Pasquali, Bernice: 134, 111.
Depero, Fortunato: (D) 348, 42.
Depew, Chauncey M.: (W, A) 322, 15.
De Porto-Riche, George: 122, 110.
Depression And Theatre: 360, 15.
"De Profundis (Wilde) (B): 51, iii.
"Depths, The": (R'25) 289, 16.
De Putti, Lya: 306, 37; 308, 40; 310, 35; 318, 45; 320, 45; (W) 325, 26; 358, 33.
"Der Gute Ruf": (R'13) 153, xxiv.
"Der Lebende Leichnam" (see also "Redemption): (R'16) 190, 355.
"Der Rosenkavalier": (OP) 154, 200.
De Ramey, Pierre: 292, 32.
De Reamer, Rubye: 192, 101.
"Derelict, The": 114, 56.
"Derelicts": 114, 54.
De Remer, Ruby: 210, 89; (A) 214, 379; 217, 189; 223, 196; 225, 328; 240, 198.
De Rennes, Brander (W): 127, 92; 128, 128.
De Reszke, Edouard: (A) 3, 1: 10, 28; 62, 108; 70, 342; 231, 367.
De Reszke, Jean: 3, 1; 17, 23; 62, 108; 79, xiii; 231, 367.
De Revere, F. Vance: (W) 300, 12.
Dereyne, Fely: 87, 142; (A) 121, xvi.
Derickson, Charles: 213, 273.
Derimo, Lillian: 116, 116.
Derit, R.E.: (W) 157, 128; 158, 192.
"Derniere Torture, La": 54, 202.
Derny, Madge: 226, 395.
De Rohan, Pierre: (W) 343, 21.
Derohe, Charles: 271, 30.
De Roincee, Viviane: 166, 269.
De Rosa, Vera: 151, 96.
Derr, Dorothy: 51, 115.
De Rue, Beatrice: 208, 363.
Derwent, Clarence: 351, 35.
Desboro, Dana: 202, 353.
Desclee, Aimee: 150, 42.
De Segurola, Andrea: 157, 116; 169, 119; 308, 38; (D) 330, 29.
De Sellem, Elaine: 52, 148.
"Desert Flower, The": (R'24) 287, 19; (R'26) 311, 18; (F) 335, 28; (F) 340, 59.
"Deserters, The": (R'10) 117, 134.
Desha: 245, 91; 258, 159; 298, 6.
Deshion, Florence: 187, 139.
Deshoulieres, Antoinette: 27, 116.
Deshon, Frank: 150, 69.
Design (see Costumes; Scene Design).
"Desire Under the Elms": (R'24) 286, 22; (S) 291, 26; 292, 20; 295, 7; 302, 12.
Deslys, Gaby: 128, 112; 129, 156; (A) 136, xix; 138, 45; 145, 66; 152, 136; 159, 272; 163, 142; 165, 227; 178, 279; 180, 59; 181, 144; (D) 219, 267; (D) 222, 78; 256, 34.
Desmond, Mae: 335, 40.
Desmond, Mona: 41, 170.
Desmond, Paula: 52, 152.
Desmond, William: 192, 97.
De Sousa, May: 29, 180; 40, 149; 104, 130; 116, 127; 122, 117; 152, 111; 153, vi; 154, c; 177, 234.
Despa, Estelle: 156, 63.
Despres, Suzanne: 131, 18; (D) 156, 83; 206, 208.
De Stefani, Joseph: 242, 331.
Destinn, Emmy: 88, 151;

93,308; 94,335; 95,25; 97,71; 98,109; 107,12; 111,159; 119, 4; 121,82; 129,154; 130,188; 133,79; 134,111; 135,iv; 141, 140; 144,51; 153,149; 157, 117; 166,270; 178,286.
De Swirsky, Thamara: 119,27.
De Sylva, Buddy: 285,27; 331, 27.
Detective Plays: 336,17; 337, 31; 344,34; 351,16.
"Detective Sparkles": (R'09) 104,107; 104,127.
De Tell, Sylvia: 210,77.
Detling, Rene: 163,114; 171, 256; 227,23; 230,254.
"Detour, The": (R'21) 248,313; 248,319.
Detroit Theatre: 157,140; 309,42; 331,20.
Deuel Sisters [Dorothy and Eleanor]: 305,25.
Deutsch, Babette: (W) 281,12.
Devaux, Leo: 105,138; 119,8; (A) 120,xvi.
"Development of Scenic Art and Stage Machinery, The": (B) [Gamble]: 327,3.
De Vere, Elise: 28,156.
De Vere, Mitty: 320,24.
Devereaux, William: 188,193.
Deverez, Mildred: 107,5.
De Vescovi, Lucille: 276,35.
Devi, Ragini: 276,23.
"Devil, The": (R'08) 92,256; (S) 92,266; 92,269.
"Devil to Pay, The": (F,R) 359, 48.
"Devils": (R'26) 303,18.
"Devil's Disciple, The": 268,17; (R'23) 268,20; (D) 292,12.
"Devil's Garden, The": (R'15) 180,65; 180,68.
De Voe, Frank: 287,36.
De Voi, Bessie: 80,270.
De Von, Hattie: 105,154.
Devore, Dorothy: 323,27.
De Vries, David: 110,108.
De Vries, Henry: 60,26; 60,27; 62,91; 72,33.
De Vries, Sol: 299,23.
"Dew Drop Inn": (R'23) 268,16.
De Wagstaffe, William (W): 11,10; 12,13; 13,13; 14,12; 15,20; 16,10; 17,9; 19,22; 20,20; 21,20; 22,22; 23,22; 154,189; 175,117; 177,243; 180,80; 181,140; 237,356.
Dewey, Arthur: 278,30.
Dewey, Bernice: 233,60.
De Witt, Daisy: 192,101; 207, 303; 220,347.
De Wolfe, Drina: 29,178; 35,c; 36,47; 37,69; 44,254; 46, 311; 49,65; 56,256; 56,257; 169,135.
De Wolfe, Elsie: 3,2; 3,3; 3,4; 10,12; 10,3; 10,4; 27,109; 36,47; (W) 46,302; 284,52; 290,29.
Dexter, Elliot: 49,60; 146,100; 154,188; 202,408; 165,204; 219,304.
Deyo, [Miss] Blanche: 22,10; 34, 300; 64,161.
D'Harville, Madeline: 134,136.
Diaghileff, Serge: 178,294.
"Dial of Love": (D) 294,22.
"Diamond Lil": (R'28) 327,65; 328,38.
"Diana of Dobson's: (R'08) 92,xxi; 92,261.
"Dibbuk, The" (see "Dybbuk, The").
Dibley, Arthur: (W) 189,286.
"Dice of the Gods, The": (R'23) 267,16.
Dick, Hilda: 68,269.
Dickens, Charles: 115,76; 132,46; 166,300.
Dickerson, Jennie: 176,170.
Dickey, Paul: 99,149.
Dickinson, Thomas: (W) 78,213; 143,27.
Dickson, Charles: 7,14; 43,216.
Dickson, Dorothy: 164,162; 197,23; 205,139; 206,231; (C) 218,203; (D) 219,267; 223,183; 226,381; (D) 227, c; 228,126; 229,210; 231, 407; 232,501; 233,50; 234,123; 235,212; 239,100; 242,357; 244,45; 257,73.
Dickson, Lydia: 212,208.
Dickson, W. Lee: (W) 234,100.
"Dictator, The": (R'04) 39,111; 39,121.
"Dictionary of the Drama, A" (Adams) (B); 46,xiv.

Didjah, Belle: 338,19.
Didur, Adamo: 80,267; 93, 309; 129,155; 132,50; 138, xii; 147,140; 156,66; 178, 285; 190,345.
"Die Gluckliche Hand": (OP) (D) 349,41.
Dieck, Herman L. (W): 86,98; 150,61.
Diegelmann, Wilhelm: 142,191.
Diegre, Leonard: (W) 327,32.
Diers, Dippy: 201,287.
Dietrich, Mary: 274,22.
Dietrichstein, Leo: 52,133; 357, 21.
Dietz, Howard: (W) 359,20.
Dietz, Linda: 54,189; 171,234.
"Diff'rent": (R'21) 241,261; 242, 343.
Diggs, Dudley: 220,363; 221,23; 222,80; 230,265; 232,503; 232,520; 237,347; 239,101; (W) 241,266; 241,267; 242, 319; 244,21; 244,31; 247, 224; 265,18; 267,30; 274,14; 278,28; 291,8; 304,14; 304, 31; 307,32; 309,27; 311,14; 323,40; (D) 325,45; (D) 327, 31; 327,37; 327,38; 339,44; 333,45.
Dika, Juliette: 162,80.
Dilley, Dorothy: 325,79.
Dilling, Mildred: 303,35.
Dillingham, Charles B.: 46, xix; 58,xxv; 67,227; 82,xxvi; 106,xxxvi; 115,68; 139,69; 163,141; 175,110; 179,15; 180,66; 184,332; 187,126; (W) 191,10; 199,122; 223,144; 234,84; 246,166; 258,147; 294,7; 306,15; (D) 315,13; 353,37.
Dillingham, [Mrs.] Charles B: 218,227; 219,294.
Dillman, Hugh: 190,374; 191,32; 219,272; 227,19.
Dillon, Adrienne: 172,300.
Dillon, Charles: 146,128.
Dillon, Enrica: 303,24.
Dillon, Maureen: 319,23.
Dillon, Olive: (W) 342,45.
Dilson, John: 210,69; 242,331.
Dinehart, Alan: 212,208; 224, 242; 229,167; 241,247; 270, 8; 302,21; 306,14; 328,34; 356,24.
"Dinner Is Served": (R'29) 343, 42.
"Dinner of Herbs, A": 98,117.
Dion, Hector: 33,273.
"Diplomacy": 3,2; 4,1; 4,3; 71,19; (R'10) 117,xi; 117,150; 165,214; (R'14) 166,262; 166,266; 209,10; 325,39.
"Diplomat, The": (R'02) 14,8.
Dippel, Andreas: 61,82; 85,xvi; 107,14; 119,9.
<u>Direction:</u> 223,142; 224,240; 260,289; 317,32; 359,45.
<u>Direction - Film;</u> 320,18.
<u>Directors - Film:</u> 310,38.
<u>Directors, Stage:</u> 65,186; 212, 202; 234,110; 259,244; 281, 9; 333,48; 345,20.
Dirkens, Anna: 72,36; 103,100.
"Discovering America": (R'12) 140,xv.
"Disengaged": (R'09) 98,xii.
Dishon, Frank: 173,3.
"Dishonored Lady": (R'30) 349, 43; (D) 350,c; 350,43.
"Disraeli": 124,205; (R'11) 129, xiii; (F,R) 248,324; (F) 346, 57.
"District Leader, The": (R'06) 64,141.
Dithmar, Edward A.: 7,12; 231, 362.
Ditrichstein, Leo: 15,2; 20,4; 59,6; 75,116; 87,ix; 117,131; 152,122; 152,123; 163,98; 165,209; 165,244; 166,c; 166, 259; 171,243; 171,261; 178, 275; 178,277; 179,18; 179,19; 180,90; 195,270; 198,79; 203,6; 203,22; 204,97; (C) 209,22; 214,347; (A) 214, 379; 215,26; 217,135; 228, 75; (W) 234,82; 243,411; 245, 83; 253,219; 52,133; 357,21.
Ditza, Mado: 177,225; 257,92.
"Divorce": 97,100; (R'09) 107,6.
"Divorcons": (R'07) 76,146; 76, 164; (R'07) 79,xi; 117,xvii; (R'13) 147,130; 147,131.
Dix, Beulah Marie: 177,230.
Dix, Lillian: 118,199.
Dix, Richard: 263,35; 284,32;

286,31; 289,33; 292,34; 307, 37; 321,35; (W) 338,28; 346, 31; 358,48; 360,48.
Dixey, Henry E.: 15,4; 29,161; 57,275; 66,207; 88,145; 88, 146; 88,161; 95,7; 98,114; 118,199; 125,13; 132,58; 156, 61; 167,8; 167,10; 172,307; 186,61; 189,297; 202,337; 257,101; 269,18.
"Dixiana": (R, F) 356,48.
Dixon, C.E.: 61,xv.
Dixon, Jean: 345,33; 347,34; 357,35; (C) 358,2.
Dixon, Thomas Jr.: (W) 59,20.
Dixon, Thomas: 176,174; 216, 79.
Doane, Frank: 13,7; 13,8; 35, 18; 137,10; 141,155; 150,71.
Doche, Eugenie: 8,14; 61,64; 204, 95.
Dockerill, Marion: 227,10.
Dockrill, [Mde.] William H.: 54, 193.
Dockstader, Lew: 36,38; 150,52; 189,278.
Dockstader's Minstrels: 42,ii.
"Dr. Claudius": 173,30.
"Dr. De Luxe": (R'11) 123,x; 123,144.
"Doctor Faustus": (R'07) 76, 148; (R'10) 111,xxv; (D) 220,337.
"Dr. Jekyll and Mr. Hyde": (F) 230,315.
"Doctor's Dilemma, The": (R'15) 171,228; (R'27) 323,38; 323, 40.
Dodd, Emily: 60,48.
Dodd, Lee Wilson: 273,26.
Dodd, Loring Holmes: (W) 303, 31.
Dodge, Beth and Betty: 341,41.
Dodge, Wendell Phillips (W) (see also "Actor in the Street, The"): 105,140; 107,20; 113, 30;118,170; 131,15; 133,81; 135,146; 137,10; 139,89; 140, 103; 141,150; 143,12; 144,62; 148,176; 149,22; 160,296; 164,160; 186,70.
Dodson, J.E.: (A) 3,17; 5,12; 9,8; 10,10; (W) 10,12; 21,10; 30, 206; 44,249; 46,320; 51,125; (A) 52,131,f; 57,266; 58, 291; 63,126; 63,127; 99, 135; 100,167; 101,20; 107,20; 127,76; 132,47.
Dodsworth, Edna: 88,155; 97, 90.
Doenges, Schweldler: 90,207.
Dohnanyi, Erno: 267,37.
"Doing Our Bit": 202,343; (R'17) 202,392.
"Doing Their Bit": (F) 211,185.
Dolan, Peggy: 229,169; 233, 28.
"Dolce": (R'06) 64,140.
Dolci, Alessandro: 217,137.
Dole, Miriam: 203,31.
"Doll Girl, The": (R'13) 152, xiii; 152,114.
"Dollar Mark, The": 104,131.
"Dollar Princess, The": (R'09) 104,xii; 105,157; 105,163.
Dolls, Theatrical: 254,302.
"Doll's House, A" 18,3; 25,71; (R'04) 37,60; (R'05) 52,133; 73,72; 78,218; 86,91; 114, 41; (R) 208,358; 209,8; 222, 102.
Dolly, Roszika (see also Dolly Sisters): 153,156; 155,31; 172,321; 173,c; 173,3).
Dolly, Yancsi (see also Dolly Sisters): 155,31; 160,293.
Dolly Sisters (see also Dolly, Yancsi; Dolly, Roszicka): 140,123; 143,14; 181,125; 183,317; (C) 188,214; 188, 215; (D) 188,226; 199,149; 200,227; 204,c; 206,242; 209,19; (D) 219,267; 224, 213; 264,42.
"Dolly Madison": 123,167; 126,67.
"Dolly Varden": 12,5; (R'02) 13,11.
Doloretes: 204,78.
Dolores: 209,27; 212,217; 226, 387; 228,117; 240,176; 240, 193; (D) 253,217; 254,340.
"Don,": (R'09) 108,35; 108, 48.
"Don Caesar de Bazan": 6,2; 8,8.
"Don Caesar's Return": 8,7; (R) 8,9.
"Don Carlos": (R'06) 63,112.

"Don Juan": 248,289; (R'01) 248, 340; (F) 307,40.
"Don Q, Jr.": (R'26) 301,66.
"Don Quichotte": (OP) (R'14) 157,116.
"Don Quixote": (R'08) 86,117; 87, 125.
Donahue, Jack: 229,187; 260, 313; 298,27; (D) 327,21; 343,18; (D) 346,27; 347,45; 349,28.
Donaghey, Frederick: 326,44.
Donalda, Pauline: 71,8; 73,83.
Donalde, Laure: 81,304.
Donaldson, Ethel: 88,155.
Donar, Kitty: 279,36.
Dondo, Mathurian: 236,268; 236,269.
Donenger, Lina: 90,207.
Donlin, Mike: 124,196.
Donn, Marion: 160,326.
Donnay, Maurice: 146,103; 161,32.
Donnelly, Dorothy: 14,2; 16,18; 41,171; 41,174; 41,175; 49, 56; 51,108; 80,262; 80,263; 82,334; 103,70; 109,71; 109, 72; 109,81; 123,166; 135,147; 139,69; 155,25; 168,77; 169, 131; 183,272; 183,294; 210, 84.
Donnelly, Edward: 348,13.
Donnelly, Henry V.: 23,6; 24, 39; 24,41; 28,135; 101,11.
Donnelly, Leo: 140,113; 152,133; 199,151; 228,99.
Donnelly, Ruth: 217,163; 232,521; 237,349; 240,175.
Donovan, Mike: 299,22.
"Donovan Affair, The": (R'26) 308,16; 308,19.
"Don't Tell": (R'20) 237,370.
"Don't Weaken": (R'14) 156, 100.
Doraine, Lucy: 265,13.
Doraldina: 185,11; 202,343; (D) 219,267.
Doran, Charles: (W) 86,108.
Dore, Demaris: 328,39.
Doremus, [Mrs.] Charles A.: 73, 84.
Dorfman, Nat N.: (W) 283,24; (W) 323,20; 331,48.
Dorgere, Arlette: 121,102; 121, 104.
Dori, Adrienne: 238,25; 327,26.
Doria, Augusta: 94,345.
"Dorian Gray": (R'28) 328,38.
Doro, Marie: 18,13; 27,108; 46, 319; 49,56; 54,c; 70,338; 77,177; 79,228; 80,274; 82, 325; 83,16; 85,70; 91,249; 98,124; 111,171; 118,165; 127, 77; 131,24; 134,127; 135,149; 137,c; 139,68; 149,15; 159, 242; 159,250; 165,214; 167, 11; 175,110; 176,177; 180, 74; 181,127; 184,345; 197,6; 198,74; 199,123; 202,408; 211,133; (D) 213,289; 231, 363; 249,363; 252,181; 253, 252.
Dooley, Gordon: 202,395; 280, 37.
Dooley, Johnny: 217,161; 281,17.
Dooley, Ray: 202,395; 222,80; 295,29; 304,35; 308,9; 337, 19.
Doone, Allen: 200,213.
"Door, The": 209,31.
"Dorothy Vernon of Haddon Hall": (R'04) 35,3; 35,7.
Dorr, Charles H. (W): 246, 162; 257,104.
Dorr, Dorothy: 12,4; 18,2; 26, 88; 49,54; 81,vii; 121,81; 151,83; 75,116.
Dorr, Olga: 92,266; 92,267; 92,268.
Dorrian, Cecil I. (W): 162,77.
D'Orsay, Lawrence: 25,54; 25,58; 27,108; 28,146; 62,84; 62, 85; 81,307; 160,298; 313,20.
Dorsha: 266,21; 305,31.
Dorziat, Gabrielle: 165,210; 165, 246; 167,11; 170,193; 170, 194.
Dos Passos, John: 303,16.
Doty, Carlotta: 122,136.
"Double Exposure": (R'18) 212, 212.
"Double Life, The": (R'06) 72, 33.
Doucet, Paul: 188,193.
Doucet, Theodore: 218,209.
Dougherty, Grace: 155,7; 262, 20.
Douglas, Byron: 107,7.

Douglas, Gilbert: 116,99; 176,181; 249,376.
Douglas, Katherine: (W) 72,55.
Douglas, Kenneth: 166,280; 168, 84; 224,220; 228,91; 246, 152.
Douglas, Leon Forrest: 205,194.
Douglas, Tom: 245,108, 334,25.
Douglass, James M: (W) 48,52.
Douthitt, Wilfried: 167,7.
Dove, Billie: 264,35; 307,35; 320,25; 339,26; 345,72.
"Dove, The": (R'25) 289,15; 291, 39.
"Dove of Peace, The": (R'12) 142, xviii.
"Dover Road, The": 252,143; (R'21) 252,168; (D) 252,169; (S) 255,360.
Dovey, Alice: 42,190; 98,113; 107, 30; 113,3; 122,132; 122,134; 126,68; 151,80; 157,112; 162, 62; 180,64; 183,293; 186,87.
Dowling, Eddie: 268,24; 304,35; 312,18; 337,19.
"Down to Earth": (F,R) 199,176.
"Down to the Sea in Ships": (F,R) 266,66.
Downey, Fairfax: (W) 328,16.
"Downstream": (R'25) 300,15.
Doyle, Arthur Conan: 70,317; 108,xiv.
Doyle, Deidre: 109,81; 166,279; 242,343; 243,398.
Doyle, Miriam: 204,97; 251,83; 308,19.
Doyle, John T.: 360,34.
"Dracula": 321,5; (R'27) 321, 84; (F) 342,23.
"Dragon's Claw, The": (R'14) 165,255.
Drake, Josephine: 249,363; 255, 371; 274,29.
Drake, O.W.: 26,99.
Drake, Stanley; 65,185.
Drake, William A.: 331,49; (W) 361,42; 361,43.
<u>Drama</u> (<u>see</u> <u>Playwriting</u>).
<u>Drama</u>, <u>State of the</u> (<u>see also</u> <u>Theatre, Economics of</u>; <u>Playwriting</u>; <u>Managers, Theatre</u>): 210,86; 211,128; 219,266.
Drama League of America: 122, 137; 124,210; 126,ix; 157, 119; 193,150; 257,74; 153, 171.
Drama Players, The: 128,vii; 130,185; 138,63.
Drama Society: 154,xxx.
"Drama To-Day, The" [Andrews] (B): 162,92.
"Dramatic Criticism -- What It Is and What It Should Be" [Symposium]: 167,12.
"Dramatic Incidents in the Lives of Eighteenth Century Players" <u>by</u> A. Lanston:

1. Episode of the Pantheon, The - 32,257;
2. Death of Peg Woffington, The - 33,287;
   Play House, The - 34,317;
3. "Perdita" - 36,46;
4. The Blue Eyed Bellamy - 37,65;
5. Unforseen Denouments - 38,101;
6. Sarah Siddons - 45,281;
   Anne Oldfield - 64,148.

"Dramatic Index, The": (B) 112,xii.
"Dramatic Values" (Montague) (B): 127,vi.
<u>Dramatists</u> (<u>see</u> <u>Playwrights</u>).
<u>Dramatists' Guild</u>: 303,11.
"Dramatists of To-Day" (Hale) (B): 54,ii.
Dramatists' Theatre: 306,53.
<u>Dramaturgy</u> (<u>see</u> <u>Playwriting</u>).
<u>Dransfield, Jane</u>: (W) 253,228.
Draper, Ruth: 185,10; 241, 262; 241,265; 257,92; 269, 40; 284,36; 335,27; 349,26; 351,28.
Draughn, Marion: 50,82.
Draycott, Wilfred: 120,62.
Drayton, Alfred: 298,14.
"Dream City": (R'06) 72,xv.
"Dream Girl, The": 282,14; (R'24) 283,16.
"Dream Maker, The": (R'21) 251,99.
Dreamland (New York): 54, 199.
"Dreams of Three": (R'19) 223,149.
Dreher, Virginia: 10,17; 10,

18; 52,151.
Dreiser, Theodore: 197,56; 203, 23; 204,75; (W) 317,7.
"Dressed to Kill": (F) 325,12.
Dresser, Louise: 95,26; 100,xv; 102,54; 137,24; 152,133; 156, 77; 163,142; 165,233; 168, 53; 169,130; 169,162; 172, 323; 175,110; 175,126; 178, 299; 181,169; 183,294; 187, 147; 197,36; 209,31; 209,39; 323,46.
Dressing Rooms: 8,20; 215,26.
Dressler, Eric: 307,27; 334,25; 344,25.
Dressler, Marie: 13,7; 13,8; 39,117; 41,175; 46,320; 60, 31; 66,221; 101,3; 112,174; 112,187; 136,191; 146,xv; 150,69; 158,199; 171,258; 176,174; 200,249; 224,222; 290,46; 308,4; 322,50; 333, 40; 354,39.
Drew, Frank: 43,231.
Drew, Georgianna: 287,25.
Drew, John: PG,24; 6,3; 8,1; 8,2; 8,3; 10,10; 10,11; 10, 17; 20,3; 22,26; 29,174; 32, 240; 33,263; 34,306; 37,73; 38,102; 41,174; 43,230; 44, 242; 44,243; 52,151; 53,175; 54,188; 56,251; 58,301; 68, 263; 70,xvi; 79,228; 79,230; 80,265; (C) 82,xxiv; 90,205; 92,255; 94,330; 95,24; 105, 134; 105,155; 106,188; 107, xxiv; 111,142; 116,107; 126,65; 127,76; 128,111; 128,114; 131,12; 139,67; 140,98; 140, 100; 145,viii; 145,74; 148,192; 149,16; 150,54; 151,78; 152, 109; 152,110; 153,143; 160, 281; 160,319; 161,15; 163,98; 164,159; 164,160; 164,195; 169,142; (A) 174,73; 176, 176; 178,287; 179,9; 179,14; 185,9; 187,124; 190,354; 201,283; 230,269; 230,271; 231,383; 232,517; 235,168; 247,219; 248,319; 260,320; 269,18; 276,21; 286,10; 293, 40; 313,20; (C) 314,19.
Drew, John Sr.: 43,230.
Drew, [Mrs.] John: 43,231; 149, 16; 155,32; 231,397; (D) 232,507.
Drew, Louise: 12,10; 37,73; 58,301; 93,292; 97,94; 103, 75; 120,42; 165,246; 166, 309.
Drew, Margaret: 20,7.
Drew, Roland: 325,50.
Drew, S. Rankin: 175,128; 210, 120.
Drew, Sidney: 52,143; 69,x; 103, 73; 103,76; 210,69; 211, 144; 213,321; 216,70; 219,325; 231,363.
Drew, [Mrs.] Sidney: 210,69; 213,321; 216,70.
Drew Family, The: 43,230; 174, 72; 361,14.
"Drifting": 252,155; (R'22) 252,166; (D) 252,169.
"Drink": 32,239; (R'03) 32, 244; 42,ii.
Drinkwater, John: 187,131; 225, 310; 228,97; 243,394; 243, 416; 270,12; 288,54; 340, 16.
"Driven": (R'14) 167,44; (F,R) 266,66.
"Drone, The": (R'12) 144,xxvii.
Douet, Robert: 24,33; 48,49; 59,15; 75,136; 90,205; 99, xiii; 99,162; 113,29.
Drown, Hope: 271,33; 283,25; 341,42.
Druce, Hubert: 140,100; 188, 204; 216,76; 343,43; 349, 44; 351,35; 356,18.
Drumier, Jack: 123,160; 123, 161.
Drummond, A.M.: 313,44; 328, 45.
"Drums of Jeopardy, The": (R'22) 257,95.
Drury, Norma: 271,37.
Drury Lane Theatre: 30,193.
Drysdale, Robert: 260,300.
Duane, Eleanor: 86,iii.
"Du Barry": 12,1; (S,R) 12,4; 14,11; 17,8; 19,9; 30,207; (F) 169,126; 231,351.
Dubarry, Gwen: 132,43.
Dubois, Theodore: 34,307.
Du Bois, W.E. Burghardt: (W) 268,12.

Du Brey, Claire: 214,393.
Duchene, Maria: 168,65.
"Duchess, The": (R'11) 130,xiv.
"Duchess of Dantzic": (R'05) 48,34.
"Duchess of Devonshire, The": 69,307.
"Duchess of Newcastle": 154, 194.
Ducker, Geneva: 261,383.
Dudley, Adeline: 125,6.
"Duell, The": 56,262; (R'06) 61,54.
"Duenna": 291,25.
Dupau, Jenny: 181,134.
Duff, James A: 331,80.
Duff, James C.: 29,173.
Duffalt, Jean: 107,12.
Duffey, Henry: 220,345.
Duffey, J.H.: 136,175; 311,31; (D) 323,23.
Duffield, Blanche: 134,105; 137, 3; 147,139.
Duffield, Malcolm: 319,23.
Duffy, Gertrude: 162,67.
Duffy, Henry: 215,29; 334,30.
Dufour, Elise: 181,144.
Dufranne, Hector: 86,112; 97,89; 107,11; 121,83; 134,111; 142, 182; 203,39; 239,111.
Du Fre, Ethel H.: 7,7.
Dufwin Theatre (Oakland): 334, 31.
Duggan, Walter: 300,23.
"Duke of Killicrankie, The": (R'04) 44,242; 44,243; 176, 168; (R'15) 176,198.
Duke of York's Theatre (London): 83,18; (D) 142,175.
Dukes, Ashley: 297,25.
"Dulcy": (R'21) 247,234; 247, 237; (D) 248,332; (S) 249, 372.
Dumas, Alexandre: 8,14; 8,16; 49,xviii; 61,64; 67,231; (D) 266,10.
Du Maurier, Gerald: 187,131.
Du Maurier, Guy: 98,131.
"Dumb Girl of Portici, The": (F) 178,305.
Dumbrille, Douglass: 326,41.
Dumeny, M.: 24,47.
"Dummy, The": 159,224; (R'14) 160,282.
Dumont, Daisy: 112,177.
Dunbar, Dorothy: 308,35.
Dunbar, Janet: 114,49; 115,88; 121,75; 121,93; 157,140; 163,106; 165,225; 183,293; 202,357.
"Dunbar in Kinemacolor, The": (F) 133,xv.
Duncan, Anna: 293,13; 301,46; 316,13; (D) 347,28.
Duncan, Augustin: 103,96; 221, 23; 226,363; 240,163; 260, 320; 261,368; (D) 277,38; 302,15; 303,17; 303,52; 358,40.
Duncan, Evelyn: 249,363.
Duncan, Isadora: 44,255; 48, 36; (D) 91,230; 92,iii; 94, 324; 98,vii; 104,116; 128,122; 171,225; 338,4.
Duncan, Lisa: 293,13.
Duncan, Malcolm: 80,263; 164, 165.
Duncan, Mary: 252,157; 295, 23; 322,12.
Duncan, Sarah: 30,184.
Duncan, William: 208,399; 208, 405.
Duncan Dancers: 269,37.
Duncan Sisters [Vivian & Rosita]: 202,343; 221,19; 222,82; 244, 17; 287,16; 292,31; 294,21; 305,25.
"Dunce Boy, The": (R'25) 291,17.
Dundas, Clementine: 138,39.
Dundy, Elmer: 50,99.
Dunlap, Maurice: (W) 84,53.
Dunlap, Orrin E.Jr. (W): 314,23; 325,35; 328,40.
Dunlap, William; 42,191; (D) 189,276.
Dunmore, Eveleen: 135,164.
Dunn, Arthur: 29,163; 45, 269.
Dunn, Emma: 72,48; 72,49; 84, 48; 85,72; 97,81; 97,84; 111,146; 119,21; 140,103; 172,302; 190,374; 191,28; 193,168; 195,283; 198,65; 247,217.
Dunn, J. Cunningham: 186,80.
Dunn, John: 340,25.
Dunn, Joseph F.: 202,358.
Dunn, Malcolm: 136,171.

Dunn, Violet: 339, 23.
Dunne, Irene: 304, 46; 360, 48.
Dunning, James Edmund: (W) 142, 170.
Dunning, Philip: 310, 33; 328, 29; 333, 49; (W) 335, 20.
Dunsany, Lord: 185, 18; 192, 96; 226, 388; 237, 382; (W) 328, 7.
Dunsford, Alice: (W) 57, 286.
Dunsmure, John: 57, 287; 236, 281.
Dupont, Mary: 40, 158.
Dupont, Paul: 357, 45.
Dupre, Fanny: 33, 274.
Dupree, Minnie: 21, 9; 25, 56; 45, 274; 73, 62; 76, 147; 156, 77; 196, 329; 221, 25; 236, 258; 260, 296; 293, 20.
Duquette, Yolande: 212, 213.
Durand, Edouard: 117, 159; 187, 149; 255, 357; (D) 255, 375.
Durant, Basil Napier: 181, 165; 253, 232.
Durante, Jimmy (see also Clayton, Jackson and Durante): 335, 38; (C) 341, 23; (W, C) 343, 39.
Durbin, Maud: 40, 139; 44, 252.
Durieux, Tilla: 275, 18; 276, 19.
Durka, Geneva: 274, 11.
Durkin, Junior: 339, 49.
Durland, Kellog: (W) 58, 315.
Durozat, Jean: 118, 194.
Durrand, Edouard: 152, 123.
Duse, Eleanora: 6, 4; 8, 15; 10, 19; 11, 12; 12, 18; 18, 1; 18, 18; (A) 20, 13; 22, 6; 59, 8; 62, 104; 75, xii; 80, 286; 87, xvi; 94, 321; 102, 48; 131, 20; 189, 286; 204, 95; 238, 10; 254, 284; 258, 137; 271, 7; 272, 20; 274, 16; 275, 39; 276, 9; 279, 67; 282, 20; 285, 22; 285, 23; 291, 23; 310, 12; 353, 18.
Du Souchet, H. A.: 55, 227.
Duss, J. S.: 17, 24.
Dutch Theatre: 138, 48.
Dux, Claire: 250, 26; 251, 129; 284, 35; 359, 36.
Dwyer, Ada: 73, 77; 120, 58; 159, 224.
Dwyer, Phil: 169, 110.
Dyas, Ada: 54, 188.
"Dybbuk, The": (R'25) 300, 15; 251, 91; 254, 295; 308, 20; (R'26) 311, 15.
"Dynamo": 336, 70; 337, 47; (R'29) 338, 45.

--E--

Eadie, Dennis: 187, 131.
Eagle, Oscar: 33, 288.
Eagles, Jeanne: 153, 155; 183, 284; 195, 275; 201, 276; 201, 281; 209, 15; 212, 193; 213, 287; 216, 98; 230, 258; 230, 270; 243, 432; 255, 391; 263, 28; (C) 270, 19; 275, 66; 296, 23; 298, 12; 306, 14; (D) 315, 15; 315, 25; (W) 322, 20.
Eagle, Joseph: 197, 16.
Eames, Clare: 208, 359; 209, 20; 238, 5; 242, 318; 243, 301; 248, 309; 254, 283; 276, 33; 277, 18; 279, 13; 297, 9; 299, 17; 304, 31; 306, 33; 309, 27; (W) 310, 20; 311, 14; 332, 29; 334, 33.
Eames, Emma: PG, 9; 10, 30; 22, 37; 59, 26; 70, 342; 71, 9; 82, 337; 185, 25; 231, 367.
Earl, Maud: 203, 18.
Earl, Virginia: 35, 3.
"Earl and the Girl, The": 53, 165; 54, 184; (R'05) 58, xviii.
Earl Carroll Theatre (New York): 246, 143.
"Earl Carroll's Vanities" (see also "Vanities of - -"): 332, 46.
"Earl of Pawtucket, The": 25, 54; (R'03) 25, 58.
Earl of Roslyn: 20, 4.
Earl of Yarmouth: 46, 314.
Earle, Edna: 208, 402; 208, 406.
Earle, Estelle: 38, 85.
Earle, Marion: 208, 363.
Earle, Virginia: 10, 14; 54, 191.
"Early American Dramatists" by M. J. Moses:
1. Royall Tyler: (D) 188, 208;
2. William Dunlap: (D) 189, 276;
3. Mrs. Mercy Warren: (D)

4. Mrs. Anna Cora Mowatt: (D) 193,142;
5. John Howard Payne: (D) 195,294;
6. The Philadelphia School: 197,14.

"Earth": (R'27) 314,21.
"Earth, The": (R'16) 182,193.
"Earth Bound" (F): 232,534; (R) 235,194.
"Easiest Way, The": 97,81; 143, 21; 183,283; 210,91; 231,351; 249,363.
"East Is West": (R'18) 216,78; 216,95; 223,189.
"East of Suez": (R'22) 260,299; (S) 261,380; (F,R) 288,32.
East-West Players: 193,149; 206,219; 216,112; 227,20; 233,30.
"Easter": (R'16) 182,198; (R'26) 303,16.
"Eastener, The": (R'08) 86,xii; 86,109.
Eastman, Gretchen: 219,291; 272, 35.
Easton, Florence: 197,31; 205, 147; 254,331; 264,37; 276, 35; 300,35.
Easton, Ruth: 334,25.
"Easy Come, Easy Go": (R'25) 298,16.
"Easy Dawson": (R'05) 56,245; 56,252.
"Easy Street": (R'24) 283,15.
"Easy Virtue": (R'25) 299,16.
Eaton, Mary: 219,283; (A) 226, 438; 233,26; 256,25; 263,33; 275,38; 277,17; 280,27; 290, 13; 303,36; 315,7; 315,56; (D) 318,7; 324,74; 325,44; 331,74.
Eaton, Walter Prichard (W); 194, 218; 195,292; 198,80; 209, 30; 237,346; 271,9; 274,9; 292,12; 330,48; 333,16; 337, 15; 347,4; 353,56.
"Eben Holden": (R) 10,4; 10,20.
Eberle, E.A.: 57,285; 59,24.
Eburne, Maude: 159,245; 160, 321; 164,171; 176,174; 188, 204b; 201,265; (W) 224,230.
Ebyrock, Helyn: 311,25.
"Echo, The": (R'10) 116,xiii.
Echols, Weyland: 331,45.
<u>Economics of Films</u>: 171,244.
"Ed Wynn Carnival": (R'20) 231,403.
Eddinger, Wallace: 80,279; 95, 33; 97,80; 100,175; 107,15; 107,28; 116,100; 118,199; 133,85; 137,10; 151,81; 153, 161; 175,105; 176,181; 184, 359; 200,213; 227,13; 231, 358; 233,36; 248,293; 252, 155; (D) 252,169; 256,37; 290,19.
Eddy, Arthur Jerome: 123,173.
Eddy, El Nino: 54,192.
Edeson, Robert: 3,11; 13,3; 14,2; 14,6; 22,22; 31,213; 37,71; 37,77; 43,232; (D) 45,288; 49,55; 49,58; 49,59; 55,c; (W) 65,178; 79,228; 80,279; 92,xxiv; 92,273; 103, 70; 105,37; 105,161; 113,17; 127,90; 130,222; 131,12; 136,189; 137,11; 142,194; 163,110; 175,127; (A) 183, 300; 184,345; 188,203; 196, 355; 201,294; 210,75; 229, 187; 256,37; 262,20; 310,39; 323,46; 335,36.
Edeson, [Mrs.] Robert: 156,77.
"Edgar Allan Poe": (R'25) 297, 70.
Edgar, Randolph (W): 216,86.
Edgard, Lewis: 153,143; 195, 267.
Ediss, Connie: 81,295; (C) 82, xxiv; 156,69.
Edison, Charles: 175,157; 179, 12.
Edison, Thomas A.: 95,14; 137,18; 150,72.
"Editha's Burglar": (R'16) 192,86.
Edler, Grace: 290,45.
"Edmund Burke": (R'05) 57, xii; 57,267.
Edney, Florence: 189,273.
"Education of Mr. Pipp, The": (R'05) 49,60.
Educational Alliance of New York, The: 42,207; 76,154; 196, 344.
Educational Films: 208,392.
<u>Educational Theatre (see also</u>

Little Theatre; Schools, Drama): 161,34.
Edvina, Louise: 146,104; 177, 248; 180,85.
Edwardes, George: 44,252; 68, vii.
Edwardes, Paula: 29,177; 35,4; 36,c; 73,78.
Edwards, Alan: 240,159.
Edwards, Bobby: 198,93; 222,89.
Edwards, Cliff: 286,37.
Edwards, E. Henry: 154,173.
Edwards, Gus: 81,xiv: 195,290.
Edwards, Harold (W): 176,176.
Edwards, H. Sutherland: 5,3.
Edwards, Julian: 13,11; 111, xxvi.
Edwards, Robert: 171,259.
Edwards, Sam: 143,24.
Edwin, Walter: 220,340; 319,23.
Edwin Forrest Home: 114,54.
'Efficiency'': (R'17) 203,22; 203, 35.
Egan, C.C.: 252,187.
Egener, Minnie: 190,345.
Egerton, Evelyn: 214,361.
Eggert, Mme.: 81,311.
'Egoist, The'': (R'22) 264,19.
'Egoists: A Book of Supermen'' (Huneker) (B): 100,x.
Egri, Lajos: 315,36.
Ehren, Kathe: 160,305.
Ehret, Louis: 161,36.
Eibenschutz, Camillia: 126,59; 132,54.
Eide, Egil: 258,141.
'Eighteen Miles From Home'': 54,207.
'Eileen'': 195,276; (R) 195, 277.
'Eileen Asthore'': (R'06) 70,xxvii.
Eisenberg, Emanuel (W); 338, 30; 345,35; 350,30.
Eisenstein, Sergei: 352,16.
El Capitan Theatre (Hollywood): 334,31.
Elaine, Mildred: 149,11.
'Elder Son, The'': (R'14) 165, 254.
Eldred, Arthur: 238,27.
Eldridge, Florence: 251,93; 253, 215; 254,293; (D) 254,309; 263,18; 267,38; 267,48; 285, 14; 301,19.
Eldridge, Louisa: 59,iii.
'Electra'': 41,164; (R'08) 85, 60; (OP) 98,128; (OP) 109,74; 114,59; 119,10; 140,105; (R'18) 205,152. 206,211.
'Electricity'': (R'10) 118,xix; 118,165.
'Elektra'' (see 'Electra'').
'Elevating a Husband'': (R'12) 133,75; 133,97.
Eley, Helen: 177,240; 281, 38.
Eliscu, Edward: 288,38.
Eliscu, Fernanda: 25,59; 51, 112; 65,180; 74,109; 96, 38; 128,124; 278,14.
Elitch's Gardens (Denver): 30,201.
'Eliza Comes to Stay'': 156,63; (R'14) 156,96.
'Elizabeth the Queen'': 356,27; (D) 357,c; 357,30; (R'30) 358,66.
Elizabethan Stage Society: 71, 23.
Elizabethan Theatre: 108,45; (D) 112,195; (D) 137,32; 139,93; (D) 182,206; 329,36; 330,39.
Ellerbe, Harry: 335,47.
Ellers, Sally: 351,60.
Ellin, Dorothy: 257,77.
Elliott, Arthur: 12,10; 240,181.
Elliott, Frank: 336,31.
Elliott, Gertrude: 30,199; 34, 312; 38,81; 70,316; 73,74; 73,75; 73,76; 75,133; 124,186; 127,87; 129,151; 134,134; 135, 165; 151,84; 153,iii; 153,142; 153,168; 155,13; 155,24; 161, 15; 161,21; 173,25; 187,131; 222,102.
Elliott, Harold: 272,18; 296,26.
Elliott, Maxine: PG,25; PG,26; 3,6; 4,6; 4,7; 19,c; 23,6; 23,7; 31,231; 33,270; 33,283; 36,40; 40,148; 46,320; 48,x; 50,100; 56,244; 56,255; 57,c; 67,xiii; 73,76; 75,118; 81,ii; 83,3; 84,34; (W) 90,202; 93, 286; 94,325; 96,41; 96,47; 97,xviii; 97,xx; 97,xxvi; 109, 69; 109,92; 111,154; 111,171;

113, 5; 119, xxi; 122, 133; 129, xxix; 132, 61; 142, 196; 146, 126; 157, 133; 157, 161; 161, 21; 165, 215; 191, 16; 192, 74; 192, 75; 196, 349; 198, 80; 198, 108; 199, 180; 200, 250; 204, 99; 212, 226; 214, 355; 222, 102; 229, 155; 231, 383; 255, 366; 258, 176; 286, 12; 290, 29; 293, 30; 293, 40.

Elliott, William: 82, 349; 84, 34; 109, 65; 109, 81; 122, 132; 122, 134; 166, 265; 192, 122; 193, 141; 195, 274.

Ellis, Charles: 250, 35; 291, 26.

Ellis, Diane: 334, 35.

Ellis, Edith: 91, 230; 99, 152; 176, 192; 295, 21.

Ellis, Edward: 91, 231; 117, 141; 153, 143; 159, 224; 201, 276; 324, 40; 344, 34.

Ellis, John: 223, 169.

Ellis, Kenneth M.: 359, 39.

Ellis, Mary: 230, 262; 284, 25; 293, 27; 300, 15; 300, 19; 301, 22; 304, 5; 310, 30; 311, 58; 315, 26; 316, 47; 322, 19; 327, 33; 338, 46; 339, 9; 347, 14; 349, 33; 352, 21; 361, 25.

Ellis, Melville: 76, 167; 171, 239; (A) 176, 203.

Elliston, Grace: 11, 5; 46, 296; 58, 287; 59, 24; 66, 221; 69, 290; 79, 256; 90, 216; 92, 269; 103, 71; 112, 175; 130, 222; 160, 302; 169, 121.

Ellsler, Effie: 84, 42; 156, 62; 256, 24.

Ellsler, Fanny: 52, 145.

Ellsler, John: 32, 258.

Ellyson, John Regnault (W, V): 226, 394.

Elman, Mischa: 94, 341; 121, 83; 170, 184; 185, 25; 270, 37; 290, 43; 332, 27.

"Elmer Gantry": (S) 330, 26; (R'28) 331, 40.

Elmore, Ruth: 333, 32.

Elocution: 8, 17; 9, 17.

Elsie, Eric: 187, 131.

Elsie, Lily: 90, 207; 128, 136.

Elsom, Isobel: 327, 6; 328, 24.

Elstner, Anne: 269, 13; 269, 31; 271, 26.

Eltinge, Julian: 127, 105; 128, 113; 136, 191; (W) 150, 56; 158, 171; 159, 227; 159, 240; 166, 284; 176, 168; (A) 181, 157; 195, 289; 198, 101; 201, 325; 203, 59; 204, 124; 209, 18; 218, 250; 244, 15.

Elvidge, June: 207, 329; 213, 273.

Ely, Edgar Atchinson: 94, 324.

"Embarrassment of Riches, The": (R'06) 64, xi; 65, 185.

"Embassy Ball, The": (R'06) 62, 84.

"Embers": (R'26) 301, 66.

Emens, Homer: 21, 16.

"Emerald Isle, The": (R'02) 20, 7.

Emerson, E. A.: 148, 179.

Emerson, Hope: 353, 33.

Emerson, Isabelle: 160, 283.

Emerson, John: 109, iii; 113, 29; 145, 86; 147, 148; 234, 98; 245, 76; 293, 20.

Emerson, Lillian: 204, 101.

Emery, Edward: 101, 12; 146, 105; 167, 35; 180, 73; 184, 361; 204, 73; 347, 48; 348, 33.

Emery, George M.: (W) 232, 506.

Emery, Gilbert: 249, 378; 255, 351; 267, 17; 272, 14; 273, 29; 282, 64.

Emery, Louis: 257, 83.

Emlay, Earle: 276, 8.

Emmett, Elizabeth: 40, 155.

Emmett, Katherine: 85, 80; 102, 44; 102, 46; 147, 132; 161, 8; 167, 15; 170, 189; 211, 155; 212, 195; 266, 17; 277, 25.

Emmons, Earl H.: (W) 337, 29.

"Emperor Jones, The": 238, 8.

Empire Stock Co. (Columbus, Ohio): 50, xii.

Empire Theatre (Japan): 127, 86.

Empire Theatre (New York): 38, 91; 47, 16f; 172, 285.

Emprey, Arthur Guy: 205, 191; 206, 264.

Emander, Hilma: (W) 298, 7.

"Enchanted April, The": (R'25) 295, 70.

"Enchanted Cottage, The": 267, 17; (R'23) 267, 19; (F) 278,

31.
"Enchantment": (F) 251,94.
"Enchantress, The": (R'11) 130, xiv; 130,217.
"En Deshabille": (R'13) 153, xvii.
"End of the World, The": 296,72.
"Endless Chain, The": (R'22) 260, 340.
Enderman, Jacob: 64,161.
Enders, Elvia: 336,52.
Endowed Theatre (see also Art Theatre; National Theatre; New Theatre; Progressive Stage Society): 4,10; 5,12; 6, 13; 11,9; 12,14; 15,16; 16, 23; 25,76; 38,87; 45,290; 61,61; 63,124; 65,194; 66,202; 78,202; 86,92; 98,111; 102, 58; 168,60; 251,90; 258,131.
Endres, Alice: 200,221.
"Enemy, The" (see also "Stronger Than Love"): (R'25) 297,18; 297,19; (S) 300,26.
"Enemy of the People, An": (R'27) 321,42; (C) 321,84.
"Enemy Sex, The": (F,R) 282,32.
"Enemy to the King, An": 23, 17; 143,22.
Enesco, Georges: 273,37.
"Engaged": (R'25) 294,15.
Englander, Ludwig: 16,5; 20,9.
Englander, Lewis (W,V): 22,33.
"English Comic Drama" [Bateson] (B): 342,2.
"English Costume Painted and Described" [Calthrop] (B): 76,xviii.
"English Daisy, An": 36,34.
English Pony Ballet: 39,112.
English Singers, The: 335,39.
"English Stage of To-Day," The" [Borsa] (B): or,xviii.
English Lheatre (see also Ervine, St. John (W); Grein, J.T. (W): 46,317; 60,46; 63,132; 77,188; 82,321; 82,326; 83,18; 86,91; 98,111; 98,131; (D) 110,125; 125,15; 126,62; 136,192; 139, 92; 146,111; 156,81; 162,74; 168,84; 227,6; 283,12; 305, 24; 307,20; 324,17; 330,21; 335,52; 340,16; 346,43; 349, 30; 351,30; 352,30; 353,30; 356,13; 358,37; 359,30; 360, 44.
"Englishman's Home, An": 98, 131; (R'09) 99,137.
"Enigma, The": (R'08) 86,90.
Enright, Florence: 183,283; 189, 269; 202,347; 203,15; 205, 159.
"Enter, Madame": (R'20) 235, 240; 236,267.
Enters, Angna: 306,8; (D) 335, 53; (D) 345,29; 357,43.
Entriken, Knowles: 184,349.
Entwistle, Peg: 317,13; 346, 11.
"Episode": (R'25) 289,18.
Equity (see Actors' Equity Association).
Equity Players: 263,25; 265,15; 269,16.
"Erdgeist": (R'25) 292,16; 292, 23.
Eric, Fred: 86,iii; 90,219.
Erlanger, Abraham L. (see also Klaw and Erlanger): 43,226; 97,xxxii; 137,x; 145,75; 155, 36; 231,379; 244,6; 245,74; 258,145; 306,53.
Erlich, Martha: 194,211.
"Erminie": 149,17; (R'21) 240, 158.
Ernst, Otto: 21,12.
Errol, Leon: 191,10; 198,83; 210,74; 213,270; 240,176; 244,8; (A) 250,63; 256,28; 285,24; 290,34; 290,46; 291, 16; (C) 313,17; 313,32; (C) 335,34.
Errolle, Ralph: 285,35; 298,35.
Erskin, Chester: (C) 339,22; 349,27; 351,26; 353,14.
Erskine, Gladys Shaw: 359,40.
Erskine, James (Pseud. of Earl of Roslyn, q.v.).
Erskine, John (W): 321,38.
Erskine, Lloyd Wheeler (W): 301,12.
Erskine, Lucile: (W) 142,186.
Erskine, Wallace: 120,36; 208, 349.
"Erstwhile Susan": (R'16) 181,123; 181,153; (F,R) 227,41.
Ervine, St. John (W): 230,257; 271,12; 296,9; 299,12; 301,

20; 302,12; 303,20; 304,30; 307,30; 309,22; (C) 333,33; 336,19; 337,4; 337,37; 338,4.
Erway, Ben: 335,47.
"Escape, The": (R'13) 153,xvii; 153,156; (F,R) 161,48; 322, 40; (C) 323,70; (F) 352,46.
Esden, Alice: 197,25.
Esler, Lemist: (W) 349,50.
Esmond, Annie: 95,30; 135,165.
Esmond, Henry V.: 12,12; 23,7; 81,ii; 156,63.
Esmonde, Merceita: 200,223; 238,27.
Espero, Sidonia: 211,133; 213,271.
"Essay on the Drama, An" [Lamb] (B): 82,v.
Esterbrooke, Howard: 141,143.
"Eternal City, The": 20,6; 22, 7; (R'03) 23,9; 24,44; (F) 168,69; (F) 273,31; 40,xiv.
"Eternal Feminine, The": 48,49.
"Eternal Magdalene, The": (R'15) 177,227; 178,227.
"Eternal Temptation, The": (R,F) 203,57.
Ethel, Agnes: 25,65; 52,151; 126,64; 173,26; 195, 263; 195,265.
Ethier, Alphonz: 108,33; 192,73; 240,160; 301,11; 303,27.
Ethiopian Art Theatre: 268,12.
Etting, Ruth: 310,56; 334,49; (C) 337,35; 338,52; 339,56; 343,56.
Eubank, Lilian: 153,148.
Eubanks, L.E.: (W) 161,43.
"Eugene O'Neill, The Man and His Plays" [Clark] (B): 340,4.
"Eugenically Speaking": (R'15) 170, 207.
"Euranthe" (OP): 168,64.
Eustace, Jennie: 26,98; 70,321; 83,13; (W) 202,366; 227,7.
Euwer, Anthony H. (W): 136,192.
"Eva": 143,xxii; (R'12) 144,xiv; 144,37.
"Eva the Fifth": (R'28) 332,48.
"Evangeline": (R'13) 153,147.
"Evagelist, The": (R'07) 81,292.
Evans, Charles E.: 28,138; 43, 232; 45,271.
Evans, Edith: 286,26; 307,21.
Evans, Greek: 207,284; 287,14.
Evans, Kathryn: 240,162.
Evans, Madge: 203,53.
Evans, Marianne: 312,42.
Evans, Millicent: 124,204; 136, 196; 163,114.
Evansville Players (Wisconsin): 212,230.
Evell, Lois: 81,313.
Evelyn, Fay: 233,17.
Everall, Harry: 137,11.
Everett, Leolyn Louis: (W,V) 259,218.
Everhart: 41,viii.
Everton, Paul: 137,10.
"Everyman" (see also "Jedermann"): (R'02) 21,4; 22,31; 146,iii; 272,40; (R'23) 274, 19.
"Everything": 212,199; (R'18) 212,212.
"Everything's Jake!": 348,13; (R'29) 348,46.
"Everywoman": 118,ii; (S) 122, 118: 122,119; 124,195; (F) 226,402.
"Eve's Daughter": (R'17) 202, 350; 202,361; (F) 205,191.
Evesson, Isabelle: 36,39; 46, 316.
Evett, Robert: 166,265.
"Evidence": (R'14) 165,252; 166, 292.
Ewell, Lois: 152,131; 154,183; 163,103; 165,213.
"Exceedingly Small": (R'28) 333,81.
"Excess Baggage": (R'28) 324, 38.
"Excursions Through An Old Scrapbook" by William Sykes:
1. Lola Montez (D) 188,210;
2. Adah Isaacs Menken (D) 189,294;
3. Dan Bryant (D) 192,104.
"Excuse Me" (see also "Toot Toot"): (R'11) 121,x; 121,73; 206, 220.
Exhibits: 135,166; 167,28.
"Exile, The": (R'23) 267,16.
"Experience": (R'14) 166,264; 166,265.
"Explorer, The": (R'12) 136, 170.

"Expressing Willie": (R'24) 279, 15; 280,14; (S) 281,26.
Extras: 63,120; 101,26; 101,27; 130,208; 162,75; 187,134; 195,284; 220,350; 327,32.
"Eye for Eye": (F,R) 216,144.
"Eyes of the Heart, The": 51,112; (R'05) 51,113.
"Eyes of Youth": 199,121; 200, 203; (R'17) 200,206; 207, 304.
Eysoldt, Gertrude: 126,60; 142, 191.
Eytinge, Rose: 11,5; 11,8; 22, 15; 25,64; 288,25.
"Eyvind of the Hills": (R'21) 241,261.

--F--

Faber, Jane: 130,223.
Faber, Leslie: 66,204; 68,259; 134,133; 135,147; 140,101; 166,266; 169,111.
Fabiano, Fabian: 258,190.
Fabregas, Virginia: 107,31.
"Fabricus": 23,8.
"Face Value": (R'21) 252,167.
Fachionette, Marie: 112,187.
"Facing the Music": (R'03) 29,161.
"Fads and Fancies": 170,167; (R'15) 170,171.
Fagan, Barney: 256,27.
"Failures, The": 274,14; (R'23) 275,16.
Fair, Florence: 235,212; 283,14; 308,38.
Fair, Joyce: 161,16; 164,173.
Fair, Phyllis: 288,37.
"Fair and Warmer": (R'15) 178, 279; 179,16.
"Fair Circassian, The": (R'21) 251,132.
"Fair Co-Ed, The": (R'09) 97, xiii; 97,93.
"Fair Exchange, A": (R'05) 59, xii; 59,10.
Faire, Virginia: 244,39; 263, 35; 291,43.
Fairbanks, Douglas: 38,106; 91, 246; 92,261; 92,277; 93,287; 128,137; 129,178; 131,13; 136,190; 143,15; 146,116; 151,81; 156,78; 163,100; 164,156; 165,207; 168,58; 169,132; 171,258; 174,79; 177,238; 180,62; 183,286; (A) 185,30; 193,167; 194, c; (W) 194,220; (D,A) 194, 255; 197,10; 199,183; 203, 60; 206,264; 207,329; 209,57; 211,183; 228,106; 228,107; 239,114; 243,424; 246,167; 246,175; 248,324; 253,232; 257,86; 259,243; 260,320; 276,33; 279,7; 279,30; 293, 33; 294,30; 298,33; 308,37; (W,V) 321,24; 323,28; (A,D) 332,71; 333,24; 336,29.
Fairbanks, Douglas Jr.: 275,30; 345,69; 360,59.
Fairbanks, Gladys: 145,72.
Fairbanks, Madeleine: 319,19.
Fairbanks Twins (Madeline & Marion): 224,243; 244,17; 244,30; 256,33; 266,43; 267, 42; 279,38; 305,25; 316,64.
Fairchild, Roy: 89,197; 153,161.
Fairfax, Marion: 40,144; 79, 238; 196,353.
Fairleigh, Harry: 89,180; 38,95.
Fairman, Austin: 275,17.
"Faith Healer, The": (R'10) 109,vi; 109,81.
"Faithful, The" (Mansfield) (B): 182,184.
"Faithful, The": (R'19) 225, 348; 226,363; 241, 267; (D) 292,12.
Faithful, Doris: 215,37; 228,86.
"Fake, The": 283,9; (R'24) 285, 62.
Falconer, Helen: 149,11; 174, 90; 205,161.
Falk, B.J.: 290,49.
"Fall Guy, The": (R'25) 290, 34; (S) 294,26; 296,12; (F,R) 352,47.
"Fall and Rise of Susan Lenox, The": 233,7; 233,29.
"Fall of a Nation, The": (R) 185, 12.
"Fall of Babylon, The": (F) 222,111.
"Fall of Eve, The": (R'25) 296,16.
"Fall of the Romanoffs": (F)

199, 175; 199, 178; (R, F) 200, 245.
"Fallen Angels": 292, 22; 294, 20.
"Fallen Idol, The": (R'15) 169, 111.
Fallon, Eva: 76, 148; 79, 249; 129, 177; 150, 60; 158, 182; 217, 145.
Fallon, Thomas F.: 59, 4; (W) 297, 20.
"False Gods": (D) 117, 160.
Families, Theatrical (see also "Famous Families..."): 132, 132; 149, 16; 155, 32; 161, 21; 162, 67; 172, 298; 174, 72; 175, 128; 199, 148; 209, 39.
"Family, The": 101, 11; (R'10) 117, xvi.
"Family Affairs": (R'29) 347, 49.
"Family Cupboard, The": (R'13) 152, x; 152, 117; 152, 130.
"Family Exit, The": (R'17) 201, 279; 201, 281.
"Family Upstairs, The": (R'25) 295, 15; (S) 296, 26.
"Famous Families of American Players" by M. J. Moses: (B) 69, ix;
1. The Booths, 39, 114;
2. The Jeffersons 41, 177;
3. The Drews 43, 230;
4. The Sotherns 45, 284;
5. The Hacketts 47, 13;
6. The Boucicaults 49, 72;
7. The Wallacks 51, 118;
8. The Davenports 55, 231.
"Famous First Nights" by J. Kaye: 338, 15; 339, 16; 340, 38; 341, 26.
"Famous Mrs. Fair, The": (R'19) 228, 98.
Famous Players Film Co.: 147, 157; 186, 101.
"Famous Women Who Have Been Dramatized by A. Bell:
1. Cleopatra 130, 219;
2. Nell Gwyn 133, 96;
3. Charlotte Corday 137, 26;
4. Adrienne Lecouvreur 138, 61;
5. DuBarry 139, 86.
"Fan, The": (R'21) 249, 424.
"Fan and Two Candlesticks, A": (R'15) 175, 139.
"Fanatics, The": 322, 40.
Fanchon: 234, 94; 246, 161.
Fanchon and Marco: 245, 97.
Fanchonetti, Marie: 176, 170.
"Fancy Free": (R'13) 146, xvi; 147, 155; (R'18) 207, 316.
Fang, Mei Lan: 262, 38; 349, 21.
"Fanny": (R'26) 308, 15.
"Fanny Hawthorne": 257, 83; (R'22) 257, 94.
"Fanny's First Play": (R'12) 140, xv; 141, 149; 143, 16.
"Fantana": 45, 273; (R'05) 48, xi; 52, xiv.
"Fantasticks, The" (see also "Les Romanesques"): 10, 9; 133, 90.
Fantasy: 88, xii.
"Far Cry, The": (R'24) 285, 15.
"Far Flung Battle Line, The": (F, R) 211, 183.
Farber, Irene: 215, 33.
Farber, Constance: 222, 87.
Farce (see Comedy).
Farleigh, Harry: 58, 95; 89, 180.
Farleigh, Margaret: 204, 83; 207, 301; 208, 359.
"Farewell to Arms, A": 356, 17.
Farfariello: 215, 32.
Farkoa, Maurice: 33, 276; 72, 34; 140, 123; 168, 57; 179, 28; 183, 308.
Farley, Morgan: 204, 76; 209, 41; 240, 160; 240, 173; 250, 25; 278, 17; 278, 29; 284, 11; 309, 29; 312, 29.
Farlow, L. S.: (W) 82, 332.
Farmer, Eda: 218, 200.
Farmer, Harcourt (W): 226, 401; 257, 76.
"Farmer's Wife, The": (R'24) 285, 19.
Farnham, Joe: 316, 40.
Farnum, Dustin: 36, 32; 36, 34; 40, 133; 49, c; 55, 215; 67, c; 68, 272; 79, 228; 80, 259; 80, 269; 86, xv; 102, 37; 108, xiv; 110, 126; 127, 84; 129, 176; 145, 78; 148, 171; 163, 110; 199, 176; (A) 253, 269.
Farnum, Frank: 265, 42.
Farnum, William: 63, 127; 91, 250; 127, 84; 129, 176; 139,

91; 161,81; 166,274; 201, 325; 203,57; 204,128; 205, 191; (A) 226,438; 227,41; 228,106; 231,416.
Farrar, Geraldine: 57,280; 69,288; 71,26; 74,111; 82,348; 82, 352; 93,309; 94,335; 94,346; 97,76; 107,11; 107,19; (A) 111,xli; 111,135; 114,63; 118,xxv; 118,xxx; 118,173; 119,c; 120,46; 121,93; 123, 148; 123,152; 129,154; 131,7; 132,51; 134,120; 135,144; 141,138; 142,166; 144,39; 153, 149; 154,182; 155,35; 158, 178; 159,229; 166,270; 167, 16; 169,118; 172,291; 173, 49; 175,130; 178,c; 178,275; 180,74; 186,87; 187,143; 189, 300; 190,345; 191,42; 194, 219; 203,63; 205,167; 207, 310; 209,42; 211,158; 212, 200; 212,205; 214,335; 215, 62; 219,297; 222,108; 224, 234; 242,327; 252,170; 257, 88; 290,43.
Farrell, Charles: 309,2; 310, 37; 317,39; 322,50; 323,6; 328,36; (D) 330,29.
Farrell, Glenda: 341,37.
Farrell, Margherite: 185,11.
Farren, George: 48,28; 51, 129; 134,116; 194,201.
Farren, Nellie: 33,276; 71,25.
Farrington, Frank: 140,123.
"Fascinating Flora": (R'07) 77, iii; 77,185; 79,255.
"Fascinating Mr. Vanderbilt, The": (R) 61,59; 61,69.
"Fascinating Widow, The": (R'11) 128,113.
"Fashion": 27,117; 193,142; (S) 193,143; (R'24) 277,16; 277,18.
"Fashions For Men": (R'22) 263, 19.
"Fashions of 1924": (R'23) 270, 15.
Fassett, Edith: 6,15; 36,33.
Fassett, Malcolm: 179,19.
"Fast And Grow Fat": (R'16) 188,204c.
"Fata Morgana": (R'24) 278,15; 278,17; 280,59.
"Father, The": (R'12) 135,140; 136,176.
"Father and Son": (R'08) 94,xv.
"Father and the Boys": 85,83; (R'08) 86,xi.
"Fatted Calf, The": (R'12) 134, xiii.
Fauchois, Rene: 101,5; 300,31.
Faucit, Helen: 71,25.
"Faun, The": 120,37; 120,40; (R'11) 121,74.
"Faust" (OP): 7,7; 50,85; 86,108; 112,190; (D) 220, 337.
"Faust": 114,39; (R'28) 333,45; 359,43.
Faust, Gracie: 40,147.
Faust, Henrietta: 185,20.
Faust, Lotta: 34,304; 47,c; 73,59; 76,146; 84,54; 87, xvi; 91,227; 98,130; 101,3; 103,c; 109,80.
Faversham, William: PG,4; 3,2; 3,4; 4,1; 4,3; 8,8; 8,9; 22,10; 23,7; 34,307; 41,175; 43,221; 44,244; 44, 262; 53,177; 90,205; 91, 247; 94,315; 94,339; 97,92; 103,71; 106,xxxi; 106,170; 106,181; 120,37; 120,40; 121,74; 125,28; 127,77; 131, 12; 142,162; 142,169; 142, 172; 145,75; 154,204; 157, 111; 157,112; 159,237; 161, 15; 165,204; 165,211; 167, 10; 168,79; 169,142; (A) 170,182; 172,307; 177,240; 182,222; 187,129; 190,358; 190,374; 191,33; 195,292; 200,213; 201,264; 202,341; 203,27; 205,178; 211,157; 212,226; 215,14; 231,365; 233,38; 234,115; 238,11; 240,188; 263,42; 290,18; 293, 43; (A) 319,61; 325,39; 329, 40; 330,42; 357,21.
Faversham, William Jr.: 221,27.
Favieres, Guy: 215,16.
Fawcett, George: 4,16; 18,5; 51,115; 52,136; 53,159; 110, 109; 119,12; 147,142; 150, 46; (C,D,W) 325,32; (W) 336,32.

Fax, Reuben: 73,77.
Fay, Elfie: 54,204.
Fay, Eva: 66,218.
Fay, Frances C. (W): 144,48; 146,103; 147,138; 148,164; 152,124; 154,202; 156,72; 157,120; 159,242.
Fay, Frank: 285,37; 286,36.
Fay, Maude: 118,183; 206,237.
Fay, W.G.: 154,176; 155,50.
Faye, Julia: 235,234; 296,40.
Fazenda, Louise: 192,97; 204,123; 282,31; 319,33; 330,38; 346, 24.
Feally, Maude: 8,17; 16,7; 27, 129; 32,257; 33,c; 33,273; 70,340; 83,12; 186,83.
"Fear": (R'13) 146,xvi; 147, 155.
"Fear Market, The": 181,123; (R'16) 181,125; 183,285; (F,R) 229,190.
Fears, Peggy: 305,23.
"Feast of Adonis, The": (R'05) 50,88.
Fechter, Charles: 14,21; 150,vi; 182,217; 191,7; 244,28.
Fedak, Sari: 329,21.
"Fedora": (R'05) 53,159; 254, 310.
Feigl, Jane Maudlin: 68,265.
Feindel, Suzanne: 179,28.
Feinhals, Fritz: 118,182.
Feininger, Karl: 88,150.
Feist, Leo: (W) 226,374.
Feld, Victor: 179,11.
Feldman, Gladys: 175,118.
"Felice": (R'13) 153,xvii.
Felix, Hugo: 184,351.
Fels, Roderick: 17,17.
Fender, Harry: 291,16.
"Fenris, The Wolf": 69, 309.
Fenton, Alva: 248,308.
Fenton, Charles: 27,130.
Fenton, Mabel: 64,161; 160, 317.
Fenwick, Irene: 115,65; 117,158; 122,108; 122,128; 143,15; 152,117; 153,169; 158,172; 168,77; 169,156; 172,303; 176,193; 182,194; 184,334; 186,102; 187,163; 188,c; 188,193; 195,283; 197,27; 199,151; 204,98; 249,365; 234,90.
Ferber, Edna (W): 316,41; 328,29.
Ferenczy Opera Company, The: 26,104.
Ferguson, Elsie: 94,331; 96, iv; 96,69; 104,106; 104, 109; 105,c; 105,152; 111, 171; 112,183; 123,167; 126, 67; 133,93; 139,69; 145,c; 148,171; 149,9; 151,80; 154, 179; 155,6; 155,8; 158,214; 162,59; 167,26; 169,141; 175,111; 181,124; 183,299; 184,335; 186,62; 190,347; 192,99; 197,19; 199,183; 200,c; 200,253; 202,394; 202,408; 204,121; 210,115; 213,321; 214,335; (A) 214, 379; (D) 219,c; 219,298; 221,65; (A) 226,438; 229, 165; 230,258; 231,369; 233, 20; 233,47; 242,364; 245, 107; 246,149; (D) 247,253; 250,46; (A) 250,63; 251, 75; (D) 251,101; 258,157; 260,320; 263,14; 264,12; 283,32; 286,8; 290,13; 300, 12; (A) 322,3; 342,16; (C) 344,4; 344,24.
Ferguson, Helen: 261,389; 291, 43; 307,36; 320,33.
Ferguson, Hilda: (D) 294,c.
Ferguson, John: 245,77.
Ferguson, R.V.: 11,5; 11,8.
Ferguson, William J.: 5,3; 28, 133; 37,75; 80,263; 87,129; 104,104; 104,105; 105,149; 148,179; 153,156; 240,162.
Feriel, M.A.: 42,203.
Fermier, Mary: 43,vi.
Fernandez, Bijou: PG,21; 62, 89; 188,203; 206,235.
Fernandez, E.L.: 218,225.
Fernandez, Escamilio: 99,138; 100,174.
Ferrari, Rudolph: 83,11.
Ferrari-Fontana, Eduardo: 156, 66; 224,231.
Ferriday, Carolyn: 252,157.
"Festival of Bacchus, The": (R'17) 203,22.
Fetes D'Orange: 19,26.

Fetter, Selena: 36,47.
Fevrier, Henri: 96,xvi.
"Fiddlers Three": (R'18) 212,242; 213,293.
Field, B.A.: 38,99.
Field, Ben: 232,528.
Field, Ethel: 40,147.
Field, Eugene: 89,194.
Field, Grace: 145,80; 180,76; 205,174.
Field, Sylvia: 310,28; 327,48; 329,46; 335,40; 361,12.
"Field God, The": 316,19.
Fielder, Max: 93,310.
Fielding, Caryl: 96,40.
Fielding, Edward: 108,38; 239, 109.
Fielding, Maggie: 60,26.
Fielding, May: 22,26; 62,151.
Fields, Herbert: 222,89; 33, 127; (W) 348,41; 361,37.
Fields, Lew: (A) 16,19; 47,8; (A) 51,i,f; 56,239; 57,273; 57,273; 68,xiii; 73,81; 81, 289; 81,295; (C) 82,xxiv; 83, c; 89,178; 101,3; 107,30; 113, 4; 121,xi; 121,71; 129,ix; 129, 175; 130,xxxiii; 133,74; 149, xx; 149,2; 154,xvi; 164,154; 164,157; 168,69; (W) 169,125; 185,6; 185,11; 186,87; (W) 186,90; 196,341; 200,249; 221, 16; 222,82; 222,89; 231,363; 245,99; 323,41; (C) 336,15; 337,30.
Fields, William A.: 331,48.
Fields, William C.: (D) 247,211; 272,19; 272,29; 279,58; 287, 51; 292,30; 295,32; 307,19; 317,59; 320,45; (C) 330,9; (W) 331,44; 331,75.
"Fiesta": (R'29) 344,68.
"Fifty Miles from Boston": (R'03) 85,62.
"Fifty Million Frenchmen": (R'29) 346,49; (F) 361,3.
"Fifty Years of an Actor's Life": (Coleman) (B): 46,xiv.
"Fight, The": (R'13) 152,111; 152,116.
"Fighting Caravans": (F,R) 360,48.
"Fighting Hope, The": (R'08) 93,284; 93,288; 93,291; (S) 95,18.
Figman, Max; 9,6; 11,8; 18,3 24,31; 24,33; 37,62; 44,262; 46,320; 65,188; 111,146; 132, 46; 132,48; 134,124; 299,11; 306,62.
Figman, Oscar: 286,18.
Filkins, Grace: 5,3; 37,62; 51,108; 51,117; 61,56; 98, 120; 104,102; 151,94; 154, xv; 154,188; 285,52.
Filmore, Russell: 235,23.
<u>Films</u> (<u>see also Hollywood</u>): 199, 173; <u>and monthly thereafter</u>.
<u>Films</u> -- <u>Color</u>: 205,194; 342, 63; 263,34.
<u>Films</u> -- <u>Early</u>: 43,viii; 53, xiii; 92,264; 126,47; 128,vi; 133,xv; 136,xii.
<u>Films</u> -- <u>Silent</u> (<u>see also</u> "Unwinding The Reel"): 95,14; 135,34; 137,18; 140,112; 147,156; 150,72; 156,88; 160, 311; 163,110; 164,161; 165, 227; 166,274; 167,18; 168, 68; 169,126; 171,244; 172, 295; 174,62; 176,176; 178, 309; 180,75; 184,356; 186,86; 188,218; 194,218.
<u>Films</u> -- <u>Sound</u>: 251,108; 254, 282; 296,22; 299,32; 302,32; 319,11; 319,21; 322,41; 324, 41; 328,18; 329,28; 331,26; 331,36; 331,50; 332,24; 332, 35; 334,63; 335,71; 336,32; 339,35; 340,26; 341,21; (C) 343,44; 343,45; 344,37; 348, 24; 349,40; 350,8; 357,32; (C) 358,27.
<u>Films, State of the</u>: 226,401; 276,30; 322,24; 350,22.
<u>Films Vs. Stage</u>: 169,126; 176, 176; 177,241; 178,309; 184, 344; 216,122; 219,290; 296, 22; 301,32; 312,16; 318, 41; 322,23; 323,22; 326,25; 335,32; 340,20; 346,30; 348, 37; 354,33.
"Final Balance, The": (R'28) 334, 46.
Findlay, Else: 340,23.
Findlay, John: 57,271; 105,150; 105,151; 128,124; 136,190.
Findlay, Ruth: 117,144; 211, 129; (D) 218,c; 230,263;

238,11; 239,94.
Findlay, Thomas: 177,235; 201, 275; 227,29.
"Fine and Dandy": 354,23; 356, 28; (R'30) 357,64.
"Fine Feathers": 142,194; (R'13) 144,34.
Finlay, Vera: 110,104; 129,175; 131,10; 144,53; 160,310.
Finley, Genevieve: 46,320.
Finley, Murrel: 320,61.
Finney, James Lee: 14,5; 21,6; 28,134; 39,124; 51,117; (A) 52,131f; 57,269; 65,189; 80, 261; 95,29; 120,58; 127,vi.
"Fioretta": 337,24; 337,45; (R'29) 337,46; 339,31.
"Fire and Water": (R) 177,222.
"Firebrand, The": (R'24) 285, 16; 286,21; (S) 290,26.
"Firefly, The": (R'12) 143,3.
"Fires of Fate": 102,41; (R'10) 108,xiv.
Fireside Players (New York): 253,248.
Firkins, Oscar W.: (W) 152, 118.
"Firm of Cunningham, The": (R'05) 52,135; 52,136.
"First Duchess of Marlborough, The": (R) 9,10; 9,11.
"First Fifty Years, The": 254,283; (R'22) 255,373; (S) 256, 18.
"First Lady in the Land, The": (R'11) 131,x.
"First Lady with the Camelias, The": 8,14.
"First Love": (R'26) 311,16.
"First Man, The": (R'22) 254, 308.
"First Mrs. Fraser, The": (R'29) 347,49; 348,45; (S) 353,32.
First Nights: 44,xii; 23,11; 106, 184; 119,12; 149,32; 171, 232; 171,242; 178,281; 190, 346; 191,38; 195,270; 197,28; 216,84; 237,376; 245,74; 245, 78; 282,19; 302,9; 309,10; 324,23; 332,28; 338,15.
"First Year, The": 238,27; (R'20) 238,30; (S) 243,402.
Firth, Ivan: 360,40.
Fischer, Alice: 12,4; 19,4; 20, 6; 20,8; 51,118; 66,200; 75,119; 121,85; 185,11; 214, 335.
Fischer, Betty: 160,305; 304, 20.
Fischer, Fred: 179,26.
Fischer, Margarita: 203,59; 302,20; 208,405; 208,406.
Fischer, Robert A.: 93,298; 179,16; 191,18; 164,165; 242, 346.
Fish, Denison (W): 225,308; 226,392.
Fisher, Alfred: 15,5.
Fisher, Charles: 22,26; 52,151; 105,147; 126,65; 193,146.
Fisher, Edna: 177,242.
Fisher, Florence: 84,39; 88, 162; 88,163; 101,11; 136, 194.
Fisher, Grace: 220,335.
Fisher, Harry: 57,273.
Fisher, Harry A.: 216,69.
Fisher, Irving: 205,137; 240, 176.
Fisher, Lola: 154,xxv; 164, 172; 166,290; 183,295; 189, 293; 191,37; 197,c; 215,29; 221,31; 232,529; 247,262; 248,293; 249,370; 261,374; 292,5.
Fisher, Sallie: 53,180; 88,163; 89,188; 99,148; 113,32; 125, 23; 132,69; 132,71; 143,24; 144,37; 149,29.
Fiske, Harrison Grey: 7,10; 43,226; 67,227; 94,xxxii; 103,71; 106,xxxvi; 154,xxviii; 166,313; 193,165; 202,411; 274,39; 275,64.
Fiske, Minnie Maddern Fiske: PG,29; 4,4; 4,13; 7,10; 9,1; 9,6; 9,7; 9,20; 11,8; 11,9; 11,c; (D) 16,9; 17,6; 18,3; 19,2; 22,5; 22,13; 22, 15; (W) 22,27; 23,4; 32,246; 33,266; 43,225; 46,292; 47, 7; 47,23; 48,27; 51,112; 53, 160; 64,140; 65,188; 67,227; 70,325; 78,211; 79,228; 84, 31; 84,33; 90,205; 90,206; 91,228; 95,19; 96,c; 96,54; 102,40; 107,2; 110,97; 111, xxx; 111,131; 111,139; 113,

22; 114,43; 118,176; 122, 106; 123,142; 123,143; 123, 146; 124,197; 127,76; 127,85; 127,104; 129,148; 130,192; 133,73; 134,133; 139,66; 141, 147; 143,5; 145,75; 148,182; 151,79; 156,86; 163,98; (A) 166,273; 170,191; 181,124; 181,153; 183,276; 185,31; 187,175; 190,361; 190,415; 193,165; 201,327; 203,20; 203, 24; 204,70; 205,133; 207, 305; (C) 209,21; 211,146; 212, 198; 218,217; 219,289; 220, 358; 220,360; 222,102; (A) 231,347; 231,368; 232,508; 235,173; 240,155; 242,325; 248,294; 271,5; 272,22; 272, 17; 273,12; 274,39; 275,64; 286,14; 286,30; 288,26; 326, 10; 340,17; 46,320.

Fiske, Stephen (W): 106,197.

Fitch, Betty: 257,97.

Fitch, Clyde: 3,5; 3,10; 7,5; 9,13; 9,14; 10,3; 10,18; 11,2; 11,4; 11,8; 11,10; 22, 10; 24,29; 25,55; 26,92; 27, 124; 28,133; 33,264; 33,271; 37,72; 45,267; 46,299; 48, 32; 49,54; 53,164; 55,227; 56,243; 56,255; 59,6; 65, 186; 67,xiii; 70,320; 71,xiii; 71,14; 72,30; 72,31; 74,104; 82,v; 84,33; 87,vii; 95,5; 95, 11; 99,xi; 99,136; 104,112; 105,158; 106,176; 106,187; 107,ix; 108,34; 114,x; 118, 198; 119,12; 149,xx; 169,132; 187,136; 193,150; 197,24; 201,274.

Fitch, Margaret: 241,249.

Fitzallan, Adelaide: 4,9.

Fitzgerald, Cissy: 302,25.

Fitzgerald, George: 190,374; 191,32; 315,26.

Fitzgerald, Lillian: 280,37.

Fitzgerald, William G. (W): 60, 38; 79,244; 82,326.

Fitzgerald, W. H.: 13,23.

Fitzhugh, Venita: 153,145; 155, 31; 162,76; 178,282.

Fitziu, Anna: 181,154; 203,41; 219,309; 248,317; 267,36; 271,37.

Fitzmaurice, George: 238,286.

Fitzpatrick, Amy: 183,276.

"Five Frankforters, The": (R'13) 146,98; 146,105.

"Five Million, The": 222,103; (R'19) 223,149.

"Five O'Clock": (R'10) 225,354.

"Five Star Final": 360,25.

"Fixing Sister": (R'16) 189, 326.

Flack, Nanette: 153,155.

"Flag Lieutenant, The": (R'09) 104,105; 104,113.

Flagg, James Montgomery: (W) 328,5; 333,74.

Flahaut, Marianne: 87,142; 96, 42; 107,6; (A) 112,ii; 118, 164; 145,77.

Flaherty, Hughie: 49,74.

"Flaherty V.C.": (R'20) 234, 108.

"Flame, The": (R'16) 188,204,c; 189,285.

"Flame of Love": (R'24) 280, 16.

Flanagan, Hallie: 326,47; 335, 4.

Flanders, Ralph: 88,167.

Flateau, Georges: 207,305; 208, 354; 246,142.

Flaven, Aileen: 112,188.

Flavin, Lucille: 10,20; 50,85.

Flavin, Martin: 272,26; 308, 29; (W) 346,40.

"Fleet of the Emigrants, The": 77,179.

Fleischer-Edel, Katharina: 69, 289.

Fleming, Una: 224,243; 237, 353.

<u>Flemish Theatre</u>: 327,19.

Flemming, Claude: 140,123; 147,150; 165,206; 177,234.

Fleta, Miguel: 272,36; 274, 37.

Fletcher, Cecil: 178,308; 204, 79.

Fletcher, Janita: 197,23.

Flexer, Dorothea: 334,43.

Flexner, Anne Crawford: 9,6; 44,248.

Fleury, Fernando: 35,15.

"Flight": (R'29) 337,47.

"Flo-Flo": (R'17) 204,87; 204,93.

Flood, John: 3,11; 59,10; 95, 33; 104,102; 195,287; 226, 365.
Flood, Redmond: 111,142.
"Flora Bella": (R'16) 188,246; 189,280.
"Floradora": 4,15; 22,11; 231, 404; (R'20) 232,573; 283, 52; (D) 349,36.
Florence, Evelyn: 17,5; 17,15.
Florence, Katherine: 36,45; 41,175; 55,220; 59,6; 80, 260; 96,40.
Florence, Mildred: 295,14.
Florence, William J.: 74,100; 86,98; 126,64; 168,73; 241, 260.
Florence, [Mrs.] William J.: 78,222.
"Florist Shop, The": (R'09) 103, xi; 103,75.
"Flossie": (R'24) 281,15.
Flower, Eva: 131,8.
"Flower Boat, The": (R'07) 76, 147.
"Flower of the Palace of Han, The": (R'12) 135,138; 135,151.
"Flower of the Ranch, The": 88,i; (R'08) 88,vi; 88,147; 88,154.
"Flower of Yeddo, A": (S, R'01) 6,15.
Flowerton, Consuelo: 256,33; 331, 59.
"Fluffy Ruffles": 92,vi; (R'08) 92, xxi.
Flunger, Ann: 15,11; 106,192.
"Fly By Night": 327,39.
"Flying Dutchman, The": (OP) 84, 40.
"Flying High": (C) 350,37; (R'30) 350,43; 350,44.
Flynn, Kitty: 263,33.
Flynn, Marie: 151,101; 153, 155; 194,231; 198,77; 217, 135.
Flynn, Rose: 45,280.
Flynn, Ruth: 333,39.
Foch, Dirk: 261,390.
Foerster, Else: 158,200.
"Fog": (R'27) 313,18.
"Fog, The": (R'14) 167,9.
Fokina, Vera: 229,174; 257, 69; 282,5; 293,41.
Fokine, Michael: 229,174.
<u>Folk Music</u>: 359,44.
<u>Folk Theatre</u> (<u>see</u> Carolina Playmakers).
"Follies, The" [London]: 103,84.
"Follies of --" (<u>see also</u> "Ziegfeld Follies of ..").
"Follies of 1908": 90,199; (R'08) 90,201; 90,211; 90, 212; 94,334.
"Follies of 1909": (R'10) 114,35; 114,45.
Follis, Dorothy: 97,90; 100, 195; 214,353; 235,179; 238,281.
Follis, Nellie: 35,12.
"Follow Me": 191,20; (R'16) 191,24.
"Follow the Girl: 206,216; (R'18) 206,220.
"Follow Thru": (R'29) 336,51; 342,40.
Folsom, Bobby: 277,37.
Fonariova, Eugenie: 195,289; 230, 262.
Fonda, Henry: 354,50.
Fontaine, Evan Burrows: 211, 137; 246,161.
Fontanne, Lynn (<u>see also</u> Lunt and Fontanne): 191,18; 195, 267; 195,295; 195,311; 217, 149; 223,184; 241,279; 243, 404; 247,237; 249,372; 249, 379; 252,183; 252,197; 269, 11; 271,17; (D) 273,10; 285, 6; 285,46; 288,43; 296,5; 299,30; 301,17; 301,44; 310, 29; 311,17; 311,24; 312,20; 315,12; (D) 323,c; 323,40; 325,40; 336,51; 359,28.
"Fool, The": (R'22) 261,420; (S) 264,28; 286,26.
"Fool and a Girl, A": 81,291.
"Fool and His Money, A": (R'03) 27,107.
"Fool Hath Said There Is No God, The": (R'08) 86,xiv.
"Fool There Was, A": (R'09) 59,135; 99,164.
"Foolish Virgin, The": 117,152; (R'10) 120,34.
"Fool's Revenge, The": (R'05) 59,xiii; 88,169.
"Foot-Loose": (R'20) 232,526.
Foote, Courtenay: 124,205; 134, 127; 190,365.

Foote, Elroy (W): 169,112; (V) 208,344.
Foote, Sterling T.: 198,89.
"Footlights Across America" (Macgowan) (B): 346,4.
"Footlights--Fore and Aft, The" (Pollock) (B): 133,xvii.
"For All of Us": (R'23) 274, 58.
"For Goodness' Sake": (R'22) 254,334.
"For Husbands Only" (F) 212,247.
"For the Defense": (R'19) 228, 100; 228,103.
"For Value Received": (R'23) 268, 19.
Foran, William: 303,28; 329,24.
Forbes, Edward S.: 216,69.
Forbes, Ralph: 284,18; 297,14; 359,46.
Forbes-Robertson, Beatrice: 105, 144; 105,145.
Forbes-Robertson, Ian (W): 194, 228.
Forbes-Robertson, John (see Robertson, John Forbes).
"Forbidden Fruit": (R'15) 172, 282; (F,R) 241,270; (F) 241, 272.
"Forbidden Land, The": 49,74.
"Forbidden Roads": (R'28) 327, 39.
Ford, Alexander Hume: 21,24; (W) 40,146.
Ford, Bickie: 235,175.
Ford, Dick: 113,30.
Ford, Edward Ellis: 147,155.
Ford, Harriet: 161,18; 170,188; 276,29.
Ford, Harrison: 41,170; 176,186; 334,31.
Ford, Helen: 260,330; 261,387; 270,27; 280,27; 283,11; (D) 297,c; 297,17; 315,19.
Ford, Hugh: 203,58; 208,398.
Ford, Inez: 260,305.
Ford, James L. (W):231,362; 233, 6; 236,264; 240,154; 265,358; 258,142; 285,9; 291,9.
Ford, Jean: 124,203.
Ford, John: 287,32; (W) 313,23.
Ford, John T.: 58,302; 74,100; 87,129.
Ford, Mabel: 283,37.
Ford, Stanley G.: 132,71; 222, 82; 292,21.
Forde, Harold H.: 130,217; 152, 127; 236,281.
Fordham Theatre (Minnesota): 252,186.
Ford's Theatre (Washington, D.C): 37,66; 148,179.
Foreign Actors: 129,163; 170, 193; 219,288; 275,24; 282, 20; 284,7; 308,40; 326,32; 342,19.
"Forever After": 213,271; (R'13) 213,312.
"Forest Lovers, The": 8,13.
Foret, Augette: 202,363.
Forman, Ada: 200,217; 225, 311; 247,229; 250,13; 279, 6.
Forman, Justus Miles: 172,284.
Forman Sisters: 361,29.
Formes, Carl: 197,31.
Fornardo, Carlo De: 260,306.
Fornaroli, Lucia: 123,148; 132, iii; 144,49.
Foster, Phoebe: 186,c; 186,59; 186,104; (A) 186,109; 199,135; 203,19; 294,91; 217,183; 226, 369; 243,411; 308,19; 319, 10; 322,28; 322,29; 343,20; 349,44; 351,34; 360,24; 360, 52.
Foulke, Gwendolyn: 184,349.
"Fountain, The": (R'14) 157,114; 157,119; (D) 296,13; 299,4; (R'25) 299,15.
"Fountain of Youth, The": (R'18) 207,287.
"Four Horsemen of the Apocalypse, The": (F) 242,349; (F,R) 243,424.
"Four Walls": 320,22; (R'27) 320, 72.
"Fourberies de Scapin, Le": (R'17) 203,21.
"Fourth Estate, The": (R'09) 105,135; 105,137; (F) 184, 356.
Fovieri, Adoni: 154,176.
Fowler, Edwin: 49,57.
Fowler, Margaret: 209,41.
Fowler, Mary: 244,33; 264, 31.
Fowler and Tamara: 301,31.

Fox, Beth: 226,375.
Fox, Della: 201,292; 201,293; 235,184.
Fox, George L.: 134,126; 195, 264.
Fox, Harry: 206,216.
Fox, Lucy: 220,390; 243,425.
Fox, Virginia: 323,23.
Fox, William: 135,vi; 108,397; 231,484; 319,11.
Fox Studios: 319,54; 323,6.
Foxe, Earle: 323,6.
"Foxy Grandpa": 7,18.
Foy, Eddie: 16,5; 36,36; 58, xviii; 75,xix; 76,152; 96, xv; 115,xiv; 115,85; 132,40; 189,267; 191,38.
Foy, Eddie Jr.: 325,4; (C) 341, 23.
Foy, Gloria: 263,23.
Frame, Virginia (W): 54,162; 65,175; 68,264; 72,42; 74, 94; 75,132; 79,238; 86,106; 89,175.
Francell, Fernand: 329,23.
Francell, Jacqueline: 329,23.
Frances, Beverley: 124,187.
"Francesca da Rimini": 7,4; 12,7; 12,8; 14,20; 16,8; 17,12; (S) 18,18; 21,18; (OP) 192, 94; 205,133.
Francis, Adeline: 147,xx.
Francis, Alec: 307,37; 312,36.
Francis, Alma: 155,3: 155,3; 208, 393.
Francis, Charles: 183,296; 251, 75; 252,164.
Francis, Dorothy: 248,312; 253, 241; 289,5.
Francis, Emma: 41,iv.
Francis, Eva: 101,23.
Francis, J.O.: 164,164.
Francis, Noel: 318,29; (C) 341,23.
Frank, Adrien: 189,289.
Frank, Art: 289,37.
Frank, Keenan: 85,78.
Frank, Zella: 40,43.
Frankfort Opera House (Germany): 66,202.
Frankl, Walter: 183,283.
Franklin, Dwight: 229,176.
Franklin, Grace: 35,23.
Franklin, Irene: 76,167; 115,82; 175,139; 176,184; 180,72; 187,145; 196,335; 196,363; 209,9; 211,155; 212,200; (W) 214,336; 230,290; 242,345; 249,415; 250,63; 252,193; 264,43; 332,57; 333,37; (W) 340,26; (D) 343,23; 353,21.
Franklin, Maurice: 105,135.
Franklyn, Beth: 183,275; 253,215.
Fraser, Vivienne: 79,233.
Fraser, Winifred: 154,197.
"Fraulein Josette--Meine Frau": (R'13) 147,xii.
Frawley, Paul: 181,125; 226, 385.
Frawley, T.D.: 9,19; 50,85.
Frayne, Frank: 63,119.
Frazee, Harry H.: 167,14; 305,48.
Frazier, Sudworth: 292,17.
Frazin, Gladys: 264,49; 269, 26; 272,43.
"Freddy": (R'29) 342,41.
Frederic, William: 132,39.
Frederici, Blanche (see Friderici, Blanche).
Frederick, Helena: 28,134; 50,94.
Frederick, Pauline: 54,206; 75,115; 80,275; 85,79; 89, 181; 94,xxvi; 94,xxviii; 94, 333; 99,161; 104,c; 144,34; 145,94; 146,c; (W) 148,172; 51,99; 158,173; 162,69; 164,157; 164,190; 168,69; 168,82; 170,77; 175,127; (W) 177,241; 182,229; 184, 351; 185,46; 186,88; 194, 210; (A) 196,365; 198,74; 199,177; 199,182; 204,121; 205,189; 207,328; 219,297; 223,180; (A) 226,438; 230, 278; 231,410; 234,114; (A) 238,72; 255,366; 260,287; 265,12; 282,31.
Fredericks, E. Arline: 149,36.
"Free Lance, The": 64,143; (R'06), 64,x.
Freed, Frank H.: 307,30.
Freedley, Vinton: 291,36; 360, 31.
Freedman, David: (W) 336,28.
"Freedom": 214,339; (R'18) 214,345.

"Freedom of Suzanne, The": (R'05) 52,134.
Freeman, Bettina: 163,102; 165,213.
Freeman, Don: (C) 338,37; (C) 339,41; (C) 341,23; (C) 343,44; (C) 345,26.
Freeman, Doris: 289,46.
Freeman, Grace: 125,8.
Freeman, Helen: 154,175; 157, 138; 220,357; 221,23; 226, 376; 250,11; 295,36; 321, 60.
Freeman, Max: 27,109; 62,101.
Freeman, R.F.: 103,75.
Freiberger, Edward: (W) 124, 198: (W) 132,69.
Fremstadt, Olive: 33,285; 60, 53; 70,341; 73,71; 97,76; 98,130; 108,39; 118,167; 188,173; 129,154; 131,5; 132, 69; 134,111; 141,140; 142, 166; 147, 135; 150,65; 153, 149; 155,14; 157,116; 178, 286.
French, Edna: 256,25.
French, Eva: 171,234.
French, H. Delmar: 28,133.
"French Doll, The": (R'22) 254, 308; (D) 255,375.
French Drama Society: 155,42; 156,102; 163,141.
"French Leave": 238,11; (R'20) 238,32.
French Opera: 86,108; 136,177.
French Opera Company (New Orleans): 38,86.
French Theatre (see also Basque Theatre; Grand Guignol; Scribe, H.S. (W); Theatre du Vieux Colombier; Theatre Francais; Theatre Parisien; Wilson, B.F. (W): 12,16; 15,13; 38,96; 40,153; 41, 162; 44,263; 45,xvii; 45,268; 48,39; 54,202; 75,xxvii; 83,v; 86,108; 91,240; 91,254; 99, 140; 100,191; 119,xviii; and monthly thereafter; 138,54; 148, xii; 148,169; 150,40; 151, 104; 152,xvii; 156,72; 159, 242; 171,257; 174,75; 177,225; 179,11; 189,288; 194,222; 206, 208; 210,92; 226,396; 261, 378; 266,22; 266,68; 279, 12; 279,16; 281,22; 284,9; 294,29; 311,34; 335,52; 336, 57; 338,22; 340,41; (C) 345, 44; 346,39; 357,22.
Frear, Fred: 24,30.
Frenyear, Mabel: 112,186; 118, 192; 127,105.
"Freshman, The": (F,R) 297, 32.
Freund, Frank E. Washburn (W): 125,24.
Friars Club: 79,254; 80,i,f; 95, xvii; 183,272; 231,399; 231, 478.
Fricken, Roy Henri (W): 312, 24; 313,10; 314,7; 315,20; 316,21; 319,41; 321,18; 325,25; 326,37; 327,23; 330, 45; 331,50; 336,46.
Friderici, Blanche: 249,392; 250,16; 253,215; 283,14; 289,14.
Friebus, Theodore: 137,8.
Friede, Samuel M.: 64,ii.
"Friend at Court, A" (Moffat) (B): 49,xv.
"Friend Indeed": (R'26) 304, 15.
"Friend Martha": (R'17) 199, 133.
"Friendly Enemies": 210,87; (R) 211,143.
Friends of the Drama: 351,41; 358,44.
"Frier Bacon and Frier Bungay": 66,ix.
Friganza, Trixie: 17,5; 34,314; 76,153; 76,167; 80,274; 83, 6; 150,51; 156,77; 158,199; 176,174; 191,16; (C) 343,40.
Friml, Rudolph: 184,351; 303, 36; 344,42.
"Frivolities of 1920"): (R'20) 229,182.
"Friquet": (R'04) 49,56.
Frisco, Joe: 285,37; (C) 333, 40; 357,61.
"Frisky Mrs. Johnson, The": (R'03) 25,55; 25,56; 26,90; 42,ii.
"Fritz in Tammany Hall": (R'05) 57,xiii.
"Frocks and Frills": 12,3; 12,4;

13,6.
Froerlich, Bianca: 34,322.
Frohman, Charles: (A) 3,1; 3,4; 7,3; 11,6; 21,4; 22, 29; 31,212; 31,218; 31,236; 34,291; 39,118; 40,152; 41, 161; 43,214; 43,226; 46, xxi; 49,76; 51,115; 58,xxi; 58,xxiv; 62,100; 67,226; 70, xxv; 79,239; (W) 82,324; 91, 228; 91,229; 94,xxxiv; 97, xii; 98,xiii; 100,xi; 100,175; 101,x; 102,ix; 103,70; 103, 72; 103,73; 106,xxxv; 107, xxiv; 108,viii; 111,xx; 112,xi; 115,xiii; 115,66; 118,xxxiv; 123,xiii; 127,76; 129,170; 135,xvii; 135,153; 137,11; 139,66; 139,89; 142,xxv; 144, vi; 144,vii; 145,75; 151,79; 153,160; 154,xxvii; 154,xxxii; 155,38; 157,132; 163,98; 165, 214; 166,312; 171,229; 171, 284; 173,8; 175,108; 175,117; 178,339; 181,122; 187,126; 187,175; 199,122; 199,184; 200,191; 211,130; 212,202; 214,338; 223,144; 231,379; 234,84; 246,166; 258,149; 270,7; 282,7; 283,39; 289,26; 294,7.
Frohman, Daniel: (A) 3,1; 9,2; 30,184; 43,226; 62,101; 75, 118; 84,42; (W) 106,174; 106,187; 109,72; 111,xx; 111, 151; 115,71; 115,86; 116,ii; 116,105; 127,x; 127,86; 132, 69; 133,xviii; 147,156; 163, 112; 167,35; 172,307; 177, 249; 178,309; 203,7; 208,394; (W) 225,294; (A) 231,346; 231,379; (W) 231,382; 261, 386; 262,38; 266,38; 271,38; 288,28; (W) 290,18; 299,38; (C) 315,33; 323,44; 324,44; 330,42; (W) 333,30; 339,38; 351,27.
"From Broadway to the Bowery": 74,109.
"From Morn to Midnight": 257,71; (R'22) 257,94.
"From out the Flood": (F) 184, 357.
"Front Page, The": (S) 329,24; 329,25; (R'28) 331,40; (C) 336,15; 340,15.
Frost, Leila: 213,275.
Frost, Lorraine: 101,12.
Frothingham, G.B.: 13,23; 136,173.
"Frou-Frou": (R'02) 17,3.
Fry, Horace B.: (W) 5,12; 15,18.
Frye, Dwight: 266,31; 312,66.
Fuchs, George: 126,57.
Fueher, Robert: 98,115.
Fueher, Lillie: 98,115.
Fuertes, Rosa: 31,222.
"Fugutive, The": (R'17) 195, 277; 195,293.
Fulda, Ludwig: 13,2; 14,2; 46,299; 61,68; 62,xiii.
"Full House, A": 172,280; (R'15) 172,282.
Fuller, Hector: (W) 356,45.
Fuller, Jeanne: 281,37.
Fuller, Loie: 99,165; 107,13; 138,iii; 161,28.
Fuller, Mary: 140,112; 166,274; 172,c; 172,277; 176,185.
Fuller Sisters: 172,300; 191, 11.
Fuller, Rosalind: 231,405; 234, 90; 247,229; 266,27; 288,5.
Fulop, Ilona: 238,18.
Fulton, Maude: 76,167; 77,178; 100,193; 194,216; 195,276; 196,354.
Fumade, Harrie: 185,21.
"Funabashi": (R'08) 84,x.
Funk, J. Clarence (W): 162, 51.
"Funny Face": (R'27) 323,58.
"Furie, La": 100,191.
Furnace, Howard H. Jr. (W): 182,212; 293,9.
Furniss, Grace Livingston: 20,6; 24,32; 55,227; 66,200; 68, 265; 81,301; 125,29.
"Furs and Frills": 201,275; (R) 202,349.
Furtwangler, Wilhelm: 288,34.
"Fuss and Feathers": (F,R) 215, 62.
<u>Futurists:</u> 294,22.
Fyles, Franklin: 6,8; 7,14.
Fyles, Vanderheyden (W): 115, 84; 116,127; 146,114; 165,

214; 167,34; 169,132; 170, 193; 187,136.
Fysher, A. Nilson: 179,28.

--G--

Gable, Clark: 332,47.
Gabrelli, Marie: 240,171.
Gabriel, Gilbert W. (W): 299, 9; 302,9; 310,9; (C) 333, 33.
Gabriel, Master: 49,66.
"Gabriel Schilling's Flight": (R'13) 146,101.
Gabrielle, Ida: 17,5; 79,233.
Gabrielle, Pearl: 79,233.
Gabrilowitch, Ossip: 21,28; 70, 342; 170,184; 178,286; 296, 35; 332,27.
"Gaby": (R'11) 124,183.
Gadski, Johanna: 74,110; 81,314; 110,127; 117,140; 118,173; 121,83; 129,154; 130,216; 133, 78; 141,140; 144,40; 153,149; 154,184; 157,116; 159,247.
Gaeter, Lillian: (D) 329,4c.
Gagliardi, Cecilia: 141,140.
Gahagan, Helen: 261,367; 263, 49; 272,14; 272,27; 280, 13; 291,27; 298,19; 299,28; (W) 305,10; (D) 307,c; 313,20; 325,39; 342,47; 358,24; 359, 15.
Gaige, Crosby: 231,494; (W) 332,13.
"Gaities and Gravities" by A. Patterson: 316,34; and monthly thereafter.
Gaiety Theatre (Manchester): 146,111.
Gaillard, Eva Ryman (W): 81, 294.
"Gala Night": (R'30) 349,64.
Galanta, Kitty: 199,175.
Galbraith, Jean: 151,xx.
Galdos, Perez: 41,164.
Gale, Alice: 76,147; 151, 105; 154,178.
Gale, Marguerite: 179,31.
Gale, Marie: 242,331.
Gale, Minna: 105,164; 37,62.
Gale, Zona: 143,27; (W) 317, 11.
Galeffi, Carlo: 239,111.
Gall, Yvonne: 217,137; 239, 111.
Gallagher and Shean: (C) 262, 26; 302,24.
Gallagher, Donald: 40,147; 64, 142; 188,216; 200,203; 218, 209; 233,36; 293,36.
Galland, Bertha: 3,c; 6,3; 8,12; (W,V) 8,13; 8,20; 9,2; 26, 93; 27,123; 33,267; 35,3; 35,7; 41,160; 96,50; 54,185; 99,xx; 99,156; 111,164; 113, 24; 340,27.
Gallatin, Alberta: 90,210.
Gallendre, Herbert: 300,23.
Galli, Rosina: 134,111; 167,17; 193,180; 212,207; 238,35; 279,35.
Galli-Curci, Amelita: 192,90; 192,91; 193,190; 198,67; 202,369; 203,41; 206,232; (D) 207,278; 228,94; 239,111; 265,36; 265,38; 272,37; (C) 286,15; 301,48; 337,36; 351, 36.
Gallimore, Catherine: 323,40.
Gallo, Fortune: 235,238.
Gallois, Gemaine: 77,196.
"Galloper, The": (R'06) 61, xiii.
"Gallops": (R'06) 61,56.
Galloway, Katherine: 185,8.
Galloway, Louise: 48,38; 68, 271; 90,i; 113,14.
Gally, David Brainard: 47,18.
Galsworthy, John: 75,114; 107, 2; 107,4; 127,89; 135,158; 156,81; 183,296; 189,280; 195,277; 261,364; 261,371; 342,22.
Gambarelli, Maria: 236,289; 259,221; 317,41.
Gamble, Warburton: 104,101; 201,291; 252,151; 254,301; 290,35.
"Gamblers, The": 117,135; (R'10) 118,164; 344,49.
"Gamblers All": (R'17) 192,87.
"Gambling": (C,R'19) 343,42; 351,25.
"Game of Love, The": (R'09) 101, 4.
"Game of Love and Death, The": 346,46; (R'29) 346,48.

"Gammer Gurton's Needle": 185, 21; 192,93.
Gamut Club: 164,183.
Ganes, Marjory: 79,233.
"Gang War": (R'28) 331,41.
"Gang's All Here, The": 360, 27; 361,36; 361,38.
Ganjiro, Nakumura: 220,362; 292, 8.
Gantvoort, Carl: 147,133; 156, 59.
Ganz, Rudolph: 261,391.
"Gaol, The": 166,267; (R'14) 166, 300.
Garbo, Greta: 297,30; 305, 38; 319,25; (W) 321,36; 345, 40.
Gard, Sumner: 51,129.
"Garden of Allah, The": (R'05) 54,184; 126,63; 128,132; 129,148; 130,iii; (R'11) 130, 184; 130,213; 131,15; 135, 168; 137,vii; (F) 318,42.
"Garden of Lies, The": 112,194.
"Garden of Paradise, The": (R'14) 167,47.
Garden, Mary: 57,280; 81,315; 82,341; 82,351; 84,45; 85, 67; 86,113; 93,309; 94,c; 95,xvi; 95,34; 96,xxiv,f; 97, 77; 98,103; 98,130; 108,183; 106,202; 108,xix; 108,57; 109,91; 111,c; 111,161; (A) 115,viii; 119,9; 120,41; 121, 76; 124,182; 129,147; 130,c; 130,191; 130,214; 137,17; 142,177; 146,102; 148,170; 155,29; 162,66; 191,14;195, 262; 197,16; 198,102; 199, 180; 203,41; 203,64; 207,324; 219,281; 228,94; 236,261; 237,361; 239,111; 241,265; 245,79; 252,153; (D) 254,287; 265,9; 288,35; 304,35; (A) 318,59.
Gardiner, Jack: 115,94.
Gardiner Trio, The: 220,340.
Gardner, Amelia: 122,107; 183,295.
Gardner, Helen: 168,69.
Gardner, Jack: 112,179; 112, 180.
Garland, Ruth: 222,32.
Garner, James: 24,31.
Garon, Pauline: 223,159; 232, 524; 249,363; 252,157.
Garratt, Edward: 68,269.
Garrick, David: 34,317; 77,189; 104,124; (D) 113,26; 182, 217; (D) 193,158; 198,72; 221,8.
Garrick, Helena Collier: 133,74.
Garrick, Thomas: 131,32.
Garrick, Yvonne: 181,132; 191, 41; 216,97.
"Garrick Gaities of 1925": (R) 305,15; (D) 305,29.
"Garrick Gaities of 1926": (R) 305,15; (D) 305,29.
"Garrick Gaities of 1929": 352,42.
"Garrick Gaities of 1930": (R'30) 353,24.
Garrick Theatre (Chicago): 124,198.
Garrick Theatre (New York): 244,6.
Garrick Theatre (Philadelphia): 37,78.
Garrison, Mabel: 203,42; 228,94.
Garrott, George: (W) 348,38.
Garry, Charles: 191,25.
Garside, Frances L. (W): 205, 168; 211,158; 213,274; 219, 286; 224,244.
Garvia, Edward: 55,225.
Gates, Eleanor: 149,xi; 165, 256.
Gates, Helen: 258,175.
Gates, Lucy: 197,31; 251,89.
Gateson, Marjorie: 222,99; 238, 14; 257,77; 321,58.
Gatti-Casazza, Giulio: 89,194; 116,108; (A) 120,52; 129, 154; 143,12; (C) 159,254; 178,294; (C) 286,15.
"Gaucho, The": (F) 323,28.
Gaudsmith Brothers: 290,45.
Gaul, George: 139,iii; 205,163; 206,213; 207,284; 215,29; 216,74; 217,155; 218,199; 229,167; 232,519; 235,183; 235,191; 248,323; 254,290; 310,37; 333,46.
Gaunt, Frances: 146,123.
"Gaunlet, A": (R'03) 26,101.
Gauthier, Eva: 278,35.
Gauthier, Henri: 189,289.

Gautier, Judith: 139,70; 150,59.
Gavrilov, Alexander: 303,10.
Gaxton, William: 321,43; 323, 41; 348,30.
Gay, Alden: 222,75.
Gay, Charles A.: 66,219.
Gay, Delphine: 27,116.
Gay, John: 341,4.
Gay, Maria: 76,166; 93,308; 95, 34.
"Gay Hussars, The": (R'09) 103,74; 103,85; 113,25.
"Gay Life, The": 96,45; 99, 141; (R'09) 100,170.
"Gay Musician, The": 88,149; (R'08) 89,174.
"Gay Paree": (R'25) 295,70.
"Gay White Way, The": 81,xvi; 81,289.
Gayer, Echlin: 301,38.
Gaynor, Janet: 309,2; 310,37; 320,13; 322,12; 322,12; 328, 36.
Gaythorne, Pamela: 122,109; 128, 115; 132,59; 134,106; 136, 183; 148,180; 151,90.
Gear, Luella: 274,29; 274,44; 306,c; 309,21; 309,47; 317, 19; 333,56.
Geary, Lalla: 224,217.
Gebuehr, Otto: 93,290.
Geddes, Alice Spendor: (W) 144, 59.
Geddes, Virgil: 351,8.
Geer, Charlotte (W) (see Radio).
Geffen, Yetta D. (W) (see also "Some Recent Hits"): 166, 291; 167,30; 186,76.
"Geisha, The": (R'13) 147, xii; 147,129; 147,133.
"Geisha and the Cavalier, The": 41,167.
Geller, James J.: (W) 302, 24.
Geltzer, Katrina: 130,199.
Gemier, Firmin: 24,47; 284,9; 285,29; 286,62; 287,27; 295, 6.
Gendron, Pierre: 263,24.
Genee, Adeline: 77,192; 83,24; 85,65; 85,80; 87,128; 93,302; 103,78; 106,xv; 106,179; 107, 17; 115,70; 127,92; 129,166.
"General Crack": (F) 348,61.
"General John Regan": 154,176; (R) 154,177.
"General Post": 204,79; (R'17) 204,87.
"Genesee of the Hills": (R'07) 73,xvii.
"Genius, The": (R'06) 69,287.
"Genius and the Crowd": (R'20) 236,280; 236,283.
"Gentile Wife, The": (R'18) 216, 77.
Gentle, Alice: 117,138; 236, 271; 267,37.
"Gentleman from Gascony, A": 31,229.
"Gentleman from Mississippi, A": (R'08) 93,286; 93, 287.
"Gentleman of France, A": 11, 11; (R'02) 12,10; 23,16.
"Gentleman of Leisure, A": (R'11) 128,115; 128,137.
"Gentlemen Prefer Blondes": 309,12; (R'26) 309,16.
George, Carl: 91,236.
George, Charlotte: 46,315.
George, Gladys: 127,77; 215, 21; 335,47.
George, Grace: PG,13; 5,2; 10,5; 11,15; 12,c; 17,3; 23,8; 25,55; 26,83; 27,109; 39,124; 50,103; 57,274; 58, 298; 58,299; 59,14; 63,135; 68,c; 255; 69,294; 76,143; 76,146; 76,164; 78,216; 79, xi; 83,16; 91,229; 98,xviii; 98,126; 98,127; 99,160; 100, 194; 103,71; 107,8; 108,63; 114,38; 123,156; 132,42; 133,99; 139,67; 140,116; 147, 131; 151,80; 153,144; 159, 233; 160,295; 160,324; 176, 180; 177,232; 178,288; 179,5; 182,193; 183,273; 183,312; (W) 184,337; 190,349; 199, 121; 199,125; 201,264; 202, 350; 202,361; 203,13; 214, 335; 228,81; 229,183; 231, 363; 241,258; 250,5; 277,12; (D) 277,13; 289,16; 290,29; 346,12; 348,45; 352,32.
George, Lilian (W,V): 159,244.
George, Mlle.: (D) 142,179.
George, Yvonne: 263,27; 267,31.

"George": 268,13.
"George Bernard Shaw" (Chesterton) (B): 113,xi.
"George Bernard Shaw / His Life and Works" (Henderson) (B): 136,xiii.
"George Daudin": (R'24) 279, 19.
"George Washington": 230,247; (R'20) 230,272.
"George Washington, Jr.": (R'06) 61,xii; 62,86.
"George White Scandals" (see also "Scandals of 19--": (R'23) 269, 15; (R'25) 294,15; (R'26) 305,15; 330,27; (R'28) 330, 36; (R'28) 331,41; (D) 344, 22; (R'29) 344,70; 345,19.
Georgian, Grace: 173,24.
Georgie, Leyla: 284,14.
Gerald, Ara: 336,37.
Gerald, Vere: 37,68.
Gerard, Frederic: 118,198.
Gerard, Teddy: (D) 236,295.
Gerardy, Jean: 11,24; 13,27.
Gerhardt, Elena: 133,80; 134, 119; 166,272; 263,36.
Gerhauser, Emil: 22,34.
"German Drama of the Nineteenth Century, The" (Witkowski) (B) 103,iv.
German Films: 295,33.
German Opera: 88,151.
German Theatre: (see also Cohen, Bella (W): 13,18; 17,16; 35,4; 35,28; 40,156; 49,iii; 51,122; 62,xiii; 81,xxi; 81, 292; 81,311; 82,xxiii; 93, 289; 114,52; 120,42; 126, 56; 128,140; 137,5; 154,xx; 165,219; 221,30; 274,22; 316,50; 335,52; 336,35.
"Germania": (OP) 121,82.
Germanova, Maria: 259,216.
Germon, Effie: 78,222.
Gerrard, Alfred: 217,135; 238, 33.
Gerrard, Douglas: 70,337.
Gershwin, George: 276,la; 278, 34; 285,27; (W) 290,30; 299, 34; 300,52; 310,6; (W) 312, 14; (C) 341,23.
Gerson, Paul: (W) 69,308; 70,i.
Gerstenberg, Alice: 145,78; 176, 192; (W) 199,142.
Gervais, Blanche: 242,336.
Gerville-Reache, Jeanne: 82,351; 83,11; 93,309; 94,345; 95,12; 109,74; 110,iii; 120,56; (W) 134,123; 147,137; 153,167; 168,61.
Gest, Lillian: 256,28.
Gest, Morris: 202,340; 238,8; (C,W) 259,223; 264,12; 265, 38; (D) 266,10; 273,79; (W) 276,9; 276,29; (C) 278,11; 285,23; (C) 316,27; (C) 339, 41.
"Get-Rich-Quick Wallingford": (R'10) 117,xiii; 117,141; 201,284.
Getwell, Anetha: 246,176; 249, 433.
"Getting a Polish": (R'10) 118, xvii; 119,12.
"Getting Even": (R'29) 343,42.
"Getting Gertie's Garter": (R'21) 247,233; 247,239.
"Getting Married": 89,iv; 191, 27; (R'16) 190,358; 190,374; (S) 191,32.
"Getting Together": 207,283; (R'18) 207,286.
Geva, Tamara: 332,12; (C) 337, 35; 358,43.
Gheen, Gertrude: 54,186.
"Ghost of Jerry Blunder, The": (R'13) 154,xxii.
"Ghost Train, The": (R'26) 308,16.
"Ghosts": (R'03) 26,100; 55,218; 66,219; 196,340; (R'17) 196, 343; 206,226; (R'23) 274, 16; 303,19.
"Gianetta's Tears": (R'13) 145,67.
Giannini, Dusolina: 289,35.
Gibbons, Grace: 6,15.
Gibbs, Clayton E.: (W) 181,143.
Gibbs, E. Payton: 208,357.
Gibbs, Nancy: 246,169.
Gibbs, Robert Payton: 52,133; 109,70.
Gibson, Hoot: (A) 255,405; 309,48; 320,54.
Gibson, Lillian: 335,15.
Gibson, Madeline: 343,28.

Gibson, T.W.: 191,29; 199,151.
Gibson, Wynne: 335,23.
Giddens, George: 76,159; 120, 61; 144,57; 193,148.
Gieseking, Walter: 296,35;332,27.
Gifford, Electra: 11,24.
Gigli, Benjamino: 264;37; 279,35; 288,35; 300,35.
Gilbert, Anne Hartley (see also Gilbert, [Mrs.] G.H.): PG,4; 6,18; 11,1; 11,15.
Gilbert, Dolly: 330,36.
Gilbert, (Mrs.) G.H. (see also Gilbert, Anne Hartley): 22,26; 42,185; 46,xvi; 46,319; 47,8; 50,91; 52,150; 52,151; 62, viii; 126,65; 141,136; 169, 136; 171,234; 231,397; 235, 168.
Gilbert, Gladys: 200,209; 204,84.
Gilbert, Grace: 129,175.
Gilbert, Henry F.: 199,152.
Gilbert, John: 16,13; 238,28;247, 244; 294,33; 297,33; 297,50; 304,48; 305,53; 306,38; 306, 40; 312,40; 320,45; 324,34; 337,22.
Gilbert, Maud: 121,92; 134,133.
Gilbert, W.S. (see also Gilbert and Sullivan): 25,60; 82,ii; 86,91; 125,ix; 229,158;
Gilbert, William: 22,26; 52,151.
Gilbert and Sullivan (see also Gilbert, W.S.): 28,145; 159, 254; 200,195; 216,86.
Gilchrest, W. Forrest: 205,166; (W) 209,10.
Giles, Corliss: 204,125.
Gilfoil, Harry: 211,176.
Gilibert, Charles: 117,ii.
Gill, Basil: 140,98; 156,75.
Gill, Robert S.: 171,230.
Gillett, William: PG,3; 7,3; 8,13; 9,14; 17,22; 18,3; 35,1; 41, 174; 51,116; 55,227; 59,1; 60, 51; 64,167; 67,229; 70,xxiii; 70,338; 91,234; 93,295; 94,332; 94,333; 106,187; 118,xix; 122, 122; 151,78; 165,214; 166,266; 167,10; 175,110; 193,145; 200, 213; 216,77; 216,81; 216,84; 217,156; 220,351; (D) 222,84; 251,99; 346,11; (D) 346,38; 358,39.
Gillette, Viola: 10,6; 136,170; 137,3; 149,2.
Gilliam, Florence (W): 243, 396; 250,28; 266,22; 272,10.
Gillingwater, Claude: 118,176; 130,197; 190,390; 202,353; 215,9; 216,94; 249,395.
Gills, Gabrielle: 194,229; 214, 341.
Gilly, Dinh: 105,138; 129,155; (A) 134,xviii; 144,39; 145,69.
Gillyn, Allyn: 252,157.
Gillmore, Margalo: 226,366; 229,166; 246,150; 251,83; 253,231; 263,31; 292,25; 299,43; 303,32; 304,31; 309, 27; 310,27; 311,14; 316,18; 317,35; (D) 325,45; 326,15; 327,38; 330,56; 339,44; 341, 15; 346,32; (D) 347,2; 351, 39.
Gillmore, Ruth: 242,346.
Gilman, Katherine: 57,285.
Gilman, Lawrence: (W) 21,26.
Gilman, Mabelle: 22,8; 22,9; 23,12; 29,c; 42,vii; 75,133; 288,25.
Gilmore, Brian: 351,39.
Gilmore, Douglas: 300,42; 355, 48.
Gilmore, Ethel: 52,145.
Gilmore, Frank: 58,307; 62,87; 66,200; 73,62; 76,160; 94, 319; 104,109; 112,178; 117, 144; 131,25; 136,190; 137,10; 181,121; 224,222; 245,76; 248, 296; (W) 251,102; (W) 269, 25; (W) 278,7; 342,34.
Gilmore, Helen: 255,263.
Gilmore, Lowell: 335,47.
Gilmore, Mabel: 52,145.
Gilmore, Paul: 55,224.
Gilmore, Ray: 100,195.
Gilmour, J.H.: 14,2; 70,337; 216,69.
Gilpin, Charles S.: 238,8; 310, 10.
Gilson, Lottie: 302,25.
Giltner, Leigh Gordon (W): 27, 127.
"Gingerbread Man, The": (R'05) 60,ix.
"Gingham Girl, The": (R'22) 261,377; 261,387.

"Gioconda, La": (R'02) 22,6.
Giordano, Umberto: 80, 266.
Girard, Harry: 79,233.
Girard, Maxime: (W) 345,45.
Girard, Pearl: 79,233.
Girardot, Etienne: 51,112; 63, 136; 144,35; 269,18.
Girdlestone, Madge: 68,263.
"Girl and the Governor, The": (R'07) 73,61; 74,99.
"Girl and the Judge, The": 11,1; (R'02) 11,4.
"Girl and the Kaiser, The": (R'10) 119,xii; 119,5.
"Girl and the Pennant, The": 154, xxv; 154,203; (R) 154,xii.
"Girl and the Wizard, The": (R'09) 105,137; 105,141.
"Girl Behind the Counter, The": (see also "Step This Way"): (R'07) 81,289; 81,295; (C) 82,xxiv; 89,178.
"Girl Behind the Gun, The": 213,271.
"Girl Crazy": 357,26; (R'30) 357, 64.
"Girl Friend, The": (R'26) 303, 50.
"Girl from Brazil, The": (R'16) 188,204b; 189,280.
"Girl from Dixie, A": 33,277; (R'04) 35,4.
"Girl from Home, The": 232,505.
"Girl from Kay's, The" (see also "Belle of Bond Street, The"): 40,151.
"Girl from Montmartre, The": (R'12) 139,xi.
"Girl from Utah, The": (R'14) 164,157; 164,167.
"Girl He Couldn't Leave Behind Him, The": (R'10) 110,102.
"Girl in the Coffin, The": 203, 15; (R'17) 203,23; (R'20) 229,222.
"Girl in the Limousine, The": 225,315.
"Girl in the Spotlight, The": (R'20) 234,105; 234,107.
"Girl in the Train, The": (R'10) 117,xv; 118,176.
"Girl in Waiting, The": 114,34.
"Girl of My Dreams, The": (R'11) 127,79; 127,89.
"Girl of the Golden West, The": (R'05) 58,291; 59,18; 59,19; 102,65; (OP) 167,21; (F) 169,129; 231,349; (F) 356, 57.
"Girl of Today, The": 213,328.
"Girl O'Mine": (R'18) 205,151; 206,231.
"Girl on the Film, The": (R'14) 156,59; 156,69.
"Girl Patsy, The": (R'06) 65,171.
"Girl Who Has Everything, The": 64,139; 64,142; (R'06) 71, xiii; 71,2.
"Girl Who Smiles, The": (R'15) 175,113; 176,170.
"Girl with the Green Eyes, The": (R'03) 24,29; 169,132.
"Girl Question, The: (R'08) 91,x; 91,236; 91,239.
"Girlies": (R'10) 113,x; 114,42.
"Girls": (R'08) 87,vii; 87,131.
"Girls of Gottenberg, The": (R'08) 92,261; 92,281.
Girls' Collegiate School (Claremont, Calif.): 67,249.
"Girls Will Be Girls": 43,217; (R'04) 44,248.
"Girofle-Girofla": 34,307; 293,17.
"Giselle": 118,178; 130,198; 130, 200.
Gish, Dorothy (see also Gish Sisters): 207,323; 210,120; 216,123; 236,287; 251,108; 256,39; 269,34; 269,35; 272, 30; 275,32; 277,30; 283,31; (C) 286,15; 287,32; 297,33; 309,3a; 320,14; (W) 320,15; 321,32; 350,17; (D) 351,18; 351,45; 352,21.
Gish Sisters: 164,161; 250,37; 256,28; 261,385; 306,40.
Gitchell, Virginia: 183,277; 204, 101.
"Give Me Yesterday": 361,12.
Given, Susan": 232,518.
Given, Thelma: 215,11.
"Glad of It": (R'03) 36,32.
Glad, Gladys: 306,21; 314,49; 315,31; 339,64.
Gladney, Kitty: 213,273.
Glamis Castle (Scotland): 48, 47; 49,viii; 52,iv.

Glaser, Lulu: PG, 20; 9, 22; 12, 5; 13, 11; 18, c; 44, 245; 44, 257; (W) 52, 140; 55, 220; 56, 241; 73, 60; 80, 274; 80, 286; 84, 35; 93, x; 93, 284; 95, 28; 111, 144; 112, 203; 113, 17; 119, xii; 119, 5; (A) 128, xviii; 134, 132; 284, 52.
Glaser, Vaughan: 110, 126; 145, 80.
Glass, Bonnie: 179, 31; 230, 292.
Glass, Everett: 203, 35; 208, 359.
"Glass Slipper, The": (R'25) 297, 18.
Glass, Gaston: 262, 35.
Glass, Julia: 261, 391.
Glaum, Louise: 192, 97; 203, 64; 216, 119.
Gleason, James: 289, 17; 293, 18; (W) 296, 12; 302, 21; 303, 32; 322, 39; 323, 47.
Gleason, James A.: 165, 206.
Gleason, James W.: (W) 231, 478.
Gleason, Lucille Webster: 341, 32; (W) 341, 33.
Glecker, Robert: 331, 30.
Glendale High School (Calif.); 292, 44.
Glendinning, Ernest: 116, 125; 117, 158; 154, xxvi; 154, 197; 167, 31; 168, 77; 172, 279; 203, 19; 218, 209; 226, 379; 238, 18; (A) 238, 72; 242, 337; 338, 32.
Glendinning, Jessie: 164, 159; 221, 12.
Glendinning, John: 52, 133.
Glendon, J. Frank: 212, 253.
"Glikering Gloria": 42, ii.
"Glittering Gate, The": (R'15) 170, 211.
"Glittering Gloria": 37, 57; (R'04) 37, 58.
Globe Theatre: (D) 182, 206.
"Gloria" 85, iii; 85, 66.
Gloria, Adelaide: 221, 17.
"Glorianna": 214, 339; (R'18) 214, 378.
"Gloria's Romance": 186, 66; (F) 188, 220.
"Glorious Betsy": 76, 157; (R'08) 92, xxiv; 92, 256.
"Glory of the Morning": 143, 27.
Glose, Augusta: 31, 217.
Glover, Amelia: 203, 27.
Gluck, Alma: 110, 107; 119, 31; 129, 155; 131, 4; 192, 95; 234, 98.
Gluck, Elizabeth: 126, 47.
Gluck, Senia: 304, 29.
Glyn, Elinor: 247, 244; 279, 32; (W) 319, 16.
Glynde, Rita: 282, 38.
Glyndon, Virginia: 10, 5.
Glynne, Derek: 344, 40; 344, 56.
Glynne, Mary: 298, 22.
"Go Easy, Mabel": (R'22) 256, 32.
"Go to It": 190, 354; (R'16) 190, 392.
"Go West, Young Man": (F, R) 217, 191.
"Goat Song": (R'26) 301, 16; 301, 17.
Gobbi, Caterina: 298, 35.
"God of Vengeance, The": (R'23) 265, 20; 269, 25.
Goddard, Henry P. (W): 66, 206; 69, 295; 72, 45; 74, 100; 81, 298; 91, 237; 120, 63; 139, 82; 150, 70.
Goddard, Paulette: 301, 13.
"Goddess of Liberty, The": (R'09) 108, xvi.
"Goddess of Reason, The": 97, 72; (R'09) 98, 105.
Godowsky, Dagmar: 282, 33.
Godowsky, Leopold; 141, 140; 170, 184; 185, 25.
"Gods of the Lightning": (R'28) 334, 47.
"Gods of the Mountain, The": (R'16) 191, 23; (R'19) 217, 144.
Goethe, Wolfgang: 63, 124; 63, 126; 112, 190.
"Goetz von Berlichingen": 84, iii.
Goff, Jerry: (C) 348, 36.
Goff, Marie: 223, 148; 330, 41.
"Goin' Home": 332, 47.
"Going Some": (R'09) 99, viii; 99, 138.
"Going Up": (R'17) 204, 88; 204, 93.
Gold, Daniel: 117, 141.

"Gold": (R'21) 245,97.
"Gold Circle, The": (S) 256, 42.
"Gold Diggers, The": 226,370; (R'19) 226,436; (D) 228,85; (F,R) 272,32.
"Gold Diggers of Broadway, The": (F) 344,71.
"Gold Rush, The": (F,R) 296,30.
Goldberg, Maurice: 290,49.
"Golden Butterfly, The": (R'08) 93,xiii; 93,283.
Golden, Beatrice: 54,206.
Golden, Bernice: 33,280.
Golden, Ernie: 295,37.
Golden, John L.: 184,351; 246, 166; 248,292; 258,149; (W) 269,22; 275,39; (W) 276, 22; 281,39; 283,39; 283,42; 292,29; 306,15; (W) 312,7; (D) 318,31; (W) 333,13; 359, 39.
Golden, Richard: 48,38; 80,260; 103,ix.
Golden, Sylvia B.: (W) 306, 35; 319,44; (W) 330,24; (W) 331,20; (W) 334,48; (W) 350, 22; 352,18; 353,18; 354,18; 356,21; 357,39; 358,21; 358, 40; 359,18.
"Golden Days": (R'21) 250,64.
"Golden Doom, The": (R'19) 217, 144.
Goldfaden, Abram: 11,16.
Goldfinch, Mrs.: 51,117; 52,146.
"Goldfish, The": 256,21; (R'22) 256,31.
Goldfish, Samuel (see also Goldwyn, Samuel): 203,55.
Goldknopf, Abraham: 143,6.
Goldsmith, Frank: 146,105; 199, 135.
Goldsmith, Oliver: 76,158; 145, 74.
Goldsmith, Ted (W): 359,21; 360,30; 361,37.
Goldwyn, Samuel (see also Goldfish, Samuel): 336,38; 340, 34; 354,31.
Goldwyn Pictures: 201,316.
Goldwyn Stars: 199,180.
"Golem, The": (F,R) 246,174; (F) 246,175.
Gollan, Campbell: 14,6; 45, 275; 46,325; 80,275.
Golschmann, Vladimir: 285,34.
Gombel, Minna: 162,77; 165, 216; 205,137; 205,148; 225, 309; (D) 331,19; 338,17; 348,25; 348,46.
Gondre, Mona: 267,31; 280,35.
Gong, Charles: 29,170.
"Good Bad Woman, A": (R'19) 220,344; 220,345.
"Good Boy": (R'28) 333,78.
"Good Fellow, The": (R'26) 309, 18.
"Good Gracious, Annabelle!": (R'16) 190,358; (F) 217, 185.
"Good Hope, The": (R'07) 73,58; 74,105; 293,46; (R'27) 322,70.
"Good Little Devil, A": (R'13) 144,xiv; 144,35.
"Good Men Do, The": (R'18) 209,22.
"Good Morning, Dearie": (R'21) 250,32.
"Good Morning, Judge": (R'19) 217,144; 217,163.
"Good News": 329,39.
"Good-Night, Paul": 200,203; (R'17) 200,207.
"Good Old Days, The": (R'23) 271,19.
"Good Times": (R'20) 235,242.
Goodal, Edythe: 232,528.
Goodall, Elizabeth: 124,187.
Goodall, Grace: 218,225.
Goodman, Edward (W): 160, 299; 162,72; 166,290; 196, 327; 235,162; 291,36; 292,7; 303,16.
Goodman, Jules Eckert: 115,81; 115,82; 179,17; 188,198; (A) 231,346; 231,395.
Goodman Memorial Theatre (Chicago): 303,37.
Goodner, Carol: 352,33.
Goodrich, Arthur: 204,75.
Goodrich, C.W.: 279,18.
Goodrich, Charles C.: 197,37.
Goodrich, Edna: 69,287; 72,47; 86,109; 125,28; 151,81; 153, 147; 156,77; 186,87; 192, 100; 201,317; 202,405; 203, 59; 204,128; 205,195.

Goodrich, Marc (W) (see also "Those Who Sit in Judgment"): 296,9; 296,24.
Goodson, Katharine: 170,184.
Goodwin, Gloria: 192,84.
Goodwin, Henrietta: 334,45.
Goodwin, Nat C.: PG,26; 3,6; 4,6; 4,7; 5,4; 23,6; 23,7; 32,248; 33,270; 36,40; 46,296; 47,11; 49,vii; 56,328; 63,116; 69,287; 86,xii; 86,109; 134,xiii; 134,127; 135,167; 168,104; 171,233; 178,288; 186,87; 204,103; 205,157; (C) 209,22; 214,360; 217,173; 231,363; 231,397.
Goodwin, Ruth: 256,40; 330,36; 336,27.
"Goose Hangs High, The": (R'24) 277,15.
Gootsched, Louise: 27,116.
Gorcey, Bernard: 269,17.
Gordin, Jacob: 11,18; 101,xi.
Gordon, Charles K.: 233,18.
Gordon, Claire: 64,161.
Gordon, Diana: 263,33.
Gordon, Dorothy F.: 181,127.
Gordon, Eleanor: 135,164; 190,347.
Gordon, Elsie Mae: 361,40.
Gordon, Frances: 91,244; 91,246; 105,134.
Gordon, Grace: 186,67.
Gordon, Jeanne: 227,45; 242,335; 267,37; 276,35; 300,35.
Gordon, Kate: 218,228.
Gordon, Kitty; 58,313; 61,72; 105,141; 108,c; 111,154; 117,142; 117,159; 122,107; 123,172; 130,217; 136,189; 145,78; 149,13; 159,272; 177,243; 178,330; (A) 178,337; 179,35; 179,47; 184,c; 184,329; (A) 194,237; 195,299; (A) 197,49; 199,167; (A) 201,305; 205,172; 209,39; 210,82; 224,256; (A) 226,425; 229,202; 259,250.
Gordon, Leon: 213,275; 214,363; 276,26.
Gordon, Letitia: 88,155.
Gordon, M.: 35,12.
Gordon, Maude Turner: 108,41; 158,172.
Gordon, Maxim (W): 294,22.
Gordon, Melanie: 235,182.
Gordon, Mitzi: (A) 180,107.
Gordon, Paul: 177,231; 266,18.
Gordon, Richard: 110,102; 113,20.
Gordon, Roy: 192,84.
Gordon, Ruby: 200,193.
Gordon, Ruth: 202,361; 204,76; 205,161; (C) 209,22; 271,13; 289,39; 299,33; 306,25; 314,22; 316,24; (C) 318,25; 318,33; (C) 319,72; 329,33; 336,50; 337,54; 339,38; 350,14; 351,44; 357,29;
Gordon, Vera: 202,348; 217,152.
Gordon, William C.: 304,19; (D) 323,23.
Gorham, Mercy (W): 167,21.
"Gorilla, The": 292,14; (R'25) 292,15; (F) 357,61.
Gorin, Bernard (W): 11,16; 42,204.
Goritz, Otto: 118,173; 135,162; 142,166; 156,68.
Gorki, Maxim: 49,xvi; 58,ii.
Gorman, George: 112,187.
Gorman, Ross: 296,37.
Gorst, Edmund (W): 115,88.
Gosnell, Evelyn: 217,140; 222,110; 223,196; 234,83; 240,194.
Gosnell, Vivian: 168,66.
Goose, Edmund: (W,V) 15,15.
Gossens, Eugene: 274,36.
"Gossipy Sex, The": (R'27) 315,24.
Gotthold, Rozel (W): 174,78; 180,82; 210,100; 171,248.
Gottschalk, Ferdinand: (A) 3,17; 13,12; 15,5; 38,86; 44,243; 62,103; 69,xiii; (C) 82,xxiv; 105,144; 105,145; 107,9; 109,93; 118,172; 159,226; 176,168; 188,204; 226,375; 255,351; 264,21; 268,28; 281,14; 229,15.
Gottschalk, Robert: 192,73.
Gould, (Mrs.) George: 86,106; 209,17.
Gould, Harold W.: 198,89.
Gould, Howard: 14,5; 134,127; 171,236.
Gould, Jay: 115,76; 115,78.

Gould, Norma: 329,29.
Gould, Rita: 181,146.
Goudal, Jetta: 266,49; 307,37; 316,38; 320,66; 321,75; 322, 6; 323,21.
Goudiss, C. Houston (W): 205,178.
Gounod, Charles Francois: 182, 220.
Gouraud, Yvonne: 197,35.
"Governor's Boss, The": (R'14) 160,320.
"Governor's Lady, The": (R'12) 140,100; 140,103; 140,104; 161,8.
"Governor's Son, The": (R'06) 65, 170.
"Goyescas": (OP) 181,154.
"Grab Bag, The": (R'24) 285,70.
Grady, Alfred: 99,158; 145,71; 145,73.
Graham, Annie: 86,iii.
Graham, Benjamin: 140,118.
Graham, George: 117,136; 165,207; 283,25; 349,45.
Graham, Gertrude: 51,112.
Graham, Martha: 357,45; 360, 38.
Graham, R.E.: 81,313.
Graham, Richard (W): 240,174.
"Grain of Dust, The": 129,177; (R'12) 132,xi; 132,72; (F) 208,395.
Grainger, Percy: 178,286; 202, 363.
Gran, Albert: 273,18.
Granados, Enrique: 181,154.
"Grand Army Man, A": (C) 82, xxiv; (R'07) 82,318; 82, 349.
"Grand Duchess and The Waiter, The": (R'25) 297,15.
"Grand Duke, The": 250,25; (R'21) 250,29; (D) 250,33.
"Grand Hotel": (R'30) 358,25; 358,28; 359,31; (S) 359,33; 360,30; 361,42.
"Grand Mogul, The": (R'07) 75, 116; 75,141.
Grand Opera House (Memphis): 61, xiv.
Grand Rapids High School (Michigan): 124,212.
"Grand Street Follies, The": (R'24) 282,15; (R'25) 294, 15; 294,21; (R'26) 305,15; 316,19; (R'29) 340,42.
Grand Theatre (Cadiz, Spain): 109,90.
Grand Theatre (Owensboro, Ky.): 65,xii.
Grand Guignol, The: 30,191; 54,202; 76,xiii; 82,xi; 88, 170; 269,7; 269,20; 270,13; 273,70.
"Grande Duchesse, La": (D) 134,129.
Grandin, Elmer: 77,191.
Grandin, Ethel: 168,69.
Grandpre, Marie: 68,274.
Granger, Maude: 63,123; 80, 279; 165,214; 189,277; 331, 80.
Granier, Jeanne: 36,vi; 54,203.
"Granny": (R'04) 46,294; 46, 319.
"Granny Maumee": (R'17) 195, 280.
Grant, Earle: 162,72.
Grant, Lawrence: 104,113; 193, 145.
Grant, Percy Stickney (W): 15,10; 208,342.
Grant, Valentine: 188,201.
Granville, Bernard: 129,177; 201,294.
Granville, Charlotte: 120,36; 130,183; 261,374; 338,48; 339,29.
Granville, Taylor: 55,213.
"Grass": (F, R) 291,32.
"Grasshopper": (R'17) 195,280.
Grassi, Amata: 278,37.
Grasso, Giovanni: 250,14; 250,15; 325,47.
Grattan, Lawrence: 284,24;
Grattan, Stephen: 83,2.
Grau, Maurice: (A) 3,1; 3,14; 10,28; 17,23; 75,xxv; 115,76; 135,153; 168,75; 231,379.
Grau, Robert (W): 112,184; 116,117; 119,7; 122,135; 124, 195; 134,126; 135,153; 137, 14; 150,68; 159,254; 161, 28; 170,191; 171,244; 172, 307; 173,25.
Grauer, Ben: 289,14.
Graves, Ralph: 242,350; 351, 66.

Gray, Eden: 263,33.
Gray, Gilda: 223,148; 253,213; 259,253; 266,3; 268,48; (A) 269,57; 277,64; 281,1; 281, 21; 282,65; 286,51; 287,23; 289,46; 294,31; 297,42; 297, 46; 297,50;303,c; 312,49; 314,69; 315,47; 317,59; 319, 71; 331,60; 337,53; 339,38; 345,61.
Gray, Jane: 133,94.
Gray, Larry: 327,4b; 354,46.
Gray, Maude: 129,175.
"Great Actors of the Eighteenth Century" (Mantzius) (B): 100,xi.
"Great Adventure, The": 153,142; (R'13) 154,179; 242,343.
"Great Broxopp, The": (R'21) 251,128.
"Great Caesar's G'oats' ": 271, 10.
"Great Catherine": (R'16) 191,21.
"Great Day!": 343,16.
"Great Divide, The": (R'06) 69, 283; 69,285; 188,200; (R'17) 193,152; 231,349; (F,R) 289, 32.
"Great Gatsby, The": 301,19; (R'26) 301,64.
"Great God Brown, The": (R'26) 301,18; 301,23; (S) 308, 26; 308,28.
"Great John Ganton, The": (R'09) 100,168.
"Great Lover, The": 178,275; (R'15) 178,277; 179,19.
"Great Match, The": (R'05) 56,243.
"Great Moment, The": (F,R) 247, 244.
"Great Music": (R'24) 285,76.
"Great Name, The": (R'11) 121, 79; 129,150; 129,168.
"Great Necker, The": (R'28) 326,41.
"Great Pursuit, The": (R'16) 183,274.
"Great Question, The": (R'08) 94, x; 94,315.
"Great Scott": (R'29) 344,47.
"Great Temptations, The": (R'26) 305,15; 305,19.
"Greater Love, The": (R'06) 63, x; 63,122.
"Greatest Notion, The": 182,230.
"Greatest Thing in Life, The": (F,R) 216,124.
Greaza, Walter: 344,47; 345,49.
"Greed": (F,R) 287,30.
Greek Drama: 39,123; 175, 116; 249,398; 327,15.
Greeley, Evelyn: 199,177; 210, 120; (D) 221,c; 245,114.
Green, Al: 357,48.
Green, Burt: 180,72.
Green, Doris: 255,372.
Green, Dorothy: 172,289; (A) 189,311.
Green, Ethel: 123,144; 124,188.
Green, Harry: 270,34.
Green, Lillian: 5,5.
Green, Marion: (D) 251,101; 255,365.
Green, Millicent: 337,27.
Green, Mitzi: 360,48.
Green, Yetta Dorothea (W): 152,126.
"Green Beetle, The": 283,14; (R'24) 284,19.
"Green Coat, The": (S) 144,50.
"Green Cockatoo, The": (R'10) 111,xxix.
"Green Derby, The": (S) 297,22.
"Green Goddess, The": (R'21) 240,224; 241,255; (F) 350,63.
"Green Grow the Lilacs": 360, 26; (R'30) 361,26.
"Green Hat, The": 290,10; 294, 14; (R'25) 296,15.
"Green Knight, The": 132,64.
"Green Pastures, The": 349, 15; 349,16; 350,28; (S) 350, 32; (R) 350,46; 351,13; 351, 23; (D) 357,16; 360,14.
"Green Ring, The": (R'22) 255, 374.
"Green Room Book, The" (Hunt) (B): 66,x.
"Green Stockings": (R'11) 129, 148; 129,171.
Greenburger, Sanford J. (W): 305,12.
Greene, Charles N.: 192,73.
Greene, Clay: 6,10; 83,30.
Greene, Daisy: 6,14.
Greene, Evie: 47,3.
Greene, J.H.: 200,209; (W,V) 206,235.

Greene, Jeanne: 337,46; 338, 48.
Greene, Margaret: 140,113; 161,29; 187,147; 195,290.
Greene, P. Clayton: 166,280.
Greene, Paul: 259,245.
Greene, Rosalind: 359,40.
Greene, Walter: 68,271; 107,7.
Greene's Opera House (Cedar Rapids): 63,xv.
Greenroom Club, The: 33,279.
Greenstreet, Sidney: 81,308; 129,172; 161,6; 184,359; 221,9; 353,34.
Greenwall, Harry J. (W): 152, xvii; 162,74; 171,257; 174, 75.
Greenwich Village: 198,93; (D) 223,143; 281,48; (D) 292, 36.
"Greenwich Village Follies": 222, 75; 222,89; (R'19) 223,152; 223,153; 236,259; (R'20) 236,279; 237,375; (R'21) 248,314; 250,27; 251,82; (D) 259,256; 260,293; (R'22) 260, 299; (R'23) 272,54; (D) 283, 27; (R'24) 284,64; (R'25) 300,18; 304,25.
Greenwich Village Players: 208, 356; 208,359.
Greenwich Village Theatre: 203, 22; 203,35; 282,7; 294,7.
Greenwood, Barrett: 206,231.
Greenwood, Charlotte: 155,31; 227, 20; (C) 263,11; 280,27; 290, 46; (C) 318,37.
Greer, Howard (W):218,216; 222, 78; 227,22; 235,176.
Greet, Ben: 28,132; 38,82; 38, 99; 41,163; 41,179; 42,211; 57,xi; 58,xix; 61,70; 74,xiii; 90,iv; 94,320; 111,xxv; 111, 142; 137,9; 139,78; 170,197; 207,295.
Gregory, Elizabeth Hiatt (W): 192,78; 193,156; 196,338.
Gregory, Eva: 305,46.
Gregory, George: 80,270.
Gregory, Gilbert: 29,181; 76, 169.
Gregory, Heathe: 25,78.
Gregory, J.P. (W): 293,12.
Gregory, Lady: 29,167; 29,168.
Gregory, Paul: (C) 337,35.
Greig, Evelyn: 199,157.
Grein, J.T. (W): 82,ii; 285, 3a; 286,26; 288,20; 292,22; 294,20; 296,20; 297,24; 298, 22.
Greneker, C.P.: 331,49.
Grenelle, Helen: (D) 275,27.
Grenville, Lillian: 119,9; 122, 114.
Grehsam, Herbert: 187,132.
Gretchaninoff, Alexander: 338, 43.
"Gretna Green": 24,31; (R'03) 24,32.
Greuze, Lillian: 177,225; 178, 289; 179,50; (A) 179,52; 184, 338.
Grey, Alexander: 274,29.
Grey, Eden: 286,21.
Grey, Jane: 117,131; 145,86; 151,104; 153,159; 157,141; 159,250; 166,265; 184,353; 200,197; 207,308; 217,135; 243,400; 295,19.
Grey, John: 152,124; 152,125; (W,V) 174,85.
Grey, Katherine: 3,3; 15,22; 40,136; 45,270; 45,286; 52, 136; 62,88; 74,86; 75,117; (W) 78,210; 86,94; 103,86; 138,49; 147,142; 158,170; 159,239; 172,307.
Grey, Lita: 279,33.
"Grey Fox, The": (R'28) 334,60.
"Greyhound, The": (R'12) 134, xv.
Gribble, Henry Wagstaffe: 249, 378.
Gribbon, Harry: 357,61.
Gribbon, Marie Louise: 72,53.
Gribunin, Vladimir: 259,217.
Grieg, Edward: 73,66; 81,316.
"Grierson's Way": (R'06) 61, 57; 61,75.
Griffen, Alfred: 243,452.
Griffen, Gerald: 98,120.
Griffen, Marie Louise: 77,178.
Griffes, Ethel: 284,18.
Griffin, Russell: 337,27.
Griffith, Corinne: 216,123; 227, 44; 245,113; 274,33; 279,33; 282,33; 288,32; 298,32; 306, 52; 319,44; 321,26; 331,33;

(D) 337, c; 347, 23.
Griffith, David Wark: 160, 311; 161, 48; 170, 212; 171, 244; 188, 217; 203, 58; 208, 398; 216, 121; 217, 191; 219, 300; 220, 400; (D) 220, 401; 231, 389; 231, 488; (D) 238, 72; 244, 38; 250, 38; 251, 108; 276, 32; 277, 32; 278, 30; 287, 32; 295, 32; 309, 40; (D) 318, 25; (W) 319, 21.
Griffith, Eleanor: 241, 263; 245, 101; 277, 63; 294, 46; 315, 25.
Griffith, Linda: 199, 181.
Griffith, Raymond (D): 293, 4; 297, 30.
Griffith, William (W): 74, 97.
"Griffith Gaunt": (D) 134, 130.
Grimm, Lores: 40, 147.
Grimwood, Herbert: 235, 192; 268, 14.
Grinell, Helen: 249, 380.
"Gringo": (R'22) 263, 19.
Grippon, Eva: 104, 114.
"Griselda": 110, xvi.
Grismer, Joseph R.: 34, 306; 255, 354.
Griswold, Grace: 149, vi.
Griswold, Mabel: 230, 268.
Griswold, Putna: 46, 315; 114, 54; 131, 6; 134, 109; (A) 137, xiv; 146, 106.
Groff, Catherine Louise (W): 301, 30.
Groody, Louise: 207, 303; 213, 269; 230, 275; 232, 497; 233, 9; 280, 27; 291, 11; 298, 17; 316, 11; 325, 21.
Gropper, Milton Herbert: 277, 29.
Gropper, William: (C) 308, 25.
Gros, Ernest: 90, 204.
Gross, Bessie: 160, 285.
Gross, Samuel Eberle: 17, 13.
Grosser, Kurt: 93, 289.
Grosses Schauspielhaus (Berlin): 237, 372.
Grossman, C. Edwin Booth: (W) 53, 179.
Grossmith, George: 13, 12; 44, 246; 156, 69; 197, 40.
Grossmith, Lawrence: 172, 297; 252, 152; 352, 34.
Grossmith, Weldon: 21, 6.
"Grotesques": (S) 184, 349; (R) 244, 60.
"Grounds For Divorce: (R'24) 285, 16.
Grove, Fred: 156, 63.
Grove Street Theatre (New York): 303, 24.
Grover, Jane: 135, 148.
Grover's Theatre (Washington, D.C.): 47, 16.
Grube, Max: 125, 24.
"Grumpy": (R'13) 155, 48; 160, 310; (F, R) 267, 34.
Grunberg, Alfred (W): 178, 298; 186, 82; 189, 298.
Grundy, Sidney: 12, 3.
"Guardsman, The": (R'24) 285, 15; 287, 17; 288, 23.
Guenther, Mizzi; 90, 207; 160, 305.
Guenther, Virginia: 185, 34.
Guerite, Laura; 76, 167; 98, 130.
Guerreri, Giovanni: 339, 49.
Guerrero, Maria: 44, 259.
Guerrero, Rosario: 37, 60.
"Guest of Honor, The": (R'20) 238, 76.
Guett, Lucienne: 123, 177; 123, 178; 124, 214.
Guhl, Edward J.: 228, 389.
"Guibour": 241, 239; (R'21) 241, 298.
Guild Theatre (New York): (D) 286, 9; 287, 27; 291, 17; 292, 12.
Guild Thacher H.: (W, V) 126, 43.
Guilbert, Yvette: 41, iv; 46, 303; 60, 36; 60, 46; 61, 78; 62, xiv; 83, v; 176, 187; 179, 10; 185, 6; (W) 190, 366; 241, 298; 242, 385; 255, 359.
Guilford, Nanette: 269, 36; 278, 35; 303, 35.
"Guilty": (R'03) 23, 8.
"Guilty Man, The": 188, 193; (R'16) 188, 204a.
Guimard, Madalene:)D) 178, 314.
Guinan, Frances: 353, 23.
Guinan, Texas: 201, 321; (C) 284, 8; 330, 16.
Guinness, [Mrs.] Benjamin: 196, 339.
Guion, Raymond: 297, 26; 350, 46.

Guitry, Lucien: 24,49; 36, vi; 110,116; 112,185; 136, 174; 163,118; 261,379; 264, 24.
Guitry, Sacha: 143,23; (C) 163,118; (D) 239,82; 259, 224; 264,25; 266,19; 266, 20; 281,22; 309,33; 312, 19; 312,21; (W) 312,32.
Gulda, Gerda: 212,199.
Gullan, Campbell: 129,153; 325, 39.
"Gum Shoe Girl, The": 100,176.
Gumbinner, Paul G. (W): 321, 25; 324,27; 329,16; 333,36.
Gunning, Louise: 22,20; 45,276; 71,4; 75,119; 81,320; 83,1; 91,245; 93,288; 93,304; 94, 328; 121,74;122,c; (A) 125, xiv; 125,13; 126,66; 132,58.
Gunsbourg, Raoul: 240,169.
Gurney, Edmund: 166,309.
Gurney, [Mrs.] Edmund: 166, 262; 190,374; 201,291.
Gustafson, William: 279,35.
Gustine, Harriet: 284,26.
Guthrie, Phoebe: 360,37.
Guthrie, William N.: 140,122.
Guy Sisters: 305,19.
Guzman, Pearl: 46,315.
Gwynn, Nell: 111,136; 142,175; (D) 275,10; (D) 354,18.
"Gypsy, The": (R'12) 142,xx; 142,181.
Gypsy Actors: 33,294; 34, 294.
"Gypsy Jim": (R'24) 276,66.
"Gypsy Love": (R'11) 130,x.
"Gypsy Trail, The": 203,19; (R'17) 203,22.

--H--

"H.M.S. Pinafore": (R'11) 125, 4; 125,11; 125,13; 132,58; 159,223; 159,254; (R'14) 159,259; (R'26) 303,50.
Habima Players: 308,20; 311,15.
"Habit": (R'18) 205,151; 205, 159.
Hackathorne, George: 252,175.
Hackett, Albert: 100,189.
Hackett, Arleen: 190,374; 191, 32.
Hackett, Carlo: 217,136.
Hackett, Charles: 276,35; 298, 35.
Hackett, Dollie: 186,102.
Hackett, Jeanette: 269,43; 281, 37.
Hackett, James Henry: 14,21; 47,13; 68,275; (D) 149,16; (D) 193,146; 211,150.
Hackett, James Keteltas: PG,3; 3,3; 6,c; 6,2; 7,3; 8,7; 8,9; 10,10; 13,7; 16,4; 17, 9; 22,25; 23,9; 23,17; 26, 83; 32,238; 34,318; 36,48; 41,175; 41,182; 47,4; 47,13; 47,15; 57,277; 61,59; 67, 228; (W) 68,275; 79,228; 79,229; 82,xxvi; 83,23; 84, 34; 93,vii; 127,77; 129,177; 132,xi; 132,72; 146,114; 149,16; 180,62; 181,123; 197, 9; 228,91; 231,365; 240,153; 240,214; 260,285; 357,21.
Hackett, Karleton (W): 130,214; 134,120; 141,141; 145,84.
Hackett, Norman: 37,80; 66, 211; 81,293.
Hackett, Raymond: 105,151; 297,26.
Hackett, Stephen: 16,1; 16,5.
Hackett, W.A.: 70,320.
Hackney, Mabel: 100,iii; 108, 34; 111,131.
Hadaway, Tom: 99,158.
Haddon, Noel: 177,222; 194, 223.
Hadfield, Henry J.: 70,336.
Hading, Jane: 8,15; 24,49; 36, vi; 130,223; 130,226; (D) 146,103.
Hadley, Grace T. (W): 218,212.
Hadley, Henry: 205, 147; 229, 173; 278,34.
Hageman, Richard: 215,26.
Haggert, John: 316,19.
Haggin, Ben Ali (see also Tableaux): (D) 213,289; 214,354; (W) 231,393; 241, 263; 246,168; 247,223.
Haggin, (Mrs.) Ben Ali: 201, 270.
Hagman, Harriet: 353,28.
Haid, Liane: 263,35.
Haig, Emma: 186,71; 198,90; 210,85; 259,237; 278,23.

Haight, George (W): 341,48.
"Hail and Farewell": 266,18.
Haines, Genevieve G.: 16, 2; 16,23; 55,227; 68,264.
Haines, Robert: 8,4; 9,7; 27, 115; 48,42; (A) 54,183f; 68, 255; 69,294; 76,164; 100, 189; 106,198; 172,301; 256, 21; 308,19; 359,25.
"Hairy Ape, The": 254,283; (R'22) 254,305; 255,370; (S) 257, 80; 257,102; (C) 346,39.
Haisley, Wayne (W): 315,18.
Hainsman, Irene:174,88; 218,217.
Hajos, Mitzi (see also Mitzi): 123,172; 143,14; 148,174; 156,63; 156,104; 158,192; 170,193; 182,196; 186,64; 186,73.
"Hakuba and Hekuba": (R'27) 315, 26.
Halbe, Max: 17,17; 137,5.
Halbert, Ruth: 43,vi.
Hale, Alan: 326,77.
Hale, Betty: 221,14; 230,268.
Hale, Chester: 250,9; 253,243; 257,89; 294,17.
Hale, Creighton: 154,177; 177, 230.
Hale, Helen: 64,164; 79,249; 95,6.
Hale, Louis Closser: 36,39; 50, 103; 63,112; 83,6; 107,7; 137,29; 167,35; 170,176; 180, 62; 193,165; (W) 218,214; 241,268; 263,31; 265,18; 280,14; 286,38; 304,27.
Hale, Marion: 151,88.
Hale, Philip: 76,158; 76,159.
Hale, Richard: 304,64; 305,33; 332,47.
Hale, Walter: 28,136; 28,137; 83,6; 88,157; 145,78.
Hales, Ethelbert: 275,17.
Haley, Jack: 337,30.
"Half a Widow": (R'27) 320,24.
"Half an Hour": (R'13) 153, 146; 154,xxv.
"Half Caste": (R'26) 303,18.
"Half Gods": (R'29) 347,66.
"Half Moon, The": (R'20) 238, 30.
"Half Shot at Sunrise": (F,R) 357,50.
Hall, Adelaide: 295,21.
Hall, Alfred: 221,7.
Hall, Al K.: 275,37.
Hall, Anna: 80,273.
Hall, Artie: 129,175.
Hall, Bettina: (D) 323,23.
Hall, Blanche: 119,19.
Hall, Donald: 80,270; 118,176.
Hall, Dorothy: 297,45; 328,46; 336,52; 337,60; 359,24.
Hall, Franklin: 228,103.
Hall, Georgie Lee: 308,19.
Hall, Grace: 235,182.
Hall, Howard: 132,39; 145,72; 145,73; 149,vi; 171,260.
Hall, Laura Nelson: 29,160; 77,186; 82,xvii; 87,131; 91, 252; 97,80; 102,45; 103,72; 118,181; 122,118; 122,119; 122,121; 123,c; 125,29; 145, 73; 156,77; 157,141; 187, 145.
Hall, Marion E.: 335,46.
Hall, Mary: 221,21; 245,89.
Hall, Pauline: 31,234; 37,70; 136,173; 149,17; 221,19; 254,299.
Hall, Porter: 334,25; (C) 344,44.
Hall, Spalding: 189,269.
Hall, Thurston: 93,302; 166, 263; 243,301; 348,13.
"Hall of Fame, The": (R'02) 13,7; 13,8.
Hall Sisters (Bettina & Natalie): 344,53; 351,17; 352,41; 353,55.
Hallam, Basil: 109,66.
Hallams, The: 19,18; 112,181; 136,198.
Halland, C.M.: 68,263.
Halle, Jeanne: 267,47.
Halleck, Grace: 142,165.
Halliday, John: 270,8; (D) 315,23; 315,25; 334,46; 335, 30.
Halligan, William: 263,43.
Halliley, Reginald: 314,25.
Hallor, Edith: 200,203; 201, 289; 212,257; 217,147; (A) 238,72.
Halloran, John: 352,32.
Halperin, Nan: 200,217; 289, 37.
Halstead, Lenore: 107,4.

Halton, Charles: 133,97; 229, 167; 232,519; 289,14.
Halton, George: 357,36.
"Ham Tree, The": (R'05) 56, vii.
Hamburger, Estelle (W): 230, 256; 237,376; 239,108.
Hambourg, Mark: 170,184.
Hamer, Gerald: 170,197; 233,23.
Hamill, Kathryn: 356,1; 356, 39.
"Hamilton": (R'17) 201,277; 201, 281.
Hamilton, Aileen: 257,111.
Hamilton, Clayton (W): (C) 193,138; 196,332; 200, 191; 208,360; 209,30; 217, 134; 270,9; 301,10; 317,62; 346,36.
Hamilton, Cosmo: 223,147; 231,395; 241,282; (W) 250, 8.
Hamilton, Elsie: 96,63; 101,15.
Hamilton, France: 37,60.
Hamilton, Hale: 117,141; 140, 109; 159,245; 213,328; 333, 46.
Hamilton, Henry B.: 62,96.
Hamilton, Ida: 22,14.
Hamilton, John F.: (D) 277,38; 280,28.
Hamilton, Laura: 151,89.
Hamilton, Ross: 246,171.
Hamilton, Virginia: 122,136.
"Hamlet": 7,3; 24,28; (R'03) 24, 31; 25,66; (R'03) 28,136; (R'04) 38,82; 39,viii; 43, 234; 47,18; 49,58; (R'05) 58, 290; 74,94; 101,1; 111,147; 124,211; 126,60; (R'12) 143, 4; 147,iii; 149,20; 151,84; 152,119; (R'13) 153,142; 153, 168; (F) 160,328; 161,15; 182, 217; 191,7; (R'18) 207,316; 208,360; (R'18) 215,18; (R'18) 216,78; 221,8; 221, 21; 221,24; 232,514; 237, 366; 247,238; (F) 248,352; (R'22) 262,21; 262,22; 263, 5; (D) 263,10; 296,21; (R'25) 297,15; 297,24; (R'25) 298, 16; 298,38; 324,16; (R'30) 350,48.
Hamlin, George: 197,31; 230,262.
Hammer, [Mrs.] Borgny: 233,18.
Hammerstein, Arthur: 278,27; 295,48; (W) 334,27.
Hammerstein, Elaine: 156,61; 157,161; 227,42; 230,278; 233,39; 234,114; 239,116.
Hammerstein, Oscar (see also Manhattan Opera): 5,1; 5,2; 13,12; 37,iv; 43,227; 53,158; 62,xi; 62,108; 64,iv; 67, 232; 69,288; 75,138; 76,169; 80,266; 86,xvi; 86,112; 94, 318; 94,344; 95,xvii; 96,70; 101,32; 103,xii; 117,138; 118,165; 127,81; 131,22; 132,60; 149,3; 166,281; 184, 351; 224,278; 265,9.
Hammerstein II, Oscar: 277, 29; (W) 290,14; 331,27; 339, 16.
Hammerstein, Reginald: 333,49.
Hammerstein's Roof: 90,201.
Hammond, C. Norman: (C) 321, 84.
Hammond, Charles: 36,45.
Hammond, Dorothy: 38,83; 50, 98.
Hammond, Harriet: 238,41.
Hammond, Lawrens: 264,34.
Hammond, Percy: (C) 268,21; (D) 314,12;
Hammond, Ruth: 314,22.
Hammond, Virginia: 82,319; 99,150; 116,122; 185,36; 188,211; 219,277; 232,524; 233,49; 288,14; 289,24.
Hampden, Burford: 203,25; 204, 84.
Hampden, Charles: 170,176.
Hampden, Walter: 79,256; 81, 299; 87,140; 89,188; 108,55; 114,50; 206,213; 207,286; 207,316; 208,360; 208,361; 215,18; 221,21; 227,9; 230, 247; 238,17; 243,391; 244, 10; 244,29; 245,104; 267, 27; 269,18; 270,7; 270,9; 274,7; 274,16; 274,23; 277, 22; (W) 280,9; 286,39; (D) 288,22; 288,39; 288,62; 297, 15; 309,15; 309,17; 317,17; (D) 321,42; (C) 321,84; (D) 324,16; (W) 325,19; (D) 333,35; 336,36; 347,47;

361, 16.
Hamper, Genevieve (see also Mantell, [Mrs.] Robert): 151, 91; 169, 123; 171, c; 171, 225; 179, 6; 186, 72; 188, 196; 196, 337; 209, 41; (A) 214, 379; 215, 31; (A) 226, 438; 227, 31; 231, 356; (D) 243, c; 245, 75; 245, 119; 248, 285; (A) 250, 63.
Hampton, Hope: 228, 120; 231, 388; 231, 422; (D) 234, c; (A) 238, 72; 244, 40; (A) 250, 63; 252, 189; 282, 33; 289, 54; 291, 43; 294, 38; 317, 10; 325, 59; 348, 60.
Hampton, Mary: 56, 261; 80, 261; 245, 77.
Hanaford, Maude: 187, 147; 220, 353; 223, 150; 235, 192.
Hancock, Carolyn: 257, 71; 308, 33.
Hancock, Helen: 99, 141.
Hand, John: 213, 272.
"Hands Up": (R'15) 175, 139.
Handyside, Clarence: 115, 67; 143, 7; 150, 51.
Hanford, Charles B.: 49, 78; 119, 3.
"Hangman's House": (F) 328, 4b.
"Hanky Panky": (R'12) 139, xi.
Hanley, Jack: 243, 407.
Hanley, Millicent: 271, 69.
Hanley, Winifred: 227, 7; 312, 20.
Hanlon, Alma: 184, 348.
Hannah, Muriel: (D) 292, 29.
Hanneford, "Poodles": 224, 217; 236, 273; 276, 37.
"Hannele": 6, 10; (R'10) 111, xxx; 111, 139; 114, 51.
Hanray, Laurence: 261, 370.
Hanse, Elna: 261, 383.
Hansel, Howell: 11, 11; 93, 291; 245, 100.
"Hansel und Gretel" (OP): 59, 25; 154, iii.
Hansen, Cecilia: 269, 37; 301, 37.
Hansen, Kate: 90, 207.
"Hans, the Flute Player" (OP): 117, 138.
Hanson, Gladys: 86, 104; 99, 150; 106, 171; 108, 52; 124, 208; 137, 14; 139, 77; 140, 103; 140, 110; 142, 199; 173, 13; 174, 81; 179, 7; 188, 211; 201, 268; 210, 79; 235, 192; 241, 257; 306, 14.
Hanson, Joseph M. (W): 178, 300.
Hanson, Lars: 312, 23.
Hapgood, [Mrs.] Emilie: 195, 280; 196, 339.
Hapgood, Harry: 35, 15.
Hapgood, Norman: 5, 16; 7, 12.
"Happiest Night of His Life, The": (R'11) 122, 108.
"Happiness": (R'14) 158, 171; 158, 174; 194, 228; 204, 73; (R'17) 204, 85.
"Happy": (R'27) 323, 40.
"Happy Days": 244, 217; (D) 228, 85.
"Happy Ending, The": (R'16) 188, 204a.
Happy Endings (see also Audiences, Tastes Of): 38, 88; 188, 84; 324, 31; 326, 23.
"Happy Go Lucky": 236, 267; (R'20) 236, 279; (R'26) 309, 18.
"Happy Husband, The": (R'28) 328, 37.
"Happy Marriage, The": (R'09) 99, xi.
"Happyland": (R'05) 57, 266; 57, 287.
Harbach, Otto A.: (W) 296, 10; 331, 27.
Harboe, Paul (W): 47, 9.
Harbour, J. S.: (W) 114, 64.
Harbury, Charles: 70, 325; 134, 127.
Harch, Frederick: 118, 199.
Harcourt, Cyril: 207, 284; 213, 281; 215, 9.
Harcourt, William: 4, 16; 37, 62; 52, 136; 66, 200.
"Hard Man, The": (R'14) 157, 113.
Hardenberg, Frank: 171, 234.
Hardie, Russell: 345, 42.
Harding, Alfred: (W) 321, 34.
Harding, Ann: 250, 40; 273, 13; 273, 18; 284, 11; 297, 29; 298, 5; 311, 11; 320, 22; 320, 76; 321, 29; (D) 322, c; 325, 56; 345, 37; 351, 22; 353, 47; 353, 54; (W) 354, 37;

356, 57.
Harding, Jane: 104, xvi.
Harding, Lyn: 134, 127; 144, 36; 153, 142; 159, 250; 180, 68; 184, 332; 184, 335; 184, 352; 197, 25; 202, 356; 231, 363; 324, 40; 331, 45.
Hardy, Doris: 97, xxii.
Hardy, Helen Avery: (W) 74, 95.
Hardy, Sam B.: 39, iv; 47, 15; 151, 94; 177, 250; 178, 302; 201, 265; 235, 165; 244, 36; 251, 105; 321, 45.
Hare, Arthur: 62, 87.
Hare, George: 221, 9.
Hare, Gilbert: 35, 9.
Hare, John: 33, 276.
Hare, Lumsden: 98, 119; 104, 113; 190, 374; 191, 32; 214, 344; (D) 252, 169.
"Harem, The": (R'24) 287, 16; 288, 14.
Harger, Burt: 317, 11.
Hargarve, Roy: 315, 25.
Harkins, D. H.: 15, 2.
Harkness, John S. (W): 299, 10.
Harlam, Macey: 49, 59; 97, 100; 156, 64; 157, 129; 170, 187; 200, 204; 216, 95.
"Harlem": (R'29) 338, 46; 339, 47; (C) 339, 22.
"Harlequinade, The": (R'21) 245, 98; 246, 145.
Harling, Lugarda: 305, 33.
Harlow, Jean: 355, 48.
Harmon, Henry: 193, 148.
Harmon, Lucille: 246, 157.
Harmony, Henry: (C) 82, xxiv.
Harned, Virginia: PG, 30; 5, 14; 10, 23; 11, 6; 11, 7; 21, 6; 25, 68; 38, 93; 40, 148; 46, c; 46, 320; 47, 23; 50, 94; 52, 133; 59, 13; 67, 243; 69, 282; 80, 259; 81, 309; (C) 82, xxiv; 90, 205; 94, 325; 106, 180; 159, 237; 185, 28; 290, 12; 340, 134.
Harney, Nora (W) (see "Personality Pictures").
Harold, Lizzie: 78, 223.
"Harp of Life, The": (R'16) 191, 22.
Harper, Andrew: 186, 63.
Harper, Belle: 18, 26.
"Harriet's Honeymoon": (R'04) 36, 33.
Harrigan, Edward: 24, 30; 30, 186; 32, 259; 67, 252; 96, 69; 125, xiii; 203, 27.
Harrigan, William: 89, 197; 232, 520; 291, 39; 301, 23; 306, 32; 308, 28; 327, 4c.
Harriman, Borden: 271, 23.
Harriman, Josephine: 192, 105.
Harringer, William: 100, 175.
Harrington, Alice: 85, ii.
Harrington, Helen (W): 231, 414.
Harrington, John: 153, 147; 223, 169.
Harrington, Ruth: 221, 27.
Harris, Averell: 301, 27.
Harris, Caroline: 111, 134.
Harris, Edward Peyton: 353, 43; 356, 39.
Harris, Henry B.: 67, 228; 70, xxvi; 82, xxvi; 104, vi; 118, xxxvi; 126, vi.
Harris, [Mrs.] Henry B.: 319, 27.
Harris, Jed: 344, 29.
Harris, Katherine: 134, 126; 152, 135; 166, 265.
Harris, Lenore: 106, 169; 124, 191; 195, 287; 195, 299; 197, 23;
Harris, Marcia: 220, 390.
Harris, Marion: 181, 125; 260, 335.
Harris, Mary: 80, 273.
Harris, Mildred: 221, 61; 231, 489; 325, 50.
Harris, Paul (W): 354, 14.
Harris, Peggy: 292, 41.
Harris, Roy: 356, 43.
Harris, Sam (see also Cohan and Harris): 121, 72; 195, 272; 223, 172; 234, 84; 246, 165; 246, 196; 249, 435; 258, 145; 260, 320; 262, 50; 262, 67; (C) 276, 11; 278, 64; 290, 93; 294, 7; 301, 6; 309, 75; 323, 34; 353, 38.
Harris, Val: 276, 37.
Harris, William: 184, 332; 234, 84; 258, 149; (C) 283, 13; 299, 23.
Harris, William Fenwick: (W) 255, 380; 256, 38.
Harris, Winifred: 187, 149.

Harrison, Bertram: 164,166; 333,49.
Harrison, Lee: (A) 16,19; 231,363.
Harrison, Louis: (A) 54,183f; 77,185.
Harrison, Maude: 84,43.
Harrison, Richard B.: 350,33; 351,23; 352,20; (C) 357,16.
Harrison, Robert: 281,14.
Harrison, Stanley: 185,10; 213, 275.
Harriss, John (W): 361,14.
Harrold, Orville: 110,106; 118, 165; 118,166; 163,102; 165, 212; 165,213; 229,230; (W) 265,9.
Harrold, Patti: 233,9; 241,254.
Harron, Robert: 207,323.
Hart, Albert: 16,5; (A) 54, 183f.
Hart, Flo: 160,285.
Hart, Jerome (W): 242,326.
Hart, Joseph: 7,18; 14,11.
Hart, Lorenz: 331,27; 361,37.
Hart, Mary: 332,18.
Hart, Moss: 353,31; 357,34; 359,32.
Hart, Vivian: 336,27.
Hart, William S.: PG,16; 55, 218; 132,41; 192,97; 195, 285; 199,177; 201,325; 203, 59; 204,127; 205,190; 205, 196; 209,60; 213,323; 216, 128; 223,180; 229,193; 237, 378; 237,380; 245,79; 394; 250,38; 251,101; 275,32; 279,32.
Hart House Theatre (see also Toronto, University of): 304, 40.
Hartje, Mary Louise: 271,23.
Hartley, Emily Wakeman: 163,113.
Hartley, Randolph (W): 14,16; 107,16; 112,190; 114,52; 115,81.
Hartman, Gretchen: 95,6; 202, 405.
Hartmann, Louis: 187,132; 350, 8.
Hartridge School (New York): 182,227.
Hartwig, Walter (W): 227,6; 230,246; 305,42.
Harty, Veola: 165,216.
Hartz, Fanny: 147,153.
Hartzell, Harold: 205,142.
Harvard University: 11,13; 12,16; 36,43; 48,43; 53,160; 65,173; 78,v; 82,345; 90, 219; 100,xiii; 101,8; 102, 38; 108,56; 135,154; 151, 98; 159,249; 181,122; 183,276; 199,132; 206,230; 220,380; 229,194; 232,538; 233,66; 241,274; 257,105; 257,106; 279,19; 292,43; 304,39.
"Harvest Moon, The": (R'09) 106,167; 106,193.
"Harvester, The": (R'04) 40,138; 44,252; 45,268; (R'04) 45, 270.
Harvey, Dorothy: 11,23.
Harvey, Gladys: 141,149; 143, 16.
Harvey, J. Clarence: 112,187; 177,234; 202,399; 221,7.
Harvey, Jackson (W):344,34; 345, 33; 349,24; 354,20.
Harvey, Martin: 6,6; 22,8; 22,9; 30,200.
Harvey, Morris: 303,21; 305, 14.
Harvey, Muriel Martin: 188, 201; 236,267.
Harvey, Paul: 261,372; 308,19.
Harwood, Harry: 37,71; 81,300; 120,53; 154,176; 200,209.
Harwood, John: 188,204; 188, 216; 190,374.
Hasoutra: 308,8.
"Hassan": 282,12; 282,13.
"Hassard Short's Ritz Revue": (R'24) 284,70.
Hassell, George: 152,112; 155,6; 168,69; 188,204b; 217,163; (C) 321,33; (C) 336,15.
Hassen, Nicholas: 171,237.
Hassett, Kate: 7,4.
Hasson, Adele: 194,219.
Hast, Marjorie: 225,306.
Hastings, Cary: 49,57.
Hastings, Cuyler: 85,72.
Hastings, Ernest: 3,11.
Hasty Pudding Club (see Harvard University).
Haswell, Percy: 11,14; 22,

27; 27,122; 34,302; 52, 135; 75,130; 86,103; 89, 187; 109,iii; 127,84; 129,176.
Hatch, Frank: 4,16; (A) 226, 438.
Hatch, Robert H. (W): 204,72.
Hatch, W.R.: 102,47; 137, 10; 137,11.
Hathaway, Ann: 27,126.
Hatsuse, Nami-Ko: 161,31.
Hatteras, Richard: 208,375.
Hatton, Fanny: 183,286; 193, 165; (W) 197,7.
Hatton, Frederic: (W) 123,173; 146,119; 183,286; 193,165; (W) 197,7.
Hatton, Raymond: 322,50.
"Haunted House, The": (R'24) 284, 19.
Haupt, Ulrich: 275,24; 275,62; 277,39.
Hauptmann, Gerhardt: 6,10; 17,16; 23,7; 46,299; 49,iii; 50,104; 62,xii; 73,xiv; 110, xvi; 111,139; 137,5; 146, 101.
"Havana": 97,vii; (R'09) 98,107; 98,115.
"Have a Heart": 192,84; (R'17) 192,128.
Haver, Phyllis: 319,17; 322,6; 323,4b; 324,8; 325,81.
"Havoc": (R'24) 284,16; 284, 18.
"Havoc, The": (R'11) 120,33; 121,94.
"Hawk, The": 165,204; 165, 210; 165,211.
"Hawk Island": (R'29) 344,72.
Hawkes, J. Kerby: 349,35.
Hawkesworth, Margaret: 181, 165; 183,313; 191,39; 199, 156.
Hawkins, Iris: 155,9; 155,50.
Hawkins, Jack: 342,26.
Hawkins, Stanley: 17,7.
Hawks, J.G.: 262,35.
Hawks, Wells (W) (see also "How Theatres Are Managed"): (V) 29,178; 172,285.
Hawley, Dudley: 65,185; 113,10; 176,71.
Hawley, Irene: 88,155.
Hawley, Wanda: 219,303; 233, 39; 245,122; 276,33.
Hawley, William: 90,203.
Haworth, Joseph: 23,2; 23,4; 25,58; 26,94; 32,258; 245, 96.
Hawthorne, Grace (W): 71,24.
Hawthorne, Lola: 63,114.
Hawthorne, Nell: 26,103; 41,162.
"Hawthorne of the U.S.A.": (R'12) 142,164; 143,15.
Hawthorne Sisters: 26,103.
Hawtrey, Charles: 9,2; 9,3; 32,240; 33,274; 39,111; 115,xii; 135,137.
Hawtrey, William F.: 68,xiii; 120,36.
Hay, Julia: 88,162; 88,163; 173,18; 124,iii; 176,188; 213,275.
Hay, Mary: 228,90; 240,176; 270,27; 337,41.
"Hay Fever": 296,20; (R'25) 297,18.
Hayakawa, Sessue: 201,323; 203,63; 242,348; 280,32; 301, 16; 301,33.
Hayden, Eleanor: 335,46.
Hayden, Ethyl: 342,47.
Hayden, Katharine (W,V): 231, 380.
Haydn, Carl: 57,287.
Hayes, Albert: 341,42.
Hayes, George: 216,93; 334, 37.
Hayes, Grace: 305,14.
Hayes, Helen: 212,195; 216, 76; 216,77; 217,156; (D) 220,361; 223,145; 225,317; 226,365; 238,26; 238,27; 240,202; 240,203; 246,150; 249,370; 250,55; 253,212; 256,23; (D) 278,38; 281,18; 283,2; 283,17; 284,29; 287, 27; 288,38; 291,17; 291,19; 292,47; 297,36; 299,19; 299,27; 304,13; 307,29; 308,32; 313,30; 320,36; 323, 24; 323,25; 330,c; 340,51; 353,12; 357,57; 359,12; (C) 359,22; 361,c.
Hayes, Irene: 210,97.
Hayes, Rich: 270,35.
Hayes, Sheelagh: 319,23.
Hayman, Alfred: 11,14; 223,144.

Haymarket Theatre (London): 48, ix.
Haynes, Gertrude: 46, 310.
Haynes, Minna Gale: 171, 233; 200, 209; 231, 363.
Hays, Will: 254, 282; (C) 317, 23; (W) 326, 25.
Hayward, Grace: 48, 52.
Hazelton, George C.: 9, 16; 20, 10.
Hazle, Lillian: 40, 147.
Hazzard, John E.: 40, 144; 189, 280; 200, 224; 221, 7; 247, 213; 260, 293.
"He and She": (R'20) 230, 269; 230, 275.
"He Came From Milwaukee": (R'10) 117, xiv; 117, 153.
"He Comes Up Smiling": 163, 100; 164, 156; (R'14) 165, 207; (F, R) 212, 250.
"He Didn't Want To Do It": (R'18) 212, 242.
"He Loved the Ladies": (R'27) 316, 20.
"He Who Gets Slapped": 252, 141; (R'22) 252, 168; 253, 231; (D) 253, 237; (F, R) 287, 30.
Head, Helena: 88, 169.
"Head Over Heels": 209, 11; (R'18) 212, 212.
"Heads Up!": (R'29) 346, 49.
Healy, Betty: 271, 35.
Healy, Ted: 282, 36; 360, 27; 361, 36; (C) 361, 38.
"Heard Here and There" by A. Hornblow: 184, 332; 185, 6; 186, 62.
"Heard on Broadway" by L'Homme Que Sait: 258, 166; and monthly thereafter.
Hearst, William Randolph: 33, 288; 241, 244; 242, 372.
"Heart of Humanity, The": (F, R) 216, 124.
"Heart of Wetona, The": (R'16) 182, 194; 182, 197; (F, R) 216, 124.
"Heartbreak House": (R'20) 238, 31; 239, 91.
"Hearts Aflame": (R'02) 16, 2; 18, 2; 20, 7; (F) 264, 35; (F, R) 265, 70.
"Hearts Courageous": (R'03) 33, 269; 33, 273.
"Hearts of the World": (F) 207, 323; (F) 208, 396.
"Heartstrings": (F, R) 229, 190.
Heath, T.K.: 56, 248.
"Heaven Tappers, The": (R'27) 314, 20.
"Heavy Traffic": (R'28) 332, 78.
Hecht, Ben: 194, 213; 199, 143; 264, 19; (W) 339, 18.
Hector, Frank: 236, 267.
Hector, Louis: 275, 14.
"Hedda Gabler": 29, 164; 33, 266; (R'03) 33, 267; 46, 292; (R'06) 70, xxi; 78, 219; (R'18) 207, 287; 208, 349; 301, 14; (R'26) 301, 15; (R'28) 327, 65.
Hedden, Irene: 37, iv.
Hedman, Martha: 141, c; 141, 144; 146, iii; 146, 99; 151, 103; 154, 177; (D) 155, c; 161, 7; 161, 21; 165, 246; 168, c; 168, 53; 170, 170; 170, 193; 170, 195; 175, 105; 176, 181; 176, 208; 177, 243; 177, 261; 184, 360; 188, 197; (A) 189, 313; 194, 206; 210, 93; (A) 222, 123; 231, 375; 232, 519; 232, 546; 237, 362; 244, 27; 253, 239; 263, 48; 282, 36; 290, 45; 303, 36.
Hegeman, Alice: 101, 23.
Hegeman, Maurice: 101, 32.
Heggie, O.P.: 169, 110; 170, 196; 183, 296; 194, 217; 204, 73; 236, 267; 255, 351; 255, 357; (D) 255, 375; 258, 157; 285, 18; 295, 18; 311, 6.
Heifitz, Jascha: 202, 334; 249, 391; 261, 391; (C) 325, 43.
"Heights, The": (R'10) 109, vii.
"Heimath": (R'01) 12, 2.
Heims, Else: 126, 58.
Hein, Sylvio: 184, 351.
Heinrich, Julia: 178, 284; 180, 85.
Heinrich, Tina: 90, 207.
"Heir to the Hoorah, The": (R'05) 51, 111; 52, 149.
Heitland, Wilmot: 185, 21.
Helburn, Teresa: (W) 160, 284;

(D) 258,167; 269,23; (W) 274,9; (W) 286,9; 309,27; (W) 339,20.
Held, Anna: 9,9; 23,c; 23,21; 24, 32; 30,208; 34,288; 45,267; 46,320; 60,41; 71,28; 72,29; 75,119; (W) 77,180; 79,c; 83,6; 92,xxiii; 95,c; 96,59; 101,30; 129,163; 156,104; 158,199; 175,127; (W) 178, 290; 188,239; 191,16; 191, 20; 191,24; 192,110; (A) 192,119; 211,176; 231,397.
Held, John Jr. (C): (W) 193,138; 264,17; 284,20; 306,27;332,30.
"Helen of Troy, N.Y.": (R'23) 269, 15.
Helena, Edith: 125,12; 127,105.
"Helena's Boys": (R'24) 279, 16.
"Helena's Husband": 177,222; (R'15) 177,223.
"Hell": (R'11) 124,183.
"Hell Bent for Heaven": (R'24) 277,19; (D) 277,38; (S) 280, 26.
"Hell Cat, The": (F,R) 215,62.
Heller, George: 316,19.
Helleu, Paul: 239,97; 239,145.
"Hello Alexander": (R'19) 225, 354.
"Hello Broadway": 168,53; (R'14) 168,101; 195,272.
"Hello, Daddy!": (C) 336,15.
"Hello Yourself": (R'28) 334, 60.
"Hell's Angels": (F,R) 355,47; 355,48.
"Helmet of Navarre, The": (R) 10,5; 11,5; (R'02) 11,6.
"Help Wanted": 157,114; (R'14) 157,150.
Helton, Percy: 134,118; 165,217; 176,178; 215,27; 295,26;
Heming, Percy: 240,157; 251,77.
Heming, Violet: 110,118; 124, 200; 148,169; 165,221; 168, 83; 174,81; 175,113; 177, 228; 188,182; 188,190; 189, 258; 201,285; 204,93; 209, 57; 211,135; 212,213; 212, 232; (D) 216,c; 217,183; 221, 25; 230,296; 234,115; 241, 249; 249,375; 254,301; 255, 354; 256,23; 256,46; 257, 101; 258,156; (A) 261,413; 268,3; 274,17; 276,39; 301, 11; 302,2; 312,59; 317,20; 325,33; 332,17; 333,32; (A) 337,62; 343,13; 343,26; 344, 39; 344,49; 354,24.
Hemmick, [Mrs.] Christian: 207, 297; 208,364.
Hempel, Frieda: 141,139; 144, 40; 145,69; 147,151; 153, 149; 155,15; 156,68; 166, 270; 168,64; 182,195; 230, 290; 243,436; 270,37; 297,35.
Hemus, Percy: 197,31.
Henderson, Archibald (W): 117, 146; 118,182.
Henderson, Beatrice Golden: 80,272.
Henderson, Grace: 39,122; 204, 83.
Henderson, Helen: 259,201.
Henderson, Isaac: 20,4.
Henderson, Jack: 91,239.
Henderson, Ray (W): 216, 88; 326,21; 331,49.
Henderson, William J.: 7,14; 33,264; 22,36; 36,53; 167, 13.
Henderson Players: 208,358.
Hendricks, Ben: 116,99; 215,15.
Hendricks, John: 201,287.
Hengler Sisters: 29,157; 32, 145.
Heniger, Minnie Herts: 161,34.
Hennings, Betty: 25,70; (A) 67,238.
"Hen-Pecks, The": (R'11) 121, xi; 121,71.
Henri: 247,221.
"Henrik Ibsen-- The Man and His Plays" (Moses) (B): 95,xxiv.
Henry, Eleanor: 150,66; 162, 61; 170,200; 224,264.
Henry, Mabel: 196,335.
"Henry, Behave": (R'26) 307,66.
"Henry Dunbar": (D) 134,130.
"Henry IV": (D) 112,195; (R'16) 183,276.
"Henry V": 8,17; (R'12) 141, 130.

"Henry VIII": 118,197; 182, 193; (R'16) 183,275; 183, 275; 183,286; 301,20.
"Henry Irving" (Craig) (B): 356,8.
"Henry of Navarre": 98,111.
Henry Miller Theatre (New York): 290,17.
Hensel, Heinrich: 124,193; 130, 190.
Henshaw, John E.: 107,30.
Hepburn, Katharine: 358,25; (C) 359,2.
"Her Cardboard Lover": (R'27) 314,22; 315,25.
"Her Country": (S) 206,206; 206, 207; (R'18) 206,219.
"Her Family Tree": 240,159; (R'20) 240,180.
"Her First Affaire": (R'27) 319, 23.
"Her First Divorce": (R'13) 148, xi.
"Her Friend the King": (R'29) 345,68.
"Her Great Match": 56,244; 56, 245.
"Her Honor, The Mayor": (R'18) 209,22.
"Her Husband's Wife": 112,175; (R'10) 112,176; 192,79; (R'17) 192,88.
"Her Lord and Master": 13,2; 287,52b.
"Her Master Mystery": (F,R) 214,392.
"Her Own Money": (R'13) 152, x; 152,112.
"Her Own Way": (R'03) 33, 264; 33,271; 33,283.
"Her Past": 74,109.
"Her Regiment": (R'17) 203,51.
"Her Salary Man": (R'21) 251, 100.
"Her Sister": 83,9; (R'07) 84,33; 95,26.
"Her Soldier Boy": (R'16) 191, 24.
"Her Unborn Child": (R'28) 326,40.
Herald Square Theatre (New York): 110,121; (D) 290,50.
Herbert, Evelyn: 228,96; 298,4; 304,14; 313,15; 329,41; 337, 74; (D) 360,c.
Herbert, Henry: 208,349; 221, 23; 235,191; 236,260; 236, 275; 268,31; 269,28.
Herbert, Holmes E.: 154,xxv; 195,276; 230,279.
Herbert, Jayne: 152,132.
Herbert, Joseph W.: (A) 52, 131f; 61,61; 85,75.
Herbert, Sidney: 20,4; 28,150; 70,336; 81,297; 104,125; 141,150.
Herbert, Victor: 30,188; 56, 244; 60,v; 72,xv; 74,87; 92,xxiv; 94,xii; 95,2; 95, 11; 105,xiv; 118,165; 122, 114; (A) 127,v; 152,xii; 157,118; 167,13; (A) 186,91; 196,334; (A) 231,346.
Herbert of Cherbury, Lord: (D) 314,7.
"Here and There" by A. Hornblow; 189,267; 191,42; 192, 126.
"Here Comes the Bride": 201, 265; (R'17) 201,278; (F,R) 217,191.
Hereford, Beatrice: 94,342; 324, 40.
Herendeen, Helen: 229,178.
"Here's Howe!": 328,39.
Hergesheimer, Joseph: (W) 317,7.
Heribel, Renee: 303,42.
Herlein, Lillian: 105,136.
Herman, C.D.: 112,193.
Herman, Charles: 145,96.
Herman, Selmar: 50,104.
Hermits' Club (Cleveland): 81,310; 97,102.
Herndon, Richard: 302,21; 306, 15; 308,6; (W) 337,13.
Herne, Chrystal: 27,114; 57,271; 66,220; 78,206; 78,209; 85, 69; 96,58; 112,200; 117, 150; 122,107; 123,143; 125, 16; 133,94; 145,78; 153,141; 155,10; 157,131; 161,21; 162,65; 167,15; 170,c; 170, 167; 170,176; 173,13; 195, 287; 196,329; 206,235; 216, 71; 228,103; 230,267; 244, 36; 280,8; 280,14; 280,24; 292,16; 298,29; 299,43; 301,

26; (W) 307,9; 310,60; 334, 40.
Herne, James A.: 5,6; 50,80; 85,vii; 138,45.
Herne, Julie: 50,80; 55,227; 56,240; 68,265; 161,21; 199, 135.
"Hero, The": 209,41; (R'21) 242, 370; (S) 250,16.
"Hero of Santa Maria, The": (R'17) 194,213; 194,223.
"Herod": 106,xxviii; (R'09) 106, 169; 106,181.
Henrick, Newbold: 86,iii.
Herrick, Robert (W): 318,9.
Herrick, William Hamilton (W): 178,294.
Hershey, Burnet (W): 280,22.
Hersholt, Jean: 328,33.
Herts, B. Russell (W): 137, 30; 143,27; 145,92.
Herts, Henry B.: 34,296.
Hertz, Alfred (see also Opera): 22,34; 129,154; (C) 159, 254.
Hervieu, Paul: 37,72; 46, 299; 48,39; 59,3; 70,323; 80, 271; 85,ix; 86,91.
Herz, Ralph C.: 56,241; 86, 100; 87,124; 110,110; 112, 180; 115,94; 123,x; 123, 144; 180,65; 190,406; 200, 203.
Herzberg, Max J. (W): 193, 158.
Herzceg, Ferenc: 329,20.
Herzl, Theodore: (W) 133,98.
Hess, Myra: 273,37; 337,36.
Hewes, Theo: 255,349; 271, 3a.
Hewitt, Muriel: 296,21.
Heyer, Grace: 37,62; 41,161; 52,156; 85,79; 226,375; 269,30.
Heyes, Herbert: 214,393.
Heyner, Herbert: 330,23.
Heyse, Paul: 19,12.
Heyward, Dorothy: 328,29.
Heyward, Du Bose: 328,29.
"Hiawatha": 91,253.
Hibbard, Edna: 209,31; 219,277; 236,266; 242,336; 242,355; 247,218; 255,363; 288,17; 289,23; 309,13; 309,49.
Hichens, Robert: 54,184; 54, 185; 129,148, 126,63.
Hickman, Alfred: 52,133; 56, 247; 76,167; 85,72; 108,42; 199,175.
Hickman, Charles: 341,25.
Hickman, Howard: 208,399.
Hickok, Guy (W): 279,12.
Hicks, Eleanor: 128,114.
Hicks, Russell: 332,47; 356, 35.
Hicks Theatre (London): 83,18.
"Hidden": (R'27) 321,43.
"Hidden Truth, The": (F,R) 217,191.
Higgins, Billy: 295,21.
Higgins, David: 201,281.
"Higgledy Piggledy": 45,267; (R'04) 46,297.
"High Cost of Loving, The": (R'14) 164,157.
"High Gear": (R'27) 321,43.
"High Hatters": (R'28) 328,63.
"High Jinks": (R'13) 155,46.
"High Road, The": (R'12) 143,2; 143,5; (R'28) 332,46; 332,48.
High School Theatre (see Amateur Theatre).
"High Stakes": (R'24) 284,19.
"Highway of Life, The": 166, 264; (R'14) 166,300.
"Highwayman, The": (R'17) 196, 343.
Higley, Philo: (W) 353,15.
Hilburne, Betty: 215,21.
Hilder, J. Chapman (W): 157,135; 265,22.
Hildred: 231,405.
Hildreth, Melvin D. (W): 313, 33.
Hill, Arthur: 18,5; 25,61; 82, vii; 201,287.
Hill, Barton: 13,4.
Hill, Gladys: 166,267.
Hill, Ira L.: 207,319; 290,49.
Hill, J. Leubrie: 157,135.
Hill, James M.: 288,28.
Hill, Josephine: 213,323; 232, 536.
Hill, Mabel: 171,239; 330,36.
Hill, Victor (W): 311,30.
Hillebrand, Fred: 219,293.
Hillhouse, Lewis J. (W): 65, 190.

Hilliard, Robert: 24,34; 54, 195; 66,200; 99,164; 106, 183; 140,127; 144,41; 147, 154; 149,31; 151,xx; 172,307; 181,145; (W) 202,354; 286, 13.
Hinckley, Allen: 95,36.
Hinckley, Isabel: 102,67.
"Hindle Wakes": (R'12) 143,2.
Hindu Drama: 43,236.
"Hindu, The": (R) 255,374; (D) 255,375.
Hines, Dixie: 332,82.
Hines, Elisabeth: 226,371; 226, 386; 243,408; 264,48; 280, 27; 284,23; 284,46; 299, 31; 317,27.
Hinsdell, Oliver: 270,41; 322,55; (W) 333,52; 351,51.
Hinshaw, William: 134,109; 159, 223; 215,27.
Hinter, Guy: 247,224.
"Hip! Hip! Horray!": (R'07) 81,xiv; 177,221; 179,15; 180, 84.
Hippodrome Theatre [1853]: 19, 21.
Hippodrome Theatre (New York): (D) 42,iv; 50,vii; 50,99; 53, 173; 60,28; 61,66; 62,90; 65,171; 72,43; 72,53; 74,vii; 76,144; 77,183; 83,xiv; 87, 121; 88,148; 90,209; 93, xiv; 93,305; 94,340; 104,108; 105,140; 116,xv; 116,110; 117,152; 128,xiv; 128,125; 140,xv; 140,107; 152,xiv; 152, 129; 164,151; 164,195; 169, 150; 177,221; 178,342; 188, 246; 188,254; 200,242; 201, 290; (D) 202,409; 208,367; 212,199; 212,212; 224,217; 226,444; 235,164; 235,242; (D) 238,73; 275,36; 282,54; 284,37.
"Hippolytus": 124,201.
Hirsch, Louis: 184,351; (W) 219,282.
Hirsch, Marie: 40,147.
Hirschfield, Al: (C) 344,26.
Hirschfeld, Max: 188,206.
Hirsh, N. Morrell: (W) 88, 158.
"His Bridal Night": (R'16) 187,140; 188,215.
"His Chinese Wife": (R'20) 232, 527; 232,529.
"His First Command": (F) 345,65.
"His Grace de Grammont": 57, 283.
"His Honor, Abe Potash": 225, 315; (R'19) 226,440.
"His Honor The Mayor": (R'06) 65,171.
"His House in Order": 62,ii; (R'06) 68,254; 68,263; 95, 24.
"His Little Widows": (R'17) 196,343.
"His Majesty": (R'06) 63,xi.
"His Majesty, Bunker Bean": 179,8; 181,152; (R'16) 189, 284; 190,365; (F,R) 207, 324.
His Majesty's Theatre (London): 69,308.
"His Name on the Door": (R'09) 107,6; 107,7.
"His Widow's Husband": 202, 347; (R'17) 202,352.
Historical Drama: 212,216; 220,358; 243,394; 255,384.
"History of the Boston Theatre, The" (Tompkins & Kilby) (B): 96,xii.
"History of the Harlequinade, The" (Sand) (B): 178,314.
"History of the London Stage from 1576 to 1903" (Baker) (B): 47,ii.
"History of the Theatre in America, A" (Hornblow) (B): 228,148.
Hitchcock, Raymond: 16,6; 17,8; 38,90; 38,95; 41, iv; 55,214; 56,252; 76,148; 79,i; 79,249; 91,243; 105, 134; 130,xii; 145,79; 155,12; 160,282; 160,289; 171,258; 189,284; 197,22; 198,83; (W) 200,192; (C) 209,21; 209,23; 210,85; 211,155; 212, 200; 238,33; 245,83; (D) 247,211; 301,38; 309,49; (D) 322,21.
Hitchcock, Walter: 68,277.
"Hit the Deck": (R'27) 316,18;

(F) 342, 65.
"Hit-The-Trail Holliday": (R'15) 176, 198; 177, 219.
"Hitchy-Koo": (R'17) 197, 22; 198, 83.
"Hitchy-Koo, 1918": (R'18) 209, 23.
"Hitchy-Koo, 1920": (R'20) 238, 29; 238, 33.
Hite, Mabel: 40, 145; 56, 240; 76, 169; 82, 328; 83, 8; 85, 68; 88, vi; 89, 174; 106, 200; 113, 10; 119, 18; 124, 183; 124, 196; 125, 30.
"Hits of the Month": 152, 117; 153, 156; 154, xxv; 155, 50; 157, 160; 159, 267; 160, 321; 161, 46.
Hitz, Gertrude: 141, 152.
Hoag, George: 300, 19.
Hoagland, Benjamin: 348, 13.
Hoban, Margaret: 159, 236.
Hoban, Stella: 141, 155.
Hobart, George V.: 20, 9; 29, 159; 84, ix; 159, 230; 174, 80; 196, 353; (W) 252, 146; (W) 253, 226.
Hobart, Rose: 347, 13.
Hobbes, Halliwell: 274, 29; 333, 48.
"Hobohemia": (R'19) 218, 205; 218, 209.
Hoboken (New Jersey) Theatre: (see Throckmorton, Cleon).
Hobson, Irene: 15, 23; 29, 173.
"Hobson's Choice": 178, 274f; (R'15) 178, 278.
Hoctor, Harriet: 220, 355; 318, 36; 324, 13; 330, 49; 333, 57; 341, 10; (W) 350, 40; 350, 41.
Hodge, William T.: 14, 8; 30, 194; 44, 258; 54, 207; 81, 290; 82, 329; 83, vi; 95, ii; 95, 5; 176, 169; 200, 209; 206, 220; 206, 231; (A) 214, 379; 293, 42; 294, 25; 306, 14; 310, 31; 313, 50; (W) 316, 5; 333, 23.
Hodges, Harrison Blake: 124, 211.
Hodkinson, William: 171, 245.
Hoey, Evelyn: 339, 23; 347, 41.
Hoey, [Mrs.] John: 195, 263; 246, 164.
Hof Theatre (Munich): 51, 122; 112, 190.
Hopburg Theatre (Vienna): 66, 203.
Hofer, Ella: 81, 311.
Hofflund, Bertha (W): 128, 122.
Hoffman, Gertrude: 90, 200; 90, 201; 98, 130; 125, 3; 126, c; (A) 126, xii; 139, 65; 143, 6; 145, 79; 195, 290; (A) 214, 379; 223, 157; 233, 21.
Hoffman, Laura: 249, 433.
Hoffman, Llora: (W) 304, 34.
Hoffman, Maude: 10, 16.
Hoffman, Olga: 94, xxii.
Hofmann, Ernst: (D) 276, 27.
Hofmann, Herman: 90, 207; 92, 267.
Hofmann, Josef: 10, 34; 11, 23; 13, 27; (W) 46, 323; 122, 116; 133, 80; 154, 184; 170, 184; 290, 43; 347, 31.
Hogarth, Leona: 301, 23; 308, 28; 308, 54.
Hohl, Arthur E.: 189, 269; 191, 29; 194, 223; 196, 340; 197, 15; 202, 347; 205, 159; 206, 231; 207, 289; 228, 77; (D) 229, 161; 320, 22; 320, 76.
"Hoity-Toity": (R'01) 9, 8.
"Hokey Pokey": (R'12) 133, xii.
Hokison, Helen (D): 268, 26; 274, 25; 276, 13; 279, 25; 281, 29; 282, 29; 291, 13; 295, 25; 299, 36.
Holbrooke, William: 223, 153; 261, 383.
Holcomb, Helen: 280, 44.
Holcomb, Willard (W): 269, 19; 273, 24.
Holcomb, Wynn (see Wynn).
"Hold Everything": (R'28) 334, 60; 342, 40; (F) 352, 59.
Holden, William: 118, 199; 190, 347; (W) 205, 134.
Holder, Mary: 334, 37.
Holding, Thomas: 184, 351; 201, 325.
Hole, Dora: 68, 269.
"Hole in the Wall, The": (R'20) 231, 403; 232, 519.
"Holiday": 335, 51; (R'28) 335, 78; 337, 18; 340, 15; (F, R) 353, 47.

Holladay, Mildred: 238,19.
Holland, Clifford: 323,6.
Holland, E.M.: 3,2; 3,3; 10,5; 10,20; 20,6; 33,265; 83,2; 96,57; 98,120; 108,48; 108,64; 111,167; 122,109; 122,129; 144,36.
Holland, George: 231,363; 331, 48.
Holland, John: 168,72.
Holland, Joseph: 4,16; 8,9.
Holland, Maurice: 255,357.
Holland, Mildred: 23,13; 36,49; 102,60; 112,177.
Holland, Peggy: 303,21.
Holles, Anthony: 325,39.
Hollicus, Otto: 294,21.
Holliday, Carl (W): 195,295.
Holliday, John: 215,9.
Hollis, Lillian: 40,143.
Hollis, Marjorie: 230,247.
Hollmann, Hermine: 93,290.
Holloway, Baliol: 323,40; (D) 325,45.
Holloway, Sterling: 274,14; 293,19; (D) 305,29; 352,42; 353,25.
Holls, Violet: 54,204.
Hollywood: 212,254; 277,24; 352, 36.
Hollywood Playhouse (Los Angeles): 314,28.
Hollywood Theatre: 229,197.
Holman, Libby: 340,50; 350,57; 357,19; 357,33; 359,55; 361, 29.
Holmes, Burton: 216,85.
Holmes, Dorothy: 332,18.
Holmes, Helen: 123,160; 171, 260; 216,95.
Holmes, John Haynes (W): 304, 18.
Holmes, Phillips: 345,51.
Holmes, Robert: 296,21.
Holmes, Taylor: 116,127; 117, 158; 162,57; 165,234; 171, 243; 179,8; 181,152; 190, 365; 200,249; 205,195; 231, 496; 235,183.
Holmes, [Mrs.] Taylor: 206, 261.
Holmes, Walter: 301,38.
Holstein, Harold: 247,231.
Holt, Ada: 61,66.
Holt, Edwin: 28,135; 65,189; 128,116.
Holt, Jack: (D) 294,1.
Holt, Ruth: 49, 76.
Holtz, Lou: 281,36.
Holubar, Allan: 217,188.
"Holy City, The": (R'03) 30, 205; 54,iii.
Holzman, Ben F.: 331,48.
Homans, Robert E.: 107,3; 107,9; 117,132; 117,152.
"Home Again": (R'18) 214,380.
"Home Fires": (R'23) 271,16.
"Home Folks": (R'05) 48,xii.
"Home of the Free, The": 196, 344; (R'18) 208,355.
"Home Towners, The": (R'26) 307,66.
Homer, Charles: 163,101.
Homer, Louise: 10,32; 34, 320; 37,69; 74,111; 106, 202; 110,106; 120,48; 129, 155; 133,78; 134,109; 141, 140; 142,166; 147,140; 153, 149; 154,182; 185,25.
Homes of Actors (see also "Prominent Players in Their Homes"): 10,10; 43,223; 67,242; 95,10; 111,168; 112, 189; 157,137; 170,178; 173, 32; 174,76; 184,345; 196, 353; 220,339; 235,171; 312, 22; and monthly thereafter.
Hone, Mary: 262,18; 262,31.
Honegger, Arthur: 332,27.
"Honest Jim Blunt": (R'12) 140,xvii.
"Honest Liars": (R'26) 307,15.
"Honey Girl": 232,505; 232, 521; (R'20) 232,527.
"Honeydew": 236,281; (R'20) 236,332.
"Honeymoon Express, The": (R'13) 145,66; 147,147.
"Honeymoon Lane": (R'26) 308, 15.
"Honeymooners, The": 79,232.
"Honor of the Family, The": 85,59; (R'08) 86,88; 86, 103.
"Honor System": (F) 194,219.
"Honorable Cad, An": (F) 217,

183.
"Hon. John Grigsby, The": (R'02) 13,3; 13,5.
"Honors Are Even": (R'21) 247, 236; 248,293.
Hood, Basil: 12,11.
Hood, Charles Newton (W): 329, 15.
Hooker, Brian: 134,109; 275, 29.
Hoops, Arthur: 11,7; 93, vii.
"Horray for the Girls": (R'18) 215,20.
Hoover, Herbert: 203,52; 333, 18.
Hoover, Herman: 333,48.
"Hop O' My Thumb": 155,9; (R'13) 155,46.
Hope, Flossie: 80,270.
Hope, Gloria: 211,181.
Hope, Lelia: 220,399.
"Hope Chest, The": (F,R) 216,124.
Hopkins, Arthur: 153,viii; 153,147; 165,256; 199,168; 200,256; 209,8; 211,130; 212,194; 224,222; 234,84; 258,149; 263,60; (W) 273, 11; 273,48; 294,7; 299,6; (W) 331,15.
Hopkins, Charles: 164,163; 167,35; 169,114; (W) 360, 18.
Hopkins, [Mrs.] Charles: 167, 35; 169,114; 179,9.
Hopkins, Christine: (W) 211,162.
Hopkins, Mae: 97,90.
Hopkins, Miriam: 309,29; 321, 19; 326,52; 339,12; 340,24; (A) 344,59; 349,17; 352, 12; 353,35; (C) 354,11; 360, 26.
Hopkins, Peggy (see also Joyce, Peggy Hopkins): 215,7; 215, 9; 218,209; (D) 220,361.
Hopp, Julius: 47,xiii; 54,185; 125,viii.
Hopper, De Wolf: 3,4; 15,18; (A) 16,19; 22,20; 25,57; 40,vi; (W) 57,284; 57,287; 84,43; 95,23; 112,177; 132, 48; 132,58; 137,1; 137,10; 137,13; 148,xii; 148,163; 150,52; (W) 155,9; 155,48; 171,227; 172,282; 173,7; 178,305; 183,292; (W) 200, 194; 212,207; 213,270; 217, 149; 231,363; 231,299; 233, 24; 240,166; 241,242; 245, 99; 287,26; 289,26.
Hopper, Edna Wallace: 4,15; 8,21; 16,17; 21,12; 22, 11; 26,84; 28,c; 70,322; 91,243; 104,128; 137,11; 159,238; 183,311; 186,64; 261,392; 290,23.
Hopper, Hedda; 215,29; 216, 89; 255,392.
Hopping, Irene: 122,126; 175, 118.
Hopwood, Avery: (W) 62,96; (W) 63,120; 69,298; 114, 62; 115,82; 118,166; 123, 156; 153,150; 193,136; (W) 231,368; 231,395; (W) 238, 6; 246,143; 247,212; 261,360; 264,12; (W) 277,10; 286,15; 290,19; 330,72.
Horgan, Paul (W): 304,24; 318, 14.
Horkeimer Brothers: 202,404.
Hornblow, Arthur (see also "Editor's Chair, The"; "Heard Here and There"; "Here and There"; "Stage Whispers") (W): 36,38; 38,87; 47,16f; 50,87; 68,xvi; 75,xxix; 76, xviii; 88,ii; 100,i; 106, xxxi; 120,xxviii; 142,xvi; (C) 177,220; 188,191; (C) 193, 138; 193,176b; 202,336; 204, 71; 205,133; 207,272; 209, 8; 219,266; 228,148; (V) 231,344; 247,210; 270,39; 275,la; 290,7; 283,9; (C) 286,15; 291,40; (C) 296, 15; 311,3a.
Hornblow, Arthur Jr.: 282,7.
Horne, C. Morton: 121,99.
Hornick, Ethel: 4,3; 33,263.
Horniman, [Mrs.] A.E.F.: 146, 111.
Hornsby, Hubert: 79,237.
Horowitz, Vladimir: 326,45; 347,31.
Horton, Agnes: 205,163.
Horton, Edward Everett: 293,

32; (W) 341,22.
Horton, Fanny: 9,iv.
Horton, Jeanette: 126,62; 164, 168.
Horton, Walter: 159,240.
Hosford, Maud: 63,112; 189,277.
"Hospitality": (R'22) 262,21.
"Hot Chocolates": 341,43.
"Hotbed": (R'28) 334,46.
"Hotel de L'Quest, L' ": 54, 202.
"Hotel Mouse, The": 254,283; (R'22) 254,334.
Hotel Stratford (Chicago): 46,324.
"Hotel Universe": (R'30) 351, 43; 351,44.
"Hottentot, The": (R'20) 230,309.
Houdini, Harry: 205,136; (A) 226,438; (A) 238,72; (A) 250,63; 264,27.
Houghton, Genevieve: 200,223.
House, Roy Temple (W): 193, 162.
"House Afire": (R'30) 350,72.
"House Beautiful, The": 361,17.
"House Next Door, The": (R'09) 99,viii; 99,135; 100,xviii; 100,167.
"House Party": (R'29) 344,47.
"House of a Thousand Candles, The": 83,2; (R'08) 84,xvi.
"House of Bondage, The": (R'14) 157,158.
"House of Burnside, The": (R'05) 48,31.
"House of Fear, The": (F) 167, 18; (R'29) 345,68.
"House of Glass, The": (R'16) 167,167; 177,235; 189, 268; 195,270; (F) 205,193.
"House of Mirth, The": (R'06) 70,320.
"House of Silence, The": (R'06) 61,58; 61,59.
"House of Usher, The": (R'25) 300,15.
"Houseboat on the River Styx, The": (R'28) 335,82.
Houk, Violet: 59,5.
Housom, Robert: (W) 143,21.
Houston, Ethel: 170,192.
Houston, George Fleming: 332,41.
"How He Lied to Her Husband": (R'04) 45,270.
"How Theatres Are Managed": by W. Hawks: 38,90; 39, 126; 40,151; 41,165; 42, 195.
"How to Produce Amateur Plays" (Clark) (B): 201,310.
"How to see a play" (Burton) (B): 172,276; 344,6.
Howard, Booth: 260,298.
Howard, Bronson: 10,18; 22,25; 22,27; (W) 28,137; 29,162; (A) 34,288; 37,72; 55,227; 62,99; 91,232; 197,24.
Howard, Cordelia: 36,44.
Howard, Esther: 202,361; 232,531; 255,369; 269,17; 270,17; 270,43.
Howard, Ethel: 171,259.
Howard, Eugene: 173,27; (C) 262,27; 286,36; 331,39; (C) 344,22.
Howard, Frances: 251,93; 283, 25; 287,13; 287,46; 290,xi; 297,48.
Howard, George: 36,44; 52, 137; 92,256; 101,11; 159, 245.
Howard, Harold: 37,62.
Howard, Jean: 273,38.
Howard, John Tasker (W): 361, 21.
Howard, Kathleen: 152,131; 163,103; 197,31; 287,35; 300,35.
Howard, Leslie: 255,351; 260, 313; 264,21; 269,14; 270, 17; 292,21; 315,25; (W) 318,24; 321,47; 322,40; (C) 323,70; 326,21; 342,19; 344, 17; 344,24; 345,16; 346,32; (C) 347,2; (W) 351,38; 352, 20.
Howard, Madeline: 174,81; 184, 342.
Howard, Mary M.: (W) 88,151.
Howard, Olin: 328,34.
Howard, Paul (W): 55,228.
Howard, Sidney: 249,378; 294, 10.
Howard, Tom: 326,40; (W) 331, 28; (C) 361,38.
Howard, Willie: 173,27; (C) 262,27; 286,36; 292,30; 293,44; 331,39; (C) 344,22.

"Howdy King": (R'26) 311,15.
Howe, Flo: 180,79.
Howe, Frank Jr.: 37,78; 232, 508.
Howe, Ida: 160,285.
Howe, Walter T. (W): 211, 140.
Howell, George: 129,150; 254, 304.
Howell, Helen: 317,11.
Howell, Lois: 162,68.
Howell, Maude: 244,27; (W) 335, 45.
Howell, Virginia: 359,25.
Howells, William Dean: 26, 100.
Howland, Allen: 296,21.
Howland, Jobyna: 60,42; 162, 70; 166,284; 187,142; 216, 76; 216,106; 263,21; 277, 17.
Howland, Olin: 260,315; (D) 316,34.
Howlett, Stanley: 277,18.
Howman, Margaret: 184,34.
"Hoyden, The": (R'07) 82,xvii.
Hoyt, Julia: 245,108; 255,359; 271,23; 289,24; 297,48; 317, 9; 327,48; 337,54.
Hoyt, Vonnie: 88,155; 101,14; 160,285.
Huara, Helba: 316,35.
Huban, Eileen: 173,14; 197, 23; 197,25; 200,219; 202, 341; 219,265; 256,45; 257, 83.
Hubbell, Raymond: 137,10; 184, 351; 188,206.
Hubel, Carl: 332,18.
Huberdeau, Gustav: 107,75; 122,114.
Huberman, Bronislaw: 249,391.
Hubert, Harold: 180,71.
"Huckleberry Finn": (F,R) 230, 278.
Hudson, Alfred Jr.: 108,38.
Hudson, Hazel: 232,536.
Hudson, Kate (W): 123,162.
Hudson, Robert: 213,275; 225, 309.
Hudson Theatre (New York): 30, 193; 34,296; 39,126; 110, 121.
Hudspeth, Marie: 154,197.
Huey, Richard: 357,27.
Huff, Forrest: 133,103; 140, 123.
Huff, Grace: 111,160.
Huff, Louise: 205,191; 208,402; 208,404; 211,185; 233,41.
Hughes, Annie: 61,55; 62,101; 170,176; 183,284; 242,343.
Hughes, Donald: 359,39.
Hughes, Edwin: 266,37.
Hughes, Gareth: 177,230; 178,302; 185,9; 188,193; 197,25; 208, 359.
Hughes, Hatcher: 283,10.
Hughes, J. Early: 70,318.
Hughes, J.J. (see Adelaide and Hughes).
Hughes, Leila: 172,279.
Hughes, Leanore: 191,39; 220, 370; 287,48.
Hughes, Lloyd: 210,117; 297,42.
Hughes, Rupert: 22,14; (W) 35,18; 44,248; 55,227; 62, xiii; (W) 111,147; 124,188; 196,353; 198,91; 198,109; (W) 206,222; 207,282; (A) 231,347; 231,395; 277,30; 289,32.
Hughston, Regan: 137,10; 268, 14.
Hugo, Victor: 15,13.
Hulbert, Jack: 300,29; 302,19.
Hulett, Otto: 340,42.
Hulette, Gladys: 141,143; 171, 237.
Hulicius, Otto: 300,19.
Hull, Henry: 152,135; 189, 285; 191,18; 219,277; 224, 215; 245,89; 253,215; 259, 243; 267,38; 271,17; 271, 21; 288,27; (A) 322,3; (W) 335,35; 347,46; 348,47; (C) 351,4; 358,28; 359,34.
Hull, Josephine: 278,17; 359,24.
Hull, Shelley: 156,79; 181, 137; 183,281; 185,29; 195, 281; 199,135; 200,213; 211, 135; 212,219; 216,93; 216, 114; 217,183.
Hull House Dramatic Players: 127, 89; 151,xix; 165,229.
Hullman, Charles: 344,53.
Humbert, George: 337,27.

Hume, Edward: 88,154.
Hume, Sam: 167,28; 196,333; (D) 220,337.
Hummel, A.H.: 37,74; (W) 46,314.
"Humoresque": (F) 232,534; (F,R) 233,38; (F) 235,194; (R'23) 266,16.
Humperdinck, Engelbert: 116, 108; 120,46.
Humphrey, Doris: 337,41; 338, 19; 357,45.
Humphrey, William: 61,65.
Humphreys, Haroldine: 304,14.
Humphreys, Mary Gay (W): 90,203.
"Humpty Dumpty": (R'04) 46, 298; 48,35; (D) 134,126; 134,131; (R'18) 213,280; 213,287.
"Hunchback, The": (R'02) 17,2; 146,115.
"Hunchback of Notre Dame, The": 115,86; (F,R) 272,30; (F) 275,39.
"Hundred Years Old, A": (R'29) 345,50.
Huneker, Diane: 70,321.
Huneker, James: (W) 3,17; 7,13; 43,216; (W) 48,39; (W) 50,89; 100,x; (W) 111, 142; (A) 231,347; 241,308.
Hungarian Theatre: 305,12; 329, 20.
Hungerford, Mona: 214,359.
"Hungry Hearts": (F,R) 263,70.
"Hunky Dory": 266,300.
Hunt, Frank Walcott: (W,V) 31, 214.
Hunt, Homer: 133,97.
Hunt, Ida Brooks: 51,129; 91, 232; 92,263; 105,159.
Hunt, Phoebe: 217,159.
Hunt, William S. (W): 42,191.
Hunter, Edna: 189,293.
Hunter, G.H.: 35,17.
Hunter, Glenn: 181,143; 226, 365; 258,139; 263,17; 266, 35; 272,33; 272,59; 298, 19; 299,26; 301,48; 304, 12; 318,61; 321,78; 323, 29; 337,43; 339,38; 347, 24; (C) 348,4.
Hunter, Harrison: 59,15; 130, 220; 191,20; 211,131; 223, 169.
Hunter, Ian: 299,11; 333,47.
Hunter, Kenneth: 142,172; 181, 123; 266,17; 278,14.
Hunter, Louise: 274,37; 281,35.
Hunter College: 221,37; 233, 61; 271,42.
Huntington, Agnes: 193,157.
Huntington, Florence: 203,31.
Huntington, Wright: 43,viii.
Huntley, G.P.: 32,240; 112, 183; 117,151; 197,40; 309, 13.
Huntley, G.P. Jr.: 359,25.
"Hurdy Gurdy Girl, The": (R'07) 81,xv.
Huret, M. Jules: 31,217.
Hurlbut, Gladys: 244,14; 327, 39.
Hurlbut, William J.: 95,18; 101,32; 115,81; 115,83; 125, 29; 307,32.
Hurst, Brandon: 83,12; 119, 23; 235,191; 324,49.
Hurst, Catharine: 199,157.
Hurst, Fannie: 239,97; (W) 313,7; 315,32; (W) 341,14.
Hurst, Vera: 251,77.
"Husband and Wife": (R'15) 177,224.
"Hush": (R'16) 189,326; 190, 365.
Huss, Henry Holden: 21,26.
Hustings, Lucille: 242,331.
Huston, Walter: 277,25; 291, 26; 299,4; 303,14; 306,28; 343,32; 344,24; 351,46; 354, 61; 356,47.
Hutcheson, David: (C) 350,47.
Hutcheson, Ernest: 181,134; 335, 39.
Hutchison, Josephine: 335,23; 345,32; (D) 346,29; 359,14.
Hutchison, Kathryn: 17,7.
Hyams, Leila: 323,45.
Hyde, Douglas: 29,168.
Hyde, James Clarence (W): 19,18.
Hyde, Walter: 136,173.
Hyem, Constance: 44,246.
Hyland, Peggy: 186,68; 206, 261; 208,393; 211,188; 224, 253.

Hyman, John: 39,112.
Hymes, Imogene: 88,160.
"Hyphen, The": (R'15) 172,280; 172,301.
"Hypocrites, The": (R'06) 68, 255; 68,258; 68,259; 74, 106.
"Hypocrites" (F): 166,275; 169, 127; 209,59.
Hyson, Carl: 211,149; 231,407; 292,41.

--I--

"I. O. U.": (R'18) 214,348.
"I Love You": (R'19) 220,342; 220,363.
Ibsen, Henrik: 5,16; 6,5; 7,8; 11,17; (C) 15,15; 18,3; 18,22; 22,27; 24,45; 25,70; 26,100; 33,267; 39,112; 46, 299; 47,9; 47,23; 48,49; 50,82; 51,iv; 57,vii; 62,xv; 65,ix; 65,177; 66,viii; 66, 219; 67,238; 69,290; 72,56; 74,86; 76,149; 79,231; 81, 288; 81,290; 84,32; 91,248; 102,48; 111,131; 112,viii; 114,41; 206,217; 208,358; 258,140; (D) 266,10; 290, 32; 301,15.
Ibsen, Lillebil: 265,21.
"Icebound": (R'23) 265,20; (S) 266,28.
Ichikawa, Ennosuke: 220,362.
Ichikawa, Sadanji: 109,83.
"Iconoclasts" (Huneker) (B): 51,iv.
Ide, Idalia: 181,127.
Ide, Leonard: 81,297.
"Ideal Husband, An": (R'18) 213, 278; 213,281.
"Idle Inn, The": 230,260; (R'21) 252,165.
"Idols": (R'09) 106,xiii; 106, 168.
"If": (R'17) 193,192; (R'27) 322, 40.
"If I Was King": (R'26) 308,18.
"If I Were King" (see also "Vagabond King, The"): 8,6; (R'01) 9,2; 9,5; 10,7; 184, 333; (F,R) 233,38.
"If Winter Comes": 267,18; (R'23) 267,19.
"Il Tabarro" (OP): 216,72; 216,73.
"'Ile": (R'18) 208,356; 208, 359; 253,270.
Ilidor: 199,175.
"I'll Be Hanged If I Do": (R'10) 119,xiii; 120,49.
"I'll Say She Is": (R'24) 281,16.
"Illicit": (F) 359,3.
Illington, Margaret: 14,5; 35,6; 39,124; 42,193; 42,194; 48,30; 58,315; 67,227; 68,263; 69, 290; 78,204; 80,257; 81,297; (C) 82,xxiv; 82,334; 95,28; 115,84; 130,212; 131,c; 131, 2; 131,27; 133,xx; 135,141; 149,19; 151,90; 162,73; 168, 56; 170,199; 171,258; 174, 60; (A) 176,190; 186,64; 187,127; 191,20; 191,21; 202,408; 206,214; 206,215; 220,345; 220,368; 231,363; 331,46.
Illinois Theatre (Chicago): 124, 198.
Illinois Theatre: 219,305.
Illinois, University of: 66,ix; 89,176; 243,428; 359,49.
"Illusion of Beatrice, The": 70, 340.
"Imaginary Invalid, The": 194, 201; (R'17) 124,214.
"Immoral Isabella?": (R'27) 322,40.
"Immortal Thief, The": (R'26) 309,15; 309,17.
Imperial Alexander Theatre (St. Petersburg): 161,21.
"Importance of Being Earnest, The": (R'02) 15,4; 304,14; (R'26) 304,15; 360,50.
"Impossible Catherine": (F) 222,135.
"Imposter, The": (R'10) 120, 37; 120,62.
"Imprudence": (R'03) 23,7.
"In a Garden": (R'25) 298,15.
"In Abraham's Bosom": 316,18; (S) 317,24.
"In After Years": (F) 137,20.
"In April": (R'15) 172,282.
"In Dahomey": (R'03) 26,96; 26,97; 30,186.
"In for the Night": 192,84;

(R'17) 192, 88.
"In Hayti": (R'09) 104, xv.
"In His Arms": (R'24) 285, 76.
"In His House": 133, 86.
"In Love With Love": (R'23) 271, 19.
"In The Bishop's Carriage": 55, 217; (R'07) 74, 88.
"In The Days of Shakespeare" (Jenks) (B): 49, xv.
"In The Fool's Bauble": 60, 35.
"In The Land of the Head Hunters": (F) 167, 20.
"In The Long Run": (R'09) 107, xi.
"In The Next Room": (R'23) 275, 19.
"In The Night Watch": (R'21) 241, 264.
"In The Zone": 202, 347; (R'17) 202, 352; (R'24) 286, 22.
"Inca of Perusalem, The": (R'16) 191, 21.
Ince, Ralph: 319, 39.
Ince, Thomas H.: 171, 244; 208, 398; 211, 186.
Inchbald, [Mrs.]: 128, 134.
"Inconstant George": (R'09) 105, 134; 105, 155; 106, xxx.
"Incubus, The": (R'09) 100, xii.
"Indestructible Wife, The": 205, 137; (R'18) 205, 149.
"Indian Summer": 154, 177; (R'13) 154, 178.
Indian Theatre: 84, 53; 87, xiv; 115, 90; 353, 39; 356, 45; 211, 165; 248, 322; 331, 56.
Indians--American: 62, 88; 83, 30; 88, 148; 114, 54; 122, 125; 122, 129; 179, 32; 185, 14; 185, 19; 298, 30.
"Indiscretion": (R'29) 338, 45.
"Indiscretion of Truth, The": (R'12) 143, 4.
Inescort, Elaine: 169, 111.
Inescourt, Frieda: 255, 351; 268, 32; 269, 26; 273, 17; 304, 33; 313, 20; 321, 47; (C) 323, 70; (D) 333, c; 343, 27.
"Infanta, The": 203, 31.
"Inferior Sex, The": (R'10) 109, 69; 109, 92.
"Infinite Shoeblack, The": 346, 15; 349, 44; (R) 349, 47.
"Information, Please": (R'18) 213, 278; 214, 349.
Ingenues: 88, 162; (D) 223, 143.
Ingersoll, William: 61, 56; 77, 172; 87, 118; 98, 98; 215, 9; 278, 17.
Ingham, Esther: 204, 93.
"Ingomar": 76, 154.
Ingram, Georgie: 305, 31; 306, 22; 306, 46.
Ingram, Rex: 262, 35; 270, 33; 281, 31; 313, 49; (W) 322, 24.
"Inner Man, The": (R'17) 199, 134; 199, 135.
"Innocent": 164, 157; (R'14) 164, 196.
"Innocent and Annabel": (R'21) 245, 98.
"Innocent Eyes": (R'24) 281, 15.
"Innocent Idea, An": 233, 23.
"Insect Comedy, The" (see "World We Live In, The").
"Inside the Lines": (R'15) 170, 172; 170, 187.
"Inspector General, The": (R'23) 268, 20; (R'30) 359, 26.
"Inspector Kennedy": (R'29) 347, 68.
Inter-Theatres Arts School (New York): 282, 68.
"Interference": (S) 322, 28; (R'27) 322, 40.
"Interior": (R'15) 170, 207.
International Alliance of Theatrical Stage Employees: 336, 45.
"International Cup, The": 116, 110.
International Film Arts Guild: 302, 32.
"International Marriage, An": (R'09) 96, xv.
"International Revue, The": (C) 350, 2.
"Interviews With Authors"
by G. H. Tower:
Frank Pixley: 56, 253;
Augustus Thomas: 58, 304;
Bronson Howard: 62, 99;

by A. Patterson:
Charles Klein: 64, 157;
David Belasco: 67, 247;

Clyde Fitch: 71,14;
George Broadhurst: 75,128;
Edwin Milton Royle: 79,240;
Grace Livingston Furniss: 81,301;
Percy MacKaye: 82,338;
Eugene Walter: 92,272;
Edith Ellis: 99,152;
Martha Morton: 104,126.
"Intimate Strangers": (R'21) 250, 30; 251,73.
"Intolerance": 188,216; (F) 191, 48.
Intropidi, Emilie (W): 243,420.
Intropidi, Ethel: 173,36; 204, 93.
"Intruder, The": (R'09) 105, xv; (R'16) 189,283.
"Invader, The": 90,i.
"Invisible Foe, The": 216,69; (R'18) 216,79.
Inyoka, Nyota: 276,23.
"Iolanthe": (R'13) 148,xii; 149,2; (R'26) 303,50; 304, 19; 308,17; (D) 323,23.
"Iole": 156,56; 156,59; (R'13) 156,106.
Ioucelli, Vincenzo; 205,159.
Iowa State University: 28,151; 271,42; 272,42; 283,42.
"Iphigenia in Aulis": (R'21) 243,415.
"Iphigenia in Tauris": 173,12; 173,13; (OP) 191,30; (D, OP) 220,337.
"Irene Wycherley": 82,321; (R'08) 85,63.
"Iris": 9,8; (R'02) 21,5.
Irish, Annie: 3,11; 4,6; 8,4; 9,6; 9,7; 10,11; 13,12; 21,10; 32,249; 43,222; 45,277; 64,159.
Irish Drama: 48,x; 343,6.
Irish Players, The: 128,xvi; 129,157; 131,11; 131,28; 145,68; 154,185; 323,58.
Irish Theatre: 29,158; 29,167; 57,xii; 141,xviii; 159,276; 173,14; 234,108; 350,74.
"Irishry": 173,14.
"Iron Cross, The": (R'17) 194, 213.
"Iron House, The": (F,R) 287, 32; 287,33.
"Iron Mask, The": (F) 336,29.
Iroquois Theatre Fire: 36,36.
Irving, Dorothy: 245,94.
Irvin, F. (W): 48,51; 54, 202.
Irving, [Sir] Henry: PG, 31; 5, 5; 7,3; 9,6; 9,17; 11,14; 19,14; 27,112; (D) 29,158; 29,159; 33,275; 41,iv; 46, xxii; 55,219; 57,ii; 57,264; 58,iii; 58,293; 60,49; 70,ix; 87,139; 89,xii; 106,180; (D) 114,39; (A) 115,92; 130,208; 132,70; 135,ix; 139,76; 139, 94; 146,128; 149,16; 150,51; 150,70; 182,128; (D) 182,217; 183,272; 187,136; 196,347; 256,14; 287,64.
Irving, Henry Brodribb: 43,215; 45,xiii; 66,204; 66,205; 69, 282; 69,283; 98,122; 149,16.
Irving, Isabel: 4,5; 20,4; 24, 48; 29,163; 33,273; 52,143; 61,80; 83,14; 93,285; 101, 25; 110,124; 116,107; 135, 165; 152,123; 172,307; 231, 363; 281,14; 290,23.
Irving, Laurence: 8,4; 82,347; 99,134; 108,34; 111,xxx; 111, 131.
Irving, Margaret: 233,27; 235, 209; 236,298; 260,307; 294, 43; 318,51; 342,52.
Irving Place Theatre: 81,311; 93,289.
Irwin, Beatrice: 20,4.
Irwin, John: 284,38.
Irwin, May: 46,298; (W) 52, 140; 56,258; 67,248; 70,318; 77,186; 93,xi; (A) 109,viii; 113,17; 119,12; 136,188; 142, 196; 146,101; 146,123; 148, 175; 174,60; 176,169; 177, 236; 188,203; 290,46; 302, 25; 316,50.
Irwin, Thomas: 167,15.
Isaacson, Charles D. (W) (see also "Music For Everyone"): 206,232; 237,348; 227,33; 228,102; 238,22; 262,15.
"Isabel": (R'25) 288,64.
Isham, Frederic: 238,15.
Ishikawei, Ennosuke: 280,23.
Isis Theatre (San Diego): 68,

xvii.
"Isle of Lost Ships, The": (R, F) 268, 58.
"Isle of Spice, The": 43, 237; (R'04) 44, 246.
"Israel": (S) 96, 58; (R'09) 106, 169; 106, 177; 326, 41.
Issachenko, Claudia: 295, 13.
"Is Matrimony a Failure?": (R) 104, 104; 104, 105.
"Is Zat So": 289, 17; (R'25) 289, 18; 308, 62.
"It All Depends": (R'25) 295, 16; 295, 19.
"It Can Be Done": (R'14) 157, 114.
"It Happened in Nordland": 47, 5; (R'05) 47, 8; 56, 239.
"It Happens to Everybody": (R'19) 220, 344.
"It Is the Law": (R'22) 263, 19.
"It Is to Laugh": (R'28) 324, 40.
"It Pays to Advertise": (R'14) 164, 159; 165, 155; (F, R) 361, 47.
Italian Theatre (see also Sicilian Theatre): 16, 25; 89, 174; 215, 32; 291, 20; 294, 22; 302, 20.
Ithaca Conservatory of Music; 213, 300.
Itow, Michio: 199, 132; 237, 367; 252, 150; 318, 39; 337, 41.
"It's a Wise Child": (S) 343, 33; (R'29) 343, 41; (C) 344, 44; 345, 33.
"It's All Your Fault": (R'06) 63, xi; 63, 112.
"It's Up To You": (R'21) 243, 460.
Iturbi, Jose: 347, 31.
Ivan, Rosalind: 85, 68; 136, 176; (W) 287, 20; (W) 288, 9.
Ivans, Elaine: 168, 69.
Ives, Alice: 73, 84.
Ives, Charlotte: 112, 178; 119, 18; 122, 107; 203, 11.
Ivogun, Maria: 280, 35.
"Ivory Door, The": (R'27) 322, 38.
"Izzy": (R'24) 284, 70.

--J--

Jacchia, Agide: 163, 102.
Jack, E. B.; 137, 10.
Jack, John: 132, 48.
"Jack and Jill": (R'23) 266, 16; 270, 18.
"Jack and the Beanstalk": (F, R) 199, 176.
"Jack O'Lantern": (R'17) 202, 392.
"Jack Straw": (R'08) 92, xiii; 92, 255; (S) 94, 330.
"Jack's Little Surprise": (R'04) 44, 246; 44, 256; 45, iv.
Jackson, Alfred: 70, 318.
Jackson, Charles: 57, 285; 77, 185.
Jackson, Ethel: 80, 258; 81, 312; 81, 313; (C) 82, xxiv; 82, 330; 84, 44; 90, 207; 95, 10.
Jackson, Joe: (D) 294, 29.
Jackson, Thomas: 137, 11; 194, 201.
Jacobson, Clarence D.: 299, 23.
Jacobson, Norman: (D) 294, 27.
Jacoby, Josephine: 61, 82; 113, 15; 137, 3; 159, 223; 216, 94.
"Jacquerie, La": (OP) 239, 11.
Jacques, Eugene Leslie: 59, xiii.
Jacques, Nanon: 108, 46.
Jadlowker, Hermann: 120, 46; 129, 154; 132, 50; 132, 51; 133, 78.
Jaffe, Sam: 207, 289; 358, 28; 359, 29; 359, 35.
James, Agnes: 300, 23.
James, Aphie: 66, 211; 79, 252; 104, 122; 125, 27.
James, Charles (W): 140, 122.
James, Gardner: 311, 49; 312, 39.
James, Henry: 86, 91.
James, Horace: 145, 96.
James, Louis: 9, 12; 19, 22; 41, 175; 52, 143; 58, 301; 65, 169; 67, 246; 78, c; 78, 207; 79, 254; 90, 225; 104, 122; 110, iv; 120, 64; 193, 146; 212, 202; 231, 363; 231, 397.
James, Mary: 280, 44.
James, Millie: 3, 4; 3, 11; 25, 76.
James, Walter: 259, 227; 260, 313.
Janacek, Leo: 287, 34.

Janauschek, Fanny: 31,228; 58,xiii; 66,206; 78,223; 232, 508.
Jane, Mary: (D) 336,27; (C) 337,35; (D) 341,31.
"Jane Clegg": 230,265; (R'20) 230,269; 241,267.
"Jane Eyre": (F) 250,39.
Janice, Dorothy: 280,18.
"Janice Meredith": 5,15.
Janin, Jules: 61,64.
Janis, Elsie: 54,208; 82,xviii; 83,26; 97,93; 97,95; 106, c; 118,193; 125,29; 132,70; 135,c; 142,193; 146,127; 164, 181; 171,254; 173,26; 177,224; 177,237; 178,287; (A) 183, 319: 185,16; 191,10; 191,17; 192,109; (D) 193,c; 193,169; (A) 193,171; (W) 196,336; 197,16; 197,38; 198,79; 200, 210; 200,211; 200,216; 204, 112; (W,V) 206,204; 209, 39; 211,132; 215,27; 221,5; (W,V) 227,14; 227,41; 229, 209; 232,512; 254,281; 257, 96; 262,37; 276,25; 278,21; 288,26; 289,18; 289,21; 290, 46.
Janney, William: 314,17.
Jannings, Emil: 244,38; 244,39; 266,72; (D) 319,42; (W) 319, 43; (C) 334,24.
Jansen, Marie: 149,17; 201,293; 241,260; 286,13.
Janvier, Emma: 86,111; 95,6; 159,232.
Janvier, Henry: 5,11.
Janvier, Jean: 194,222.
"Japan By Night": (R'03) 30, 184; 30,186.
"Japanese Honor": 140,117.
"Japanese Nightingale, A": 6,18; (R'04) 35,4; 35,6.
Japanese Theatre: 6,15; 41,167; 47,20; 79,250; 109,82; 136, 180; 156,84; 189,290; 207, 298; 220,362; 258,161; 280,22; 306,30; 323,13; 342, 6; 349,20; 350,74.
Jardin De Paris: 77,iv; 79,232.
Jardon, Dorothy: 123,172; 132,43; 191,38; 200,217; 217,137.
Jarnagin, Jerry: 340,26.
"Jarnegan": 331,41; (R'28) 333,78.
Jarrell, Irma: 266,21.
"Jaunts Into Brightest England" by C. Miles:
G.B. Shaw: 259,213;
John Galsworthy: 261,364;
A.N. Pinero: 265,25;
A.A. Milne: 268,25.
"Java Head": (F,R) 265,72.
Jaynes, William Burton: 41,159.
Jazz: 309,20; 312,14; 344,42.
"Jazz Singer, The": 302,23.
"Jealous Moon, The": (R'28) 334,45.
"Jealousy": (R'28) 334,45; 334, 46; (S) 335,30.
"Jeanne D'Arc" (see also "Joan of Arc"): 69,309; 70,315; 73,c; (R'07) 73,59; 73,80.
Jeans, Isabel: 170,197; 307, 21.
Jeayes, Allen: 320,28.
"Jedermann": (R'27) 323,58.
Jefferson, Cornelia: 41,177.
Jefferson, Joseph: PG,4; (A) 7,1; 13,14; 15,17; 41,174; 41,176; 52,139; 53,c; 53, 179; 53,180; (A) 58,300; 61,i,b; 66,214; 70,329; 74, 100; 74,108; 77,187; 81, 294; 104,119; 126,64; 141, 136; 145,74; 168,72; (D) 182,261; 231,397; 237,366; 258,142; 301,70.
Jefferson, [Mrs.] Joseph Jr.: 117,144.
Jefferson, Thomas: 41,176; 57,268; 118,xxi; 167,11.
Jefferson, William: 74,108.
Jefferson Theatre (Goshen, Indiana): 63,xv.
Jeffreys, Ellis: 48,29; 50, iv; 50,80; 50,83; 51,109; 51,110; 61,69; 68,xv; 68,254; 74,91; 76,158.
Jelenko, N.L.: 6,15.
Jenbach, Bela: 299,20.
Jenkins, Allen: 329,24.
Jenks, George C. (W): 69, 297; 76,166; 77,192; 83,18; 89,186; 90,209; 96,66; 97,

92; 101,33; 102,44; 103, 98; 107,27; 109,95; 110,118; 116,105; 125,33; 126,47; 137, 4; 139,74; 141,156; 149,16; 150,48; 157,152; 162,79; 220, 350; 224,240; 235,190; 236, 256; 237,366; 240,156; 242, 334.
Jennings, De Witt: 108,54; 117, 135; 164,154.
"Jenny": 345,15; (R'29) 345,48.
Jensen, Eulalie: 320,20.
Jeppson, Agnes: 185,34.
Jepson, Eugene: 57,285.
Jergens, Alice: 186,67.
Jeritza, Marie: 250,26; 262,43; 266,37; 272,37; 287,35; 336, 39.
Jerome, Jerome K.: 105,134.
Jerome, William: 179,26.
Jerrold, Mary: 87,122.
"Jerry": (R'14) 159,225.
"Jerry For Short": (R'29) 343,41.
"Jersey Lily": (R'03) 32,241.
Jessel, George: (W) 302,22; 302,23; (W) 323,22; (A) 350, 74; (C) 358,44.
"Jest, The": (R'19) 219,324; 220,336; (S) 220,352; 220, 353; 220,358; 223,150; 301, 11.
"Jesters, The": (R'08) 84,ix; 84, 33.
Jew In Drama (see also "Yellow Ticket, The"; Yiddish Theatre): 96,58; 98,xi; 122,ix; 139, 76; 157,112; 158,212; 159,275; 211,154; 246,146.
Jewel, Betty: 257,75; 281,30.
Jewel, Izetta: 108,38.
"Jewel of Asia, The": (R'03) 25, 60.
Jewell, Violet: 88,155.
"Jewelled Tree, The": (R'26) 309,68.
"Jewels of the Madonna, The": (OP) (R) 134,110; 154,183.
Jewett, Henry: 48,41; 58,309; 301,36.
Jewett, Sara: 25,63; 54,189; 126,65; 171,232; 202,338; 245,96.
Jewish Theatre, The (Toronto): 104,132.
Jewish Art Theatre: 251,91.
"Jim Bludsoe": 15,9; (R'03) 24,34.
"Jim Jam Jems": (R'20) 238, 76.
"Jim The Penman": (R'10) 112, ix; 112,iii; 112,173.
"Jimmie": (R'20) 238,74.
"Jimmy The Carrier": (R'05) 51,112; 52,153.
Jitney Players, The: 289,42.
"Jitta's Atonement": (R'23) 264,16.
"Joan O' The Shoals": (R'02) 13,11.
"Joan of Arc" (see also "Jeanne D'Arc"): 101,8; 101,27; (R'09) 102,38; 103,81; (F) 189,300; 214,343; 245,102.
Joeffries, Fleurette: 270,35.
Joel, Clara: 158,190; 191, 17; 199,125; 200,204; 200, 221; 200,228; 201,269; 242, 324.
Johaneson, Bland (W) (see also Vaudeville): 259,238; 260, 316; 262,36; 270,10.
Johann, Zita: 331,37; 332,47; 334,32; 360,33.
Johannes, "Count": 103,78.
"Johannes Kreisler": (R'22) 263,15; (D) 264,17.
"Johannesfeuer": (R'05) 47,2.
Johannson, Ronny: 267,23; (D) 347,28.
John, Alice: 90,216; 111,139; 122,136; 128,115; 159,225; 165,221; 188,204; 238,40; 266,17; 304,33.
"John Bull's Other Island": (R'05) 57,264; 57,271.
"John Ermine of the Yellow-stone": 34,318.
"John Ferguson": 220,363; (R'19) 221,13; 221,23; 241, 267; 245,77.
"John Gabriel Bjorkman": 109, 82; (R'15) 172,281; (R'26) 301,15.
"John Glayde's Honor": (S) 76, ix; 83,21; (R'07) 84,34.
"John Henry": (R'03) 29,159.
"John Hudson's Wife": (R'06) 69,xiii; 69,310.

"John Murray Anderson's Almanac" (see "Almanac").
John Street Theatre (New York): 19,18; (D) 136,197; 243,419.
"John The Baptist": 70,312; (R'07) 73,xvi.
John, The Orange Man: 62,94.
"Jonathan Makes a Wish": 213, 269; (R'18) 213,312.
"Johnny Get Your Gun": 193,153; (R'17) 194,216.
Johns, Florence: 243,301; 271, 14; 272,29; 283,25; 284, 23; 302,27; 307,29.
Johnson, Alice: (D) 249,389.
Johnson, Arthur: 161,44.
Johnson, Ben: 87,130; 105,144; 105,145; 107,9; 107,24; 118, 169; 122,129; 129,162; 150, 54; 42,190; 182,201.
Johnson, Edith: 169,129.
Johnson, Edward: 85,75; 228, 96; 239,111; 280,35; 289, 35; 299,35; 339,30; 361,23.
Johnson, Ethel: 42,188; 49,74; 69,293; 71,22.
Johnson, Howard: 202,358.
Johnson, Julian (W): 168,67.
Johnson, Kay: 304,27.
Johnson, Margaret: 230,275.
Johnson, Marion Pollock: 20, 10; 78,220.
Johnson, Martin: 270,33.
Johnson, Mary: 134,136.
Johnson, Moffat: 324,40.
Johnson, Molly: 284,18; 285,46; 292,26.
Johnson, Naomi: 326,50; 331, 53; 332,c.
Johnson, Orrin: 11,1; 25,59; 30,185; 33,273; 38,85; 66, 207; 70,319; 118,181; 123, 160; 123,161; 128,114; 148, 183; 154,181; 158,170; 183, 276.
Johnson, Owen: 85,72; 271,59.
Johnson, Renita: 235,195.
Johnson, Robert Underwood (W): 181,130.
Johnson, Selena: 44,242; 50, 103; 51,108; 91,252; 104,131; 108,46; 144,41; 150,44; 214,344.
Johnsrud, Harold: 324,39.
Johnston, Alfred C.: 290,49.
Johnston, Colin Keith: 296,21.
Johnston, Fanny: 5,8.
Johnston, John Leroy (W): 348, 37.
Johnston, Julanne: 308,36.
Johnston, Moffat: 263,18; 268, 31; 273,17; 290,35; 324,40.
Johnston, William (W): 132,66.
Johnstone, Daisy: 55,225.
Johnstone, Gordon: 96,38.
Johnstone, Justine: 120,64; 173, 17; 183,278; 189,293; 196, 357; 198,81; 204,89; 222,93; 234,128; 238,50; (D) 244,48; 284,36.
Johnstone, Lucy Jane: 85,64.
Johnstone, Mary: 23,6.
Johnstone, Menifoe: 6,17.
Jolivet, Rita: 131,1; 137,25; 151,98; 152,115; 156,61; 157,118; 185,26; 201,269; 210,95.
"Jolly Bachelors, The": (R'10) 108,xiv.
"Jolly Roger, The": (R'23) 271,76.
Jolson, Al: 145,67; (W) 152, 134; 165,255; 166,281; 182, 196; 206,227; (W) 207,290; 219,281; 246,151; 249,424; 250,12; 256,28; 257,96; 264, 40; 270,29; (A) 277,55; 278, 10; 286,10; 288,19; (W) 297, 20; 305,46; 307,19; (W) 319,9; 332,35; 335,38; (A) 335,63; 337,38; (W) 340, 43; 343,29.
Jolson Theatre (New York): 257, 99.
"Jonathan Makes a Wish": 213, 269; (R'18) 213,312.
Jones, Buck: 228,147.
Jones, Frederick: 270,18; 293, 36.
Jones, George (see Johannes, "Count").
Jones, Henry Arthur: 15,6; 44, vii; (W) 68,268; 71,28; 74, 106; 78,v; 81,292; 113,12; 133,74; 134,135; 168,56; 181,151; 197,24; 239,97; (W) 282,9; 357,10.
Jones, Isham: 282,23.

Jones, John Price: 329,39.
Jones, Nard: 322,46; (W) 327, 15; 328,32; 329,36; 330, 39.
Jones, Nina M.: (W,V) 155,32.
Jones, Robert Edmond: (D) 171, 248; (D) 184,336; 188,199; (W,D) 195,266; (D) 220,337; (D) 224,236; 228,94; 231,361; 241,298; 244,10; 250,19; (D) 260,290; 260,306; (D) 262,22; 296,13; 299,15; (D) 330,35; 344,35; (D) 349,41; 351,21; (D) 361,41.
Jones, Sybil Eliza: (W) 254,318.
Jones, [Mrs.] W.G.: 12,12; 79, vi; 28,132.
Jones, Walter: 116,125; 183, 275; 191,20; 199,151; 217, 152; 308,14.
Jones, Winifred Arthur: 135,143.
"Jonesy": (R'29) 339,45.
"Jongleur De Notre Dame, Le" (OP): 83,23.
Jordan, Dorothy: 352,47.
Jordan, Eben: 88,167.
Jordan, Frances: 120,36.
Jordan, [Mrs.] J.H.: 11,5.
Jordan, Jessie: 41,178.
Jordan, Mary: 152,131.
Jordan, Walter C.: 53,164.
Jorn, Carl: 98,109; 106,202; 129,155.
"Josef Suss": (R'30) 348,44.
Joselito: 209,38.
"Joseph and His Brethern": 144, 33; 144,34; (R'13) 144,37; 145,94; 149,xx; 151,xii; 162, 75.
"Joseph Entangled": (R'04) 45, 266; 46,269.
"Joseph Jefferson" (Wilson) (B): 67,x.
"Josephine": (R'18) 205,149; 205,153.
Josephine, Lois: 151,89; 156, 76; 159,244; 169,138.
Journet, Marcel: 22,38; (A) 132, xiv.
"Journey's End": 339,6; (R'29) 339,43; 339,45; 340,14; (D) 340,21; (S) 342,25; (D) 344, 19; (F) 349,31; 350,21; (F, R) 352,44; 353,27.
Jouvet, Louis: 202,342; 204, 86.
Joy, Gloria: 214,393.
Joy, Helen: 200,223; 335,47.
Joy, Leatrice: 211,181; 273, 30; 293,31; 305,13; 306, 38; 307,38; 308,37; 320,66; 321,75; 322,6; 323,4b; 323, 30; 324,8; 325,81; 341,20.
"Joy of Living, The": (R'02) 22,13.
Joyce, Alice: 140,112; 147, xvii; 165,227; 207,325; 210, 106; 213,323; 215,55; 223, 177; 233,39; 235,196; 246, 176; 270,33; 287,63; 288,46; 289,48; 343,46.
Joyce, Peggy Hopkins (see also Hopkins, Peggy): 270,15; 270, 27; 282,39; 298,44.
"Juarez and Maximilian": (R'26) 309,14; (S) 309,26; 309,27.
Juarez Theatre (Guanajuato): 107,31.
"Jubilo": (F,R) 228,106.
Judd, Dr. [pseud. for George W. Stevens, Sr.] (W): 26,99; 30,202; 36,44; 40,139; 41, 173; 42,200.
Judels, Charles: 185,11; 238,33.
"Judge and the Jury, The": (R'06) 68,xv.
"Judgement House, The": (F) 201,323.
"Judge's Husband, The": (R'26) 309,18.
"Judith of Bethulia": (B) 47,iii; (R'05) 47,3.
"Judith Zaraine": (R'11) 121, xiii.
"Judy": (R'27) 313,19.
"Judy Forgot": 117,130; (R'10) 117,133.
"Judy O'Hara": 125,27.
Jukes, Bernard: 321,60.
"Julie": (R'27) 316,20.
"Julie Bonbon": 60,25; 60,26; (R'05) 60,30.
"Julien": (OP,R'14) 158,178.
Juliet, Miss: 183,286; 267,43.
"Julius Caesar": (R'03) 23,3; 63,131; (R'12) 142, 162; 142,169; 142,172; 161, 15; 196,337; (R'18) 207,

286; (R'27) 317,18.
"Jumping Jupiter": (R'11) 122, xiii.
June, Roma: 183,278; 184, 342.
"June Love": (R'21) 244,30.
"June Madness": 138,63; (R'12) 141,x; 141,134.
"June Moon": 345,33; (R'29) 345, 47; (D) 346,c; (S) 347,32; 351, 28; 351,47.
"Jungle, The": (R'07) 76,146.
Junior, John: 131,32; 356,35.
Junior League: 86,iii.
"Juno and the Paycock": 301,9; (R'26) 302,15; 303,17.
"Just a Minute": 226,391; (R'19) 226,426.
"Just a Wife": (R'10) 109,vi.
"Just a Woman": 181,122; (R'16) 181,124.
"Just Around the Corner": (R'19) 217,144.
"Just As Well": (R'14) 158,171; 158,175.
"Just Because": 255,379.
"Just Boys": (R'15) 176,200.
"Just Fancy": 322,38.
"Just Herself": (R'14) 168,99.
"Just Like John": (R'12) 139,xi.
"Just Married": 244,9; (R'21) 244,30.
"Just Out of College": (R'05) 57,267; 57,285.
"Just Outside the Door": (R'15) 176,200.
"Just Suppose": 238,7; (R'20) 238,30.
"Just the Other Day": (F) 340,26.
"Just to Get Married": (R'12) 132,42.
"Justice": 127,89; 183,272; (R'16) 183,272; (S) 183,296; 186, 77; 188,200; 198,63.

--K--

"K Guy, The": (R'28) 333,81.
Kabuki Theatre (Japan): 220,362.
Kaelred, Katherine: 99,xvi; 99, 164; 100,174; 101,13; 110, 109; 110,119; 120,35; 120, 36; 121,95; 140,109; 175, 136; 185,32; 201,291; 208, 369; 220,345; 229,187.
Kahn, Florence: 4,12; 8,7; 8,9; 8,17; 8,18; 51,106.
Kahn, Maud: 182,243.
Kahn, Otto: 86,92; 124,195; 184,336; 287,27; (C) 344,26.
Kain, Gail: 144,c.
Kalish, Bertha: 11,16; 46,316; 53,157; 53,158; 57,265; 58,309; 68,253; 78,199; 79, 228; (C) 82,xxiv; 82,318; 82,340; 82,341; 86,87; 86, 88; 89,172; 93,306; 94,319; 99,157; 102,35; 106,183; 109, 67; 110,100; 127,91; 138,37; 153,151; 155,6; 155,8; 158, 191; 158,214; 159,237; 164, 161; 170,193; 171,230; 173, 26; 184,355; (W) 212,214; (A) 214,379; (C) 215,35; 216,104; 217,177; 224,231; 286,27; 287,52b; 301,16; 302,13.
Kamman, Emmerich: 297,25.
Kamerny Theatre: 268,22; 293, 16; 293,17.
Kampf, Leopold: 84,xii.
Kanders, Helen: 230,262; 231, 360.
Kandt, Elizabeth: 297,35.
Kane, Diana: 287,56.
Kane, Gail: 135,152; 140,102; 143,31; 144,c; 153,156; 153,161; 157,152; 163,122; 165,217; 166,291; 172,301; 173,23; 191,17; (A) 195,315; 205,195; 210,107; 217,157; 221,25; 234,83; 236,299; 254, 324; 255,400.
Kane, Genevieve: 103,99.
Kane, Helen: 332,49.
Kane, Whitford: 173,14; 208, 359; 246,145; 252,151; 257, 83; 278,14.
Kappeler, Alfred: (D) 263,11.
Karasz, Ilouka: 238,18.
"Karen": 204,83; (R'18) 205, 152.
Karkoa, Maurice: 141,146.
"Karl and Anna": (R'29) 345, 48.
Karlash, Nicholas: 257,81.
Karolevna, Ilona: 302,29.
Karolik, Maxim: 351,14.

Karsavina, Tamara: 127,94; 130,201; 176,166; 178, 294; 178,295; 284,34; (D) 347, 29.
Kartousch, Luise: 160,305.
"Kasernenluft": (R'13) 153,xxiv.
"Kassa": (R'09) 97,72; 97,101.
Katchaloff, Vassily: 259,216; 264,14.
"Katinka": 180,65; (R'15) 180, 66.
"Katja": (R'26) 310,18.
Katzin, Olga: 319,23.
Kauffman, Joe: 137,11.
Kaufman, Alfred: 152,132; 163, 102.
Kaufman, George S.: 268,40; 271,21; 328,29; 333,49; (W) 345,24; 354,27; (W) 357,46; (C) 358,2.
Kaufman, S. Jay: (C) 286,15.
Kauser, Alice: 46,xi; 53,163.
Kavanaugh, Lucille: 157,141.
Kawamura, Kikue: 161,31.
Kaye, A.P.: 200,209; 240, 181; 254,291; 254,304; (D) 254,309; 266,14.
Kaye, Joseph (W): 306,17; 308, 22; 311,10; 338,15; 339,16; 340,38; 341,26; 342,29; 343, 47; 344,33; 347,36; 348,31.
Kayser, Dora: 319,50.
Kean, Charles: (A) 58,302; 139, 96; 146,128; (D) 149,20; 182, 217; 232,502.
Keane, Doris: 51,129; 56,242; 58, 295; 68,258; 68,259; 68,280; 78,204; 89,173; 95,28; 99, 153; 99,154; 100,xiv; 100, xvi; 100,xx; 103,74; 104,125; 112,196; 117,151; 124,191; 141,131; 143,30; 145,65; 146, 112; 148,c; 150,iii; 161,8; 163,125; 183,302; 205,176; 216,85; 230,279; 242,341; 249,370; 253,211; 253,235; (D) 253,237; 254,321; 256,28; (D) 278,38; 280,21; 285,38; 288,46; 289,30; 301,36; 314, 33.
Kean, Edmund: 39,114; 46,320; 86,99; 97,86; 109,87; 125, vii; 182,217; (D) 223,166; (D) 232,506; 280,62.
Keane, Robert Emmett: 209, 11; 233,23; 288,37; (W) 342,34; 343,23.
Kearney, Eileen: 101,14.
Kearney, John L.: 183,275.
Kearns, Allen B.: 306,49; 328,39.
Keaton, Buster: 272,32; 273, 32; 281,23; 291,34; 298, 30; (C) 318,25.
Keefe, Zena: 232,533; 245,115.
Keeler, Ruby: 337,38; 340,13; 341,23; 360,27.
Keen, Malcolm: 282,12; 282, 13.
Keenan, Frank: 12,5; 13,3; 13,5; 49,xvi; 50,87; 50,95; (A) 51,i,f; 59,18; 65,187; 84,48; (W) 85,78; (W) 90, 221; 102,36; 105,135; 142, 172; 166,286; 166,287; 217, 192; 275,29.
Keenan, Harry G.: 42,212.
Keenan, Hilda: 163,117.
Keene, Laura: 124,186; 205, 166.
Keene, Mattie: 226,389.
Keene, Tom: 32,244; 232,502.
Keene Twins [Elizabeth & Margaret]: 259,237; 279,38.
Keener, Mary: 155,19.
"Keep Her Smiling": 210,69; (R) 211,144.
"Keep It to Yourself": (R'18) 216,80; 216,95.
"Keep Kool": (R'24) 281,15.
"Keep Shufflin' ": (R'28) 326,41.
"Keeping Up Appearances": (R'10) 118,xxii; (R'16) 191,21.
Keers, Helen: 242,331.
Keeshon, Grace: 215,33; 227,26.
Keggeris, R.B.: 113,20.
Kegley, Howard C.: (W) 236,274.
Keightley, Cyril: 92,259; 117, 136; 145,89; 168,77; 187, 149; 206,221; 208,375; 216, 81; 230,257; 239,101; 244, 21; 263,21; 266,17.
Keightley, Mabel Shambleau (W): 69,307; 142,198; 169, 122.
Keim, Adelaide: 34,302; 44,

260; 53,168; 67,228.
Keith, A. Paul: 231,485.
Keith, Benjamin F.: 49,xiv; 231, 408; 231,485; 250,36; 255, 347.
Keith, Ian: 255,357; 255,372; 258,150.
Keith, Robert: 301,23.
Keith-Johnson, Colin: 338,45; 342,26; (D) 344,19.
Keith's Union Square Theatre: 38,iv.
Kelcey, Herbert: PG, 3; 13,2; 14,8; 15,20; 44,245; 61,67; 70,319; 144,36; 189,277; 247,232; 287,52b.
Kellard, Ralph: 122,112; 128,112; 200,203; 208,345; 208,369; (A) 214,379; 239,105; 247, 231.
Keller, Helen: 224,252.
Keller, Marguerite: 168,80.
Kellerd, John E.: 10,26; 36,45; 96,40; 99,165; 130,210; (D) 143,4; 161,6; 239,105.
Kellerman, Annette: 120,xxvii; (W) 190,348; (A) 190,385; 191,17; 192,113; 193,147; 194, 240; (A) 194,249; 195,269; 197,45; (A) 203,1.
Kelley, Alice: 112,194,
Kelley, Ethel Amorita: 150,41; 165,230.
Kelly, Anthony Paul: 214,363.
Kelly, Desmond: 83,9; 84, 36; 105,155; 167,31; 168, 88; 324,40.
Kelly, Dorothy: 198,70.
Kelly, E.H.: 110,127.
Kelly, George: 191,38; 277, 29; 281,10; 286,36; 306, 32; 308,29; 347,25.
Kelly, Gregory: 111,139; 185, 21; 192,93; 202,361; 205, 163; 206,225; 209,22; 213, 269; 224,215; 247,237; 298, 27.
Kelly, Harry: 94,327; 102,53.
Kelly, John T.: (A) 16,19; 113,10; 124,196; 133,74; 231,363.
Kelly, Margot: 191,18; 195, 295; 201,267; (A) 214,379; 241,254; 292,23.
Kelly, Paul: 123,160; 272,14; 357,28; 358,33.
Kelly, Patsy: (C) 342,14; 343,43; 353,24.
Kelly, Peggy: 285,32.
Kelly, Renee: 100,194; 131, 14; 141,134; 141,152; 165, 216.
Kelly, Robert: 204,83; 262,31.
Kelly, William J.: 64,142; 108,44; 110,104; 182,194.
Keltie, Madeleine: 236,271.
Kemarskaya, Nadiezhda: 294,13.
Kemble, John Phillip: 58,300; 73,73; (D) 149,20; 182,217; 221,8.
Kemp, Barbara: 265,37; 276,35.
Kemp, Harry (W): 314,32; 349,22.
"Kempy": (R'22) 256,30; 257, 83; (S) 259,230; 261,388.
Kendal, Madge: 168,72.
Kendall, Ezra: 22,25; 28,134; 44,247.
Kenebel, Frank: 83,4.
Kenmore, Octavia: 250,24.
Kennan, Frank: 160,293.
Kennedy, Charles Rann: 87, 140; 95,8; 103,91; (W) 182, 128; 209,33; 214,359; 288,18.
Kennedy, Elizabeth: 66,212; 69, 286.
Kennedy, Joseph P.: 319,11.
Kennedy, Katherine: 38,85; 38, 92.
Kennedy, M.A.: 21,6; 286,13.
Kennedy, M. Bratton: 119,19.
Kennedy, Madge: 141,152; 143, 16; 164,164; 164,170; 173, 11; 178,279; 179,16; 180,79; 191,41; 192,c; 198,102; 199, 180; 222,114; 227,44; 229, 190; 231,412; 236,262; 239, 109; 240,186; 243,404; 245,87; 249,411; 272,27; 281,38; 288,13; 304,33; 304,44; (A) 322,3; (D) 326,13; 327,48; 329,19; 330,56; (D) 352,52.
Kennedy, Mary: 281,49; 291, 14; 293,36; 322,39; 338,52; 340,25; 342,49.
Kennedy, Merna: 304,47; 305, c; 325,50.
Kent, Barbara: 313,39.

Kent, Craufurd: 122,132; 152, 127.
Kent, Edgar: 120,61.
Kent, Eleanor: 10,8; 104,119.
Kent, Harriet (W): 211,138; 212,220; 213,286.
Kent, Helen: 118,170.
Kent, Maud: 88,155.
Kent, S. Miller: 9,22.
Kent, William: 207,289; 215, 16; 218,228.
Kentucky, University of: 235, 199.
Kentucky Theatre: 315,49.
Kenyon, Doris: 196,349; 210, 115; 225,315; 226,408; 228, 69; 230,255; 231,442; 238, 37; 242,332; 247,228; 247, 250; 248,331; 249,384; (D) 279,30; 284,30; 289,55; 310, 48.
Kenyon, Leslie: 133,97.
Keogh, Thomas J.: 6,17.
Ker, Paul: 184,360.
Kerey, Marion: 90,226; 127, 78;206,207; 213,267; 249, 382; 270,17; 340,23; 359, 44.
Kerker, Gustav: 184,351.
Kern, Cecil: 132,68; 160,292; 210,95.
Kern, Grace: 341,35; 356,25.
Kern, Jerome: 184,351; 280, 10; 285,27; 357,48.
Kerr, Caroline V. (W): 106, 172; 120,50.
Kerr, Frederick: 109,66; 239, 112; 255,372.
Kerr, Geoffrey: 238,7; 268,32; (W) 304,10; 309,12; 359,25.
Kerr, Molly: 310,25.
Kerrigan, J.M.: 129,157; 257,71; 268,3; 269,31; 278,26.
Kerrigan, Kathleen: 122,119.
Kerry, Anita: 322,40; 345,63.
Kershaw, Willette: 98,113; 102, 60; 116,124; 128,126; 128, 139; 147,155; 156,77; 215, 7; 261,357.
Kesler, C.: 11,17; 11,18.
Kessel, Adam Jr.: 171,244.
Kessel, Gaby: 138,35.
Kessler, D.E. (W): 102,62; 103,77.
Kessler, David: 168,81.
Kesslere, G.M.: 290,49.
Kessner, Rose: 207,289.
Kester, Paul: 9,15.
Key, Kathleen: 276,29.
Key, Pierre V.R. (W) (see also "Music and Musicians"): 218,202.
Keyes, Katherine: 28,156; 44,256.
Keys, Nelson: 281,17; 281,27; 286,36.
Kibbee, Guy: 356,35; 359,29.
"Kibitzer": (R'29) 337,45; 337, 46; (S) 338,26; 340,15.
"Kick In": 166,265; (R'14) 166, 304.
"Kick Me Again": (F,R) 360,48.
"Kid, The": (F,R) 241,270; (F) 241,272.
"Kid Boots": (R'23) 276,70; 277, 17.
"Kid Is Clever, The": (F,R) 211,183.
Kidder, Augusta Raymond (W): 285,26.
Kidder, Edward E.: (W,V) 5,6; 9,15; 14,5; 55,227; (W) 214, 338; (W) 253,240; (W) 302, 38.
Kidder, Kathryn: 98,107.
Kiefer, Edmund J. (W): 313, 22; 318,18; 319,32; 326,23.
Kienzl, Wilhelm: 147,135.
Kiernan, Thomas: 4,15.
"Kiki": (R'21) 251,97; (D) 251, 101; 251,105; 253,212; 254, 303.
Kilborn, Orson: 293,45.
Kilgour, Joseph: 35,22; 40, 155; 51,117; 97,82; 98,125; 140,113; 249,363; 340,24.
Killigrew, Thomas: (D) 314,8.
"Killing the Goose": 239,86.
Kimball, Ed. M.: 147,xix.
Kimball, Frank: 49,57.
Kimball, Grace: 37,75; 56, 243; 61,56.
Kimball, Louis: 247,239; 283, 14.
Kincaid, Z.: (W) 161,31.
Kindler, Hans: 278,35.
"Kindling": (R'11) 131,2; 131, 27; 135,141.

Kinetoscope (see Films).
King, Ada: 240,160.
King, Alice: 155,19; 180,90; 205,174.
King, Allyn: 181,125; 198,87; 199,155; 235,182; 238,20.
King, Alta: 233,27; 246,160.
King, Anita: 178,310; 202,395.
King, Carlotta: 335,28.
King, Charles: 39,128; 228, 96.
King, Claude: 225,305; 228,91; 254,291; (D) 254,309; 255, 357; 288,8.
King, Dennis: 265,31; 269,38; 298,13; 326,41.
King, Edith: 220,335; 229,201; 251,83; 251,103; 268,49.
King, Eileen: 315,44.
King, Hamilton: 210,62; (D) 231,c.
King, Helen: 238,51.
King, Henry: 211,188.
King, Jane: 244,17.
King, John: 191,29.
King, Joseph: 324,29.
King, Mary: 244,17.
King, Mollie: 40,147; 151,89; 151,107; 162,79; 171,252; 212,197; (A) 214,379; 218, 232; (D) 220,361; 222,89; 242,341; 242,364.
King, Olive: 218,221.
"King, The": (R'17) 203,22; 204, 97.
"King Argimenes and the Unknown Warrior": (R'19) 217,144.
"King Dodo": 5,3; 16,6.
King Edward's Theatre: 17,6.
"King John": (R'03) 26,82; 78,224; (R'09) 98,104.
"King Lear": 29,160; 48,51; 75, 120; (R'11) 123,xi; 209,41; (R'18) 215,18.
"King of Cadonia, The": 108,iii; (R'10) 108,38.
"King of Kings": (F) 310,39; 315,45; 315,76.
"King of Nowhere, The": (R'16) 183,304.
Kingdom, Edith: 53,175; 193,157.
"Kingdom of God, The": (R'28) 336,49.
"Kingdom Within": (F,R) 265,72.
"King's Carnival, The": 4,2.
"King's Highway, The": 40,vi; 48,49.
"King's Messenger, The": 6,18.
"King's Musketeer, The": 8,18.
Kingsbury, George A.: 159,219.
Kingsbury, Lillian: 41,iv.
Kingsford, Walter: 208,349; 348,48; 349,34; 356,19; (C) 359,2.
Kingsley, Mona: 196,363; 200, 209; 205,139; 323.53.
Kingsley, Walter J.: (D,W) 317, 21; 331,49.
Kingston, Gertrude: 193,150,
Kingston, Morgan: 152,131; 163,103; 165,212; 276,35.
Kingston, Natalie: 313,39.
Kingston, Winifred: 181,144.
Kingstone, Cecil: 117,135.
Kinkead, Cleves: 177,228.
Kinsella, Kathleen: 63,122.
Kiper, Miriam: 184,349.
Kippen, Manart: 265,31.
Kirchner, Raphael: (D) 223, 158.
Kirkby-Lunn, Louise: 85,85; 121, 83.
Kirke, Donald: 344,47.
Kirkland, Alexander: 353,45; 356,41.
Kirkland, Hardee: 6,17; 58, 291; 132,47; 164,157.
Kirkland, Muriel: 324,40; 335,47; 344,20; (C) 345, 4; 346,19; 347,57; 352,21; 354,28; 359,24.
Kirkwood, James: 204,121; 248, 287; 262,31; 264,28; 288, 17.
Kirman, Patrick: 82,327.
Kirwin, Lenora: 83,vi; 83,28.
"Kismet": 127,85; 131,1; (R'11) 132,40; 133,101; 133,102; 134,122; 134,134; 135,168; 231,351; (F) 239,113; (F,R) 239,114; (F) 357,32; (F,R) 358,47.
"Kiss Burglar, The": (R'18) 208, 356; 208,357.
"Kiss for Cinderella, A": (R'16) 192,86; 192,89.
"Kiss in a Taxi, The": (R'25) 295,70.

"Kiss in the Dark, The": (R'14) 157,114.
"Kiss Me Quick": (R'13) 152, xiv.
"Kiss Waltz, The": 128,112; (R'11) 129,xv.
Kissel, Marry: (W) 294,24.
"Kissing Time": (R'20) 237, 414.
"Kit Carson": 6,8.
Kitchen, Karl K. (W): 122,113; 134,117; 138,40; 141,144; 147,143; 158,161; 160,305; 161,21; 162,64; 163,118; 237,372.
"Kitty Grey": (R'09) 97,xiii.
"Kitty Mackay": (R'14) 156,59.
"Kitty's Kisses": (R'26) 304, 16.
"Kivalina of the Ice Lands": (F,R) 294,30.
Klaer, Adele: 206,207; 252, 173; 273,23; 293,14; 332,19.
Klauber, Adolph: (W) 104,120; 111,150; 167,14; 209,13; 234, 84; 294,64.
Klaw, Joseph: 212,205; 234,84.
Klaw, Marc (see also Klaw and Erlanger): 43,226; 147,156; 153,160; (W) 201,263; 231, 379; 234,84; 238,73.
Klaw and Erlanger: 41,160; 43, 227; 46,xix; 46,xxiv; 46, 298; 49,76; 65,188; 67,228; 70,xxvi; 74,99; 81,xxi; 91, 229; 94,xii: 94,xxxi; 106, xxxiii; 116,x; 118,xxxv; 130, xxxiv; 135,153; 139,68; 142, xxii; 151,80; 154,xxvii; 178, 342; 187,126; 190,413; 199, 122; 202,409; 223,144; 234, 84; 302,38.
Klaw Theatre (New York): (D) 242,345; 243,319.
Klein, Charles: 13,3; 22,20; 25,57; 55,227; 64,157; 71, 3; 81,xiii; 82,324; 106,187; 108,36; 111,150; 111,151; 115,71; 116,ii; 143,vii; 145, 75; 153,150; 159,230; 167,12; 172,284; 172,293; 178,276; 181,152; 198,64.
Klein, Hermann (W): 61,79; 72,44.
Klein, Josef: 147,160.
Klein, Manuel: 22,20; 25,57.
Klein, Olive: 202,372.
Klein, Sybil: 48,46; 72,35.
Kleine, George: 171,245.
Klemperer, Otto: 297,34.
"Kleptomania": (S) 233,10.
Klewer, Dorothy: 217,147.
Kline, J.C.: 216,69.
Kline, Virginia: 26,100; 111, 139.
Kling, Saxon: 206,231; 207, 289; 208,345.
Knapp, Dorothy: 306,21; 310, 46; 312,66; 315,41; 331, 53; 338,11.
Knell, Grace: 233,23.
Knepler, Paul: 299,20.
Knickerbocker Theatre (New York): 121,90.
"Knife, The": (R'17) 196,342; 196,355; 199,130.
Knight, Frank: 359,40.
Knight, Percival: 153,145; 190,354.
Knight, Walter: 206,206.
"Knight for a Day, A": 76, 169; (R'07) 84,xi.
Knipper, Olga: 259,216.
Knoblock, Edward: 175,134; 246, 167.
Knoch, Ernst: 163,103.
Knoelke, Clara: 79,249.
Knote, Heinrich: 60,53.
Knott, Roselle: 33,282; 69,307.
"Know Thyself": (R'09) 108,xv; 108,35.
Knowles, Priscilla: 132,67; 149, 27; 318,38.
Knowlton, Maude: 70,321.
Ko, Fuji: 68,266.
Kobbe, Gustav (W): 19,25; 46, 318; 59,13.
Kober, Arthur: (W) 316,12; 331,48; (W) 351,23.
Kober, Leo: (D) 307,11; (D) 309,25.
Koch, Frederick H.: 235,200; 239,118; 259,246; 281,44; (W) 290,52; 298,40; 353,51.
Kochanski, Paul: 249,391; 279, 35.
"Koenigskinder": (OP) 120,46.
Koffe, Dorothy: 197,39; 210,

Kohana: 326,36.
Kohler, Fred: 335,44.
Kohlman, Leon: 45,274.
Kohlmar, Lee: 152,133; 178, 299.
Kohne, Wayne: 305,31; 311,8.
Kolker, Henry: 49,59; 58,309; 70,333; 86,88; 97,100; 114, 39; 121,79; 122,135; 129, 168; 158,176; 192,79.
Komisarjevsky, Theodore: 261, 269.
Komisarzhevsky, Vera F.: 86, 91; 86,100; 89,vii.
Kondo, Naae: 289,21.
"Kongo": 303,14; (R) 303,18; (S) 306,26.
Konig, Josef: 160,305.
Konstantin, Leopoldine: 132,54; 133,81.
Koonen, Alexandra: 268,22; 268,23.
Kopernak, Salina: 246,153; 254, 304.
Kopp, Norma: 25,58.
Koralli, Vera: 130,200.
Korenieva, Lydia: 262,14.
Korff, Arnold: 277,25; 333,47.
Korff, Mara: 93,289.
Kormendy, John: 329,20.
Korngold, Erich Wolfgang: 250, 19.
Koroleva, Lina: 133,92.
Korolewicx, Jeanne: 119,9.
Kosary, Emmy: 299,20.
Koshuba, Valentina: 338,19.
Kosloff, Alexis: 248,299.
Kosloff, Theodore: 202,405; 213, 269; 276,30.
Kosta, Tessa: 160,289; 220, 335; 231,407; 252,149; 268, 24; 292,17; 300,5;304,c; 305,52.
Kotchetevsky: 258,148.
Kouns, Nellie: 199,149; 210, 85.
Kouns, Sara: 199,149; 210,85.
Kouns Sisters (Nellie & Sara): 229,169; 278,25; 289,37.
Kousnezoff, Maria: 177,248.
Koussevitzky, Serge: 277,34.
Kovak, Stephanie: 243,403.
Koven, Joseph: (W, FI) 227, 34; 228,78.
Kowalski, Henri: 87,137.
Krall, Clare: 143,24.
Kramer, RoseMary: 156,68.
Kramer, Wright: 49,56; 50, 95; 65,189; 73,82; 76,147; 77,191; 90,205; 324,40.
Kraus, Ernst: 118,183.
Krause, Werner: 276,17.
Krehbiel, H.E.: 7,13.
Kreidler, Louis: 154,183; 163,103; 165,213.
Kreisler, Fritz: 12,21; 12,22; 13,27; 112,188; 152,xxiv; 170,184; (A,D) 184,365; 185,25; 186,62; 249,391.
Krembs, Felix; 160,283; 190, 354; 208,345; 210,87; 227,19; 236,260;295,19.
Kremer, Theodore: 42,192; 55, 227.
Kremler, Felix: 175,113.
Kreutzbeg, Herald: 338,41; (D) 347,29.
"Kreutzer Sonata, The": (R'06) 67,xv; 68,253; (R'24) 280, 15.
Krieghoff, Bertha: 30,188.
Krolow, Olga: (C) 344,44.
Kruger, Elsa: (D) 347,28.
Kruger, Otto: 171,260; 191, 18; 195,270; 201,265; 211,149; 226,375; 244,21; 324,29; 344, 18; 346,46.
Krum-Nathansen, Gerda: 90,207.
Krummer, Clare: 241,265.
Krummer, Marjorie: 241,265.
Krutch, Joseph Wood (W): 335, 19; 346,28.
Kubelik, Jan: 7,6; 10,34; 11, 23; 12,21.
Kummer, Clare: 241,265; 242, 342; (W) 242,344; 307,29.
Kun, Stanislawa: 130,202.
Kupfer, Gerthe: 9,10.
Kurlov, Sonia: 357,27.
Kurt, Melani: 166,271; 170, 185; 178,286; 189,274.
Kurton, Peggy: 253,241.
Kutner, Nanette: (W) 316,22.
Kyasht, Lydia: 151,iii; 156, 73.
Kyle, Howard: 41,178; 51,126; 62,90; 63,122; 98,106; 109, 90; 142,192; 167,15; 185,9;

194,201; 199,132; 201,269; 207,286; 268,42.
Kyra: 246,169; 252,171; 276,23.
Kyrels, Harvey: 344,36.

--L--

Labadie, Harriet: 138,64.
Labia, Maria: 91,233; 93,308; 94,335; 94,344; 95,34; 96,52.
"La Boheme": (OP) 136,177; (F) 297,33.
L'Abri Theatre (Paris): 210,92.
"Labyrinth, The": (R'05) 59,3; 59,17; 80,271.
"Lace Petticoat, The": (R'27) 312,21.
Lachman, Marc: 331,48.
Lackaye, Helen: 39,120; 55, 225; 134,126; 164,169; 187, 145.
Lackaye, James: 112,178.
Lackaye, Wilton: PG,21; (W) 6, 13; (A) 6,14; 8,7; 15,4; 15, 5; 25,56; 26,92; 35,10; 39, 119; 44,249; 52,133; (W) 56,250; 67,225; 81,17; 72,32; 89,179; 94,325; 96,iv; 96, 49; 96,57; 112,iii; 112,173; 98,120; 125,29; 127,77; 132, x; 132,39; 136,191; 142,196; 147,134; 148,174; 161,15; 169,127; 171,230; 171,242; 171,243; 175,127; 177,220; 177,239; 179,6; 183,292; 199, 134; 199,135; (W) 199,144; (W) 221,32; 226,389; 244,34; 253,216; 259,227; (C) 316, 31; 322,34.
Lackland, Ben: 314,17.
Lada: 233,21.
Ladd, Margot: 191,42.
Ladd, Schuyler: 96,45; 192, 105; 194,201; 194,244.
"Ladder, The": (R'26) 309,72; 332,15; 336,70.
Ladella, Tony: 201,287.
"La Donne Curiose" (OP): (R) 132,50; 132,56.
"Ladies All": 354,24; (R'30) 354,25.
"Ladies First": (R'18) 214,378.
"Ladies Leave": (R'29) 345,68.
"Ladies' Night": 234,83; (R'20) 235,185.
"Ladies of the Evening": (R'24) 288,15; 288,17.
"Ladies of the Jury": (R'29) 345,50.
"Lady, The": 275,17; (R'23) 275,18.
"Lady Audley's Secret": (D) 134,129.
"Lady, Be Good": (R'24) 287,16.
"Lady Billy": (R'20) 239,107.
"Lady Bug": (R'22) 256,30.
"Lady Clara": (R'30) 351,72.
"Lady Cristilinda, The": (R'22) 263,15; 264,21.
"Lady Frederick": (R'08) 94,xi; 94,311; 95,26.
"Lady from Lane's, The": (R'07) 80,xv; 80,273.
"Lady from Lobster Square, The": (R'10) 111,xxvi.
"Lady from Oklahoma, The": (R'13) 147,xiv.
"Lady from the Sea, The": (R'11) 130,186; 131,30; (R'23) 274,16.
"Lady Godiva": (R'02,S) 18,8.
Lady Gregory: 29,167; 29,168; 129,157.
"Lady in Love, A": (R'27) 313, 60.
"Lady Jim": (R'06) 68,xv.
"Lady Luxury": (R'14) 168,60.
"Lady Margaret": (R'02) 13,6; 13,12.
"Lady of Coventry, The": (R'11) 131,xi.
"Lady of Dreams, The": (R'12) 134,107; 134,115; 134,116.
"Lady of Lyons, The": 16,2; (R'02) 16,3; 57,270.
"Lady of the Camellias, The": (R'17) 204,85.
"Lady of the Lamp, The": (R'20) 235,188; 235,191.
"Lady of the Orchids, The": (R28) 335,50.
"Lady of the Slipper, The": 142, 193; 145,iii; 145,79.
"Lady of Venice, The": 34,306.
"Lady Patricia": (R'12) 134, 108; 134,133.
"Lady Rose's Daughter": (R'04) 35,6.

"Lady Shore, The": 50,94; (R'05) 51,108.
"Lady Teazle": (R'05) 48,34.
"Lady Windermere's Fan": (R'14) 159,259; 160,291; 216, 84; (F) 298,33.
"Lady's Name, A": (R'16) 185, 8; 185,10.
"Lady's Virtue, A": (R'25) 299, 16.
Laemmle, Carl: 171,245; 216, 122; 319,11.
Lafayette Square Opera House (Washington, D.C.): 27,123.
"L'Affaire Des Poisons": (S) 84, 37.
Laffargue, Antoinette: 199,132.
La Follette, Fola: 89,174; 121, 85; 153,159; 157,141.
La Gattuta, Joseph: (W) 360,28.
Lagier, Suzanne: 95,iv.
Lagner, Lawrence: 294,7.
La Gue, Mildred: 218,211.
Lahey, Richard (D): 266,11; 267,11; 268,21; 269,21.
Lahr, Bert: 337,30; 340,42; (C) 350,37; 353,32.
Laidley, Alice: 288,46.
"L'Aiglon": PG,11; PG,12; 31,224; (R'24) 286,20; (R'28) 324,62.
Laine, Elizabeth: 164,162.
Laite, Charles: 211,131.
Lake, Alice: 54,192; 203,59; 231,496.
Lake, Harriette: (C) 361,27.
Lake, [Mrs.] William: 54,192.
"La La Lucille": 221,7; (R'19) 221,16; 222,82.
"Lally": (R'27) 313,20.
Lalor, Frank: 157,160; 175,112; 183,294.
La Marr, Barbara: 270,33; 273,31; 274,32; 277,33; (A) 284,53.
"Lamb, The": (F,R) 177,238.
Lamb, Gladys: 179,31.
Lambart, Ernest: 142,181; 165,234.
Lambert, Alexander: 3,16.
Lambert, Charlotte: 66,211.
Lambert, Marie: 58,303.
Lambs Club: 33,279; 60,44; 100,175; 133,ix; 137,10; 159,230; 173,3; 173,7; 184, 332; 197,40; 217,149; 231, 398; 231,466; 247,279; 271, 38; 272,7; 315,24.
Lamison, Norah: 3,5; 39,130; 202,361.
Lamon, Isabelle: 124,203.
Lamond, Frederick: 267,37.
Lamont, Clifford; 40,147.
Lamont, Jennie: 179,25.
"L'Amore Medico" (OP): (R) 159,228.
Lamp, William: 52,136; 131, 32.
Lamy, Charles: 63,137.
Lancaster, A.E. (W): 25, 62; 29,182; 46,305; (V) 47, 8; 54,187.
"Lancers, The": 81,307; (R'07) 83,xi.
"Land of Heart's Desire, The": (R'03) 29,159.
"Land of Joy, The": 203,9; (R'17) 203,23; 204,78.
"Land of Nod, The": (R'07) 75, xx.
"Land of Opportunity, The": (F,R) 299,190.
"Land of Promise, The": 156, 79; (R'13) 156,99; (D) 157, 125.
"Land of the Free, The": 201, 273; (R'17) 201,328.
Lander, Frank: 38,85.
Landford, Elsie: 322,28.
Landi, Elissa: 356,17.
Landolf, Bluch: 200,204; 201, 287.
Landor, Edward: 146,111.
Lane, Charles: 80,269; 87, 123; 88,166; 165,207; 286, 33; 308,36.
Lane, Dorothy: 148,163.
Lane, Grace: 136,171; 136,195.
Lane, Harry (W): 294,24.
Lane, Leona: 332,49.
Lane, Lupino: 239,112; 292,17; (D) 312,38; 312,49; (W) 329,28.
Lane, Mary: 231,405.
Lang, Alois: 255,378; 352,39.
Lang, Anton: 15,10; 106,190; 107,26; 116,112; (A) 117, 147; 255,377.

Lang, Fritz: 316,40.
Lang, Hanns: 352,39.
Lang, Harry L.: 82,329.
Lang, Howard: 238,12; 250,7.
Lang, Matheson: 70,337; 108, 64; 109,93.
Lang, Peter: 47,15; 223,169.
Langdon, Harry: 35,15; 310,36; (D) 312,1f; (W) 321,22; (D) 322,7.
Lange, Sven: 49,iii.
Langford, Edward: 105,149;163,101.
Langford, R. Helen: 136,194.
Langlen, Paula: (D) 323,23.
Langner, Lawrence: 201,279; (W) 276,22; (W) 290,25; (W) 291,18; (W) 292,18; 294,7; 309,27.
Langsner, Clara: 320,22.
Langtry, Lily: 5,c; 17,14; 24, 33; 25,73; 31,209; 32,241; 46,314; 128,127; 179,6; 182, 192; 232,508; 242,345; 244, 28; 256,34; 293,30; 337, 33; 356,21; 357,39.
Language, Stage (see also Terminology, Stage): 29,159; 222,96; 291,12; 341,39; 344, 19.
Lanner, Katti: 83,17.
Lanston, Aubrey (W) (see also "Dramatic Incidents in the Lives of Eighteenth Century Players"): 46,317; 48,42; 136, 178.
Lantelme, [Mlle.]: (A) 124,218.
Laparra, Raoul: 208,371.
La Pierre, Irma: 10,15; 28,152; 59,16; 78,220; 99,165; 122, 135.
"La Piste": (S) 66,ii.
La Plante, Laura: 306,35; 307, 36; 307,49; 312,39; 313,39; 320,37; 336,34; 340,37.
La Prade, Malcolm (D): 238,9; 239,85; 241,241; 242,321; 246,148; (W) 247,246; 252, 172; (W) 259,247.
Lardner, Ring: 342,20; 345, 27; 352,27.
Larimore, Earle: 309,27; 311, 14; 323,40; 339,44.
Larkin, John Jr. (W): 302,32.
La Rocque, Rod: 280,33; 307, 38; 307,48; 311,37; 313,40; 320,66; 321,75; 322,6; 323, 4b; 324,8; 325,81; 356,33.
Larrimore, Francine: 147,155; 153,166; 175,112; 219,281; 222,124; 223,147; 226,370; 242,333; 244,22; 277,8; 287, 13; 303,29; 304,31; 310,5; 311,54; 312,20; (C) 316,31; 337,14; 339,29.
Larsen-Todsen, Nanny: 285,35.
La Rue, Florence: 61,66.
La Rue, Grace: 111,136; 138, 47; 150,xiii; 179,14; 198, 83; 222,87; 241,259; 277, 36; 277,37.
La Salle, Katherine: 146,100; 151,xx; 166,309; 191,20.
La Scala Opera House: 142,170.
Lascelles, Ernita: 156,65; 252, 151; 254,290; 255,371.
La Shelle, Kirke: 43,227; 52,ix; 231,379.
Lasher, Marie: 208,363.
Lasky, Edith Deblois (W,V): 273,20.
Lasky, Edward: 273,29.
Lasky, Jesse L.: 171,244; (A) 198,105; 208,397; 210,114; 261,392; 319,11.
Lasky Studio (Hollywood): 208, 400.
Lassalle, Robert: (A) 122,xvi.
"Lassie": (R'20) 231,401; 231, 407.
"Lassoo, The": (R'17) 199,134; 199,135.
"Last Appeal, The": (R'02) 15,2.
"Last Laugh, The": (R'15) 175,112; (F,R) 289,31.
"Last Mile, The": 349,18; (R'30) 349,43; 350,30; 351,14; 353,25.
"Last Night of Don Juan": (R'25) 298,15.
"Last of Mrs. Cheney, The": (R'25) 295,15; 299,19.
"Last of The Duanes, The": (F,R) 227,41.
"Last Resort, The": (R'14) 158, 212.
"Last Straw, The": (R'17) 194, 213; 194,223.

"Last Waltz, The": (R'21) 244, 64; 245,101.
"Last Warning, The": (R'22) 261, 420; 262,24.
L'Atelier L'Oeuvre: 336,57.
Latell, Alfred: 181,124.
"La Tendress": (R'22) 260, 342.
Latham, Cynthia: 180,65.
Latham, Hope: 68,263; 95,6; 106,169; 119,14; 138,59; 149,34.
Lathrop, Elise (see also "Where Shakespeare Set His Stage") (W): 27,123; 28,142, 36, 52; 46,312; 49,64; 50,86; 52,144; 55,212; 57,273; 57,232; 68,261; 69,iv; 71, 26; 72,40; 73,83; 76,149; 76,169; 77,174; 83,22; 83, 23; 84,52; 85,73; 94,328; 95,52; 99,143; 102,42; 102, 56; 108,58; 110,115; 119, 31; 163,104; 179,32; 180, 91.
Latimer, Edyth: 166,264; 191,9; 215,9.
"La Tosca" (OP): 146,102.
Latscha, Albert: 117,144.
Lauder, Harry: 94,322; 94,325; (A) 163,147; 202,363; 203, 17; 205,157; 207,279; 302, 25; 352,8.
Lauder, Jean: 86,99.
Laudner, Odette: 291,11.
Laudouska, Yona: 167,18.
"Laugh, Clown, Laugh": (R'23) 275,15.
"Laughing Husband, The": 157, 113; R'14) 157,156.
"Laughing Lady": (R'23) 265, 16; 266,17.
Laughlin, Anna: 19,8; 29,177; 82,vii; 135,164.
"Laughter of the Gods, The": (R'19) 217,142; 217,155.
"Launcelot and Elaine": (R'21) 248,340.
"Launzi": (R '23) 273,16.
Laurel, Jane: 51,116; 95,29; 96,xx; 105,155; 116,107; 121,93.
Laurell, Kay: 171,257; 174,66; 210,101; 214,337; (A) 214, 379; (A) 220,369; 260,322; 282,16.
Lauri-Volpi, Giacomo: 267,37.
Lavalliere, Eva: (A) 126,52; 203,33.
Lavedan, Henri: 56,262; 61,54; 146,103.
La Verne, Lucille: 181,137; 234, 83; 249,382; 269,13; 270, 17; 271,26; 295,35; 334, 19.
"La Vestale" (OP): 300,20; (D) 300,21.
Law, Arthur: 21,8.
Law, Evelyn: 246,157; 290,81; 320,41.
Law, Ruth: 191,11.
"Law and the Man": (R'06) 72,32.
"Law of the Land, The": 166, 207; (R'14) 165,208; (F,R) 199,176.
"Law of the North, The": (F,R) 212,250.
"Lawbreakers, The": (R'22) 253,262.
Lawford, Ernest: 45,282; 66, 222; 85,79; 110,102; 128, 177; 164,158; 179,5; 204, 103; 224,220; 248,319; 304, 19; 308,17; 311,31; 336,31.
"Lawful Larceny": (R'22) 252, 167.
Lawlor, Anderson: 335,47.
Lawlor, Andrew: 212,195; 212, 205.
Lawlor, Andrew Jr.: 323,26.
Lawlor, Mary: 309,21; 323,15; 329,39; 332,49; 337,64; 338,57.
Lawlord, Amber: 63,117.
Lawrence, Atkins: 69,301.
Lawrence, Basil (W): 292,10.
Lawrence, Georgia: 15,5; 100, 188; 110,127; 164,163.
Lawrence, Gerald: 63,127.
Lawrence, Gertrude: 276,18; 279,46; 279,61; 280,13; 281,17; 283,19; 296,11; 299,44; 301,67; 308,36; 311, 5; 311,47; 312,46; 317,48; 331,29; 341,49; 342,18; 344, 17; 344,24; 348,23; 348,57; (C) 350,2; 356,37; 360,22; 360,41; (C) 361,2; 361,52.
Lawrence, Lillian: 5,7; 24,38;

184,351.
Lawrence, Margaret: 121,74; 122,126; 213,276; 214,349; 221,43; 227,13; 229,180; 231, 358; 240,181; 241,278; 243, 404; 253,225; 264,31; 288,13; 289,46.
Lawrence, Vincent: 273,29; 277, 36.
Lawrence, W.J. (W): 87,139; 121,91; 125,12; 127,82; 190, 368; 191,44.
Lawrence, Walter N.: 52,135; 67, ix; 143,22.
Lawrence, William: 81,294.
Lawrenceville School: 220,378.
Lawson, Eleanor: 104,109.
Lawson, Elsie: 283,17; 305,48.
Lawson, John Howard: (D) 268, 9; 289,21.
Lawton, Mary: 53,168; 111,152; 141,137; 156,65; 159,234; 255,369.
Lawton, Thais: 95,22; 105,144; 105,145; 108,62; 128,111; 200, 193; 250,7; 312,30; 312,31; 349,42.
Laye, Evelyn: 303,21; 344,14.
Lazaro, Hipolito: 189,279; 205, 147.
"Lazarus Laughed": 328,42.
"Lazybones": (R'24) 285,70.
Lea, Elizabeth: 42,189.
Lea, Emily: 129,166; 136,198; 155,31; 201,289; 215,23.
Leach, George: 89,197;329,25.
"Lead, Kindly Light": (R'13) 145,xxix.
Leaf, Mildred: 308,46.
League of New York Theatres: 357,15; 360,31.
"Leah Kleschna": (R'05) 47,4; 47,7; 53,160; (R'24) 280,16.
Lean, Cecil: 89,184; 110,104; 184,361; 231,376; 253,229; 301,38.
"Learned Ladies, The": 130, 183; 130,184; (R'11) 130, 185; 144,63.
Leary, Gilda: 216,87.
Leary, Thomas C.: 71,7.
"Leave It to Jane": 200,203; (R'17) 200,242.
Le Bargy, Simone: 109,78.
Le Baron, Louise: 51,129; 112, 176; 124,204; 147,150.
Le Baron, William: 204,75; 249, 378.
Lebedeff, Ivan: 328,33.
Leblanc, Georgette: 118,xvi; 118,194; 128,128; 133,87; 240,174.
Leblang, Joe: 351,62; 357,17; 358,63.
Le Breton, Flora: 289,38; 328, 19.
Le Burt, Estelle: 79,254.
Le Clercq, Carlotta: 191,8.
Le Clercq, Charles: 22,26; 52, 151.
Lecocq, Alexander Charles: 124, 193.
Lecouvreur, Adrienne: 85,70.
Lederer, George W.: 116,xiv; 151,83; (W) 360,43.
"Le Donne Curiose" (OP): 132, 50.
Ledova: 287,37.
Lee, Auriol: 104,101; 153,159; 157,141.
Lee, Belden (W): 151,100.
Lee, Betsy: 331,24.
Lee, Davey: 338,31.
Lee, Dorothy: 261,383; 284,6.
Lee, Dorris: 219,302.
Lee, Etta: 289,32.
Lee, Frances: 313,39.
Lee, Gwen: 330,20.
Lee, Joseph: 337,27.
Lee, Kendall: 287,48.
Lee, Kenneth: (W, FI): 17,20; 18,24; 19,27; 23,19.
Lee, Lila: 209,53; 217,170; 276,31; 293,50; 295,23; 344,43.
Lee, Lillian: 121,71.
Lee, Lois: 227,42.
Lee, Louise: 231,436.
Lee, Merri (W): 342,15.
Lee, Norma: 247,237; 295,26.
Lee, Phoebe: 246,159.
Lee, Virginia: 222,75; 230, 295; 236,305; 256,54.
Leech, Al: 43,217.
Leedom, Edna: 272,35; 324,56; 324,62.
Leeds, Dorothy: 211,159; 217, 147.

Leesugg, Catherine: 47,13.
Leet, Marjorie: 292,30.
"Left Overs": 273,29.
Leftwich, Alexander: (W) 183, 294; 333,49; (W) 359,45.
"Legacy, The": 134,xvi.
Le Gallienne, Eva: 183,284; 180, 71; 186,61; 187,136; 189, 297; 201,265; 206,229; 208, 375; 232,523; 234,126; 244, 31; 247,226; 253,221; 254, 286; 254,303; 266,12; 268, 3; 270,5; (D) 273,10; 273,12; 273,14; (D) 275,20; 290,27; 298,21; 299,58; 300,12; 307,5; (C) 308,11; 310,18; 311,29; (C) 312,27; (W,C) 313,12; 313,13; 315,40; 323,44; 324, 25; 327,65; (W) 334,15; 336, c; 344,23; 346,28; (D) 346,29; 350,29; 352,27; 361,26.
"Legend of Lenora, The": (R'14) 156,58; (D) 157,125.
Leginska, Ethel: 153,159; 270, 37.
Legouve, Ernest (W): 75,124.
Le Guere, George: 129,151; 184,342; 226,389; 229,187; 260,296.
Lehar, Franz: 82,330; 83,29; 126,vii; 127,xi; 162,64; 297,25; 299,20.
Lehman, Benny: 40,147.
Lehman, Elsa: 338,19.
Lehmann, Lilli: 10,33; 13,28; 242,327.
Lehrian, George C.: (D) 323, 23.
Lehrman, Henry: 231,489.
Leiber, Fritz: 144,58; 185, 15; 208,345; 216,78; 216, 93; 229,175; 240,222; 244, 40; 248,297; 350,26; 350,48.
Leigh, Clifford: 27,106.
Leigh, Dorma: 156,69.
Leigh, Grace: 176,170.
Leigh, Leslie: 124,187.
Leigh, Lisle: 247,231.
Leigh, Lois: 219,291; 221,11.
Leigh, Mercedes: 60,46.
Leigh, Ora V. (W): 97,88.
Leigh, Philip: 201,291; 276,14; 278,29; 290,35; 311,14; 323, 40; 325,40.
Leighton, Isabel: 245,94; 265, 21.
Leitzel, Lillian: 263,43.
Lejune-Gilibert, [Mrs.] Charles: 75,140.
Leland, Lea: 186,68.
Leland, Pauline: 234,93.
Lelaunay, Louis: 77,181.
"L'Elevation": (S) 203,12; 203,13; (R'17) 203,21.
Lely, Durward: 136,171.
Lely, Madeleine: 136,174.
Le Maire, Charles (D): 253, 217; 254,287.
Le Maire, George: 151,89; 223,159; 292,30.
Lemmers, Laura: 11,15.
Lemoine, Rose: 77,187.
Lemon, Courtenay: 315,38.
Le Moyne, Sarah: 6,16; 9,10; 9,11; 122,118.
Le Moyne, W.J.: 58,xix; 62,101; 84,43.
Lengyel, Melchior (W): 252, 170; 273,20.
Leni, Paul: 305,38; 305,48; 314,49.
Lenihan, Winifred: 215,21; 228,103; 252,143; 252,157; 274,14; 275,5; 276,14; (D) 278,38; 279,20; 279,21; 295,36; 310,27; 334,39.
Lennox, William: 237,365.
Lenora, [Mlle.]: 101,33.
Lenormand, H.R.: 275,29; 286, 62; 287,9.
Lenormant, Edouard (W): 26, 88; 31,214.
Lenox, William: 219,272.
Lent, Sylvia: 273,37.
Leon, Edward Chin: 318,42.
Leonard, C.A.: (W) 339,22.
Leonard, Eddie: (D) 228,85; 270,29; 273,33; 285,37.
Leonard, Ernst: 138,53.
Leonard, O. (W): 106,188.
Leonard, Robert: 208,399.
Leonard, William E.: 143,27.
Leoncavallo, Ruggiero: 69,289; (C) 159,254.
Leonidoff, Leon: 324,21.
Leontovich, Eugenie: 353,44; 358,28; 358,36; 359,28; 359,34.

"Le Petit Cafe": (F, R) 360, 48.
Le Petit Theatre Du Vieux Carre (New Orleans): 255, 385; 255, 386; 270, 40; 270, 41; 324, 53: 324, 55; 340, 44.
"Le Poilu": (R'16) 192, 394.
Leraas, Margit: 226,393; 241,243.
Lerch, Georgia: 283, 21; 306, 21.
Lerner, Jacques: 300, 13.
Lerner, Tina: 146, 121; 153, 159; 157, 141; 170, 184.
Leroux, Xavier: 217, 173.
Leroy, Hal: (C) 361, 38.
Leroy, Maud: 138, 60.
Lertora, JosephM 214, 339.
Leslie, Edgar: 285, 27.
Leslie, Elsie: 28, 134; 29, 159; 80, 261; 107, 28; 124, 205; 127, 100.
Leslie, Ethel: 6, 7.
Leslie, Frances: 126, 47.
Leslie, Gladys: 207, 333; 211, 188; 248, 303.
Leslie, Jack: (D) 352, 4.
Leslie, John: 232, 513.
Leslie, Lawrence: 344, 47.
Leslie, Marguerite: 148, 183; 156, 75; 156, 81; 161, 21; 167, 26; 172, 299; 178, 283; 179, 49; 181, c; 181, 119; 181, 138; 181, 139; 191, 17; 191, 45; 195, 295.
Leslie, May: 181, 125; 211, 155; 220, 347; 221, 51.
Leslie, Richard (W): 174, 89.
Leslie, Stacie: 88, 155.
"Les Miserables": (F) 202, 399; (F, R) 203, 57.
Le Soir, George: 23, 9; (W) 47, 8.
"Les Plaidures": 11, 13.
"Les Romanesques": (S) 5, 10.
Lesser, Amy: 77, 182; 131, 14.
Lesser, Theodore J.: (W) 341, 11.
Lessing, Gotthold E.: 78, viii.
Lessing, Madge: 32, 260; 201, 293; 241, 253.
"Lesson in Love, A": (R'23) 272, 75.
Lester, Florence: 69, 298.
Lester, Frances: 100, 188.
Lester, John T.: (W) 182, 226.
Lester, Kate: 60, 28; 123, 142.
Lestina, Adolph: 87, 138.
L'Estrange, Julian: 96, 47; 120, 53; 134, 115; 134, 116; 151, 90; 156, 64; 184, 335; 213, 281.
"Let and Sub-Let": (R) 352, 42.
"Let Us Be Gay": (S) 339, 28; 340, 15.
"Let's Beat It": 219, 269.
"Letter, The": (S) 320, 28.
"Letter of the Law, The": (R'20) 230, 312.
"Letters of Henrik Ibsen" (B): 62, xv.
"Letters to Actors I Have Never Seen" by M. Moone:
Charles Richman: 36, 48;
Robert Edeson: 37, 77;
John Drew: 38, 102;
Edward Sothern: 39, 118;
J. K. Hackett: 41, 182;
William Faversham: 44, 262.
"Letty": (R'04) 44, 240; 44, 244.
Levenson, Lew: 331, 48.
Levey, Ethel: 45, ix; 62, 86; 86, 91; 125, 15; 158, 199.
Levick, Ida: 38, 104.
Levis, William: 83, 15.
Levitski, Mischa: 216, 73; 271, 37; 282, 35.
Levy, Arthur J.: 331, 49.
Levy, Bert: 224, 217.
Lewers, William: 48, 33; 85, 86; 100, 183.
Lewes, Miriam: 250, 7.
Lewinson, Paul (W): 283, 12.
Lewis, Ada: 13, 7; 13, 8; 64, 160; (W) 67, 251; 77, iii; 77, 185; 99, 154; 107, 30; 133, 74; 203, 27; 219, 296.
Lewis, Arthur: 68, 258; 156, 58; 164, 157; 173, 27; 179, 19.
Lewis, Earl R.: 299, 23.
Lewis, Edgar: 212, 249; (A) 212, 256; 231, 391; 231, 414.
Lewis, Eric: 187, 131.
Lewis, Fanny Ward: 75, 122.
Lewis, Frederick: 26, 100; 51, 106; 85, iii; 93, 285; 99, 150; 105, 135; 108, 35; 118, 161; 180, 73.
Lewis, Gene: 335, 47.

Lewis, Hazel: 137,8; 142,184.
Lewis, James: 22,26; 52,151; 53,175; 63,123; 126,65; 235, 168; 243,414; 286,12.
Lewis, Jeffreys: 71,17; 85,79; 111,131; 114,37; 165,214; 188,204.
Lewis, Mary: 258,135; (D) 293, 11; 298,36; 301,35; (A) 320,61; 351,37.
Lewis, Ralph: 77,179.
Lewis, Ruby: 101,15.
Lewis, Sheldon: 31,212; 111, 139; 215,59; 216,125; 220, 390; 220,391; 220,393.
Lewis, Sinclair: 218,205; 218, 227; 304,7.
Lewis, Ted: (C) 314,21.
Lewis, Tom: 88,165.
Lewis, W.A. (W): 63,134; 64,149.
Lewis, Walter: 233,36.
Lewisohn, Adolph: (A) 231, 347; 330,24.
Lewisohn, Alice: 192,93; 279, 29.
Lewisohn, Edna May: 179,12.
Lewisohn, Irene: 246,167.
Lewisohn, Ludwig: (W) 269, 9; (W) 279,10; 283,33.
Lewisohn Stadium (New York): 172,283; 268,37; 330,24.
Lhevinne, Josef: 132,52; 272, 37; 338,43.
"L'Homme Et Ses Fantomes": (R'24) 286,62; 287,9.
"Liar, The": (F,R) 217,191.
"Liars, The": (R'05) 52,137.
"Libation Pourers, The": 87, iii; 87,xv.
"Liberty Bells, The": 75,133.
"Liberty Belles, The": 8,5; (R'01) 9,13.
"Liberty Hall": 146,iii; (R'13) 146,99.
Liberty Theatre: 30,193.
Liddell, Marguerite: 46,315.
Lido, Joan: 322,50.
"Lie, The": (R'14) 168,56; 168, 59.
Lieb, Francis: 142,181; 154, 174.
Lieb, Lora: 105,134.
Lieber, Fritz: 101,12; 240, 157; 269,38; 280,13; 316,19.
"Lieber Augustin": (R'13) 152, xiii; 152,xvii; 152,111.
Liebler and Co.: 18,3; 46, xix; 67,229; 115,67; 163, 100.
Liebler Brothers: 67,229.
Liebling, Estelle: 11,21; (W) 351,36.
Liebling, George (W): 332,45.
Liebling, Leonard (W): 114, 57.
Liedtke, Harry: 93,289.
Liedtke-Proft, Hanne: 93,289.
"Life": (R'02) 15,5; (R'14) 166,306; 167,27.
"Life of Augustin Daly, The" (Daly) (B): 205,180.
"Life of Man, The": 181,163; 193,137; (R'17) 193,149; 199, 120.
"Life of the Party, The" (F): 356,5; 357,49.
Light, James: 242,343.
"Light Eternal, The": 71,2.
"Light from St. Agnes, A": (R'05) 51,113.
"Light of Asia, The": (R'28) 333,47.
"Light of the World, The": (R'20) 228,142.
"Light That Lies In Woman's Eyes, The": (R'04) 37,60.
Lightfood, Helen V.: (W) 99,146.
Lighting: 21,17; 71,10; 102,63; 151,xii; 187,132; (D) 209,36; 211,153; 218,212; 221,36; 232,539; 251,80; 287,20; 340,4; 350,8; 352,23.
Lightner, Winnie: 356,5; 357, 49; (C) 359,3.
"Lightnin' ": 212,203; (R'18) 212,209; 236,272; 248,292; (F,R) 359,48.
"Lightning Conductor, The": 61, 67.
"Lights O' London, The": (R'11) 124,182; 124,191.
"Lights Out": (R'22) 259,268.
"Like A King": (R'21) 249, 424.
"Likes O' Me, The": 95,28.
"Lilac Domino, The": (R'14) 166,267; 167,7.

"Lilac Room, The": (R'07) 75, 117.
"Lilac Time": 193,145; (R'17) 193,152.
Lilienthal, David E.: (W) 232, 542.
"Lilies of the Field": 249,363; (R'21) 249,416; (F) 347, 23.
"Liliom": 244,5; 244,7; (R'21) 244,29; 244,31; (S) 247,220; (F,R) 357,50.
Lillie, Beatrice: 276,18; 281, 17; 297,24; 308,36; 312,6; (D) 324,51; (D) 331,51; (C) 334,40; (A) 339,55; 347, 26; 356,37; 358,31.
"L'Illusioniste": (R'26) 312,20.
"Lily, The": (R'09,S) 108,42.
"Lily and the Prince, The": 23, 13.
"Lily Sue": (R'26) 311,18.
Limedorfer, Eugene (W): 7,8.
"L'Imperatrice": 100,172.
"Lincoln": 62,92; (R'06) 63, 114; 63,123.
Lincoln, Abraham: 47,16; 62,92; 87,130; 148,179; 231,466; 286, 10.
Lincoln, Elmo K.: 202,399; 205, 187.
Lincoln, Eugene: 202,347; 205, 159; 242,343.
Lincoln, Florence: 135,155.
"Lincoln At The White House": 97,xvi.
Lincoln Stock Company: 184,362.
Lincoln Theatre (New York): 184, 362.
Lindahl, Alice: 138,56; 159, 267; 193,163; 194,242.
Lindahl, Tulle: 215,33.
Lindbergh, Charles: 316,26.
Linden, Margaret: 252,151.
Linder, Max: 193,167.
Lindley, David Howell: 181,124.
Lindo, F. Newton: 82,321; 104, 105.
Lindo, Olga: 294,20.
Lindroth, Helen: 119,19.
Lindroth, Nellie: 89,174.
Lindsay, Howard: 247,237; 308, 33; 333,48.
Lindsay, Vachel (W): 317,7.
Lindsay, Ben B. (W): 188,192.
Ling, Richie: 74,99; 105,164; 117,151; 122,108; 137,10; 152,123; 315,30.
"Linger Longer Letty": (R'19) 227, 20.
Link, Adolph: 230,247; 287,14.
Link, Helen: 242,324.
Linnell, Gertrude (W): 218,218.
Linthicum, Lotta: 29,182; 165,216; 200,209; 341,42.
"Lion and the Mouse, The": 58, 288; (R'05) 59,4; 59,24; 66,201; 69,290; 80,264; 82,324; 115,71; 116,ii; 231, 351.
"Lion Tamer, The": (R'26) 309,18.
Lipkowska, Lydia: 105,139; 107, 12; 142,iii; 246,141; 248, 293; 249,401.
Lipman, Clara: 9,8; 43,233; 50, 96; 60,25; 60,26; 60,30; 61, c; 67,246; 107,23; 115,xiv; 115,68; 116,110; 127,77; 139, 90; 193,166; 233,24.
Lisa, Mona: 206,253; 240,187.
Lissner, Edward (W, FI): 34, 301.
"Listen Lester": (R'18) 216,80; 216,87.
Lister, Francis: 272,17; 350,43.
Liszt, Franz: 67,240.
Littell, Robert: (C) 335,42; (W) 344,19; (W) 351,18.
Little, Ann: 209,57; 215,61.
Little, Crosby: 99,138.
Little, Julian: 179,19.
"Little Accident": (R'28) 333,46.
"Little Bit of Fluff, A": (R'16) 188,204a.
"Little Blue Devil, The": (R'19) 226,424.
"Little Boy Blue": 131,iii; (R'11) 131,3; 131,29.
"Little Brother, The": 215,9; (R'18) 215,17.
"Little Brother of the Rich, A": (R'09) 108,xiii; 108,35.
"Little Caesar": (F) 360,59; (F,R) 361,60.
"Little Cafe, The": (R'13) 154, xii; 155,3.
"Little Cherub, The": (R'06) 67,xv; 67,226.

"Little Clay Cart, The": 310,4.
"Little Damozel, The": (R'10) 117,136.
"Little Duchess, The": 23,21.
"Little Eyolf": (R'10) 112, viii; 112,201; (R'26) 301, 15.
"Little Face": 166,267; (R'14) 166,400.
"Little Father of the Wilderness, The": (R'05) 64,143; 64,151.
"Little French Girl, The": (F) 290,36.
"Little Gray Lady, The": (R'06) 61,60; 61,65.
"Little Jessie James": (R'23) 271, 52.
"Little Johnny Jones": (R'04) 46, 298.
"Little Journey, A": (R'18) 216,77; 216,81.
"Little Lady in Blue": 191,25; (R'16) 192,85.
"Little Lord Fauntleroy": (F,R) 249,394; 249,395.
"Little Man, The": (R'17) 194, 215; 194,217.
"Little Mary": (R'04) 36,34.
"Little Michus, The": (R'07) 73, xvii.
"Little Millionaire, The": (R'11) 129,xvi; 129,174.
"Little Minister, The": 50,91; 115,86; (F) 174,89; 181,141; (F) 252,175.
"Little Miss Bluebeard": (R'23) 271,50.
"Little Miss Brown" (see also "Kitty's Kisses"): (R'12) 140,xi; 140,119; 151,100.
"Little Miss Fix-It": (R'11) 123, ix; 123,145.
"Little Miss Hover": (F,R) 216,124.
"Little Nemo": 9r,vii; (R'08) 94,xii; 94,327.
"Little of Everything, A": (R'04) 41,161.
"Little Old New York": (R'20) 236,278; 237,357.
"Little Orchid Annie": (R'30) 351,47.
Little Princess, The": 25,77; 76,156; 161,34; (F,R) 202, 394.
"Little Show, The": 340,41; (R'29) 340,42; 343,c; 356, 25.
"Little Simplicity": (R'18) 214, 347; 215,15.
"Little Sister": 154,185.
"Little Stone House, The": (R'19) 227,20.
"Little Stranger, The": (R'06) 68,xii; 68,269,
"Little Teacher, The": 205,142; (R'18) 205,150.
Little Theatre (see also Amateur Theatre): 54,202; 64,167; 89,174; 133,84; 143,27; 145, 84; 145,87; 150,61; 164,163; 164,166; 174,64; 175,139; 175,157; 181,143; 184,349; 192,92; 195,292; 196,332; 197,32; 197,33; 198,82; 214, 352; 224,214; 232,530; 235, 162; 237,358; 243,396; 257, 76; 280,25; 287,12; 290,17; (C) 309,11; 315,32; 327, 4c; 344,51; 346,21; 348,50; 349,50.
Little Theatre [Ames]: (D) 133, 77; 134,iii; 134,108; 136, 182; 142,xv; 146,122; 151,80; 174,64; 192,92.
Little Theatre [Philadelphia]: 174, 64; 209,33.
"Little Water on the Side, A": 156,60; (R'14) 156,62.
"Little Whoper, The": 226,391.
"Little Women": 141,142; 141, 143; (F,R) 214,392.
"Littlest Rebel, The": 129,176.
Liveright, Horace: 291,36; (W) 298,18; 306,15.
"Living Corpse, The": 152,122; (R'29) 347,46.
"Living In": (R'22) 263,20.
"Living Mask, The": (R'24) 276, 68.
Living Pictures (see Tableaux Vivants).
Ljunberg, Gota: 273,37.
Lloyd, Alice: 91,244; (A) 129, xviii; 134,c; 160,293.
Lloyd, Doris: 233,25.
Lloyd, Florence: 116.
Lloyd, Frank: 262,35.

Lloyd, Harold: 297,32; 314, 39; 352,26.
Lloyd, Jefferson: 281,14.
Lloyd, Jessie: (W) 338,35.
Lloyd, Marie: 158,199.
Lloyd, Rollo: (W) 296,12; (D) 303,30.
Loasby, Alice: 79,233.
Lobel, Malvine: 168,81.
Lobero Theatre (Santa Barbara): 301,40.
"Lobetanz" (OP): (R) 130,189.
"L'Occident": (S) 159,244.
Locheimer, Louis L. (W): 294, 36.
Locke, Edward: 99,ix; 103,94; 172,288; 173,9.
Locke, Lydia: 183,280.
Locke, William J.: 83,14.
"Locked Door, The": (R'24) 281,16.
Locker, Robert: 171,259.
Lockford, Nara: 255,355.
Lockford, Zita: 255,355.
Lockhart, Gene: 302,14.
Lockhart, Grace: (W) 340,32.
Lockwood, Harold: 167,19; 207, 331; 213,327.
Lockwood, W.S.: (W) 116,122.
"Lodger, The": (R'17) 192,88; 194,231.
Loeb, Philip: 293,19; (D) 305, 29.
Loew, Marcus: 135,vi; 157,139; 160,293; 278,27.
Loew's Delancey St. Theatre (New York): 157,139.
Loew's State Theatre (New York): 253,395.
Loew's State Theatre (St. Louis): 294,56.
Loff, Jeannette: 324,22; 337,32.
Loftus, Cecilia [Cissie]: 6,16; 9,3; 9,5; 9,13; 10,8; 14, 20; 24,31; 24,37; 25,c; 44, 241; 75,118; 81,307; 83, xi; 113,4; 147,iii; 232,512; 247,232; 274,34; 274,35; 292,30; 325,39.
Loftus, Gladys: 160,285.
Logan, J.D.: (W) 39,112.
Logan, Jacqueline: 310,39; 324,8; 325,81; 330,67.
Logan, Stanley: 315,25.
Loge, Marc (W): 149,4; 161, 32; 164,177.
"Lohengrin" (OP): 67,240; (D) 241,241.
Lohr, Marie: 100,169; 116, 98; 255,371; 359,30.
"Lola From Berlin": (R'07) 81,xviii.
"Lollipop": (R'24) 276,68.
Lomas, Herbert: 238,7; 257, 83; 341,24.
Lombard, Carol: 336,48.
"Lombardi, Ltd.": (R'17) 201, 279; 201,281.
London, [Mrs.] Jack: 223,177.
London, Louis: 136,172.
"London Assurance": 50,iv; (R'05) 51,109; 51,110; 51, 111; 95,24; 126,66.
London Opera House: 127,81.
London Theatre (see English Theatre).
"Lone Wolf, The": (F,R) 199, 176.
"Lonely Lives": (R'03) 23,7.
"Lonely Romeo, A": (R'19) 221,16; 211,35; 222,82.
Lonergan, Lester: 186,77; 216, 95; 261,368; 278,14; 312,34.
"Lonesome Like": 173,14; (R'18) 208,355; 208,359.
Long, Elitch: 30,201.
Long, John Luther: 23,2; 55, 227.
Long, Kate: 13,5.
Long, Nicholas: 194,223.
Long, Nick Jr.: 278,23.
Long, Ralph W.: 299,22.
Long, Sally: 233,9.
"Long Dash, The": (R'18) 214,348.
"Long Road, The": (R'30) 356, 26.
"Long Voyage Home, The": (R'24) 286,22.
Longacre, Frank: 194,223; 203, 19; 205,148.
Longacre Theatre (New York): 148,162.
Longfellow, Malvina: 100,170; 111,149.
Longman, Edward: 69,301.
Lonnon, Alice: 39,131; 53, 169; 59,23.

Lonsdale, Frederick: (C) 270,26; 271,38; 286,25; 354,31.
"Look Who's Here": (R'20) 230, 309; 230,312.
Loos, Anita: 298,36; 305,16; (W) 316,41; 320,45; (D) 351,53.
"Loose Ankles": (R'26) 307,14; 307,23.
"Loose Ends": (R'26) 310,15; 310,25.
Lopez, Vincent: 271,37; (W) 275, 12; 282,23; 300,37.
Lopoukowa, Lydia: 125,2; 127,94; 130,198; 130,202; 134,107; 140,c; 147,152; 153,159; 155, 18; 157,141; 158,181; 159, 222; 159,270; 160,287; 160, 315; 168,99; 170,171; 178, 279; 181,128; 242,329.
"L'Oracolo" (OP): 169,107.
Loraine, Robett: 4,4; 12,1; 41, 183; 56,247; 56,249; 61, 70; 62,c; 64,xiv; 117,134; 231,365; 283,9.
Lorber, Martha: 259,235; 282, 18; 316,15; 339,23; 352,41; (D) 353,c; 357,54; 357,55.
Lord, Helen: 13,6; 14,22.
Lord, Leonard: 335,46.
Lord, Marion: 262,31.
Lord, Pauline: 132,45; 181,150; 206,229; 220,345; 229,167; 251,85; 252,162; 254,303; 273,12; 273,13; 284,36; 285, 5; 287,19; 288,18; 289,20; 293,26; 297,8; 297,9; (C) 308,11; 313,20; 316,26; 318, 21; (D) 327,21.
"Lord and Lady Algy": 35,5; (R'17) 204,86; 222,102; (F,R) 227,41.
"Lord Chumly": 290,18.
Lorenze, Mercedes: 206,216.
Lores, Ethel: 235,181.
Loretto College (Missouri): 238, 46; 247,272.
Lorimer, Wright: 38,84; 39,110; 40,vi; 69,291; 71,c; 79,230; 236,276.
"Lorna Doone": 6,4; (F,R) 263, 70.
Lorne, Marion: 92,267; 103,75.
Lorraine, Harry: 179,16.
Lorraine, Hollis (W): 30,195.
Lorraine, Lillian: 105,154; 113, c; 114,45; 132,42; 142,184; 148,iii; 155,31; 157,132; 184, 346; 199,148; 209,25; 227, 26.
Lorraine, Lola: 160,285.
Lorraine, Robert: 27,124; 46,298f; 55,221.
Lorraine Sisters: 288,37.
Lorrell, Lily: 31,236; 51,129.
Lortat, Robert: 194,229.
Lory, Jane: 215,25.
Los Angeles Theatre: 144,42; 186,86; 293,22.
Losch, Tilly: 346,16.
Losee, Frank: 145,96; 146,105.
Losee, Harry: 338,19.
"Lost Co-Respondent, The": (R'15) 172,282.
"Lost in London": (D) 134,129.
"Lost Lady, The": (F,R) 289, 32.
"Lost Leader, The": (R'19) 226, 368; 227,23.
"Lost Sheep": (R'30) 352,41.
"Lost World, The": (F,R) 290, 37.
Loth, Ila: 262,16.
Lothian, J.M.: 77,191.
Loti, Pierre: 139,70.
Lotta (see Crabtree, Charlotte).
"Lottery Man, The": 107,iii; (R'09) 107,5; 108,53.
Loud, Marguerite: 315,38.
Loughton, Frances: 196,333.
"Louie the Fourteenth": (R'25) 290,32; 291,16; 285,24.
"Louise": (OP): 77,174; 77,175.
"Louisian Lou": 129,177.
Louisiana Theatre: 210,100; 309,43.
Louisville Players: 315,49.
Louisville, University of: 211, 164; 334,50.
Lou-Tellegen (see Tellegen, Lou).
"Love": (R'21) 242,340.
Love, Bessie: 192,97; 198,78; 203,63; 216,125; 298,32; 307,38; 308,36; 312,49.
Love, Montagu: 170,170; 183, 274.
"Love Among the Lions": 115, 66; 116,67; (R'10) 115,69.
"Love and the Man": (R'05)

50, 81.
"Love Birds": (R'21) 242, 342; 243, 421.
"Love Child": (R'22) 262, 21.
"Love City, The": (R'26) 301, 16.
"Love Cure, The": 100, xxii; (R'09) 104, 102; 104, 111.
"Love Dreams": (R'21) 249, 416.
"Love Drive, The": (R'17) 202, 352.
"Love Duel, The": (R'29) 339, 44.
"Love 'Em and Leave 'Em": (R'26) 301, 64; (S) 302, 26; 308, 82.
"Love for Love": (R125) 291, 15; (D) 296, 13.
"Love Habit, The": (R'23) 266, 15.
"Love, Honor and Betray": (R'30) 350, 42.
"Love Hungry": (F) 327, 4b.
"Love in a Mist": (R'26) 303, 50; 304, 33.
"Love in Idleness": (R'05) 49, 58.
"Love Is Like That": (R'27) 315, 25.
"Love Laughs": (R'19) 221, 13; 221, 35.
"Love Leash, The": (R'13) 154, xv; 154, 188.
"Love Letter, The": (R'06) 69, xiii; (R'21) 249, 388.
"Love Lotion, The": (R'19) 227, 21.
"Love O' Mike": 192, 84; (R'17) 193, 149.
"Love of a Geisha, The": 68, 266.
"Love of One's Neighbor": 171, 259.
"Love of Three Kings, The": (OP) 156, 66.
"Love Route, The": 70, 314; 72, 43.
"Love Song, The": (R'25) 289, 16.
"Love Watches": (R'08) 92, xiv; 92, 259; (S) 93, 292.
"Lovely Lady, The": (R'28) 324, 62.
"Lover's Lane": 3, 3; 3, 4; 3, 11; 3, 12; 3, 13.
"Lover's Luck": (R'16) 189, 263; 189, 269.
"Love's Lottery": (R'04) 45, 268; 45, 276; 45, 282.
"Loves of Carmen": (F) 320, 6.
"Love's Pilgrimage": (R'04) 39, 111.
Lovett, Helen: 221, 19.
Lovett, Josephine: 8, 10; 8, 11; 69, 290; 78, 226; 154, 181.
Loving, Pierre (W): 255, 384; 263, 22.
Lowe, Edmund: 195, 271; 233, 15; 310, 49; 311, 36; 321, 45; 323, 6; 325, 12; 346, 61.
Lowe, Florence: 215, 15.
Lowe, Isabel: 212, 217; 216, 87; 227, 32.
Lowell, Helen: 44, 258; 108, 53; 144, 52; 187, 133; 237, 365; 260. 298; 279, 18; 282, 28; (C) 344, 44.
Lowelly, Berthe: 152, 138.
Lowenberg, Selma H. (W): 220, 336.
Lowenberg, Walter A. (W): 226, 372; 230, 260; 233, 8; 235, 166; 240, 182.
"Lower Depths, The": 264, 14; (R'23) 264, 15.
Lowrie, Jeannette: 64, 143.
Lowry, Hazel: 205, 161.
Lowry, Judith: 192, 93; 205, 163; 248, 323.
Lowry, Kathleen: 334, 25.
Loy, Myrna: 323, 42; 338, 34; 359, 6.
"Loyalties": 261, 366; 261, 370; 261, 371; (S) 262, 28.
Loyo, Dora: 254, 299.
"Luana": (R'30) 356, 26.
Lubell, Lily: 246, 145.
Lubetty, Madeleine: 255, 383.
Lubin, Siegmund: 171, 244.
Lubin Stock Company: (F) 137, 19; 137, 22.
Lubitsch, Ernst: 295, 32.
Lubovska, Desiree: 200, 229; 201, 302; 211, 137; (W) 213, 294; (A) 214, 379; 225, 311; 242, 342; 244, 7.
Lucan, Halane: 41, 162.
Lucas, Daisy: 79, 233.
Lucas, George: 104, 114; 107, 12.
Lucas, Wilfred: 39, 128.
Lucchesi, Josephine: 271, 37; 296, 35.
Luce, Claire: 301, 13; 305, 23;

321,27; (A) 322,3; 328,48; 328,59; (C) 344,4; 344,56; 345,39; 345,57.
"Luck of Macgregor, The": (R'08) 88,146.
"Lucky": (R'27) 315,26.
"Lucky Break, A" (see also "Rainbow Rose"): (R'25) 295, 16.
"Lucky Devil, The": (F,R) 295,34.
"Lucky Dog, The": 72,44.
"Lucky Miss Dean": (R'06) 61,60.
"Lucky One, The": (R'22) 262, 19.
"Lucky O'Shea": (R'17) 200,207.
"Lucky Star, A": (R'10) 109, vi; 110,114.
Lucy, Arnold: 141,149; 170,197.
Luders, Gustav; 16,16; 26,101; 40,143.
Ludlow, Godfrey: 294,34.
Ludlowe, Henry: 85,60; 86,90; 86,104.
Ludmilla, Anna: 226,373; 237, 367; 241,243; 254,311.
Ludwig, Josephine: 7,7.
Lugne-Poe, Alexandre: 206,208.
Lugosi, Bela: (C) 263,11; 266, 25; 321,5; 342,23.
Lukin, Jacob: 257,81.
"Lullaby, The": (R'23) 272,15; 272,18.
"Lulu Belle": (R'26) 301,15; 313,18.
"Lulu's Husbands": 111,133; (R'10) 112,177.
Luna Park (see Coney Island).
Lunn, Kirkby: 44,240; 46,315; 70,342.
Lunt, Alfred (see also Lunt and Fontanne): (D) 202,348; 202, 353; 226,365; 228,91; 251, 73; 261,374; 268,14; 269,10; 277,14; 278,26; 279,33; 290, 13; 309,27; 309,28; 311,14; 316,18; (C) 321,33; 323,40; (D) 325,45; 327,38.
Lunt and Fontanne (see also Fontanne, Lynn; Lunt, Alfred): 281,8; 283,39; 285,15; 287, 17; 288,23; 291,45; 291,46; 304,31; 334,17; 346,44; 347, 48; 348,32; 353,37; 356,27; 357,30; (D) 358,c.
Lupino, Stanley: 309,23.
"Lure, The": (R'13) 151,xi; 151,83; 152,116; 152,117; 152,124.
Lusk, Norbert (W): 161,44.
"Lusmore": 226,375.
Luther, Anne: 218,256.
Luttrell, Gladys (W): 26,102.
Luzhsky, Vassily: 262,14.
Lyceum Theatre (London): 30, 193; 50,90.
Lyceum Theatre (New York): (D) 231,352; 290,17.
"Lydia Gilmore": (R'12) 133,74.
Lydig, [Mrs.] Philip: 196,339.
Lydy, Beth: 189,280; 193,148; 207,277; 208,373.
Lyle, Carl: 141,133.
Lyman, George C.: 179,8.
Lynch, Gertrude (W): 122,122; 132,54; 136,182; 138,54.
Lynd, Helen: 340,7.
Lynd, Rosa: 206,207; 206,229.
Lyne, Felice: 132,60; 166,272; 176,191; 265,63.
Lynn, Agnes: 33,282.
Lynn, Sharon: 334,28.
Lynton, W. Mayne: 193,145.
Lyon, Ben: 293,39; 317,39.
Lyon, Esther: 48,38; 120,62.
Lyon, Wanda: 260,305; 265,49.
Lyons, Edmund D.: 5,7.
Lyons, Edward E.: 132,46; 208,347.
Lyons, Gretchen: 14,2; 16,18.
Lyons, James: 286,23.
Lyons, Ruth: (D) 332,11.
Lyric Theatre (New York): 30, 193; 110,121.
"Lysistrata": (S) 148,189; 294,13; (R'25) 299,15; (R'30) 353,26; (S) 353,33; 354,13.
Lytell, Bert: 193,137; 199,151; 199,176; 201,324; 231,496; 233,40; 235,197; 238,39; 258, 157; 270,30; 279,31; 302,33; 338,21.
Lythgoe, David: 17,5.
Lytton, Genevieve: 286,13.

--M--

"M.G.M. Revue": (F) 353,20.
"Ma Gosse": (R'10) 108,xvi.
Mab, Queenie: 213,287.
Mabie, Carmen Crittenden (W):

135,161.
Mac, Nila: 194,219; 208,349.
Mcadoo, William: 305,32.
Mcallister, Hall: 61,56.
Mcallister, Mary: 313,39.
Mcallister, Paul: 29,162; 79, 252; 92,266; 92,267; 125,27.
Macart, Will H.: 190,390.
Macarthur, Charles: 313,30; 340, 34.
Mcarty, Grace: 83,8.
Macauley, Barney: 155,36.
Macauley, Joseph: 203,31; 203, 35; 208,359; 276,14; 278,29; 304,23; 326,41.
Macauley, Thurston (W): 285,12; 330,46.
Mcavoy, Daniel: 13,7; 20,10; 25,58.
Mcavoy, J.P.: 306,27.
Mcavoy, May: 245,105; 251,96; 256,40; 272,33; 272,59; 278, 31; 294,32; 320,35; 326,20.
"Macbeth": 48,47; 49,viii; 52, iv; (R'05) 58,290; (D) 105, 142; (D) 113,26; 115,91; 118, 161; (R'10) 119,3; (D) 129, 173; 156,84; (R'16) 181,123; 182,128; (F) 182,182; (D) 182, 213; 189,290; (R'18) 207,286; 240,153; 240,214; (D) 241, 241; 241,250; (R'21) 241,298; 243,391; 244,10; (R'21) 244,29; 245,89; 258,150; (R'24) 278, 16; (D) 332,23; (R'30) 350,48.
Macbeth, Florence: 151,82; 155, 30; 163,102; 165,212; 180, 85.
Macbeth, Helen: 114,59.
McBride, Emily Raymond (W): 122,125.
McCabe, Lida Rose (W): 62, 103; 212,198; 236,268.
McCahill, Angela: 240,163; 245, 77; 261,376.
McCall, Robert: 299,23.
McCann, Thomas: 212,195.
McCarthy, Justin Huntley: 4,8; 8,6; 9,2; (W) 10,7; (A) 10, 9; 23,2; 25,68; (W,V) 34,291; 48,x.
McCarthy, Lillah: 169,110; 170, 196; 171,251; 172,283; 173, 12; 187,131.
McCarthy, Nellie: 304,46.
McCarthy, Rector: 114,56.
McCarthy Sisters: 230,312.
McClendon, Rose: 317,25; (A) 322,3.
McClintic, Guthrie: 252,176; 291,22; 291,36; 331,34.
McClintock, Marjorie: 202,347; 203,15.
McClintock, Walter: 114,54.
McCloskey, John: 84,35; 117,159; 132,43.
McCloy, June: 330,36.
McClung, Littell: (W,V) 118,195.
McClure, William: 237,357.
McCollum, H.H.: (D) 275, 27.
McComas, Carroll: 40,145; 136, 198; 153,145; 153,156; 155,31; 164,165; 170,137; 172,304; 187,139; 205,143; (A) 228, 127; 238,14; (A) 238,72; 240, 181; 242,324; 246,155; 269, 5; 269,18; 272,38; 274,23; 295,36.
McConnell, Gladys: 313,39.
McConnell, Lulu: 235,192; 333, 40.
McCord, Mary: 253,232.
McCormack, Frank: 213,267; 259,227; 292,14.
McCormack, John: 110,107; 122,114; 159,248; 166,272; 179,12; 185,25; 198,95; 208, 81; (W) 290,42.
McCoy, Bessie (see also Davis, Bessie McCoy): 52,146; 90,c; 90,222; 91,xi; 91,245; 91,246; 115,77; 126,39; 126, 40; 202,363; 222,89.
McCoy, Gertrude: 168,69; 198,69.
McCoy, Mildred: 343,34; (C) 344,40; 349,57.
McCoy, Nellie: 49,68.
McCoy, Tim (W): 327,28.
McCoy Sisters: 33,272; 52, 145.
McCrea, Henrietta A. (W): 100,172.
McCree, Junie: 91,239; 97, 100.
McCue, Betty: 266,21.
McCulloch, Campbell (W): 314, 28; 319,11; 333,24.

McCullough, John: 13,22; 62, 93; 145,74.
McCullough, Paul (see Clark and McCullough).
McCurdy, James Kyrle: 44,262.
McCutcheon, George Barr: 123,173.
McCutcheon, Wallace Jr.: 86, 109.
McDermott, Marc: 140,122.
McDermott, William F. (W): 352,38.
MacDonald, Christie: 71,6; 84, 35; 84,36; 86,102; 113,15; 114,49; 119,iii; 120,xv; 120, 59; (A) 124,xvi; 125,29; 127, c; 136,191; 143,iii; 151,80; 152,xii; 152,110; 156,77; 235, 236.
MacDonald, Cordelia: 105,160; 182, 230.
MacDonald, Donald: 143,22; 168, 83; 191,63; 209,33; 217,161; (W) 224,218; (W) 229,160; 356,26; 361,25.
McDonald, Eva: 122,136; 128, 139.
MacDonald, Flora: 216,69.
McDonald, Francis: 208,359.
McDonald, Jeanette: 266,73; 321,60; 337,52; 356,48.
McDonald, Katherine: 206,264; 218, 249; 231,413; 231,489.
MacDonald, Mary: (W,V) 154, 188.
MacDonald, W.H.: 13,23.
MacDonell, Kathlene: 123, 143; 167,27; 181,129; 181, 145; 191,64; 218,209; 262, 18; 273,13; 322,30.
Macdondo, Margaret: 157,141.
McDonough, Glen: 22,8; 30, 188.
McDonough, Harry: 40,145.
MacDougall, Duncan: 222,83.
MacDougall, Rex: 95,30; 118, 162; 124,195; 189,273; 203, 20.
MacDowell, Edward: 21,26; 73,66.
McDowall, Ethel: 172,289.
McDowell, Melbourne: 71,17; 207,332.
Mace, Fred: 72,56.
Mcentee, Frank: 225,313.
Mcentee, James F.: 299,23.
Mcevers, Veda: 120,36; 123, 142.
Mcevoy, J.P.: (C,W) 332,30.
McFadden, Elizabeth A.: 135, 155.
McFarland, Marie: 161,21.
McFarland, Mary: 161,21.
MacFarlane, Elsa: 291,24.
MacFarlane, George: 125,11; 125,13; 140,127; 147,139; 152,111; 158,182; 171,243; 189,280.
MacFarlane, Ian: 283,14.
McFarlane, John M.: 197,23; 226,375.
McGarry, George A.: 143,22.
McGhie, John: 188,206; 216, 86.
MacGibbon, Harriet: 331,30.
McGill, Earle: 315,38.
McGilvray, Laura: 66,200.
McGlinn, Francis D.: 133,85.
McGlynn, Frank: 228,88; 228, 89; 277,7; 344,35.
McGowan, Jack: 238,33.
McGowan, John: 331,27.
MacGowan, Kenneth: (W) 164, 173; (W) 167,28; 252,201; (W) 260,239; (W) 263,25; 263,40; (C) 267,11; (W) 289,9; 305,6; (W) 316,10; 347,4; 353,38.
McGowan, Roxana: 214,391.
McGrath, Thomas: 39,121.
MacGregor, Edgar (W): 257, 90.
MacGregor, Edward: 333,48.
MacGregor, Harmon: 240,160; 240,163.
MacGregor, Helen: 58,307.
McGuire, Dorothy: 254,50.
McGuire, Katherine: 232,536; 320,45.
McGuire, William Anthony: 123, 173; 249,378; 331,27; (C) 341,23.
"Machinal": (R'28) 332,46; 332,47; 334,20; (S) 334,32; 336,70.
MacHugh, Frank: 338,48.
Macintire, Elizabeth Jelliffe: (W,V) 140,120.
McIntosh, Burr: 10,5; 52,133;

171,243; 236,287.
McIntosh, Hattie: 26,96.
McIntosh, Louise: 224,222.
McIntyre, Frank J. (see also McIntyre and Heath): 80, 279; 91,231; 127,88; 128, 139; 137,11; 139,91; 141, 155; 188,204c; 233,35; 280,18; 306,14; 309,21.
McIntyre, James: 56,248.
McIntyre, Leila: 127,89; 127,90.
McIntyre, Molly: 156,57; 159, c; 159,268; 159,270; 160, 315; 280,14.
McIntyre and Heath: 56,248; 104, xv; 225,354.
Mack, Andrew: 6,14; 8,10; 8, 11; 25,59; 46,298; 109,xii; 100,127.
Mack, Catherine: 185,34.
Mack, Charles (see Moran and Mack).
Mack, Georgia: 7,18; 134,124; 183,294.
Mack, Willard: 187,144; 201, 275; 214,339; 222,103; 242, 342; 296,16; (W) 313,21; 323,44; 327,34.
Mack, William B.: 35,266; 47,7; 117,135; 118,198; 167,15; 222, 103; 307,27.
Mackaill, Dorothy: 274,30; 306, 13; 308,40; 329,4b; 333,28; 342,35; 356,6.
Mackall, Lawton (W): 284,24; 288,10; 320,43.
McKay, Beatrice: 101,22.
Mackay, Edward: 51,129; 119, 2; 119,3; 146,105.
Mackay, Elsie: 179,23; 196, 345; 213,291; 218,207; 226, 365; 240,172; 241,277; 242, 333; 250,50; 266,14.
Mackay, F.F.: 13,22; 37,62.
McKay, George: 232,521.
McKay, Morris: 217,155.
McKay, Neil: 288,37.
Mackay, Robert: 89,185.
Mackaye, Dorothy: 199,129; 226,386; 247,239; 289,46.
Mackaye, Hazel: 82,339; 153,171.
Mackaye, Percy: 28,150; 69,309; 73,59; 80,282; 82,318; 82, 338; 93,285; 101,vii; 103, 91;108,56; 135,154; 136,184; 145,87; 165,222; 178,298; (W,V) 182,214; 182,269; 185,8; (W) 206,203; 288,9.
Mackaye, Steele: 92,338; 82, 339; 84,42; 89,184.
McKee, Frank: 43,227.
Mackeller, Helen: 187,139; 213,267; 218,221; 223,145; 225,309; 230,255; 246,150; 257,87; 264,49; 285,38; 340, 35.
McKenna, "Boots": 302,14.
MacKenna, Kenneth: 253,215; 262,20; 273,17; (D) 278,38; 295,14; 304,14; 311,48; 331, 331,31; 332,33; 335,26.
MacKenzie, Compton: 143,26.
McKenzie, Gertrude: 38,86.
MacKenzie, Max: 108,46.
MacKenzie, Tandy: 270,36.
Mackin, Clara: 215,16.
Mackin, John: 16,4.
Mackinder, Lionel: 92,281.
McKinnel, Norman: 144,45; 150, 51.
McKinney, E.L.: (W,V) 148, 188.
McKinney, MargaretM 14,14.
Mackintosh, Louise: 104,104; 104,105; 105,149; 261,372.
McKovor, Mary: 186,67.
Macklyn, Frederick: 119,3.
McLaglen, Victor: 323,6.
MacLaren, Donald: 59,10.
MacLaren, Ian: 242,343; 243, 398; 246,145; 264,18; 276, 14; 278,29; 303,13; 349,31.
MacLaren, Mary: 218,258.
McLaughlin, J.M. (W): 287,10.
McLaughlin, Millicent: 38,99.
McLaughlin, Robert H.: 177, 227.
McLaurin, Kate: 79,256; 88,163.
McLean, Dolores: 77,182.
McLean, Edward: 340,23.
MacLean, Joan: 238,7; 242, 332; 318,13.
MacLean, Josephine: 221,29; 259,207; 267,41.
MacLean, R.D.: 26,82; 27,117; 49,71; 49,75; 157,111.
McLellan, C.M.S.: 55,227.
MacLennan, Francis: 44,240.

McLeod, Donald (W): 219,270.
McLeod, Keith: 290,47.
MacMahon, Aline: (D) 312,25.
McMahon, Helen: 102,53.
McMahon, Tom: 163,101.
MacManamy, Sue: 224,239.
McManus, Joseph: 195,287.
McMechan, F.H. (W): 8,17.
MacMillen, Francis: 249,391.
McMillen, Violet: 79,237.
McNabb, Anna: 40,145.
McNally, J.J.: 55,227.
McNally, Marie (W): 171,240; 177,225; 179,23.
McNamara, Edward J.: 323,6; 344,56; 345,48.
McNamee, Graham: 291,37.
McNaughton, Charles: 222,82; (D) 320,4d.
MacNaughton, Tom: 120,59; 166, 265.
McNeel, Sally: 38,95.
Macnez, Umberto: 144,39.
Macomber, Master: 166,309.
Maconda, Charlotte: 22,38.
Mcowen, Bernard: 209,20.
Macowen, Norman: 349,44.
MacQuarrie, George: 349,43.
McQuire, Kathryn: 261,389.
Macrea, Bruce: 34,290; 48,43; 60,37; 62,101; 65,185; 68, 271; 81,vii; 84,38; 103,74; 104,103; 104,113; 106,198; 108, 42; 110,127; 118,162; 118,165; 119,28; 132,62; 144,36; 146, 119; 152,124; 152,125; 169, 121; 186,87; 193,167; 200, 213; 213,287; (W) 217,160; (A) 224,216; 226,370; (A) 226,438; 228,96; 231,368; 261, 372; 283,18.
Macray, Elsie: 168,85.
Mcrae, Maurice: 309,27.
Macready, George: 300,22.
Macready, William Charles: (A) 58,302; 95,iv; 139,96; (D) 149,20; 182,217.
McSween, J. Sidney: 140,112.
Mactammany, Ruth: 221,17.
Macullum, Barry: 240,163.
"Macushla": (R'20) 232,527.
McVay, William: 87,138; 105, 144; 107,9; 108,48; 135, 165.
MacVicars, Frank: 71,3.
McVicker, James Hubert: (D) 124,198.
McVicker, Julius: 94,315.
McVicker, Mary: 39,115.
McVicker, Sarah: 91,231.
McVine, Olive: 40,147.
McVoy, Celeste Aymond (W): 205,154.
McWade, Edmond: 6,17.
McWade, Edward: 158,177.
McWade, Margaret: 181,124.
McWade, Robert: 140,103; 187, 149; 202,353; 260,296.
Macy, Alfred: 86,iii.
"Mad Lover, The": (F,R) 202, 394.
"Mad Week, The": (S) 148,170.
"Mad Woman, The": (F) 217, 183.
"Madame Butterfly" (OP): 69, 302; (R'06) 70,313; 74,111.
"Madame Moselle": (R'14) 161,37.
"Madame Pierre": (R'22) 253, 236; 254,301; (D) 254,309.
"Madame Pompadour": 286,19; (R'24) 286,19; 289,21.
"Madame President": (R'13) 153,xxiv; 153,156.
"Madame Sand": 203,20; (R'17) 203,24.
"Madame Sans-Gene": (OP) 169, 118; (R'24) 286,20; (F) 286, 33; (F,R) 292,32.
"Madame Sherry": 112,179; 112, 180; 115,94; (R'10) 116,xiv.
"Madame Troubadour": (R'10) 117,xvii.
"Madame X": 98,iv; 101,6; 109, 65; (R'10) 109,66; 109,71; 109,85; (F,R) 234,114.
"Madcap, The": (R'28) 326,41.
"Madcap Duchess, The": 154,174; (R'13) 154,178.
"Madcap Princess, A": (R'04) 44,245; 44,257.
Maddern, Merle: 181,123; 244, 20; 280,14; 280,21.
"Madeline": (OP) 157,116.
"Madelaine and the Movies": (D) 254,309; (R'22) 254,336; 255,379.
"Mlle. Baby": 156,104.
"Mlle Josette, Ma Femme":179,11.

"Mademoiselle Marni": (R'05) 50, 82.
"Mlle. Mischief": (R'08) 93,x; 93,296.
"Mlle. Modiste": 57,266; 58, 292; (R'05) 60,v; 60,33; 62,86.
"Mlle. Napoleon": 30,208; (R'04) 35,7.
"Mlle. Sallie": (R'05) 71,xv.
Madison, Maud: 186,80.
Madison Square Theatre (New York): 25,64; 52,135; 62,93; 62,101; 71,10; 84,42.
"Madonna of the Future, The": 205,137; (R'18) 205,149.
"Madras House, The": (R'21) 251,98; 252,151.
Mae, Ada: 275,38.
Maeterlinck, Maurice: 18,4; 19, 16; 26,98; 54,iii; 58,289; 59,11; 72,55; 105,142; 115, 92; 116,97; 118,194; 118, 195; 128,128; 172,282; 194, 213; 215,17; 218,200; 227, 12; 230,249; (A) 231,346.
"Magda": 12,2; (F,R) 201,316; (R'26) 301,16.
Magee, Eithne: 131,11.
Magee, Virginia: 261,389.
"Maggie Pepper": 123,147; 127, 99; (R'11) 128,116.
"Maggie the Magnificent": (R'29) 345,68.
Magic: 150,62; 183,300; 205,136; 240,156.
"Magic": (R'17) 194,215; 194, 217.
"Magic Flute, The": (OP) 143, 13.
"Magic Knight, The": (R'06) 72,xv; 72,34.
"Magic Melody, The": (R'19) 226,368; 227,23.
"Magic Ring, The": (R'23) 272,75.
"Magical City, The": 183,273; (R'16) 183,277; 187,128; 189,278.
Maginn, Bonnie: 26,82; 33,274.
"Magnanimous Lover, The": (R'19) 227,21; (R'20) 229, 222.
Magrane, Thais: 112,194; 132, 65; 151,96.
Magrauth, Joseph Walker (W): 341,11.
Maguire, Edward J.: 148,190.
Mahan, Frances: 258,148.
Maharashtra Company: 115,90.
Mahler, Gustav: 81,314; 120, 48; 182,198.
Mahoney, Will: 322,47; 328,41; (C) 342,14.
Mahr, Claire: 300,25.
Mahuron, Charlotte: 289,11.
"Maid and the Mummy, The": (R'04) 43,216; 43,233.
"Maid in America": (R'15) 170,211; 171,238; 171,239.
"Maid in Germany": (R'13) 148, x.
"Maid Marian": (R'02) 13,4; 13,23.
"Maid Mistress, The": (R'17) 196,343; 197,31.
"Maid of France, The": (R'18) 208,356; 208,359.
"Maid of the Mountains, The": 213,271; (R'18) 280.
"Maids of Athens": (R'14) 159, 261.
"Main Street": 249,365; (R'21) 249,387; (D) 250,33; (F) 268,35.
Maine Theatre: 233,33.
Mainwaring, Mary: 41,180.
Maitland, Sybil: 171,253.
"Maitresse Du Roi": (R'26) 311,16.
Majeroni, Georgia: 117,132; 166,266.
Majeroni, Mario: 67,228; 153, 141; 303,14; 312,66.
Majestic Theatre (New York): 25,72.
Major, Clara Tree" 205,159; 301,33.
"Major Andre": (R'03) 34, 290; 34,291.
"Major Barbara": 58,viii; 60, 30; 179,5; (R'15) 179,7; 179, 9.
"Major Pendennis": 190,354; (R'16) 190,356.
Majori, Antonio: 16,25; 17,6; 22,12.
Makalif, Edmund: 225,311; 244,25.

Makara: 113,28.
Make Up: 44,249; 107,20; 129, 172; 172,310; 179,38; 191, 14; 193,168; 212,227; 213, 297; (D) 252,172; 304,23; 319,37; 353,56.
Make Up--Film: 174,89.
"Maker of Dreams, The": (R'15) 170,211.
"Makers of Light,": (R'22) 257, 93.
"Making Good": (R'12) 133,xiv.
"Makropoulos Secret, The": (R'26) 301,18.
Malaguenita, La: 136,178.
Malcolm, Nellie: 66,210.
"Male and Female": (F) 225, 319; (F,R) 227,41.
Malevinsky, Moses L. (W): 304,34.
Maley, Denman: 208,357.
Maley, Stephen: 292,14.
Malibrau, Madame: 34,317.
Malo, Gina: 353,24; (C) 361, 38.
Malone, Andrew E. (W): 301,9.
Malone, Dudley Field: 324,48.
Malone, Florence: 139,73; 200,193; 202,357.
Malone, Geraldine: 87,138; 128, 121.
Malone, J.W. (W): 94,341.
Malone, John: 15,19.
Malone, Walter: 81,293.
Maloney, May: 129,175.
"Malvaloga": (R'22) 261,373; 261,376.
"Mama Loves Papa": (R'26) 302,16.
"Mama's Baby Boy": (R'12) 137,2.
"Mamma's Affair": (R'20) 229, 181; 229,187.
Mamoulian, Rouben: 323,37; 333,48; 344,29.
"Man and His Angel": (R'06) 69,xii.
"Man and Superman": 42,186; 56,viii; (R'05) 56,238; 56, 247; 56,249; 57,v; 57,vi; 348,49.
"Man and the Masses": (R'14) 279,15; 353,49.
"Man from Blankly's The": (R'03) 32,240; 33,274.
"Man from China, The": (R'04) 40,137.
"Man from Cook's, The": (R'12) 135,xiv.
"Man from Home, The": 82, 329; (R'08) 92,260; (F) 165, 227.
"Man from Mexico, The": (R'09) 100,171; 100,173.
"Man from Now, The": (R'06) 68,xii; 68,260.
"Man in Possession, The": (R'30) 358,25.
"Man in the Box, The": (R'05) 57,267; 57,275.
"Man in the Making": (R'21) 249,438.
"Man in the Sky": (F) 357, 48.
"Man Inside, The": 154,175; (R'13) 154,179.
"Man of Destiny, The": (R'04) 38,86; (R'25) 299,16; 299, 17.
"Man of God, The": (R'27) 315, 26.
"Man of Honor, A": (R'11) 128,xi; 129,iii; 129,162.
"Man of the Hour, The": 71,3; (R'06) 71,6.
"Man of the People, A": (R'20) 236,280.
"Man on the Case, The": (R'07) 80,xii; 80,261.
"Man Proposes": 38,83; (R'04) 38,84.
"Man Who Came Back, The": (R'16) 188,204c; 189,285; (F,R) 360,47.
"Man Who Laughs, The": (F) 324,49.
"Man Who Married a Dumb Wife, The": 169,115; (D) 171, 248; 195,266; (D) 296,13.
"Man Who Owns Broadway, The": (R'09) 105,xiv; 105, 134.
"Man Who Stayed Home, The": (R) 208,356; 208,369.
"Man Who Stood Still, The": (R'08) 94,312.
"Man Who Was, The": 60,29.
"Man Who Was Killed, The":

(F) 230, 279.
"Man with a Load of Mischief, The": 296, 20; 297, 14; 300, 7.
"Man with Three Wives, The": (R'13) 145, xxix.
"Man, Woman and Marriage": (F) 241, 269.
Managers, Theatre (see also Actors' Equity Association): 43, 226; 51, 114; 52, ix; 62, 89; 63, v; 65, 186; 66, 200; 67, 230; 92, xii; (C) 133, 98; 135, 153; 137, 14; 141, 156; 143, 18; 145, 74; 147, 156; 153, 160; 155, 19; 182, 230; 188, 191; 194, 199; 198, 63; 203, 7; 204, 71; 207, 272; 209, 8; 211, 138; 217, 134; 225, 314; 231, 379; 262, 7; 264, 7; 272, 12; 273, 11; 276, 22; 297, 7; 299, 7; (D) 303, 22; 310, 32; 330, 15; 331, 36; 361, 18.
Mandel, Frank: 329, 34; 331, 27.
Maney, Richard: 331, 49.
Mangasarin, Christine: 160, 289; 160, 324.
"Manhattan Mary": (R'27) 321, 44.
Manhattan Opera House (see also Opera): (D) 62, 108; 75, 138; 76, 169; 81, 310; 81, 314; 82, 350; 85, 84; 97, 76; 102, ix; (D) 290, 50.
Manhattan Stock Company: 7, 10.
Manhattan Theatre (New York): 21, 17; 101, 28.
Manion, Lucille: 219, 271.
Mann, Bertha: 175, 123; 223, 148.
Mann, Frances: 327, 29.
Mann, Louis: 9, 8; 25, 59; 43, 223; 46, 298; 47, 8; 50, 96; (A) 51, i, f; 60, 25; 60, 30; 67, 246; 73, 59; 74, xiii; 76, 146; 93, 298; 93, 299; 94, 312; 95, 11; 114, 33; 114, 34; 114, 37; 127, 77; 132, 70; 133, 75; 133, 97; 139, 68; 155, 46; 158, 199; 171, 228; 193, 166; 200, 216; 210, 87; 211, 128; (A) 214, 379; (W) 222, 88; 231, 383; 233, 24; 237, 373; 268, 27; (W) 340, 19.
Mann, Margaret: 326, 26.
Mannering, Mary: PG, 5; PG, 6; 5, 14; 5, 15; 6, 2; 8, 20; 10, 10; 16, 2; 16, 3; 17, c; 17, 9; 22, 6; 22, 25; 38, 82; 41, 175; 47, 13; 50, 79; 50, 85; 56, 237; 57, 277; 57, 279; 58, c; 61, 59; 72, 54; 76, 157; 80, 276; 81, c; 92, 256; 94, 323; 106, xxiii; 106, 197; 109, 68; 109, 72; 116, 128; 118, 192; 129, 148; 130, 213.
Mannering, Robert (W): 158, 186.
Manners, Diana: 242, 347; 264, 26; 275, 21; 276, 17; 276, 29; 302, 47.
Manners, J. Hartley: 193, 165; 194, 228; (D) 213, 289; (A) 231, 347; (W) 234, 92; 253, 233.
Manners, Jane: 233, 18; 338, 48.
Manners, Muriel: 239, 104.
Mannheimer, Jennie: 86, vi.
Manning, Alice: 271, 35.
Manning, Natalie: 214, 362.
Manning, William T.: (W, A) 324, 15.
Mannion, Katherine: 233, 28.
Manola, Adelina: 83, 8; 105, 158.
Manola, Antoinette: 92, 277.
Manon, Marcia: 219, 301.
"Manon Lescaut" (OP): 3, 6; 135, 144; 142, 166; (F, R) 161, 48.
"Manru" (OP): (R, S) 5, 17; 10, 32; 10, 33; (R) 13, 24.
"Man's Estate" 339, 44.
"Man's Friends, A": (R'13) 147, xiv; 147, 142.
"Man's Man, A": (R'25) 297, 70.
"Man's Name, The": (R'21) 250, 32.
"Man's World, A": (R'10) 109, 68.
Mansfield, John: (D) 182, 184; 225, 348.
Mansfield, Martha: 211, 159; 217, 147; 221, 15; 223, 188; 228, 107; 230, 277; 237, 390; 239, 113; 242, 366; 254, 323; 257, 103; 266, 48; 275, 39.
Mansfield, Richard: PG, 30;

(A) 3,1; 3,4; 3,13; 4,c; 4, 17; 8,17; 8,18; 9,12; 10,1; 27,128; 11,4; 23,5; 23,5; 33,271; 37,66; 37,69; 38,83; 41,175; 44,249; 50,85; 51,vi; 51,106; 51,116; 52,iv; 52, 131; 55,iv; 57,277; 62,88; 62, 102; 63,v; 63,112; 65,c; 65,190; 67,244; 72,49; 73,x; 74 86; 78,iii; 80,282; 82,323; 94, xxx; 95,31; 98,x; 104,112; 112,195; 120,63; 127,85; 139,78; 141,136; 150,52; 154, 174; 155,32; 62,58; 172,298; 181,122; 195,283; 199,126; 200,200; 211,146; 212,198; 231,348; 231,397; 237,368; 284,68; 293,38; 297,36; 302, 36; 356,40.

Mansfield, Richard Jr.: 195,289.

Mansfield Theatre (New York): 301,66.

Manship, George: 125,21.

Mantell, Ethel Charlotte: 147, vi; 175,128.

Mantell, Robert Bruce: 23,18; 35,6; 47,19; 58,290; 58,305; 66,197; 67,246; 69,c; 70, xx; 70,312; 77,171; 79,228; 84,51; 88,143; 91,228; 95, 27; 98,104; 98,108; 98,121; 122,106; 123,xi; 124,189; 127,77; 139,69; 143,11; 145, 75; 150,70; 160,301; 161,16; 163,101; 167,10; 169,122; 169,142; 174,61; 175,129; 179, 6; (A) 179,33; (A) 182,222; 186,80; (W) 188,194; 196, 337; 196,342; 209,41; 211, 135; 214,333; (A) 214,379; 215, 18; 218,228; (A) 226,438; 231,357; (A) 238,72; 244,7; 245,75; 245,119; 250,63; 253, 214; 267,28; 284,66; (A) 322, 3; 330,72.

Mantelli, Eugenia: 75,134.

Manthey, Lottie: 108,37.

Mantle, Burns: (C) 193,138; (C) 270,11; (W) 335,42.

Manville, Lorraine: 282,21.

"Many Waters": (R'29) 344,68; 343,18; 345,50.

Mapes, Victor: 6,2; 6,3; 6,15; 54,187; 65,194; 78,200; (W) 78,202; 199,134.

Maple, Audrey: 113,20; 116, 114; 143,3; 149,11; 201, 289.

Mara, Hanna: 44,240.

Marbe, Fay: 217,135; 219,271; 232,531; (D) 233,c; 235, 204; 275,43.

Marberg, Lili: 51,123.

Marble, Anna: (W,V) 70,326; 88, 166.

Marble, Mary: 36,29; 38,ii.

"Marble Heart, The": (R'09) 101,2.

Marburg, Guido: (W) 18,14.

Marbrugh, Bertram: 121,81; (W,V) 130,184; 152,110; 172, 301; 213,275.

Marbury, Elizabeth: 3,17; 53,163; 71,14; 88,162.

Marbury, Jane: 98,107; 103, 76.

Marc, Agnes: 137,4.

Marceil, Isador: 199,135.

Marceline: 52,136; 82,336; 83,i; 104,108; 235,191; 276,37.

"Marcelle": (R'08) 93,288; 93, 304; 94,328.

Marcelle, Lucille: 125,16; 193, 145.

Marcellus, Irene: 222,75; 258, 25.

"March Hares": (R'21) 247,274.

Marchesi, Blanche: 46,xx.

Marcin, Max: 177,228; (W) 189,268; 288,12.

Marco, Maria: 203,9.

"Marco Millions": 324,38; 325, 45; 353,49; 359,42.

"Marco Polo" 298,5.

Marcoux, Vanni: 146,104.

Mardones, Jose: 281,35.

"Margaret Schiller": 181,124; (R'16) 181,126.

"Margery Daw": (R'16) 191,64.

Margolies, Edward: 257,96.

Margules, Annette: 276,26.

"Maria Marten": 346,43.

"Maria Rose": (R'14) 157, 114; 160,308.

Marie Bonnie: 208,354.

Marie, Frances: 30,188.

"Marie Antoinette": (R'21) 251,

98.
"Marie Dressler's All Star Gambol": (R'13) 146, xv.
"Marie-Odile": (R'15) 169, 111; 169, 131; 170, 174; 170, 175; 174, 78.
"Mariners": 315, 26.
Marinetti, F.T.: 294, 22.
Marini, Luigi: 153, 148.
Marinoff, Fania: 100, xix; 100, 174; 157, 161; 165, 204; 175, 123; 184, 348; 187, 141; 203, 11; 203, 35; 204, 83; 207, 301; 213, 285; 228, 86; (D) 236, 273; (A) 238, 72; 248, 310; 249, 414; 250, 16; 255, 389; 267, 38; 273, 18; 275, 26; 305, 45.
Marinsky Theatre (Russia): 158, 181.
Mario, Queena: 236, 271; 267, 37; 275, 35; 301, 35.
Marion, Frances: 203, 64.
Marion, George: 65, 188; 187, 132; 209, 11; 218, 204.
Marion, Suzanne: 229, 178.
"Marion De Lorme": 77, 181.
Marionettes (see Puppet Theatre).
"Marionettes, The": (R'11) 131, 3; 131, 25.
Marischka, Hubert: 160, 305; 304, 20.
"Marjolaine": (R'22) 253, 268.
"Marjorie": (R'24) 283, 15.
"Mark of the Beast, The": (R'15) 178, 324.
"Mark of Zorro, The": (F, R) 239, 114.
Markey, Enid: 188, 235; 205, 187; 266, 50.
Markey, Irene: 150, 49.
Markham, Kirah: 161, 26.
Markham, Pauline: 209, 16; 340, 38.
Markham, Phyllis: 197, 34.
Markova, Sonia: 202, 405.
Marks, [Mrs.] J. Christopher: 337, 42.
Marks, Sallie: 54, 193.
Marley, Mlle.: 249, 381.
"Marlowe" (Peabody) (B): 60, 55.
Marlow, Heinrich: 81, 292; 81, 311; 154, xx.
Marlowe, Babe: 233, 26.
Marlowe, E.H.: 53, viii.
Marlowe, Ethel: 106, 182.
Marlowe, James C.: 165, 217; 238, 33.
Marlowe, Julia (see also Sothern and Marlowe): PG, 1" PG, 2; (A) 3, 1; 3, 5; 4, 17; 7, 15; 8, 21; 9, 12; (A) 10, 15; 11, 2; 15, 18; 20, 17; 22, c; 22, 18; 22, 19; 22, 21; 23, 1; 23, 5; 25, 61; 26, 87; 40, 149; 41, 174; 47, vi; 47, 1; 50, c; 50, 93; 55, 210; 58, 291; 62, 106; 65, 186; 65, 187; 67, 242; 69, 305; 70, 312; 70, 313; 71, 10; 72, 45; 73, 58; 72, 80; 75, 132; 79, 228; 79, 229; 83, 2; 85, iii; 85, 66; 93, 73; 94, 323; 96, 67; 97, c; 98, 130; 100, 194; 104, 101; 105, 144; 105, 145; 106, 184; 109, 72; 113, 23; 118, 163; 121, 78; 125, 12; 126, 45; 127, 76; 128, 127; 139, 67; 142, 196; 142, 198; 142, 199; 145, 75; 145, 93; 150, 63; 151, 78; 152, iii; 152, 120; 160, 308; 170, 191; 174, 61; 175, 144; 176, 175; 177, 249; 182, 225; 185, 7; 189, 286; 191, 16; 196, 329; 214, 335; 225, 298; 227, 25; 231, 383; 232, 514; 242, 317; 249, 361; 277, 22; 290, 12; 290, 29.
Marmein, Irene: 251, 79.
Marmein, Miriam: 251, 79.
Marmein Sisters: 222, 101; 267, 43; 277, 5.
Marmont, Percy: 203, 20; 216, 69; 298, 33.
Marne, Lily: 342, 48.
Marolda, Dina: 86, 109.
Marquees, Theatre: 110, 121; 121, 90; 202, 344.
Marquis, Don: 260, 306; 307, 29; (W) 321, 15.
"Marquis De Priola, The": (R'19) 217, 141.
"Marquise, The": (R'27) 323, 38.
Marr, Graham: 165, 213.
Marr, Paula: 30, 207; 110, 114; 120, 49; 152, 113; 156, 60.
"Marriage": (F, R) 214, 392.
"Marriage a la Carte": 120, iii;

120,44; (R'11) 120,xv; 121, 99.
Marriage And Stage: 214,360; 224,244; 233,24; 320,26; 329,22.
"Marriage Certificate, The": (D) 134,129.
"Marriage De Figaro, Le": (R'18) 214,347.
"Marriage Game, The": 9,13; (R'02) 11,2; 11,3; (R'13) 154,176; 154,181; (R'14) 156,104.
"Marriage Market, The": (R'13) 153,xxii; 153,145; 153,156.
"Marriage-Not, The": (R'12) 136,xii.
"Marriage of a Star, The": (R'10) 115,xiv.
"Marriage of Columbine, The": (R'14) 166,306; 167,35.
"Marriage of Convenience, A": 208,343; (R'18) 208,355; 220,358.
"Marriage of Kitty, The": (R'04) 35,3; 35,9.
"Marriage of Reason, A": (R'07) 75,115.
"Marriage of William Ashe, The": 58,i; 58,298; 58,299; (R'05) 59,3.
"Marriage Price, The": (F,R) 218,253.
"Marriage Proposal, The": 326, 46; 326,47.
"Married in Hollywood": (F) 344,48.
"Married Woman, The": (R'16) 192,85.
"Marrow of Tradition, The": 26,96.
"Marrying Mary": (R'06) 68, 260.
"Marrying Money": 159,232; (R'14) 159,262; 159,268.
Mars, Leo: 61,58.
Mars, Mlle.: (D) 142,179.
Mars, Orilla: 122,136.
Marsh, Helena: 280,35.
Marsh, Howard: 287,14.
Marsh, Lucile (W): 305,30; 357,44; 360,37.
Marsh, Mae: 164,161; 199,c; 199,180; 213,327; 221,67; 269,34.
Marsh, Peggy: 254,299.
Marshall, Armina: 278,17; 339, 44.
Marshall, Boyd: 209,11.
Marshall, Charles: 242,335.
Marshall, Edward: 201,294.
Marshall, Herbert: 360,33.
Marshall, Irby: 219,293; 315, 21.
Marshall, Madeline: 273,13.
Marshall, R.E. (W,V): 130, 220; 156,83.
Marshall, [Capt.] Robert: 20,5; 24,28.
Marshall, Tully: 86,105; 87, 130; 108,55; 109,88; 132, 45.
Marshall, Virginia: 89,180; 101,15.
Marston, John: 325,30.
Marston, Lawrence: 11,6; 90,i; 199,121.
"Marta of the Lowlands": (R'03) 33,268; 33,269; 86, 88.
Marteau, Henri: 290,43.
Martens, Carl: 112,180.
Martin, Beth: 214,363; 232, 518.
Martin, Boyd: 315,49; (W) 155, 36.
Martin, Ethel: 307,23.
Martin, Isabelle (W): 166, 283.
Martin, [Mrs.] Jacques: 215, 21; 249,382; 337,48; 346, 47.
Martin, Kathlyn: 253,249.
Martin, Muriel: 192,101; 197, 39.
Martin, Neil: 205, 163; 211, 149.
Martin, Paul R.: (W) 139,76.
Martin, Rea: 124,203.
Martin, Riccardo: 82,352; 106, 202; 129,155; 134,109; 146, 107; 176,191.
Martin, Vivian: 87,118; 124, 210; 133,85; 135,143; 139, 84; 154,181; 154,186; 161, 8; 184,348; 201,317; 201, 320; 209,57; 215,60; 220,

399; 236,285; 244,9; (D) 246,184; 247,228; 304,43.
Martin, Willis: 50,103.
Martin Beck Theatre (New York): (D) 287,27; (D) 290, 17.
Martindell, Edward B.: 45, 271; 46,322; 79,233; 80, 280; 106,198; 132,43; 195, 276.
Martine, Stella: 61,66.
Martinelli, Giovanni: 153,149; 169,119; 170,183; 190, 345; 192,94; 264,37; 264, 38; 272,37; 281,35; 288, 35; 330,23.
Martinetti, Ignacio: 112,180.
"Martinique": (R'20) 232,526.
Martinot, Sadie: 3,13; 7,6; 11,2; 11,3; 46,314.
Martyl, Nelly: 125,36.
Martyn, Edward: 29,167; 29, 168.
Martyn, Kathlene: 230,253; 242, 364; 244,53; 245,122; 256, 25; 287,46.
"Maruxa": (R'19) 220,343.
Marvenga, Ilse: 287,13; 287,14.
Marx, Graucho: 307,19; (C) 334,11.
Marx Brothers: 281,16; 281, 25; 299,14; 308,70; 334,36; 334,48; 356,47.
"Mary": (R'20) 238,32; 238,33.
"Mary and John": (R'05) 56, vii.
"Mary Goes First": (R'14) 166, 300.
"Mary Jane McKane": (R'23) 276,19.
"Mary Jane's Pa": (R'08) 95, 4; 95,7.
"Mary Magdalene": (R'10) 119, 2; 119,3.
"Mary, Mary, Quite Contrary": (R'05) 60,30; 272,17; (R'23) 272,18; (D) 273,44; 274, 39.
"Mary of Magdala": (S) 19,12; 21,14; 22,5; 22,13; 22,14; 22,15; 22,16; (R'03) 23,4; 42,ii.
"Mary Rose": 240,155; (R'20) 240, 177.
"Mary Stuart": (D) 134,129; (S) 242,318; 243,301; 243, 394; (R'21) 243,416.
"Mary the Third": (R'23) 265,20.
"Mary's Ankle": (R'17) 199,133; 199,151.
"Mary's Lamb": (R'08) 89,v.
Mascagni, Pietro: 6,6; 20,24; 21,28; 96,70; 116,108; 147, 159; 339,16.
Mascagno, Eva: 274,35.
"Mascot, The": (R'09) 99,xxi.
Masefield, John: (D) 142, 176; (A) 288,9.
Mashir, Marie: 257,81.
"Mask and the Face, The": (R'24) 284,62.
Mask And Wig Club (see also Pennsylvania, University of): 148,x; 163,128.
"Mask of Hamlet, The": (R'21) 248,340.
Mask Playhouse: 246,142.
"Masked Ball, The": 216,84.
"Masked Woman, The": (R'22) 263,16.
"Maskerade": (R'06) 62,xiii.
Masks: 239,92; 264,22; 301, 23.
Maslova, Vlasta: 244,25.
Mason, Adelaide: 177,229.
Mason, Ann: 228,103; 232, 510; 262,24.
Mason, Dan: 203,61.
Mason, Edith: 178,285; 180, 85; 277,35.
Mason, Edward T. (W,V): 84,50; 130,193.
Mason, Ellen (W): 312,32.
Mason, Florence: 269,32.
Mason, Gregory (W): 168,81.
Mason, John: 37,59; 47,7; (A) 51,i,f; 70,325; 81,309; (C) 82,xxiv; 83,13; 89,182; 110, 109; 111,151; 111,152; 122, 107; 139,66; 141,150; 145, 75; 146,iii; 151,79; 154,177; 163,99; 168,77; 175,111; 176,171; 178,288; (W) 190, 350; 216,114.
Mason, Kitty: 117,155.
Mason, Louise Hurlbut (W): 85,76; 97,86.
Mason, Redfern (W): 30,198;

150,49.
Mason, Reginald: 137,10; 150, 51; 181,137; 199,135; 203, 25; 205,143; (D) 252,169; 255,360; 268,28; 312,20.
Mason, Richard: 252,143.
Mason, Ruth: 316,19.
Mason, Shirley: 192,105; 211, 180; 218,256; 226,400; 228, 147; 229,191; (D) 230,c; 230,309f; 231,416.
Mason, Warren (W): 172,295.
"Masque of Vanity, The": 67, 249.
"Masque of Venice, The": (R'26) 302,18.
"Masquerader, The": 200,193; (R'17) 200,208.
Massachusetts Theatre: 164,166; 228,110; 244,43; 303,39.
Massagner, Conrado: (C) 263,11.
Massalitinoff, Nikolai: 259,216.
Massary, Fritzi; 289,28.
"Masse Menche" (see also "Man and the Masses"): 274,22; 279,22.
Massen, Louis: 56,247; 90,i; 104,127; 117,151;
Massenet, Jules: 87,137; (D) 100, 196; 139,vii.
Massey, Edward: 196,349.
Massin, Leonid: 178,297; 181, 128.
Massingham, Dorothy: 334,37.
Masso, Leonora: 209,29.
"Master, The": 191,9; (R'16) 191,24; (R'18) 206,219.
"Master Builder, The": (S) 79, 231; (R'07) 81,288; 81, 299; (R'15) 299,58.
"Master Key, The": (R'09) 105, xv.
"Master Mind, The": (R'13) 146,100.
"Master of the House, The": (R'12) 140,xiii; 140,118.
"Masterpieces of Modern Drama, The" (Pierce) (B): 182,184.
Masterson, Kate: (W) 10,17.
Matchabelli, Princess: 295,5.
Mate, C.S. (W): 182,212.
"Mater": (R'08) 93,285.
"Maternity": (R'15) 168,56; 168,61.
"Matinee Hero, The": (R'18) 214,347.
Mathews, Charles: 96,xiii; 195,264.
Mathews, Dorothy: 361,34.
Mathews, Frances Aymar: 68, 264.
Mathews, Irene: 222,75.
Mathewson, Anna: (W,V) 29, 163.
Mathewson, Christy: 153,152.
"Matilda": (R'06) 72,xv.
"Matinee Hero, The": (R'18) 214,347.
"Matinee Idol, A": (R'10) 112, 177.
Matinee Idols (see Star System).
"Matriarch, The": (R'30) 350,46.
"Matrimonial Bed, The": (R'27) 321,80.
Matsui, Shoyo (W): 79,251.
Matsui, Sumo-Ko: 161,31.
Matsumoto, Koshiro: 207,298.
Matthews, A.E.: 115,66; 115, 67; 116,126; 117,158; 243, 407; 252,155; 274,17; 299, 19; 322,30; (W) 332,26; 348, 45; 352,32.
Matthews, Brander: 28,134; 45, xii; 68,270; 139,92; (W) 182,214; 183,272; (W) 195, 263; (W) 196,346; (W) 197, 30; 215,34; (W) 216,83; 217,150; (W) 226,362; (W) 227,28; (A) 231,346; 231, 347; 246,144; (W) 247,240.
Matthews, Jessie: 313,15; 348, 17.
Matthews, Peggy: 252,147.
Matthison, Edith Wynne: 21, 5; 21,10; 28,131; 28,132; 28,136; 28,139; 38,99; 41, 179; 46,298f; 64,156; 70, 337; (W) 71,23; 85,76; 86, 89; 90,217; 95,9; 110,99; 111, 143; 111,145; 112,191; 118, c; 118,169; 120,54; 121,74; 121,84; 122,107; 122,129; 135,151; 135,159; 142,199; 145,89; 157,141; 167,10; 173, 12; 174,82: (A) 178,303; (W) 179,22; 180,74; 182,c; 182, 189; 183,286; 184,386; 185,

9; 201,269; 205,151; 205, 155; 206,219; 208,349; 209, 33; 212,198; 215,21; 246, 178; (W) 249,398; 258,170; 258,171; 292,30.
Mattray, Ernst: 163,109.
Maturin, Eric: 86,111; 93, 286; 109,73.
Matzenauer, Margarete: 130, 189; 134,125; 153,148; 190, 345; 203,42; 300,35.
Maubourg, Jeanne: 123,148.
Maud, Bonnie: 96,46; 111,148; 140,125.
Maude, Beatrice: 146,125; 171, 250; 211,147; 213,269; 217, 155; 223,161.
Maude, Charles: 156,65.
Maude, Cyril: 151,77; 153,165; 154,xxii; 154,176; 155,48; 159,252; 161,48; 169,134; 169,142; 182,192; 186,87; 190,358; 212,221; 214,364; 215,14; 215,26; 217,183; 231,351; 267,18; 267,19; 268,5; 269,14; 270,28; 298, 14; 352,9; 352,29.
Maude, Margery: 153,165; 161, 16; (A) 178,338; 189,295; 192,83.
Maugham, W. Somerset: 91, 228; 92,xiii; 92,278; 94, xi; 105,137; 107,xii; 116,98; 156,99; 248,300; 269,27; 312,28; 359,30.
Maunsell, Charles: 341,24.
Maurel, Barbara: 292,17.
Maurel, Victor: 189,320; 193, 146.
Mauret, Virginie: 246,161.
Maurey, Max: 54,202.
Maurice [Mouvet]: 134,136; 167,30; 167,37; 190,373; 191,17; 198,69; 214,343; 225, 300.
Maurice, Eleanora Ambrose: 330, 19.
Maurice, Mary: 205,191.
"Mauricette": (S) 66,205.
Mauresette: 221,14.
"Mauvais Bergers, Les": (R'18) 206,219.
Mawson, Edward R.: 28,153; 71,4; 84,46.
Mawson, Harry P. (W): 13, 18; 18,10; 21,14; 24,38; 27,118; 28,148; 35,10; 66, 208; 70,338; 74,103; 80, 282; 82,322; 114,49; 126, 42; 132,46; 134,129; 137, 18; 149,27.
Maxeville, Maurice: (C) 287, 29.
"Maxims of the Stage" by F.F. Schrader: 60,i,b; 66,xi; 78,viii.
Maxine Elliott Theatre (New York): 96,46; 127,102.
Maxon, Eric: 247,213.
Maxwell, Edwin: 235,191; 308, 19.
Maxwell, Elsa: 98,xii; 181, 127.
Maxwell, Marguerite: 260,305; 274,27.
Maxwell, Perriton (W): 186, 73; 187,132; 188,198; 191, 14; 311,3a; 335,42; 336, 20; 341,30.
Maxwell, Vera: 126,40; 196, 335.
Maxwell-Conover, Teresa: 36,42; 122,109; 140,103; 201,276; 205,137; 227,13; 238,14.
May, Ada: 216,87; 218,221; 239,100; 304,43; 280,17; 280,27; 303,46; 304,35; 310,60; 313,15; 314,6; (D) 320,c; (A) 322,3; 339,19.
May, Ailleen: 44,260; 55,234.
May, Ann: 219,295; 234,115.
May, Charles H.: 61,xv.
May, Doris: 222,109.
May, Edna: 3,7; 43,214; 44, 246; 45,c; 55,226; 56,259; 57,276; 66,223; 183,286; 183,311; 201,293.
May, Florence: 61,xv.
May, Lola: 93,287; 151,83.
May, Margaret: 6,17.
May, Olive: 6,5; 34,306; 82, 321.
"Maya": (R'28) 325,41.
"Maybe It's Love": (F) 357, 3.
Mayborn, Amelia: 126,67.
Maycliffe, Ruth: 88,162; 88, 163; 99,xviii; 99,166; 112,

193; 121,100; 133,85; 135, 143; 195,289; 201,265.
Mayer, David: 299,23.
Mayer, George: 111,xviii.
Mayer, Louis B.: 319,11.
Mayer, Morris E.: 75,xxv.
Mayer, Virginia Janet: 173, 30.
Mayfield, Cleo: 180,109; 181, 136; (A) 182,259; 230,312; 231,376; 231,460; 233,58; 253,229; 256,33; 311,46.
Mayhew, Kate: 251,103; 303, 28; (D) 351,18.
Mayhew, Stella: 66,221.
Maynard, Dorothy: 180,70; 316, 33.
Mayne, Clarice: 95,20.
Mayo, Christine: 196,338.
Mayo, Deronda: 26,88; 117, 144; 136,190.
Mayo, Edna: 88,155; 172,295; 177,242; 180,105.
Mayo, Frank: 17,19; 64,149; 83,26; (A) 247,265.
Mayo, Margaret: 68,264; 116, 103; 136,189; 145,75; 153, 150; 176,192; 186,64; 193, 165; 200,248; 217,170; (A) 231,347; 251,98.
"Mayor of Tokyo, The": 55, 225; (R'05) 59,6.
Mayr, Guido: 255,376; 352,38.
May's Opera House (Ohio): 61,xiv.
"Maytime": (R'17) 200,205; 200,221.
Mazarin, Mariette: 106,202; 109,74; 109,75.
Mazza, Desdemona: 264,34.
MC-- (Entries beginning with MC are listed as if spelled MAC).
Meade, Ada: 220,335.
Mead, Sue Belle: 38,106.
Meade, Tommy: 187,133.
Meader, George: 275,35; 289, 35.
Meads, E.F.: 109,92.
Meakins, Charles: 131,29; 189, 280.
"Meanest Man in the World, The": 237,349; (R'20) 237, 422.
"Measure of a Man, The": 61,i; (R'06) 70,xxvii.
"Mecca": 237,349; (R'20) 237,369.
"Medal and the Maid": (R'04) 36,31; 36,33; 37,75;
Medbury, Lew: 192,93.
"Medea": (R'18) 206,217; (R'20) 231,403.
Medieval Theatre: 328,32.
Meehan, Edward J.: 40,vi.
Meehan, Ginger; 353,23; 353,28.
Meehan, J.J.: (W,V) 103,84.
Meehan, John: 242,346.
Meehan, William E.: 188,205; 188,216.
Meek, Donald: 302,27; 333,46; 346,48; 359,16.
Meek, Kate: 109,66.
"Meet My Sister": (R'30) 360, 60.
"Meet the Prince": 338,46.
"Meet the Wife": (R'23) 275, 16.
Meffing, Mathilde: 86,104.
Megrew, Kanet: 246,160; 266,48.
Megrue, Roi Cooper: 166,276.
Mehaffey, Blanche: 336,34.
Mei Lan-Fang (see Lan-Fang, Mei).
Meier, Nellie Simmons (W): 29,174.
Meighan, Thomas: 83,8; 239, 116; 245,106; 268,35; (D) 291,2; 293,32; 295,38; 316, 38; 321,50; 337,38.
Meiningen Players: 125,24.
Meiser, Edite: 285,43; 306, 45.
"Meister Manoli": 50,102.
Meitschik, Anna: 105,139.
Melba, Nellie: 72,39; 75,139; 81,314; 93,309; (A) 116, ix; 116,109; 154,184; 231, 367; 242,345.
Melchior, Lauritz: 297,35; 339,30.
"Melinda and Her Sisters": 181,127.
Melis, Carmen: 107,10.
Melledge, Edgar Cecil: 351, 41; (W) 358,44.

Meller, Raquel: 272,24; 285, 8; 300,17; 303,18; 306, 40.
Meller, Tina: 346,45.
Mellish, Fuller: 39,121; 52, 153; 70,337; 97,99; 134,127; 166,269; 180,74; 201,275; 287,14.
Mellish, Fuller, Jr.: 328,39.
Mellish, Mary: 265,37.
Melodrama: 42,192; (D) 134, 129; 199,130; 218,198; (D) 223,143; 236,254; 317,14.
"Melody of Youth, The": (R'16) 182,194.
Melrose, Wilson: 107,7.
"Melting of Molly, The": (R'18) 216,80; 216,87.
"Melting Pot, The": (S) 96,58; (R'09) 104,106; 104,132.
Meltzer, Charles Henry (W): 9,10; 111,139; 170,198; 203, 7; 231,361; 239,88; 241,238; 266,12; 268,9; 270,12; 271, 24; 275,10; 276,20; 281,22; 282,12; 291,20; 322,43; 324, 20; 327,17.
Meltzer, Harold: 177,222; 203, 35; 208,359.
Melven, Sidney: 124,191.
Melville, Emelie: 41,iv; 143,7.
Melville, Frank: 54,193.
Melville, Rose: 83,28.
Melville Family: 54,192.
Melvin, G.S.: 278,37.
"Men Who Write The Hits, The" by C. Bird:
1. George Kelly: 281,10;
2. Lynn Starling: 282,10;
3. Hatcher Hughes: 283,10;
4. Martin Brown: 284,10;
5. L. Stalings & M. Anderson: 285,28.
6. Max Marcin: 288,12.
"Menace": (R'27) 314,21.
Mencken, H.L.: 114,41; 329,37.
Mende, Lola: 299,44.
"Mendel, Inc.": (R'29) 347,67.
Mendelssohn, Felix: 182,220.
Mendes, Catulle: 20,16; 56, 262; 72,54; 97,iv; 100,172.
Mendez, Lucila: 275,11; 296, 25; 319,39.
Mendoza, David: 330,47.
Mendum, Georgia: 16,8; 57, 285; 91,239; 174,72.
Mengelberg, William: 238,35; 266,37; 290,40; 333,25.
Menjou, Adolphe: 278,32; 287, 32; 291,34; (D) 295,2a; 298, 32; 320,45.
Menken, Adah Isaacs: (D) 189, 294; 209,16.
Menken, Grace: 309,45.
Menken, Helen: 205,161; 249, 369; 262,5; 266,26; (D) 267,6; 273,12; 294,6; 308,5; (C) 308,11; 309,14; 309,44; 310,30; 310,37; 311, 22; 311,23; (D) 312,27; 317, 20; 334,46; 335,58; (W) 336, 37; 346,15; 349,44; 351, 57.
Menuhin, Yehudi: 323,33.
"Mercenary Mary": 297,7.
Mercer, Beryl: 185,10; 193, 148; 194,231; 197,25; 213, 287; 220,345; 237,347; 242, 328; 288,38.
"Merchant, The": (R'02) 14,7.
"Merchant of Paris, The": 340,22.
"Merchant of Venice, The": 3, 6; 4,6; 4,7; 5,4; 21,19; (R'03) 29,160; 50,86; (R'05) 52,137; (R'05) 58,290; 60, 52; (R'08) 86,90; 139,76; 184,331; (R'16) 184,335; (R'18) 205,151; 207,295; (R'21) 244,60; (R'22) 263, 16; (R'23) 264,18; (F) 291, 33; 326,33; 334,19.
"Merchants of Glory": (R'25) 300,18.
"Mere Man": (R'12) 143,4.
Meredith, Ann: 120,64; 121,93; 145,79; 154,186; 157,109; 158,170; 158,216; 187,139; 200,197; 202,343;
Meredith, Charles: 212,208.
Meredith, Jane: 239,90.
Meredith, Lois: 157,114; 160, 294; 196,329; 210,113; 255,372.
"Merely Mary Ann": 35,18; (R'04) 36,34.
Meriden, Orson (W): 172,283; 173,16; 174,62; 176,185; 179,27; 185,35.

Merington, Marguerite: 9,16; (W) 48,50; 68,265.
Merivale, Philip: 166,262; 173, 12; 236,255; 264,18; 315, 28; (C) 317,31; 318,17; 347, 13.
Merkel, Una: 324,59.
Merlyn, Iva: 27,110; 30,205; 144,35.
Merman, Ethel: 357,26; 361,28.
Merrick, Gladys: 168,88.
Merrill, Beth: 288,17; 289,23; 321,37; (A) 322,3; 337, 23.
Merritt, Grace: 38,89; 77,187; 89,vii; 116,116.
"Merry Christmas, Daddy": (R'16) 192,86.
"Merry Countess, The": (R'12) 140,99; 140,123.
"Merry Death, A": 189,269; (R'16) 189,283; 197,33.
"Merry-Go-Round, The": 88, 144; (R'08) 88,147; 89, 195; (R'27) 317,18.
"Merry Malones, The": (R'27) 320,74.
"Merry, Merry": (R'25) 297, 16.
"Merry Whirl, The": (R'10) 113,4.
"Merry Widow, The": 79,252; 81,iv; 81,312; 81,313; (C) 82,xxiv; (R'07) 82,330; (R'08) 84,ix; 84,35; 87, 119; 90,207; 91,iii; 231, 349; 248,293; (D) 293,11; (F,R) 296,60.
"Merry Wives of Gotham": (R'24) 276,66; 277,12; (D) 277,13.
"Merry Wives of Windsor, The": 60,47; 66,211; (R'10) 118, 162; 118,169; (D) 137,32; (R'16) 183,276; (R'16) 185, 8; 185,27; 192,73; (R'17) 192,87; 193,146; (R'28) 326,76.
"Merry World, The": (R'26) 305,15.
Mersereau, Violet: 172,295; 200,247; 277,33.
"Merton of the Movies": (R'22) 262,25; 263,17; 271,30; (F,R) 284,32.
Mertons, Ivy: 335,47.
Mery, Andree: 177,225.
"Message from Mars, A": (R'01) 9,3.
Messager, Andre: 99,134; 213, 268.
"Messaline": (OP, R'01) 13,24.
"Messenger Boy, The" 8,6.
"Messin' Around": (R'29) 340, 41.
Messingham, Dorothy: 296,21.
Messmer, Otto: 322,32.
Mestayer, Emily: 302,37.
Mestayer, Harry: 121,79; 121, 88; 153,156; 205,153; 207, 273; 227,29; 255,379.
Mestayer, Louis: 302,37.
Metales, Georgios: 39,123.
Metcalfe, James S.: 15,18; (D) 49,76; 53,159; 66,vii; (C) 193,138; (W) 241,248; (W) 272,9; (W) 282,19.
"Meteor": 347,48; (S) 348, 32; (R'29) 348,45; 349,8.
Methot, Mayo: 344,32; 356,35.
Metro-Goldwyn-Mayer Studios: 319,12.
Metropolitan Opera [House] (see also Opera; "Opera, At The"): 3,14; 52,144; 60, 34; 64,xii; 69,288; 71,8; 73,70; 75,118; 81,314; 85, xvi; 100,vi; 122,114; 123, 148; 124,193; 134,109; 134, 124; 141,138; 143,12; 158, 178; 159,228; 166,270; 168, 66; 190,344; 279,7; 284,7; (D) 287,24; (D) 297,21; 345, 21.
Metropolitan Theatre (Los Angeles): 282,54.
Metternich, Pauline: 79,255.
"Mexicana": (R'06) 61,xvi; 61, 61.
Mexico Sisters: 91,243.
Mexican Theatre: 18,15; 107, 31; 124,206; 239,96; 335, 29.
Meyer, Bror: 204,112.
Meyer, George: 285,27.
Meyer, Grete: 90,207; 154, xx.
Meyer, Josephine: 171,259.

Meyer, Louis: 291,40; (W) 349,36.
Meyer, Paul: 291,40; 338, 36.
"Meyer & Son": (R'09) 98, xi.
Meyerhold, Wsewolod: 281,12.
Meyers, Carmel (see Myers, Carmel).
Meyers, Charles W.: 55,225.
Meyers, Jo: 353,23.
Miami University: 236,292.
"Mice and Men": 24,30; (R'03) 25,56.
"Michael and Mary": (R'29) 347,45; 347,46; 348,47; (C) 351,4.
"Michael Arlen": 290,10.
Michelena, Beatrice: 166,274; 201,323.
Michelena, Theresa: 189,285.
Michelena, Vera: 39,116; 89, 185; 118,176; 219,293; 271, 34.
Michey, Alice: 281,37.
Michigan, University Of: 266, 46; 275,68; 299,39; 306, 41; 313,42; 354,8.
Michigan Theatre: 274,42.
"Mid-Channel": (R'10) 109,68; 109,73.
"Middle Watch, The": 345,47; (R) 345,50.
Middlebury College: 127,106.
Middlemass, Robert: (D) 352, 4.
Middleton, George: 274,24; 277,37; (W) 285,22; 319, 27.
"Midnight": 359,24; (R'30) 360, 25.
"Midnight Follies": 292,41; 301, 71.
"Midnight Girl, The": 158,182; (R'14) 158,212.
"Midnight Romance, A": (F,R) 218,249.
"Midnight Rounders, The": (R'20) 234,93; 234,108.
"Midnight Rounders of 1921": (R'21) 241,264.
"Midnight Sons, The": (R'09)101, 2; 101,17.
"Midsummer Madness": (F,R) 240,186; 240,188.
"Midsummer Night's Dream": (R'03) 34,289; 35,11; (R'06) 69,xii; 69,301; 170,196; 323,38.
Mielziner, Jo: 287,27; 351,20.
Mielziner, Leo Jr.: 225,313.
Migliaccio, Eduardo (see Farfariello).
"Mignon": (OP) 213,272.
"Mikado, The": (R'10) 113,4; 113,15; (R'13) 148,163; 292, 17; 320,29; (R'27) 320,72.
"Milady's Boudoir": (R'14) 166,306.
Milburn, Mary: 236,260.
"Mile-A-Minute Kendall": (R'16) 191,23.
Miles, Beatrice: 287,31.
Miles, Carlton (W): 252,158; 254,284; 258,164; 267,22; 271,12; 283,20; 334,30.
Miles, Emily: 185,20.
"Milestones": 138,33; 139,85; 140,101; (R'12) 141,130; 142,ix; 352,15.
Milford, Mary Beth: 261,349.
"Military Mad": (R'04) 44, 247.
Millar, Gertie: 92,281; 93,294; 179,19.
Millard, Evelyn: 100,184.
Millay, Edna St. Vincent: 246, 177; 254,340.
Miller, Agnes: 34,307; 168,74; 175,129.
Miller, Alice Duer: 236,273.
Miller, Dorothy: 226,385.
Miller, Gilbert: 175,128; 234,84; 258,149; 264,13; 266,38; (W) 273,11; 282,7; 296,38; 302,6; 353,38.
Miller, Henry: 11,6; 12,9; 12, 10; (D) 15,7; 26,81; 34,307; 38,83; 39,108; 45,269; (W) 51,130; (A) 52,131f; 52,154; 58,314; 61,75; 62,101; 65. 187; 69,285; 71,13; 74,89; 80,c; (A) 94,xxxii; 109,81; 111,xx; 111,144; 112,174; 120,33; 121,94; 134,xv; 134,108; 138,c; 139,69; 140, 113; 142,xxi; 169,135; 169, 142; 170,193; 172,307; 175,

128; 193,137; 195,292; 199, 123; 199,168; 207,287; 208, 343; 210,79; 214,344; 219, 285; 220,358; 231,365; 234, 84; 246,166; 264,13; 266,5; 269,12; 272,22; 273,26; 276,39; 280,39; 290,19; 301,66; 352,28.
Miller, Hugh: 316,23.
Miller, Ivan: 242,331.
Miller, Jane: 254,293.
Miller, Marilynn: 162,78; 165, 239; 165,240; 169,140; 173, 27; 174,87; 191,37; 194, 239; 21p,102; 210,106; (D) 212,c; (A) 214,379; 222,73; 238,21; 238,57; 240,176; 240,179; 241,246; 248,303; 255,363; 256,28; 257,110; 259,240; 265,26; 284,66; 285, 25; 286,19; 286,48; 305,17; (D) 321,16; (A) 322,3; (D) 329,6; 340,28; 346,41; 346, 59; 353,22; 353,38; 356,52; 356,55; 357,c.
Miller, Miriam: 239,102; 270, 21.
Miller, Mizzi: 90,207.
Miller, Nellie Burget: (W) 261,396.
Miller, P. Ralph: (W) 303,12.
Miller, Patsy Ruth: 273,33; 307,36; 307,49; 311,35; 313,39; 321,23; (A) 360, 58.
Miller, Ray: 282,23.
Millership, Florrie: 238,33.
Millholland, Marchal: (W) 327, 19.
Milliken, Sandol: 24,30; 37, 71.
Milliman, Virginia: 281,19.
"Million, The": (R'11) 130, 187; 130,206.
Millman, Bird: 247,229; 278, 37.
Millman, L'Estrange: 247, 231.
Milloy, May: 138,53.
Mills, Constance: 50,88.
Mills, Florence: 255,355; (D) 263,11; 295,20.
Mills, Frank: 10,4; 52,143; 74,102; 85,64; 127,78; 195, 273; 231,363; 284,52.
Mills, Grace: 111,142.
Mills, Grant: 357,35.
"Mills of the Gods, The": (R'07) 74,89; 75,121; 75, 136.
Millward, Charles A.: 89, 188; 97,101; 111,131; 120, 42.
Millward, Jessie: 3,2; 4,1; 4,3; 7,4; 20,4; 26,81; 38,88; 67,230; 68,258; 68,259; 74,106.
Milne, A.A.: 245,79; 246, 152; 263,238; 254,306; 268, 25; 271,38.
Milne, W.S. (W): 275,41.
Miltern, John: 115,66; 164, 157; 182,197; 183,281; 229,183; 307,27.
Milton, Barbara: 228,103.
Milton, Ernest: 345,49; 352, 20.
Milton, Maud: 112,183; 120, 42; 188,204; 202,341.
Milton, Robert: 187,132; 235, 178; (W) 252,144; 261,368; 265,12; (W) 281,9; 282,7; 291,36; 294,7; 299,30; 322, 34.
Milton-Waldeck, Minnie: 90, 207.
"Mima": (R'28) 335,49; 336, 24.
"Mimic World, The": (R'08) 91,200; 91,iii; 92,227; (R'21) 247,279.
Mimicry (see Burlesques).
"Mind-The-Paint Girl, The": (R'12) 140,98.
"Mind Your Own Business": 191,38.
Mindlin, Michael: (W) 328, 18.
"Minick": (R'25) 285,16; 285, 18.
Minjer, Harold: 303,13.
Minneapolis Theatre: 242,330; 332,18.
Minnesota, University of: 244, 41; 244,42; 300,39.
Minstrel Shows: 60,52; 66, 224; 88,168; 104,118.
Minter, Mary Miles: 129,176; 195,285; 201,317; 207,325;

211,188; 222,89; 224,248; 228,106; 230,278; 233,38; 234,113; 246,176.
Minty, Mado: 156,77.
"Minute's Walk, A": (R'20) 234,108.
"Miquette et Sa Mere": (R'16) 192,128.
"Miracle, The": (S) 132,44; (D) 135,163; 138,34; (F,R) 146,xv; 147,160; 163,109; 267,12; 267,13; 268,40; (D) 275,8; 275,21; (R'23) 276,15; 276,17; 279,24; 281,39; (C) 286,15.
"Miracle Man, The": (R'14) 165,205; 165,217; (F) 224,254.
"Miracle of St. Anthony, A": (R'15) 172,282; 172,286.
Miracle Plays (see also Religious Drama): 241,239.
"Mirage, The": (R'20) 237,414.
"Miranda of the Balcony": (R'01) 9,6; 9,7.
Mirbeau, Octave: 30,190; 37,72; 206,219.
Mirou, Joseph: 35,4.
"Mirrors": (R'28) 324,39.
"Misalliance": (R'17) 201,280; 201,291.
"Misanthrope, The": (R'05) 51,106; 52,131; 52,132; (R'19) 219,274.
"Miserables, Les" (see also "Law and the Man, The"): 67,225; 71,17.
Mishka, Olga: 219,272; 236,270.
"Misleading Lady, The": (R'13) 155,7; 155,21.
"Miss Caprice": 153,156.
"Miss Daisy": 165,201; 165,206.
"Miss Dolly Dollars": 56,241; (R'05) 56,244.
"Miss Dundlesack": 134,132.
"Miss Elizabeth's Prisoner": (R'04) 35,5.
"Miss Hook of Holland": (R'07) 84,xii; 84,35.
"Miss Information": (R'15) 177,223.
"Miss Innocence": 97,90.
"Miss Innocence Abroad": 34,306.
"Miss Jack": 128,iii; (R'11) 128,113.
"Miss Lulu Bett": (R'20) 240,180; 240,181.
"Mis' Nelly of N'Orleans": (R'19) 217,143; 218,217; 219,289.
"Miss 1917": (R'17) 202,350; 204,71.
"Miss Nobody from Starland": 110,110.
"Miss Patsy": 110,110; (R'10) 166,102; 116,119.
"Miss Phoenix": (R'13) 154,xv.
"Miss Pocahontas": (R'07) 82,xix.
"Miss Princess": (R'12) 144,xii; 144,38.
"Miss Simplicity": (R'01) 13,4; 13,6.
"Miss Springtime": 189,280; (R'16) 189,282; (D) 202,367.
Mississippi State College For Women: 253,245.
Mississippi Theatre: 138,48.
"Mr. and Mrs. Daventry": (R'10) 110,xii.
"Mister Antonio": (R'16) 189,281; 189,285.
"Mr. Barnum": 213,287.
"Mr. Bluebeard": 25,60; 27,121; 36,36.
"Mr. Buttles": (R'10) 109,xii.
"Mr. Faust": (R'22) 253,266.
"Mr. Hamlet of Broadway": 96,vii; (R'08) 96,xv.
"Mr. Hopkinson": (R'06) 61,55; 61,56.
"Mr. Lazarus": 186,61; (R'16) 188,204d; 189,297.
"Mr. Lode of Koal": (R'09) 106,xviii.
"Mr. Moneypenny": (D) 330,35; (R'28) 333,45; 333,46.
"Mr. Myd's Mystery": (R'15) 176,200.
"Mr. Pickwick": (R'02) 22,20; 132,48.

"Mr. Pim Passes By": 242,319; (R'21) 242,339; (S) 246, 152; 247,266.
"Mister Pitt": (R'24) 277,16.
"Mr. Preedy and the Countess": (R'10) 118,xix.
"Mister Romeo": (R'27) 320,24.
"Mr. Wife's Millions": (R'03) 32,242.
"Mr. Wu": (R'14) 166,263; 166,279; (F) 313,36.
Mistinguette: 119,xxii; 151, vi; 225,326; 275,11; 276, 29; 281,15.
"Mrs. Avery": (R'11) 130,xv.
"Mrs. Battle's Bath": (R'05) 52, 136.
"Mrs. Black Is Back": (R'04) 46,298.
"Mrs. Bumpstead-Leigh": 118, 176; 123,142; 123,143; (R'11) 123,146; (R'29) 340, 42.
"Mrs. Dane's Defense": 71,28; 169,148; 325,48.
"Mrs. Dering's Divorce": 31, 209.
"Mrs. Dot": 109,66; (R'10) 109,70.
"Mrs. Gorringe's Necklace": 47, 4; (R'05) 47,6.
"Mrs. Jack": (R'02) 20,6; 20, 8.
"Mrs. Jimmie Thompson": (R'20) 231,402.
"Mrs. Leffingwell's Boots": 48,30; (R'05) 48,31.
"Mrs. Moonlight": 357,28; 358, 30; (D) 359,c.
"Mistress Nell": 3,2; 4,2; 4,8; 30,195; 216,84.
"Mistress of the Inn, The": (R'23), 274,19.
"Mrs. Partridge Presents": (R'25) 288,16.
"Mrs. Peckham's Carouse": (R'08) 93,xi.
"Mrs. Temple's Telegram": (R 05) 49,57.
"Mrs. Van Vechten's Divorce Dance": 86,106.
"Mrs. Warren's Profession": 58,296; 28,298; 66,198; 74,xii; 75,137; (R'18) 206, 218.
"Mrs. Wiggs of the Cabbage Patch": 33,288; 41,159; (R'04) 44,244; 100,178; (F) 168,69.
"Mrs. Wilson": (R'06) 70,318.
Mitchell, Abbie: 26,97.
Mitchell, Dodson: 57,271; 207, 273.
Mitchell, Doris: 28,154; 98, 112; 174,86; 220,363.
Mitchell, George: 118,176.
Mitchell, Grant: 93,286; 117, 141; 164,155; 200,209; 201, 274; 215,26; 240,181; 242, 337; 244,21; 257,83; 260, 320; 304,27; (W) 305,10; 311,24.
Mitchell, Julian: 65,186; 65, 189; 171,238.
Mitchell, Langdon: 130,192; 185,6.
Mitchell, Louise D. (W): 77, 183; 88,148; 100,178.
Mitchell, Maggie: 198,109; 231,397.
Mitchell, Norma: 192,79.
Mitchell, Thomas: 214,359; 245,77; (D) 251,101; 302, 31; 303,26; 319,27; 327, 39.
Mitti, Germaine: 246,153; (D) 247,211; 247,227.
Mitzi (see also Hajos, Mitzi): 209,11; 212,212; 213,283; 214,340; 234,101; 237, 362; 239,100; 239,107; 243,393; 243,413; 257,77; 274,13; 291,11; 299,48; 302,47; 303,36; 305,21; 316,17; 323,46; 328,34.
Miura, Tamaki: 177,224; 197, 9; 271,37.
Mix, Tom: 234,114; 293,34.
"Mix-Up, A": (R'14) 168,60.
"Mixed Marriage": (R'20) 239, 107; 240,163.
"Mizpah": (R'06) 69,284.
"Mob, The": (R'20) 237,422.
"Moby Dick": (F) 354,59; (F,R) 355,47.
Mock, Alice: 334,43.
"Mock Doctor, The": (OP) 197,31.

"Mocking Bird, The": (R'02) 22,8; 23,12; 288,25.
"Model, The": (R'12) 140,xii; 140,102.
Models, Theatrical (see also Toy Theatres): 287,11.
"Modern Crusoe, A": (R'03) 27,110.
"Modern Eve, A": 172,279; (R'15) 172,281.
"Modern Girl, A": 165,221; (R'14) 165,254.
"Modern Magdalen, A": (R'02) 15,3; 15,5.
"Modern Marriage": (R'11) 128, xiii.
Modernwell, Hiram K. (W): 140, 105; 185,33; 187,128; 201, 286.
"Modest Suzanne": (R'12) 132, xii; 132,71.
Modjeska, Helena: PG,7; (A) 3,17; 11,12; 51,v; 52,160; 91,237; 99,133; (A) 99, 139; 100,181; 109,90; 114,41; 121,xv; 138,44; 142,199; 182, 225; 222,102; 231,397; 242, 338.
Moeller, Helen C.: 174,84; (W) 192,82; 261,358; 265, 11.
Moeller, Philip: 204,75; 219, 295; 309,27; 333,49; 356, 27.
Moffat, Elizabeth: 255,359.
Moffat, Graham: 135,150; 237, 361.
Moffat, Jessie Emerson: 49, xv.
Moffat, Katie: 135,150.
Moffat, Sanderson: 129,152; 135,150.
Moffat, [Mrs.] William: 135, 150.
Moffett, Cleveland (W): 5, 10; 11,14; 15,13; 96,iv.
Mogout, Endja: 265, 13.
Mogulesko, Sigmund: 157,115; 168,81.
Moissi, Alexander: 126,59; 126, 60; 142,191; 309,32.
Moliere: 12,16; 51,106; 130, 185; 144,63; 149,10; (D) 223,166; (D) 246,144; (D) 256,5; 256,38.
"Moliere": (R'19) 219,273; 219, 285.
"Moliere" (Chatfield-Taylor) (B): 73,xiii.
"Moliere" (Mathews) (B): 257, 126.
Molineux, Roland B.: 26,82.
"Mollusc, The": (R'08) 92, 257; 92,279; 95,x; (R'09) 101,2; 169,135.
"Molly May": (R'10) 111,xxvi; 111,132.
"Molly O'"; (R'16) 185,11.
Molnar, Ferenc: 92,256; 92, 266; 152,115; (D) 246,143; 247,219; 273,16; 273,39; 286,25; 297,18; (D) 305, 12; 311,9; 324,36; (W) 333,41; 334,57.
"Moloch": (S) 177,230; 183, 283.
"Moment Before, The": (F) 184,351.
"Mona"(OP): 124,ix; 134,109; (R) 135,144.
Monaco, James V.: 179,26.
"Money from Home": (R'27) 314,22.
"Money Lender, The": (R'28) 332,78.
"Money Makers, The": 48, 31; (R'05) 48,33; 165, 208; (R'14) 165,253.
"Money Moon, The": 148,183.
"Mongolia": (R'28) 324,40.
"Mongrel, The": (R'24) 287,62.
"Monkey Talks, The": 300,13; (R'25) 300,16.
"Monna Vanya": (R'02) 18,4; (S) 19,16; (R'05) 58,289; 58,308; 58,309; 59,11; (OP) 158,167; (OP,R) 158,179.
Monologues: 338,30.
Monrath, Anna: 27,117.
Monroe, Carrie: 164,162.
Monroe, Ed Thayer: 290,49.
Monroe, Frank: (W) 97,100; 108,41; 181,124; 222,103.
Monroe, George: 82,xxiii.
Monroe, George W.: 129,175.
"Monsieur Beaucaire" (see also "Beaucaire"): 9,12; (R'01) 11,4; (R'12) 134,xiii; 135,

157; 136,195; 227,5; 278, 32; 278,33; (F,R) 283,30.
"Monster, The": (R'22) 259,225; 259,227.
Montague, Harry J.: 205,166; 244,28.
Montaigue, M.J.: (W) 182, 226.
Montana, University of: 273,41.
Montclair Players: 222,107.
Monte Carlo (Monaco): 121,101; 240,169.
"Monte Carlo": (F,R) 356,48.
"Monte Cristo": 191,8.
"Monte Cristo, Jr.": 218,201; (R'19) 218,208.
Montegut, Maurice: (W,FI) 82, 342.
Monteil, Annette: 229,166.
Montemezzi, Italo: 156,66; 156,67; 276,34.
Monterey, Carlotta: 172,296; 181,150; 193,180; 214,361; 218,209; 219,279; 225,293; 227,46; 234,99; 250,21; 254, 303; 256,9; 257,80; 259,219; 259,249; (D) 271,45; 278, 43; 285,38; 286,28; 289,48; 296,67; 297,48; 299,30.
Monteux, Pierre: 198,95; (C) 273,27.
Montez, Lola: 40,139; (D) 188,210.
Montford, May: 112,187.
Montgomery, David (see also Montgomery and Stone): 25,60; 40,136; 69,293; 137,11; 176, 176.
Montgomery, Douglass: 330,41; 337,48; 346,71; 348,33.
Montgomery, Gladys: 248,308.
Montgomery, H.W.: 171,234.
Montgomery, James: 141,154; 240,162.
Montgomery, Scamp: 117,141.
Montgomery, Walter: 69,295; 186,79.
Montgomery, William: 139,80; 145,vi.
Montgomery and Stone: 18,5; 25, 60; 69,293; 103,72; 108, xv; 137,11; 142,193; 166, 265; 166,304; 176,176; 231, 349; 256,26.
"Month in the Country, A": (R'30) 350,42; 350,45; 351,21.
Montmartre: (D) 227,22; 345, 45.
"Montmartre": (R'22) 253,264.
Montrose, Beula: 80,273.
Moody, William Vaughn: 69,283.
Mooers, [Mrs.] Edward D.: 271,23.
Moon, Bill: 280,59.
"Moon Flower, The": (R'24) 278,19.
"Moon Is a Gong, The": (R'26) 303,16; 303,33.
"Moon Lady, The": 185,21.
"Moon of the Caribees, The": (R'21) 244,60; (R'24) 286,22.
"Moondown": 171,259.
Moone, Millicent (W) (see "Letters To Actors I Have Never Seen").
Mooney, Gypsy: 208,363.
Mooney, Helen: 147,146.
Mooney, Martin: 331,48.
"Moonlight and Honeysuckle": 226,371.
"Moonlight Mary": (R'16) 181, 125.
"Moonshine": 58,xviii.
Moore, Alfred: 95,33.
Moore, Charles: 323,33; 350, 32.
Moore, Colleen: 268,34; 276, 33; 282,30; 282,33; 287,33; 288,30; 291,34; 293,32; 309,35; 319,35; 320,7; (D) 321,c; 332,37; (D) 334,67; 337,71; 339,61; (D) 341,59; 356,33.
Moore, Dennie: 336,27; 356,35.
Moore, Eva: 156,63.
Moore, Florence E.: 137,28; 139,80; 145,vi; 185,20; 191,41; 204,93; 229,187; 231, 374; (W) 235,172; (D) 249, 389; 250,34; 258,157; 308, 14; 308,16; 311,24; 326,24.
Moore, George: 29,167; 121, 96; 141,157.
Moore, Gladys: 130,187.
Moore, Grace: 248,298; 253, 251; 254,313; 274,29; 287,

38; 289,44; 326,45; 359, 47.
Moore, Irene: 79,243; 95,24; 98,104; 122,112; 125,32.
Moore, Jill Esmond: 341,25.
Moore, John: 22,26; 52,151.
Moore, Lucia: 314,22.
Moore, Mabel: 87,136; 221, 21.
Moore, McElbert (W): 337, 31.
Moore, Mary: 47,4; 109,66.
Moore, Matt: 216,127; 294,32.
Moore, Owen: 228,108.
Moore, Percival: 91,231; 283, 14.
Moore, Tom: 233,40.
Moore, Victor: 60,26; 83,4; 122,108; 211,161; 288,36; 329,31; 346,49; 354,28.
Moores, Clara Louise: 181,152; 206,231; 207,284; 214,361; 230,275; 232,554; 234,103.
Moorhead, Natalie: 334,30.
Morality Plays (see also "Everyman"): 60,50; 82,xvi; 123,175.
Morality In Films: 162,50; 184,356; 222,109.
Morality In Theatre (see also Sensationalism; Sex Appeal; Sex In Theatre): 22,25; 30,206; 48,48; 60,vii; 66, 199; 93,297; 129,168; 177, 227; 192,71; 193,140,197,34; 205,134; 209,34; 221,26; 228, 74; 238,6; 249,390; 269,25; 294,16; 294,52; 312,5; 324, 15; 325,48; 327,5; 328,12; 339,27.
"Morals": (R'25) 299,16; 299, 21.
"Morals of Marcus, The": (R'07) 83,5.
Moran, George (see Moran And Mack).
Moran, Joseph: 335,46.
Moran, Lois: 294,19; 310,40; 312,36; 319,29; (A) 322,3; 322,12; 324,50; 327,4b; 328,17; 339,34; 359,25; 361, 55.
Moran, Neil: 80,261.
Moran, Polly: 322,50; (W) 327,20.
Moran And Mack: 304,25; 353, 48.
Morand, Paul (W): 357,22.
Morant, Fanny: 202,338.
Mordant, Edwin: 171,236.
Mordaunt, Edmund: 69,301.
Mordaunt, Frank: 10,16.
Mordkine, Michael: 110,107; 110,115; 118,179; 118,180; 127,92; 128,119; 130,198; 130,200; 130,203; 285,21; 320,29.
Morehouse, Marion: 332,54.
Morehouse, Ward (W): 357,17.
Moreland, Beatrice: 113,10.
Moreland, Margaret: 134,136; 201,270.
Morely, Malcolm: 194,212.
Morena, Berta: 81,314; 99,143; 129,154.
Morena, Cormelia: 108,37.
Moreno, Antonio: 235,234; 280,32; 294,48; 298,32; 305,38; 306,40; 308,52; 317,40;
Moretti, Eleanor: 116,101; 117, 133.
Morey, Harry: 183,286; 213, 328.
Morgan, Beatrice: 70,332; 76,150.
Morgan, Edward J.: 5,8; 22, 7; 34,307; 55,209; 56, 257; 231,365.
Morgan, Frank: 209,31; 212, 203; 222,103; 240,159; 249, 371; 272,18; 286,21; 290, 26; 349,44; 350,42; 351,33; 351,34.
Morgan, Helen: (D) 342,13; (D) 343,23; 344,24.
Morgan, Kate: 173,14; 201,281; 203,15.
Morgan, Leone: 266,49.
Morgan, Marion: 188,213; (D) 199,140; 209,37; 219,287; 241,269; 242,313; 258,136; 346,59.
Morgan, M.E. (W): 311,32.
Morgan, Mary (W): 110,104; 116,103; 143,9; 147,146; 161,12; 171,242; 229, 185.

Morgan, Matt: 286, 53.
Morgan, Mona: 157, 141.
Morgan, Pauline: 229, 198.
Morgan, Ralph: 99, 166; 166, 290; 179, 16; 183, 294; 211, 149; 231, 354; 247, 219; 271, 17; 280, 13; 361, 25.
Morgan, Sydney J.: 131, 11.
Morgana, Nina: 281, 35; 303, 35.
Mori, Ritsu-Ko: 161, 31.
Morin, Pilar: 94, 319; 116, 104.
Morini, Erika: 242, 335; 249, 391; 272, 37.
Moritzen, Julius (W): 25, 71.
Morley, Catherine: 90, 210.
Morley, Christopher (W): 333, 15; 343, 37.
Morley, George: 299, 23.
Morley, Malcolm: 201, 291; 203, 31.
Morley, Victor: 40, 143; 230, 309; 275, 17.
Mormon In Drama: 167, 6; 196, 343.
Morningside Players (see also Columbia University): 192, 126; 196, 344.
"Morocco": (F, R) 359, 47.
Morosco, Oliver: 134, xv; 137, 14; 144, 42; 153, viii; 153, x; (A) 154, xxix; 154, xxxii; 167, 36; 187, 172; 187, 177; 193, 150; (W) 197, 8; 202, 411; 229, 181.
Morosco, Walter: 306, 52.
Morosco Theatre (New York): 202, 345.
Moroseff, Sergeii: 130, 202.
"Morphia": (R'23) 266, 16.
Morran, William: 229, 167.
Morris, Chester: 340, 18.
Morris, Clara: 8, 15; 16, 14; (W) 22, 17; 25, 63; 25, 64; (W) 34, 313; 39, 107; 39, 125; (W) 42, 206; (W) 46, 303; 52, 150; 52, 152; 64, vii; 98, iv; 106, 180; 126, 64; 127, 88; 195, 265; 204, 95; (W) 231, 377; 238, 28; (A) 287, 25; 288, 26.
Morris, [Mrs.] Felix: 190, 374.
Morris, Frances: 335, 47.
Morris, George: (W) 177, 227.
Morris, Lily: 290, 44; 290, 45.
Morris, McKay: 185, 21; 192, 93; 218, 204; 227, 16; 248, 323; (D) 250, 33; 259, 227; 266, 17; 268, 3; 269, 18; 269, 38.
Morris, Margaret: 136, 192; 149, iii.
Morris, Mary: 277, 18; 287, 21; 291, 26; 292, 20.
Morris, Nina: 93, vii; 104, 119; 205, 142.
Morris, Patricia: 236, 266.
Morris, Paul (W): 185, 25; 192, 96; 196, 358; 198, 70; 199, 130; 203, 8; 207, 274; 309, 20.
Morris, Ramsey: 21, 10.
Morris, William: 4, 3; 38, 88; 49, 57; 100, 189; 104, 105; 105, 149; 116, 117; 117, 131; 135, vi; 140, 119; 152, 130; 187, 149; 202, 341; 218, 209; 236, 255; 272, 14.
"Morris Dance, The": (R'17) 194, 213.
Morrison, A. B.: 61, xv.
Morrison, Abby: 283, 35.
Morrison, Adrienne: 168, 61; 218, 223; 290, 5; (D) 353, 40.
Morrison, Anne: 251, 93; 268, 31.
Morrison, Charles P.: 159, 240.
Morrison, E. W.: 90, 219.
Morrison, James W.: 175, 140.
Morrison, Lewis: 69, 308; 78, 222.
Morrison, Mabel: 53, 177; 34, 191; 136, c.
Morrison, Mary Horne: 227, 7.
Morrison, Rosabel: 78, 222.
Morrissey, Grace: 116, 122; 157, 140.
Morrissey, James W. (W): 115, 76; 116, 113; 119, 17.
Morse, Beryl: 40, 147.
Morse, Edwin H.: 255, 360.
Morse, Grace: 218, 209.
Morse, Lee: 286, 37.
Morse, Salmi B.: 6, 10.
Mortimer, Dorothy: 164, 175;

204,77; 204,97; 225,321; 225,322; 248,312.
Morton, Betty: 223,186; 233, 27.
Morton, Charles: 323,6.
Morton, Harry K.: 236,281; 292,21.
Morton, Lew: 333,48.
Morton, Martha: 9,16; 14,7; 14,8; 25,55; 35,i,f; 55, 227; 68,265; 73,84; 80,xi; 104,126; 145,75; 153,150; 156,64; 240,162.
Mosby, John S. Jr. (W): 148, 179.
Mosconi, Verna: 264,43.
Moscovitch, Maurice: 348, 28.
Moscow Art Theatre: 162,56; 250,28; 259,215; 259,216; 263,7; 264,14; 264,15; 264, 39; 266,7; 274,19; 282,20.
Moscow Art Theatre Musical Studio: 294,12; 296,14; 299, 15.
"Moses": (R'10) 114,49.
Moses, Montrose J. (W) (see also "Early American Dramatists"; "Famous Families Of American Players"; "Stage History Of Famous Plays"): (V) 36,43; 41,177; 42,190; (V) 46,319; 47,23; 50,88; 59,23; 69,ix; 92,264; 94,320; 95, xxiv; 102,64; 106,190; 108, 45; 131,28; 133,xvii; 136, 197; 137,27; 139,92; 142, 176; 143,26; 145,87; 153, 158; 164,164; 171,232; 173, 12; 180,92; 182,210; 203, 16; 208,346; 227,12; 253, 238; 254,300; 286,10; 339, 6; 347,8.
Moses, Myrtle: 180,85.
Maskovina, Mascotte: 238,13; 240,228.
Moskvin, Ivan: 259,217; 262, 14; 264,14; 308,40; 311, 37.
Moss, Arthur (W): 255,372.
Moss, Theodore: 168,82.
Moss And Fontana: 300,27; 336,41.
Moss And Frye: 273,35.
Mossi, Alexander: 323,19.
"Most Striking Episode In My Life, The" [Symposium]: 212, 200; 213,270; 214,340; 215, 14; 216,98; 217,164; 218, 228; 219,296.
"Moth, The": (S) 159,242.
"Mother": 111,146; (F) 204, 127; (R'10) 116,xiii; 179,17.
"Mother, The": (R'03) 26,100.
"Mother Carey's Chickens": (R'17) 201,278; 201,291.
"Mother Goose": (R'04) 35, 7.
"Mother's Cry": (F) 357,50; 358,57.
"Mother's Liberty Bond": (R'18) 211,143.
Motion Pictures (see Films).
Moto-Girl, The: 26,103.
"Motor Girl, The": (R'09) 102,36; 102,63.
Motts, Robert T.: 83,27.
Moulan, Frank: 24,30; 28, 146; 28,152; 75,141; 109, 96; 173,3; (W) 229,158; 229,159; 301,38.
Moulin Rouge: 303,12.
Moulin Rouge Theatre (New York): 135,140.
Moulton, Zita: 256,47; 262,48; 275,43.
Mounet, Paul: 77,181.
Mounet-Sully, Jean: 37,74; 38, 97; 139,79; 182,187.
Mount Vernon Stock Co. (New York): 195,318.
"Mountain Climber, The": 62, 83; (R'06) 62,84; 64,150.
"Mountain Man, The": (R'21) 251,128.
"Mountebank, The": (R'23) 268, 18; 268,19.
"Movers, The": (R'07) 80,xi; 80,262; 80,263.
Moving Pictures (see Films).
Mowatt, [Mrs.] Anna Cora: (D) 193,142.
Mower, Jack: 199,179.
Mower, Margaret: 183,273; 186,75; 194,223; 196,340; 206,205; 211,153; 213,285; 217,155; 218,199; 223,161; 236,266; 238,20; 243,399;

253,239; 280,44; 286,29.
Moyer, Gertrude: 33,282.
"Mozart": (R'26) 311,16; 312, 19; 312,21; 312,50.
"Much Ado About Nothing": (R'04) 38,86; 38,88; (R'04) 46,292; 142,189; (R'12) 143, 5; 152,109; 152,110; (D) 182, 215.
Muck, Karl: 69,289; 141,140; 178, 286.
Mudd, A.I. (W): 47,16; 53, 180; 57,288.
Mudie, Alan: 109,96.
Mudie, Leonard: 344,40.
Mueller, Gerda: 289,29.
Mueller, Maria: 301,35.
Muenster, William F.: 299,22.
"Muggins": (R'18) 209,24.
Muhlmann, Adolph: 118,173.
Muir, Esther: 344,54.
Muir, Gavin: 237,352; 241, 247.
Muira, Tamaki: 296,35.
Mulcahy, Edmund: 154,174.
Muldoon, William: 137,11.
Muldowney, John Humphrey: (C) 338,37.
Mulhall, Jack: 312,49; 320,45.
Mulkins, Katherine: 96,60; 110,114.
Mullen, Joseph: (D) 285,13; 298, 36.
Mullen, Sadie: 242,366.
Mumford, Ethel Watts: 207,297.
"Mummy and the Hummingbird The": 20,3; (R'02) 20,4.
Muni, Paul: 357,38; 359,29.
Municipal Theatre (see Civic Theatre).
Munson, Ona: 264,43; 311,47; 313,15; 327,11; 333,66; (D) 338,c; 338,67; (A) 359,7.
Munz, Mieczyslaw: 265,37; 278, 35.
Muratore, Lina C.: (A) 214, 379.
Muratore, Lucien: 177,248; 198,98; 198,99; 203,39; (D) 207,278; 208,352; 210, 81; (A) 214,379; 242,327.
Muray, Nickolas: 290,49.
"Murder on the Second Floor": 344,34; 344,46.
"Murderess, The": (R'19) 219,274.
Murdie, Leonard: 242,319.
Murdoch, Helen: 335,46.
Murdoch, James E.: 13, 22; 14,22; 46,305; 58,xiii; 139,94.
Murdoch, Jean: 126,69.
Murdock, Ann: 105,160; 118, 165; 122,112; 133,91; 135, 156; 136,184; 144,64; 155, 31; 159,245; 161,20; 163, c; 163,95; 163,142; 164, 158; 165,246; 168,76; 171, 233; 174,76; 182,245; 182 248; 186,81; 187,c; 187,138; 188,204; 192,105; 199,173; 199,184; 202,401; 203,20; 205,176; 207,333; 231,363.
Murnau, F.W.: (W) 322,41.
Murphy, George P.: 99,158.
Murphy, Ralph: 191,29.
Murphy, Tim: 127,88; 179,17; 216,94; 239,101.
Murray, Bonnie: 305,25; 306,49.
Murray, Charles A.: 143,24.
Murray, Elizabeth: 100,171; 112,180; 131,16; 156,77; 159,237; 164,176; 200,203.
Murray, J. Harold: 246,169; 263,24; 279,14.
Murray, James: 317,39; 325,34.
Murray, John T.: 246,169.
Murray, Marjorie: 163,107.
Murray, Mae: 79,233; 105, 154; 162,77; 173,17; 180, 74; 182,229; 192,105; 197, 20; 201,321; 202,408; 208, 399; 208,404; 212,259; 220, 395; 223,167; 226,357; 230, 278; 230,279; 233,37; (A) 233,55; 236,286; 240,187; (D) 242,c; 244,50; 247, 205a; 257,87; 259,253; 263, 35; 285,33; 296,30; 298,30; 307,37; 315,71.
Murray, Olive: 180,71.
Murray Hill Theatre (New York): 24,38.
Murray Sisters (Marjorie & Bonnie): 305,25.
Muse, Ophelia: 184,362.
Musgrave, Kenyon: 180,67; 188,204.

Music And Concerts (see also "Music For Everyone"): 3,16; 10,33; 11,23; 12,21; 13, 26; 20,27; 23,25; 24,51; 25,77; 33,284; 35,24; 47, 26; 58,316; 59,25; 60,53; 61,81; 62,110; 69,288; 70, 341; 80,iii; 170,184; 178, 286; 191,30; 194,230; 215, 10; 216,72; 227,33; 260, 318; and monthly thereafter; (D) 295,31; 339,25; 354, 30; 356,42.
Music And Films: 274,30.
"Music And Musicians" by P.V. R. Key: 215,10; 216,72; 217,136; 219,268.
Music And Theatre: 356,30.
"Music Box Revue of 1921": 249,367; (R'21) 249,387; (D) 249,389; 250,34.
"Music Box Revue of 1923": 269,3; 272,2; (R'23) 272, 54.
"Music Box Revue of 1924": (R'23) 287,19.
"Music Box Revues": 275,22.
Music Box Theatre (New York): 249,396.
"Music For Everyone": 202, 369; 203,40; 204,105; 205, 146; 206,237.
"Music Master, The": (R'04) 45,269; 45,274; 57,273; 73,63; 88,150; 190,359; 231, 348; 231,349; (F) 312,36.
Musical Comedy: 25,60; 28,145; 31,212; 31,217; 38,85; 56, vii; 56,253; 82,xix; 82,330; 88,vi; 150,69; 160,305; 186, 90; 188,206; 196,334; 200, 222; 201,292; 202,346; 210, 78; 212,204; 220,398; 224, 218; 236,264; 249,368; 250, 34; 257,90; 275,22; 290,14; 296,10; (D) 304,11; 319,14; (D) 322,25; 329,34; 335,37; 337,24; 349,38; 353,20; 358, 42; 359,45.
Musson, Bennet: 36,35.
Muybridge, Eadweard: 137,19.
Muzio, Claudio: 202,382; 209, 39; 216,73; 218,226; (A) 226,438; 286,35.
"My Beginnings" by:
Viola Allen: 62,93;
Margaret Anglin: 58,314;
Blanche Bates: 52,138;
Edmund Breese: 75,135;
George M. Cohan: 72,52;
Arnold Daly: 83,25;
Frank Daniels: 55,216;
Jefferson de Angelis: 54,205;
Robert Edeson: 65,178;
Katherine Grey: 78,210;
James K. Hackett: 68,275;
Anna Held: 77,180;
DeWolfe Hopper: 57,284;
Frank Keenan: 85,78;
Wilton Lackaye: 56,250;
Ada Lewis: 67,251;
Carlotta Nillson: 79,236;
May Robson: 81,305;
Otis Skinner: 63,118;
Blanche Walsh: 53,181;
David Warfield: 60,41;
Joe Weber: 73,81.
"My Best Girl": 140,iii; 140, xiv.
"My Cinderella Girl": 112,180.
"My Country": (R'26) 307,16.
"My Cousin": (F,R) 215,62.
"My First Lines" (Symposium): 169,142; 171,258.
"My Friend Teddy": (R'13) 145, 67.
"My Girl": (R'24) 286,64.
"My Girl Friday": (R'29) 337,47.
"My Golden Girl": (R'20) 229,220.
"My Lady Friends": 227,13; (R'19) 227,61.
"My Lady Molly": (R'04) 36, 33.
"My Lady Peggy Goes to Town": (R'03) 23,8; 28, 136; 28,137.
"My Lady's Dress": 166,268; 166,269.
"My Lady's Maid": 69,292.
"My Lady's Man": (R'06) 69, xiv.
"My Little Friend": (R'13) 149,xx.
"My Little Sister": 151,vi.
"My Mamie Rose": 85,69.
"My Man": (R'10) 117,x; (F) 336,73.

"My Official Wife": (F) 174, 89.
"My Own United States": (F,R) 205,194.
"My Son": (R'24) 285,64.
"My Wife": (R'07) 80,261; 80, 265; (C) 82,xxiv.
"My Wife's Family": (R'08) 93,x.
"My Wife's Husbands": 36,42.
Myers, Carmel: 227,23; 228,115; 280,31; 280,33; 301,47; 301,49; 318,23; 331,42; (W) 335,32.
Myers, Ernestine: 222,101; 235,175; (A) 240,201.
Myers, Henry: 255,381; 331,27.
Myers, Marguerite: 268,14.
Myers, Vera: 247,221.
Myers and Hanaford: 263,43.
Myra: 273,35.
Myrio, Jean: 344,36.
Myrtil, Odette: 173,20; 181, 125; 275,37; 279,14; 280, 27; 289,39; 306,14; 308, 27.
Myrtill, Marcelle: 121,87.
"Myself--Bettina": (R'08) 93,xiii; 93,286.
<u>Mystery Plays (see Detective Plays)</u>.
"Mystery Ship, The": (R'27) 314,22.
"Mystery Square": (R'29) 341,43.

--N--

Nadworny, Devora: 292,37.
Nagel, Conrad: 213,271; 213, 276; 272,33; 309,35; 312, 23; 318,44; 337,69; (D) 351,29.
Nagele, Margaret: 132,59.
Nagle, Claire: 219,277; 221, 31; 241,254; 243,445.
Nagy, Izabella: 329,20.
Nahm, Ida C.: 109,72.
Nairn, Ralph: 177,234; 183, 275; 310,14.
Nakamura, Ganziro: 258,161.
"Naked": (R'24) 286,20; 360,28.
"Naked Truth, The": 118,199; (F) (R'14) 161,48.
Naldi, Nita: 212,217; 217,147; 226,406; 232,510; 236,260; 242,336; 248,301; 266,49; 271,33; 275,33; 275,36; 286,44; 288,51; 291,43.
Namara, Marguerite: 178,279; 179,23; 181,144; 183,290; 203,42; 214,353; 220,339; 221,48; (A) 226,438; 228, 116; 231,421; 243,433; 249, 396; (D) 250,45; 288,21; 288,44; 288,58; 292,17; 292,38; 297,48.
Namirovitch-Danchenko, Vladimir; (C) 294,12; 299,34.
"Nancy Ann": (R'24) 279,19.
"Nancy Brown": (R'03) 26,83.
"Nancy Lee": (R'18) 207, 286; 208,369.
"Nancy Stair": (R'05) 50,82; 50,85.
"Nancy's Private Affair": (R'30) 348,45; 348,46.
Nannery, Edward (D): 254,309; 352,4.
Nansen, Betty: 169,128.
Napier, Nina: 149,2.
Narodny, Ivan: (W) 295,12.
"Narrow Path, The": (R'09) 101, 4.
Nash, Florence: 75,127; 85,72; 92,263; 116,119; 119,20; 124,200; 129,177; 134, 128; 143,16; 148,168; 159, 221; 161,21; 169,135; 171, 249; (A) 184,377; 186,105; 195,283; 197,16; 199,123; 201,273; 215,28; 215,29; 216,98; 238,18; (A) 250,63; (W,V) 252,170; 263,17; 299, 13; (A) 300,62; 312,48; 313, 52b.
Nash, Frances: 296,35.
Nash, George: 32,243; 39,121; 83,13; 117,135; 133,85; 159,227; 159,238; 165, 217; 173,18; 173,25; 212,213; 212,221; 216,95; 310,21; 320,23.
Nash, Mary: 128,116; 129,170; 134,128; 148,168; 151,83; 160,293; 161,21; 168,60; 171,249; 177,232; 178,306; 178,327; 179,9; (A) 188, 219; 189,285; 191,6; 195,

299; 197,16; 198,79; 211, 139; 213,302; 214,339;(A) 214, 379; 234,97; 238,20; 239, 83; 239,123; 249,373; 252, 155; (D) 252,169; 256,23; (D) 258,c; 275,17; (A) 285,51; 290, 23; 299,13; 299,43; (A) 300, 62; 301,c; 304,43; 312,48; 320,24; 321,57; (A) 322,3; 323,39; (D) 325,27; (A,D) 326,67; (A) 327,63; (D) 328, c.

Nashimoff, Mme.: 58,xi.

Nathan, George Jean: (W) 121, 93; (W) 131,12; (W) 142, 183; (W) 193,135; (C) 193, 138; (C) 269,21; (C) 284,20; 317,28; 329,37.

"National Athem, The": (R'22) 253,233; 253,250.

National Art Theatre (see also Endowed Theatre; National Theatre: 27,114; 28,153; 29,162; 30,186; 31,216; 35,2; 38,i; 40,ix; 41,163; 54,185.

National Sylvan Theatre (Washington, D.C.): 197, 9.

National Theatre (see also Endowed Theatre): 24,28; 24,35; 25,74; 26,86; 27, 114; 28,133; 58,294; 59,7; 150,38; 206,203; 208,364; 264,7; 268,39.

National Theatre (Mexico): 107,32; 124,206; 335,29.

National Theatre (New York): 51,119.

National Theatre (Washington, D.C.): 27,122; 87,120.

National Vaudeville Artists Association: 231,480; 238,75; (D) 269,41.

National Vaudeville Club: 231, 491.

National Vaudeville Home: 222, 94; 222,126.

"Natoma": (OP) (R'11) 122, 114.

Nattowa, Natacha: 300,6.

"Natural Law, The": (R'15) 171,230; 171,260.

Naudain, May: 88,163; 95,26; 180,65.

"Naughty Anthony": 294,16.

"Naughty Cinderella": (R'25) 298,16.

"Naughty Marietta": (R'10) 118,165; 118,166.

"Naughty Riquette": 309,23.

"Naughty Wife, The": (R'17) 203,51; 204,93.

Navarro, Ramon: 262,35; 267,35; 273,33; 352,47.

"Nazareth": (R'01) (S) 6,10; 6,11; 15,12.

Nazimova, Alla: 71,12; 73,72; 76,c; 76,145; 76,151; 78, 218; 78,219; 79,231; 81, 288; 81,299; 82,331; 84, 33; 84,39; 89,x; 102,48; 107,18; 111,132; 111,168; 112,201; 114,61; 127,77; 129,163; 130,185; 131,3; 131,25; 136,169; 139,66; 142,163; 142,186; 149, 26; 156,77; 163,99; 166,261; 167,11; 169,116; 169,142; 170,193; 174,61; 175,111; 177,240; 180,88; 192,70; 193,144; 194,225; 206,217; 206,223; 207,273; 207,287; 207,310; 208,349; 208,358; (C) 209,21; 209,33; 213, 270; 213,327; 216,123; 216, 124; 220,394; 223,179; (D) 224,c; 228,108; 234,116; 238,39; 245,107; (D) 245, 117; 246,143; 259,211; (C) 263,10; 266,13; 266,49; 267,43; 274,24; 282,30; 286,32; 292,34; 305,21; 333, 17; (W,D) 337,18; (D) 340, c; 350,45; 352,57.

Negri, Pola: 240,185; 250,38; 261,392; 265,38; (D) 275, 31; 278,32; 280,30; 284, 30; 285,33; (C) 286,15; (D) 290,v; 291,34; 291,62; 292,39; 296,31; 298,31; 303, 47; 308,40; 312,22; 315, 48; (D) 320,39.

Neal, Robert Wilson: (W,V) 116, 116.

"Near Santa Barbara": (R'21) 241,262.

"Nearly a Hero": (R'08)

86,xii; 86,91; 89,193.
"Nearly Married": (R'13) 152, 112; 152,124; 152,125.
"Necken, The": (R'13) 148,163.
"Ned McCobb's Daughter": 311, 14; (R'26) 311,15.
Nedbal, Oskar: (D) 160,305.
Nedd, Edythe: 260,293.
"Ne'er-Do-Well, The": (R'12) 140,102; 140,109; 143, vi.
"Neglected Lady, The": (R'14) 157,113.
Negro Actors: 26,96; 59,20; 66,224; 83,27; 85,xii; 184,362; 195,280; 196, 350; 238,8; 268,12; 295,20; 338,50; 351,23.
Negro Little Theatre: 338,50.
Neighborhood Playhouse (New York): (D) 170,198; 181, 143; 185,18; 191,21; 192, 92; 251,98; 258,166; 294, 64; 300,13; 303,13; 306, 53; 315,24; (R'15) 170,211.
"Neighbors": (R'23) 276,19.
Neil, Nelly: 307,27.
Neilan, Marshall: 231,489.
Neill, R.R.: 5,15; 37,62.
Neilson, Adelaide: 50,93; 54, 189; 78,222; 103,82; 106, 174; 138,44; 140,128; 150, vi; 150,52; 182,225; 243, 414.
Neilson, Alice: 56,255; 185,45.
Neilson, Julia: 117,145; 118, 190; 187,172.
Neilson, Louise: 86,iii.
Neilson, Oda: 170,194.
Neilson-Terry, Dennis: 298,22.
Neilson-Terry, Phyllis: 163,104; 163,105; 165,223; 167,8; 167,32; 170,170; 170,172; 171,243; 173,11; 176,c; 176, 161; (A) 177,257; 183,274; 184,332; 184,348.
Nelis, Sylvia: 240,157; 241,257; 251,77.
Nelma, Mabel: 31,216.
Nelmes, Harry S.: (W) 294,24; 299,22.
Nelson, Edgar: 188,205.
Nelson, Elizabeth: 140,113; 143,32; 148,181; 163,115; 173,35.
Nelson, Ethel M.: (W,V) 128, 122.
Nelson, Frank: 36,35; 89,197; 188,205.
Nelson, George Merwin (W): 173,19; 179,34.
Nemeroff, Maria: 252,147.
Nemeth, Juliska: 261,365.
"Nemisis": 243,395; (R'21) 243,416.
"Neptune's Daughter": 72,53.
Nerney, Joseph Mackin: 345,42.
"Nero": 61,61; 62,94; (R'07) 83,4.
"Nerves": (R'24) 284,16.
"Nervous Wreck, The": (R'23) 273,68.
Nesbit, Wilbur D.: 123,173.
Nesbitt, Cathleen: 183,296; 194,217; 195,273; 215,7; 282,13.
Nesbitt, Evelyn: 34,295; 158, 199; 193,166; 203,18; 215, 63.
Nesbitt, Miriam: 35,12; 62,84; 140,112.
Nesbitt, Tom: 240,155.
Nesmith, Ottola: 163,106.
"Nest, The": 253,215; (R'22) 253,235.
"Nest Egg, The": (R'10) 119, x; 119,19.
"Net, The": (R'19) 218,206; 218,209.
Nethersole, Olga: PG,24; 8,15; 8,19; 46,314; 55, 211; 58,288; 59,3; 59,7; 59,17; 60,34; 68,276; 70, 323; 72,c; 77,194; 82,324; 83,15; 85,xi; 85,61; 86, 91; 90,205; 96,44; 100, xviii; 100,170; 100,189; 101,26; 103,80; 110,xiii; 119,2; 119,3; 126,49; 127, 85; 129,166; 146,114; 156, 77; 158,199; 197,24; 204,95; 294,16; 338,15.
"Nettie": (R'14) 167,44; (R'19) 219,274.
Nevendorff, Adolf: 81,292.
Neuendorff, Mme.: 103,76.
Neuman, Franklin: (W) 329,18.
Nevada, Emma: 184,342.

Nevada, Mignon: 130,211.
"Never Homes, The": (R'11) 129,ix; 129,175.
"Never Say Die": (R'12) 142, xx; 143,18; 151,96.
"Never Trust to Strangers": 96, 41.
"Nevertheless": (R'16) 191, 23.
Neville, Harry: 203,31.
New Aeolian Hall (New York): 145,76.
New Amsterdam Theatre: 30, 193; 35,20; 41,160; 181, 122; 202,344; 290,16.
"New Brooms": (R'24) 287,16.
"New Clown, The": (R'02) 20,9.
New Comedy Theatre (New York): 127,102.
"New England Folks": (R) 10,6; 10,16.
"New Englander, The": (R'24) 277,19.
"New Generation, The": 93, 298; 93,299.
New Hampshire Theatre: 213,299.
"New Henrietta, The": (R'13) 156,61; 156,78.
New Jersey Theatre: 338,33; 339,44.
"New Lady Bantock, The": (R'09) 97,xv.
"New Marriage, The": 130,192.
New Mexico Theatre: 267,46.
"New Moon, The": (F) 220, 397; R'28) 332,80; 342,50; (F) 359,47.
New Orleans Opera: 35,26; 136, xi.
New Orleans Theatre: 255,385; 270,41.
New Park Theatre (New York): (D) 231,352.
"New Poor, The": (R'24) 276, 70.
New Rochelle College: 182,227.
"New Secretary, The": (R'13) 145,68.
"New Sin, The": (R'12) 141,xvi; 183,283.
"New South, The": 34,306.
New Theatre (Chicago): 62,88; 67,xi; 78,200; 78,202; 79, xiii; 82,324.
New Theatre (New York) (See also Endowed Theatre): 66,202; 79,235; 86,92; 87, xiii; 91,xii; 100,xxii; 101,vi; 102,58; 102,59; 104,viii; 104,xv; 105,144; 105,145; 106,ii; 106,166; 106,194; 107,9; 108,49; 113,2; 113,26; 115,67; 118, x; 118,162; 120,ix; 120, 38; 122,xiv; 122,106; 123, 142; 124,xi; 124,190; 168, 63; 170,198; 175,111; (D) 249,396; 252,144.
"New Toys": (R'24) 277,19.
"New Word, The": (R'17) 196,344; 197,25; (R'18) 208,355.
"New York": (R'10) 118,xxii; 118,181.
"New York Idea, The": 70,325; (R'06) 71,2; (R'15) 177, 224.
New York Theatre: 19,20.
New York University: 59,13; 221,58; 241,300; 251,110; 259,247; 267,44; 271,40; 277,42.
"New Yorkers", The": (R'01) 9,8; 10,5; (R'27) 314,21; (C) 360,32.
"New York's Historic Theatres" by Charles Burnham:
1. The Old Bowery (D) 205,160;
2. Booth's Theatre (D) 206,236;
3. Niblo's Garden & Wallack's Museum (D) 207,294.
Newberry, Barbara: 308,9; 309,53; 329,41; 331,16; 332,56; 341,7; 341,23.
Newbold, Robinson: 218,201; 219,272; 235,191; 292,17.
Newcomb, Helen: 254,311.
Newcomb, Mary: 226,369; 230,255; 271,13; 271,18; 288,13.
Newcombe, Caroline: 117,152.
Newcombe, Jean: 230,247.
Newcombe, Warren A.: 268,58.
"Newcomes, The": 66,207; 199,120.
"Newly-Married Couple, The": (R'18) 207,288.

"Newlyweds And Their Baby, The": (R'09) 99,xxi; 99,158.
Newman, E. M.: 143,3.
Newman, Horace: 112,187.
Newman, "Red": 246,171.
Newman, Walter: 218,256; 220,390.
Newport Casino Theatre: 353,44.
Newport (Rhode Island) Theatre: 19,19.
Newton, Peter: 194,201.
Newton, Theodore: (D) 352,4.
"Next of Kin, The": 107,15; (R'09) 108,36; 115,74.
Ney, Elly: 245,79.
Niblo, Billy: 78,213.
Niblo, Fred: 137,11; 184,361; 294,38; (W) 326,32; (W) 341,39.
Niblo's Garden (New York): 19, 18; 78,213; 137,27; (D) 207,294.
Nicander, Edward: 299,21.
Nicander, Edwin: 104,127; 173,6; 193,143; 206,216; 216,95; 217,164; 295,14.
Nice, Freddie: 151,89.
"Nice People": (R'21) 242,339.
"Nice Wanton": 125,175; 182, 227.
"Nice Women": 341,42; (R'29) 341,43.
Nichols, Anne: 269,23; 279, 39; (W) 280,19; 291,10; 293,43; 293,44; 316,7.
Nichols, Beatrice: 212,203; 213, 291; 239,90.
Nichols, Dorothy E.: (W) 308, 30.
Nichols, Guy: (W) 231,399.
Nichols, Humphrey T.: 198, 89.
Nicholson, Kenyon: (W) 340,20.
"Nic-Nax": (R'26) 307,16.
Nicoll, Arthir: 299,23.
Niday, Kathleen: (D) 352,4.
Nielsen, Alice: PG,24; 60,42; 103,77; 166,282; 180,91; 199,127; (W) 238,10; 56, 255; 185,45.
Nielsen, Christine: 113,15; 114, 49; 132,43; 136,170.
Nielsen, Karen: 100,194.
Nielson, Alma: 287,36; 290,45.
"Nifties of 1923": (R'23) 272,54.
"Nigger, The": 107,3; (R'09) 107,4.
"Night": (R'17) 193,150.
"Night at an Inn, A": 185,18.
"Night Bell, The": (OP) 197,31.
"Night Boat, The": (R'20) 229,220; 230,275.
"Night Call, The": (R'22) 256,31.
<u>Night Clubs</u> (see also <u>Cabarets</u>): 276,12; (D) 276,13; 281, 48; 291,13; (D) 306,29; 311,20.
"Night Duel, The": (R'26) 301,66.
"Night Hostess": 335,20.
"Night in Avignon, A": (R'19) 217,142; 217,155.
"Night in Paris, A": (R'26) 300, 18.
"Night in Venice, A": 342,42.
"Night in Spain, A": (R'27) 316,20.
"Night Lodging": (R'19) 228, 100.
"Night of Snow": (R'15) 177, 222.
"Night of the Party": (R'02) 21,6.
"Nightcap, The": (R'21) 247, 236.
"Nightie Night": 224,225.
"Nightingale, The": (R'27) 312,21.
"Nightshade": 233,23; R'20) 233,31.
Nijinsky, Vaslav: 102,51; 127,93; 127,94; 178,296; 191,42; 223,153; (D) 264, 10.
Nikisch, Arthur: 133,80.
Nikisch, Mitja: 271,36.
Nikolas, Lucile: 332,32; 332, 33.
Niles, Doris: 248,299; 262, 29; 333,39.
Niles, John J.: 340,23; 359, 44.
Nillson, Carlotta: PG,21; 33, 266; 37,62; 40,140; 43, 217; 44,244; 46,308; 57,275; (W) 70,324; 70,333; (W) 79,236; 87,116; 92,xxi; 97, 79; 98,106; 102,49; 108, 37.

Nilsson, Anna Q.: 179,23; 208, 395; 235,195; 276,33; (A) 283,63; 285,32; 288,30; 296,57; 319,45; 323,46.
Nilsson, Christine: 115,76; 115, 80.
"Nina Rosa": 356,16; (R) 356, 26.
"Nine O'Clock Town, The": (F,R) 211,183.
"Nineteenth Hole, The": (R'27) 321,42.
"Ninth Guest, The": 356,24.
"Ninety and Nine, The": (R'02) 21,10; 21,11.
"90 in the Shade": 169,120; (R'15) 169,150.
Nirdlinger, Charles Frederic: (W) 163,124.
Nirska: 234,94.
"Nirvana": (R'26) 302,16.
Nissen, Greta: 286,32; 292, 35; 295,34; 296,32; 305, 23; 318,45.
Nitter, Erna: 93,290.
Nixon, Marion: 305,47; (D) 313,41; (A) 361,56.
"Nju": 195,273; (R) 195,278.
"No Foolin' ": 305,23.
"No More Blondes": 228,99; (R'20) 228,144.
"No More Women": (R'26) 307,16.
"No, No, Nanette": 305,17; (F) 348,63.
"No Other Girl": (R'24) 283,16.
"No Trespassing": (R'26) 308, 18.
"Noah's Ark": (F) 333,44; (F) 338,63; (F) 339,63.
"Noah's Flood": 123,175.
"Noble Spaniard, The": (R'09) 105,137; 105,160; 105,161.
"Nobles, Milton (W): 185,31; 186,79.
"Nobody Home": (R'15) 172, 280; 172,297.
"Nobody's Child": (D) 134,129.
"Nobody's Daughter": (R'11) 121, x; 122,109.
"Nobody's Money": (R'21) 247, 274; 248,293.
"Nobody's Widow": 118,162; (R'10) 118,166; 119,16; 119,28; 231,368.
"Nocturne": (R'18) 209,24.
Noel, Margaret: (W,V) 65,193.
Noel-Noel: (C) 345,44.
Noftzger, M.: (W) 156,88.
Noguchi, Yone (W): 41,167; 47,20.
Noizeux, Paulette: 203,11.
Nolan, Boyd: 145,73.
Nolan, Mary: 322,44; 337, 28.
"None So Blind": (R'10) 109,x.
Noni: 274,35.
"Noose, The": (R'26) 309,70; 310,21.
Norcross, A.F.: (W) 302,37.
Norcross, Hale: 238,27.
Nordau, Max: 26,101.
Nordica, Lillian: 62,108; 79, ii; 81,315; 108,39; 121,82; 126,61; 128,127; 131,22; 160,322; 183,300; 231,367.
Nordstrom, Clarence: 309,21; 314,17.
Nordstrom, Marie: 98,112; 129,169; 160,283.
Noria, Jane: 105,138.
Norman, Beatrice: 8,17.
Norman, Christine: 96,68; 100,184; 107,28; 111,147; 118,199; 122,135; 143,7; 145,88; 150,50; 178,302; 179,25; 193,163; 217,157; 219,308.
Norman, Gertrude (W): 12,6; 48,36; 49,67; 51,122; 52, 147; (W) 55,219; 62,104; 122,110; 126,52; 131,18.
Norman, Henry: 22,20; 117,153; 132,48.
Norman, Thyrza: 144,45.
Normand, Christine: 254,322.
Normand, Florence: 248,314.
Normand, Mabel: 192,97; 199,180; 200,247; 205, 176; 206,255; 207,331; 234, 116; 262,35.
Norrie, Elsie: 244,17.
Norrie, Florence: 244,17.
Norris, William: 12,6; 82,xv; 82,319; 96,46; 112,180; 144,35; 173,25; 200,221; 321,43.
North, Bobby: 104,110; 114,45.

North, Clyde: 251,75.
North, Olive: 41,163; 54,204.
North, Wilfred: 3,5; 29,163; 51,117; 136,183; 138,59.
North Carolina Theatre: 213, 298; 235,200.
North Carolina, University of (see also Carolina Playmakers; Koch, Frederick F.): 239, 117; 239,118; 242,353; 269, 45; 280,40; 298,40; 310, 42; 328,45; 342,44; 351,51.
North Dakota, University of: 187,131; 212,229; 222,129.
Northampton (Massachusetts) Theatre: 164,166.
Northrup, Harry: 212,253.
Northway, Madeline: 318,50.
Northwestern University: 297, 41.
Norton, Barry: 323,6.
Norton, Edgar: 184,342; 194, 212; 262,20.
Norton, Lillian: 79,233.
Norton, Ruby: 143,3; 205,161.
Norton, W.A.: 196,355.
Norton, William G.: 299,23.
Norwegian Theatre: 258,140.
Norwood, Adelaide: 8,6; 35, 22.
Norwood-Brandt, Adelaide: 69, 302.
Norworth, Jack (see also Norworth and Bayes): 114,35; 189,278; 199,148.
Norworth and Bayes: 112,i; 114,v.
Nory, Alice: 120,xxii.
"Not Herbert": (R'26) 302,18.
"Not So Fast": (R'23) 269,16.
"Not So Long Ago": (R'20) 232,525; 254,286.
"Not With My Money": (R'18) 214,378.
Note, Jean: 94,345; 97,76; 110,108; (A) 116,xx; 145, 76.
"Nothing But Lies": (R'18) 214, 346; 214,349.
"Nothing But Love": (R'19) 225, 356.
"Nothing But the Truth": (R'16) 188,246; 189,285.
"Notre Dame": (R'02) 14,4.
"Nouvelle Idol, La": (R'18) 205,152.
Nova, Hedda: 204,127; 212, 253.
Nova, Marta: 263,13.
Novaes, Guiomar: 202,372; 216,73.
Novak, Eva: 268,53.
Novarro, Ramon: 278,32; 288, 31; 304,47; 306,38; 322, 26; (W) 322,27.
Novasio, Lenora: 207,277; 215, 33.
Novelli, Ermete: 32,262; 43, 213; 73,ix; 73,67; 74,96; 75,xxiii; 78,iv; 83,4; 92, 271; 189,286.
Novello, Ivor: 264,35; 270, 33; 356,30; 360,24.
"Novice and the Duke, The": (R'29) 347,46.
Novikoff, Laurent: 284,17.
"Now-A-Days": (R'29) 343, 41.
Nowak, Adelaide: 72,49; 79, 238; 106,193; 112,188; 141, 134.
Noyes, Beatrice: 126,67; 130, 222; 222,103.
Noyes, Florence Fleming: 145, 90; 161,3; 197,9; 201,268.
Nudity On Stage: 222,74; 272,7; 284,12.
Nugent, Elliott (see also Nugent Family): 257,83; 292,15; 295,26.
Nugent, J.C.: 257,83.
Nugent, Maude: 302,25.
Nugent, Ruth: 257,83; 296, 26.
Nugent Family: 261,388.
"Number 7": (R'26) 308,18.
"Nur Ein Traum": (R'13) 154,xx.
"Nurse Marjorie": (R'06) 69, 287; 70,320.
Nybloc, Margaret: 159,267.
"Nydia" (Boker): (B) 343,6.

--O--

"O Nightingale": (R'25) 292, 16.
Oaker, Jane: 49,60; 115,67; 115,69; 213,276.

Oakland, Dagmar: 287,14.
Oakland, Ethelmary: 196,359; 204,101.
Oakland, Vivienne: 232,505; 235,175.
Oakley, Florence: 89,198; 112, 194; 199,129.
Ober, Margarete: 153,148; 154, 182; 156,68; 158,180; 168, 65; 170,183.
Ober, Robert: 61,65.
Oberammergau: 15,10; 106, 190; 107,26; 114,44; 116, 112; 117,146; 117,149; 140, 122; 255,376; 349,10; 352,38.
"Object Matrimony": (R'16) 190, 392.
O'Brien, Alice: 125,35.
O'Brien, Eugene: 101,7; 120, 42; 120,45; 141,137; 171, 233; 174,82; 192,79; 200, 203; 217,191; 226,403; 228,106; 231,363; 231,410; 237,380; 254,297; 307,40; 308,40; 309,2; 323,6; 338, 63.
O'Brien, Geraldine: 163,101; 165,217; 180,68; 181, 129.
O'Brien, Gypsy: 176,188; 180, 71; 187,149; 220,363; 237, 388; 295,23.
O'Brien, Jack: 221,63.
O'Brien, John S.: 234,98.
O'Brien, Marietta: 236,270; 304,42; 351,53.
O'Brien, Neil: 23,7.
O'Brien, Nora: 54,191.
O'Brien, Pat: 356,26; 359, 29.
"O'Brien Girl, The": (R'21) 249,440.
O'Brien-Moore, Erin: 336,52; 337,27; 338,53; 343,55.
O'Bryan, Arthur: 42,209.
O'Casey, Sean: (A) 301,9.
O'Connell, Bland: 255,372; 280,11.
O'Connell, Hugh: 357,35; (C) 358,2; 359,29.
O'Connor, Adeline: 151,98; 215, 27.
O'Connor, Eileen (W): 179,18; 180,77; 181,138; 183,300; 189,296; 201,296; 202, 368; 204,78; 210,84; 337,42.
O'Connor, Evelyn: 112,186; 132, 57.
O'Connor, James Owen: 103, 80; 138,36.
O'Connor, Jeremiah: (W) 37, 66.
O'Connor, Kathleen: 222,109.
O'Connor, Robert: (D) 253,237; 260,296.
Oda, Madame: 76,149.
O'Day, Molly; 326,31.
"Odd Man Out": (R'25) 293, 15.
O'Dear, Bonna: 284,27.
Odell, Maude: 94,xxiv; 95, 22; 107,29; 116,99; 136, 190.
O'Denishawn, Florence: 209,20; 227,11; 237,387; 239,102; (D) 247,211; 249,380; 257, 91; 274,38.
Odilon, Helene: 3,4; 13,20; 15, 15.
O'Donnell, Irene: 55,225.
O'Donovan, Fred: 146,110.
"Oedipus": 126,56; (R'11) 128,112; (D) 133,84; 149, 21; 273,3a; (R'23) 273,15; (OP) (D) 361,41.
Oehman, Martin: 285,35.
Oerlichs, [Mrs.] Hermann: 194, 228.
"Off Chance, The": (R'18) 206, 218; 206,221.
"Off Key": (R'27) 313,18.
"Officer 666": (R'12) 133,xi; 133,85.
O'Gatty, Packey: 331,30.
Ogden, Angsla: 40,140; 66, 214.
Ogden, Vivia; (W) 16,14; 32, 258; 50,103; 87,138; 138, 53.
Ogle, Charles: 276,31.
Oglebay, Kate: (W) 282,41.
"Oh, Boy!": (R'17) 194,214; 194,227; 199,157; (F) 220,398.
"Oh, I Say!": (R'13) 154,xx.
"Oh! Oh! Delphine": (R'12) 141,x; 141,155; 150,71.
"Oh Lady! Lady!!": 205,143;

(R'18) 206, 220.
"Oh, Mama!": 295, 14; (R'25) 295, 15.
"Oh, My Dear": 215, 37.
"Oh, Promise Me": 359, 16.
"Oh, What a Girl!": (R'19) 223, 151; 224, 220.
O'Hara, Fiske: 142, 190; 243, 407; 304, 35.
O'Hara, John D.: 147, xix.
O'Hara, Shirley: 348, 33.
O'Higgins, Harvey: 170, 188.
Ohio State University: 214, 368.
Ohio Theatre: 50, xii; 247, 230.
Ohmer, Ted: 323, 50.
Oland, Warner: 136, 176; 329, 35.
Olcott, Chauncey: PG, 31; 22, 12; 22, 16; 35, 4; 36, 32; (A) 54, 183f; 54, 204; 56, c; 57, 267; 73, 63; 82, 320; 83, xiv; 95, 5; (W) 192, 76; 208, 369; (A) 214, 379; 216, 79; 216, 87; 216, 98; 232, 527; 242, 360.
"Old Country, The": (R'17) 202, 352.
"Old Country Lane": 202, 341.
"Old Curiosity Shop": 132, 46; 132, 47; 132, 48.
"Old Dutch": (R'09) 107, xi; 107, 30; (F) 168, 69.
"Old English": 286, 26; (R'24) 288, 16; 288, 24; (S) 292, 26; (F, R) 356, 47.
"Old Friends": (R'17) 196, 374; 197, 25.
"Old Heidelberg" (see also "Student Prince, The"): (R'03) 33, 266.
"Old Homestead, The": 81, 294; 89, 192; 185, 33.
"Old Lady, The": (R'19) 223, 149.
"Old Lady Shows Her Medals, The": (R'17) 196, 374; 197, 25.
"Old Lady 31": 191, 28; 193, 168; (R'16) 199, 357; (F, R) 233, 38.
"Old New Yorker, An": (R'11) 123, ix.
"Old Soak, The": 260, 296; (R'22) 260, 301.
"Old Town, The": (R'10) 108, xv; 109, 86.
"Old Town Limerick": (R'02) 22, 16.
Old Vic: 276, 20; 305, 24.
"Old Wives Tale, The": 127, 106.
Oldfield, Anne: 64, 148.
Oldham, Elsie: 120, 40.
Olitzka, Rosa: 153, 16.
Olive, Edyth: 144, 45.
"Olive Latimer's Husband": (R'10) 108, xvi.
Oliver, Clarence: 151, 94.
Oliver, Edna May: 254, 304; 296, 19; 297, 27.
Oliver, Olive: 97, xxii; 118, 172; 121, 84.
"Oliver Twist": (R'05) 38, xvi; 58, 291; 132, 46; 132, 47; (D) 132, 49; (R'12) 134, xi; 134, 127; 135, 167; 137, vii; 231, 363; (F, R) 262, 34.
Olivette, Nina: 337, 30.
Olivier, Laurence: (C) 344, 46.
Olly, Marietta: 97, 72; 111, xxv; 111, 134; 111, 141; 114, 43; 170, 195.
Olms, Louis: 299, 23.
Olmsted, Gertrude: 307, 36; 318, 44; 322, 60.
Olney, Channez: 5, 3; 285, 52.
Olonova, Olga: 288, 38.
Olsen, George: 278, 27.
Olsen, Moroni: 282, 22.
Olsson, Doris: 245, 100.
Olszewska, Maria: 330, 23.
"Olympe": (R'04) 36, 31; 37, 77.
"Olympia": 333, 47; (R'28) 333, 80.
O'Madigan, Isabel: 182, 197.
O'Malley, Rex: 327, 26; 349, 45.
"Omar, the Tentmaker": (R'14) 156, 104.
O'Mara, Emmet: 274, 35.
O'Mara, Joseph: 96, 41.
O'More, Colin: 271, 37.
Omura: 283, 6.
"On Approval": (R'26) 309, 74.
"On Baile's Strand": 145, 78.
"On Parole": (R'07) 74, 87.
"On the Art of the Theatre": (Craig) (B): 136, xiii.
"On the Eve": (R'07) 84, xii;

105,135.
"On the Hiring Line": 225,309; (R'19) 226,368.
"On the Spot": (R'30) 358,68; 359,26.
"On Trial": (R'14) 164,154; 164,160; 164,169; 195,272; 231,348; 231,349.
"On with the Dance": 202,341; (R'17) 202,351; (F,R) 230,278.
"On with the Show": (F) 342, 63.
"Once in a Lifetime": (R'30) 357,26; (S) 357,35; (C) 358,2.
"Once to Every Man": (F) 213,324; 217,191.
"Once Upon a Time": (R'05) 48,32; 48,42; (R'18) 207,316; 208,369.
"One": (R'20) 236,277; 237, 359.
"One Day More": (R'26) 303,16.
"One Exciting Night": (F) 259, 243.
"One for All": (R'27) 316,19.
"One Night In Rome": (R'19) 227, 21.
"One of the Family": (R'25) 300,66; (S) 304,26; 304, 27.
"One of Us": (R'18) 213,280.
"One Way Street": (R'28) 335, 49.
O'Neal, George (W): 282,22.
O'Neal, William: 333,43.
O'Neal, Zelma: 325,49; 338, 11; 348,70; (C) 361,38.
Onegin, Sigrid: 262,43; 339, 30.
Ongley, Byron: 176,179.
O'Neil, Nance: 42,187; 47,2; 47,23; 49,62; 91,236; 97, 91; 108,42; 113,21; 125,9; 131,21; 139,68; 145,75; 158, 199; 193,134; 193,141; 199, 175; 217,183; 229,183; 230, 259; 231,355; (W) 232,516; (A) 250,63; 278,36; 320, 33.
O'Neil, Peggy: 154,180; 177,242; 189,285; 189,309; 197,27; 211,161; (A) 214,379; 219, 283; (A) 219,317; 220,381; (D) 222,c; 225,324; 230, 290; 232,543; 234,97; 247, 262,266,49.
O'Neil, Raymond: 268,12.
O'Neil, Annie: 12,11; 12,15.
O'Neill, Eugene: 202,352; 208, 358; 230,264; 245,73; 245, 97; 250,29; 250,31; 254,308; 261,360; (A) 261,361; 266, 39; (D) 268,9; 278,16; 279, 8; 279,9; 279,19; 286,22; (C) 289,12; 289,40; 290,20; 298,7; 299,12; 299,15; 301, 18; 302,12; 306,27; (C) 307,30; 308,29; 317,10; 323,12; 323,15; 325,39; 328, 29; 338,45; 340,4; 342,37; 349,22.
O'Neill, James: PG,14; 9,18; 9,19; 36,49; 51,110; 81, 289; 81,292; 86,101; 105, 136; 137,4; 137,11; (W) 202,338; 237,402.
O'Neill, Maire: 154,185.
"O'Neill of Derry": (R'07) 83, xiv.
"Only Girl, The": 166,263; (R'14) 166,303.
"Only Law, The": 103,iii; (R'09) 103,73.
"Only Son, The": (R'11) 130, xiii; 130,197.
"Only 38": (R'21) 249,422; 251,103.
"Only Way, The": (R'02) 22,9.
Onoe, Baiko: 207,298.
Onofrei, Demetri: 283,35.
Onslow, Alexander: 206,207; 238,11; 249,392; 360,25.
Onuji, Haruko: 192,100.
"Oolah, The": 286,13.
"'Op O' Me Thumb": 49,53; (R'05) 49,55; (D) 49,55.
Opening Nights (see First Nights).
"Opera Ball, The": (R'12) 133, xi.
Opera Comique: 96,62.
Opera, English Language: 8,6; 36,50; 114,54; 134,109; 197, 31; 213,272; 314,25; 332, 45.
Opera (see also "Opera, At The"; Review Of The Year--Opera):

12,21; 46,306; 59,7; 60, 53; 61,81; 62,108; 69,288; 70,341; 71,8; 72,37; 73, 64; 74,110; 75,138; 79, ii; 79,244; 80,xviii; 80,266; 81,314; 82,332; 82,350; 83, xiv; 83,10; 83,23; 85,84; 86,112; 88,167; 90,xii; 93,308; 94,335; 94,343; 94, 344; 95,12; 95,34; 95,42; 96,70; 99,146; 102,67; 104, 114; 105,138; 106,201; 107, 10; 108,39; 109,74; 109,84; 110,106; 116,108; 117,140; 118,182; 121,82; 122,114; 123,149; 123,150; 123,151; 124,195; 129,154; 131,4; 130,188; 131,4; 141,41; 147, 140; 149,3; 152,131; 154, 192; 156,66; 159,228; 163, 146; 165,212; 166,270; 167,16; 167,21; 168,64; 169,118; 176, 191; 189,274; 190,344; 202, 391; 207,278; 213,272; 215, 10; 216,72; 218,202; 219,297; 225,308; 227,33; 228,102; 229,230; 231,366; 237,348; 238,22; 242,326; 265,9; 300, 20; 303,24; 322,43; 332,45; 351,36.

"Opera, At The": 71,8; 72,36; 73,64; 74,110; 82,10; 84,40; 143,8; 144,39; 145,69; 153, 148; 155,14; 157,116; 170, 183.

Opera, State Of The: 7,18; 17,23.

Opera, Touring: 11,20.

Operetta (see Musical Comedy).

Opp, Francis: (W) 85,72.

Opp, Julie: 8,9; 8,12; 24,35; 41,175; 43,221; 82,344; 94, 339; 95,xx; 97,xviii; 97,xxvi; 102,42; 106,167; 106,181; 109,c; 115,83; 120,37; 125, 28; 143,25; 147,149; 151, 81; 154,204; 161,15; 162, 88; 167,10; 177,240; 236, 276; 243,452.

Oppenheimer, Francis (W) 87,134; 88,150; 95,14; 135,166.

"Opportunity": 234,111; (R'20) 235,188.

"Optimist, The": (R'06) 64,ix.

O'Ramey, Georgia: 108,40; 118,198; 147,155; 164,174; 179,21; 189,280; 201,289.

Orchestras, Theatre: 31,212; 138, 46; 235,190; 327,17.

"Orchid, The": (R'07) 75,xix; 76,152; 76,153; 76,167.

Ordynski, Richard: 202,407.

"Orfeo E Eurydice": (OP) 108,39.

Oregon, University of: 330,50.

Orleneff, Paul: 58,315; 71, 13; 133,92.

Orlova, Katusha: 245,108.

Ormonde, Eugene: 27,124; 99, 157; 105,151.

Ormsbee, Helen: 65,174.

Ornstein, Leo: 181,134; 206, 237; 356,42.

O'Rourke, Eugene: 80,270.

O'Rourke, G.A.: 129,157; 131,11.

Orpheum Stock Company: 87,118.

Orpheum Theatre (San Francisco): 138,51.

"Orpheus": 305,33.

Orr, Anna: 160,289; 160,324; 161,46; 184,342; 202,357.

Orr, Forrest: 89,180.

Orridge, Theodora: 130,189.

Orton, Adelaide: 103,75.

Orton, Josie: 197,55.

Osborn, Erastus W.: 322,37; (C) 335,43.

Osborn, Lincoln: 269,28.

Osborn, Robert: 20,26.

Osborne, Hubert: 122,119.

Osborne, Vivienne: 253,152; 274,29; 290,57; 293,5.

Osipova, Sophia: 257,81.

Os-Ko-Mon, Chief: 233,18.

Osten, Eva Plaschke-Von Der: 154,200.

Osterle, Edith: 81,297.

Ostermann, Kathryn: 132,71.

Osterson, Blanche: 247,221.

Ostlere, Edith: 89,185.

Ostrovsky, A.N.: 42,203.

O'Sullivan, Denis: 85,xiv.

O'Sullivan, John: 217,137.

"Otello" (OP): 36,50; 107, 10.

"Othello": (R'03) 28,135; (R'05) 47,3; 55,235; (R'05) 58,290; 74,96; 157,111;

(R'14) 157,112; 163,105; 246,148; 260,285; (F,R) 266, 72; 270,9; (R'25) 288,62.
"Other Days" (Winter) (B): 98, xiv.
"Other Fellow, The": (R'10) 118,xxi.
"Other Girl, The": (R'04) 36,31; 36,47.
"Other House, The": (R'07) 80, xvii; 80,260.
"Other Man, The": 143,20.
"Other Men's Wives": (R'29) 346,46.
"Other Players, The": 207,288.
"Other Rose, The": (R'23) 275, 15.
Otis, Elita Proctor: PG,21; 3,7; 3,8; 3,9; 5,3; 39,124; 44,249; 152,133; 171,233; 231,363; 285,52.
Ott, Janet: 159,236.
Ott, Mildred: 330,36.
Otterman, Marie: 90,207.
Otto, Frank: 203,61; 345, 33; 347,34.
Oudart, Felix: (D) 293,11.
"Ouija Board, The": (R'20) 231,401; 232,519.
Oukrainsky, Serge: 198,71; 240, 171; 242,329; 245,71; 251, 79.
Oulukanoff, Nicolai: 334,43.
Oumansky, Alexander: 225,355; 232,513; 236,289.
"Our American Cousin": 84, 32; 84,55; (R'08) 85,61; 87, 130; 179,7.
"Our Betters": (R'17) 195,277; 195,287.
"Our Boston Museum Days" (Ryan) (B): 178,314.
"Our Children": (R'15) 176, 167.
"Our Gang": (F) 308,48.
"Our Little Wife": 191,20; (R'16) 191,21.
"Our Miss Gibbs": (R'10) 116, 101; 116,126.
"Our Mrs. McChesney": 178,307; (R'15) 178,320.
"Our Mutual Friend": (D) 132,49.
"Our Mutual Girl": (F) 170,180.
"Our Pleasant Sins": (R'19) 220,342; 220,345.
"Our Wives": (R'12) 142,xviii.
"Our World": (R'11) 121,xiii.
"Ourselves": (R'13) 154,xviii.
Oursler, Fulton: (W) 329,5.
"Out of a Clear Sky": (F,R) 213,320.
"Out There": 195,267; (R'17) 195,279.
"Outcast": (R'14) 166,303; 167, 26.
<u>Outdoor Theatre (see also Pageantry)</u>: 125,18; 328,20.
"Outrageous Mrs. Palmer, The": (R'20) 238,29.
"Outside Looking In": (R'25) 296,16.
"Outsider, The": 278,14; (R'24) 278,15; (D) 278,38; (S) 328,24.
"Outward Bound": (R'24) 276, 68; 277,14; (W) 278,26.
"Over a Welsh Rarebit": (R'03) 29,161.
"Over Here": (R'18) 213,280.
"Over Night": (R'11) 120,xi; 121,74; 151,100.
"Over the Hills to the Poor-House": (F,R) 237,378.
"Over the 'Phone": (R'17) 201,277.
"Over the River": (R'12) 132,xii; 132,40; 134,136.
"Over the Top": 204,89.
Over There Theatre League: 212,205.
Overman, Lynne: 244,9; 246, 151; 352,22; 354,25; 354, 33.
"Overruled": (R'17) 193,150.
"Overtones": 181,143.
"Overture": (R'30) 359,24.
Owen, Catherine Dale: 303,52; 310,14; 310,47; 328,4c.
Owen, Orville: 123,176.
Owen, Reginald: 304,14; 310, 14; 344,17; (C) 359,22.
Owen, Senna: 177,238.
Owen, William F.: 14,4; 202,356.
Owens, John Edward: 15,24.
Owin, Rita: 239,102.
Oxenford, John: 20,9.
Oy-Ra: 156,69.
Oyra, Jan: 325,40.

--P--

Pachmann, Vladimir De: 269, 37.
Padden, Sarah: 159, 254; 188, 212.
Paderewski, Ignace: 5, 17; 12, 24; 13, 24; 14, 24; 15, 26; 69, 289; 79, 239; 88, 160; 130, 196; 154, 184; 261, 391; (D) 276, 27; 279, 34; 290, 43; 81, 316.
"Padre, The" (see also "His Own Way"): (R'26) 312, 21.
"Pagan Lady": 358, 20.
"Paganini": (R'16) 188, 204d; 189, 295; (OP) 299, 20.
Page, Ruth: 232, 513; 243, 403; 253, 243; 257, 89; 260, 315; 265, 41; 357, 45.
Page, Will. A. (see also "Stage Anecdotes"): 72, 43; 80, viii; (W) 87, 120; 94, 340; (W) 140, 114.
"Page from Yesterday, A": 211, 134; 213, 296.
Pageantry: 79, viii; 82, 326; 91, 253; 103, 88; 118, 197; 120, 43; 125, 21; 145, 94; 153, 171; 186, 76; 188, 211; 200, 199; 201, 268; 221, 38; 228, 84; 242, 352; 248, 327.
Paget, Frolliott: 62, 87; 98, 119; 143, 24.
"Pagliacci": (OP) (R'14) 157, 116.
Pagnol, Marcel: 352, 27; 354, 32.
"Paid": (R'25) 299, 18.
"Paid in Full": (R'08) 86, 88; 86, 105; 171, 235.
Paine, Frances: 171, 259.
Paine, Lou: 22, 20.
"Painted Woman, The": (R'13) 146, 100.
Painter, Eleanor: 166, 263; 167, 7; 168, 87; 175, 111; 177, 250; 179, c; 179, 3; 180, 110; 185, 53; 199, 123; 214, 339; 215, 14; 216, 87; 217, 145; 235, 236; 245, 101; 252, 145; 268, 33; 313, 6.
"Pair of Petticoats, A": 207, 283; (R) 207, 285.
"Pair of Queens, A": (R'16) 188, 204b.
"Pair of Silk Stockings, A": (R'14) 166, 263; 166, 280; 168, 64; 180, 82.
"Pair of Sixes, A": (R'14) 159, 226; 159, 245; (R'26) 308, 66.
"Pair of White Gloves, A": (R'13) 153, xv.
"Pajamas": (F) 321, 12.
Palace Theatre (London): 296, 38.
Palace Theatre (New York): 147, xviii.
Paley, William S.: 356, 39.
Pallo, Imre: 329, 21.
"Palm Beach Nights": 301, 12.
Palmer Albert M.: (W) 4, 10; (A) 4, 17; 25, 62; 39, 118; 50, 101; 51, 115; 68, 275; 84, 42; 112, ix; 126, 69; 168, 74; 195, 263; 202, 366; 231, 379; 286, 14; 288, 25.
Palmer, Charlotte: 50, viii.
Palmer, Clara: 55, 232; 77, 190; 95, 6.
Palmer Photoplay Corporation: 247, 206.
Palmeri, Mimi: 279, 33.
Palmer's Theatre: 25, 65.
Palmistry: 29, 174.
"Palmy Days": (R'19) 226, 367; 226, 388.
"Pals First": (R'17) 194, 215; 194, 231.
Paltrinieri, Giordano: 290, 41.
"Pan and the Young Shepherd": (R'18) 207, 287; 207, 301.
"Pansy": (R'29) 340, 42.
"Pantaloon": (R'05) 60, 32.
Panteon Theatre (London): 32, 261.
"Panthea": 159, 227; (R'14) 159, 260.
Pantomime: 134, 126; (D) 134, 131; 144, 62; 188, 209; 247, 246.
Pantomime, English: 10, 6; 110, 126.
"Pants": (F, R) 200, 245.
"Paola And Francesca": 7, 4; (R'06) 69, 282; 284, 11; (R'24) 287, 19; 288, 8; 344, 50.
"Papa": (R'19) 220, 344.
"Papa Lebonnard": (R'08) 88, 145.

"Papa's Darling": (R'14) 166,314.
Pape, Lionel: 299,19.
"Paper Chase, The": 121,92; (R'12) 143,3.
"Paradise Alley": (R'24) 279, 68.
"Paradise of Mahomet, The": (R'11) 121,ix.
Paradise Roof Garden: 5,1; 5,2; 17,5.
Paramount Studios: 239,78; 319, 12; 319,13.
Paramount Theatre (New York): (D) 310,lf; 310,62.
"Parasites": (R'24) 287,15.
"Pardon, The": (R'16) 191,23.
Parepa-Rosa, Mme.: 115,76; 115,80.
Pares, Gabriel: 41,172.
Pareto, Graziella: 289,35.
"Pariah, The": 197,15; (R'17) 197,22.
"Paris": (R'28) 333,81; (F) 344,31; (F) 344,73.
"Paris Bound": (R'28) 324,40.
Paris Conservatoire: 34,308; 140,120.
Paris Opera House: 66,202; 86,108; 338,22.
Paris Theatre (see French Theatre).
"Parisina": (OP) 147,159.
Park, John: 236,281.
Park Theatre (New York): 19,19; (D) 136,197; (D) 173,19; (D) 190,368.
Parker, Albert: 152,133.
Parker, Corinne: 40,156.
Parker, Dana: (W) 322,32.
Parker, Dorothy: 120,61; 166, 264; 337,66.
Parker, Grosvenor A.: (W) 151,xii.
Parker, Henry Taylor: 324,35.
Parker, Horatio W.: 21,26; 124,ix; 134,109.
Parker, Lottie Blair: 55,227.
Parker, Louis N.: (R) 12,8; 12,13; (W) 79,viii; 149,xx.
Parker, Madeline: 305,31.
Parker, Rena: 208,373.
Parkes, Albert L. (W): 65,196; 76,168.
Parkes, George: 22,26; 52,151.
Parks, Blanche: 185,20; 233, 26; 246,159.
"Parlor, Bedroom and Bath": (R'17) 204,88; 204,93; 205, 134.
Parola, Angelo: 93,309.
Parry, Maxwell: (W) 198,82.
Parselle, John: 25,63; 171, 232.
"Parsifal": (OP) (S) 32,251; 33,284; (OP) 36,53; (OP) 37,72; (OP) 42,189; (OP) 44,240; (OP) 45,266; (OP) 46,315.
Parsonnet, Mario: 321,52.
Parsons, George: 20,7; 59, 10; 159,245; 172,280; 201,265.
Parsons, Bill: 206,262; 206, 263; 210,119.
Partington, Phyllis: 141,160; 174,68.
"Partners Again": 256,7; (R'22) 256,29.
Pasadena Playhouse: 235,201; 253,247; 254,318; (D) 273, 42; 275,40; 277,41; 295, 42; 299,58; 300,39; 301, 41; 303,40; 308,41; 314, 43; 317,42; 320,46; 328,43; 331,55; 336,53; 348,49; 358, 49.
Paskovieskai, Stepania: 130, 202.
"Passant, Le": 90,223.
"Passers-By": (R'11) 128,ix; 128,117.
"Passing of the Idle Rich, The": (R'13) 148,162.
"Passing of Third Floor Back, The"N 105,133; (R) 105, 134; 114,51.
"Passing Show, The": 293,40.
"Passing Show of 1912, The": 139,74.
"Passing Show of 1913, The": (R'13) 151,83; 151,89.
"Passing Show of 1914, The": (R'14) 161,37; 165,230.
"Passing Show of 1915, The": 173,27; (R'15) 173,39; 174,57.
"Passing Show of 1916, The": 186,63; (R'16) 186,94.

"Passing Show of 1917, The": (R'17) 196,344; 196,345.
"Passing Show of 1918, The": (R) 211,144; 211,145.
"Passing Show of 1920, The": 232, 517; (D) 237,351.
"Passing Show of 1921, The": 240,165; (R'20) 240,177.
"Passing Show of 1923, The": (R'23) 269,15; 270,14.
"Passing Show of 1924, The": (R'24) 284,16; 284,26.
"Passion": (R) 240,184; (F) 240,185.
"Passion Flower, The": 229, 183; (R'20) 229,184.
Passion Plays (see also Oberammergau; Religious Drama): 88,153; 106,190; 107,26; 116,112; 140,122; 219,306; 236,274; 259, 272; 349,10; 352,39.
"Passport, The": (R'05) 49,57.
"Pasteur": (R'23) 266,20.
Pastor, Tony: 92,iv.
Pastoral Plays (see also Pageantry): 94,320.
Pateson, Dorothy: 291,16.
Pathe, Charles: 217,192.
"Patience": 136,iii; (R'12) 136,170; 136,171; (R'24) 288,15.
Patnode, Carlos: 194,201.
Patrick, Jerome: 156,161; 169, 131; 191,25; 203,20; 205, 137.
Patrick, Lee: 295,19.
Patricola, Tom: 273,6.
"Patriot, The": (R'08) 95,xi; 95,30.
Patson, Doris: 311,25.
"Patsy, The": (R'25) 300,66.
"Patsy on the Wing": 211,161.
Patten, Grace Bigelow (W): 128,134; 142,174.
Patterson, Ada (W) (see also "Chats With Authors"; "Gaities and Gravities"; "Thumbnail Sketches of Player-Folk"): 31,218; 33,270; 34, 297; 36,40; 37,67; 38,93; 39,117; 46,320; 50,91; 67, 247; 72,50; 88,162; 91,244; 92,262; 94,322; 95,8; 96, 64; 98,125; 100,188; 100, 192; 101,13; 104,110; 105, 152; 106,180; 107,17; 107, 24; 109,89; 110,124; 111, 134; 112,198; 113,16; 116, 118; 117,142; 119,21; 119, 24; 120,54; 121,86; 121, 90; 122,127; 122,130; 123, 158; 124,209; 125,15; 125, 30; 127,98; 128,124; 129, 156; 129,159; 130,194; 131, 8; 132,62; 133,101; 133, 104; 134,113; 135,141; 136, 180; 136,188; 137,23; 138, 43; 139,70; 140,121; 141, 159; 142,196; 143,14; 143, 28; 144,56; 145,82; 146, 119; 146,122; 147,144; 147, 154; 148,168; 148,175; 149, xii; 150,46; 153,165; 154,185; 154,198; 156,70; 156,80; 157,126; 158,184; 158,196; 159,234; 159,248; 160,290; 160,300; 161,14; 161,18; 163,106; 164,182; 165,210; 166,276; 166,286; 167,32; 167,50; 168,70; 168,84; 170, 174; 171,251; 172,302; 172, 305; 173,21; 174,72; 175,126; 176,193; 177,236; 178,292; 179,29; 181,149; 182,225; 183,292; 184,340; 185,29; 187,142; 188,202; 189,292; 190,342; 192,90; 193,162; 196,360; 198,92; 199,138; 201,274; 202,340; 203,30; 204,80; 208,364; 209,34; 210,74; 211,154; 213,290; 214, 350; 217,154; 220,358; 222, 86; 225,302; 229,168; (FI) 230,250; 233,20; 235,180; 236,272; 237,360; 238,26; (FI) 240,164; 243,418; 251,106; 253,216; 256,36; 258,154; 266,26; 268,27; 270,19; 271, 22; 273,22; 275,20; 275,64; 276,24; 277,12; 287,22; 288, 23; 290,12; 291,22; 292,20; 298,24; 299,22; 301,22; 309, 12; 311,22; 316,34; 344,49; 353,74; 361,45.
Patterson, Elizabeth: 201,281; 202,347; 339,44; 357,27.
Patterson, Frederick: (W) 89,198.

Patterson, Idelle: 197,31; 204, 106.
Patterson, Joseph Medill: 123, 173.
Patterson, Marjorie: 188,209; 190,c; 211,133; (W,V) 212, 224; (A) 214,379; (W,V) 196,328.
Patterson, "Nan": 53,159.
Patti, Adelina: 33,275; 33,286; 76,169; 98,133; 102,68; 257, 104.
Patti, Carlo: 102,68.
Patti, Carlotta: 102,67.
Pattison, Diantha: 195,287; 207, 289; 220,363; 296,46; 348, 46.
Patton, Frank: 37,75.
Pattou, Edith Elting: (W) 63, 124.
Paul, Mae: 97,90.
Paul, Morris J. (W): 182,220; 189,274; 190,344; 191,30.
"Paul and Virginia": (R'17) 193,150.
Paulding, Frederick: 94,x.
Paulin, Flora: 79,233.
Paull, H.M.: 20,9.
Paulson, Arvid: 195,281; 198, 95; 304,23; 331,45.
Pauly, William C.: 219,269.
Paumier, Alfred: 164,153.
Pauncefort, George: 281,14.
Paur, Emil: 10,33; 14,23; (W) 22,36.
Pavey, Marie: 141,143.
Pavley, Andreas: 198,71; 219, 287; 240,171; 241,235; 242, 329; 252,147; 294,17.
Pavley-Oukrainsky Ballet: 256, 3; 256,13; 280,27; 280,29.
Pavloska, Irene: 205,139.
Pavlowa, Anna: 101,24; 103, 83; 105,138; 110,115; 111,165; 118,178; 118,180; 127,92; 130,198; 130,200; 130,203; 130,220; 149,1; 153,c; 153, 162; 158,166; 161,28; 161,48; 165,226; 169,109; 169,143; 175,122; 176,191; 178,305; (A) 183,325; 185,24; 189,275; (D) 191,49; (D) 219,267; 223,153; 227,30; 235,161; 249,359a; 250,13; 256,13; 271,11; 284,17; 286,25; 293,25; 302,29.
Pavola, Tatiana: 298,23.
Pawle, Lennox: 120,61; 166,264; 269,31; 288,14.
Pawley, Edward: 292,30; 330, 26; 330,28; 339,44.
Pawlosha, Irene: 180,85.
Pawn, Doris: 226,404.
"Pawns": (R'18) 206,219.
Paxton, Marie: 319,23.
"Pay-Day": (R'16) 182,193; 182,194.
Payne, George Henry: (W, FI) 10,24.
Payne, Iden: 252,164; 305, 41.
Payne, John Howard: 58,300; (D) 195,294.
Payne, Louis: 48,30.
Payne, Nina: 196,356.
Paynter, Corone: 231,405.
Payton, Corse: 24,39; 24,40; 24,41; 150,48.
Peabody, Josephine Preston: 110,xix; 114,64; 135,154.
Peacock, Anne (W,V): 69, 305; 79,231; 82,336; 100, 181; 109,80; 111,133; 114, 42; 118,162; 125,8; 129, 172; 132,67; 144,64; 147, 148; 149,26; 152,120; 176, 175; 178,288; 231,345.
Peacock, Bertram: 216,86; 229,159; 249,367; (D) 249, 389; 292,17.
Pearl, Jack: (C) 338,37; (C) 350,2.
Pearl, Violet: 47,xiv; 51,xii.
"Pearl and the Pumpkin, The": 55,213; (R'05) 56, vii.
"Pearl Maiden, The": (R'12) 133,xv.
"Pearl of Great Price, The": (R'26) 310,16.
Pearson, Margery: 142,197; 159,270; 162,68.
Pearson, Molly: 129,152; 139,c; (A) 180,78; 194, 212; 231,407; 232,524; 252, 143; 255,362.
Pearson, Virginia: 135,142; 151,xx; 155,33; 178,306;

210,119; 212,236; 214,370; (A) 214,379; 215,47; 215, 59; 216,117; (D) 217,c; 217,190; 218,254; 220,390; 220,391; 221,64; 222,135; 223,200; 224,254; 224,286.
"Peasant Girl, The": (R'15) 170,171; 170,192; 174, 78.
Peeler, Clare P. (W): 121,76; 130,191; 143,17; 146,102; 150,65; 155,35; 170,185; 202,358.
"Peer Gynt": (S) 69,291; 72, 48; 72,49; 73,66; (R'07) 74, 86; 90,225; (R'23) 265, 15; 265,18; (D) 292,12; 295, 42.
"Peg O' My Heart": 143,7; 151, 89; (D) 157,125; 167,36; (F) 224,252; 231,351; 241,237; (R'21) 241,304; (R'12) 144, 36.
"Peggy": (R'11) 131,xi.
Peggy, Baby: 290,44.
Peggy And Cortez: 356,16.
"Peggy From Paris": 31,235; 32,241; (R'03) 32,245.
"Peggy Machree": (R'08) 96,40.
Pehlemann, Kurt: 265,6.
Peixotto, Maude: 14,14.
Pekin Colored Theatre (Chicago): 83,27.
Pelham, Laura Dainty: 151,xix.
"Pelican, The": 288,20; (R'25) 296,18.
Pelissier, Constance: 247,237.
"Pelleas And Melisande": 275, 14; (R'23) 275,15.
"Pelleas Et Melisande" (OP): 77,174; 86,112; 118,194.
Pelucchia, Annetta: 203,41.
Pemberton, Brock: 258,147; 264,13; 300,8; (W) 300,9; 311,7; (W) 334,13.
Pemberton, Stafford: 150,60; 161,16; 165,230; 171,252; 177,240; 200,213.
"Pendennis": 199,120.
Pendleton, Clara: 295,46.
Pendleton, Eleanor: 93,302; 111,160.
Pendleton, James: 303,10; 315, 29.
Pendleton, Jimmie: 307,8.
"Penelope": 96,xxvi; 98,123; (R'09) 107,xii.
Penfield, Cornelia S. (W): 208,366.
Pennarini, Alois: 44,240; 46, 315.
Pennell, Daniel: 121,94.
Pennell, R.O.: (D) 330,29.
Pennington, Ann: 160,324; 173,17; 186,71; 197,13; 198,69; 201,267; 205,195; (D) 219,267; 221,11; 221,16; 224,219; 233,19; 236,330; (D) 286,15; 312,54; 316,6; (A) 322,3; 328,6; 335,67; 342,31.
Pennington, Walter: 67,225.
"Penny Arcade": (R'30) 350, 43.
"Penrod": 212,195; (R'18) 212,211.
"Penrod And Sam": (F,R) 270,32.
Pennsylvania College For Women: 234,22; 237,385; 237,386.
Pennsylvania, University of (see also Mask And Wig Club): 137,19; 221,39; 232,538; 349,49.
"People At Play, The" (Hartt) (B): 103,iv.
People's Institute: 41,179; 87,134.
People's League: 170,186.
People's Theatre: 48,xi.
Pepito: 277,37.
Peple, Edward: 81,xv; 176, 179.
Pepys, Samuel: 142,174; (D) 309,22.
Peralta, Frances: 274,37.
Percival, Walter: 88,149; 95, 24; 126,40; 144,37.
Percy, Herbert: 69,310; 81,297; 86,104.
Percyval, T. Wigney: 120,61; 278,14.
Perdita (see Robinson, "Perdita").
"Pere Goriot": 114,60.
Perfect, Rose: 329,41.
"Perfect Fool, The": (R'21) 250,32.
"Perfect Lady, A": (R'14)

166, 266; (F, R) 215, 62.
Perier, Jean: 86, 112.
Perini, Flora: 178, 284.
"Perkins": 214, 344; (R'18) 214, 345.
Perkins, Bobby: 316, 46; (C) 337, 35.
Perkins, Edward B.: (W) 165, 219.
Perkins, Grace: (W) 334, 29.
Perkins, Osgood: 307, 23; 329, 25; (C) 336, 15; (D) 351, 18; 352, 43; 360, 35.
Perkins, Walter E.: 24, 48; 50, 85.
Perlman, Phyllis: (W) 340, 16.
Perot, Cynthia: 223, 153; 228, 99.
Perot And Taylor: 301, 31.
"Perplexed Husband, The": (R'12) 140, 98; 140, 100.
Perrier, Gabrielle: 188, 209; 190, 374.
Perrin, Ernest: 62, 98; 156, 102.
Perry, Albert: 34, 318; 132, 59; 239, 91.
Perry, Antoinette: 75, 131.
Perry, Eileen: 199, 183.
Perry, Frank: 107, 15.
Perry, Frederick: 3, 6; 35, 6; 49, 56; 71, 3; 104, 102; 119, 21; 140, 102; 164, 169; 214, 349; 244, 20; 286, 23; 314, 22; (C) 319, 72; 359, 24.
Perry, Katherine: 180, 79; 194, 204; 221, 14; 222, 121; 223, 186; 224, 265; 307, 35.
Perry, Margaret: 353, 41.
"Personal": (R'03) 32, 241; 32, 243.
"Personal Recollections of Augustin Daly" by M. Hall: 52, 150; 53, 174; 54, 188; 55, 213.
"Personal Reminiscences" by
Billie Burke 187, 123;
Robert B. Mantell 188, 194;
Jane Cowl 189, 269;
John Mason 190, 350;
Chauncey Olcott 192, 76;
Douglas Fairbanks 194, 219;
Frances Starr 196, 320;
David Warfield 198, 84;
De Wolf Hopper 200, 194;
James O'Neil 202, 338.
"Personal Reminiscenses of Henry Irving" (Stoker) (B): 70, iv.
"Personality Portraits":
No. 1 Frank McGlynn 228, 88;
No. 2 Ina Claire 229, 168;
No. 3 Eugene O'Neill 230, 264;
No. 4 Elsie Ferguson 233, 20;
No. 5 Helen Hayes 238, 26.
"Persons and Places" (Benton) (B): 60, iii.
Perugini, Signor: 34, 307.
"Peter Ibbetson": (R'17) 196, 342; 196, 345; 197, 15; 199, 130; (F, R) 250, 38; (OP) 361, 21; 361, 22.
"Peter Pan": (S) 54, 200; (R'05) 58, 288; 89, 180; 141, 146; (F, R) 279, 32; (R'24) 286, 19; (F, R) 288, 30; 334, 15; 336, c.
"Peter Weston": (R'23) 272, 19.
Peters, Fred: 80, 261.
Peters, House: 166, 274.
Peters, Rollo: 220, 363; 221, 23; (W) 224, 214; 240, 163; 251, 75; 261, 376; 264, 16; 265, 17; 269, 38; 275, 14; 277, 62; 300, 14; 304, 36; 325, 39; 331, 34.
"Peter's Mother": 214, 344; (R'18) 214, 348.
Petersen, Elsa: 292, 17.
Peterson, Dorothy: 318, 52; 321, 5; 328, 13; 344, 34; 357, 50.
Peterson, Marjorie: 258, 135; 313, 15.
Peterson, May: 184, 348.
Petit, Eugenie: 60, 39.
Petit, Margaret: 233, 14; (D) 247, c; (A) 250, 63; 258, 135; 289, 11.
"Petite Peste": 179, 11.
Petley, Frank: 341, 24.
Petra Theatre (Arabia): 176, 189.
Petrass, Sari: 189, 280; 189, 282; 193, 163.
Petrova, Olga: 159, 227; 175, 105; 177, c; 177, 211; 178,

332; 178,338; 182,253; 199, 176; 200,244; (D) 201,318; 201,325; 232,510; 244,23; (D) 265,5; 295,38; 305,21.
Petrovich, Ivan: 308,40; 321, 45.
"Petticoat Influence": 359,12; (C) 359,22.
Peyton, Jane: 32,243; 86,111; 156,62; 128,116.
"Phantom of the Opera, The": (F,R) 296,32.
"Phantom Rival, The" (see also "Tale of the Wolf, The"): 165,209; (R'14) 165,244.
"Phantom Ship, The": 306,25.
"Phantoms": (R'30) 348,72.
"Phedre": 110,xiv; 268,23.
Phelan, Florence V.; (W) 169, 136.
Phelps, Albert D.: (W) 165, 229.
Phelps, Samuel: 88,169.
Phelps, T.A.: (W) 222,112.
Phelps, William Lyon: (W) 278,41.
"Philadelphia": (R'29) 344,47.
Philadelphia Opera House: 94, 318.
Philadelphia Theatre: 37,78; 81,iv; 82,xiv; 137,16; 144, 63; 150,61; 197,14.
"Philanderer, The": 156,65; 160,310.
Philbin, Mary: 292,33; 307, 39; 308,49; 324,50; 325, 31.
Philbrick, Will: (C) 337,35.
Philbrick, William H.: 186, 63.
"Philemon Et Baucis": (OP) 25,78.
"Philip Goes Forth": (R'31) 360,24.
Philipp, Adolf: 155,20.
Philipp, Alfred O.: (W) 335, 29.
Phillips, Albert: 232,511.
Phillips, Alexandra: 49,78; 67, 249.
Phillips, Dorothy: 208,405; 208, 406; 217,188; 218,257; 308, 48.
Phillips, Edna: 13,5; 40,142; 57,267.
Phillips, Edwin: 307,33.
Phillips, Henry Albert (W): 305,24; 324,36; 328,20; 329,20; 336,35; 342,37.
Phillips, Howard: 350,30.
Phillips, John: 216,86.
Phillips, John Franklyn: (W,V) 124,195.
Phillips, Joseph: 132,43.
Phillips, Kate: 120,36.
Phillips, Mary: 260,296; 303,27; 309,31; (C) 343,42; 352,40; 359,16; 361,17.
Phillips, Nan: 236,284.
Phillips, Norma: 170,180; 170, 181.
Phillips, Stephen: 7,4; 13,7; 16,20; 32,238; 46,299; 47, ii; 66,iv; 106,170; 288,54.
Phillips, Will: 133,94.
Phinney, W.J.: 187,149.
"Phipps": (R'14) 166,267.
Phipps, Sally: 309,2; 313,39.
Phonograph Records: 150,72; 242,320.
Photographers: 290,49.
Physioc, Joseph A.: 90,203.
Piantadosi, Al: 179,26.
Piatov, Sacha: 238,13.
Piatt, Aurora: 122,118; 122, 119; 126,55.
Piccaver, Alfred: 284,35.
Pichel, Irving: (W) 324,53; 325,53.
Pickels, Master: 180,90.
Pickford, Jack: 205,191; 222, 114.
Pickford, Mary: 144,xv; 144, 35; 148, 176; 151,c; 153, 159; 155,31; 157,14; 162, 51; 164,161; 167,c; 167,3; 167,18; 170,178; 175,147; (A) 177,247; 178,305; 182, 229; 183,294; 184,376; 185, c; 185,3; 186,73; (A) 188, 242; 191,14; 197,10; 198, 75; 199,181; 200,245; 201, 325; 202,394; 202,401; 202, 408; 203,63; 205,196; 206, 259; 209,54; 209,57; 214, 387; (A) 218,253; 219,297; (A) 226,438; 229,190; 229, 192; 234,114; 245,106; 249,

394; 249,395; 253,232; 256, 40; 259,240; 269,34; 272,30; 272,33; 277,33; 277,39; 279, 7; 280,30; 293,32; 298,30; 308,37; 333,24; 339,24; 356, 33.
"Pickpockets, The": 96,38.
"Pickwick": (R) 25,57; 132,46; 319,23.
Picon, Molly: 315,37; 334,23.
Pidcock, Dorothie: 303,21.
Pigdeon, Edward Everett: 317, 34.
"Pied Piper, The": 95,vii; 95, 23.
Pierat, Marie-Therese: 125,38; 240,169.
Pierce, Edith: 240,165.
Pierce, Evelyn Miller: (W) 338,50.
Pierce, Lucy France (W): 45, 287; 65,194; 68,ix; 74,92; 87,126; 90,215; 184,349; 187,152; 192,90.
"Pierre Of The Plains": (R'08) 93,xiv; 94,331.
"Pierre Patelin": (R'16) 183, 277; 183,283; 185,5.
"Pierrot, The Prodigal": (F,R) 161,48; (R'16) 188,204d; 188, 209; (R'25) 290,34.
"Petro": (R'20) 229,182; 229, 183.
Pietsch, Walter (see Hull House Players).
"Piff, Paff, Pouf": (R'04) 39,112.
"Pigeon, The": (R'12) 134, 104; 136,182; 136,183; 253, 215.
"Pigs": (R'24) 284,72.
"Piker, The": (R'25) 288,64.
"Pilate's Daughter": 167,14; (R'14) 167,44.
Pilcer, Harry: 181,144.
"Pilgrim, The": (F,R) 266,34.
Pilgrimage Play (California): 236,274; 264,44.
"Pillars of Society": (R'04) 39, 112; (R'10) 111,131; 111, 139.
"Pin Wheel Revue, The": (R'22) 258,151.
"Pinch Hitter, A": 257,71; (R'22) 257,93.
Pinchot, Rosamond: 276,17; 277,25; 359,39.
Pinero, Arthur Wing: 9,8; 21,5; 46,299; 51,128; 51, 256; 62,ii; 67,234; 69,xviii; 86,91; 95,24; 109,68; 118,196; 120,xi; 193,135; 197,24; 217,144; 233,32; 240,214; 265,25; 267,19.
Pingree, Maud (W): 158,64; 157,115; 158,174; 159,239; 159,253; 161,34.
Pini-Corsi, Antonio: 159,228.
"Pink Lady, The": (R'11) 122,xii; 122,132; 122,134; 135,iii.
Pinkert, Regina: 67,233; 71, 9; 72,40.
"Pins and Needles": (R'22) 253,264.
Pinski, David: 238,15.
Pinto, Angelo: (D) 350,38.
Pinto, Effingham: 100,183; 101,29; 159,230; 217,145; 217,152.
Pinto, Salvatore: (D) 350,39.
"Piper, The": 110,xix; 114, 64; 121,iii; 121,70; (R'11) 121,72; 121,84; 167,35; (R'20) 231,402.
"Pipes of Pan, The": (R'17) 203,24; 203,25.
"Pippa Passes": (R'06) 70, xxiii.
Pirandello, Luigi: 263,9; 276,29; 297,24; 302,20; 360,28.
"Pirates of Penzance": (R'12) 137,2; 137,3; (R'26) 311, 18; 311,31; (D) 313,18.
"Pisanelle, La": (D) 155,10.
"Pit, The": 35,10; (R'04) 37,57; 39,119; 42,ii.
Pitcher, Georgianna: (W,V) 64, 165.
Pitkin, Robert: 200,203.
Pitoeff, Georges: 266,22.
Pitou, Augustus: 22,16.
Pitt, Charles: 97,101.
Pitt, Fanny Addison: 3,12.
Pitt, Frank Addison: 76,159.
Pitt, Margaret: 39,132.
Pixley, Frank: 16,6; 40,143;

55,227; 56,253.
Pixley, Gus: 30,188.
"Place in the Sun, A": 215,9; (R'18) 215,19.
Placide, Thomas: (D) 203,28.
Plagerism (see also Copyright): 17,13; 87,119; 143,6; 152, 122; 275,12; 315,16.
"Plain Jane": (R'24) 281,16.
Plancon, Pol: PG,9; (A) 3,17; 10,31; 70,342; 231,367.
Platt, George Poster: 105,145.
Platt, Livingston: 174,83; (W) 182,219; 205,152; 206,211.
Platt, Polly: 247,229.
Play Readers: 44,256.
"Play Without a Name, The": 336, 26; (R'28) 335,51; 336,24.
Playbill Restaurant, The: 104, 117.
Playbills (see Programs, Theatre).
"Playboy of the Western World, The": 131,11; (R'21) 244, 60; 245,77; 280,20.
Playel Building (Paris): 345, 70.
"Players And Vagabonds" (Roseboro) (B): 50, iv.
Players Club: 33,278; 91,243; 144,63; 145,viii; 217,165; 231,398; 231,399; 257,93; 269,18; 276,42; 283,40; 283,42.
"Players I Have Known" by H. P. Goddard: 72,45; 74,100; 120,63; 139,82; 150,70.
Players' Playhouse (Detroit): 309,41; 309,42.
Player's Workshop (Chicago): 199,142; 199,143.
Playgoers, The: 293,45.
Playhouse, The (London): 83, 20.
Playhouse, The (New York): 123,x; 124,viii; 127,102.
"Playhouse and the Play, The" (Mackaye) (B): 101,vii.
"Play-Making" (Archer) (B): 138,42.
"Play's the Thing, The": 310, 14; (R'26) 310,15; (S) 311, 26; 311,28; 312,50.
"Playwrights: 82,331; 115,81; 118,196; 123,173; 137,5; 145,76; 149,32; 153,150; 153,155; 154,194; 156,81; 176,179; 187,144; 188,191; 192,98; 193,135; 196,354; 199,124; 203,38; 204,102; 207,296; 210,88; 226,372; 243,418; 243,422; 252,170; 268,9; 271,9; 271,20; 276, 10; 281,7; 290,20; 300,38; (D) 305,11; 310,9; 316,28; 323,11; (C) 339,39.
Playwriting (see also Russell, John Patten (W): 9,14; 22, 32; 30,185; 34,313; 42,189; 46,299; 62,103; 64,157; 66, 198; 66,199; 66,208; 68, 264; 71,14; 74,97; 76,xv; 82,324; 93,285; 104,112; 106,176; 106,186; 156,93; 160,299; 163,115; 169,132; 181,151; 186,84; 186,148; 188,198; 188,200; 193,154; 194,199; 195,268; 196,327; 197,18; 198,63; 198,70; 199,120; 201,284; 205,138; 205,144; 208,368; 210,94; 211,160; 212,204; 212,220; 215,22; 215,36; 216,88; 222, 96; 223,162; 224,238; 227,28; 231,394; 234,92; 237,346; 239,110; 242,344; 246,144; 247,239; 258,142; 273,11; 277,10; 279,10; 298,18; 300,10; 308,22; 311,30; 312,10; 313,7; 314,16; 315, 39; 317,12; 322,46; 329,5; 333,20; 339,11; 345,23; 345, 36; 347,21; 348,41; 350, 15; 354,40; 358,14; 361,42.
Playwrighting -- Films: 172, 295; 186,88; 212,250; 320, 21; 320,32; 321,38; 325,42; 338,42; 341,14; 360,45.
"Pleasure Sound": (R'29) 337, 47; (C) 338,37.
"Please Get Married": 217,163; (R'19) 218,208; (F) 224, 251.
"Please Help Emily": (R'16) 187,138; 188,204.
"Pleasure Seekers, The": (R'13) 154,xx.
Plimmer, Harry: 266,17; 319,

23.
Plimmer, Marcus: (W) 146,126.
"Plongee, En": (S) 82,xi.
"Plots and Playwrights": (R'17) 195,278; 195,287; 197,22.
"Plough and the Stars, The": (R'27) 323,58.
Plummer, Inez: 68,277; 158, 177; 159,272; 160,288; 175, 112; 239,109.
Plunkett, Al: 246,171.
"Plutocrat, The": 349,72; 353, 42.
Plympton, Eben: 28,132; 51, 110; 82,329; 129,148; 130, 213; 168,73.
Poe, Edgar Allan: 30,191; 49, 77; 59,13; (D) 266,10.
Poel, William: 71,23.
Pogany, Willy: (D) 244,12; 244, 27; 260,320; (D) 315,58.
"Poia": (OP) 114,54.
Point Loma (California) Theatre: 128,122.
"Point of View, The": (R'03) 27,106; (R'12) 142,xvi.
Poiret, Paul: (W) 262,47.
"Poisoning Case, The": (S) 84,37.
"Pokey": (R'18) 205,151; 205, 159.
Polacco, Giorgio: 141,140; 178,284.
Polaire, Mlle.: 54,203; 154, xviii; 154,187.
Poland, Joseph Franklin: (W) 320,32.
"Poldekin": (R'20) 237,371.
Polese, Giovanni: 93,309.
Poli, S. Z.: 67,xiv.
Polini, Emelie: 153,143; 166, 267; 204,83.
Poli's Theatre" 67,xiv.
Politics and Theatre: 350,24.
Pollak, Max: (D) 347,28.
Pollard, Daphne: 177,250.
Pollard, Snub: 290,45.
Polloch, Alice Leel: 117,131.
Pollock, Allan: 197,38; 250, 17; 257,71; 258,154.
Pollock, Channing: 55,227; 61, 60; 74,88; 104,103; (W) 194,199; 196,353; 210,80; (A) 231,346; 231,395; (W) 231,400; (W) 256,11; (W) 264,8; 268,38; (C) 269,19; 272,7; 289,22; (W) 298,9; (W) 325,17; 334,40.
Pollock, Frank: 117,138.
"Polly": (D) 297,27.
"Polly of the Circus": 83,4; (R'07) 84,xi; 88,159; 93, 295.
"Polly Preferred": (R'23) 264, 17.
"Polly with a Past": 200,197; (R'17) 200,242; 210,91.
"Pollyanna": 189,277; (R'16) 189,281; (F, R) 229,190; 229, 192.
Polsky, Nina: 333,39.
"Polygamy": (R'14) 167,6; 167, 15; 187,154.
Pomada, Maxime: 319,23.
"Pomander Walk": (R'10) 120, 34; 120,61; 124,203; 221,54.
"Pomeroy's Past": (R'26) 304, 16; (S) 307,26.
"Pom-Pom": (R'16) 182,196.
Pond, Anson: 15,5.
Pond, Dorothy: 171,238.
Pondelicek, Bozena: 237,355.
Pondelicek, James: 290,49.
Ponselle, Carmela: 297,35.
Ponselle, Rosa: 215,11; 218, 226; 218,235; 264,37; 268, 37; 276,35; (C) 286,15; 299,35; 338,43.
"Pony Express, The": (F) (R'25) 297,32.
"Poor Fool, The": (R'17) 195, 278.
"Poor Little Man, The": (R'25) 295,16.
"Poor Little Rich Girl, The": (S) 145,71; 149,vi; 149,xii; 162,82.
"Poor Little Ritz Girl, The": (R'20) 235,187.
"Poor Little Thing": (R'14) 168,60.
"Poor Nut, The": 292,15; (S) 295,26.
"Poppa": (R'29) 337,46.
Poppen, Detmar: 122,119; 297, 17; 326,41.
"Poppy": (R'23) 272,19.
"Popularity": (R'06) 69,xiii;

69, 286.
Porcasi, Paul: 295, 14.
"Porgy": 321, 39; 321, 80; (R'27) 321, 82.
"Port O'London": (R'26) 301, 72.
"Porta Chiusa": (R'23) 274, 16.
Porter, H.E.: (W, V) 143, 18.
Porter, Paul: 308, 14.
Portmanteau Players (see also Walker, Stuart): 176, 139; 175, 140; 185, 21; 191, 23; 192, 92; 192, 93; 198, 82; 217, 142; 217, 144; 217, 155; 218, 207.
Porto-Riche, George (see De Porto-Riche, George).
"Possible Case, A": 286, 13.
Post, Billy: 250, 10.
Post, Guy Bates: 14, 2; 21, 9; 36, 35; 37, 60; (A) 52, 131f; 56, 255; 102, 46; 102, 47; 107, 3; 110, 100; 128, 115; 132, 59; 139, 90; 155, 10; 156, 106; 157, 115; 200, 193; 200, 213; 204, 80; 204, 81; 210, 80; (A) 214, 379; 224, 215; 231, 386; 263, 35.
Posters, Theatre: 13, 18; 34, 299; 60, 61; 61, 61; 63, 137; 74, 132; 75, 132; 84, 42; 85, 62; 88, 153; 100, 196; 101, 8; 104, 117; 142, 170; 145, 80; 165, 229; 174, 78; 175, 138; 177, 225; 189, 290; 207, 278; 210, 99; 232, 506; 262, 17; 303, 12; 338, 22; (D) 354, 44.
Posuelo, Amparo: 107, 32.
"Pot Luck": (R'21) 249, 422.
"Potash and Perlmutter": (R'13) 152, 115; 152, 133; 177, 220; 199, 136; (F, R) 285, 31; (R'26) 308, 68.
"Potemkim": (F) 311, 37.
"Potiphar's Wife": (R'28) 335, 82.
Potter, [Mrs.] James Brown: 17, 18; 96, xxvi; 168, 73; (D) 229, 186.
Potter, John S.: 26, 90.
Potter, Paul M.: 9, 16; 14, 4; 55, 227; 106, 187.
"Potters, The": (R'23) 275, 19.
Poughkeepsie Little Theatre: 257, 105; 257, 106; 327, 43.
Pounds, Courtice: 157, 113.
Pounds, Louie: 113, 20.
Pounds, Louisa: 90, 207.
Povah, Phyllis: 227, 34; 233, 22; 242, 319; 273, 13; 273, 17; 285, 18; 288, 13; 295, 8; 319, 27; 325, 24; 336, 43.
Powell, David: 169, 130; 170, 170; 172, 301.
Powell, E.S.: 94, 330.
Powell, Francis: (W) 151, 98.
Powell, Jack: 343, 43.
Powell, Lillian: 250, 13; 282, 25; 294, 35.
Powell, Michael: 318, 42.
Powell, William: 237, 352; 349, 25.
Power, Jewel: 98, 113; 98, 127.
Power, Nancy: 200, 209.
Power, Tyrone: 19, 13; 22, 5; 22, 14; 22, 16; 26, 85; 32, 239; 33, 281; 44, 249; 49, 71; (C) 51, 127; 62, 88; 66, 207; (C) 82, xxiv; 87, 136; 121, 70; 122, 106; 142, 172; 161, 16; 202, 337; 206, 202; 207, 286; 216, 93; 216, 94; 244, 35; 247, 219; 250, 7; 257, 101; 278, 37; 325, 39.
"Power of Darkness, The": (R'01) 9, 8; 228, 77; (D) 229, 161; (R'20) 229, 184; 241, 267.
Powers, Clyde W.: 77, 183.
Powers, Ethel: 38, 104.
Powers, Eugene: 252, 151; 277, 14; (D) 351, 19; 352, 43; 356, 19.
Powers, Francis: (C) 51, 127.
Powers, James T.: 3, 7; 25, 60; (A) 52, 131f; 98, 107; 98, 115; 100, 182; 136, 172; 147, 129; 187, 150; 187, 151; 188, 204b; 214, 335; (W, V) 215, 8; 257, 101; 268, 3; 268, 11; (D) 312, 162; 340, 36.
Powers, Leona: 68, 263.
Powers, Tom: 189, 297; 191, 18; 248, 323; 254, 283; 255, 357; 273, 18; 290, 35; 293,

36; 299,17; 304,33; 306,27; 310,7; 325,40; 349,45; 352, 15.
Powers, William: 90,212.
Poynter, Beulah: 168,68.
Prach, Herma: 267,23.
Pratt, Jeanette: 241,249.
Pratt, Lynn: 43,238; 70,319.
Pratt, Muriel: 146,111.
Pratt, Purnell B.: 153,161.
Pratt, Theodore: (W) 315, 39.
Pratt Institute: 281,47.
"Prayer of the Sword, The": 54,184.
Preer, Evelyn: 268,12.
Presinger, Hansi: 352,38,
Prentice, Beatrice: 91,250; 101,24; 174,90; 194,201; 218, 209; 219,293.
Presbrey, Eugene W.: 10,6; 15,19; 65,187; (W) 71,10; 84,42; 159,230.
"Present Arms": (R'28) 327, 65; 328,39.
"Preserving Mr. Panmure": (R'12) 134,xiv; 135,165.
Presidents And Theatre (see names of presidents).
"Press Agent, The": (R'05) 59,xii.
Pressagentry: 26,103; 49,74; 53,ix; 72,42; 74,104; 79, 239; 162,77; 185,13; 196, 348; 207,278; 208,362; 211, 152; 236,282; 240,154; 273, 24; 278,20; 304,32; 310, 12; 313,28; 318,32; 323,17; 331,48; 342,11.
Pressagentry -- Film: 200, 246; 201,322; 207,327.
"Press Cuttings": 133,86.
Preston, Clinton: 125,32.
Preston, Raymond: (W) 167, 31.
"Pretenders, The": 74,95; (R'07) 75,xxiii; 91,248.
Pretty, Arline: 196,335; 212, 245; 228,120.
"Pretty Peggy": 26,83; (R'03) 27,109; 27,111; 63,120.
"Pretty Mrs. Smith": 165, 206; (R'14) 165,207.
"Pretty Sister of Jose, The": (R'03) 34,289; 35,17.
Preuse-Matzenauer, Margarete: 118,182.
Previn, Charles: 219,281; 330, 47.
Prevost, Marie: 308,40; 320, 66; 321,75; 322,6; 322,42; 322,60; 329,59.
Prevost, Peggy: 301,13.
"Price, The": (R'11) 130,xii; 130,220.
Price, Alonzo; 152,135.
Price, Drew: 360,35.
Price, E.D.: 75,118.
Price, Georgie: 331,35.
Price, Mark: 57,271.
Price, W.M.: 5,11.
Price, W.T.: (W) 7,12; (W) 17,13; 44,256; 93,iii; 131, xiii; 135,xi; 232,568.
"Price of Coal, The": 185,18.
"Price of Money, The": (R'06) 68,257; 68,277.
"Pride of Jennico, The": (R'01) 8,12.
"Pride of Race, The": 181,147.
Priest, Janet: 43,233.
Prill, Arthur: (W) 157,139.
"Prima Donna, The": (R'08) 95,2.
"Primrose Path": (R'07) 76,147; 77,179.
Prince, Adelaide: 18,20; 37, 57; 82,321; 83,8; 96,61; 105,155; 118,162; 125,29; 136,188; 199,151; 201,270.
"Prince and Pauper: (F) 180,74; 238,11; (R'20) 238,31.
"Prince Chap, The": 56,i; (R'05) 56,240; 56,243; (F) 235,195.
"Prince Consort, The": (R) 50,80; 50,83.
"Prince Igor": (OP) 180,89.
"Prince of Bohemia, The": (R'10) 109,xii; 110,127.
"Prince of India, The": 59,iv; 63,127; (R'06) 69,285.
"Prince of Parthia": 215,36.
"Prince of Pilsen, The": (R'03) 26,81; 26,85; 40,143.
"Prince There Was, A": 217,163.
"Princess and the Butterfly,

The": 143,22.
"Princess April": (R'24) 287, 16.
"Princess Beggar": (R'07) 72, xiii.
"Princess Flavia": 298,4.
"Princess Ida": 292,17.
"Princess Lontaine" (see "Lady of Dreams, The").
"Princess of Kensington, The": (R'03) 32,242.
"Princess Pat, The": (R'15) 177,223; 177,259.
Princess Players, The": 146, xvi; 147,155; 148,186; 153, xv; 153,143; 157,113; 166, 267; 167,9; 181,143.
"Princess Shows": 280,10.
Princess Theatre (New York): 148,186; 149,2; 163,101; 199,122.
Princess Theatre (San Francisco): 138,51.
"Princess's Nose, The": (R'02) 15,6.
Princeton University: 76,148; 114,59; 192,80; 192,81; 227, 37; 240,189; 240,191; 252, 180; 258,169; 265,45; 275, 40; 278,41; 278,42; 302, 39; 310,41; 312,43; 324, 54; 351,49.
Pringle, Aileen: 294,39; 306, 39.
Pringle, Jessie: 212,203; 226, 393.
Printemps, Yvonne: 281,22; 309, 33; 312,21.
Prinzregenten Theatre (Munich): 51,122.
Prior, Allan: 284,27.
"Prisoner, The": 324,39; (R'28) 324,62.
"Prisoner of Zenda": 93,vi; (F) 147,156; (F,R) 262,56.
Pritchard, Frances: 172,308; 175,131; 177,242; 180,76; 217,147.
"Private Account, A": (R'17) 194,213.
"Private Lives": 360,22; 360, 41; (C) 361,2; (R'31) 361, 25.
<u>Private Theatres:</u> 20,18; 76, 169; 87,126; 94,342; 197, 37; 257,104; 269,46.
"Privilege Car": 361,26.
Prize Play Competition: 25,55; 26,78; 26,80; 35,i,f; 34, 316; 37,56.
"Probation Wife, The": (F,R) 218,253.
Probert, George: 72,30; 151,83; 152,117; 183,275.
<u>Problem Plays:</u> 26,100; 56, 246; 61,54; 152,124.
"Processional": (R'25) 288,19; 289,14.
Proctor, Catherine: 69,301; 97,94; 179,21; 204,73; 304,14; 307,27.
Proctor, F.F.: 63,xiii.
Proctor's Opera House (Troy): 63,xiv.
Proctor's Stock Company: 53,x.
"Prodigal Husband, The": 164, 159; 164,160; (R'14) 164,195.
"Prodigal Son, The": (R'05) 56, 241; 56,256; 56,257.
<u>Producers</u> (<u>see also</u> <u>Managers, Theatre</u>): 161,6: 162,68; 203,34; 281,9; 295,7; (D) 309,25; 312,12; (C) 312,15; 326,27; 332,13; 351,24; 353,13; 360,42.
<u>Producers -- Film:</u> 348,24.
Producing Managers' Association: 223,172; 256,6; 259, 220; 268,39; 278,64.
<u>Profanity:</u> 183,279; 332,38.
Profeit, Leopold: 141,133.
Professional Woman's League: 164,183.
"Professor's Love Story, The": 194,212; (R'17) 194,215.
<u>Programs, Film:</u> 92,265.
<u>Programs, Theatre:</u> 12,18; 14,25; 19,18; 33,275; 36, 37; 58,293; 58,300; 78, 222; 86,98; 86,99; 90,219; 94,342; 104,118; 148,179; 171,232; 173,19; 178,276; 190,368; 198,68; 221,30; 310, 22; 341,26.
Progressive Stage Society: 45,286; 47,xiii; 58,293.
<u>Prohibition:</u> 212,196; 222,86;

(D) 231,381; 231,400; 236,256; 306,24.
"Prominent Players In Their Homes":
1: Frances Starr 157,137;
2: Marguerite Clark 158,189;
3: David Warfield 159,243;
4: Billy Burke 160,303;
5: Laurette Taylor 161,22;
6: Viola Dana 162,83;
7: Lillian Russell 163,119;
8: Elsie Janis 164,181;
9: Louise Dresser 165,233;
10: Frank Keenan 166,287;
11: Julia Dean 167,29;
12: William Faversham 168,79;
13: William Courtenay 169,139;
14: Pauline Frederick 170,177;
15: Mary & Florence Nash 171,249;
16: Irene Fenwick 172,303;
17: Ruth Chatterton 175,137;
18: Alla Nazimova 180,88;
19: Marguerite Leslie 181,138;
20: Marguerite Namara 183,290.
Propaganda Producing Company: 206,206.
Properties: 227,8; 287,10; 310,22.
"Proud Laird, The": (R'05) 52,136.
"Proud Prince, The": 33,264; 33,265; 42,ii.
"Proud Woman, A": (R'26) 311,18.
Prouty, Jed: 189,280.
Provincetown Players: 242,340; 244,60; 306,42.
Provincetown Playhouse: 198, 92; 234,108; 279,19; 282, 7; 294,7; 306,53.
Provincetown Theatre: 268, 16.
"Provoked Husband, The": 168, 86.
Provost, Jeanne: 189,288.
Prue, Edwina: 308,44; 309,67.
Pruette, William: 17,4; 44, 257; 60,33; 66,208; 92, 263; 105,159; 113,15; 118, 184.
"Prunella, Or Love in a Garden": (R'13) 154,174; 154,197; 188,200; (F) 205, 196.
Prussing, Louise: 232,536; 260, 305.
Pryor, Arthur: 102,62; 103, 77.
Pryor, Roger: (D) 318,25; 344,13; 350,48.
Pryor, Ruth: 281,37.
Pryor, Sara Sherman (W): 296,43.
Pseudonyms: 201,296; 223,146.
"Public Defender, The": (F,R) 201,316.
Publicity (see Pressagentry).
Puccini, Giacomo: (A) 27, 125; 69,289; (A) 69,302; 72,44; (A) 100, 198; 116,108; (A) 119,1; (A) 120,52; 135,iv.
Puchol, Luisita: 203,9.
Puck, Eva: 326,35.
Puget, S.A.: 189,289.
Pulitzer Prize: 198,63; 280, 39; 292,7; 304,7; 326,9; 353,32.
Pulitzer, Walter (W): 24,46.
Punch And Judy Theatre (New York): 166,306; (D) 167, 35; 172,306; 174,64.
"Punch, Judy & Co.": 30,184.
Puppet Theatre: 65,175; 65, 240; 187,152; 199,138; 217,162; 236,268; (D) 266, 24; 271,24; 303,13; 318, 49; 324,43.

"Puppets": (R'25) 290,34.
"Puppets of Passion": (R'27) 314,21.
"Puppy Love": (R'26) 301,66.
Purcell, Charles: 189,280; 200,221; 209,13; 219,295; 227,23; 235,183; 246,151; 297,17.
Purcell, Gertrude: 255,381.
Purdue University: 211,163.
Purdy, Charles: 162,72.
"Purloined Letter, The": (F) 180,74.
"Purple Mask, The": 228,75; (R'20) 228,142.
"Purple Road, The": (R'13) 147, 131; 148,162; 148,185.
Purviance, Edna: 270,30.
Putnam, Alice: 144,36; 146,119.
Putnam, Boyd: 38,88; 48,41.
"Puzzles of 1925": (R'25) 289,18.
"Pygmalion": (R'14) 166,262; (R'26) 310,15; 311,17; 312, 20.
Pyle, Wynne: 202,370.
Pyne, Mary: 204,83.
"Pyramids": (R'26) 307,16.

--Q--

"Quaker Girl, The": (R'11) 130, xiii; 186,70.
"Quality Street": 8,3; (R'01) 9,5; 10,1; 10,2; 10,3; 42, ii.
Qualters, Tot: 236,265; 240, 165; 245,115.
"Quarantine": (R'24) 287,62; 288,38.
Quartaro, Nena: 323,4b.
Quartermaine, Charles: 261, 370; (C) 262,32.
Quartermaine, Leon: 166,269; 342,25; (D) 344,19; 356,12; (C) 359,2.
"Queen Elizabeth": (F) 138, 34; 138,35.
Queen Elizabeth of Roumania: 50,102; 55,215.
"Queen Fiametta": (S) 20,16; 22,18; 22,19; 22,21.
"Queen High": 309,21; (F,R) 355,48.
"Queen of Hearts": (R'20) 233,31; (R'22) 261,377.
"Queen of Sheba, The": (OP) (R'05) 59,9; (F,R) 244,38.
"Queen of the Moulin Rouge, The": 95,4.
"Queen of the Movies": (R'14) 156,96.
Queen Victoria: 35,i.
"Queen Victoria": (R'23) 274, 15; 274,18.
"Queen's Enemies, The": (R'16) 191,21; 192,93.
"Queen's Husband, The": (S) 326,28.
"Question, The": (R'12) 144, xxvii.
Quimby, Margaret: 268,43.
"Quincy Adams Sawyer": (R'02) 19,7.
Quinlan, Gertrude: 5,2; 110, 110; 113,20; 115,80; 116, 119; 122,126.
Quinn, Jane: 155,21.
Quinn, Louise: 335,47.
Quinn, Rose: 171,238; 234, 93.
"Quinneys": 178,276; (R'15) 178,278; 178,308.
Quirk, Leslie W: (W) 29, 181.
Quive, Mary: 129,177.
"Quo Vadis" (1901): PG,21; 123,149; (F) (R'13) 148, x; (F) 150,38; 150,39.

--R--

"R.U.R.": (R'22) 261,375; 262, 18.
Raabe-Burg, Emmy: 81,292; 81,311.
Rab, Pol: 313,c; 313,3a.
Rabaud, Henri: 215,10.
Rabb, Kate Milner: (W) 248, 322.
Rabbette, Leo: (W,V) 156, 78.
"Rabensteinerin, Die": 93,289.
Rabinoff, Max: 155,16; (W) 202,360.
"Rachel": 155,6; (R'13) 155, 8.
Rachel, Lydia: 120,42.
Rachel, [Mlle.]: 75,124; (D) 142,168; 154,195.

Rachmaninoff, Sergei: 216,73; (D) 276,27.
Racine: 11,13.
"Rack, The": (R'11) 129,xvi.
"Racquet, The": 323,39.
Radcliffe, W.H.: (W) 150,62.
Radcliffe College (see also Harvard University): 53,xiii; 281,45.
Radclyffe, Cecilia: 154,197; 202, 341; 275,17.
Radeef, Vladimir: 257,81.
Radier, Alice: 195,287.
Radio: 262,15; 270,24; 278,39; 280,7; 284,24; 288,7; and monthly thereafter; 296,74; 314,23; 325,35; 328,40; 353, 42; and monthly thereafter.
Radisse, Lucienne: 349,56.
Radnor, Leona: 96,46.
Rae, Maud: 204,123.
Rae, Newton: 86,iii.
Raeburn, Eleanor: (W) 140,111; (W,V) 146,98; (W) 154,194.
"Raffles": (R'03) 34,290; 42,ii.
Rafter, Adele: 13,23; 55,218.
Ragina: 318,36.
Rahn, Kathryn: 199,157.
"Rain": (R'22) 262,25; (S) 263, 28; 270,19; 302,10; 350, 27.
"Rain or Shine": 329,38.
"Rainbow": (R'28) 334,60; (R'12) 134,xv; 134,108.
"Rainbow Girl, The": 207,277; (R'18) 207,316.
"Rainbow Rose": (R'26) 302,15.
Raine, Luis: 276,17.
Raines, Nettie: 256,17.
Rainey, Ada: (W) 146,115.
Rains, Claude: 252,160; 330,41; 340,25.
Raisa, Rosa: 203,41; 205,147; 217,137; 288,35.
Raison, Milton: 331,49.
Rale, M.W.: 133,85.
Raleigh, Evangeline: 321,56; 325,49.
Ralph, Jessie: 157,114; 265, 31.
Ralph, Phillis: 82,327.
Ralston, Esther: 305,36; 324, 42.
Rambaud, Paul: 134,123.
Rambeau, Marjorie: 167,8; 179, 23; 180,73; 183,292; 186, 107; 187,149; 188,233; (D) 189,c; 197,16; 199,121; 200, 203; 200,228; 201,268; 204, 108; 204,109; 211,127; 218, 225; 219,315; 224,233; 227, 19; 245,85; 249,365; 256, 21; 258,144; 259,231; 279, 68; 300,55; 301,29; 303, 32; 334,31.
"Rambler Rose": (R'17) 201, 277; 201,281.
"Ramblers, The": (R'26) 308, 15; 310,19.
Rambova, Natacha: 315,35; 317, 46; 320,23.
Ramon And Rosita: 316,29.
"Ramona": (F) 325,50.
Ranck, Edwin (W): (V) 153, 155; 159,249; 174,83; 195, 283; 198,74; 199,152; 200, 218; 201,288; 204,104; 206, 226; 207,292; 208,368; 210, 92; 211,148; 212,216; 221,24; 223,162; (V) 225,298; 233,10; 237,358; 238,36; 241,240; 298, 20.
Rand, Rosa: 120,53.
Rand, Sally: 313,39.
Randall, Carl: 186,71; 205,143; 219,281.
Randall, John: 237,357.
Randall, Leita: 245,94.
Randall, Ruth: 186,63.
Randolph, Anders: 308,38.
Randolph, Edith: 181,129.
Randolph, Eva: 140,118.
Randolph, Louise: 88,152; 115,86; 130,197; 158,194; 303,17; 303,27.
Randolph, Renita: 308,19.
"Ranger, The": (R'07) 80,259; 80,264; 80,269.
Ranken, Frederick: 55,227; 58, xix.
Rankin, Doris: 206,221; 215,15; 224,222; 251,93; 332,34.
Rankin, McKee: 49,62; (W) 111, 157.
Ranous, Dora K.: 132,57.
"Ransom's Folly": (R'04) 36, 31; 37,71.
"Ranz Des Vaches, Le": (OP)

147,135.
Ranzenberg, Mary: 97,76.
Rapee, Erno: 330,47.
"Rapid Transit": (R'27) 315, 26.
Rapp, William Jourdan: (C) 339,22.
Rappaport, S. (see Ansky, S.).
Rappold, Marie: 59,9; 120,48; 129,155.
Rasch, Albertina: 163,102; 230, 266; 317,57; (D) 347,28; 347,42.
Rasche, William: 344,36.
Rasely, George: 202,348.
"Rasputin the Black Monk": (F,R) 200,245.
"Rat, The": (R'25) 289,18.
Ratcliffe, E.J.: 82,329; 96, 38; 112,193; 166,279.
Rath, George: 268,43.
Rathbone, Basil: 253,211; 255, 357; 273,14; 307,29; 309, 14; 311,23; 319,31; 320, 24; 323,39; (D) 327,21; 327, 49; 336,18.
Ratliff, Joseph M.: 101,17.
Raucourt, Jules: 188,204.
Rauh, Stanley E. (W): 278,24; 279,24; 281,20; 287,12; 292, 24.
Rauworth, Grace: 42,196.
Ravel, Maurice: 326,45.
Ravine, Gabrielle: 268,18; 269,31.
Ravine, George: 213,265.
Rawling, Ray: 335,46.
Rawlins, W.H.: 238,11.
Rawlinson, Herbert: (A) 251, 131; 352,68.
Ray, Allene: 291,43; 324,46.
Ray, Carol: 238,25.
Ray, Catherine: 309,46.
Ray, Charles: 192,97; 199,177; 207,332; 211,186; 215,61; (A) 226,438; 231,489; 234, 114; 242,348; 245,106; 274, 33; 277,32; 291,62; 302, 48; 306,38; 312,23.
Ray, Moira L.: (W) 29,167.
Raymond, Helen: 141,155.
Raymond, John T.: 81,298; 86, 98; 246,164; (W) 271,20.
Raymond, Maude: 64,160; 108, 46.
Raymond, Ray: 217,135; 242, 341.
Raymonde, Ruth: 308,44.
Raynal, Paul: 279,12.
Raynore, Katherine: 20,7.
Rea, Isabelle: 47,18.
Rea, Lawrence: 120,59.
Rea, Virginia: 225,320.
Reade, Janet: 358,12.
Reader, Ralph: 301,38.
"Ready Money" (see also "Oh, Look!"): (R'12) 140,100; 140,113.
"Real Thing, The": 127,iii; 127,78; (R'11) 127,79.
Realism: 22,31; 46,303; 58, 315; 70,324; 89,xii; 151, 86; 151,96; 161,6; 166,286; 207,304; 216,88; 313,21; 320, 44; 324,31; 331,17; 334,20; 337,15; 340,14; 342,12; 345,35; 349,18.
Reals, Grace: 226,389.
Reamer, Lawrence: (C) 193, 138.
"Rebecca of Sunnybrook Farm": 110,118; (R'10) 117,xiii; 117,vii; (F,R) 200,245.
"Rebellion": (R'11) 129,151.
"Rebound": (C) 349,4; (R'30) 349,42; 349,43.
"Recapture": (R'30) 348,70.
Recht, Charles: (W) 268,22.
"Reckoning, The": (R'07) 73, xvi; 75,117.
"Recollections of a Playgoer" by Brander Matthews: 195,263; 196,346; 197,30.
Records, Phonograph (see Phonograph Records).
"Rector's Garden, The": (R'08) 86,xv.
"Red Canary, The": (R'14) 160, 319.
"Red Carnation, The": (R'05) 50,85.
"Red Cloak, The": (R'15) 180, 116; 181,143.
"Red Dancer, The": (F,D) 330, 29.
"Red Darkness": (R'16) 192, 394.
"Red Dawn, The": (R'19) 223,

152.
Red Feather, Princess: 179,32.
"Red Geranium, The": (R'22) 256,32.
"Red Kloof": (R'01) 9,5.
"Red Lantern, The": (F) 220, 394.
"Red Light Annie": (R'23) 271, 15.
"Red Lights": (F,R) 272,32.
"Red Mill, The": (R'06) 69,xi; 69,293; 70,x; 70,328; 71, 22; 72,43.
"Red Moon, The": (R'09) 100,xii.
"Red Peppers": (R'22) 257,95.
"Red Peril": (F,R) 229,190.
"Red Rose, The": (R'11) 126, 40; 126,51.
"Red Rust": (R'29) 347,45; 347, 49; 349,8.
"Red Widow, The": (R'11) 130, xii; 130,186.
Red Wing (Minnesota) Theatre: 45,290.
Redd, Clarence: 303,14.
Redding, Harry: 120,40.
Redding, H.E. (W): 301,10; 302,10; 306,24.
"Redeeming Sin": (F) 337,69.
"Redemption" (see also "Der Lebende Leichnam"): (D) 220,337; 221,24; (R'18) 213, 277; (S) 214,358; 214,359.
Redlich, Marion: 90,216.
Redmond, Aleine: 33,274.
Redmond, Jack: 305,17.
"Redskin, The": 62,i; (R'06) 62, 86; 62,88; 62,89.
Reed, Albert: 155,7.
Reed, Eloise: 79,233.
Reed, Florence: 29,162; 76,161; 82,328; 92,274; 104,128; 124, 204; 134,108; 140,118; 154, 203; 156,64; 157,129; 159, 251; 169,132; 171,233; 172, 298; 194,198; 202,337; (W) 204,94; 207,324; 215,15; (W) 217,146; 231,363; 231,373; 235,169; 236,297; 239,94; 240, 199; 245,106; 257,79; 261, 380; 266,18; 269,12; 272,18; (D) 273,10; 301,5; (W) 304, 22; 304,23; 306,47; 307,29; (C) 308,11; (C) 325,16; 332, 11.
Reed, Florence P.: 315,38; (W) 317,32.
Reed, Genevieve: 79,233.
Reed, Jessie: 212,217; 217, 147.
Reed, John: 198,92.
Reed, Lillian: 51,129.
Reed Sisters, The: 79,233.
Reed, Vivian: 179,23.
Reeid, Nathaniel E.: (W) 319, 48.
Rees, Betsy: 274,35; 341,19.
Reese, Edmund: 104,119.
Reeve, Frances: 138,47.
Reeves, Billie: 90,212; 91, 243; 102,53; 114,45.
Reeves, Francis: 147,150.
Regay, Pearl: 226,385; 277, 37; 292,48.
"Regeneration, The": 89,191; 89,197; (R'08) 92,xv.
Regnier, Marthe: 121,101.
"Regular Feller, A": (R'19) 224,280; 226,379.
"Regular Girl, A": (F,R) 227, 41.
Rehan, Ada: PG,7; 10,17; 22,26; 30,203; 36,viii; 36, 30; 38,c; 52,151; 53,174; 54,189; 78,212; 126,64; 128,127; 142,198; 145,74; 169,136; 180,96; 182,225; 196,347; 231,397; 235,168; 245,96; 293,40; 358,21.
Rehearsal Club: 164,183.
<u>Rehearsal Descriptions:</u> 46,xv; 98, 108; 101,10; 107,vi; 107, 27; 114,39; 118,178; 135, 146; 137,4; 143,2; 162,75; 167,21; 188,198; 199,121; 209,12; 223,142; 226,393; (D) 271,8; 288,10; 305,20; 307,27; 327,12; 324,21; 359,27.
Reichenbach, Harry: (W) 311, 12.
Reicher, Emmanuel: 168,102; 170,204; 172,281; 172,282; 179,8; 230,260; 230,261; 246,142.
Reicher, Frank: 121,85; 136, 182; 143,32; 144,57; 157, 160; 169,131; 243,301; 253,

231; 257,71; 261,368; (W) 339,35.
Reicher, Hedwig: 81,292; 81, 311; 93,289; 100,186; 104, 107; 104,128; 105,135; 107,15; 107,22; 131,30; 140, 126; 173,21; 266,38.
Reid, James Hallack: 123,161.
Reid, Lewis: 360,40.
Reid, Opie: 27,107.
Reid, Wallace: 217,191; 222, 114; 224,254; 240,186; 240, 188; 246,174; 248,324; 250, 38; 254,297;
Reilly, Zulieka: 245,94.
Reimer, Helen: 87,118; 118,172; 122,109.
Reindollar, Maud: 11,15.
Reinhard, Delia: 265,37.
Reinhardt, Beatrice: 230,247.
Reinhardt, Max: 126,56; 132,44; 132,54; 132,57; 133,81; 138,34; 142,191;237,372; 267,13; 268, 38;268,40; 276,9; 292,40; 305, 17;323,19; (C) 323,29; 323,38; 336,78.
Reinold, Bernard: 288,38.
Reischberg, Hansi: 90,207.
Reiss, Albert: 134,109; (A) 136,xvi;197,31.
Reizenstein, Elmer L.: 164, 160; 176,179.
Rejane, [Mde.] Gabrielle: 43, 224; 46,295; 47,24; 72,vii; 74,97; 74,98; 83,15; 91, 251; 100,172; 149,4; 233, 69.
"Rejuvenation of Aunt Mary, The": (R'07) 82,xix; 83,15.
Religious Drama: 6,10;15,10; 78, viii; 88,153; 89,176; (D) 110,125; 114,50; 125,20; 228,84; 236,294; 264,45; 321,53.
Relph, George: 134,122; 142, 165; 179,6.
Relph, Phyllis: 194,231.
Remick, Jerome H.: 201,310; 214,397.
"Remmant": (R'18) 215,19; 215, 29.
"Remote Control": 344,47; (R'29) 344,74.
Rempel, Harriet: 219,291.
Renaud, Charles: 107,11.
Renaud, Maurice: 65,170; 70, 341; 71,8; 83,22; 94,345; 106,165; 121,82; 133,79; 242, 327; 265,9.
Renard, Jules: 21,8.
Renavent, George: 210,95; 210,101; 213,265; 218,204; 218,217; 236,283; 253,215; 263,21.
Rendel, Robert: 225,309.
Rendl, Paula: 255,376.
Renevant, Georges: 325,39.
Reneys, Roberta: 300,23.
Reniers, Percival (W): 229, 176; 289,12.
Rennie, James: 226,371; 241,268; 259,226; 283, 25; 292,21; 195,17; 301,19; (D) 315,41.
Rennyson, Gertrude: 7,7; 133, 80.
Reno (Nevada) Stock Company: 114,46.
"Rented Earl, The": (R'15) 169,150.
Repelsky, Eugenia: 260,13.
Repertoire Theatre: 58,294; 90,215; 100,175; 101,4; 114, 46; 124,190; 148,168; 153, 158; 160,290; 246,142; 247, 230; 250,6; 251,74; 280,9; 313,12; 340,16; 346,28; 347,18; 348,31; 359,14.
Repertory Theatre (Boston): 303,53.
"Representative American Plays" (Hobson) (B): 209, 52.
Repton, Leila: 102,47; 124,205.
Republican Guard of Paris (Band): 41,172; 42,208.
"Rescuing Angel, The": (R'17) 202,349; 202,353.
Residenz Theatre (Munich): 51, 123.
"Restless Women": (R'28) 324, 39.
"Resurrection": 24,50; (R'03) 25,58; 26,94; 28,148; 42,ii; (F) 313,40; 314,40.
Rethberg, Elizabeth: 275,35; 299,35; 331,23.
Retired Actors (see Actors'

Homes).
Retreats, Actors' (see Clubs, Actors').
Retter, Dezso: 290,45.
"Return from Jerusalem, The": (R'12) 132,39.
"Return of Eve, The": (R'09) 99,134.
"Return of Peter Grimm, The": 121,75; (R'11) 129,xi; 130, 193; 134,118; 169,148; (R'21) 249,388.
"Return to Multon, The": (R'18) 208,358.
Reuter, Florizel: 13,27.
Revalles, Flore: 188,199; 199, 155; 200,230; 230,280.
Revell, Dorothy: 47,22; 51, 128; 56,261; 58,310; 70,321.
Reveill, Nellie (W): 158,199; 159,237; 160,293; 187,144; 188,212; 189,278; 190,370; 191,38; 192,100; 193,166; 194, 224; 195,290; 196,356; 197, 36; 198,90; 199,148; 200, 216; 201,294; 202,364; 203, 18; 278,27.
Revelle, Hamilton: 5,16; 14,6; 59,7; 60,34; 71,11; 90, 205; 92,269; 93,303; 122, 108; 133,100; 179,16; 183, 292; 188,203; 218,217; 219, 296; 231,365; 256,37; 294, 16; 338,16.
"Revellers, The": 104,xiii.
Rever, M. Ernest: 3,14.
Review of the Season:
1900-01: 3,2; 5,18;
1901-02: 16,2; 16,26
1902-03: 18,4
1903-04: 31,210; 35,2; 40, 134; 41,vii
1904-05: 43,214; 51,114; 52,xv
1905-06: 55,210; 65,x
1906-07: 67,226; 77,v; 77,172
1907-08: 79,228; 89,ix; 89,172
1908-09: 91,228
1909-10: 103,70; 109,xii; 113,2; 114,vii
1910-11: 115,66; 123,142
1911-12: 127,76
1912-13: 139,66; 161,15
1913-14: 151,78
1914-15: 163,98
1915-16: 175,108
1916-17: 187,126; 197,21
1917-18: 199,122; 209,21
1918-19: 211,130; 221,6
1919-20: 223,144
1920-21: 234,84
1921-22: 246,164; 249,362; 252,174; 254,288
1922-23: 258,134; 258,145
1923-24: 270,7
1924-25: 282,7; 292,9
1925-26: 294,7
1926-27: 306,15
1927-28: 316,19; 318,4; 318,22; 329,38
1928-29: 330,36; 341,41
1929-30: 342,41; 343,15; 345,17; 349,38; 350,18; 351,14
Review of the Season -- Opera:
1901-02: 10,28; 22,34
1905-06: 65,x
1906-07: 75,138
1907-08: 77,174; 82,350
1908-09: 93,308
1909-10: 104,114
1910-11: 116,108
1911-12: 129,154; 135, 144
1912-13: 141,138; 142,166
1913-14: 178,284
1920-21: 238,34.
Revivals: 137,14; 328,5; 340, 19.
Revner, Katherine: 313,30.
"Revolt": (R'28) 334,60; (R'15) 171,229; 171,236.
"Revolt in the Arts" (Sayler) (B): 359,8.
"Revolt of the Actors, The" (Harding) (B): 345,76.
Revues (see Musical Comedy).
Reyer, Ernest: 97,ii.
Reynolds, Carrie: 61,76; 99, 158; 132,68; 148,188; 183, 275; 188,237.
Reynolds, Harrington: 57,269.
Reynolds, Thomas: 354,25.
Reynolds, Vera: 282,31; 320, 66; 321,75; 322,6; 322,50.
Reynolds, William Bartlett (W):

233,36; 261,422.
Rhea, Mlle. (W): 150,40; 151, 104; 152,137; 153,167; 287, 37.
Rhead, John: 138,33.
Rhode Island Theatre: 219,320; 306,42.
Rhodes, Billie: 209,60.
Rhodes, Lila: 129,174.
Rialto, The: 69,296; 138,57; (D) 173,19; (D) 266,10; 285,7; (C) 345,26.
Rialto Theatre (New York): 183,282; 189,328; 191,42.
Riano, Renee: 232,521; 250, 27.
Ricard, Amy: 24,33; 46,300; 54,187; 78,221; 87,131; 202,348.
Ricardo, Corona: 54,191.
Riccardi, Albert: 174,89.
Riccardo, Corona: PG,16; 31,212; 33,268; 54,191.
Ricciardi, William: 45,274; 179,19; 345,48.
Rice, Dan: 54,192.
Rice, Edward E.: 16,8.
Rice, Elmer: 266,19; 267, 30; (D) 268,9; (W) 336, 26; (C) 339,39.
Rice, Fanny: 34,306.
Rice, Florence: (D) 348,53.
Rice, Gitz: 210,98; 210,99.
Rice, John C.: 31,211.
Rice, Sidney F.: 28,156; 37, 62.
Rice, Wallace: 123,173.
Rich, Irene: 296,30; 298, 33; 301,47; 322,44; 325, 58; (W) 329,22; (D) 351, 29; 354,22.
"Rich Man, Poor Man": 190,354; (R'16) 190,392; (F,R) 207, 324.
"Rich Man's Plaything, A": (F) 202,401.
"Rich Man's Son, A": (R'12) 142,xviii.
"Rich Mr. Hoggenheimer, The": (R'06) 70,xx; 70,338.
"Rich Mrs. Repton, The": (R'04) 46,296.
Richard, George: 31,235; 186,62.
"Richard Lovelace": (R'01) 8,4.
"Richard III": (R'05) 47,3; (R'05) 58,290; 66,216; 73,x; (R'08) 86,90; (R'20) 230,309; 231,343; 232,502; (D) 296,13.
Richard, V.K.: (W) 325,51.
Richards, Cicely: 120,61.
Richards, George: 50,95.
Richards, Isabel: 179,25.
Richards, Regina: 196,335.
Richardson, Henry S.: 5,11.
Richardson, Jane: 223,165; 255, 379.
Richardson, Jazzlips: (C) 342, 36; 343,43.
Richardson, Madge: 113,10.
"Richelieu": (R'09) 99,134; 99,150; 99,151; 214,333; 347,47; (R'29) 347,49; 349,6.
Richepin, Jean: 14,11.
"Richest Girl, The" (see also "Tantalizing Tommy"): (R'09) 98,xii.
Richman, Arthur: 235,178; 250,19; 260,310; 262,12; (D) 268,9; 308,29; (W) 344, 37.
Richman, Charles: PG,22; 3,2; 4,3; 5,8; 12,12; 14,1; 24, 29; 35,16; 36,48; 61,56; 71,11; 109,68; 120,62; 124, 191; 129,169; 139,68; 229, 186; 231,365; 356,18; 269, 18; 283,25.
Richman, Harry: 318,18; 342, 27.
Richmond, Estelle: 142,184.
Richter, Hans: 80,266.
"Richter Von Zalamea, Der": (R'05) 50,80.
Ricker, Bessie Bown: 120,36.
Ricketts, Dan: 48,42.
Ridde, George: 9,17.
"Riddle: Woman, The": (R'18) 214,346; 215,35.
Rideout, Gertrude Helen: (W) 345,53.
"Rider of Dreams, The": (R'17) 195,280; (S) 196,350.
Ridgely, Cleo: 169,129.
Ridges, Stanley: 228,99; 348, 46.
Ridgeway, Fritzie: 272,35.

Ridgewell, Audrey: 170,197.
Riegel, Charles H.: 90,i.
Riegelman, Mabel: 199,132.
Riesenfeld, Hugo: 217,187; 282,8; 298,37.
Rigby, Edward: 326,30.
"Right Age to Marry, The": 302,17.
"Right Girl, The": (R) 242, 370; 243,421.
"Right of Way, The": (R'07) 82, 320.
"Right to Be Happy, The": (R'12) 135,138; 135,147.
"Right to Dream, The": (R'24) 281,15.
"Right to Happiness, The": (R'12) 132,xi.
"Right to Kill, The": (R'26) 302,16.
"Right to Love, The": (R'03) 26, 101.
"Right to Strike, The": (R'21) 250,30.
"Right You Are If You Think You Are": (R) 314,21.
Rigl, Betty: 78,223.
Rigl, Emily: 54,188.
Rignold, George: 139,82.
Rihani: 209,33.
Rikla, Helen: 214,351.
Riley, Louise: 253,243; 270, 21.
Riley, Madeline Lucette: 27, 116; 55,227.
Rimini, Giacomo: 203,39.
Rinehardt, Mary Roberts: 235,181; (W) 339,13.
Ring, Blanche: 23,13; 25,60; 26,86; 28,155; 29,161; 30,c; 41,174; 52,134; (W) 52,141; 56,239; 66,210; 81,289; 82,344; 95,21; 101,31; 109, xi; 110,113; 113,17; 115,c; 125,34; 129,167; 135,xvi; 135,139; (A) 136,xxi; 136, 190; 153,153; 157,113; 158, 196; 158,216; 160,315; 161, 21; (A) 169,133; 185,6; 187, 133; (A) 187,167; 190,387; 191,16; 192,118; 199,127; 226,395; (A) 226,438; (A) 238,72; (A) 250,63; 278,36; 285,38; 290,23; 348,36.
Ring, Frances: 67,236; 75, 127; 78,226; 83,8; 96,48; 110,110; 117,141; 118,196; 161,21.
Ring, Julie: 313,19.
Ring, Lillian: 307,14.
Ringling, Alf. T.: 135,148.
Ringling, Robert: 323,33.
"Ringmaster, The": (R'09) 103,76; 104,123.
"Ringside": (S) 331,30; (R'28) 332,47.
Rin-Tin-Tin: 294,39.
"Rio Grande": (R'16) 183, 273; 183,295.
"Rio Rita": 317,16; (F) 342, 65.
Riots, Audience: 38,101; 44, xiii; 75,xxvi; 131,28; 221, 28; 280,20.
"Rip Van Winkle": (R'05) 57, 268; 124,198; 258,142; 299, 25.
Ripley, Lon: 105,149.
"Ripples": (R'30) 349,46.
Risdon, Elizabeth: 143,16; 193,137; 200,247; 201,264; 201,291; 207,291; 216,81; 217,159; 234,85; 239,99; 248,312; (A) 250,63; 299, 31; 312,19.
Risdon, Kate: 204,127.
"Rise of Jennie Cushing, The": (R,F) 202,394.
"Rise of Rosie O'Reilly, The": (R'23) 276,19.
"Rise of Silas Lapham, The": (R'19) 227,18.
"Rising of the Moon, The": 129, 157; (R'20) 234,108.
"Rising Son, The": (R'24) 286,20.
Risley, Greta: 16,6.
Risser, Marguerite: 259,227.
Rissler, Suzanne: 360,16.
Ristori, Adelaide: 49,64; 55, 212; 69,iv; 80,285; 115, 76; 138,44; 142,198; 150, 68.
"Rita Coventry": (R'23) 265, 19.
Ritchie, Adele: 12,8; 45,273; 63,134; 64,160; 77,185.
Ritchie, Franklin: 55,234;

121, 92.
Riter, Joseph (see Corey and Riter).
"Ritornell": (R'27) 315, 25.
Rittenhouse, Florence: 274, 29.
"Ritzy": 349, 17; (R'30) 349, 47.
"Rivals, The": 116, 127; (R'12) 144, 38; 144, 57; (R'22) 257, 93; 257, 101; 268, 3; 268, 11; (R'23) 268, 15; 285, 7; 292, 5; 301, 10; (D) 312, 16a.
Riverdale County School (New York): 182, 227.
Rives, Amelie: 185, 285.
"Riviera Girl, The": 201, 265; (R'17) 201, 328.
Riviera Theatre (Chicago): 294, 56.
Rivoli Theatre (New York): 202, 403; 202, 406; 204, 118.
Roach, Hal: 293, 34; 319, 11.
Roach Studios: 319, 13.
"Road to Happiness, The": (R) 176, 169; (R'27) 316, 19.
"Road to Mandalay, The": (R'16) 182, 196; (F) 305, 37.
"Road to Rome, The": (R'27) 314, 20; (S) 315, 28.
"Road to Yesterday, The": (R'06) 72, 36; 73, 82; 76, 147.
"Roadhouse in Arden, The": (R'15) 180, 116; 181, 143.
"Roads of Destiny": 215, 15; (R'18) 215, 18.
"Roar China!": 357, 31; (D) 358, 14; 358, 26; (R'30) 358, 66; 359, 43.
Robards, Jason: 317, 39.
Robb, Lotus: 204, 103; 239, 83; 239, 112; 257, 83; 299, 31; 311, 19.
Robb, W. G.: 141, 133.
"Robbery, The": (R'21) 242, 342.
Robbins, Helen: 204, 83; 205, 167; 208, 359.
Robe, Annie: 168, 72.
Robenne, Anna: 292, 17; (D) 310, c.
Robert, Hans: 129, 162.
Robert, Renee: 254, 311; 275, 37.
"Robert E. Lee": 270, 12; (R'23) 274, 15.
"Robert Emmet": (R'02) 19, 8.
Robert, Lyda: 361, 20; 361, 28.
Roberts, Al: 301, 27; 313, 35.
Roberts, Beatrice: 324, 76.
Roberts, Casey: (W) 319, 24.
Roberts, Edith: 239, 137.
Roberts, Emma: 217, 171.
Roberts, Evelyn: 342, 25.
Roberts, Florence: 9, 19; 37, 74; 63, 113; 64, 140; 64, 140; 64, 152; 112, iii; 112, 173; 113, 32.
Roberts, George G.: 104, 123.
Roberts, Hans: 41, 163.
Roberts, Harry: 5, 7.
Roberts, James Booth: 16, 13.
Roberts, Olive: 55, 225.
Roberts, R. A.: 108, xvii.
Roberts, Theodore: 34, 318; 38, 88; 61, 53; 82, 318; 84, 57; 132, 59; 152, 117; 152, 135; 186, 87; 198, 74.
Robertson, Agnes: 49, 73.
Robertson, Aubrey: 49, 72.
Robertson, Catherine: (W) 241, 256.
Robertson, Donald: 65, 194; 90, 214; 111, xxvii; 111, 129; 112, 177; 128, vii; 130, 183.
Robertson, Helen: 77, 178; 99, 162.
Robertson, Jean: 210, 72.
Robertson, John Forbes: 30, 198; 34, 312; 37, 57; 38, 82; 44, 249; 50, 81; 70, 316; 73, 74; 75, 133; 82, 346; 87, 130; 103, 73; 104, 103; 105, 133; 106, 169; 106, 200; 114, 51; 127, 104; 146, 128; 151, 84; 151, 85; 153, 142; 153, 168; 154, 198; 155, 13; 155, 24; 158, 193; 160, 312; (D) 161, c; 161, 15; 161, 48; 165, 215; (A) 182, 216; 187, 131; 201, 264; 202, 393; 202, 400; 222, 102; 243, 424; 280, 32; 297, 76.
Robertson, [Lady] J. F.: 154, 199.
Robertson, Lolita: 92, 258;

142,194; 252,157.
Robertson, Madge: 33,276.
Robertson, Willard: 132,41; 248, 319; 329,24.
Robeson, Paul: 280,15; 293, 24; 310,11; 343,51; 353, 30.
Robie, Louis: 255,354.
"Robin Hood": (R'12) 136,170; 136,173; 145,80; 159,276; 233,46; (F) 259,243; (F,R) 262,54.
Robineau, Priscilla: 311,29.
Robins, Edward H.: 97,80; 97,83; 129,162; 181,153.
Robinson, Bill: 272,35.
Robinson, Clarence: 54,193.
Robinson, E.J.: 286,21.
Robinson, Edward G.: 205,142; 265,31; 290,26; 304,31; 309, 27; 323,39; (C) 334,11; 335, 40; 337,46; (D) 338,27; 338,40; 360,59.
Robinson, Florence: 215,29.
Robinson, Forrest: 28,132; 37,57; 105,147; 140,118.
Robinson, Grace: 274,11.
Robinson, James: 54,193.
Robinson, [Uncle] John: 54,192.
Robinson, Maria Elizabeth (see Robinson, "Perdita").
Robinson, Mary: 36,46.
Robinson, "Perdita": 77,189.
Robinson, Thomas P.: 249,378.
"Robinson Crusoe, Jr.": 182,196; (R'16) 182,238.
"Robinson's Isle": (R'04) 35,5.
Robison, Joseph: 308,19.
Roblee, Milton: 75,118.
Robson, Eleanor: 10,18; 11,11; 12,10; 15,1; 15,2; 23,10; 23,15; 28,133; 28,143; 35, 18; 35,19; 39,c; 50,93; 52,c; 52,142; 53,170; 58, 301; 64,139; 64,142; 69, 284; 70,320; 71,2; 73,77; 78,iii; 97,99; 99,159; 113, 23; 142,196; 155,32; 193, 157; 231,363; 276,29.
Robson, May: 6,6; 24,34; 34, 307; 35,7; 41,175; 48,33; (W) 81,305; 82,xx; 83,15; 83,17; 84,42; 129,158; 130, xiv; 139,94; 159,238; 166, 288; 177,239; (A) 183, 300; 361,48.
Robson, Stuart: 25,64; 27,106; 27,109; 28,137; 103,76; 111,158; 175,128; 237,368.
Robyn, Alred: 184,351.
Rocamora, Suzanne: 37,iv; (W) 42,202.
Rocco, Bertha: 35,2.
Roche, John: 240,172; 242, 343; 252,151; 262,18; 295,39.
Rochester, Claire: 195,269.
Rocholl, Theodor: 147,160.
Rock, William: 76,167; 100, 193; 186,71; 198,83; 204, 83.
"Rock-A-Bye Baby": (R'18) 209,23; 209,31.
"Rockbound": (R'29) 339,44.
Rockey, Howard (W): 353, 42; 354,42; 356,39; 357, 40; 358,39; 360,39; 361, 39.
Rockwell, Ethel Theodore (W): 310,42.
Rockwell, Florence: 7,6; 7,7; 12,11; 28,144; 29, 160; 38,88; 49,69; 57,272; 65,192; 74,87; 75,136; 77, 191; 90,i; 90,208; 103, 93; 106,182; 108,33; 148, 191; 174,74.
Rockwell, George: 329,13; (W) 341,18.
Rodeos: 327,28.
Rodgers, Charles: 134,127.
Rodgers, Richard: 331,27; 361,37.
Rodin, Auguste: 131,20.
Rodriguez, Isabel: 212,217.
Rodriguez, Luisa: 107,32.
Roebuck, Mabel: 83,2; 99, 135; 100,xviii; 106,168.
Roeder, Charlotte: 90,207.
Roeder, Ralph: 178,279; 197, 15.
Roesner, Walt: 330,47.
"Roger Bloomer": (R'23) 265,15.
Rogers Brothers: 6,18; 20, 8; 22,30; 32,245; 42,ii; 80,xviii; 109,xii.
"Rogers Brothers in Harvard":

22, 8f.
"Rogers Brothers in Ireland, The": 56, 254.
"Rogers Brothers in London, The": (R'03) 32, 245.
"Rogers Brothers in Panama, The": (R'07) 80, xviii.
"Rogers Brothers in Washington, The": 8, 2.
Rogers, Charles: 317, 39; 322, 50; 341, 28.
Rogers, Charles T. (W, V): 107, 18.
Rogers, Ferne: 156, 59.
Rogers, Ginger: 358, 41.
Rogers, Helen: 183, 276; 199, 132.
Rogers, John: 250, 24; 250, 40.
Rogers, Katherine: 168, 73.
Rogers, Max: 109, xii.
Rogers, Robert: 105, 149.
Rogers, Will: 135, xvi; 181, 125; (W) 197, 12; 210, 76; 213, 328; 228, 106; 237, 378; 237, 380; 242, 348; 250, 38; (C) 263, 11; 302, 38; 303, 36; (W) 320, 9; 333, 46.
Rohe, Alice (W): 250, 14; 258, 137; 260, 303; 263, 9; 266, 9; 269, 46; 272, 20; 289, 20.
Rohe, Margaret: 29, 161.
Roland, Frederick: 70, 337; 202, 347; 205, 159; 236, 288.
Roland, Gertrude: 177, 229.
Roland, Gilbert: 323, 46.
Roland, Mildred: 185, 34.
Roland, Ruth: 217, 192; 235, 234; 264, 41.
Rolanda, Mlle.: 204, 89.
Rolando, Rose: 242, 329; 245, 115; 253, 243; 263, 23; 282, 25; (C) 286, 15.
Rolfe, B. A.: 231, 392.
"Roll of Honor, The": 204, 82.
Rolland, Adele: 118, 170; 247, 239; 249, 382; 257, 111.
Rolland, Gustave: 237, 365; 266, 18.
Roller, Olga: 195, 276.
"Rollicking Girl, The": (R'05) 52, 135; 52, 137; 54, 197.
"Rolling Stones": (R'15) 176, 169.
"Rollo's Wild Oat": 239, 83; (R'20) 239, 105; (D) 243, 396.
"Roly-Boly Eyes": (R'19) 225, 344; 226, 371; (D) 228, 85.
"Roly Poly": (R'12) 143, 5; 144, 44.
Romain, Irene: 161, 30.
Romain, Jules: 300, 31.
Romaine, Margaret: 158, 182; 158, 212; 159, 267; 161, 21; 161, 27; 215, 11.
Roman Theatre: 176, 189.
"Romance": 145, 65; (R'13) 145, 66.
"Romance And Arabella": 202, 353.
"Romance of a Poor Young Man, The": (D) 134, 130.
"Romance of Happy Valley, A": (F, R) 217, 191.
"Romance of the Air, A": (F, R 214, 392.
"Romance of the American Theatre, The" (Crawford) (B): 159, 276.
"Romancing 'Round": (R'27) 321, 80.
"Romantic Young Lady, The": (R'26) 304, 15.
Romberg, Sigmund: 291, 23; 302, 21; (W) 333, 27; 357, 33; 360, 56.
"Romeo and Juliet": 15, 1; (R'02) 15, 2; 22, 25; (R'03) 25, 59; 25, 65; 28, 132; (R'03) 28, 143; (R'04) 46, 292; 46, 307; 46, 312; 50, 92; (R'05) 52, 136; 69, 309; 73, 78; (F) 92, 264; 113, 23; 146, 114; 163, 124; (OP) 165, 212; 179, 6; (R) 179, 10; (D) 182, 206; 263, 3; (R'23) 264, 16; (R'23) 264, 20; 265, 17; 293, 17; 319, 46; 351, 48.
Romer, Sebastian ("Buster"): (W) 189, 272.
Romer, Violet: 137, iii.
Romilly, Rita: 244, 26.
Romo, Amparo: 107, 32.
"Romola": (F) 286, 33.
Roof Gardens: 39, 134; 41, 160; 42, 188; 53, 158; 69, 170; 108, xv.

Rook, Helen: (D) 208,341.
Rooke, Irene: 146,111.
"Rooms to Rent": 72,42.
Rooney, Kate: 159,240.
Rooney, Pat: 160,317; 243, 421; 285,37.
Roorbach, Eloise: (W) 189, 290.
Roos, Joanna: 246,145; 247, 225; 258,139; (D) 351,19; 352,43.
Roosevelt, Theodore: 87,120; (W) 321,17.
Root, Ivy Ashton: 68,265.
"Rope": (R'28) 326,40.
"Rope, The": (R'18) 208,358.
"Rope's End": (R'29) 344,74.
Rork, Ann: 311,35; 323,27.
Rorke, Ina: 166,269.
Rosaire, Robert: (D) 275,27.
"Rosalind": 176,167.
"Rosander, Rose": 238,25.
"Rosary, The": (R'10) 118, xxii.
Rose, Durant: 40,147.
Rose, Edward E.: 11,6; 13,6.
Rose, Eleanor: 171,238.
Rose, Guilbert: 243,403.
Rose, Harry: 182,230.
Rose, Polly: 353,23.
Rose, Ruth: 104,128; 247,231.
"Rose, The": 51,112; (R'05) 51,113.
"Rose and the Ring, The": 71,18.
"Rose Bernd": 40,156; (R'22) 261,375.
"Rose Briar": (R'23) 264,16.
"Rose Girl, The": (R'21) 241, 304; 242,329.
"Rose Maid, The": 136,xviii; (R'12) 136,172; 136,175.
"Rose Marie": (R'24) 284,16; (F) 325,34.
"Rose O'Plymouth Town, A": (R'02) 21,9.
"Rose of Algeria, The": 105,v; (R'09) 105,xiv.
"Rose of China, The": (R'19) 227,61; 228,99.
"Rose of Kildare, The": 142, 190.
"Rose of Panama, The": (R'12) 133,xv; 133,94.
"Rose of Stamboul, The": (R'22) 254,308.
"Rose of the Alhambra, The": (R'07) 73,61.
"Rose of the Rancho, The": (R'06) 71,4; 71,11; (F) 166,275.
"Roseanne": (R'23) 276,16.
"Rosedale": (R'13) 147,xii.
Roselle, Anne: 283,35.
Roselle, William: 104,123; 159,232; 173,6.
Rosemary: 265,21.
Rosemary And Capella: 305, 19.
Rosen, James E.: 99,158.
Rosen, Max: 205,147.
Rosenfeld, Sydney: 22,8; 35,1; 55,227; 148,163; (W) 286, 12; 288,25.
"Rosenkavalier, Der": (OP) 123,170; 123,171; 124,viii; (R'14) 156,67.
Rosenthal, Harry: 345,33; 347, 35.
Rosenthal, Moriz: 68,262; 70,341; 269,37.
Roshanara: 193,143; 200,201; 206,225; 211,137; 238, 23; 284,5.
Rosmer, Milton: 146,111.
"Rosmersholm": (R'04) 39, 112; 84,31; (R'07) 84,33; (R'25) 292,16.
"Rosmunda": 106,188.
Ross, Arthur: 111,146.
Ross, Charles J.: 64,160; 95,21; 104,111; 110,120; 132,68; 137,11; 160,317.
Ross, Corinne: 349,43.
Ross, David: 111,146; 353,43; 361,39.
Ross, Douglas: 333,48.
Ross, Frances: 202,347.
Ross, Frederick: 178,308.
Ross, Herman: (D) 244,8; 245, 104;246,162; 283,27.
Ross, Lillian: 205,148; 205, 163.
Ross, Mabel: 27,130.
Ross, Richard: 173,12; 212, 195; 214,351.
Ross, Robert: (D) 346,29.

Ross, Thomas W.: 38,92; (A) 54,183f; 55,215; 59,10; 69, 286; 129,177.
Ross, Vera: 304,19; 311,31; (D) 323,23.
Rosse, Herman: (D) 246,162; 283,27.
Rossi, Tulio: 118,173.
Rossignol, Aimee: 235,175.
Rostand, Edmond: 5,10; 6,12; 17,13; 31,224; 46,299; 49,v; 56,249; 73,vi; 77,195; 94, 338; 98,134; 109,78; 116, xii; (W,V) 117,152; 122,132; 133,89; 134,107; 161,33; 215,12.
Rostand, Maurice: 122,132; 161, 33; 263,38; (D) 294,29.
Roswitha: 27,115.
Roth, Lillian: 199,135; 232,517.
Rothappel, S. L.: 202,403; 220, 393; 220,396; 289,38; 313,37; 316,40; 320,54; 324,21.
Rothschild, Zeta (W): 210,90; 212,224; 252,172.
Rothe, Anita: 110,102.
Rothier, Leon: 120,48; 123, 148; (A) 131,xiv; 131,4; 168,66; 178,285; 214,335; 225,297; (A) 226,438; (A) 238,72; 268,36; 290,41.
"Rotters, The": (R'22) 257, 95.
"Round-Up, The": 77,191; (R'07) 80,xiv; 81,300.
Rousby, Clara: 293,38.
Routman, Isaac: 57,266.
Rowan, Lansing: 69,301.
Rowland, Adele: 119,18; 121, 88; 130,207; 168,67; 172,297; 180,70; 186,83; 192,103; 192,124; 196,c; 221,17; 232, 522; 251,116; 258,157; 281, 36.
Rowland, Irene: (W,V) 14,22.
Rowland, Mabelle: 33,280; 40, 149; 41,c; 275,29.
Rowley, J. De La Mare: (W) 156,73.
Roxy (see Rothafel, S. L.).
Roxy Theatre (New York): (D) 300,36.
Roy, Walter: 260,300.
"Royal Chef, The": (R'04) 44,248.
"Royal Family, A": 11,12; (S) 324,28.
"Royal Family of Broadway, The": (F,R) 359,47; 359, 48.
"Royal Fandango, A": (R'23) 274,58.
"Royal Mounted, The": (R'08) 87,viii; 87,123; 88,166.
"Royal Rival, A": 8,9; (R'01) 8,10.
Royal Theatre (Berlin): 165, 219.
Royal Theatre (Hanover): 66,203.
"Royal Vagabond, The": 218, 201; (R'19) 218,207; 218, 227; 220,358.
"Royal Virgin, The": (R'30) 350,46.
Royalties, Author's: 50,102; 71,19; 88,iv; 88,169; 97, 92; 106,186; 149,29; 153, 150; 196,353; 291,9.
Royalty and Theatre: 101,34; 159,242; 239,84.
Royce, Brigham: 63,127; 192, 73.
Royce, Edward: 333,48.
Royce, Julian: 104,127.
Roye, Ruth: 189,278.
Royle, Edwin Milton: 32,244; 65,188; 79,240; 81,290; 121,97; 159,230; 196,353; 278,25.
Royle, Josephine: 249,377; 252,173.
Royle, Selena: 37,70; 265, 18; 265,31; 278,22; 332, 39; 357,42.
Royton, Helen: 50,104; 91, 236; 92,280.
Ruben, Jose: 189,269; 192,90; 196,340; 203,20; 230,258; 239,83; 249,371; 253,219; 301,52b; 303,19; 335,15; 191,29.
Rubens, Alma: 204,128; 229, 192; 244,35; 306,35; 328, 14.
Rubens, Paul: 32,238.
"Rubicon, The": 254,301.
Rubini, Jan: 302,46.
Rubinstein, Artur: 61,v.

Rubinstein, Ida: 125,5; (D) 155, 10.
Rubinstein, Erna: 257,92.
"Rubiyat of Omar Khayyam, The": (F) 237,379.
"Ruby Red": 206,225; (R'19) 227,21.
Ruckerts, Hilda: 177,221.
Rudami, Rosa: 322,31.
"Ruddigore": 229,159; (R'27) 316,18.
Rudersorf, Mde.: 106,197.
Ruffo, Titta: 141,130; 143,17; 158,207; 177,248.
"Rufus Le Maire's Affairs": (R'27) 315,24.
Ruggles, Charles: 176,186; 178, 302; 184,359; 193,153; 219, 277; 225,315; 309,21.
"Ruggles of Red Gap": (R'15) 180,65.
"Ruined Lady, The": (R'20) 229,181; 229,183.
"Ruint": (R'25) 291,17.
"Rule of Three, The": 158,170; (R'14) 158,172.
"Ruling Passions": (R, F) 213,320.
"Ruling Power, The": (R'04) 38,84; 38,85.
Rulowa, Shura: 273,35.
Rumann, Siegfried: 358,28; 359, 35.
Rumel, Meta: (W) 295,24.
Rumford, Kennerley: 157,141.
Rumsey, John W.: 134,x.
Rumsey, Marion: 195,318.
"Runaway, The": 129,150; (R'11) 129,151; (R'03) 28,134; 28, 135; 29,157; 29,163.
Runnells, Burnell: 54,193.
"Running For Office": (R'03) 28,134.
Rush, Cecilia: 13,22.
Rush, Peggy: 178,308; 179, 14.
Rushmore, Vivian: 143,19; 151, 106; 160,307; 234,104; 238, 51.
Rushworth, Frank: 13,23; 93,304.
Russ, Emily: 173,24.
Russ, Gianina: 69,289; 75,138; 85,84.
Russell, Alexander: (W) 341,21.
Russell, Annie: 8,20; 10,26; 11,1; 11,5; 11,10; 24,27; 27,c; 37,59; 39,120; 41, 174; 47,6; 52,153; 60,30; 67,236; 69,300; 84,43; 94,323; 95,xx; 95,xxii; 95, 3; 100,194; 109,93; 120,37; 120,62; 142,xviii; 143,5; 144,38; 144,56; 144,57; 150, c; 157,141; 161,16; (W) 164,177; 167,10; 170,191; 285,52; 290,12.
Russell, Dorothy: 58,301.
Russell, Edmund: 28,136; 221, 56.
Russell, F.C. (W): 224,218; 226,378; 228,92; 301,62.
Russell, Georgie: 61,66.
Russell, Harold: 9,11.
Russell, Henry: 88,167; 119,8.
Russell, John Patten (W): 354, 56; 356,70; 357,72; 358, 72; 359,70; 360,70.
Russell, Lillian: PG,8; 6,8; (A) 16,19; 24,c; 34,307; 46,295; 46,316; 48,44; 58,301; 67,242; 70,325; 75,118; 92,c; 92,xv; 92, 260; 93,xx; 93,xxii; 103, 71; 105,xiii; 105,148; 111, 136; 118,189; 127,101; 128, 127; 133,74; 134,114; 136, 190; 163,119; (A) 165,236; 175,236; 175,126; (W) 179, 22; 183,292; 188,202; (A) 201,304; 202,384; (A) 214, 379; 231,363; 245,96; 248, 318; 257,88.
Russell, Marie Booth: 50,90; 70,336; 98,108; 123,163; 142,199; 142,200.
Russell, Sol Smith: 16,5.
Russell, William: 205,195; 208,404; 208,406; 228,147; (A) 249,431.
Russell, Zella: 236,281.
Russian Balalaika Orchestra: 119,6.
Russian Ballet (see also Pavlowa, Anna): 102,51.
Russian Dance: 125,2; 127,92; 130,198; 139,74; 158,181; 161,30; 176,166; 178,294; 178,340; 200,205; 250,22;

295, 12; 299, 29.
Russian Films: 260, 308; 352, 16.
"Russian Honeymoon, The": 62, 101.
Russian Opera: 256, 30.
Russian Theatre (see also Kamerny Theatre; Moscow Art Theatre): 42, 203; 50, iv; 57, xi; 58, 315; 84, xii; 86, 91; 151, 108; 152, 137; 161, 21; 232, 530; 253, 236; 254, 298; 256, 28; 263, 3; 281, 12; 293, 16; 294, 12; 308, 20; 338, 35.
Russo, Dominico: 104, 114.
"Rust": (R'24) 279, 16; 279, 27.
Rustic Theatre (Quebec): 89, 189.
Ruth, Babe: 312, 38.
Ruth, Jay W.: (W) 354, 39.
Ruth, Joan: 285, 35.
Rutherford, Jack: (C) 337, 35.
Rutherford, John: 262, 18.
Rutherford, Montague: 252, 151.
"Rutherford and Son": (R'12) 144, xi; 144, 45.
Rutter, Louise: 85, 62; 128, 113; 138, 47; 139, 90; 190, 367.
Rutz-Nissen, Grethe: 278, 13.
Ryan, Don: (W) 277, 24.
Ryan, Else: 69, 292; 73, 80; 94, 316; 115, 74; 120, 44; 134, 126.
Ryan, Georgie: 240, 172.
Ryan, Manie: 42, 196.
Ryan, Mary: 49, 74; 91, 244; 102, 52; 105, 147; 108, 54; 114, c; 144, 43; 147, c; 151, xxii; 164, 169; 164, 192; 173, 28; 175, 163; 177, 235; 182, 244; 195, 270; 205, 142; 206, 214; 206, 215; (A) 226, 438; 228, 99; 248, 310; 251, 103; 272, 27.
Ryan, Nancy: 332, 48.
Ryder, John: 152, 138.
Ryley, Madeline Lucette: 23, 6; 24, 30.
Ryskind, Morrie (W, V): 189, 267; 192, 72.
Ryther-Fuller, Martha: 198, 92.

--S--

"S. S. Glencairn": (R'24) 286, 22.
"S. S. Tenacity": (R'22) 252, 166.
"Sabbatai Zewi": 104, 132.
Sabine, Martin: 180, 74.
Sacchetto, Rita: 105, 138; 106, 172; 107, 13; 114, 47.
Saccur, Alma: 90, 207.
Sackett, Albert: 155, 21.
"Sacrament of Judas, The": 35, 5.
"Sacred and Profane Love": 230, 258; (R) 230, 270.
"Sacrifiee, La": 89, 186.
Sadanji; 79, 251; 220, 362.
"Sadie Love": 179, 8; (R'15) 179, 9.
Sadler's Wells (London) 64, 159; 360, 44.
"Safe For Democracy": (F, R) 214, 392.
Safety (see Theatres).
"Safety First": 192, 80; 192, 81.
Safonoff, Wassili: 63, 138.
Sage, Stuart: 244, 33.
Saharet: 25, 74; 97, 98.
Sahary-Djeli: 179, 31.
Sainpolis, John: 146, 105.
St. Albans, Khyva: 178, 277; 179, 45: 183, 293; 213, 269.
St. Clair, Clare: 354, 25.
St. Clair, Edith: 38, 87.
St. Clair, Marguerite: 165, 232.
St. Claire, Eleanor: 126, 47; 136, 192; 171, 239; 197, 43.
St. Cyr, Dirce: (W) 59, 11.
St. Denis, Ruth (see also Denishawn Dancers): 61, 62; 65, 193; 106, 172; 127, 94; 146, 115; 156, 82; 180, 76; 181, 142; 183, c; 183, 269; 189, 278; 191, 35; 214, 343; 218, 215; 258, 165; (D) 268, 26; (D) 279, 17; 293, 6; 306, 31; 322, 13; 357, 44.
"Saint Joan": 276, 14; (R'23) 276, 14; (R'23) 276, 14; 279, 20; (D) 292, 12.
St. John, Marguerite: 59, 24; 124, 205; 135, 153; 224, 220; 269, 14.

St. Leon, Ida: 229,187.
St. Louis Exposition: 43,vii.
St. Louis (Missouri) Theatre: 165,222; 184,340; 217,167; 223,174.
"St. Patrick at Tara": 125, 21.
St. Paul (Minnesota) Theatre: 332,18.
Saint-Saens, Camille: 69,289; 70,341; 182,220.
St. Vincent's College (Chicago): 87,126.
Saker, Annie: 164,153; 166,289.
Sakharoff, Alexander: 229,179; 258,133.
Sakharoff, Clotilde: 229,179.
Saki, Marion: 212,199.
"Sakuntala": (R'04) 43,236.
"Salammbo" (OP): (R,S) 3,14.
Salaries, Actors (see also Economics of Theatre): 122,135; 197,8; 198,86; 207,274; 209,54; 308,10; 344,33.
Salazar, Manuel: 236,271; 271, 37.
Sale, Charles ("Chic"): 218, 199; 268,43; 298,27.
Saleza, Albert: PG,9; (A) 3,17.
Salignac, Thomas: 11,20; 11, 21.
Salisbury, Jane: 157,128; 162, 70.
Salisbury, Marie: 55,225.
Salisbury, Monroe: 208,405; 208,406; 218,257.
"Sally": 240,171; (R'20) 240, 178; 240,176; 253,226; (F,R) 291,34; (F(346,59.
"Sally in Our Alley": (R'02) 20,9.
"Sally of the Sawdust": (F,R) 295, 32.
"Salome": (OP) 61,79; 64,144; (OP) 73,70; 88,164; 91,235; (OP) 94,335; 95,5; (OP) 97,76; 98,130; 107,xiv; (F) 207,331; (R'18) 208,355; 208,359; (F,R) 213,320; (F,R) 264,74; 293,41.
"Salomy Jane": (R'07) 73,60; 73,77; 75,130; (F) 166, 274.
Salt Lake Theatre (Utah): 97, 88; 179,34.
Salter, Harold: (D) 255,375; 266,18.
Saltus, Edgar: (W) 9,14.
Saltzmann-Stevens, Minnie: 102,57.
"Salvation Nell": (R'08) 92,2; 95,19; (S) 96,54; 99, 144; 143,22.
Salvini, Gustavo: 17,7; 28,142; 55,218; 149,21; 181,130.
Salvini, Maud: 34,311.
Salvini, Tomasso: 17,7; 24,45; 28,142; (W) 63,116; 112, 184; 116,v; 168,74; 180,62; 181,130; (A,D) 181,130.
"Sam Abramovitch": (R'27) 312,21.
"Sam Houston": (R'06) 70, xxix.
"Samaratine, La": 59,3.
Sammarco, Mario: 67,233; 73, 64; 75,138; 74,85; 81,315; 85,85; 93,309; 96,42; 96, 43; 134,110.
Sampson, William: 120,42; 137,13; 232,519; 238,12.
Sams, William H.: 349,45.
Samson, Ivan: 250,35.
"Samson": (S) 91,234; (R'08) 94,314; 94,332; 94,333; 95,28.
"Samson and Delilah": (OP) 95,12; 238,58.
Samuels, Harold: 332,27; 338, 43.
Samuels, Maurice V.: 192,122.
San Carlo Theatre (Naples): 52,144.
San Francisco Earth Quake: 64,146; 65,184; 138,50.
San Francisco Theatre: 64,146; 138,50; 213,299; 229,195; 276,42; 276,71.
San Gabriel (California) Mission Play: 147,153; 250,19.
San Mateo Theatre (California): 301,66.
San Quentin Penitentiary: 131, 23.
Sanborn, Pitts: (W) 208, 352.
"Sancho Panza": (R'23) 275,

16; (D) 275,27.
"Sandalwood": (R'26) 308,15.
"Sandbar Queen, The": (R'18) 205, 151; 205,159.
Sanders, Mary: PG,17; 24,38; 132,48.
Sanders, Pearl: 34,304.
Sanderson, Adele: 304,19.
Sanderson, Julia: 54,195; 66, 208; 66,209; 80,270; 80, 281; 83,7; 109,96; 112,c; 125, 33; 128,120; 128,124; 139,78; 145,66; 145,67; 146,109; 149, 24; 151,93; 163,97; 164,167; 164,190; 165,c; 165,201; 169, 142; 177,240; 177,245; 181, 135; 186,62; 191,16; 199, 127; 199,155; 199,184; 201, 281; 202,357; 210,89; (A) 214,379; (A) 226,438; 238, 33; 247,213; 247,218; 250, 57; 255,365.
Sanderson, Sybil: 10,32.
"Sandro Boticelli": (R.23) 266, 15.
Sands, Anna: 204,93; 229,169.
Sands, Dorothy: 294,21; 300, 19; 303,13.
Sands, Martin: 181,141.
Sanford, Erskine: 207,295; 242,319.
Santa Barbara (California) Theatre: 301,39; 301,40; 340,47.
Santje, Suzanne: 59,7.
Santley, Fred: 173,3; 218, 201.
Santley, Joseph: 132,69; 143, 22; 151,101; 180,66; 197, 36; 215,37; 217,149; 233, 36; 249,367; 257,92; 260, 320; 281,36; 322,34.
Santley, Maude: 165,212.
Santschi, Thomas: 169,127.
"Sap, The": (R'24) 287,62.
"Sapphire Ring, The": (R'25) 291,17.
"Sappho": 60,34; 216,84; 294, 16; 338,15.
"Sappho and Phaon": (S) 80, 262; (C) 82,xxiv; (R'07) 82, 318; 82,341.
Saranoff: 186,63.
Sarcey, Francisque: 26,85.
Sardou, Victorien: 12,7; 25,73; 27,112; 37,61; 37,72; 46, 299; 54,186; 60,30; (W) 63,133; 69,xiii; 71,19; 76, 146; 79,xi; 84,37; 87,xvi; 94,317; 165,214.
"Sardou and the Sardou Plays": (Hart) (B): 160,328.
Sarg, Tony (D): 199,138; 217, 162; 249,389; 250,33; 251, 101; 252,169; 253,237; 254, 309; 255,375; 256,59.
Sargent, Franklin: 271,7.
"Sari": (R'14) 156,104; (R'30) 348,70.
Sari, Lari: 275,11.
Sarjeantson, Kate: 176,167.
Sarony, Nora: 48,35.
Saroya, Bianca: 248,317; 271, 37.
Satchel, Blanche: 320,61.
Sato, Chiye-Ko: 161,31.
"Saturday Night": (R'26) 310, 18.
"Saturday to Monday": 201,265; (R'17) 201,280.
"Saturday's Children": 314,22; (S) 316,24; (C) 319,72.
"Sauce for the Goose": (R'11) 123,x.
Sauchelli, Francesco (W): 220,364; 222,104.
"Saucy Sally": (R'04) 39,110; 39,111.
Sauermann, Carl: 145,88.
Sauganash Hotel (Chicago): 124,199.
Saunders, Gertrude: 295,21.
Saunders, Jackie: 184,356; 200,246; 209,55; 230,288.
Saunders, Louise: 213,273.
Saunders, Madge: 171,256.
Saus, Amparo: 203,9.
Savage, C. Courtenay (W): 200,220; (FI) 229,162; (FI) 224,226.
Savage, Frances: 155,21; 158, 216.
Savage, Henry W.: 26,81; 43, 226; 62,96; 67,229; 69, 302; 70,xxvi; 79,252; 82, xxii; 82,330; 91,229; 94, xxxiii; 103,70; 106,xxxiv; 118,xxiv; 126,viii; 127,78;

130, xxxii; 139, 69; 142, xxi; 151, 82; 187, 126; 190, 413; 191, 14; 202, 410; 207, 282; 214, 398; 223, 144; 246, 166; 273, 79; 294, 64; 298, 8.
Savage, Nelly: 285, 11; 289, 11; 313, 25.
Savage, Richard (W) (see also Vaudeville): 53, 235; 59, 9; 61, 77; 70, 327; 105, 149; 106, 186; 131, 26; 142, 191; 180, 75; 198, 98; 245, 76; 251, 108; 276, 13; 285, 24; 297, 12; 300, 22; 303, 24; 307, 18; 309, 24; 311, 24.
"Savages Under the Skin": (R'27) 315, 25.
Savannah (Georgia) Theatre: 69, v.
"Savelli, La": 74, 98.
Savile, Hubert (W): 198, 64; 203, 10; 204, 92; 205, 140; 216, 88; 217, 138; 217, 148; 221, 34; 223, 146.
Saville, John: 32, 243; 95, 30.
Saville, Nina: 83, 17.
"Saving Grace, The": (R'18) 213, 277.
"Saviors": (R'15) 172, 282.
Savo, Jimmy: 279, 14; 281, 17; (C) 343, 2; (C) 343, 40; 353, 30; 354, 20.
Savoy, Bert (see also Savoy and Brennan): 260, 293; 263, 26.
Savoy, Viola: 64, 142.
Savoy and Brennan: (C) 262, 26; 263, 26.
Savoy Producing Co.: 175, 110.
Sawmura, Sonosuke: 207, 298.
Sawyer, Ivy: 197, 36; 215, 37; 217, 149; 219, 312; 281, 36; 221, 19; 249, 367; 250, 34; 257, 92; 272, 3; 302, 51.
Sawyer, Jane: 170, 166; 174, 70; 201, 294; 202, 365.
Saxe-Meiningen, Duke, of (see also Meiningen): 125, 24.
Saxon, Marie: 314, 46; 330, 12; 334, 55; 345, 55.
Sayer, Margaret: 33, 274.
Sayler, Oliver M. (W): 207, 298; 259, 215; 261, 369; 264, 22; 294, 12; 347, 39; 359, 8.
Sayre, Katherine: 252, 151.
Sayre, Theodore Bort: 8, 10; 25, 59; 44, 256; 55, 227; 83, xiv.
Scaife, Gillian: 104, 101.
"Scalawag, The": (R'27) 315, 26.
"Scandal": (R'19) 225, 340; 226, 370; (R'10) 118, xx.
"Scandal Sheet": (R, F) 361, 47.
"Scandale, Le": 99, 140.
"Scandals of 1920": (R'20) 233, 29.
"Scandals of 1924": (R'24) 282, 15.
Scanlan, Walter: 217, 145.
"Scaramouche": (F, R) 273, 30.
Scarborough, George: 152, 124.
Scarborough, Harry: 111, 131.
"Scarecrow, The": 108, 56; (R'11) 121, 71; 121, 85; 136, 184.
Scarlet, Lillian: 261, 383.
"Scarlet Fox, The": (R'28) 327, 37.
"Scarlet Man, The": (R'21) 247, 279.
"Scarlet Pages": (C) 344, 4; 344, 46.
"Scarlet Pimpernel, The": 117, 129; (R'10) 118, xvii; 118, 190; 118, 191.
"Scarron": 56, 262.
"Scars of Jealousy": (F, R) 268, 34.
Scene Design: (D) 171, 248; 175, 124; 178, 316; 180, 82; (D) 182, 219; (D) 185, 33; 195, 266; (D) 206, 228; 220, 336; 231, 361; 240, 182; (D) 246, 162; 287, 41; 296, 13; 300, 32; 316, 10; (D) 348, 42; 351, 20; 36, 130.
Scene Design -- Films: 319, 24.
Scene Painting: 90, 203.
Scenery (see also Scene Design; Stagecraft): 32, 256; 50, 104; 90, 203; 108, 49; 122, 113; 155, 10; 185, 33; 187, 128; 191, 44; 198, 76.
Scenic Effects: 13, 28; 61, 57.
Schaaf, Myrtle: (A) 265, 61.
Schafer, Natalie: 334, 45.
Schaffer, Sylvester: 163, 139; 164, 195.

Schannen, Nicholas: 208,359.
Schauten, Charles: 257,92.
Scheerer, Maud: 234,109.
Scheff, Fritzi; 33,289; 35,13; 37,c; 46,297; 48,xii; (W) 52,141; 52,142; 58,292; 60,32; 60,33; 63,c; 63,128; 63,130; 93,297; 95,1; 95,2; 96,xx; 96,xxii; 113,13; 113,15; 114,55; 127,77; 129,160; 129, 166; 130,xiv; 158,199; 165, 206; 166,285; 185,22; 272, 23; 290,43; 340,10.
Scheffauer, Herman: (W) 103, 88.
Scheidemantel, Karl: 154,200.
Scheider, May: 99,166; 119, 20; 165,218.
Schell, Sherril (W): 107,31; 209,38.
Schellin, Walter: 202,353.
Schelling, Ernest: 170,184; 176, 286; 185,25; 333,25.
Schenck, Elliott: 105,145.
Schenck, Joseph M.: 319,11.
Schildkraut, Josef: 243,407; 244,5; 246,143; 247,220; 248,338; 253,219; 259,222; 263,38; 265,12; 265,18; 265,24; 267,21; 286,21; 289,63; 290,13; 290,26; 307,35; 310,39; 311,49; 320, 27; 337,32; 360,26; 360,36.
Schildkraut, Rudolf: 126,60; 144,54; 265,24; 285,38; 310, 39; 320,27.
Schiller, Frederich: 63,112; 63, 124; 92,282.
Schilling, Margaret: 348,36.
Schipa, Tito: 265,38; 331,23.
Schlusnus, Heinrich: 330,23; 359,36.
Schmidt, Kate: 177,221.
Schmolz, Helena: 130,202.
Schnebbe, Allan S.: 299,23.
Schneider, Adelheid: 93,290.
Schneider, Elizabeth: 112,190.
Schnitzler, Arthur: 73,xvi; 111, xxix; 134,xvi; 137,5; 140, 106; 201,310; 203,22; 271, 74; 297,25.
Schnitzler, Germaine: 170,184; 194,229.
Schober, Elizabeth: 74,92.
Schoedsack, Ernest B.: 316,40.
Schon, Margaret: 295,33.
"School for Husbands, The": (R'05) 51,107; 51,117.
"School for Scandal, The": (R'02) 13,8; 53,166; 100, 169; 107,8; (R'10) 108, 62; 111,167; 146,115; 269, 18; (R'25) 297,44; (R'25) 299,18.
"School Girl, The": (R'04) 44, 243; 44,246.
Schools, Drama: 45,xi; 69, 308; 70,i; 74,xix; 86,vi; 124,212; 131,xiii; 139,92; 156,88; 159,249; 184,337; 208,350; 225,318; 242,385; 266,74; 271,76; 282,68; 320,4c.
Schorr, Friedrich: 278,35.
Schrader, Fred. F. (W): 61,i,b; 66,xi; 73,79; 76, 150; 78,viii; 85,81; 91,249; (V) 161,10.
Schreiber, Georges: (C) 337, 35.
Schrode, William C.: 46,301.
Schroeder, Corona: 63,125.
Schumann, Elizabeth: 168,64.
Schumann-Heink, Ernestine: 10, 28; 12,21; 42,188; 45,268; 45,267; 69,289; 81,315; 83, 7; 129,166; 185,25; 203, 17; 231,367; 342,27.
Schwab, Charles M.: (W) 325,15.
Schwab, Laurence (W): 329, 34; 335,37.
Schwartz, Arthur: (W) 359,20.
Schwartz, Jean: 179,26.
Schwartz, Joseph: 298,35.
Schwartz, Maurice: 254,295; 265,14.
Schweid, Mark: 251,91.
"Schweiger": (R'26) 303,16.
Schweighofer, Felix: 13,20.
Scotch Theatre: 129,152.
Scott, Agnes: 48,38.
Scott, Betty: 140,108.
Scott, Clement: 8,18; 71,19.
Scott, Cyril: 37,57; 56,243; 87,ix; 87,123; 88,166; 89,c; 105,158; 107,iii; 108,53; 111,xviii; 111,151; 113,17; 190,365; 200,197; 225,309.

Scott, Edith: 339,21.
Scott, Elise: 55,236.
Scott, Grayce: 9,20; 10,16.
Scott, Henri: 104,114.
Scott, Howard: 133,97.
Scott, Ivy: 152,132.
Scott, Janet: 246,154; 247, 266.
Scott, Mabel Juliene: 212,251; 226,404.
Scott Sisters (Clara and Jean): 305,25.
Scotti, Antonio: 10,30; 85,82; 94,346; 107,10; 118,173; 129,154; 132,50; 143,8; 149, 10; 179,38; 190,345; 242,327; 288,35.
"Scouts of the Plains, The": 41,173.
"Scrambled Wives": 235,165; (R'20) 235,186.
"Scrap of Paper, A": 160,281; (R'14) 160,319; 165,229; (R'17) 201,279.
"Scrape O' The Pen, A": (R'12) 141,132; 141,133.
"Scratch My Back": (F,R) 233, 38.
Scribe, Eugene: 20,5; 75,124.
Scribe, Honore St. Simon (W): 338,22; 340,22.
"Sea Gull, The": 185,3; (R'16) 185,10; (D) 346,29; (R'30) 349,74.
"Sea Hawk, The": (F,R) 281,30; (F) 281,31.
"Sea of Dreams, A": (F) 268, 34.
"Sea of Ice, The": (D) 134, 131.
"Sea Woman, The": (R'25) 295, 15.
Seabrook, W.B.: (W) 217,162.
Seabrooke, S.: 31,233.
Seabrooke, Thomas Q.: 17,4; 61,61; 124,191.
"Sealed Hearts": (R,F) 228, 106.
"Search Me": (R'15) 175,157.
Sears, Gwen: (W) 219,298.
Sears, Lucille: 344,13.
Sears, Miriam: 226,379; 235, 179.
Sears, Zelda: 91,250; 95,6; 119,x; 119,19; 120,58; 122, 127; 159,226; 168,58; 169,132; 199,151; 215,28; 219,277; 225, 315; 243,419; 272,75; (W) 282,24.
Seastrom, Dorothy: 308,40.
Seastrom, Victor: 297,30.
Seater, Gladys: 171,238.
Seaton, Violet: 142,181.
Seaward, Sydney: 338,45.
Sebel, Frances: 359,36.
"Second Fiddle, The": (R'05) 47,6; 47,8.
"Second In Command, The": 8,1; 8,3; (R'13) 154,176.
"Second Man, The": 316,18.
"Second Mrs. Tanqueray, The": (R'02) 12,2; (R'13) 145, xxix; (R'24) 286,20.
"Secret, The": 156,75; (R'13) 156,99.
"Secret of Polichinelle, The": (R'04) 37,59; 37,75.
"Secret of the Storm Country": (F,R) 202,394.
"Secret Orchard, The": 82,321; 84,46.
"Secret Service": 64,167.
"Secret Strings": 167,5; (R'14) 168,58; 168,60.
"Secret Way, The": 194,228.
"Secrets": (R'22) 263,15; (S) 265,28.
Sedano: 287,37.
Sedgwick, Eileen: 181,127.
"See America First": (R'16) 183,276.
"See My Lawyer": 176,194.
"See Naples and Die": 344, 13; (R'29) 344,70.
"See Saw": 226,371.
Seebach, Maria: 114,52; 150, 68.
"Seed of the Brute": (R'26) 310,16.
Seegar, Miriam: 326,38; 346, 31.
"Seeing Things": (R'20) 233,31; 233,35.
Seeley, James: 34,318; 47,15; 65,189; 73,77.
Segal, Vivienne: 175,112; 183, 293; 205,139; 205,143; 222, 93; 227,32; (D) 245,117;

262,41; 262,49; 270,27; 306, 14; 308,31; 312,30; 314,49; (D) 327,35; 329,41; (D) 331, c; 343,70; 352,45.
Segond-Weber, Mme.: 15,13; 100,191.
Segovia, Andres: 326,45.
Seidel, Toscha: 208,371.
Seidl, Anton: 17,24.
Seidl, Betty: 90,207.
Seiter, Philip: 188,193.
Seitz, Don C.: (W) 303,11.
Selbini, Lalla: 224,217.
Selden, Samuel: 354,8.
Seldes, Gilbert (W): 278,10; 280, 10; 285,10; 291,10; 292,9; 293,10; 296,22; 297,10; 330,10; 300,32; 301,32; 306, 12; 308,10.
Seldon, Edward: 122,130.
Selig, W.N.: 171,245.
Sellery, William: 142,181.
Sells, Bryant: 330,41.
Selman, Joseph: 212,213.
Selten, Morton: 20,7; 116,107; 156,58; 192,89.
Selter, William: 83,21.
Selwyn, Archibald: 53,164; 231, 492; 248,334.
Selwyn, Edgar (see also Selwyn and Co.): 35,17; 45,272; 53,165; 80,281; 91,250; 93, xiv; 93,286; 94,331; 108,56; 116,103; 128,142; 129,xiv; 129,163; 136,189; 193,135; 193,165; 231,492; 260,60; (W) 276,22; (W) 289,9; 290,93; 293,42; 306,5; 306,6; 307, 27; 309,75; (W) 346,30.
Selwyn, Florence: 307,72.
Selwyn, Rae: 165,234; 176,186; 191,20.
Selwyn and Co. (see also Selwyn, Edgar): 163,100; 175,109; 178,339; 187,179; 190,414; 214,398; 223,144; 231,492; 231,493; 234,84; 246,165; 270,7; 282,7.
Selwyn Theatre (Chicago): 282, 54.
Selwyn Theatre (New York): 270,66.
Selznick, Lewis J.: 171,244.
Sembach, Johannes: 166,271; 168,64.
Sembrich, Marcella: 10,28; 13,24; 14,25; 22,35; 34, 320; 60,54; 81,314; 97, 78; 118,168; 231,367; 335, 39.
Semon, Larry: 275,33.
"Senator, The": 289,25.
"Senator Keeps House, The": (R'11) 131,2; 131,8; 131, 9.
Sennett, Mack: 208,398; 213, 319; 319,11.
Sennett Bathing Beauties: 204,123.
Sensationalism (see also Morality In Theatre): 160, 299.
Senton, Harry: 39,121.
"Septimus: (R'09) 107,7; 107, 16.
Serafin, Tullio: 280,34.
Serato, Arrigo: 170,184.
"Seremonda": (R'17) 192, 87.
"Serena Blandish": 336,50; (R'29) 337,45; 340,14.
"Sergeant Blue": 52,134; (R'05) 52,137.
"Sergeant Kitty": (R'04) 36,31; 36,32.
Sergine, Vera: 125,6.
"Serio-Comic Governess, The": (R'04) 44,241.
Sermolino, M.: (W) 221,22.
Serova, Sonia: 237,367.
"Serpent's Tooth, A": (R'22) 260,301; (S) 260,310.
Serrano, Fernando: (W) 44, 259.
Serrano, Vincent: 4,6; 4,7; 59,13; 80,262; 84,46; 108, 35; 110,102; 147,142; 151, 83; 168,59; 171,236; 182, 194; 200,197; 220,345; 290, 19.
"Servant in the House, The": 86,89; (R'08) 87,116; 87, 136; (S) 87,140; 114,50; 125,25; 208,349.
"Service": 207,305; (R'18) 208,356.
"Service for Two": (R'26) 308,18.
"Servir" (see also "Service"):

146,103.
Servoss, Mary: 213,275; 258, 146; 264,18; 273,5; 337,27.
Sessions, Roger: 356,42.
"Set a Thief": (R'27) 313,19.
Set Design (see Scene Design).
Seton, Harold (W) (see also "Theatre Thoughts"): 197,18; 198,94; 199,124; 200,202; 201,266; 202,362; 203,26; 204,74; 205,162; 206,234; 209,18; 210,78; 211,156; 212,206; 214,342; 215,22; 216,84; 218,212; 219,288; 220,354; 221,8; 222,92; 223, 164; 226,380; 227,24; 228, 75; 229,172; 232,512; 233,34; 237,350; 239,84; 246,172; 249,366; 249,371; 253,218; 258,138; (V) 251,104.
Setti, Giulio: 148,178.
Settings (see also Scene Design): 210,90.
Settings -- Film; 170,178.
"Seven Chances": (R'16) 187, 137; 187,139.
"Seven Days" (see also "Tumble In"): (R'09) 106,xv.
"Seven Days Leave": (R'18) 205, 152; 205,153.
"Seven Keys to Baldpate": 153,156; 153,161; 160,310; 187,154; (F,R) 200,245; 231,349.
"Seven Sisters": (R'11) 122, xi; 122,136.
"Seventeen": 204,76; (R'18) 205,150; 205,163; (C) 209, 22.
"Seven Up": 211,153.
"Seventh Heaven": (R'22) 262, 23; (F) 318,6.
Severn, Margaret: 236,259; 243,409; 274,35; 282,25; 293,13; 305,31.
Seville, Lillian: 48,38.
Sewell, Cissie: 232,505; 234, 85.
Sewell, Marie: 246,159.
Sex Appeal (see also Morality): 177,243; 204,94; 319,16; 332,26; 338,24.
Sex On Stage: 108,42; 217,146; 218,210; 219,278; 248,294; 252,142; 281,22; 289,15; 296,9; 302,7; 304,22; 323, 31; 335,24.
Seygard, Camille: 25,78.
Seymour, Davenport: 37,62; 38, 85.
Seymour, Jane: 300,28.
Seymour, John: 297,17.
Seymour, Madelein: 156,69.
Seymour, May Davenport: 9, 20; 78,204.
Seymour, William: 25,61; 26, 80; 65,187; 132,46; (W) 222, 90; (W) 232,502.
"Shadchen's Daughter, The": (R'18) 206,219.
"Shades of Night, The": 3,2; 3,3.
"Shadow, The": (R'15) 169, 111; 169,121; (R'22) 256, 29; (R'23) 276,19.
"Shadow of the Glen, The": 129, 157.
Shadow Plays: 79,235.
"Shadowed": (R'13) 153,xxii.
"Shadowland": 226,385.
"Shadows of Uldane, The": 208, 351.
Shadurskaya, Lora: 342,42; (W) 342,43.
Shakespeare, William (see also Bacon vs. Shakespeare; Stratford-On-Avon; "Where Shakespeare Set His Stage"): 4,5; 6,16; 22,25; 35,18; 38,82; 38,88; 38,100; 39, viii; 41,179; 42,90; 48,iii; 56,xiii; 56,xiv; 58,290; 59,23; 64,iii; 66,iv; 70,322; 71,23; 73,xii; 73,67; 75, 142; 76,150; 77,ix; 79,ix; 88, iv; 89,190; 92,264; 96,ii; 103,92; 108,45; 114,52; 116,122; 122,124; 130,ix; 137,32; 139,76; 145,74; 151, 78; 151,98; 152,118; 153,158; 159,224; 160,290; 161,15; 166,278; 170,196; 171,274; 177,220; 179,1; 180,67; 182,entire issue; (A,D) 182, 226; 184,336; 185,7; 194, 228; 202,356; 203,28; 205, 133; 206,226; 207,287; 217, 154; 226,364; 244,34; 251,

78; 251,111; 252,158; 252, 178; 262,7; (D) 266,10; 271, 41; 272,41; 277,7; 292,18; 293,9; 298,11; 325,19; 342, 6; 350,48.
Shakespeare Association of America: 283,7.
Shakespeare Memorial Theatre (England): 98,111; 114,64; 153,158; 182,221.
"Shakespeare Problem Restated, The" [Greenwood] (B): 91, xv.
"Shakuntala": 163,123; (R'19) 219,276; 219,293.
Shale, Tom A.: 140,123.
Shalek, Bertha: 57,287.
Shaler, Eleanor: 293,19; 320, 19; (C) 343,40.
"Sham": (R'09) 99,137; 99, 149.
"Shame Woman, The": 273,29; (R'23) 273,68.
Shand, John (W): 349,30; 351, 30; 352,30; 353,30; 356, 37; 359,30; 360,44.
"Shanghai Gesture, The": 301, 5; (R'26) 301,18; 304,22.
Shannon, Effie: PG,3; 3,6; 13,2; 14,7; 15,20; 44, 245; 61,67; 66,212; 70, 319; 75,134; 144,36; 146, 119; 168,55; 189,277; 212, 219; 214,395; 229,187; 248, 319; 261,392; 287,52b; 290, 29; (C) 337,35.
Shannon, Frances: 173,24.
Shannon, Frank: 252,164.
Shannon, Lavinia: 307,23.
Shannon, Winona: 3,6.
"Shannons of Broadway": (R'27) 320,74; 322,39; 323,47.
Shanor, Peggy: 207,325; 214, 387.
Shapiro, Nanthaniel S.: (W) 207,300; 234,100.
"Shark Monroe": 216,128.
Sharkey, Jack: 222,103.
Sharlow, Myrna: 180,85.
Sharon, Ula: 237,367; (D) 259,256; 268,41; 289,6; 301, 8.
Sharp, Adelaide: 42,209.
Sharpe, Robert Redington: (W) 361,30.
Sharrock, Emma: 276,37.
"Shavings": (R'20) 230,272; 230,275.
Shaw, Arthur: 91,231; 93,302; 144,62; 260,298.
Shaw, Billie: 246,167.
Shaw, Brinsley: 104,131.
Shaw, Eleanor Frances: 307,28; 307,33.
Shaw, George Bernard: 35,4; 40,141; 42,186; 46,318; 46,319; 48,30; 48,34; 51, 116; 51,121; 56,viii; (D) 56,246; 57,v; 57,264; 58, 296; 58,298; 60,vii; 60,28; 60,30; 61,72; 66,198; 67, xiv; 70,312; 73,58; 74,90; 76,163; 82,348; 89,iv; 91, 254; 133,86; 140,xv; 141, 136; 154,185; 156,81; 159, 234; (A) 159,235; 160,294; 163,117; 168,63; 171,228; 171,252; 180,62; (C) 182, 223; 183,272; 187,131; 189,267; 190,358; 191,21; 193,150; 194,200; 197,40; 199,120; 201,264; 205,140; 207,300; 229,158; 233,32; 241, 238; 254,291; 259,212; (D) 259,213; (D) 266,10; 268,20; 281,39; 285,36; (A) 290,8; (W) 290,9; 291,10; 298,16; 299,5; (C) 306,17; (C) 313, 27; 330,18; 349,15.
Shaw, Jed F.: 299,22.
Shaw, Mary: 18,21; 26,100; 41,175; 74,101; 75,137; 102, 48; 167,15; 187,145; 193, 143; 196,340; 207,289; 257, 101; 268,3.
Shaw, Oscar: 181,125; 326,17.
Shaw, Rose: 353,28.
Shaw and Lee: (C) 338,37; (C) 361,38.
Shawn, Ted (see Denishawn Dancers): 180,76; 181,142; 189,278; 214,343; 252,171; 258,165; (D) 268,26; (W) 284,12; 293,6; 295,17; (W) 306,30; 306,31.
Shay, Jessie: 11,23.
Shay, Paula: 200,223.
"She Couldn't Say No": (R'26)

308,14; (R'26) 308,16.
"She Had to Know": (R'25) 289,16.
"She Made Him Behave": (F) 232,537.
"She Stoops to Conquer": (R'05) 52,132; 52,142; 74,91; 76,158; 76,159; 111,140; 111,142; 125,32; (R'12) 142,xviii; 231,363; (R'24) 281,16.
"She Walked in Her Sleep": (R'18) 211,176; 213,275.
Shean, Al (see also Gallagher and Shean): 177,250.
Shearer, Norma: 274,27; 293,31; 299,46; 306,38; 307,38; 308,35; 317,36; 327,22.
Sheehan, John: 337,30; (C) 361,27.
Sheehan, Joseph F.: 7,7.
Sheehan, Winifield: 208,397.
Sheffield, Flora: 215,21; 237,352; 247,218; 286,23.
Sheffield, Reggie: 166,292; 183,276; 188,192; 214,351; 215,21.
Shelby, Juliet: 133,104.
Shelby, Martha: 270,6.
Sheldon, Charles: (D) 266,6; (D) 267,6.
Sheldon, Edward: 107,4; 121,vii; 135,154; 143,xxi; 95,2; 96,40; 115,81; 115,83; 145,66; 145,75; 168,58; 206,230; 263,12; 122,130.
Sheldon, H.S.: 123,173.
Sheldon, Suzanne: 9,3; 74,105; 134,127.
"Shelf, The": (R'26) 309,16; 310,24.
Shelley, Elsa: 331,13; 340,39.
Shelley, Hazel: 302,14.
Shelly, Patsey: 163,116.
"Shelter": (R'26) 301,16.
Shelton, Hassell: 335,46.
Shelton, Marie: 258,174.
Shem, Aldova: 49,58.
Shepard, Pearl: 217,189.
Shepherd, Mabel: 80,273.
"Shepherd in the Distance, The": 171,259.
"Shepherd King, The": (R'04) 39,110; 42,ii.
Shepley, Ruth: 92,277; 128,137; 152,124; 161,30; 164,155; 167,36; 176,181; 178,330; 181,167; 223,145; 226,375; 226,407; 227,27; (D) 229,c; 231,430; 236,262; 270,8; 271,43; 292,25; 295,36.
Sheppard, Heloise: 147,147.
Sheridan, Frank: 87,130; 92,260; 107,15; 114,56; 121,72; 132,39; 134,124; 149,26.
Sheridan, Helen: 265,18.
Sheridan, Mary: 102,61.
Sheridan, Richard Brinsley: (D) 46,317; 53,166; (W) 111,144; 145,74.
Sheridan, Sybil: 234,115.
Sheridan Square Theatre: 198,92.
"Sherlock Holmes": 51,116; 346,11; 346,36; (R'29) 347,68.
Sherman, Cecile: 314,25.
Sherman, Jane: 353,23.
Sherman, Lowell: 179,21; 182,197; 188,193; 196,355; 207,283; 225,302; 228,99; 232,520; 236,287; 264,31; 271,13; 272,13; 290,13; (W) 294,24; 310,30; (C) 311,12; 311,24; (C) 316,31.
Sherrick, Johanna: (W) 146,111; 152,122.
Sherriff, Robert Cedric: 340,36.
Sherrill, Jack: 212,259; 213,317.
Sherrill, William: 208,397.
Sherry, [Mrs.] E.P.: 143,27.
Sherry, Jr. Barney: 206,264.
Sherwin, Louis: (C) 193,138; (W) 199,120; 206,254.
Sherwood, C. Blythe (W): 210,98; 238,16.
Sherwood, Henry: 360,25.
Sherwood, Joseph: 71,17.
Sherwood, Mimi: 255,383.
Sherwood, Phyllis: 84,54.
Sherwood, Robert E.: 328,29.
"She's a Good Fellow": (R'19) 220,343; 221,19.
"She's in Again": 173,6; (R'15)

173,7.
Shields, Sarah: 193,143.
Shields, Sydney: 181,123; 193, 137; 195,276; 196,357; 204, 91; 204,93; (D) 255,375; 257,77; 257,111.
"Shifting Scenes of the Modern European Theatre" [Flanagan] (B): 335,4.
Shine, John L.: 122,119; 250, 25.
Shinkman, Paul (W): 342,19; 343,25; 345,23; 346,43.
"Ship, The": (S) 86,110.
Shipley, Joseph T.: (W) 282, 20.
Shipman, Helen: 210,89; 230, 254; 241,254; 265,48; 268, 24; (D) 276,46.
Shipman, Louis Evan: 12,9.
Shipman, Samuel: (W) 218, 198; 261,386; 276,39; (W) 314,14; (D) 314,15.
Shirley, Blanche: 39,vii; 43,v.
Shirley, Florence: 179,8; 181, 152; 205,143; 206,229; 225, 299; 227,48; 231,359; 231, 442; 261,402.
"Shirley Kaye": 190,347; (R'16) 192,85; (F) 203,61.
"Sho-Gun, The": 42,209; 45, 270; 45,271; (R'04) 45,272.
Shoemaker, Anne: 301,23; 308, 28; (D) 313,31; 327,4c.
Shone, Hermine: 189,278.
"Shoo-Fly Regiment, The": (R'07) 79,xi.
Shore, Lois: 294,21.
"Shore Acres": 78,201; (R'22) 259,225; 259,226.
Shorrock, Polly: 234,104.
Short, Hassard: 38,83; 66, 200; 82,329; 100,175; 104, 131; 116,107; 117,144; 143, 7; 150,48; 158,175; 179,25; 199,148; 223,189; 237,361; (W) 275,22; 301,38; 358, 42.
Shotwell, Margaret: 340,27.
Shotwell, Marie: 189,293; 271, 23.
"Show Boat": 323,58; 326,35.
<u>Show Boats</u>: (D) 195,296.
<u>"Show Girl"</u>: (C) 341,23; 342,9; (R'29) 342,39; (D) 344,c.
"Show Girl, The": (R'02) 16, 8; 17,7.
"Show of Shows, The": (F) 347, 59.
"Show of Wonders": (R'16) 199, 357.
"Show-Off, The": (R'24) 277,16; (D) 278,38; 279,18; (S) 282,26.
"Show Shop, The": (R'14) 168, 57; 168,58; 174,79.
Shubert, J.J.: (W) 294,9; 308,33.
Shubert, Lee (<u>see also</u> Shubert Brothers): 94,ii; 105,145; 145,75; 153,160; (W) 155, 22; (W) 277,9; (C) 281, 11; 297,6; 308,33.
Shubert, Samuel L. (<u>see also</u> Shubert Brothers): 43,227; 52,ix; 135,153.
Shubert Brothers: 17,3; 56, xiii; 63,113; 65,189; 67, 228; 73,67; 94,xxxii; 103, 72; 106,xxxvi; 127,76; 127, 78; 128,xii; 139,68; 151,79; 163,99; 175,108; 187,126; 199,122; 211,130; 223,144; 245,75; 246,196; 258,147; 274,12; 306,15.
"Shubert Gaities of 1919, The": (D) 223,152.
Shubert New Theatre (Joplin, Mo.): 85,xiv.
Shubert Theatre (New York): 153,146; 290,17.
"Shuffle Along": (R'21) 245, 98.
"Shulamite, The": 66,215; (R'06) 70,xxi; 82,321.
Shumlin, Herman: 360,30.
Shurr, Louis: (W) 356,44.
Shutta, Eddie: 357,50.
Shutta, Ethel: 299,46; 337,11.
Shy, Gus: 337,30; (C) 361, 27.
Siagrist, Winnie: 33,282.
"Siberia": (OP) (D) 80,266.
Sibiriakoff, Leon: 119,8.
Sibley, Rose: 138,33.
<u>Sicilian Theatre</u>: 86,96; 88, 153; 95,xiv; 95,4.
Sick, Carl: 93,289.

"Sick-A-Bed": 206,216; (R'18) 206,218.
Siddons, Sarah: 45,281; 52, 150; 66,206; 78,222; 109, xvii; 139,94; 150,54; 195, 265; 205,133.
"Sidewalks of New York": (R'27) 321,44.
Sidney, George: 168,58; 169, 132; 170,200; 236,283; (D) 237,351; 241,247; 246,146.
Sidney, Sylvia: 307,33; (D) 318, 25; 341,42: (D(342,33; 356,25; 357,28.
Siebel, George: (W) 335,52.
Siedle, Edward: 167,21.
Siedlowa, Julia: 130,205.
"Siege": (F,R) 295,34.
Siegel, Al: 357,26.
"Siegfried": 295,33; (F,R) 296, 32.
Sienkiowicz, Henryk: 79,248; 107,90.
Sierra, G. Martinez: 304,15.
"Sign of the Cross, The": (F) 166,274: 166,275: (F) 170, 181; (R'09) 102,61; (R'11) 129,xiv; 156,104; 173,7.
"Sign of the Door, The": 228,99; (R'19) 228,101.
Silberta, Rhea: 337,36.
"Silence": 286,23; (R'24) 286, 58.
"Silent Enemy, The": (R'30) 352,68.
"Silent Voice, The": 168,56; (R'14) 168,59.
"Silent Witness, The": (R'16) 187, 138.
"Silks and Satins": (R'20) 234,105.
Sills, Milton: 98,113; 101,7; 117,150; 140,103; 154,175; 159,227; 233,40; 239,115; 293,39; (A) 295,65; 321,20; 322,60; 329,4b; 335,36.
"Silver Box, The": (R'07) 75,114; 75,129.
"Silver Cord, The": (R'26) 311, 58; 312,19; 312,50.
"Silver Fox, The": (R'21) 248, 314; (S) 252,152.
"Silver Girl, The": (R'07) 81,xv.
"Silver Slipper, The": (R'02) 22,11.
"Silver Star, The": (R'09) 106, xv.
"Silver Wedding, The": (R'13) 151,83; 151,105.
Silvernail, Clarke: 161,16; 214, 343; 307,72.
Silvester, Richard: 203,31.
Simon, Robert A. (W): 225, 314; (V) 245,78.
"Simon Called Peter": (R'24) 286,22.
"Simon The Cyrenian: (R'17) 195, 280.
"Simone": (S) 88,viii.
Simone, Madame: 110,116; 127, 75; 128,118; 129,xii; 129, 159; 130,186; 132,37; 132, 39; 134,107; 134,115; 143,1; 143,3; (W) 155,18; 156,99; 160,284; 170,193; 277,23; 279, 16; 284,58; 285,29; 286,20; 286,45.
Simonsen, Lee: (D) 187,128; (D) 220,337; 230,257; 241, 267; 255,381; 279,15; 351,20; 359,42.
Simonson, Selli: 188,206.
"Simple Simon": (R'30) 349, 46; (D) 351,c.
Simpson, Cheridah: 17,8; 47, 68.
Simpson, Elizabeth (see Inchband, Mrs.).
Simpson, Ivan F.: 241,255; 245,88; 292,28.
"Sin Flood, The": (F,R) 262, 54.
"Sin of David, The" [Phillips] (B): 47,ii.
"Sinbad": 206,227; (R'18) 207,316.
Sinclair, Ada: 231,407.
Sinclair, Arthur: 324,59; 353,37.
Sinclair, Eleanor: 210,85.
Sinclair, Upton: 76,146.
Sinclair, Walter: (D) 344,51.
Sindelar, Pearl: 127,85.
Singer, Helen: 48,46.
Singer, Joseph: 203,31.
"Singer of Seville, The": (F) 352,47.

Singer's Midgets: 349, 46.
"Singing Fool, The": (F) 332, 35.
"Singing Jail Birds": 335, 50; (R'28) 335, 82.
"Single Man, A": 128, 111; (R'11) 128, 114.
Singleton, Amy: 129, 153.
"Sinners": 168, 88; (R'15) 168, 101.
Sinnott, Helene: 172, 294.
"Sins of Society, The": 103, 72; (R'09) 104, xiv.
Sipperly, Ralph: 217, 163; 237, 349; 248, 291; 249, 392; 294, 28.
Sircum, Arthur: 292, 30.
"Sire": (R'11) 121, xi.
"Siren, The": (R'11) 128, xii; 128, 120.
Sisk, Robert F. (W) 313, 28; 331, 49; (W) 343, 27; 347, 43.
Sisson, Wesley: 62, 101.
Sissons, William: 61, 66.
"Sister Beatrice": (R'10) 110, xx; 110, 98; 110, 99; (S) 112, 186; 113, ix.
"Sisters of Susanna": 189, 269; (R'16) 189, 283.
"Sit Tight": (F) 359, 3.
Sitgraves, Beverly: 27, 107; 28, 156; 52, 149; 105, 144; 105, 145; 107, 9; 152, 112; 156, 102; 179, 19; 180, 73.
"Sitting Pretty": (R'24) 279, 19; 280, 18.
"Six Characters in Search of an Author": (R'22) 262, 23; 263, 18.
"Six Cylinder Love": 248, 291; (R'21) 248, 313; 251, 103.
"Six Little Stenographers, The": 38, 88.
"Six Who Pass While the Lentils Boil": 175, 113; (R'15) 175, 139; 185, 21; (R'16) 191, 23.
Skelly, Hal: 319, 22; 320, 24; (A) 322, 3; 322, 8; 327, 41; 330, 34; 349, 47.
"Sketch Book": (C) 342, 14; (R'29) 342, 39.
"Skidding": (R'28) 328, 39.
"Skin Game, The": 238, 7; (R'20) 238, 29.
Skinner, Cornelia Otis: 251, 113; 275, 23; 341, 40.
Skinner, Maud Durbin (W): 34, 294; 168, 56.
Skinner, Olive: 40, viii.
Skinner, Otis: 4, 4; 4, 14; 7, c; 7, 4; 7, 5; 12, 7; (W) 14, 19; 15, 18; 19, 6; 22, 6; 29, 174; 34, 287; 35, 8; 36, 30; 38, 94; 40, 138; 41, 162; 44, 252; 45, 268; 45, 270; (W) 46, 311; (W) 51, v; 54, 189; 57, 283; 61, 54; 63, c; (W) 63, 118; 67, 245; 79, 228; 85, 59; 86, xvi; 86, 89; 86, 103; 87, c; 88, 156; 90, 200; 96, xvii; 103, 74; 106, 183; (W) 106, 184; 108, 37; 108, 38; 108, 52; 109, 95; 111, 151; 111, 152; 120, 63; 121, xi; 121, 89; 126, 43; 127, 77; 131, 1; 132, c; 133, 101; 134, 134; 139, 68; 139, 78; 142, 196; 145, 75; 151, 80; 163, 99; 168, 56; 169, 142; 170, 191; 171, 233; 173, 11; 174, 61; 176, 176; 179, 37; 180, 67; (W) 182, 208; 184, 361; (A) 187, 155; 189, 281; 189, 285; 200, 200; 201, 315; 212, 221; 213, 280; 213, 287; (A) 214, 379; 215, 26; 220, 359; (W) 221, 18; 229, 183; 230, 257; 231, 363; 233, 24; 238, 27; 239, 113; 239, 114; 250, 24; (A) 250, 63; (W) 253, 242; 265, 34; (D) 275, 27; 299, 30; (A) 322, 3; 325, 4; 338, 36; 342, 19; 343, 14; (W) 357, 32.
Skinner, [Mrs.] Otis: 37, 70.
"Skipper & Co., Wall Street": (R'03) 28, 132; 28, 156.
Skipworth, Allison: 49, 56; 70, 336; 154, 181; 202, 348; (W) 221, 26; 249, 363; 260, 298; 260, 313; 281, 40; (D) 342, 32.
Skirvin, Marguerite: 138, 63; 144, 50.
Skolsky, Sidney (W): 317, 8; 326, 27; 331, 48; 343, 22; 352, 2.
"Skull, The": (R'28) 328, 38.
"Sky Farm": 13, 7; (R'02) 14,

5; 14,8.
"Sky High": (R'25) 290,34.
"Skylark, A": 111,xxvii.
"Skylark, The": 247,213; (R'21) 247,233.
"Skyscraper": (F) 326,77.
"Skyscrapers" (Ballet): 302,34; 302,35.
"Slacker, The": (F,R) 199,176.
Slang, Stage (see also Terminology, Stage): 213,288; 339,33.
Slater, Gladys: 197,39; 212, 197.
Slavik, Adelyn: 235,196.
Slavin, John: 18,4; 71,28; 76, 169; 100,175.
Sleath, Herbert: 75,116; 76,159.
Sleeper, Martha: 313,39.
"Sleeping Partners": (R'18) 214,347.
"Sleepless Night, A": (R'19) 218,206; 218,209.
Slezak, Leo: 102,42; 105,138; 107,10; 107,25; 120,48; 129,154; 133,80; 136,185; 155,16; 166,272.
"Slice of Life, A": (R'12) 133, xii; 133,75.
"Slim Princess, The": (R'11) 120,x.
Sloan, A. Baldwin: 22,8; 184, 351.
Sloan, J. Balding: (D) 220,336.
Sloan, Fred: 310,38.
Sloane, Paul: (W) 331,26.
Slobodskaja, Oda: 266,36.
Slosson, Pauline: 46,325.
Small, William Jr.: 168,64.
"Smiles": (D) 358,16.
Smiley, Robert: 159,245; 242, 331.
"Smilin' Through": 227,10; (R'19) 228,97.
"Smiling Irish Eyes": (F) 339, 67.
Smirnoff, Dimitri: 120,48.
"Smith": (R'10) 116,98; 116, 107.
Smith, Alfred E.: (A) 231, 346; 287,27; (W) 321,17; (A) 333,18.
Smith, Ben: 335,51.
Smith, C. Aubrey: 129,150; 156, 58; 166,292; 168,59; 272, 17; 327,24.
Smith, Charles Sprague: 41, 179; 87,134.
Smith, Ethel M. (W): 145, 90; 153,71.
Smith, G. Albert: 323,26.
Smith, Gladys: 122,136.
Smith, H. Reeves: 3,12; 45, 272; 61,60; 66,200; 109, 73; 129,171; 143,7; 158, 174; 178,292; 179,25; 193, 167; 228,96.
Smith, Harry B.: 6,18; 12,4; (W) 86,100.
Smith, Harry J.: (W) 206,230.
Smith, Henry C.: 198,89.
Smith, Herbert: 63,112.
Smith, Jackson: (W) 225,314.
Smith, John Talbot: (W) 221, 32.
Smith, Joseph C.: 95,4; 155, 26; 156,61.
Smith, Joseph Lindon: 200,199.
Smith, Kaj: 272,11.
Smith, Lewis Worthington: (W, V) 104,124.
Smith, Lilie: (D) 347,29.
Smith, Mark III: 97,80.
Smith, Pauline: 204,97.
Smith, Queenie: 183,277; 196, 349; 219,287; (D) 228,85; 270,27; 280,18; 282,18; 304,21; 307,29; 344,28.
Smith, Rex (W): 325,23; 330, 22; 334,24; 337,22.
Smith, Richard P.: 197,14.
Smith, Sol: 30,204.
Smith, [Mrs.] Sol: 105,144; 110,104; 140,124; 167,11.
Smith, Virginia: (D) 255,c.
Smith, Winchell: 93,295; (W) 190,364; 196,353; 248,292; 259,254; 333,49.
Smith College: 43,236; 64, 162; 74,94; 91,248; 182, 227; 236,290; 257,107; 269, 45; 270,42; 284,40; 296, 44; 301,30; 329,42.
"Smoldering Flame, The": (R'13) 153,xxii.
"Smooth As Silk": (R'21) 242, 342.
"Smouldering Fires": (F,R) 291,

32.
Smythe, Ella: 119,14.
Smythe, William G.: 136,191.
"Snapshots of 1921": (R'21) 245, 97; 245,99; (D) 245,116.
Snarks, The": 268,46.
Snell, Olive: 351,40.
"Snobs": (R'11) 128,115; 128, 139.
"Snow Shop, The": 169,132.
"Snow White": 76,155.
"Snow White and the Seven Dwarfs": (R'12) 142,xx; 142,195.
Snowden, [Mrs.] Albert A.: 337,42.
Snowden, Elsie: 108,50; 111, ix.
Snowdon, Eric: 166,269.
Snyder, Ella: 5,13; 10,6; 80, 278.
Snyder, Georgie: 80,273.
Snyder, [Rev.] John: 58,306; 60,viii.
Snyder, Mabel: 100,195.
Snyder, Maida: 70,xix.
Snyder, Thomas: 275,29.
"So Big": (F) 287,33; (F,R) 288,30.
"So Long Letty": (R'16) 190, 355.
"So Much for So Much": (R'14) 167,48.
"So This Is London": (R'22) 260,340.
"So This Is Politics?": (R'24) 281,16.
"So Was Napoleon": (R'30) 347,74.
Soanes, Jack: 359,39.
Sobel, Bernard (W): 184,356; 211,163; 236,282; 246,170; 250,34; 318,32; 340,29.
"Social Significance of the Modern Drama, The" (Goldman) (B): 163,145.
"Social Whirl, The": (R'06) 63, 113; 63,134; 64,160; 64, 161.
Societe Des Instruments Anciens: 194,229.
"Society and the Bulldog": (R) 85,xii.
Society and Theatre: 20,18; 66,202; 86,106; 176,182; 181,127; 187,130; 192,78; 193,156; 196,338; 197,11; 220,334; 220,350; 231,406; 241,276; 271,23; 313,14; 342,32; 353,74.
Society of American Dramatists and Composers: 146,101.
Society of American Singers: 213,272.
Society of Dramatic Authors, The: 73,84.
Sodero, Cesare: 293,37.
Soffray, Anne Marie: 278,35.
"Soft Living": (F) 324,12.
Sokol Hall Company: 137,31.
Sokoloff, Nikolai: 146,111.
Sokolova, Lydia: 178,294.
Sokoloff, Wladimir: 323,38; 324,59; 325,49.
"Solange": 99,142.
"Solid Ivory": (R'25) 298,16.
"Soldiers and Women": 343,13; (S) 344,39; (R'29) 344,45.
"Soldiers of Fortune": 14,2; (R'02) 14,6; 22,22; 42,ii.
"Solid South": (R'30) 357,27.
"Some Baby": (R'15) 176, 168.
"Some Night": (R'18) 213,279.
"Some Time": (R'18) 214, 346.
"Somebody's Luggage": (R'16) 188,204b.
"Somebody's Sweetheart": (R'18) 216,78; 217,145.
"Someone in the House": 213,275; (R'18) 213,279.
Somerset, Pat: 278,14.
Sommes, George: 248,323.
"Son Daughter, The": (R'19) 227,17; 227,29.
"Son Homme": 179,11.
"Son of the People, A": (R'10) 110,98; 110,109.
"Song and Dance Man, The": (R'23) 276,16.
"Song of Songs, The": (R'14) 168,58; 168,77.
"Song of the Flame": (R'25) 300,16; (F) 350,67; (F) 351,56.
Song Pluggers: 80,x.
"Song Writer, The": (R'28)

332, 78.
Song Writers: 179, 26; 179, 27; 184, 351; 200, 222; 201, 266; 202, 358; 210, 98; 275, 12.
Song Writing: 226, 374; 341, 29.
Sonnenthal, Adolph: 179, 18.
"Sonny": (R'21) 247, 236.
"Sonny Boy": (F) 338, 31.
"Sons O'Guns": (D) 346, 27; (R'29) 346, 49; 347, 45; (D) 348, c; 348, 21.
"Son's Windhund": (R'13) 153, xvii.
"Sonya": (R'21) 247, 274.
"Sophie": 230, 247; (R'20) 230, 272.
"Sorcerer, The": (R'15) 173, 7.
"Sorceress, The": 37, 61; (R'04) 45, 267.
"Sorciere, La": 27, 112.
Sorel, Cecile: 301, 24; 301, 25; 303, 48; 311, 16; 311, 27.
Sorel, Felicia: 256, 13; 304, 29.
Soroya, Bianca: 283, 35.
"Sorrows of Satan": (F) 306, 37.
Soss, Wilma: (W) 309, 30.
Sothern, E. A.: 45, 284; 58, 300; 76, 162; 78, 222; 84, 55; 106, 174; 126, 64; 139, 82; 141, 136; 145, 74; 149, 16; 187, 136; 209, 10.
Sothern, Edward H. (see also Sothern and Marlowe): PG, 31; (A) 3, 18; (W) 4, 10; 4, 11; (A) 4, 12; 7, 2; 8, c; 8, 4; 8, 18; 9, 3; 9, 5; 10, 7; 10, 10; 23, 17; 24, 28; 24, 31; 25, 66; 28, 150; 33, 264; 38, 93; 39, 118; 45, iv; 45, 284; 46, 322f; 50, 92; 58, 290; 58, 297; (A) 58, 300; 62, 106; 65, 187; 67, 243; 72, 32; 79, 228; 79, 229; 82, x; 82, 317; 82, 347; 84, 32; 84, 55; 85, 61; 86, xiv; 86, 117; 87, 125; 99, 134; 99, 150; 99, 151; 105, 144; 105, 145; 114, 53; 118, 161; 119, 13; 126, 44; 127, 76; 130, ix; 132, 69; 139, 76; 142, 161; 145, 75; 149, 16; 151, 79; 152, 120; 152, 121; 170, 191; 172, 298; 173, 26; 174, 59; 177, 219; 177, 220; 177, 240; 178, 287; (W) 178, 290; 179, 7; 180, 61; 182, 222; 184, 333; 184, 360; 189, 292; 195, 280; 198, 108b; 201, 269; 208, 346; 208, 347; 209, 2; 214, 335; 224, 221; 231, 346; 231, 365; 232, 51; 251, 111; 252, 178; 253, 214; 281, 40; 290, 18; 290, 22; 294, 5; (W) 313, 5; (W) 316, 32.
Sothern, Eve: 338, 44.
Sothern, Harry: 324, 59.
Sothern, Henry: 175, 129.
Sothern, Sam: 120, 36; 216, 81.
Sothern and Marlowe (see also Marlowe, Julia; Sothern, Edward H.): 46, 292; 46, 307; 57, 268; 62, 107; 69, 309; 70, xxiv; 70, 312; 70, 315; 73, xiv; 73, c; 73, 59; 74, 102; 79, 229; 79, 239; 90, 205; 101, 1; 101, 4; 106, 166; 107, 9; 119, 3; 119, 13; 119, 15; 127, 105; 142, 189; 145, 79; 151, 78; 152, 118; 152, 119; 152, 121; 161, 15; 161, 17; 183, 287; 226, 364; 231, 348; 232, 514; 250, 32; 256, 34; 273, 19; 273, 25.
Sothern Family: 45, 284.
"Soul Kiss, The": 85, 80.
Sound Effects: 82, 332; 280, 59.
"Souper D'Adieu": (R'03) 34, 291.
"Sour Grapes": (R'26) 308, 18.
"Source, The": (F, R) 212, 250.
Sousa, John Philip: 64, x; 102, 62; 103, 77; 146, xv; 181, 140; 184, 351; (A) 193, 193; 200, 215; 202, 363; (A) 202, 389; 209, 13; (D) 257, 68.
Soussanin, Nicholas: 338, 34.
Southampton, Earl of: 182, 184.
Southard, Harry D.: 233, 7.
Southerland, Lawrence: (W) 195, 286.
Southern, Alice: 319, 23.
Southern, Sara: 262, 31; 264, 30; 296, 48.
"Southerners, The": (R'04) 41, 161; 41, 169.
Southwark Theatre (Philadelphia):

137,16.
"Souveraine, La": (R'18) 207, 288.
"Sowing The Wind": 34,307.
Spachner, Leon: 299,23.
Spadora: 288,37.
Spalding, Albert: 178,286.
"Spanish Love": (R'20) 235,242.
Spanish Theatre: 44,259; 136, 178; 204,78; 220,343; 220, 357; 223,149; 251,99; 340, 32.
Spanuth, August: (W) 10,28.
Sparkes, Lenora: 123,148; 147, 141; 157,117.
Sparks, Joseph: 32,259; 57, 271.
Sparks, Ned A.: 163,101.
Sparling, H.: 132,46.
Speare, Edith: 56,240.
Specht, Paul: 282,23.
"Speckled Bank, The": (R'10) 119,xiii.
Speculators, Ticket: 4,2; (C) 74,103; 86,vi; 150,68; 203,8; 215,6; 248, 290; 275,9; 292,24; 297,20; 299,5; 318,30; 321,18; 323, 20; 354,21; 358,16; 359,21.
"Speed": (R'11) 128,xii; 128, 114.
Speers, Marta: 174,67; 174,70.
"Spell, The": (R'07) 81,xviii.
"Spellbinder, The": (R'04) 44,247.
Spelterini, Maria: 76,168.
Spelvin, George (sic): 212, 203; 325,37.
Spencer, Bernadette: 306,21.
Spencer, Lillian: 176,170; 187,139; 203,50.
"Spendthrift, The": (R'10) 111,xxix; 112,194.
Sperr, Ilona: 90,207.
Sperry, Robert M.: 100,ix.
"Spice of Life, The": 213,273.
"Spice of 1922": (R'22) 258, 151.
"Spider, The": (D) 315,23; (R'27) 315,24; 315,25; 317, 33.
Spink, George: 72,33; 117,144.
Spinnelly: 234,94.
"Spiritualist, The": 146,98; (R'13) 147,132.
"Spitfire, The": (R'10) 112,174; 112,913.
Spitzley, Florence Hayward: 43, 238.
"Splendid Sinner, The": (F,R) 207,324.
"Spoilers, The": (R'07) 74,xii; 74,93; (F,R) 356,48.
Spong, Hilda: 10,14; 12,3; 14, 4; 45,269; 63,116; 69,310; 112,204; 180,71; 190,374; 191,32; 201,264; 216,81; 227,19; (W) 233,32; 249,375; 273,14; 277,28; 280,24.
Spooner, [Mrs.] B.S.: 24,40; 24,41.
Spooner, Cecil: 23,8; 23,14; 28,136; 28,137.
Spooner, Edna May: 78,215.
"Sport of Kings, The": (R'26) 304,15.
"Sporting Days": (R'08) 93, xiv.
"Sporting Life": (F,R) 212,250.
"Sporting Thing to Do, The": (R'23) 265,19.
Spottswood, James: 88,146; 159,240.
"Spread Eagle": (R'27) 315, 24.
Spreckles Theatre (San Diego): 141,145.
Spring, Helen: 297,17.
"Spring Chicken, The": 71,20.
"Spring Cleaning": 274,17; (R'23) 274,19; (S) 279,26.
"Spring Fever": (R'25) 295, 16; 295,17.
"Spring Is Here": (R'29) 338, 47; (F) 347,24.
"Spring Maid, The": (R'10) 120, xv; 120,59.
"Spring Time a la Carte": (F,R) 211,183.
"Springboard, The": (R'27) 321,44.
"Springtime": (R'09) 106,170; 106,186.
Sproston, F. Manning: 260,300.
Spurin-Calleia, Joseph: 358, 29.
"Spy, The": (R'13) 144,xv; 145; 89; (F,R) 199,176.

"Squab Farm, The": 207,283; (R'18) 207,285.
"Squall, The": (R'26) 310,18; (F) 338,34.
"Square Crooks": (F) 326,6.
"Square Deceiver, The": (F,R) 203,57.
"Squaw Man, The": 53,177; (R'05) 58,293; 61,53; 79, 240.
"Squealer, The": (R'28) 334, 46.
Squire, Ronald: 195,271; 195, 287; 359,30.
Stace, Arthur W.: (W) 124, 212.
Stafford, Marie: 233,25.
Stage Door Johnnies: 210,96; 232,532; (C) 289,8; 294, 36; 304,34; 343,47.
Stage Doormen: 121,93; (D) 298, 25; 304,10.
Stage Effects (see also Scenic Effects): 21,11; 62,94; 82, 332; 102,55; 105,140; 131, 15; 132,53; (D) 280,12; 280,59.
Stage Fright: 9,20; 9,21; 46,xviii; 46,320; 306,18.
Stage Hands: 242,334.
"Stage History of Famous Plays" by M.J. Moses:
1. "Romeo and Juliet" 50,92;
2. "The School for Scandal" 53,166;
3. "The Lady of Lyons" 57,270;
4. "La Dame Aux Camillias" 61,64;
5. "Diplomacy" 71,19;
6. "She Stoops to Conquer" 76,158;
7. "The Fool's Revenge" 88,169.
Stage Managers: 107,27; 219, 270;332,43.
Stage Mothers: 307,18.
Stage Names (see Pseudonyms).
"Stage Scenery and Lighting" (Selden & Sellman) (B): 354,8.
Stage Society of New York: 167, 28.
"Stage Whispers": 179,6; 180,62; 181,122; 182,183; 183,272.
Stagecraft: 21,14; 42,195; 71,23; 90,203; 108,49; 167, 22; 167,28;186,65; 211,153; 216,82; 217,150; 254,315; 293,12.
Stagers, The: 291,15; 292,7; 294,7; 303,16.
Stahl, Bernard (W): 110,112.
Stahl, John M.: 128,114.
Stahl, Rose: 45,280; 65,176; 69, 298; 71,21; 77,c; 81,308; 83,7; 94,325; 106,168; 123, 147; 124,181; 127,98; 136,190; 155,17; 181,125; 181,126; 337,40.
Staley, George: 13,5; 106,198.
Stallard, Ernest: 73,62; 108, 54; 134,133.
Stallings, Laurence: 285,28; 308,29; (W) 313,5.
Stamford [Connecticut] Theatre: 163,113.
Stamper, Dave: 285,27.
Stamper, F. Pope: 105,163.
Stanard, Ethel: 200,223; 216, 75; 216,95.
Stanbury, Douglas: 297,37.
Standing, Guy: 3,2; 8,3; 8,12; 61,54; 70,314; 104,106; 161,17; (D) 163,108; 172, 307; 198,69; 345,15; 357, 28; (W) 358,30; (W) 361,44.
Standing, Herbert: 36,39; 56, 245; 91,238; 118,199.
Standon, Harriet: 113,32; 133,82.
Stanford, Henry B.: 5,2; 8,13; 12,11; 12,15; 97,99; 105, 144; 105,145; 135,157; 221, 9.
Stanford University: 271,42; 284,42; 291,43; 296,42; 302,40; 315,48; 331,57; 338,51; 341,46; 346,50; 356,49.
Stanhope, Allen (W): 324,43.
Stanislavsky, Constantin: 162,56; 259,215; 264,14; 265,27; 265,38; (D) 226,10; 268,38; 276,9.
Stanley, Charles: 98,127.

Stanley, Eric: 342,26; (D) 344,19.
Stanley, Helen: 155,16; 180, 85; 208,371; 286,35.
Stanley, Polly: 80,273.
Stanley, S. Victor: 339,49.
Stanley, W.A.; (W) 199,126; 200,200.
Stannard, Anna: 54,190.
Stanton, Gertrude: (W,FI) 31, 230.
Stanton, Mable: 249,382.
Stanton, Richard: 205,191.
Stanwood, Rita: 140,iii; 203, 25; 204,91.
Stanwyck, Barbara: 313,9; 319, 22; 320,24; 320,52; 327,41; 356,46; 359,3.
Star System: 66,201; 78,202; 85,xvi; 89,198; 93,307; 102,ix; 108,41; 131,12; 133,xviii; 195,283; 214, 342; 217,158; 219,290; 221,24; 229,172; 237,364; 268,7; 270,21; 273,58; 353, 15; 357,20; 358,37.
Star Theatre (New York): (D) 231,352.
Starbuck, Betty: 337,17; 344,21; 301,31.
"Starbucks, The": (R'03) 27, 107.
Starhill, Madeline: 260,277.
Stark, Pauline: 272,30; 295, 35; 310,49; 313,49; 314, 49; 317,40; 323,35.
Starlets: 198,78; 249,364; 259,238.
"Starlight": (R'25) 290,32.
Starling, Lynn: 277,29; 282,10.
Starr, Frances: 61,56; 65,176; 71,1; 71,11; 72,50; 74,c; 76,156; 79,228; 79,229; 80, v; 83,7; 84,47; 96,51; 97, 81; 97,82; 99,v; 100,181; (A) 105,xxi; 115,95; 127,76; 129,161; 139,68; 141,iii; 141,137; 142,196; 143,9; 150,47; 151,78; 156,75; 156, 99; 157,137; 158,214; 159, 270; 160,309; 160,315; 163, 99; 167,10; 169,131; 170, 174; 170,175; 170,215; 174, 78; (A) 175,135; 176,176; 185,46; 186,74; 187,127; 189,266; 191,16; 191,25; 192,106; 195,269; 195,283; (W) 196,320; 196,329; 196, 330; 206,209; 210,79; 215, 29; 216,91; 216,106; 217, 164; 219,286; (A) 226,438; 233,4; 237,359; (D) 238,c; (A) 238,72; 247,209; 247, 249; 249,363; 259,226; 261, 386; 262,33; 292,6; 308, 23; (W) 310,24; (D) 322, 16; (W) 322,17; 325,39.
Starr, Muriel: 129,iii; 129, 162; 132,39; 134,124.
Stauber, Mary: 334,25.
Staunton, Virginia: 102,44; 112,188.
Stavely, W.R.: 156,65.
"Steadfast Princess, The": (R'20) 233,31.
Stechhan, H.O.: (W) 169, 126.
Stedman, Myrtle: 186,80; 209,55; 228,108.
Steel, John: 222,80.
Steele, Asa: (W) 37,78.
Steele, Bernard: 333,48.
Steele, Charles: 208,347; (W) 213,284.
Steele, Vernon: 166,264; 180, 67; 221,65; 292,21; 304,14.
Steele, Willis (W): 26,86; 33, 278; 55,227; 84,42; 88,153; 90,205; 99,165; 103,78; 106, 176; 109,87; 114,60; 117, 152; 118,174; 124,184; 126, 62; 136,174; 140,117; 143, 23; 144,50; 148,169; 151, 92; 166,260; 167,24; 168,63; 173,34; 174,85; 175,124; 181,151; 195,288; 203,38; 215,12.
Steep, Miriam: 321,52.
Steger, Harry: 57,273.
Steger, Julius: 7,18; (A) 51, i,f; 165,221.
Stehli, Edgar: 185,21; 206,
Steil, Ferdinand: 93,289.
Stein, Geoffrey: 218,209.
Steinbach, Hattie L.: 112,188.
Steingruber, Franzi: 85,75.
Steinway, Theodore E.: 198,89.
Stembler, Sallie: 42,212.

Stengel, Hans (D): 272, 8; 275, 13; 280, 25; 305, 11; 306, 29; 307, 25; 309, 11; 310, 13; 311, 21; 312, 15; 313, 29; 314, 13.
Stengel, Leni: 334, 45.
Stengel, Madelen: 280, 27.
"Step This Way": (R'16) 185, 11.
"Stepdaughters of War": 356, 23; (R'30) 357, 28.
"Step-Sister, The": 81, vii; (R'07) 81, xiii.
Stephens, Harvey: 350, 43; 360, 35.
Stephens, Yorke: 120, 61.
Stephenson, Edgar (W): 99, 155; 101, 5.
Stephenson, Henry: 152, 110; 170, 187; 180, 71; 183, 296; 227, 10; 283, 17; 284, 29; 320, 24; 354, 33; 356, 18; 359, 12; (C) 359, 22.
"Stepping Stones": (R'23) 274, 58.
Sterling, Frances [Fanny]: 71, 24.
Sterling, Nora: 247, 231.
Sterling, Richard: 49, 59; 280, 14.
Sterling, Suissabell (D): 323, 23.
Sternberg, Sadie Hope: (W) 301, 24.
"Steve": (R'12) 141, xii.
Stevens, Ashton: 272, 66; 318, 20.
Stevens, Edwin: 3, 2; 4, 3; 17, 4; 36, 45; 91, 246; 92, 266; 92, 267; 92, 268; 93, c; 119, 16; 136, 173; 149, 26.
Stevens, Emily: 42, 204; 51, 112; 70, 325; 107, 16; 116, 120; 154, 178; 162, 63; 167, 22; 175, 110; 177, 220; 178, 292; (A) 183, 301; 195, 293; 199, 123; 205, 137; 206, 214; 206, 215; 216, 78; 230, 247; 230, 273; 232, 503; 233, 48; 241, 258; 278, 17; 280, 21; 301, 14.
Stevens, Frances: 51, 117.
Stevens, George W., Sr. (see Judd, Dr.).
Stevens, Ivy: 356, 34.
Stevens, Mary: 265, 38.
Stevens, Ogden: 112, 180.
Stevens, Thomas Wood: 200, 199; (W) 208, 350; 218, 230; 218, 231; (A) 231, 346; (W) 256, 42; (D) 303, 37.
Stevenson, Charles A.: 49, 70; (C) 51, 127; 93, 285; 101, 7; 117, 135; 121, 98; 215, 15.
Stevenson, Henry: 154, 188.
Stevenson, Richard: 276, 26; 303, 14; 306, 28; 324, 40.
Stevenson, Robert C.: 299, 22.
Stevenson, [Mrs.] W. Yorke: 144, 63.
Steves, Emily: 179, 25.
Stewart, Anita: 166, 274; 173, 16; 179, 3; 227, 44; 231, 415; 231, 489; 236, 296; 239, 129; 241, c; 250, 48; (A) 250, 63.
Stewart, E. Burton (W): 24, 47.
Stewart, Donald Ogden: 335, 23; (W) 338, 18; 348, 44; (C) 349, 4; 349, 43.
Stewart, Grant: 22, 20; 87, 122; 132, 46; 216, 81; 217, 156; 224, 222; (W) 296, 12; 336, 31.
Stewart, Harrison: 83, 27.
Stewart, Helen: 203, 31.
Stewart, Henry T. (W): 53, 163.
Stewart, Katherine: 45, xv; 128, 139; 143, 3; 247, 266.
Stewart, Melville: 56, 241; 114, 37.
Stewart, Rosalie: 291, 36.
Stickney, Dorothy: 313, 35; 352, 15; 353, 17.
Stickney, Robert: 54, 192.
Stift, Magnus: 93, 290.
"Stigma": (R'27) 313, 60.
"Still Waters": (R'26) 302, 16.
Stillman, Henry: 228, 77.
Stillwell, George: 335, 23.
"Stingy": (R'19) 217, 142.
Stinton, Albert: 353, 43.
Stires, Ernest Milmore: (W) 216, 68.
Stires, Louise Homer: 277, 35.
Stirling, Richard: 103, 75.
"Stitch in Time, A": (R'18) 214, 348.

Stock (see also Repertoire Theatre): 7,10; 24,38; 101, 33; 126,42; 126,64; 132,67; 149,27; 150,48; 197,8; 203, 30; 216,96; 242,330; 245, 100; 250,12; 290,18; 322, 49; 329,12; 332,38.
Stockbridge, Henry: 38,88.
Stockdale, Eugene: 206,213.
Stockham, Edith: 210,97.
Stocking, M.A.: (W,D) 159,125.
Stoddard, George E.: 221,27.
Stoddart, James H.: 4,12; 8,3; 9,11; 25,63; 84,43; 171,232; 209,10.
Stodola, Gilbert I.: (W) 266,24.
Stoker, Bram: 11,14.
Stoker, H.G.: 261,370.
Stokes, John: 106,193; 147, 155; 286,23.
Stokes, Marion: 235,196.
Stokes, Sybil: 246,159.
Stokowski, Leopold: 266,37; (C) 273,27.
"Stolen Fruit": (R'25) 297,15.
"Stolen Orders": (R'15) 177,252.
"Stolen Story, The": (R'06) 69, 286.
Stoll, Horatio F. (W): 125, 18; 138,50; 147,153.
Stone, Allene: 348,29.
Stone, Amelia: 16,8; 76,167; 77,173; 88,149; 91,244; 91, 245; 100,185; 256,26.
Stone, Dorothy: 275,23; 275, 29; 289,21; 298,43; 333,46; 334,c; (A) 337,62; 342,50; 343,31; 348,29.
Stone, Fred A. (see also Montgomery and Stone): 25, 60; 69,293; 125,29; 137, 11; 172,311; 176,176; 202, 361; 204,127; 205,157; 211,188; 238,33; 268,6; 275,29; 289,40; 312,13; 316, 34; 325,44; 348,29; 349, 46; (C) 350,47.
Stone, Janet: 226,385; 237,367.
Stone, John Augustus: 197,14.
Stone, Lewis: 112,194; 132,59; 155,21; 170,187; 180,71; 183,292; 195,276; 231,413; 291,34; 301,49; (D) 315, 41; 346,25.
Stone, Marmion: 112,181.
Stone, Paula: 342,50; 348,29.
Stone, Stuart B.: (W) 129,162.
Stoneham, Catherine: 270,21.
Stonehouse, Ruth: 172,295.
"Stonewall Jackson's Way": (F) 167,19.
"Stop! Look! Listen!": 180, 59; (R'15) 180,66; 181, 180.
"Stop Thief": (R'12) 144,xi; 144,43.
Storer, Capp: 126,47.
Storey, Bobby: 276,18.
Storey, Edith: 191,17.
Stork, Clifford: 94,331.
Storm, Otto: 160,305.
"Storm, The": 225,309; (R'19) 225,350; 238,74.
"Storm Center": (R'27) 323, 40.
Story, Belle: 164,174; 218,213; 224,217; 225,299; 235, 191; 257,87.
Story, Rex: 223,153.
"Story of My Life, The" (Terry) (B): 98,xiv.
"Story of the Rosary, The": 164,153; (R'14) 164,196; 166,289.
Stout, Kate: 204,93.
Stow, Charles (W): 54,192.
Stowe, Leslie: 331,45.
Stowe, Vira: 81,293.
Stowell, William: 223,182.
Stowitts, Hubert: 227,30; 238,19; 245,90; 249,380.
Stracciari, Riccardo: 203,39.
Strachey, Lionel (W): 30,206; 38,88; 43,224; 46,324.
Strahl, Juliet: 240,165.
"Straight Road, The": (R'07) 72,31; 72,35.
"Straight Thru The Door": (R'28) 333,80.
Strakosch, Avery (W): 179,38.
Strand Theatre (New York): 184,369.
Strandin, Ebon: 272,10.
Strange, Michael: 260,295; 286,25; 303,36; 324,62.
Strange, Robert: 191,29; 202, 347; 203,15; 205,159; 206, 231; 207,289; 220,363; 261,

374; 271,17; 292,14; 359, 24.
Strange, Stanislaus: 13,11.
"Strange Interlude": (R'28) 325, 39; 325,40; 361,25.
"Strange Woman, The": (R'13) 155,6; 155,8.
"Stranger, The": (R'11) 132, x; 132,39; (R'17) 193,150.
"Stranger Than Fiction": 194,212; (R'17) 195,280.
Stransky, Josef: 126,54; 130, 190; 178,286; 266,38.
Strassmann, Julius: 93,290.
Stratford-On-Avon (England): 52, iii; 96,ii; 171,274; 172, 289; 182,202; 182,204; 325, 6; (D) 330,45.
Straton, [Rev.] John Roach: (W) 228,74; 230,248.
Stratton, Clarence (W): (V) 118,181; (V) 121,93; (V) 122,124; (V) 131,31; (V) 138,60; 172,289; 182, 221; 224,272; 226,398; 227, 39; 228,111; 229,196; 230, 284; 231,417; 232,539; 256, 59; 283,41; 284,41; 285,41; 286,41.
Strauss, Johann: 194,230.
Strauss, Oscar: 85,xi; (W) 349,40.
Strauss, Richard: 33,286; 61, 79; 64,144; 73,70; 98,128; 109,74; 110,103; 123,170; 154,200; 255,399.
Stravinsky, Ivor: 289,34.
"Straw, The": (R'21) 250,31.
"Strawberry Blonde, The": (R'27) 313,20.
Strawbridge, Edwin: 204,83.
Street, Lawrence (W): 182,223.
"Street, The": 160,308.
"Street Scene": (R'29) 336,50; (S) 337,26; (C) 341,34; (D) 342,c; 350,20.
"Street Singer, The": (R'29) 344, 72.
"Streets of New York": (D) 134,130.
"Strength of the Weak, The": (R'06) 64,140.
"Strictly Dishonorable": 344, 20; (R'29) 344,45; (C) 345, 4; 345,33; 345,48; 348,20; 351,28.
"Strife": (R'09) 107,2; 107, 9; 113,27.
"Strike Up The Band": (C) 348, 36; (R'30) 348,48.
Strikes, Theatrical (see also Actors Equity Association): 60,34; 189,298; 223,172; 225,314.
Strindberg, August: 50,89; 135,140; 136,xv; 142,197; 154,202; 161,27; 182,228; 233,30; 314,16; 348,38.
"String Beans": (F,R) 216, 124.
Stringer, Arthur: (W,V) 127, 84.
"Strollers, The": 5,2.
Strong, Austin (W): 335,26.
Strong, Jay: 202,347; 203,15; 205,159.
"Strong Man's House, A": (R'29) 344,47.
"Stronger Sex, The": 83,12; (R'08) 95,xi.
"Stronger Than Love"(see also "Enemy, The"): (R'25) 300,16.
"Strongheart": (R'05) 49,55; 49,59.
Strozzi, Kay: 332,21.
"Struggle Everlasting, The": (R'07) 81,290; 81,303; (F,R) 207,324.
Stryker, Muriel: 289,11.
Stuart, A.H.: 94,315.
Stuart, Clinton (W): 27,122.
Stuart, Grant: 96,58.
Stuart, Iris: 313,39.
Stuart, Judson D. (W): 171, 238.
Stuart, Leslie: 184,351.
Stuart, Muriel: 244,25.
Stuart, Ralph: 6,17; 11,15; 74,93; 78,225; 104,109.
Stuart, Suzette G. (W): 207,302.
"Stubborn Cinderella, A": 97, 74; (R'09) 97,75.
"Stubbornness of Geraldine, The": (R'02) 22,10; 23,11.
Studebaker Theatre (Chicago): 124,199.
"Student King, The": 71,7;

(R'06) 72,35.
"Student Prince, The": 287,14; (R'24) 287,15.
"Studies In Stagecraft" (Hamilton) (B): 172,276.
"Study of the Drama, A" (Matthews) (B): 115,vii.
Sturges, Preston: 344,20.
Sturmfels, Fritz: 134,105.
Stutton, Ada Stewart: (W,V) 116,101.
Stuyvesant Theatre (New York): 82,318.
Susscription Theatre: 347, 18.
"Suburban, The": 27,106; (R'03) 27,111.
"Subway, The": 336,50; (R'29) 337,47.
"Subway Express": 344,34; 345,34; 345,35; (R'29) 345, 66.
"Success": 205,141; (R'18) 205,150.
"Successful Calamity, A": 193, 145; (R'17) 193,152.
"Such a Little Queen": (R'09) 104,103; 104,109.
"Such Is Life": (R'16) 191,22; 220,336.
"Sudden Jim": (F,R) 199,176.
Sudermann, Hermann: 17,16; 22,13; 46,299; 47,2; 61, iii; 62,xii; (R'07) 73,xvi; 76,147; 137,5.
Suffrage: 99,xiii; 150,38; 157, 141; 181,127.
"Sugar House, The": 189,269; (R'16) 189,283.
Sullivan, Arthur: 20,7.
Sullivan, Joe J.: 256,27.
Sullivan, John T.: 27,124; 33, 273.
Sullivan, Pat: 322,32.
"Sultan of Sulu, The": 24, 30; (R'03) 24,34; 27,105.
Sumers, Amy: 72,30.
Summer Theatre: 329,18; 341,48; 353,44.
"Summer Widowers, The": 113,3; (R'10) 113,4.
Sumner, Charles: 172,288.
Sumner, John S. (W): 273,9; 304,18; (A) 326,11; 327,7.
"Sumurun": (S) 132,54; 175,160.
"Sun Dodgers, The": (R'12) 143,4.
"Sun Up": (R'23) 268,16; 269,13; (S) 271,26; (F) 295, 35.
"Sunday": (R'04) 46,297.
"Sunken Bell, The": (R'07) 73,xiv; 320,46.
"Sunkist": (R'21) 245,97.
"Sunny": (R'25) 297,16; (F) 354,16.
"Sunny Days": (R'28) 325,41.
"Sunny Side of the Street" (Wilder) (B): 55,v.
"Sunshine": (R'26) 307,15.
Sunshine, Beulah: 204,123.
Sunshine, Marion: 232,522.
"Sunshine Girl, The": (R'13) 145,66; 145,67; 149,24; 151,93.
Supernumaries (see Extras).
"Superstition of Sue, The": (R'04) 39,112; 39,128.
Superstitions, Stage: 101,31; 192,74; 220,356; 289,25; 306,18; 361,14.
Supervia, Conchita: 177,248.
"Suppressed Desires": (R'18) 205,151; 205,159; (R'20) 229,222.
"Sure Fire": (R'26) 309,72.
Surrat, Valeska: 73,68; 126, 41; 126,50; 126,51; 136, 198; 152,140; 159,237; 178,309; 202,401; 264,33.
"Susan In Search of a Husband": (R'06) 71,xiv.
Susman, Harold (W): 195, 272.
"Suspense": 352,30; (R'30) 354,26.
"Suspicion": (F,R) 214,392.
Sutherland, Anne: 38,87; 70, 321; 92,280; 104,105; 105,149; 187,149; 188,216; 301,26.
Sutherland, Evelyn Greenleaf: 13,11.
Sutherland Sisters, The Seven: 63,vi.
Sutro, Alfred: 56,262; 61,63; 76,ix; 84,34.
Sutton, Vida: 105,144; 105,

145.
"Suzanne": (R'10) 120,x; 120, 53.
"Suzi": 166,265; (R'14) 166, 303.
"Svengali": (F) 361,47.
Swain, Charles: 28,156.
Swain, Eva: 148,170; (D) 156, 85; 183,277.
Swan, Arthur (W): 128,131; 134,118.
Swan, Paul: 159,231; 197,35; 203,33; 219,301; 238,19.
"Swan, The": 273,14; (R'23) 273,15; (S) 277,26; (F,R) 291,34.
Swanson, Gloria: 209,60; 215, 63; 216,123; 219,304; 222, 109; 225,319; 228,105; 231, 411; 247,244; (D) 247,252; 271,32; 271,33; 273,32; 275,30; 279,32; 280,31; 283,32; 284,33; 285,31; (C) 286,15; 287,30; 289,31; 292,32; 297,31; 302,45; 308, 38; 308,39; 312,38; 315,52; (C) 321,33; 343,24.
Swanson Sisters [Marcella & Beatrice]: 279,38.
Swartz, Edward: 128,131.
Swartz, Jeska: 113,8.
Swartz, Maurice: 251,91; 267, 5; 268,20.
Sweatman, Willis: 151,xxiii.
Swedish Ballet: 272,10.
Swedish Theatre: 132,66.
Sweeney, Benny: 176,178.
"Sweeney Todd": (R'24) 282,15.
Sweet, Blanche: 164,161; 169, 127; 211,182; 212,253; 213, 318; (D) 215,c; 215,64; 216, 120; 216,127; 229,190; 230, 278; 259,240; 274,33; 281, 33; 307,48; 309,48; 322,60; 348,40.
"Sweet Adeline": (D) 343,23; (R'29) 344,45; (D) 345,c.
"Sweet and Low": (C) 358,44.
"Sweet and Twenty": (R'02) 12,11.
"Sweet Anne Page": PG,20.
"Sweet Kitty Bellaires": (R'04) 35,2; 36,45; 36,41.
"Sweet Land of Liberty": (R'24) 276,70.
"Sweet Little Devil": (R'24) 276,70.
"Sweet Nell of Old Drury": 268,14; (R'23) 268,15; 269, 10.
"Sweet Seventeen": (R'24) 278,19.
"Sweetheart Shop, The": 236, 281; (R'20) 236,334.
"Sweetheart Time": (R'26) 301, 18.
"Sweethearts": (R'13) 152, xii; (R'29) 344,72.
Swete, E. Lyall: 200,198; 208,375; 214,339; 218, 200; 219,293.
Swift, Lena: 97,90.
Swinburn, Algernon: (W) 182, 201.
Swinburne, Ann: 136,173; 141, 157; 147,150; 154,174; 160,297; 173,25; 177, 228.
Swinburn, Nora: 272,17.
Swirskaya, Thamara: 214, 359; 218,197.
Swiss Theatre: 92,282.
"Switchboard, The": (R'13) 146,xvi; 147,155.
"Sword of the Kings, The": 21,5.
Swordplay: 23,17; 50,iii; 216, 96.
"Swords": (R'21) 248,316.
"Sybil": (R'16) 181,125; 181, 135.
Sydney, Basil: 259,229; 262,18; 269,38; 298,16; 301, 11; 315,26; 317,20; 326,7; (D) 328,11; 338,46; 347, 14; 348,48; 349,32; 361,25.
Sydney, Midge: 353,23.
Sydney, Sylvia: (D) 315,41; 358,33.
Sykes, Ethel M.: 174,68.
Sykes, Gladys M.: 174,68.
Sykes, Jerome: 21,11; 24,34.
Sykes, William (W) (see "Excursions Through an Old Scrapbook").
Sylphe, La: 221,12.
Sylva, Carmen (pseud. for Queen Elizabeth of Roumania,

q.v.).
Sylva, Gertrude: 74,112; 76, xv.
Sylva, Marguerite: 8,19; 63, 114; 97,102; 103,77; 104, 114; 108,61; 119,9; 129,c; 130,x; 131,xi; 130,xviii; 133, iii; 208,371; 213,272; 218, 213; 240,162; 247,213; 247, 228; 247,233; 253,221.
Sylvester, Frank: 155,51; 179, 17.
"Sylvia Runs Away": (R'14) 164, 195.
Symons, Arthur: 49,67.
Syndicate, The (see also Trust, The): 56,xiii; 85,81; 86, 93; 119,7; 155,19; 185,2.
Synge, John M.: (D) 124,202; 129,157; 159,276.
"Synthetic Sin": (R'27) 321, 44; (F) 334,67.
"System of Dr. Tarr, The": 30, 191; 50,95.
Szamosy, Elza: 69,302; 69, 303; 70,311.
Szirmai, Albert: 297,25.
Szold, Bernard: 322,54.

--T--

Taafe, Alice: 186,67.
Taber, Richard: 195,281; 331, 30; 331,32.
Taber, Robert: 38,vii.
Tableaux Vivants: 86,106; 209, 35; 214,354; 222,77; 247, 223.
"Tabloid Hamlet, The": 117, 144.
Tacoma Theatre (Washington): 65,xii; 125,22.
Tacon Theatre (Havana): 74, 112.
Taft, William H.: 134,117.
Taggart, Jack: 66,210.
Tai, Jue Quon: 265,43.
"Tailor-Made Man, A": 200, 209; (R) 200,242.
"Tainted Philosophy": 143,6.
Tairoff, Alexander: 268,22.
Taiz, Lillian: 338,14.
"Take It From Me": (R'19) 219,275; 219,293.
"Take My Advice": (R'11) 131, xi; 131,32.
"Taking Chances": (R'15) 171, 230; 171,246; 174,78.
Talbott, Jack: 60,52.
Talchekar, H.A.: (W) 115,90.
"Tale of the Wolf, The": (R'25) 297,18.
"Tale of Two Cities, A": (see "Only Way, The").
"Tale the Ticker Told, A": (F) 95,16.
"Tales of Hoffman, The": (OP) 145,69.
Taliaferro, Edith: 44,247; 91, 244; 117,vii; 117,137;123, 158; 136,188; 141,156; 150, 45; 156,70; 161,21; 169, 127; 171,258; 191,15; 191, 47; 197,27; 199,125; 201, 291; 202,359; 217,163; 238,14.
Taliaferro, Mabel: 30,194; 33,288; 41,159; 42,c; 42, 197; 71,5; 83,4; 85,74; 88,158; 93,295; 103,71; 104,129; 106,186; 111, 153; 116,117; 136,188; 150, 45; 142,196; 156,70; 161, 21; (A) 214,379; 218,213.
"Talk About Girls": (R'27) 317,18.
"Talk of New York, The": (R'07) 83,xii.
"Talker, The": (R'12) 132,38; 132,45.
"Talkies, The" [Krows] (B): 358,8.
Talking Films (see Films -- Sound).
Tallant, Hugh: 34,296.
Taliard, Ernest: 94,319.
Talley, Marion: 297,36.
Tallman, George: 45,276; 105, 159.
Talma, Mme.: 45,xvi.
Talma, Francois Joseph: (D) 142,179.
Talma, Zola: 218,217; 219, 283; 318,19.
Talmadge, Constance: 199,179; 222,113; 222,116; 229,193; 231,489; 235,193; (D) 236, c; 237,378; 241,270; 256,

39; 271,33; 273,32; 280, 33; 289,32; 307,40; 309, 38; 309,39; 323,46.
Talmadge, Natalie: 229,193.
Talmadge, Norma: 167,19; 193, 187; 194,238; 195,285; 198, 78; 200,238; 201,323; 212, 259; 220,397; 226,405; 228, c; 229,193; 229,210; 231, 387; 231,489; 234,114; 234, 115; 241,271; 244,38; 256, 39; 262,35; 268,34; 268, 35; 271,33; 279,31; 279,33; 286,31; 296,32; 307,37; 309, 38; 309,39; 314,36; 322,48; 339,42.
Talmadge, Richard: 310,35.
Tamamoto, T.: 218,225.
Tamar, Amera: 283,37.
Tamara: 298,44.
"Taming of Helen, The": 26,81; (R) 27,108; 29,178.
"Taming of the Shrew, The": (R'03) 28,134; 36,viii; (R'04) 36,30; (R'05) 57, 268; 62,107; R'13) 151,xi; (R'14) 159,224; 170,173; (D) 182,205; (R'23) 273,19; 300,14; (R'25) 300,15.
Tamiris: 333,39; 357,44.
"Tangerine": 247,213; (R'21) 247,234.
Tanguay, Eva: 17,6; 98,130; 147,143; 156,77; 160,293; 197,36; 201,321; 210,95; 222,87; 242,317; 276,36; 289,36; 302,25.
Tannehill, Edward: 286,13.
Tannehill, Myrtle: 137,24; 216, 81; 239,109.
Tannen, Julius: 178,299; 307, 19.
Tansey, Harry: 129,168.
Tansey, John: 98,106; 98,113.
"Tantalizing Tommy": (R'13) 141,xv; 143,23.
"Tante": 154,173; (R) 154, 174.
"Tantrum, The": (R'24) 284,15.
Tapley, Rose: 39,122.
"Taps": (R'04) 44,242; 44,245; (R'25) 292,15.
Tarasova, Nina: 225,311; 238, 18; 289,35.
Tarbue, Marion: 287,37.
Tarkington, Booth: 106,170; 230,257; 263,38; (W) 318, 12.
"Tarnish": 273,18; (R'23) 273, 70; (S) 275,26.
"Tartarin": (S) 151,92.
Tarver, Jim: 199,179.
"Tarzan of the Apes": (F) 205,187; (F,R) 205,194.
Tashman, Lilyan: 243,440; 247,255; 249,370; 197,29; 217,147; 268,47; 327,14.
Tasker, Ann: 135,164.
"Tatooed Man, The": (R'07) 74,87.
"Tavern, The": (R'20) 237,370; 237,373; 351,42; (D) 352,4; (R'30) 352,41.
Tawde, George: 306,25.
Taxes, Theatre: 276,7; 323,44.
Taylor, Clarence: (W) 330, 40.
Taylor, Deems: 361,21.
Taylor, Estelle: 238,40; 280, 33; 302,47; 311,52; 322, 36; 335,70.
Taylor, Ethel C. (D): (W) 190,371; (W) 223,143; 231,381; 234,102; (D) 235, 163; (D) 236,257; (D) 237, 351.
Taylor, Eva: 284,24.
Taylor, J.F.: (W) 254,298.
Taylor, Julia Marie: 76,170.
Taylor, L. Stoddard: 313,33.
Taylor, Laurette: 100,169; 101,22; 108,41; 110,126; 114,34; 115,89; 122,136; 132, 39; 132,59; 133,c; 133,90; 141,153; 143,7; 143,20; 145, 82; 150,67; 158,174; 158,175; 159,270; 160,c; 160,315; 160, 328; 174,60; 175,119; 181, 149; 183,312; 187,127; 191, 22; 191,27; 193,165; 194, 225; 195,267; 195,283; 196, 363; 202,339; 204,73; 204, 86; 207,287; 207,299; (C) 209,21; (D) 213,289; 217,149; 227,15; 227,21; 231,351; 241,237; 241,244; 242,322; 253,234; 253,250; (A) 253, 260; 255,381; 256,28; 256,34;

262,35; 265,34; 268,14; 268, 29; 279,27; 284,33; 290,5; 290,34; 297,9; 300,11; 305,5; 317,20; 323,36; (W) 203,32.
Taylor, Marion: (W) 151,84.
Taylor, Ruth: 209,28; 321,50; 326,22.
Taylor, Tom: 88,169; 145,74.
Taylor, Valerie: 359,22.
Tchernichowa, Lubov: 181,128.
"Tea for Three": (R'18) 213,277; 214,349.
Teal, Ben: 65,186.
Teall, Gardner: (W) 91,240.
Teare, Ethel: 203,59.
Tearle, Conway: 50,103; 133,97; 159,233; 179,9; 184,360; 195,293; 199,175; 205,157; 224,222; 236,288; 244,36; 251,116; 262,35; 285,33.
Tearle, Noel: 218,209; 267,17; 280,13.
"Tears of the Sea": (F) 248, 352.
Teasdale, Sara: (W,V) 125,12.
Teasdale, Verree: 307,47; 311, 45; 312,11; 314,60; 330,55; 333,54; 338,54; 343,13; 359,24; 359,52.
"Teaser, The": (R'21) 247,233.
Teatro Argentina: 86,110.
Teatro De La Paz [Mexico]: 107,31.
Teatro Del Piccoli: 271,24.
Theatro Juarez [Mexico]: 18, 15.
Teatro Marti [Havana]: 138, 41.
Teatro Nacional De Costa Rica: 18,14.
Teatro Nationale [Bulgaria]: 98, 129.
Teatro Nacional [Mexico]: 107,32; 124,206; 335, 29.
Teatro Olimpico [Italy]: 91, 242.
Teatro Sperimentale [Rome]: 294,23.
Techern, Lubov: 178,296.
"Telegrapher's Daughter, The": (F) 184,357.
Television: 328,40.
Tell, Alma: 207,283; 207, 284; 210,67; (D) 211,c; 225,302; 230,279; 231,370; 233,7; 234,127; 240,175; 249,365; (D) 250,33; 251, 83; 251,115; 252,199; 269, 14; 270,26; 298,14.
Tell, Olive: 163,106; 176, 178; 182,193; 183,284; 199,184; 201,270; 204,79; 205,c; 205,169; 212,257; 218,221; 226,371; 227,32; 231,371; 231,413; 243,395.
Tell, Sylvia: 218,211; 248, 317.
"Tell Me More": (R'25) 292,16.
Tellegen, Lou: 150,xv; 157, 124; 167,5; 168,60; 171, 246; 174,78; 175,132; 180, 74; 182,193; 187,143; 203, 20; 203,24; 205,157; 207, 310; 210,81; (A) 214,379; 224,234; 248,289; 248,340; 259,222; 269,43; 293,34; 308,40.
Telva, Marion: 268,37; 274,37; 290,41.
Temianka, Henri: 334,43.
"Temperamental Journey, The": (R'13) 152,114; 152,122; 152,123.
"Tempest, The": 42,207; (R'16) 184,334; 184,353.
Tempest, Marie: 35,3; 35,9; 51,109; 52,134; 98,123; 107,xii; 107,1; 108,60; 112,183; 120,34; 120,39; 127,76; 166,264; 167,6; 168,70; (A) 168,71; 172,307; 175,111; 176,167; 176,168; 177,233; 183,274; 185,10; 185,45; 186,69; 191,41; 192,79; 201,293; 258,144; 260,302.
Temple, Elaine: 319,23.
"Temple Maiden, The": 193,143.
Temple, Olive: 61,55; 65, 192; 101,24; 132,38; 159, 236.
Templeton, Fay: 3,4; 15, 19; (A) 16,19; 31,222; 42, 201; 60,26; 73,63; 133, 74; 137,23; 192,100; 231, 363.

Templeton, Mercer: 232, 505.
"Temptation": (R'11) 124, 183.
"Temptress, The": (F) 305, 38.
"Ten Commandments, The": (F) 274, 31.
Ten Eyck, Melissa: 271, 35.
"Ten of Diamonds, The": (F, R) 200, 248.
"Tenderfoot, The": (R'03) 29, 180; (R'04) 38, 85.
"Tenement Tragedy, A": (R'06) 71, xiv.
Tennant, Dorothy: 41, 170; 44, 240; 45, 289; 65, 189; 81, 293; 98, 127; 118, 196.
Tennant, Gertrude: 116, 119.
Tennyson, Jean: 275, 38; 292, 30; 333, 21.
"Tenor, The": (R'15) 180, 116.
Tent Theatre: 348, 31.
"Tenth Avenue": (R'27) 319, 22.
"Tents of the Arabs, The": 196, 332; 203, 31; (R'19) 218, 207; 328, 8.
"Terence": (R'04) 36, 32.
Ternina, Milka: 10, 30; 70, 341.
"Terre D'Epouvante": 83, v.
"Terrible Meek, The": (R'12) 135, 139.
Terrill, Charles Moesser: 211, 142.
Terris, Norma: 317, 3; (C) 321, 33; (D) 325, 18; 329, 41.
Terriss, Tom: 107, 5.
Terry, Alice: 267, 35; 273, 74; 274, 33; 285, 33; 298, 32; 307, 38; 307, 40; 313, 49; 318, 42.
Terry, Beatrice: 34, 298; 208, 371; 271, 14; 272, 27.
Terry, Edward: 47, 6; 49, 58.
Terry, Eleanor: (C) 343, 40.
Terry, Ellen: PG, 31; 33, 275; 55, 219; 64, 166; 66, 205; 46, 320; 67, xi; 67, 237; 73, 59; 73, 69; 74, 105; 76, 162; 77, 173; 82, xx; 119, 34; 128, 127; 135, 161; 142, 198; 144, 64; 155, 32; 167, 10; 172, 288; 182, 225; 185, 6; 187, 131; 330, 72.
Terry, Ethel Grey: 211, 177.
Terry, Ethelind: 236, 281; 239, 94; 302, 46; 318, 15.
Terry, Fred: 117, 129; 118, xvii; 118, 190; 118, 191.
Terry, Kate: 271, 38.
Terry, Muriel: 105, 156.
Terry-Lewis, Mabel: 269, 14; 270, 28.
Terwin, Johanna: 142, 191.
"Tess of the D'Urbervilles": (F) 156, 86; 216, 84; (F) 281, 33; (F, R) 283, 30; 297, 24.
Tesseman, Robert: 80, 261.
Tessier, Valentine: 215, 25.
Tester, Ruth: 302, 14; 311, 25; 313, 18; 353, 36; 361, 28; (C) 361, 38.
"Tethered Sheep": (R'15) 170, 211.
Tetrazzini, Luisa: 67, 233; 83, 5; 85, 73; 85, 84; 93, 308; 94, 346; 129, 154; 131, 4; 149, 8; 150, 58; 265, 9.
Tew, Whitney: 10, 34.
Texas, Franz Marie: 234, 85.
"Texas Nightingale, The": (R'22) 262, 19; 263, 21.
Texas Theatre: 300, 40; 338, 50.
Texas, University of: 291, 44.
Texsmith, Vaughan: 4, 15.
Teyte, Maggie: 131, 26; 146, 128; 152, 137; 157, 141; 176, 191; 213, 272.
Thalia Theatre: 123, 168.
"Thais": (OP) 77, 175; (OP) 77, 175; 121, 70; (R'11) 122, xiii; 122, 106.
"Thank You": (D) 249, 389; (R'21) 249, 438; 251, 103.
Tharp, Norman: 140, 113; 180, 73.
"That Awful Mrs. Eaton": (R'24) 285, 19.
"That Man and I": (R'04) 37, 60.
"That Sort": 166, 261; (R'14) 166, 307.
"That's Gratutude": (R'30) 356, 24; (D) 357, 2.
Thaule, William: 38, 102.
Thayer, Edith: 184, 342.
"Theatre, The" (Cheney) (B): 345, 6.

Theatre An Der Wein (Vienna): 160,305; 165,219.
Theatre Antoine: 24,47; 80,258; 83,v; 88,186.
Theatre De Charmilles (France): 141,158.
Theatre Des Funambules (Paris) (D): 239,82.
Theatre Des Mathurins: 54,202.
Theatre Du Chatelet, Le: (D) 174,75.
Theatre Du Vieux Colombier (see also Copeau, Jacques): 204,86; 205,151; 205, 152; 206,219; 213,292; 214, 347; 215,19; 217,143; 219,274; 218,206.
Theatre, Economics of (see also Actors' Equity; Angels; "How Theatres Are Managed"; Royalties, Authors: Strikes): 18,2; 25,55; 38,90; 39, 126; 43,217; 51,114; 70, 321; 85,82; 94,340; 97, 92; 106,186; 110,118; 115, 94; 122,135; 124,195; 145,74; 155,22; 171,260; 188,202; 191,12; 243,396; 259,223; 272,12; 277,9; 284,54; 294, 9; 308,7; 312,17; 337,24; 344,15; 360,15; 300,9; 334, 42; 361,18.
"Theatre Everywhere, The": 50, xii; and monthly thereafter.
Theatre Francaise (Paris): 38,96; 94,ii; 95,14; 142, 180; 165,219; 177,225; 179,43; 181,164; 192,128.
Theatre Guild: 220,342; 221, 12; 221,23; 224,214; 225, 348; 229,184; 230,269; 237,369; 241,266; 241,267; 244,6; 244,29; 252,144; 254,305; 258,149; 261,369; 269,7; 270,7; 271,9; 274, 9; 287,7; 289,26; 292,12; 294,7; 295,9; 298,5; 298, 16; 301,16; 304,31; 306, 53; 309,27; 315,24; 339, 20; 343,27; 347,4; 347, 18; 353,37; 359,42.
Theatre Guild Studio: 347,43.
Theatre Libre (see Theatre Antoine).
"Theatre Management" [Stanton] (B): 345,76.
"Theatre of Tomorrow, The": [Macgowan] (B): 254,340.
Theatre Parisien: 226,396; 227,61.
Theatre Rejane (Paris): 149, 6.
Theatre, State of the (see also Managers, Theatre): 221, 32; 223,162; 230,256; 249,326; 251,74; 255,380; 264,8; 273,20; 278,12; 285,9; 290,7; 295,9; 297, 10; 301,30; 303,31; 304, 9; 304,18; 313,5; 316,16; 318,16; 319,18; 322,17; 328,30; 329,7; 330,11; 336, 19; 337,13; 338,20; 339,13; 340,9; 345,38; 346,13; 346, 17.
"Theatre Thoughts" by H. Seton: 205,140; 211,156; 215, 22; 216,88; 217,148; 220, 360; 222,88; 230,276; 234, 112; 235,180; 237,350; 241, 252.
Theatre Workshop: 203,30; 203,31.
Theatres (see also "New York's Historic Theatres"): 5,8; 19,18; 30,193; 33,296; 36,36; 44,ii; 58,xix; 86, 98; 98,117; 106,914; 108, xv; 110,121; 123,169; 124, 184; 125,18; 127,102; 136, 197; 137,16; 137,27; 138, 50; 149,2; 153,146; 172,283; 184,336; 187,146; 206,212; (D) 231,352; 244,6; 250, 42; 253,212; 257,98; 264, 62; 278,10; 275,7; 279,7; 290,16; 296,75; 297,7; 303, 24; 324,53; 325,53; 344,15.
Theatres -- Film: 144,59.
Theatres (Philadelphia): 37,78.
Theatrical Women's Exchange: 255,356.
"Theatron" [Stratton] (B): 336,4.
"Theodora": 175,133; (F,R) 250,38; (F) 251,107.
Theodore, Belle: 183,275.

"Theory of the Theatre" [Hamilton] (B): 113, xi.
"There and Back": (R'03) 28, 134; 28, 138.
"There's Many a Slip": 20, 4; (R'02) 20, 5.
Theresa, Maria: 302, 8.
"These Charming People": (R'25) 297, 18; 298, 14.
"These Few Ashes": 334, 45; (R'28) 334, 47.
"These Modern Women": (R'28) 325, 40.
"They All Want Sympathy": (R'26) 309, 68.
"They Knew What They Wanted": (R'24) 287, 19; 288, 18; 292, 7; (S) 293, 26; 294, 10; 304, 7.
"They Never Grow Up": (R'30) 351, 48.
Thibaud, Jacques: 33, 284; 265, 37; 297, 35.
"Thief, The": 80, 257; (R'07) 80, 258; 81, 297; (C) 82, xxiv; 93, 297; 129, xii; (R'27) 316, 20.
"Thief of Bagdad, The": (F) 279, 7; (F) 279, 30.
Thimble Theatre (New York): 175, 157; 179, 12.
Thimig, Hans: 323, 38.
Thimig, Helen: 289, 29; 298, 23.
Thimig, Herman: 323, 38.
"Things That Count, The": 155, 6; (R'13) 155, 7; (D) 157, 125.
"Third Degree, The": 95, 33; (R'09) 97, 73; (S) 97, 96; 115, 72.
"Third Paper, The": (R'14) 163, 139.
"13th Chair, The": 191, 20; (R'16) 191, 22; 199, 130.
"39 East": (R'19) 219, 275; 219, 277; (F, R) 237, 378.
"This Is New York": 359, 25.
"This Man's Town": 350, 48.
"This Thing Called Love": (S) 333, 32; (F) 346, 61.
"This Was a Man": (R'26) 311, 15.
"This Way Out": (R'17) 200, 206.
"This Woman and This Man": (R'09) 98, xi.
"This Year of Grace": 332, 74; (R'28) 334, 60.
Thomas, Allen: 245, 80.
Thomas, Ambroise: 182, 220.
Thomas, Augustus: 9, 13; 9, 14; 10, 18; 25, 58; 36, 47; 48, 31; 49, 60; 51, 115; 55, 227; 56, 249; 58, 304; 65, 188; 80, 259; 83, 2; 96, iv; 96, 58; 106, 167; 106, 187; 115, 81; 115, 83; 118, 196; 122, 108; 123, xiii; 137, 10; 137, 13; 145, 75; 153, 150; 159, 230; 169, 135; 175, 117; 181, 151; 184, 336; 196, 353; 197, 24; 206, 210; (A) 231, 347; (W) 231, 394; 259, 210; 259, 220.
Thomas, Calvin: 183, 295; 201, 275; 204, 84.
Thomas, Clara Fargo: 287, 27.
Thomas, Dorothy: 81, 296.
Thomas, Edna: 251, 89; 267, 31; 279, 27.
Thomas, Frank: 158, 172; 177, 235.
Thomas, Grace: 258, 173.
Thomas, Igor: 331, 23.
Thomas, John: 103, 75.
Thomas, John Charles: 170, 192; 173, 27; 178, 279; 193, 162; 200, 213; 212, 221; (A) 214, 379; 225, 312; 228, 96; 247, 219; 257, 114.
Thomas, [Mrs.] Leonard: 207, 297.
Thomas, Louis: 179, 12.
Thomas, Mona: 236, 283.
Thomas, Olive: 175, 118; 181, 125; 184, 374; 190, 363; 192, 101; 199, 177; 206, 261; 217, 153; 222, 110; 232, 537; 234, 115; 237, 377.
Thomas, Walter: 10, 16; 62, 94.
Thomason, Adelina O'Connor: (W) 255, 376.
Thompson, Carolyn: 217, 159; 222, 93.

Thompson, Charlotte: 68,265; 70,xiv.
Thompson, Denman: 43,218; 81,294; 89,192; 121,98; 123, xiv; 154,xxxi; 231,397; 237, 366.
Thompson, Frederick W.: 50,99; 84,xi; 93,295.
Thompson, Harlan: 298,36.
Thompson, Leonora: 206,225.
Thompson, Lydia: 197,34; 209,16.
Thompson, Margaret: 209,60.
Thompson, May: 194,231; 196, 357.
Thompson, Sydney: 232,517; 251, 89.
Thompson, Walker: 184,363.
Thompson, William H.: 26,88; 26,89; 37,75; 45,276; 51, 110; 165,217; 286,13.
Thomson, Beatrix: 311,19.
Thomson, Carolyn: 165,220; 298,13; 289,45.
Thomson, Cesar: 290,43.
Thomson, Kenneth: 292,5.
Thorndike, Russell: 94,320.
Thorndyke, Sybil: 116,107; 146, 111; 301,20; 201,21; 306, 33; 307,21; 326,42.
Thorne, Charles: 25,64; 78, 222; 111,157; 202,399.
Thorne, Fred: 117,144; 136,190.
Thorne, Grace: 32,243.
Thorne, Nellie: 10,6; 80,263; 81,304.
Thorne, Olive Harper: 132,72; 140,119.
Thorne, Robert W.: (W) 221, 10.
Thorne, Thomas: 96,45; 99,141; 104,102.
Thorne, W. L.: 222,103.
Thorner, Will: 191,42.
Thornton, Bernard: (W) 208,370.
Thornton, Frank: 136,171.
Thornton, Renee: 282,35.
"Those We Love": (R'29) 349, 47.
"Those Who Sit In Judgement" by M. Goodrich
1. Percy Hammond (D) 314,12
2. Alexander Woollcott 315,22
3. G.J. Nathan 317,28
4. Aston Stevens 318,20
5. Alan Dale 319,40
6. J. Brooks Atkinson 320,40
7. Robert Benchley 321,41
8. E.W. Osborn 322,37
9. H.T. Parker 324,35
10. Frederick Donaghey 326,44.
"Those Who Walk in Darkness": (R'29) 224,224; 224,225.
"Thou Desperate Pilot": (R'27) 314,22.
"Thousand Years Ago, A": 156,61; (R'14) 156,63; (D) 157,125.
"Three Bears, The": 203,20; (R'17) 203,51.
"Three Cheers": (R'28) 333, 46.
"Three Daughters of Monsieur DuPont, The": (R'10) 111, xxx; 111,131.
"Three Faces East": (R'18) 212,209; 212,213.
"Three Fast Men": (D) 134, 129.
"Three for Diana": (R'19) 220,341.
"Three Lights, The": (R'11) 130,xiv.
"Three Little Girls": (R'30) 351,48; 352,41.
"Three Little Maids": (R'03) 32,238; 32,240; 33,276.
"Three Live Ghosts": 237,347; (R'20) 237,371.
"Three Musketeers, The": (F,R) 248,324; (R'28) 326,39; 326,41; 328,37.
"Three of Hearts": (R'15) 173, 6; 173,18.
"Three of Us, The": (R'06) 70,316; 70,333; 72,42.
"Three Passions, The": (F) 332,29.
"Three Romeos, The": (R'11) 130,xv.
"Three Showers": (R'20) 231, 402; 231,407.
"Three Sisters, The": (R'23) 264,15; 310,17; (R) 310, 18.
"Three Twins": 90,222; (R'08)

91, xi.
"Three Weeks": (F) 279, 31.
"Three Wise Men": (R'18) 214, 345.
"Three's a Crowd": (D) 358, 13; 358, 42; 359, 20.
Throckmorton, Cleon: 323, 37; (W, C) 338, 33; 343, 37; 356, 20.
Thuille, Ludwig: 130, 206.
"Thumbnail Sketches of Player Folk" by A. Patterson: 313, 30; 314, 30; 315, 40.
"Thumbs Down": (R'23) 271, 52.
"Thunder": (R'19) 225, 347.
"Thunderbolt, The": 90, 206; (R'10) 118, 163; 118, 172.
Thurman, Mary: 209, 57; 248, 311.
Thurman, Wallace: (C) 339, 22.
Thurston, Adelaide: 32, 242.
"Thy Name Is Woman": (R'20) 238, 58; 239, 83.
"Thy Neighbor's Wife": 128, 115; (R'11) 128, 116.
Tibbett, Lawrence: 288, 35; 301, 35; 331, 23; 359, 47.
<u>Ticket Brokers</u> (see also <u>Speculators, Ticket</u>): 312, 24.
"Ticket-of-Leave Man, The": (D) 134, 129.
<u>Tickets, Theatre</u> (see also <u>Speculators, Ticket</u>): 74, 104; 137, 30; 170, 186; 171, 260; 201, 263; 235, 166; 343, 21; 347, 15; 357, 17.
"Tickle Me": (R'20) 235, 240; 236, 270.
"Tick-Tack-Toe": (R'20) 230, 272.
Tiden, Fred: 23, 7; (D) 275, 27.
"Tidings Brought to Mary": (R'22) 264, 20.
"Tiefland" (OP): 95, 25.
Tiernan, Junior: 232, 517.
Tierney, Genevieve: 279, 14.
Tierney, Harry: (W) 341, 29.
Tiffany, Annie Ward: 11, 9; 86, 98.
Tiffany, Marie: 249, 396; 262, 43.
"Tiger Cats": 283, 62; (R'24) 285, 62.
"Tiger Rose": 201, 275; (R'17) 202, 349.
"Tiger! Tiger!": (R'18) 215, 17; 215, 29; 219, 286.
Tilbury, Zeffie: 48, 41.
Tilden, Frederick: 128, 115; 256, 21.
Tilden, William: 312, 38.
"Till Eulenspiegel": (D) 296, 13.
Tilley, Vesta: 30, 192; 198, 131.
"Tillie": 116, 69; (R'19) 216, 80.
"Tillie's Nightmare": (R'10) 112, 174; 112, 187.
Tillio, M.: (D) 247, 211; 247, 227.
Tillis and La Rue: 271, 35.
Tilton, Thomas: 294, 21.
"Time": (R'23) 274, 58.
"Time, the Place and the Girl, The": (R'07) 79, x; 79, 237.
Times Square Theatre (New York): (D) 237, 361.
Timponi, Florence: 233, 17.
Tincher, Fay: 220, 389.
Tinney, Frank: 138, 59; 166, 281; 236, 270; 270, 29; 307, 19.
Tinnin, Glenna Smith: 153, 171.
"Tip Top": (R'20) 237, 424.
"Tipping the Winner": (R'14) 165, 254.
"Tired Business Man, The": (R'29) 341, 43.
"Tit for Tat": (R'04) 40, 136; 40, 155.
Titheradge, Dion: 195, 290; 310, 25.
Titheradge, George S.: 146, 126.
Tigherage, Madge: 132, 38; 132, 40; 141, 151; 143, 10.
Titkos, Ilona: 298, 23.
"Title Mart, The": (R'06) 62, 85; 62, 87.
<u>Titles of Plays</u>: 212, 224; 227, 24; 300, 24; 334, 27.
Tittell, Esther: 31, 211.
Titus, Anna: 90, 216.
"To Love": (R'22) 261, 371.
"To the Ladies": 254, 301; (R'22) 254, 307.
"Toast of the Town, The": (R'05) 59, 6; 59, 15.

Toback, Hannah: 237,349; 239, 112.
Tobin, Genevieve: 124,203; 226,389; 234,85; (D) 237, 351; 240,175; 258,157; 266,31; 292,46; 301,59; 314,3a; 346,23; (D) 349,52; 353,1.
Tobin, Thomas R. Jr.: 128,114.
Tobin, Vivian: 148,183; 158, 170; 171,231; 250,25; 268,3; 323,54; (D) 341,17; 353,52.
Tobin Sisters [Vivian & Genevieve]: 275,25; 305,25.
"Toby's Bow": (R'19) 218,205; 218,225.
Tod, Quentin: 141,149.
"To-Day": (R'13) 153,144; 154,178.
Todd, James: 324,40.
Todd, Thelma: 323,27.
"Together": (F,R) 213,320.
Tokatyan, Armand: 287,35.
"Told in the Hills": 68,271.
Toledo (Ohio) Theatre: 247, 230; 249,430.
Toler, Sidney: 314,24; 338, 32; 343,33; (C) 344,44; (W) 350,36.
Toller, Ernst: 279,22.
Toller, Rosalie: 128,117.
Tolstoi, Ilya: (W) 314,40.
Tolstoi, Leo: 24,50; 26,94; 42,203; 51,110; 55,215; 75,142; 80,260; 182,223; 190,355; 314,40.
"Tom Jones": (R'07) 82,xv.
"Tom Moore": (R'01) 8,10.
"Tom Sawyer": (F,R) 203,57.
"Tombeau Sous L'Arc De Trimphe, Le": 279,12.
Tombes, Andrew: 235,183.
"Tommy": (S) 314,24.
"Tommy Rot": (R'02) 22,9; 22,14.
"Tomorrow and Tomorrow": (R'31) 350,24; (S) 360,33.
"Tomorrow-Land": 57,i.
Tone, Franchot: 360,26.
Tonge, Ashton: 197,25.
Tonge, Phillip: 221,9.
"Tongues of Men, The": (R'13) 154,xvi.
"Tonight at 12": (R'28) 334,45.
"Tonight or Never": (R'30) 358,26.
"To-Night's the Night": 168, 57; (R'14) 168,99.
"Too Many Crooks": (R'14) 158,170; 158,177; 160,296; 199,146.
"Too Many Husbands": 224,220; (R'19) 225,347.
"Too Many Millions": (F,R) 215, 62.
"Toodles": (R'08) 87,vii.
Toohey, John Peter: 331,49.
Toole, John Lawrence: 33,276; 67,xii.
"Toot Sweet": (R'19) 220, 343; 221,17; (R'18) 206, 220; 207,282; 207,289.
"Top Hole": (R'24) 284,72.
"Top O' The World, The": 82, vii; (R'07) 82,xx.
"Top Speed": (R'29) 347,63.
"Topaze": 349,44; (R) 349, 48; 350,42; (S) 351,32.
"Topics of 1923": (R'23) 274, 16.
"Topsy and Eva": (R'24) 288,16; 292,31.
"Torch Song": (R'30) 356,24; (S) 356,34.
"Torchbearers, The": 260,298; 268,42.
"Torches, The": (R'17) 202, 351.
"Toreador, The": (R'02) 12, 9; 13,15.
Tormey, May: 163,114.
Toronto Theatre: 311,41.
Toronto, University of: 275, 41; 275,42.
Torrence, David: 3,5; 96,69; 98,118; 199,135.
Torrence, Ernest: 168,87; 201, 275; 230,275; 280,31; 294, 1; 310,39; 322,35.
Torrence, Ridgeley: 196,350.
Torriani, Gina: 118,173; 123, 162.
Torrup, Ingeborg: 333,11; 361,40.
Toscanini, Arturo (see also Opera): 90,200; 116,109; 119,4; (A) 120,52; 129,154; 301,34; 333,25.
"Toto": 243,411; (R'21) 243,458.

Totten, Edythe: 337,42.
Touring (see also "Theatre Everywhere, The"): 45,ix; 65,181; 89,186; 89,195; 93, 306; 119,17; (D) 133,86; 135,61; 195,268; 197,26; 200,218; 225,295; 239,86; 282,22; 287,22; 289,42; 301, 10; 302,10; 314,5; 316,5; 329,15; 343,27; 352,13; 358, 37.
"Tourists, The": 66,208; 66, 209; (R'06) 68,xiii.
Tourneur, Jeannette: 221,12.
Tourneur, Maurice: 199,183.
"Towards a New Theatre": [Craig] (B): 151,xvi.
Tower, Catherine: 98,116.
Tower, Grace Hortense (W) (see also "Interviews With Authors"): 65,181.
"Tower of Lies": (F,R) 297,30.
Towers, Gail Y.: 108,41.
"Town Topics": 178,301.
Towne, Charles Hanson: (W,V) 94,324.
Towse, John Ranken: 7,14; 231, 362.
"Toymakers of Nurenberg, The": (R'07) 83,xiv.
Toy Theatres: 115,88; 171,255; 229,176.
Toy Theatre (New Jersey): 339,46.
Tracey, Stella: 92,270.
Tracy, Cora Lingard: (W) 78,222; 225,320; 229,159.
Tracy, Helen: 88,146.
Tracy, Lee: 279,18; 309,19; 310,28; 311,32; 312,29; 329,25; 329,26; (C) 330,9; 359,16.
Tracy, Spencer: 338,48; 350, 30.
"Trader Horn": (F,R) 361,48.
Tragedy: 90,221; 245,104.
"Tragedy of Hamlet, The" [Frank] (B): 117,v.
"Tragedy of Nan, The": (R'20) 230,272.
"Tragic 18": (R'26) 309,68.
Trahan, Al: 354,26.
"Trail of the Lonesome Pine, The": 132,41; (R'12) 133,76.
Traill, Hester: 31,222.
"Transplanting Jean": (R'21) 240,179; 240,181.
"Trap, The": (R'15) 170, 170.
Trask, C. Hooper: 185,5; 229,187.
Traube, Shepard (W): 354,40; 359,37.
Traubel, Helen: 303,35.
"Travelling Man, The": (R'16) 192,86.
"Travelling Salesman, The": (R'08) 91,230; 91,231.
Traver, George H.: 75,117.
Travers, Henry: 226,363; 230, 265; 239,91; 273,17; 299, 17; 304,31; 311,17; 313, 35; 323,40.
Travers, Natalie: 299,45.
Traverse, Madeline: 157,141; 205,139; 209,55; 214,395; 228,147; 231,412.
Treadwell, Sophie: 342,20.
"Treasure, The": 237,347; (R'20) 237,369; 241,267.
"Treasure Island": 179,8; 179, 17; (D) 184,354; 191,27; (F) 229,191.
Tree, Ellen: 95,iv.
Tree, Beerbohm: 14,15; 15, 18; 16,23; 43,217; (D) 45, 283; 62,94; 64,166; 66,198; 69,308; 88,170; 99,165; 100,169; 103,73; 104,120; 107,7; 112,202; 118,197; 125,15; (D) 129,173; 163,105; (A) 181,148; 182,182; 182, 192; 182,217; 183,272; 183,275; 183,286; 183,287; 183,289; 184,331; 184, 335; 185,6; 185,8; 193, 167; 196,345; 197,40; 198, 100.
Tree, [Mrs.] Beerbohm: 85,60; 85,68.
Tree, Viola: (D) 45,283.
"Trelawney of the Wells": (R'11) 120,xi; 120,42; 120,45; (R'25) 293,15; (R'27) 313,19; 313,20; 327,22.
Tremaine, Beatrice: 249,384.
Trentini, Emma: 72,38; 75,140; 118,165; 118,166; 121,88;

143,3; 170,192; 171,241; 174,78; 186,73.
Trenton, Pell: 205,193.
Trevelyan, Hilda: 187,131.
Trevor, Austin: 322,40.
Trevor, Norman: 183,281; 184,334; 192,89; 193,148; 197,25; 203,24; 203,25; 207,283; 213,281; 215,9; 218,225; (W) 222,96; 226, 379; 227,19; (D) 237,351; 250,39; 268,18; 295,19; 323,45.
Trevor, Vaughan: 132,72; 153, 143; 166,267.
"Trial by Jury": (R'15) 173,7.
"Trial Marriage, The": (R'12) 144,164.
"Trial of Joan of Arc, The": (R'21) 243,415.
"Trial of Mary Dugan, The": 320,22; (R,C) 320,76; (S) 321,28; 340,15; 342,37.
"Triangle, The": (R'06) 62, xiii; 62,103.
Triangle Club (see Princeton University).
Triangle Theatre (New York): 269,46; 281,48.
Tridon, Andre (W): 72, 46; 133,92; 135,158.
"Trifles": (R'16) 191,21; 191, 29; (R'21) 244,60.
"Trifler, The": (R'05) 50,84.
"Trigger": (R'27) 323,39.
"Trilby": (R'05) 52,133; 60, 41; 169,134; (R'15) 171, 230; 171,242; 171,243; (F) 269,33.
"Trimmed in Scarlet": (R'20) 229,185.
"Trimplet, The": (R'15) 175,139.
Trini: 266,41; 287,5; 296,25; 321,13; 322,47.
"Triple Crossed": (R'27) 316, 20.
"Tristam and Iseult": 70,337.
"Triumph of Love, The": 36, 30; 37,56; (R'04) 37,62.
"Triumph of X, The": (R'21) 248,314.
"Trois Jeunes Filles Nues": (R'29) 340,41.
"Trojan Women, The": 173,12; 331,54.
"Troth, The": (R'20) 234,108.
Troubetskoy, Prince and Princess: 212,226.
Trouhanowa, Natacha: 132,44.
"Trouper, The": (R'26) 302,18.
Troutman, Ivy: 88,162; 88,163; 102,44; 116,125; 117,156; 123,165; 135,160; 150,53; 154,196; 159,245; 159,270; 171,246; 173,45; 179,36; 192,73; 201,270; 207,291.
Trowbridge, Charles: 154,181; 255,379; 262,24; 272,18; 301,26; 303,52.
"Troyka": (R'30) 350,70.
Truax, Sarah: 18,8; 32, 245; 62,100; 63,127; 78, 200.
"True Adventures of a Play, The" [Shipman] (B): 163, 145.
"True to Form": (R'21) 248,344.
Trueman, Paula: (D) 329,11; 340,42; 340,50; 352,66; (C) 358,44.
Truesdell, Frederick: 44,240; 45,289; 99,157; 123,147; 127,99; 164,169; 165, 234; 199,135; 292,14.
Truex, Ernest: 92,260; 137,11; 144,35; 159,224; 159,230; 161,46; 180,64; 183,281; 184,359; 199,129; 217,163; 228,99; 236,283; 248,291; 251,103; 290,13; 294,25; 294,26; 295,39; 302,21; 304,47; 306,27; 307,28; 342,19; 344,25; 345,50; 353,34.
Trunnelle, Mabel: 167,19.
Truscott, George: 98,111.
Trust, Theatrical (see also Syndicate, The): 7,7; 17,8; 31,236; 53,160; 57,288; 65,181; 264,7; 277,9.
"Truth, The": (R'07) 72,30; 72,33; 159,226; 159,233; (R'14) 159,265.
"Truth About Blayds, The": (R'22) 254,306; 255,351; (D) 255, 375; (S) 258,156.
"Truth Game, The": 360,24;

(R) 360, 26.
"Truth Tellers, The": (R'05) 57, 268; 58, 290.
"Truth Wagon, The": (R'12) 134, xv; 134, 124.
Tryon, Glenn: 344, 27.
Tryouts: 162, 79; 169, 132; 289, 7; 296, 12.
"Tsar Fyodor Ivanovitch": 262, 14; (R'23) 264, 15.
Tsutsui, Tokujiro: 349, 20.
Tucholsky, Johanna: (W) 79, 248.
Tucker, Florence L.: (W) 60, 51.
Tucker, Sophie: 129, 177; (A) 226, 438; 267, 42; 285, 36; 292, 30; 341, 27.
Tully, May: 68, 260.
Tully, Richard W.: 190, 414; 202, 410; 211, 121; 231, 376; 238, 84.
"Tumble In": (R'19) 219, 274; 219, 277.
Tulsa, University of: 330, 53.
Tuohy, Joseph: 90, i; 144, 41; 159, 224.
"Turandot": 142, 191.
Turck-Baker, Roschen: 163, 116.
Turgenieff, I.S.: 42, 203.
"Turn to the Right!": (R'16) 187, 140; 188, 205; 190, 364.
Turner, Alberta: 177, 229; 184, 374; 197, 39.
Turner, Jack: 30, 202.
Turnley, Harry: 99, 150.
Turner, Maidel: 159, 240.
Turney, Hazel: 204, 84.
"Turning Point, The": (R'10) 110, xii.
Turrill, Celia: 281, 35.
Tuschkan, Else: 90, 207.
Tuttle, Frank: (W) 203, 14.
Twain, Mark (see also Clemens, Samuel): 296, 70; 302, 74.
"Tweedles": (R'23) 271, 19.
"Twelfth Night": 34, 292; (R'04) 37, 56; (R'04) 38, 83; 38, 99; 90, 219; (R'10) 109, 67; 109, 93; 154, 193; (R'14) 159, 225; 161, 6; (R'14) 167, 8; (R'17) 204, 86; 221, 9; 225, 298; 300, 23; 329, 42; 356, 12; (R'30) 357, 27.
Twelfth Night Club: 98, iv; 164, 183.
"Twelve Miles Out": (R'26) 301, 72.
"Twelve Pound Look, The": (R'11) 121, xi.
"Twelve Thousand": (R'28) 326, 76.
"Twenty Days in the Shade": (R'08) 85, 64; 85, 79.
"Twiddle-Twaddle": 60, i; (R'06) 60, vi; 60, 31.
"Twin Beds": (R'14) 164, 154; 164, 163; 180, 82; 231, 349.
"Twin Sister, The": (R'02) 13, 2; (R'02) 14, 1; 14, 2.
"Twirly-Whirly": (R'02) 20, 8.
"Two Blocks Away": (R'21) 248, 344.
"Two Fellows and a Girl": 270, 8; (R'23) 270, 15.
"Two Girls Wanted": (R'26) 308, 68.
"Two Hearts in Waltz Time": (F, R) 360, 47.
"Two Is Company": (R'15) 177, 224; 177, 234.
"Two Little Brides": (R'12) 136, x; 136, 172.
"Two Little Girls in Blue": (R'21) 244, 30; 245, 99.
"Two Mr. Wetherbys, The": (R'06) 68, xiii.
"Two Noble Kinsmen, The": 35, 18.
"Two Orphans, The": 38, 100; 39, 107; (R'04) 39, 108; 39, 124; 111, 157; 231, 363; (F) 250, 37; (R'26) 303, 15.
"Two Out of Time": 133, 86.
"Two Roses, The": (R'05) 47, 8.
"Two Schools, The": 21, 7; (R'02) 21, 8.
"Two Strangers from Nowhere": (R'24) 279, 19.
"Two Virtues, The": 177, 219; (R'15) 177, 222.
"Two Women": (R'10) 119, xi; 119, 23.
"Two Women and That Man": (R'09) 106, xvii.
Tyler, Fred: 90, 219; 98, 118.
Tyler, George C.: 43, 227;

153, viii; 180, 62; (W) 183, 283; 199, 122; 201, 264; 211, 130; 223, 144; 231, 379; 258, 149; (W) 339, 11.
Tyler, Harry: 321, 60.
Tyler, Henry: 170, 188.
Tyler, Odette: 26, 82; 27, 117; 45, 286; 70, 314.
Tyler, Royall: (D) 188, 208.
Tyana, Brandon: 9, 4; 19, 8; 84, 39; 85, 86; 112, 201; 137, 11; 144, 33; 145, 94; 149, 25; 171, 243; 182, 194; 186, 84; 190. 354; 205, 141; 217, 135; 228, 75; 247, 214.
Tynan, Robert: 19, 5.
Type Casting (see Casting).
"Typhoon, The": (R'12) 134, xi; 134, 108; 136, 180; 136, 194.
"Tyranny of Love, The": (R'21) 242, 339.
"Tyranny of Tears, The": (R'13) 153, 143; 160, 314.
Tyree, Elizabeth: 17, 4; 20, 11; 24, 31; 24, 32; 25, 54.
Tyree, Bessie: 40, 156; 203, 27; 229, 186.
Tyrell, Henry (W): (V) 10, 16; 15, 19; 16, 21; 18, 18; 18, 21; (V) 19, 26; 21, 18; 25, 76; 26, 89; 30, 205; 32, 246; 34, 308; 41, 164; 42, 192; 43, 219; 45, 276; 46, 299; 47, 27; 49, 77; 50, 85; 53, 161; 54, 208; 55, 227; (V) 58, 293; 69, 309; 80, 262; 81, 293; 85, 67; 87, 137; (V) 106, 184; 109, 78; 111, 130; 114, 36; 130, 198; 29, 170; 35, 8.
Tyron, Glenn: 324, 50.
Tyrrell, Edith Wynne: (W) 28, 139.
Tyson, Grace: 114, 45.

--U--

Uart, Lottie: 112, 187.
Ulrich, Lenore: 169, 134; 173, 29; 176, 174; 182, 197; 183, 284; 186, 87; 199, 131; 201, 275; 207, c; 209, 14; 209, 15; 222, 79; 224, 267; 226, 377; (A) 226, 438; 227, 29; 230, 286; 231, 358; 234, 124; (A) 235, 223; 237, 363; 244, 13; 250, 49; 251, 81; (D) 251, 101; 251, 105; 254, 303; 256, 28; 258, 152; 261, 381; 262, 12; (A) 263, 63; 286, 17; 288, 14; 290, vii; 290, 56; 298, 12; 302, 5; (W) 306, 9; (D) 308, c; 334, 14; 352, 44; 354, 12; (D) 356, c; 356, 31; 357, 14; (W) 358, 20; 358, 52.
Ulrich, Olive: 30, 204; 117, 138; 118, 164; 140, iii.
"Ulysses": 13, 7; 14, 15; 16, 22; 31, 215; (R'03) 32, 238; 33, 281.
"Umpire, The": 72, 56.
"Unbeliever, The": (F, R) 205, 194.
"Unbroken Road, The": 99, 157.
"Unchastened Woman, The": (R'15) 177, 252; 178, 292; 179, 25.
"Uncle Sam": (R'11) 130, xiii.
"Uncle Tom's Cabin": (see also "Topsy and Eva"): 26, 102; 36, 44; 37, ix; 327, 39; 341, 26; 354, 44.
"Uncle Vanya": 303, 21; 351, 14; (C) 351, 18; 351, 20; (R'30) 351, 42; 351, 45; 352, 43.
"Under a Texas Moon": (F) 351, 59.
"Under Cover": (R'03) 32, 240; 32, 259; 161, 13; 164, 154; (R'14) 164, 155; 166, 290; 169, 132; 174, 79; 187, 154.
"Under Fire": 175, 113; (R'15) 175, 139; 180, 83.
"Under Many Flags": (R'12) 140, xv.
"Under Orders": (S) 212, 218; 212, 219.
"Under Sentence": (R'16) 189, 326; 190, 354.
"Under Southern Skies": (R) 10, 5; 11, 15.
"Under the Gaslight": 354, 44.
"Under the Greenwood Tree": 81, ii; 84, 34; (F, R) 215, 62.
"Under the Top": (F, R) 216, 124.
"Under Two Flags": 3, 4; 29, 164.
"Undercurrent, The": (R'25) 289, 18.
Understudies: 103, 98; 174, 67; 226, 380; 246, 170; 281, 19.

"Undertow, The": (R'07) 76, 145.
Underwood, Frances: 205,137.
Underwood, Franklyn: 147,150.
"Une Nuit De Noel Sous La Terreur": 143,2.
"Unforseen, The": (R'03) 24,28; 24,29.
Unger, Gladys: 291,23; (W) 300, 24.
Union Square Theatre (New York): 25,62; 250,36.
Unions, Theatre (see also Actors Equity Association): 60,34.
United Artists Studios: 319,12.
Universal Film Co.: 158,186.
Universal Peace Theatre Company: 49,vii.
Universal Studios (California): 171,244; 319,12.
"Unknown Lady, The": (S) 274,24.
"Unknown Purple, The": 213, 267; (R'18) 213,278.
"Unknown Woman, The": (R'19) 227,17; 227,19.
"Unpardonable Sin, The": (F) 216,127.
"Unsophisticates, The": (R'29) 347,70.
Untermeyer, Louis (W): (V) 78,219; (V) 87,128; (V) 106,169; (V) 146,110; 282,17; 309,32.
"Until They Get Me": (F,R) 203, 57.
"Unwelcome Mr. Hatch, The": (R'02) 11,8; 11,9.
"Unwinding the Reel": 199,178; and monthly thereafter.
"Unwritten Chapter, The": (R'20) 237,424.
"Unwritten Law, The": (R'13) 145, xxix.
"Up and Down Broadway": (R'10) 115,xiv; 115,85.
"Up and Up, The": (R'30) 356,25; 356,26.
"Up from Nowhere": (R'19) 224, 280; 226,379.
"Up in Mabel's Room": (R'19) 217,142.
"Up in the Clouds": (R'22) 253, 266.
"Up Pops the Devil": (R'30) 356, 25.
"Up the Line": (R'26) 311,18.
"Up York State": (R) 9,11.
"Upstairs and Down": (R'16) 189,282; 190,365.
"Upstart, The": 112,178; (R'10) 116,102.
Upton, Frances: (D) 331,13; (C) 337,35; (D) 339,32.
Uptown Theatre (Chicago): 300,61.
"Uptown West": (R'23) 268,20; (S) 269,28.

Urban, Joseph: (D) 175,124; (D) 183,269; 183,276; 184,351; (D) 184,336; 184, 386; 185,11; 194,248; (D) 202,367; (D) 220,337; (D) 231,361; 251,94; (D) 251,95; 278,39; 290,39; (D) 298,34.
Urlus, Jacques: 141,139; 145, 69; 155,15.
Urmy, Charles: (W,V) 94,314.
Ushers: 41,165; (D) 282,29.
"Usurper, The": 46,296; (R'05) 47,3.
Utah, University of: 217,166.
Uzalmon: 220,362.
Uzzell, Thomas H.: (W) 161,21.

--V--

Vachell, Horace Annesley: 180, 92.
Vaders, Henrietta: 82,321.
Vadie, Maryon: 233,25; 260, 288; 268,43; 283,37.
"Vagabond King, The": (R'25) 297,44; 298,13.
Vail, Francis M.: (C) 325, 75.
Vail, Leslie: 325,29.
Vail, Lester: 336,52.
Vajda, Ernest: 278,39; 279, 27; (D) 305,12; (W) 320, 21.
Vale, Louise: 121,98.
Vale, Rita: 339,29.
Valencia, Tortola: 203,29.
Valentine, Elizabeth: 64,164; 75,117.

Valentine, Ethel: 183,275.
Valentine, Grace: 142,165; 160,299; 174,67; 174,70; 197,47; 199,145; 201,281; 203,48; 206,c; 206,248; 217, 174; 218,219; 229,180; 235, 174; 235,206.
Valentine, Gwendolyn: 117,152; 118,171.
Valentine, Louiszita: 163,127.
Valentine, Sidney: 134,106; 140,121.
Valentine, William: 283,25.
Valentino, Rodolph: 254,297; 257,86; 278,32; 283,30; 284, 33; 287,32; 291,33; 295,34; 298,42; 305,46; 307,39; 307,52.
Valentinova, Valentina: 257,81.
Valerio, Edith: (W) 176,187.
Valery, Odette: 94,312.
Vallee, Rudy: 341,47; 344,30.
"Valley of Lost Hope, The": (F) 168,68.
"Valley of the Shadow, The": (S) 81,293.
Valli, Valli: 58,313; 96,38; 104,119; 105,157; 107,c; 111,166; 148,174; 148,185; 150,42; 152,c; 157,112; 158, 184; 182,194; 183,314; 183, 316; 186,68; 191,41; 218, 213.
Valli, Virginia: 200,249; 308, 36; (A) 357,58.
"Vampire, The": 96,40; (R'09) 97,74.
Vampire Women: 101,13; 107, 5; 177,246; 205,162; 211, 145; 212,258; 215,59; 217, 146; 220,389; 222,100; (D) 223,143; (D) 239,85; 240, 187; 248,318; 283,22.
Van, Billie B.: 94,327; 207, 277; 208,354; 292,30; 305, 19.
Van Bechten, Edward: 203,33.
Van Biene, Eileen: 173,6; 192,84; 311,25.
Vanbrugh, Irene: 62,ii; 307,21.
Van Buren, A.H.: 114,34; 208, 369.
Van Buren, Lotta: 279,35.
Van Buren, Mary: 9,18; 65, 179.
Van Buren, Ned: 205,189.
Van Cleve, Harriet: 182,230.
Vandamn (W): 353,44; 356, 28; 358,42; 359,42; 361,20.
Vandenhoff, Kate: 46,305.
Vander, Charles O.: (W) 331, 75; (W) 332,82.
Vanderbilt, Cornelius Jr. (W): 312,10; 313,14; 315,34; 324, 31.
Vanderbilt, Gertrude: 109,88; 130,186; 132,69; 202,365; 217,168; 217,178.
Vanderbilt, Muriel: 287,43.
Vanderbilt, W.K.: 86,92; 106, 194.
"Vanderbilt Cup, The": (R'06) 61,xiii; 61,57.
Vanderbilt University: 216,99.
"Vanderbilts and the Players, The": 20,18.
"Van Der Decken": 180,86; 180, 87; 180,88.
Van Der Stucken, Frank: 21, 26.
Vander Vere, Ethel: 114,54.
Van Doren, John (W): 247, 212; 251,76; 258,145.
Van Doren, Mme.: 215,25.
Van Dresser, Marcia: PG,30; 7,5; 12,6; 180,85; 214, 353.
Van Druten, John: 300,31.
Van Dyck, Rosina: 123,148.
"Van Dyck, The": (R'21) 249, 440.
Van Dyke, Henry: (W) 323,9.
Vane, Betty: 337,52.
Vane, Sutton: (D) 277,29.
Vanera, Lucien: (W) 209,12.
Van Gordon, Cyrenne: 180, 85; 203,41.
Van Hoogstraten, Willem; 262,42; 340,27.
Van Hoose, Helen: 251,103.
"Vanishing American, The": (R,F) 298,30.
"Vanities of 1923": (R'23) 270,15.
"Vanities of 1925": (R) 294, 15.
"Vanities of 1926": 311,3a.

"Vanities of 1930": (R'30) 353, 24.
"Vanity Fair": (R'11) 120, 34.
Van Law, H.R. (W): 113, 23.
Vanne, Marda: 344, 45; 345, 50.
Van Noppen, Leonard C. (W): 27, 126.
Van Raalte, Joseph: (W, V) 168, 104.
Van Rellin, Jane: 162, 61.
Van Rooy, Anton: 60, 53.
Van Ryker, Alice: 171, 238.
Van Sell, Elizabeth H.: 117, 132.
Van Sloan, Edward: 265, 31; 344, 47.
Van Studdiford, Grace: 12, 11; 13, 23; 28, 156; 91, 246; 93, 283; 121, 96.
Vantine, Marion: 233, 35.
Van Varseveld, Laurette (W): 83, 15.
Van Vechten, Carl (W): 201, 292; 215, 32; 293, 24.
Van Volkenburg, Edna: 255, 379.
Van Voorhees, Linn: 260, 293.
Varasi, Eurica: 34, 318.
Varden, Beth: 263, 21.
Varden, Evelyn: 119, 19; 124, 212; 219, 283.
"Varennes": (D) 41, 164.
Varesi, Gilda: 170, 194; 220, 340; 235, 189; 236, 267; (D) 237, 351; 237, 360; (A) 238, 72; 245, 93; 246, 170.
Vargas, Albert (D): 228, c; (D) 294, c.
Varian, Edward: (W) 197, 24.
Varlamoff, C.A.: 161, 21.
Varrey, Edwin: 76, xv.
"Varying Shore, The": 251, 75; (R'21) 251, 97; (D) 251, 101.
Vassar College: 246, 177; 246, 179; 257, 106; 260, 323; 326, 46; 326, 47; 341, 44; 350, 49.
Vaudeville: 37, iv; 38, iv; 39, iv; 61, x; 62, 103; 81, xxi; 94, xvi; 96, 45; 105, ii; 116, 117; 158, 199; 159, 237; 160, 293; 166, 281; 187, 144; and monthly thereafter; 222, 83; 222, 94; 231, 408; (D) 239, 108; 250, 36; 262, 36; and monthly thereafter: (D) 279, 37; (D) 282, 37; 289, 7; 294, 29; 317, 21; 325, 21; 325, 51; 327, 30.
Vaudeville, German: 120, 42.
Vaughn, Adamae: 313, 39.
Vaughn, Adele: 202, 347.
Vaughn, Alberta: 279, 33; 309, 36; 331, 24.
Vaughn, Evelyn: 74, 88.
Vaughn, Hilda: 285, 38; 310, 27; (D) 312, 27; 324, 39; 332, 44.
Vecsey, Ferenc: 249, 391.
Vedder, Dorothy: (W) 342, 32.
Veidt, Conrad: 263, 35; 310, 35; 313, 38; 320, 20; 324, 49.
Veiller, Bayard: 152, 111; 170, 188; 193, 165; 328, 29.
"Veils": (R'28) 326, 40.
Veit, Martha: 255, 376.
Velez, Lupe: 323, 28; (A) 358, 59; 360, 47.
Velie, Janet: 221, 7; 235, 174; 238, 33; 256, 17; 291, 11; 303, 45; 332, 68; 333, 11; 350, 72.
Velinkanoff, Ivan: 294, 13; 296, 14; 300, 35.
Velour, Rose: 284, 26.
"Velvet Lady, The": 217, 135; (R'19) 217, 143.
"Veneer": (R'29) 346, 45.
Veness, Amy: 207, 273; 341, 24.
"Venetian Romance, A": (R'04) 40, 136; 40, 145.
Venning, W. Gerald: 82, 327.
Ventura, Giovanni: 108, 188.
Verande, Louis P.: 45, 274.
Verdi, Francis: 292, 30.
Verdi, Giuseppe: 182, 220.
Vermell, Nancy: 207, 295.
Vermilyea, Harold: 307, 23.
"Vermont": (R'29) 336, 51.
Verneuil, Louis: 300, 31.
Vernie, Eugenie: 104, 101.
Vernille, Nitza: 290, 44.
Vernon, Frank: 48, 41.
Vernon, Grenville (W): 277, 20; 290, 20.
Vernon, Ida: 70, 325; 82, 329; 180, 77.

Vernon, Jean (W): 281,19.
Vernon, Ley: 74,88.
Vernon, Marie: 217,140.
Vernon, Shirley: 309,58.
Veronica (see Blythe, Veronica).
Veronica, Vera: 321,50.
"Veronique": 58,313.
Verse Drama (see also Phillips, Stephen; Mackaye, Percy): 165,222; 288,9.
"Versiegelt": (OP,R'12) 133, 78.
"Very Good, Eddie": (R'15) 180, 64.
"Very Good Young Man, A": (R'18) 212,209.
"Very Idea, The": 199,129; (R'17) 199,133.
"Very Minute, The": 195,273; (R'17) 196,341.
"Very Naked Boy, The": (R'19) 217,144.
"Very Wise Virgin, A": (R'27) 317,18.
"Vestale, La": (OP) 298,34.
Vestvali, Felicia: 209,16.
Vettori, Elda: 275,35.
"Via Crucis": (R'23) 274,19.
"Via Wireless": (R'08) 94,x; 94,337.
Vibert, Marcel: 318,42.
Vichnevsky, Alexander: 262,14.
"Vicissitudes of a Playwright" by L. Denig:
- 1 Eugene Walter 171,235;
- 2 Charles Klein 172,293;
- 3 Edward Locke 173,9;
- 4 Porter Emerson Browne 174,71;
- 5 Jules Eckert Goodman 179,17.

"Victim, The": 171,230.
Victor, Josephine: 84,32; 84, 46; 90,219; 96,57; 98,120; 100,185; 127,103; 143,14; 153,170; 177,223; 181,124; 190,370; 199,125; 217, 170; 232,509; (W,FI) 234,86; 238,7; 288,20.
Vidas, Raoul: 215,11.
Vidor, Florence: 208,393; 241, 269; (W) 320,26; 332,42.
Vidor, King W.: 231,489; 306, 38; 306,40; 312,39.
Viebig, Clara: 27,115.
"Vieil Homme": (D) 122,110.
"Viennese Nights": (F) 358,3; (F,R) 361,48.
Viennese Opera Co.: 108,37.
Viennese Theatre (see Austrian Theatre).
Viereck, George Sylvester: 72, x; (W) 82,331.
Vignola, Robert G.: 204,121.
"Vikings at Helgeland, The": 352,23; 352,42.
"Village Lawyer, The": (R'08) 86,xv; 86,97.
"Village Postmaster, The": 34, 307.
Villains: 306,11; 307,22.
Villani, Luisa: 155,15.
Villars, Paul (W): 98,111.
Villasana, Juan: 181,123.
Vince, Laura: 304,8.
Vincent, Eva: 61,65.
Vincent, Henry: 118,176; (C) 359,22.
Vincent, James: 93,298.
Vincent, James N.: 299,23.
Vincent, Leon J.: 35,14.
Vincent, Ruth: 58,313; 59, 12.
Vinci, Lora: 287,31.
"Vinegar Buyer, The": (R'03) 28,134.
"Vinegar Tree, The": (R'30) 358,26.
Vinton, Arthur R.: 359,26.
Vinton, Darrel: 195,281.
Vinton, Doris: 332,49.
Vinton, Horace: 6,17.
"Virgin, The": (R'26) 302,18.
"Virgin Goddess, The": 70, xiv.
"Virgin Man, The": (R'27) 312,21.
Virginia, Daisey: 151,88.
Virginia, University of: 219,318; 253,245; 253,246.
"Virginian, The": (R'04) 36, 32; 36,34; 68,272; (F) 163,110.
"Virginius": (R'07) 81,289.
"Virtue's Bed": (R'30) 351, 48.
"Virtuous Wives": (F,R) 216, 124.

Vishnevsky, Alexander: 264, 14.
"Vision of St. Agnes, The": (D) 184, 336.
"Visitor, The": 114, 36.
Viskovsky, Viacheslav: 260, 309.
Vitagraph Co.: 95, 15.
Vitak, Albertina: 301, 13.
Vitaphone Varieties: 353, 59.
Vivero, Adela: 220, 357.
Vivian, Daisy: 230, 247.
Vivian, David: 324, 59.
Vivian, George: 94, 321; 221, 9.
Vivian, Percival: 134, 127; 221, 9.
Vivian, Robert: 298, 14.
Vivian, Violet: 94, 320; 111, 140; 111, 142.
"Vivian's Papas": 31, 211; (R'03) 32, 242; 42, ii.
Vix, Genevieve: 203, 41.
Vogel, Henry: 169, 131.
"Vogues of 1924": 279, 14; (R'24) 279, 16.
"Voice from the Minaret, A": (R'22) 253, 236.
"Voice in the Dark, A": 222, 103; (R'19) 223, 151.
"Voice of McConnell, The": (R'18) 216, 79.
"Voile Du Bonheur, Le": (R'18) 215, 19.
Vokes, May: 37, 58; 74, 90; 152, 117; 172, 280; 242, 328; 259, 241; 290, 46.
Vokes, Rosina: 81, 300.
Vokes Family: 243, 414.
Vokes Theatre (Wayland, Mass.): 94, 342.
Volare, Lorna: 214, 350; 214, 351; 222, 89.
Volinine, Alexander: 125, 4; 130, 198; 239, 102.
Volksbuhne Theatre (Berlin): 274, 22; 336, 35.
Vollmer, Lula: 271, 26; 273, 29; 361, 39.
"Volpone": 327, 37; (R'28) 327, 38; 328, 35; 336, 56.
"Voltaire": 255, 367; (R'22) 255, 373.
Vom Baur, Eva Elise (W): 126, 56; 140, 106; 142, 178; 144, 46; 144, 47; 145, 88; 145, 94; 146, 112; 148, 186.
Von Busing, Fritzi: 132, 43; 144, 58.
Von Dewitz, Baroness: 164, 174.
Von Ende, Amelia (W): 27, 115; 104, 132; 102, 48; 110, 108; 120, 42; 137, 5.
Von Grona, Eugene: 337, 41.
Von Hatzfield, Olga: 88, 149; 95, 26.
Von Heldburg, Helene: 125, 24.
Von Hofmannsthal, Hugo: 85, 60; 110, 108; 137, 5.
Von Leth, Gertrude: 97, 100.
Von Mayhof, Grete: 155, 20.
Vonnegut, Marjorie: 189, 269; 191, 29; 194, 223; 203, 15; 205, 148; 205, 159; 208, 359; 248, 323; 291, 14; 294, 19; 308, 33.
Von Ostermann, Hedwig: 13, 21.
Von Possart, Ernst: 51, 122; 116, iv; 120, 50.
Von Schuch, Hofrath: 64, 144.
Von Selover, Elaine: 4, 15.
Von Sonnenthal, Adolph: 13, 21; 15, 14.
Von Stroheim, Eric: 287, 30; 296, 30; (W) 320, 18.
Von Tilzer, Harry: 179, 26.
Von Vecsey, Franz: 41, 180.
Von Waldron, Ethel: 129, 163.
Von Wildenbruch, Ernst: 97, iv.
Von Wolzogen, Ernst: 120, 42.
Von Zathwiczky, Eduard: 284, 35.
Vonzell, Harry: 359, 40.
"Vortex, The": (R'25) 296, 15; 296, 17; (S) 298, 26.
Vosburgh, Harold: 123, 160.
Vosper, Frank: 296, 21.
Vossen, Amelia: (D) 322, 25.
"Votes for Women": (R'09) 99, xiii; 99, 148.
Vreeland, Frank (W) 293, 22.
Vroom, Edward: 88, 147.

--W--

Wabash College: 140, 105.
Wadsworth, William: 327, 39.

Wagner, Billie: 222,99; 233, 25.
Wagner, Charles L.: 278,22.
Wagner, Cosima: 179,24.
Wagner, Richard: 32,252; 37, 72; 67,240; 79,244; 79,247; 118,181; 118,182; (D) 127, 80; 132,71; 179,24; (D) 266,10.
Wagner, Siegfried (C): 178, 304; 179,24; 275,34.
Wagstaff, [Mrs.] Alfred Jr.: 196,339.
Wagstaffe, Blanche: 207,297.
Wainwright, Helen: 42,212; 70,340.
Wainwright, Marie: 13,4; 169, 131; 170,191; 202,353; 216, 81; 217,164.
"Wait 'Till We're Married": (R'21) 249,426.
"Wake Up and Dream": 346,45; (R'29) 347,63.
"Wake Up, Jonathan": (R'21) 241,261.
Wakefield, Charlotte: 280,18.
Wakefield, Henrietta: 123,148.
Wakefield, Willa Holt: 166,281.
Wakeman, Emily: 111,131; 129,150.
Wakeman, Keith: 86,111.
Walbrook, H.M.: (W) 307,20.
Walburn, Raymond: 261,372.
Walcamp, Marie: 220,389.
Walcot, Charles Melton: 205, 166.
Walcott, George: 343,34; 344, 44.
Walcott, William; 177,235; 228,103.
Wald, Lillian D.: 305,32.
Waldorf, Janet: 47,14.
Waldorf Theatre (London): 53, 178.
Waldridge, Harold: 337,48.
Waldron, Charles D.: 84,48; 89,197; 90,205; 141,134; 143,5; 243,301; 243,398; 360,20; 361,35.
Waldron, Isabel: 37,62; 45,274; 111,131.
Waldrop, Oza: 97,80; 104,123; 112,193; 128,114; 149,28.
"Walk Offs, The": (R'18) 213, 312.
Walker, Ada Overton: 26,96; 66, 224; 86,97.
Walker, Antoinette: 45,274; 88, 163; 92,280; 110,104; 142, 165; 166,279; 163,294.
Walker, Charlotte: 16,1; 16,4; 16,5; 23,9; 34,318; 36,48; 47,15; 53,172; 56,256; 56, 257; 62,103; 65,185; 67, 241; 71,16; 78,201; 84,49; 88,c; 90,205; 94,313; 103, 70; 108,52; 110,123; 111, 144; 129,149; 132,41; 136, 193; 150,57; 154,192; 156, 76; 177,219; 179,30; 180, 74; 186,87; 208,369; 210, 80; (A) 214,379; 214,387; 235,170; 236,255; 238,20; 269,18.
Walker, Dan: 246,167.
Walker, Edyth: 59,25.
Walker, George W.: 26,96; (W) | 66,224; 85,xii; 86, 97.
Walker, Guy: 249,225.
Walker, Jimmy: (W) 312,5.
Walker, June: 215,21; 229, 166; 231,440; 248,291; 251,103; 289,14; 289, 23; 297,36; 306,5; 309,12; 309,13; 310,61; 317,80; (D) 325,36; 327,25; (D) 329,c; (C) 348,4; 360,26.
Walker, Laura: 171,228; 172, 277; 243,411; 245,82.
Walker, Lillian: 199,179; 204,126; 207,325; 211,184; 212,251; 212,252; 213,322; 213,327; (D) 214,c; 214, 390.
Walker, Margaret: 4,15.
Walker, Polly: 322,51; (W,D) 333,29; 336,69; 341,61.
Walker, Starr King: 101,12.
Walker, Stuart (see also Portmanteau Theatre): 175, 139; 191,13; (W) 204,76; 219,296; 248,322; 248,323; 271,72.
Walker, Walter: 335,51.
Walkley, A.B.: 43,217; 111, 150.
"Walkure, Die": (OP) 134,125.

Wall, Helen: 31,213.
Wall, Marjorie: 234,104.
"Wall Street Girl, The": (R'12) 135,xvi.
Wallace, Edgar: 356,32; 359, 30.
Wallace, Fay: 117,141; 129, 162; 140,113.
Wallace, Florence: 172,290.
Wallace, [General] Lew: 31, 226; 59,iv.
Wallace, Marie: 160,285.
Wallace, Ramsey: 167,15.
Wallace, Regina: 153,155; 190,354; 210,87; 213,291; 232,519; 254,313; 257,77; 279,18.
Wallach, Arthur: (W) 113,6.
Wallack, James W.: 15,24; 51, 118; 86,99; 168,72; 191, 8; (D) 211,150.
Wallack, Lester: 25,62; 51,118; 66,200; 71,19; 89,184; 111, 163; 113,6; 126,64; 126,65; 138,45; 140,127; 145,74; 148, xiv; 168,72; 215,38; 286,16; 289,25; (A) 358,16.
Wallack Family: 51,118; 205, 166.
Wallack's Lyceum (New York): 207,294.
Wallack's Theatre (New York): 39,127; 51,119; 168,72; 222,91; 226,362; (D) 231, 352; (D) 290,50.
Waller, Lewis: 128,132; 129, 148; 130,185; 130,213; 132, 38; 134,xiii; 135,157; 136, 171; 136,195; 139,68; 141, 130; 141,159; 161,15.
Wallis, Bertram: 84,35; 85,62.
Wallison, L.R.: (W) 31,228.
"Walls of Jericho, The": (R'05) 57,265; 57,277; 57, 279; 61,63.
Walnut Street Theatre (Philadelphia): 19,20; 37, 79; 64,xvi; 69,v; 86,99; (D) 232,506.
Walrond, Eric: (W) 295,20.
Walsh, Blanche: PG,7; 5,6; 8,2; 21,13; 25,53; 25,58; 26, c; 26,94; 28,148; 29,174; 49,54; 51,110; 51,115; (W) 53,181; 67,233; 72,35; 78, 203; 82,xxi; 94,323; 129,151; 158,199; 235,184.
Walsh, George: 205,196; 215, 61; 228,147; 277,32; (W) 325,42.
Walsh, George Ethelbert: (W) 138,48.
Walsh, Harry: 337,30.
Walsh, Josie: 208,363.
Walsh, Lionel: 103,75.
Walsh, Marie: 165,232.
Walsh, Percy: 157,128.
Walsh, Thomas (W): (V) 28, 136; 29,176; 68,278.
Walsh, Tom: 239,109; 241,268.
Walsh, Towsend (W): 164, 176; 175,138.
Walska, Ganna: 214,353.
Walter, Bruno: 286,34.
Walter, Eugene: 86,88; 88, 144; 92,272; 111,144; 121,97; 142,194; 145,75; 171,235; 181,124; 210, 79; 271,20.
Walter, Wilfred: 334,37.
Walter, William E.: (W) 36,50.
Walters, Charles: 325,41.
Walters, Harry: 250,23; 291,6.
Walthall, Henry B.: 210,120; (D) 351,29.
Walther, Edna: 120,64.
Walton, Florence: 167,30; 172,299; 173,15; 174,c; 174,57; 175,149; 190, 373; 191,17; (A) 193,130; (W) 193,168; 207,310; 213, 306; (A) 214,379; 215,14; 221,33; 222,115; 226,414; 238,47; (A) 250,63; (A) 255,346a; 256,50; 273, 34; 286,36.
Walton, Fred: 60,31; 141, 157; 176,170; 186,63; 201,287.
"Waltz Dream, A": (R'08) 85,xi; 85,75.
"Waltz of the Dogs, The": (R'28) 328,38.
"Wanderer, The": 192,122; 193,141; (R'17) 193,151; 194,198; 194,231.
"Wandering Jew, The": 250,7;

(R) 250,30.
Wanger, Walter: 330,42.
"Wania": 42,203.
War And Drama (see also "Roll of Honor, The"): 165,219; 168,78; 171,257; 175,114; 181,149; 185,12; 193,162; 195,286; 196,328; 196, 356; 197,38; 198,64; 199, 119; 200,215; 201,268; 201, 272; 202,336; 203,16; 205, 158; 206,203; 206,259; 207, 280; 207,282; 207,302; 208, 346; 209,17; 210,82; 210, 87; 210,92; 211,136; 211,148; 212,194; 213,266; 213,284; 214,335; 216,68; 218,214; 218,216; 221,30; 222,84; 252,142; 279,12; 324,24; 348,18.
"War Brides": 169,116.
"War Game, The": 199,143.
"War Nurse": (F,R) 358,48.
Waram, Percy: 335,23.
Ward, Dorothy: 245,120; 246, 153; 246,169; 248,303.
Ward, Eugene: 203,35.
Ward, Fannie: 81,291; 97,75; 162,55; 172,307; 180,74; 186,78; 202,395; 217,192; 218,255.
Ward, Fleming: 271,18.
Ward, Genevieve: 242,338.
Ward, Harry A.: 292,14.
Ward, Hugh J.: 255,354.
Ward, Ivy: 215,57.
Ward, John: 73,60; 150,54; 237, 357; 262,20.
Ward, Julia: 224,239.
Ward, Lulu: 345,43.
Ward, MacKenzie: 319,23; 332, 48.
Ward, Marion: 51,129.
Ward, William: 156,60.
Ward, Winifred: (W) 216,90.
Ward and Van: 286,37.
Warde, Frederick: 156,61.
Warde, Helen L.: 45,x.
Ware, Helen: 41,viii; 48,32; 70,340; 73,82; 76,147; 81, 304; 89,197; 90,205; 92, 275; 95,33; 98,c; 112,198; 116,112; 120,64; 127,76; 130,220; 139,81; 142,164; 152,139; 165,231; 170, 169; 173,11; (A) 183,300; (A) 184,358; 184,379; 196, 351; 197,26; 201,269; 207, 287; (A) 214,379; 244,35; 250,7; (A) 250,63; 269, 43; 282,51; 288,8; (A) 322, 3.
"Ware Case, The": 179,7; (R'15) 179,9.
Warfield, David: 3,4; 6,8; 9,4; (W) 13,16; 44,249; 44,261; 45,269; 45,274; 46,320; 47,17; (C) 50,81; 51,c; (A) 51,i,f; 51,xi; (W) 70,330; 71,6; 73,63; 79,241; 80,277; 82,c; (C) 82,xxiv; 82,319; 82,349; 88,150; 95,10; 113,18; 121,75; 127,76; 129,xi; 130,193; 131,13; 133,xii; 134,118; 139,68; 145,75; 151,80; 159,243; 161,15; 175,109; 176,176; 180,87; 180,88; 187,127; 190,359; 194,225; (W) 198,84; 214, 340; (A) 231,346; 231,348; 231,349; 231,383; 239,101; 246,151; (A) 250,63; 251, 90; 263,12; 263,16; 264,18; 267,29; (A) 312,57; 336,40.
Warfield, Irene: 152,128; 157, 140.
Warmington, S.J.: 166,269.
Warner, Charles: 33,276; 39, 124.
Warner, Genevieve: 181,125.
Warner, Henry B.: 67,237; 70,320; 71,2; 96,57; 98, 120; 103,71; 108,41; 113, 29; 118,198; 137,2; 139, 69; 141,141; 147,132; 216, 94; 235,194; 235,195; 268, 28; (W) 269,22; 286,23; 288,27; 293,43; 294,25; 312,22; (W) 323,14.
Warner, Jack L.: 319,11.
Warner, Sam L.: 319,11.
Warner Bros. Studios: 319,13.
Warren, Beatrice: 199,135.
Warren, Frank H.: (W) 238, 34.
Warren, George C.: (W) 182, 217.

Warren, [Mrs.] Mercy: (D) 191, 34.
Warren, Rebecca: 5,16; 61, 75; 111,129.
Warren, Whitney Jr.: 271, 23.
Warren, William: (D) 232, 506; 293,40.
Warren-Manley, Marian: 299,21.
"Warrens of Virginia, The": (R'07) 83,xi; 84,48; 84,49.
Warrington, Ann: 81,309.
Warrington, Jane: 253,215.
"Warrior, The": (F,R) 199, 176.
Warrum, Helen: 178,285.
"Wars of the World": 164,151; (R'14) 164,193.
Warsden, Ranchott (W): 192,92; 197,28.
Warwick, Elsie: 162,77.
Warwick, Robert: 76,157; 81, 309; 86,111; 90,205; 104, 131; 112,175; 119,23; 144, 38; 156,75; 171,233; 174, 82; 214,342; 231,363; 252, 155; 257,101; 341,42.
"Was It a Dream": (R'03) 26,82.
Washburn, Bryant: 214,393; 218,256; 238,40.
Washburn, Grace: 124,212; 148, 187.
Washington, Isabelle: (C) 339, 22.
Washington, University of: 256,41; 263,46; 273,40; 277,41; 287,40; 308,42; 332,50.
Washington Square College (see New York University).
Washington Square Players: 170,198; (R'15) 170,207; 171, 259; 172,282; 172,286; 175, 110; 177,222; 178,320; 180, 116; 181,143; 183,277; 184, 332; 185,10; 189,269; 189, 283; 191,21; 191,29; 192,92; 194,213; 194,223; 195,278; 195,292; 198,64; 198,82; 201,286; 202,347; 202,352; 203,15; 203,23; 205,151; 205,159; 206,213; 206,218; 206,219; 207,289; 208,355; 208,358; 208,359.
Washington [D.C.] Theatre: 27,122; 37,66; 236,291; 313,33; 224,247.
"Wasp, The": (R'23) 266,15.
Wassman, Hans: 142,191.
"Watch Your Neighbors": (R'18) 212,210; 213,275.
"Watch Your Step": (R'14) 167,9; 168,67; 174,78.
"Watcher, The": 109,iii; (R'10) 109,x.
"Waterloo Bridge": (R'30) 247, 70; (C) 348,4.
Waterman, Ida: 80,263; 99, 149; 132,59.
Waterous, Herbert: 216,86.
Watkins, Linda: 314,31; 339,49; 345,46; 347,32; 359,24; 359,41.
Watkins, Mary F. (W): 241, 252; 255,382; 257,100; 295, 30; 300,20.
Watkins, Polly: 234,104.
Watson, Beulah: 49,60.
Watson, Donald: 260,300.
Watson, Dorothy: 80,273.
Watson, Evelyn: (W,V) 136, 192; (W,V) 149,12.
Watson, Frederick: 106,198.
Watson, Harry: 114,45.
Watson, Harry Jr.: 278,37; 290,45.
Watson, Leona: 101,29; 100, 183.
Watson, Lucille: 39,121; 86, 111; 111,160; 242,346; 253, 215; 268,28; 303,19; 304,14.
Watson, Minor: 324,59; 331, 45; 333,32; 343,33; 344,23; (C) 344,44.
Watson, Virginia: 256,13.
Watts, James: 223,153; 224, 231.
Watts, Lionel: 252,143; 277, 14.
Watts, Richard Jr. (W): 295, 32; and monthly thereafter: 357,23.
Waxman, Percy (W): 200,222; 202,346.
"Way Down East" (F): (R) 236,286; 236,287; (D) 241,241.

"Way of the World, The": (R) 10,3; 10,4; 284, 52; 285,12; (D) 285,13; (R'24) 286,62.
"Way Things Happen, The": (R'24) 277,15.
"Way to Kenmar, The": (R'04) 46,298.
Wayburn, Ned: 71,iii; 79, x; 112,174; 147,146; 151, xi; 171,238; 175,111; 177, 229; (W) 190,362; 226,385; 226,393; (W) 231,404; 272, 42; 273,22; 287,43; 289, 40; 290,81; 291,31; (A) 296, 59; 297,66.
"Wayfarer, The": 228,84.
Wayne, Justina: 61,65; 88,162; 116,122.
"We Americans": (R'26) 309, 70.
"We Are Seven": 156,62; (R'13) 156,100.
"We Can't Be As Bad As All That": 120,35; (R'10) 120, 36.
"We Can't Have Everything": (F) 210,120.
"We Girls": (R'21) 250,64.
"We Moderns": (R'24) 278,19.
Weadick, Guy: 185,19.
"Weak Sisters": (R'25) 297,18; 351,25.
"Weak Woman, A": (R'26) 301, 16.
"Weather-Beaten Benson": 44,247.
"Weather Clear -- Track Fast": (R'27) 322,39.
Weathersby, Eliza; 209,16.
Weathersby, Helen: 146,123; 189,277.
Weaver, Alice: 257,97.
Weaver, Blanche: 70,325.
Weaver, Harry: 97,101.
Weaver, John V.A.: 289,21; (W) 291,12; (W) 293,18; 303, 36.
Weaver Brothers: 286,37.
"Weavers, The": (R'15) 179,7; 180,64.
Webb, Clifton: 165,255; 192, 84; 201,270; 210,72; 216, 87; 224,215; 275,66; 281, 17; 294,21; 337,41; 358, 43; 360,23.
Webb, Dorothy: 143,23; 161,26; 193,153.
Webb, Nella: 30,188; 56, 260; 102,66.
Webber, Frederick: 47,15.
Webber, John F.: 104,105; 105,149.
Weber, Henry G.: 323,33.
Weber, Joe M.: (see also Weber and Fields): 15,19; (A) 16,19; 46,297; 60,vi; 60,31; 65,viii; (W) 73, 81; 81,xiv; 84,ix; 84,35; 88,155; 118,xxxvi; 127,x; 133,74; 186,87; 231,363.
Weber, L. Lawrence: 294,64.
Weber, Lois: 240,186.
Weber, Lucien: 226,396.
Weber and Fields (see also Fields, Lew; Weber, Joe M.): 3,4; 9,8; 15,19; 16,19; 20, 8; 73,81; 89,vi; 133,xii; 133,74; 134,113; 137,24; 143,5; 144,44; 216,84; 231, 363; 231,474; (C) 290,97.
Webster, Ben: 50,83; 51,108; 51,110; 58,298; 58,299; 187,131.
Webster, Charles: 214,339; 356, 40.
Webster, Henry Kitchell: 138,63.
Webster, Jack: 70,340.
Webster, John: 117,158; 263, 17.
Webster, Lucile: 322,39; 323, 47.
Webster, Willard: 149,28.
"Wedding Bells": (R'19) 226, 367; 227,13.
"Wedding Day, The": (R'09) 107,8.
"Wedding Trip, The": (R'11) 132,x; 132,43.
Wedekind, Frank: 137,5.
Weed, Marion: 33,286; 70, 342; 72,37.
Weeden, Evelyn: 105,133; 114, 51.
Weedon, William Crawford: 89, 176.
Weeks, Marion: 262,37.
Weems, Hariette: 31,236.
Weer, Helen: 229,193.

Wegefarth, G. A.: 37, 80.
Wegefarth, W. D.: 39, vi.
Wegener, Paul: 307, 40.
Wegman, Dorothy: 274, 27.
Wehlen, Emmy: 121, c; 121, 99; 130, 210; 134, 126; 135, 138; 135, 140; 156, 69; 168, 57; 181, 127; 195, 285; 196, 326; 205, 176; 211, 147; 216, 119.
"Weibstenfel, Der": 178, 320.
Weidman, Charles: 357, 45; 360, 38.
Weidt, Lucie: 118, 183.
Weigert, August: 81, 292; 81, 311.
Weil, Elsie F.: (W) 151, xix.
Weil, Hermann: 124, 193; 124, 194; 130, 190; 134, 125.
Weill, Otto: 93, 290.
Weiman, Rita: 229, 173; (W) 249, 364; 257, 115; (A) 298, 54.
Weimar Theatre (Germany): 63, 125.
Weinberg, Gus: 154, 178; 176, 194.
Weiner, Hans: 330, 25.
Weingartner, Felix: 61, 82; 125, 16.
Weisenfreund, Munie: 265, 14.
Weisenthal, Grete: 135, 140.
Welch, Niles: 308, 19.
"Welcome Home": (F, R) 293, 32.
"Welcome Stranger": 236, 283; (R'20) 236, 332.
"Welcome to Our City": (R'10) 116, xv.
"Welded": (R'24) 278, 16; (D) 278, 38.
Weldon, Henry: 163, 102; 165, 212.
Weldon, Mortimer: 58, 299.
Welford, Christine: 233, 28.
Welford, Dallas: 61, 55; 85, 79; 152, 127; 228, 99; 359, 39.
Weller, Viola: 236, 265.
Welles, Georgia: 6, 17.
Wellesley, Alfred: 345, 47.
Wellesley College: 247, 247; 248, 325.
Wellington, Martha: 136, 192.
Wellman, Emily Ann: 93, 298; 114, 37; 114, 39; 133, 97; 135, 143; 188, 193; 188, 216.
Wellman, William: (W) 324, 24.
Wells, Carolyn: (W) 336, 17.
Wells, Charlotte (W): 188, 200; 211, 136.
Wells, Loretta: 93, 291.
Wells, Phradie: 274, 37.
Wells, Ruth: 119, 19.
Welsh, Scott: 105, 134; 141, 155; 292, 17.
Welsh Theatre: 164, 164.
Wemple, Julia (pseud. for Ogden, Vivia; see "Confessions of a Stage Struck Girl").
Wemyss, Francis C.: (D) 232, 507.
Wendell, Anna: 151, 88.
Wendell, Evert Jansen: 198, 89.
Wendell, Jacob Jr.: 105, 144; 107, 9; 111, 170; 117, 132; 117, 152; 118, xi.
Wenger, John: (D) 178, 316.
Wentworth, Estelle: 57, 287; 66, 209; 74, 99; 144, 61.
Wentworth, Lura: 103, 98.
Wentworth, Marion Craig: 202, 364.
Werba and Lueschier: 130, xxxiii.
Werber, Mia: 26, 104.
"Werewolf, The": (R'24) 283, 64.
Werfel, Franz: 301, 36.
Werner, Gustave: 157, 113.
Werrenrath, Reinald: (D) 198, 95; (D) 202, 370; 268, 37.
Wesley, Adelyn: 143, 24.
Wesleyan College: 265, 46.
Wesselhoff, Eleanore: 360, 40.
Wessell, Vivian: 177, 244; 191, 37.
West, Berkeley: 141, 143.
West, Beverly: 187, 139.
West, Blanche: 142, 181.
West, Dorothy: 185, 20.
West, Harold: 204, 103; 300, 19.
West, Isabel: 129, 150.
West, Louise Bronson: (W) 129, 168.
West, Mae: 216, 97; 248, 308; 327, 65; 328, 38; 330, 30; (C) 330, 43; 335, 24.

West, Mary: 198,79.
West, Olive: 123,160.
West, Percita: 49,59.
West, Roland: 214,363.
West, Teresa: 295,21.
West, Will: 86,111.
West, Willie: 290,45.
West Point Theatre: 266,44.
Western, Lucille: 78,222; 106,182.
Western College (Ohio): 335, 54.
Western Reserve University: 331,54.
Westerton, Frank: 95,30.
Westley, Helen: 181,143; 185, 5; 189,269; 191,29; 194, 223; 202,347; 203,15; 205, 159; 208,359; 213,285; 216, 89; 218,209; 220,363; 221, 23; 228,77; 230,265; 232, 503; 235,208; 237,347; 242, 319; 242,328; 244,31; 253, 221; 257,72; 265,18; 269, 28; 273,17; 278,17; 290,29; 295,18; 304,31; 309,27; 311, 24; 312,20; 325,40; 327,37; 329,9; 340,25; 349,45; 360, 26.
Westley, John: 55,217; 101, 11; 102,40; 112,178; 124, 200; 152,124; 164,163; 188,215; 220,363; 233,35; 247,237; 249,371; 249, 372; 270,17.
Westman, Nydia: 284,23; 287,22; 309,31; 338,29.
Westminster Abbey: 58,iii.
Weston, Betty: 292,14.
Weston, Lucy: 90,211; 90, 212; 127,79; 128,c; 139,84.
Weston, Sadie: 112,193.
Westover, Winifred: 231,412.
Westvay, Annette: 246,153.
Wetzler, H.H.: 33,286.
"We've Got to Have Money": (R'23) 271,50.
Whalen, Will W.: 180,90.
Wharton, Anthony P.: 82,321.
"What a Widow": (F,R) 357, 49; 357,50.
"What Am I Offered?": 183, 287.
"What Every Woman Knows": (R'08) 96,38; 98,118; (F,R) 242,348; (R'26) 303,50; 304,13.
"What Happened at 22": (R'14) 164,159; 164,165.
"What Happened to Mary": 147,xix; (R'13) 147,130.
"What Is Love?": (R'14) 165, 254.
"What It Means to a Woman": (R'14) 167,48.
"What Price Glory": 284,14; (R'24) 284,15; 285,28; 286,19; 304,7; (F) 318,6; 335,19.
"What the Doctor Ordered": (R'11) 129,xv; (R'27) 319, 23.
"What the Public Wants": 256,21; (R'22) 256,29.
"What Would You Do?": 158, 211.
"What's in a Name": 231,405; (R'20) 231,460.
"What's the Matter with Susan": (R'04) 35,6.
Wheat, Lawrence: 89,180; 94,316; 100,174; 100, 175; 110,110; 160,289.
Wheatcroft, Nelson: 58,314; 106,180; 290,18.
Wheatley, Jane: 174,67.
Wheaton, Anna: 133,76; 147, 139; 149,2; 151,101; 194,227; 195,271; 199,157; 231,407; 232,522.
"Wheel of Life, The": 263,14.
Wheeler, Bert: 263,43; 292,30; 357,30.
Wheeler, Betty: 263,43; 292,30.
Wheeler, Van Rensselaer: 12, 5; 82,319.
Wheelock, Joseph Jr.: 36, 47; 55,220; 57,110; 57, 285.
"When a Feller Needs a Friend": 215,42.
"When Claudia Smiles": (R'14) 157,115.
"When Dreams Come True": 150,xi; 151,100; 151,101; (R'13) 152,xiii; 152,117.
"When Johnny Comes Marching Home": 23,2; (R'03) 24,31.

"When Knighthood Was in Flower": 3,5; 69,307.
"When Knights Were Bold": (R'07) 80,xvii; 80,275.
"When Sylvia Runs Away": 163, 101.
"When the Clouds Roll By": (F,R) 228,108; 228,107.
"When the Young Vine Blooms": (R'15) 179,8.
"When We Are Forty-One": 54,208.
"When We Are Young": (R'20) 238,74.
"When We Dead Awaken": (R'05) 50,82; 51,106.
"When We Were Twenty-One": 12,12; (R'04) 40,xiii.
"Where Ignorance Is Bliss": (R'13) 152,115.
"Where Poppies Bloom": (R'18) 212,212.
"Where Shakespeare Set His Stage" by E. Lathrop:
(B) 69,ix
Merry Wives of Windsor 60,47
Julius Caesar 63,131
Richard III 66,216
Cymbeline 70,336
King Lear 75,120
King John 78,224
Twelfth Night 154,193.
"Where the Cross Is Made": (R'20) 233,30.
"Where There's a Will": (R'10) 109,xi.
"Where's Your Husband?": (R'27) 312,21.
Whiffen, [Mrs.] Thomas: 4,3; 118,165; 177,230; 239, 95; 241,256; 279,27; 322, 34; (D) 323,10.
"While New York Sleeps": (F,R) 236,286.
"Whims": 178,279.
"Whip, The": 141,135; (R'12) 143,5.
"Whirl of New York, The": (R'21) 245,126; 246,169.
"Whirl of the World, The": (R'14) 156,100.
"Whirlwind, The": (R'10) 111, xxv; 111,134; (R'11) 130, 186.
"Whispering Gallery, The": (R'29) 337,46.
"Whispering Wires": (R'22) 259,228.
White, Alice: 309,49; 323,46; 335,48; 342,67.
White, Carolina: 119,9; 134, 110; 155,34; (D) 158,c; 211,180.
White, Charlotte: 31,210.
White, Florence: 191,12.
White, Frances: 186,71; 188, 199; 193,166; 198,c; 198, 83; 201,270; 204,83; (D) 219,267; 237,354; 254,283; 302,25.
White, George (see also "Scandals of 19.."): 198, 90; 221,11; 257,86; 316, 22; (A) 321,69; 330,27; 356,44.
White, George R.: (W) 162,75.
White, Lillian: 257,73.
White, Lyola: 240,165.
White, Marjorie: 338,60.
White, Maud: 41,184.
White, Maude: (W) 223,168.
White, Pearl: 169,129; 185, 35; 196,329; 211,158; 214, 385; 226,404; 229,236; 236,289; 238,41; 239,122; 250,c; 259,253; 261,362.
White, Roderick: 270,37.
White, Ruth: 7,14; 248,299; 257,73.
White, Sammy: 326,35.
White, Stanford: 60,44.
"White Cargo": (R'23) 274, 19; 275,66; (S) 276,26.
"White Cat, The": (R'05) 58,xvii.
White Deer, Princess: 238,19; 265,43.
"White Eagle, The": 324,62.
"White Feather, The": 169,111; (R'15) 169,149.
"White Hen, The": (R'07) 74,xiii; 74,86; 76, 146.
"White Lights": (R'27) 321, 43.
"White Lilacs": (R'28) 332, 80.

"White Magic": (R'12) 133,76; 134,134.
"White Pearl, The": (F) 176, 177.
White Rats: 146,126.
"White Rose, The": (F) 267, 35; (R) 269,34.
"White Sister, The": 98,105; (R'09) 105,136; 105,164.
"White Villa, The": (R'21) 241,264.
"White Wings": (R'26) 309, 72.
Whitebread, T.E.: 4,15.
Whitecar, W.H.: 210,69.
"White-Headed Boy, The": (R'21) 249,386.
Whitehill, Clarence: 177,248; 274,37; 282,34; 290,41; 301, 35.
Whitelock, William Wallace (W): 15,14; 17,16; 19,12; 25,69; (V) 26,93; 29,173; 40,156; 77,197.
Whiteman, Paul: 263,11; 266,38; 276,1a; 278,34; 282,23; (C) 333,41; 337,35; 339,36.
Whiteside, Rosamond: 275,23; 294,38.
Whiteside, Walker: 80,268; 96,58; 104,118; 104,132; 134,108; 136,180; 165,203; (W) 166,278; 166,279; 172,307; 175,110; 213,295; 215,9; (D) 255,375.
"Whitewashing of Julia, The": (R'04) 35,6; 37,73.
Whitford, Annabelle: 40,145; 91,243.
Whitfield, Charles: 212,195.
Whitford, Trixie: 185,34.
Whiting, Joseph: 36,47.
Whiting, Jack: 301,38; 346, 49; (C) 361,27.
Whitman, Walt: (D) 266,10.
Whitmore, Francise: 234,93.
Whitmore, Nina: 234,93.
Whitmore, Vida: 101,15; 115, 85.
Whitmore, Virginia: 353,29.
Whitney, Celeste: 269,43.
Whitney, Claire: 188,211; 198, 75; 233,23; 234,99; 237, 380.
Whitney, Edith: 150,49; 213, 273.
Whitney, Fred C.: 43,227.
Whitney, Marion: 100,195.
Whitson, Pauline: 111,131.
Whittell, Josephine: 132,68; 154,174.
Whittemore, Henry: 333,32.
Whittier, Robert: 37,62.
Whittlesey, White: 9,18; 59, 13; 85,iii; 85,66.
Whitty, May: 187,131.
Whitworth, Grace (W): 62,91; 67,242.
Whitworth, Robert: 111,140; 111,142.
"Who Cares": (R'30) 353,26.
"Who Did It": (R'19) 222,81.
"Who Goes There?": (R'05) 50,84.
"Whole Town's Talking, The": (R'23) 271,66.
"Whoop-Dee-Doo": 33,282.
"Whoopee": (R'28) 335,50; (C) 337,35; (F) 354,32; (F,R) 357,49.
Whoops Sisters: 354,42.
"Who's Who?": (R'13) 152,xi; 152,113.
"Who's Who in the Theatre": [Parker] (B): 351,74.
"Who's Who on Broadway": 216,94; 217,152; 232,520.
"Who's Who on the Stage": (B) 72,x.
"Why Be Good?": (F) 337,71.
"Why Change Your Wife": (F) 231,411; (F,R) 232, 534.
"Why Marry?": (R'17) 204, 85; 204,103.
"Why Men Leave Home": (R'22) 261,377.
Whytal, Russ: 83,13; 85,86; 134,106; 136,183; 169, 114; 176,171; 217,152; 297,19.
Whytal, [Mrs.] Russ: 150,xiv; 273,18.
Wickes, Joseph: 139,92.
Wickham, Florence: 46,315; 104,122; 105,138; 107,10; 123,148; 136,173.
Widdecomb, Wallace: 161,6.

Wideman, Charles: 262,29.
"Widow by Proxy": (R'13) 146, 101; 146,123.
"Widowers' Houses": (R'07) 74,90.
"Widow's Might, The": (R'09) 105,xiii.
Wiehe, Charlotte: 34,290; 41, 162.
Wiesenthal Sisters: 127,95.
"Wife Decides, The": (R'11) 130, xv; 131,31.
"Wife Hunters, The": (R'11) 130,xiii; 130,187.
"Wife With a Smile, The": (R'21) 251,100; (D) 251,101.
"Wife Without a Smile, A": (R'05) 48,xii.
Wigman, Mary: (W) 358,45.
Wigs: 191,14.
Wilbur, Crane: 299,11; 305, 27; 321,68; 333,48; 358, 32; 359,26.
Wilbur, Mabel: 189,281.
Wilcox, Blanche: 335,46.
Wilcox, Ella Wheeler: 15,17.
Wilcox, Frank: 195,318.
Wilcox, Ruth: 283,21.
"Wild Duck, The": (R'18) 206,217; 207,273; (R'25) 290,32; 290,35.
"Wild Rose, The": (R'02) 16,5; 17,5; 20,18; (R'26) 310,16.
"Wildcat, The": (R'21) 251, 99; (D) 251,101.
Wilde, Oscar: 15,4; 51,iii; 60, 50; 61,79; 208,370.
Wilde, Renee: 281,24.
Wildenbruck, Ernst Von: 62,xii.
Wilder, Cyrus E.: 303,37.
Wilder, Marshall P.: 55,230; 57,284; 67,248.
Wilder, Thornton: 306,53.
"Wilderness, The": (R) 12,12; 14,13.
"Wildfire": (R'08) 92,xv; 92, 260.
"Wildflower": (R'23) 269,16; 269,17.
Wilfred, Thomas: 254,316; 352, 23.
Wilke, Hubert: 230,247.
Wilkes, Paula: 121,88.
Wilkins, Marie: 25,65; 111, 157.
"Will, The": (R'13) 153,143.
"Will Shakespeare": 252,158; (R'23) 264,20.
Willa, Suzanne: 224,225.
Willard, Catharine: 284,23; 348,13.
Willard, Edward S.: (A) 3,17; 10,18; 12,8; 12,13; 12,14; 13,c; 14,11; 49,56; 59,xiii; 59,23; 60,29; 168, 74.
Willard, Grace: (W) 175,134.
Willard, John: 283,33.
Wille, Bruno: 336,35.
Willems, Eleanor: 295,23.
Willey, Day Allen: (W) 101,18.
Willey, Leonard: 275,17.
William, Warren: 280,14; 291,14; 339,29; 356,23; 358,25.
"William Tell": 92,282.
Williams, Bert A.: 26,96; 62,xiv; 66,224; 85,xii; 86, 97; 106,xviii; (W) 220,346; 223,159; 255,355; 257,86.
Williams, Clara: 209,60.
Williams, Crafton: 156,69.
Williams, Derek: (D) 341, 13.
Williams, Dorothy: 361,29.
Williams, Earl: 215,64.
Williams, Edith Barrett (W): 49,61; 105,162.
Williams, Eugene: 224,251.
Williams, Eva: 213,275; 260,286; 260,313.
Williams, Florence: 149,11.
Williams, Frances: 343,54; (D) 344,22; 344,62; 345,19; (C) 360,32.
Williams, Fritz: 15,19; (A) 16,19; 24,49; 41,175; 195, 287; 231,363.
Williams, Hannah: (C) 358,44.
Williams, Harry: 137,11.
Williams, Hattie: 31,211; 33,269; 40,149; 48,32; 67, 226; 75,119; 80,274; 91,c; 98,112; 104,107; 104,127; 106,180; 110,102; 117,151; 127,78; 139,75; 145,81; 151,

102; 152,xiii; 152,114; 187, 136.
Williams, Herbert: 285,37; 353, 24.
Williams, Hope: 335,51; 336, 33; 340,42; (C) 349,4; 349, 20; 349,43; 357,25.
Williams, Ina: 281,17.
Williams, Irene: 241,253.
Williams, Jesse Lynch: (W) 317,7.
Williams, John D.: (W) 95,24; 187,172; 211,130; 246,196; 354,12; (C) 359,22.
Williams, Katherine: 169,127.
Williams, [Mrs.] Lottie: 26,96.
Williams, Malcolm: 88,159; 132,39; 140,118; 165,209; 307,29.
Williams, Margery: 335,47.
Williams, Margot: 166,265; 168, 88.
Williams, Mervin: 321,52.
Williams, Odell: 9,4.
Williams, Percy: 135,vi; 166, 282; 361,45.
Williams, Robert: (C) 344,4.
Willis, Suzanne: 151,83.
Williams, William: 202,353; 206,207; 241,268; 304,19; 323,23.
Williams College: 240,189; 240,192; 254,317; 271,40.
Williamson, Arleigh B.: (W) 361,50.
Williamson, Hardy: 165,212.
Willis, Jill: 319,23.
Willoughby, Peggy: 276,18.
Willow Grove Park (Philadelphia): 18,17.
'Willow Tree, The": (R'17) 194,216; 195,281; 198,96.
Wills, Ivan: 103,97.
Wills, Nat M.: 32,260; 56,252; 160,293; 180,84; 186,80; 201,287.
Wills, Sophie: 246,170.
Wills, W.G.M 71,25; 125,12.
Willy, Alan: 218,200.
Willy, Collette: 127,95.
Wilson, Alice: 120,36; 155,21.
Wilson, B.F. (W): 263,26; 269,27; 270,22; 272,24; 274,20; 275,24; 284,9; 287,9; 290,22; 295,22; 302,30; 305,16; 306,18; 310,32; 311,20; 323,34.
Wilson, Carey: 301,48.
Wilson, Catherine: 328,9; 335,58.
Wilson, Charles C.: 308,19.
Wilson, Charlie H.: 88,160.
Wilson, Edith: 295,21.
Wilson, Edwin: 103,85.
Wilson, Eileen: 228,99; 235,191; 237,354; 320,24.
Wilson, Ethel: 208,369; 272,29.
Wilson, Evelyn: (C) 344,22.
Wilson, Flora: 111,166.
Wilson, Florence: 320,28.
Wilson, Francis: 5,2; 7,17; 12,8; 12,9; 13,13; 48,33; 62,83; 64,143; 64,151; 67,244; 68,x; 79,228; 80, xvii; 80,275; 103,70; 108, xv; 108,36; 127,76; 146,98; 147,132; 149,17; 167,11; 240,167; 257,101; 268,3; 268,11; 283,52; 286,13; 287,25; 299,25; (W) 336, 42.
Wilson, G. Hepburn: (W) 159, 266.
Wilson, G.W.: 10,7.
Wilson, Gladys: 155,21.
Wilson, Imogene: 273,23.
Wilson, Izetta: 254,317.
Wilson, James: 134,124; 180, 70.
Wilson, Jane: 134,127.
Wilson, Lizzie: 256,27.
Wilson, Lois: (D) 294,1; 294,32; 305,36.
Wilson, Margaret: 257,97; 281,38; 282,43.
Wilson, Margaret Woodrow: 177, 226.
Wilson, Marjory: 192,97.
Wilson, Rufus Wilson: (W) 61,73.
Wilson, Stuart E.: 232,519.
Wilson, Tony: 256,27.
Wilson, Violet: 221,35.
Wilson, Woodrow: 195,260a; 277,7.
Wilstach, Frank: 72,viii; (W) 323,17.

Wilstach, Paul: (W) 95,31.
Wimperis, Arthur: 285,24.
Winant, Forrest: 116,124; 153, 169; 188,205; 216,95.
Winchell, Walter: (C) 333,33.
"Winchester": (S) 6,17.
Window, Muriel: 190,390; 223, 165.
"Windows": (R'23) 273,16; 273,17.
Winds, Adolf: 81,292; 81, 311.
Windsor, Claire: 259,240; 302, 33; 316,36.
Windsor Castle Theatre (London): 159,242.
"Wine, Woman and Song": 73, 63.
Wingate, James: 312,37.
"Winged Mystery, The": (F,R) 202,394.
Wingfield, Conway: 276,28.
"Wings of the Morning": (F,R) 228,106.
"Wings Over Europe": 335, 49; (R'28) 335,50; (S) 336, 30; 340,14.
"Winning His Wife": (F) 217, 183.
Winninger, Charles: 183,284; 184,361.
Winslow, B.R.: (W) 101,31.
Winslow, Helen: (W) 91,251.
"Winsome Widow, A": (R'12) 135,140.
"Winsome Willie": (R'04) 35,4.
Winston, Bruce: 321,60.
Winston, Florence: 147,160.
Winston, Nancy: 185,21.
Winter, Dale: 334,30.
Winter, William: 7,12; 25, 71; (W) 52,139;66,xi; (W) 68,280b; (W) 80,268; 112, 195; 181,126; (W) 182,204; 183,291; 198,100; 231,362; (W) 338,16.
Winter, Winona: 121,88; 248,303.
"Winter": (R'18) 206,219.
"Winter Feast, The": (R'08) 95, 3.
Winter Garden Theatre (New York): 123,xi; 123,174; 124, 184.
"Winter's Tale, A": 45,266; (R'05) 48,29; 48,41; (R'10) 111,133; 208,351; (R'21) 241,262.
Winthrop, Adelaide: 198,83.
Winthrop, Ethel: 173,18.
Wintner, Helene: 69,290.
Winton, Jane: 266,21; 334, 26.
Winwood, Estelle: 189,287; 190,365; 193,145; 195, 271; 198,97; 204,103; 205,165; 211,135; 211,166; (D) 213,c; 216,81; 219, 285; 220,359; 224,220; 225, 316; 225,326; 225,331; 226,417; 245,82; 249,403; 254,293; 254,301; (D) 254, 309; 260,316; (C) 263,11; 274,17; 280,21; 288,29; 296, 27; 300,14; 300,15; 301,52b; 304,36; 305,21; 311,13; 313,20.
Wirth, May: 135,146.
Wirth, Mizzi: 90,207.
Wisconsin Dramatic Society: 143,27.
Wisconsin Theatre: 343,49.
"Wisdom Tooth, The": (R'26) 302,16; 302,30; 302,31; (S) 303,26.
Wise, Emma: 285,18.
Wise, Thomas N.: 31,211; 49,57; 67,226; 80,xv; 89, 184; 90,i; 93,286; 93,287; 94,336; 100,175; 137,10; 137,11; 137,13; 151,105; 168,77; 183,271; 183,276; 187,147; 192,73; 193,146; 194,231; 204,79; 213,287; 217,149; 217,163; 287,8; 307,27.
Wise, [Mrs.] Thomas A.: 195, 281.
Wiseman, George H.: 162,68.
Wiseman, Harrison Gahagan: (W) 290,16.
Wisenfrend, Muni: 312,29; 320,22.
Wishaar, Grace: 47,xii.
Wistaria Grove (New York): 53,158; 65,172.
Wister, Owen: (W) 317,7.
"Witch, The": (R'10) 110,99; 110,100.

Witchie, Katharine: 180,76.
"Witching Hour, The": (R'07) 83,2; 83,13; 89,173; 89, 183; 231,351.
Withee, Mabel: 212,251; 213,317; 221,11.
Withers, Charles: 197,36; 270, 35.
Witherspoon, Cora: 204,97; 226, 366; 249,363; 261,372; 285, 43; (C) 348,4.
Witherspoon, Herbert: 60,54; 95, 36; 134,109.
"Within Four Walls": (R'23) 267,15.
"Within the Law": 138,36; (R'12) 140,xiv; 140,97; 143, 18; 231,349.
"Without Benefit of Clergy": (F,R) 247,244.
Witkowska, Marta: 134,111; 137,27.
Witmark, Julius: 20,9.
"Witness for the Defence, The": (R'11) 131,ix.
"Wives of Men": (F,R) 212,250.
"Wizard, The": (F) 323,45.
"Wizard, of Oz, The": 18,4; 25,59; (R'03) 25,61; (R'03) 39,112; 102,62; 231,349; (F,R) 292,34.
Wodehouse, P. G.: 202,368; 277,39; 280,10.
Woffington, Peg: 33,287; 34, 317; 77,188; 127,82; (D) 127,83; 129,xvii; 129,xxxi; (D) 223,166.
Wohlgemuth, Else: 298,23.
Wolf, Rennold: (C) 193,138.
"Wolf, The": (R'08) 88,144; 88,157.
Wolfe, Victoria; 261,383.
Wolff, Marjorie Helen: 148,178.
Wolff, Pierre: 122,137; 300, 31.
Wolf-Ferrari, Ermanno (W): 130,221; 132,50; 134,10.
Wolheim, Louis: 254,283; 257, 80; 258,153; 284,14; 284, 15; 298,12; (W) 318,41.
Wollersen, Florence: 185,21; 192,93.
"Wolves, The": 336,53.
"Woman" (F): 212,257; (R) 214,392.
"Woman, The": (R'11) 128,x; 128,116; 143,6; (F) 172, 295.
"Woman Disputed, A": (R'26) 309,16.
"Woman Haters, The": (R'12) 141, xv.
"Woman in His House, The": (F) 237,421.
"Woman in the Case, The": (R'05) 49,54; 51,115.
"Woman of Bronze, The": (R'20) 236,277.
"Woman of Impulse, A": (R'09) 98,105; 98,107.
"Woman of It, The": (R'13) 145,xxix.
"Woman of No Importance, A": 34,307; 143,22; (R'16) 184, 334.
"Woman on the Index, The": (R'18) 212,210.
"Woman on the Jury, The": (R'23) 271,16; 271,18.
"Woman the Germans Shot, The": (F) (R'18) 214,392.
"Woman Who Laughed, The": (R'22) 259,268.
"Woman's Way, A": (R'09) 98,104; 98,126; 98,127; (S) 99,160.
"Woman's Wiles, A": 194,228.
"Womansia": 40,vi.
<u>Women in Theatre</u>: 18,21; 27, 115; 37,69; 46,304; 47, xii; 47,23; 53,163; 54,198; 60,35; 64,162; 68,264; 74, 92; 78,216; 88,162; 102,48; 150,38; 154,194; 159,239; 161,31; 164,177; 179,22; 196, 354; 198,94; 201,282; 207, 295; 221,26; 227,34; 230, 274; 255,366; 275,10; 283, 22; 293,30; 294,24; 335, 45; 337,37; 347,30.
Women's National Theatre: 150, 38.
"Wonder Hat, The": (R'20) 233,30.
"Wonderful Night, A": (R'29) 347,72.
"Wonderful Thing, The": (R'20) 230,270.

'Wonderful Visit, The": (R'24) 278,19.
'Wonderland": (R'05) 58,xviii.
Wong, Anna May: 281,33; 284, 32; 306,48; 317,15; 327, 27; 358,23; 359,26.
Wontner, Arthur: 309,14; 322,28.
Wood, Douglas J.: 37,62; 111, 142; 152,130; 201,270; 334, 25.
Wood, Elizabeth: 83,17.
Wood, Frank J.: 173,18.
Wood, George: 272,35; 274, 34.
Wood, Leonard Jr.: 271,23.
Woods, Louise: 105,149.
Wood, Marjorie: 76,160; 89, 174; 91,250; 149,32; 219, 281.
Wood, Peggy: 149,11; 153,159; 157,134; 157,141; 173,24; 178,306; 193,163; 200,221; 201,c; 202,359; 209,13; 224, 239; 225,312; 226,409; 231, 354; 253,229; 254,293; 255, 390; 266,29; 281,14; 289, 21; 291,27; 303,36; 314,27; 324,19; (D) 326,c; 326,62; (D) 335,25; 344,38; 356,8; 356,13.
Wood, Philip (W): 230,248; 325,37; 326,14; 328,10; 329,12; 331,43; 332,43; 334,38; 337,39; 343,45; 344, 23; 345,38; 348,22.
Wood, Rose: 78,223.
Wood, William B.: (D) 232,506.
Woodburn, Joseph: 146,123.
Woodbury, Clare: 313,35.
'Woodland": 41,163; 42,210; (R'05) 47,6.
Woodland Theatre: 137,9.
Woodruff, Eleanor: 168,68; 189,285; 243,395; 244,33; 245,122; 248,330; 249,410; 253,274; 308,19; 309,31; 309,45; 322,56; 323,54; 335,58.
Woodruff, Harry: 15,3; 22,13; 22,14; 22,15; 23,18; 51, 120; (A) 52,131f; 61,75; 66,200; 136,190.
Woodruff, Henry: 62,87; 62,94; 65,180; 75,c; 106,169; 117, 144.
Woods, Al. H.: 127,x; 157, 142; 163,101; 175,109; 177,241; 178,341; 187,172; 212,194; 214,397; 223,144; 226,443; 234,84; 246,168; 254,300; (W) 255,352; 258,145; 270,16; 272,66; (W) 273,11; (C) 282,11; 292,29; 294,7; (W) 297, 20; 304,6; 306,5; (W) 340, 9; 343,15; 353,37.
Woods, Edward: 357,50.
Woods, Louise: 144,43; 151, 108; 105,149.
Woodson, Elizabeth: 38,87; 51,126.
Woodthorpe, Georgie: 138, 43.
Woodward, Eugenia: 252,151.
'Woof Woff": (R'29) 347, 63.
'Wooing of Priscilla, The": (S) 5,6; 5,7.
Woolerson, Florence: 202,361.
Woolf, Edgar Allan: 280, 36.
Woolf, Walter: 245,101; 282, 14; 306,14; 337,21; 354, 24.
Woolfe, Frank: 145,96.
Woollcott, Alexander: (C) 193, 136; (W) 256,8; (C) 266, 11; (C) 286,15; 315,22; 345,24.
Woolsey, Robert: 243,421.
Wooster, Boots: 215,21; 230, 268; 248,312; 269,26.
'Words and Music": (R'17) 204,88.
Workers' Theatre Guild: 229, 222.
'World and His Wife, The": (R'08) 94,315; 94,339.
'World of Pleasure, A": 178, 282.
'World We Live In, The": 262,21; (R'22) 262,23.
Worlock, Frederick: 263,14.
Worm, A. Toxen: 57,vii; (W) 67,238; (W) 196,348.
Worrell, Devah: 252,147.
Worrell Sisters: 78,215.
Worsley, Wallace: 110,114.

Worth, Florence: 230,281.
Worth, Helen: 353,29.
Worth, Mary: 242,328.
"Worth of a Woman, The": (R'08) 85,ix; 86,94.
Worthing, Eleanor: 52,152.
Worthing, Frank: 3,11; 4,4; 13, 12; 22,21; 23,1; 31,214; 36,47; 49,57; 61,69; 69, 294; 76,164; 98,127; 99,c; 104,104; 104,105.
Worthing, Helen Lee: 229,178; 231,405; 256,17; 256,25; 273,23; 297,48.
Worthington, Harriet: 74,93; 96, 66; 138,38.
Wouters, Francene: 265,18.
Wray, Fay: 315,42; 321,48; 336,44.
Wray, John: 248,323; 286, 23; 297,19; 300,28.
Wren, Rene: (W) 223,166.
Wright, Ethel: 88,163; 174, 68; 268,31.
Wright, Frances: 89,174.
Wright, Franklyn: (W) 210,94.
Wright, Fred: (D) 323,23.
Wright, Fred Jr.: 44,246; 46, 300.
Wright, H. Humberston: 318, 42.
Wright, Haidee: 105,135; 154, xxv; 154,xxvi; 178,302; 264, 31; 324,30; (C) 327,36; 356,38.
Wright, Harry: 27,114.
Wright, Huntley: 80,270; 80, 281.
Wright, J. Hooker: 111,131; 182,230.
Wright, Olive: 58,307.
Wright, Stephen: 283,14.
"Writing on the Wall, The": (R'09) 100,169; 100,189; 250,10.
Wullner, Ludwig: 96,70.
Wunderlee, Frank: 112,180.
Wurster, Emily: 101,12.
Wyatt, Marguerite: 307,45.
Wycherly, Margaret: 49,60; 60,28; 77,179; 117,132; 152,116; 191,20; 193,165; 230,265; 234,95; 240,163; 243,300; 255,369; 256,21; 263,18; 267,32; 293,29.
Wyndham, Olive: 82,329; 105, 144; 105,145; 108,62; 111, 170; 130,209; 134,127; 147, xix; 147,130; 151,95; 157, 141; 161,21; 191,39; 196, 355; 214,349; 222,103; 223, 141; 239,94; 241,255; 243, 300; 245,88; 290,29.
Wyndham, Charles: 46,294; 47, 4; 101,2; 168,75; 216,114; 217,160.
Wyngate, Charles: 98,107.
Wynter, Georgina: 334,37.
Wynters, Charlotte: 358,33.
Wynn [Holcomb] (D): 266,10; 267,10; 271,29; 286,15; 287,24; 288,11; 289,8; 291, 30; 294,29.
Wynn, Ed: 186,63; 214,346; 224,231; 231,403; 232,521; 250,32; 257,96; 275,29; 290,46; 298,48; 302,46; 311,40; 316,37; 321,51; (A) 322,3; 347,44; 349,27; (C) 350,47; (D) 351,c; 353,32; 358,47.
Wynn, Keenan: 324,44.
Wynne, Bessie: 110,110; 115, 88; 124,204; 161,26.
Wynne, Celeste: 5,4; 46,315.
Wynne, Gladys: 142,190; 191, 29; 194,223.
Wynne, Grace: 90,217.

--Y--

Yacco, Sada: 161,31.
Yale University: 74,95; 75, xxiii; 88,147; 96,50; 131, 28; 173,13; 186,76; 188,211; 219,274; 220,366; 269,45; 278,41; 298,20; 311,42.
Yamakawa, Uraji: 161,31.
"Yankee Circus on Mars, A": 53,173.
"Yankee Consul, The": (R'04) 38,85; 38,95.
"Yankee Girl, The": (R'10) 109,xi.
"Yankee Prince, The": (R'08) 88,145; 88,165.
"Yankee Princess, The": (R'22) 261,377.

"Yankee Tourist, A": (R'07) 79,230; 79,249; 81,306.
Yankton College (South Dakota): 178,300.
Yapp, Cecil: 107,9; 116,101; 117,132; 170,200; 226, 379.
Yarrington, Edith: 72,56.
Yates, J. Carrington: 23,7; 45,274.
Yates, Gretchen: 213,281.
Yates, Mary Ann: 239,84.
Yaworskaia, Lydia: 119,xviii.
Yeamans, Annie: 11,3; 43, 233; 116,106; 134,vi.
Yeamans, Jennie: 32,240; 32, 259.
"Years of Discretion": (R'12) 144,xii; 144,36; 146,119.
Yeats, William Butler: 29,158; 29,167; 30,186; 49,60; 129, 157; 158,176; 253,272.
"Yellow": (R'26) 308,66.
"Yellow Jacket, The": (R'12) 142,162; 142,164; (V) 144,37; 144,62; 334,18.
"Yellow Sands": (R'27) 320,23.
"Yellow Ticket, The": 156,64; (R'14) 157,112; 157,129; 158, 212; 159,275.
"Yeoman of the Guard, The": 171, 227; (R'15) 172,282.
Yershoff, Vladimir: 262,14.
"Yes or No": 204,83; (R'17) 204,88.
Yiddish Art Theatre: 265,14; (D) 311,10; 350,56.
Yiddish Theatre (see also East-West Players; People's Theatre): 9,8; 11,9; 11,16; 13,16; 21,18; 42,207; 48,33; 53,161; 93,307; 101,xi; 104,132; 114,49; 115,93; 157, 115; 157,136; 168,81; 183, 304; 206,219; 230,260; 251, 91; 308,20; 311,10; 334,53.
Yielder, Frank: 335,46.
"Yip, Yip, Yaphank": 212,222; 212,223.
Yokel, Alex: 331,48.
"Yolanda": (F,R) 278,30; (F) 278,33.
"Yolanda of Cyprus": (OP) 344, 53.
Yorke, Alice: 105,156.
Yorke, Lansing: 69,301.
Yorke, Letty: 170,192.
Yorke, Oswald: 8,3; 52,153; 60,30; 89,180; 95,3; 107, 3; 141,131; 179,17; 230, 247.
Yorska, Mme.: 208,355; 208, 359; 209,7; 216,71.
"Yosemite": (R'14) 167,48.
Yost, Herbert A.: 121,74; 122,112; 167,35; 192,84; 200,197; 246,152.
"You and I": (R'23) 265,16; (S) 268,28.
"You Never Can Tell": 48,28; (R'05) 48,30; 210,90.
Youmans, Vincent: 342,65.
Young, Brigham: 179,34.
Young, Charles M.: 182,217.
Young, Clara Kimball: 165,227; 171,237; 174,89; 186,92; 198,73; 200,243; 201,316; 201,319; 202,c; 202,396; 203,56; 203,61; 204,120; 204,125; 205,188; 205,193; 206,256; 206,258; 207,326; 207,326; 207,333; 208,387; 211,187; 212,248; 213,325; 214,388; 215,57; 215,58; 217,191; 234,144; 237,379; 256,48.
Young, Cyril: 81,299.
Young, Frank: 86,94; 177,235.
Young, J. Arthur: 142,165.
Young, James: 48,41; 56, 254.
Young, John E.: 155,3.
Young, John H.: 90,204.
Young, Lillian: 236,284.
Young, Loretta: 330,32; 345, 69; 351,40; 359,48.
Young, Mary: 152,135; 194,212; 196,360; 237,345; 238,49; 245,100; 248,309; (A) 250, 63; 251,114; 254,313; 264, 9; 281,18; 283,17; 285,43; 290,69; 293,60; 295,36; 296,45; 308,47.
Young, Phyllis: 110,114.
Young, Rida Johnson: 68,264; 111,144; 153,152; 176,192; 194,202; 196,353; 209,13.
Young, Roland: 181,143; 183,

283; 201,286; 203,19; 235, 165; 239,83; 242,337; 254, 301; (D) 254,309; 266,31; 268, 17; 281,5; 294,25; 299,19; 304,36; 326,28; 326,29.
Young, Stark: 283,33.
Young, Walter: 119,19.
"Young America": (R'15) 176,168; 176,178; 177,220.
"Young Blood": (R'25) 299,18.
Young People's Theatre, Inc.: 233, 31.
"Young Romance": (F) 169,127.
"Young Sinners": 350,46.
"Young Turk, The": (R'10) 109, xii.
"Young Visiters, The": 232, 528; 239,87; (R'20) 239, 106.
"Young Wisdom": (D) 157,125; (R'14) 156,60.
"Young Woodley": (R'25) 298, 15; 298,19; (S) 299,26.
"Younger Generation, The": (R'13) 153,145.
"Younger Mrs. Parling, The": (R'04) 37,58; 37,59.
"Youngest, The": (R'25) 288, 19.
"Your Humble Servant": (R'10) 108,37; 108,38.
"Your Uncle Dudley": (R'29) 346,46.
"Your Woman and Mine": (R'22) 254,336.
"You're in Love": (R'17) 193, 151; 194,231.
"Yours Truly": (R'27) 313,19.
"Youth": (R'11) 125,viii; (R'18) 206,219; 206,231.
Ypsilanti Players: 222,106.
Ysaye, Eugene: 141,140.
"Yum Chapab": 203,15; (R'17) 203,23.
Yun, Moo Sooy: 262,38.
Yung, Cha Pih: 191,36.
Yurka, Blanche: 105,149; 137, 29; 199,135; 211,129; 211, 131; 235,167; 248,321; (A) 250,63; 252,182; 256, 23; 258,150; 263,5; 279,5; 290,35; 290,54; 292,45; 293, 29; 293,49; 295,15; 303,52; 311,33; (D) 315,41; 319,38; 336,25; 336,66; (W) 338, 20; 340,61; 351,12; 352,23; (W) 359,50.
Yvette: 183,293.
"Yvette": (R'04) 40,136.
Yvette and Roberts: 302,29.

--Z--

Zabelle, Flora: 3,7; 38,105; 76,148; 79,249; 105,134; 129,163; 145,79; 200,226; 232,505.
Zacconi, Ermete: 266,68.
Zambelli, Carlotta: 130,204.
"Zander the Great": 267,14; (R'23) 267,20.
Zangwill, Israel: 50,112.
Zanini, Mlle.: 291,33.
Zanou, Thalia: 270,21.
Zarska, Erma: 178,285.
Zarzuela (see Spanish Theatre).
Zasloawsky, Georges: 332,27.
"Zaza": 216,84; (F,R) 273, 32.
"Zebra, The": (R'11) 121, x; 122,108.
Zell, Gladys: 138,44; 149, 11.
Zell, Violet: 88,155.
Zemach, Benjamin: 333,39.
Zenatello, Giovanni: 75,113; 81,315; 82,350; 83,10; 84,52; 93,309; 94,345; 95,35; 119,8; 176,191.
"Zeno": (R'23) 271,66.
Zentay, Mery: 202,372.
"Zeppelin": (R'29) 336,50; 337,31.
Zeppilli, Alice: 83,10; 119,9.
Zerola, Nicolo: 104,115; 106, 174.
Zhdanova, Maria: 259,217.
Ziegfeld, Florenz Jr.: 77,iv; 90,201; 135,140; 166,284; 173,32; 177,249; 184,332; (W) 191,12; 195,289; 198, 65; 218,228; (W) 223,158; 246,166; 246,186; 250,53; 253,217; 257,86; 263,38; 263,40; 265,38; 269,12; (A) 270,65; 275,1,a; (C) 277,11; 285,10; 290,19; 290,92; 292,29; 301,12;

306,7; (W) 308,9; 309,6; 311,34; 321,49; (D,A) 323, 63; (W) 341,9; 342,65; 350, 40; 354,15.
Ziegfeld, Patricia: 286,25.
"Ziegfeld Follies" (see also "Palm Beach Nights"; "Follies of 19--"): 209,8; (D) 242,358; (D) 246,184; 269,6; 318,35.
"Ziegfeld Follies of 1907": 135,x.
"Ziegfeld Follies of 1911": 126, 39; (R) 126,40; 126,46; 126,47.
"Ziegfeld Follies of 1914": (R'14) 161,37.
"Ziegfeld Follies of 1915, The": 174,66; (D) 175,124; 186,70.
"Ziegfeld Follies of 1916, The": (R'16) 185,11; 186, 71.
"Ziegfeld Follies of 1917, The": (R'17) 197,55; 198,87.
"Ziegfeld Follies of 1918, The": (R'18) 210,112; 222, 77.
"Ziegfeld Follies of 1919": (R'19) 222,81; 223,159.
"Ziegfeld Follies of 1921": (R'21) 246,168; (D) 247,211; 247, 223.
"Ziegfeld Follies of 1922": (R'22) 257,95; 258,135.
"Ziegfeld Follies of 1923": (D) 270,44; (R'23) 273,19.
"Ziegfeld Follies of 1924": (R'24) 282,15.
Ziegfeld Girls: 151,88; 160, 285; 170,200; 171,257; 172, 292; 173,17; 174,66; 181, 119; 181,125; 185,34; 186, 71; 192,101; 197,39; 198, 66; 209,25; 211,159; 217, 147; 221,14; 223,158; 231, 393; 232,532; 233,26; (D) 235,c; (D) 236,295; 238, 16; 246,159; (D) 253,217; 258,135; 258,174; 273,22; (D) 286,c; 301,13; 306, 16; 308,9; 320,61.
"Ziegfeld's Midnight Frolic" (1915): 170,200; 172, 292; (D) 176,204.
"Ziegfeld Midnight Frolic - (1916)": 181,119; 181, 125; (R) 181,126; 191, 12; (R'16) 192,394.
"Ziegfeld Midnight Frolic - (1917)": 204,83.
"Ziegfeld's Midnight Frolic - (1918)": 209,35; 217, 147.
"Ziegfeld Midnight Frolic - (1920)": (R'20) 234, 106; (R'20) 236,334.
"Ziegfeld Nine O'Clock Frolic": 241,263; (R'21) 241, 264.
"Ziegfeld Nine O'Clock Revue (1920)": 231,393.
Ziegfeld Theatre: (D) 310,23.
Ziegler, Charles F.: 5,11.
Ziegler, Edward: (W) 73,70.
Zimbalist, Efrem: 93,310; 130,190; 144,48; 166,272; 170,184; 192,95; 234, 98; 236,332; 270,37; 330, 23.
Zimmerman, J. Fred Sr.: 37, 78.
"Zira": (R'05) 57,269.
Zola, Emile: 32,244.
Zucca, Mana: 148,192; 238, 35.
Zucker, A.E.: (W) 334, 18.
Zuckerman, Augusta: 14,25.
Zukor, Adolph: 156,86; 171, 245; 202,397; 203,63; 208, 397; 281,39; (W) 290,38; 319,11.
Zwerenz, Mizzi: 160,305.
Zwink, Johann: 114,44; 117,148.

Bibliography

Ambriere, Francis. La Galerie Dramatique. Paris: Editions Correa, 1949.

Blum, Daniel. A Pictorial History of the American Theatre. 1900-1956. New York: Greenberg, 1956.

Browne, Walter and E. DeRoy Koch (eds.). Who's Who on the Stage. New York: B.W. Dodge, 1908.

Ganahl, Blanche M. "The Commercial Theatre Magazine in the United States from 1900 to 1958." Unpublished Master's thesis, Southern Illinois University, 1959.

Hiss, Sophie K. A.L.A. Rules for Filing Catalog Cards. Chicago: American Library Association, 1942.

Kolodin, Irving. The Metropolitan Opera, 1883-1935. New York: Oxford University Press, 1936.

Lang, Andre. Tiers de Siecle. Paris: Libraire Plon, 1935.

Mantle, Burns and Garrison P. Sherwood. The Best Plays of [various years]. New York: Dodd, Mead, and Company.

Melnitz, William Wolf. Theatre Arts Publications in the United States, 1945, 1952. AETA Monograph, No. 1. Dubuque: Brown, c. 1959.

Odell, George C.D. Annals of the New York Stage. New York: Columbia University Press, 1949.

Parker, John. Who's Who in the Theatre. Sixth edition. London: Pitman & Sons, Ltd. 1930.

Slonimsky, Nicolas. Baker's Biographical Dictionary of Musicians. New York: G. Schirmer. 1958.

Theatre Magazine. New York: The Meyer Brothers. 1900-1931.

Welker, David. Educational Theatre Journal, A Ten-Year Index: 1949-1958. Michigan: AETA [n.d.].